"*The Reality of Precaution* provides a nuanced, fact-based account of the various meanings and applications of the Precautionary Principle in Europe and United States. Rejecting the heated rhetoric that so often accompanies discussion of risk regulation, the editors have put together a balanced volume that ought to be essential reading for both policy analysts and policymakers on both sides of the Atlantic."
Susan Rose-Ackerman, Henry R. Luce Professor of Jurisprudence, Yale Law School and Department of Political Science; and co-editor, *Comparative Administrative Law*

"Going beyond the slogans of the precautionary principle, the authors bring together all sides of the debate in the US and Europe and provide in-depth and insightful analysis of the issues. Anyone who cares about environmental policy must read this book."
Richard D. Morgenstern, Senior Fellow, Resources for the Future; former Director of the Office of Policy Analysis, U.S. Environmental Protection Agency; and co-editor, *Choosing Environmental Policy: Comparing Instruments and Outcomes in the United States and Europe*

The Reality of Precaution

The Reality of Precaution
Comparing Risk Regulation
in the United States and
Europe

EDITED BY

Jonathan B. Wiener, Michael D. Rogers,
James K. Hammitt, and Peter H. Sand

RFF PRESS
RESOURCES FOR THE FUTURE

First published in 2011 by RFF Press, an imprint of Earthscan

Earthscan
605 Third Avenue, New York, NY 10017

Simultaneously published in the USA and Canada by Earthscan
2 Park Square, Milton Park, Abingdon, Oxon OX14 4RN

Earthscan is an imprint of the Taylor & Francis Group, an informa business

Copyedited by John Deever and Joyce Bond
Typeset by OKS Press Services
Cover design by Circle Graphics

Cover images (from left to right): "Analysis of samples" © dra_schwartz/istockphoto.com; "World Trade Center Rubble" © Terraxplorer/istockphoto.com; "Nuclear Power Plant" © Elena Aliaga/istockphoto.com; "Chemical protection" © Ivan Tykhyi/istockphoto.com

Library of Congress Cataloging-in-Publication Data

The reality of precaution : comparing risk regulation in the United States and Europe / edited by Jonathan B. Wiener ... [et al.].
    p. cm.
  Includes bibliographical references and index.
  ISBN 978-1-933115-86-3 (hardback : alk. paper) – ISBN 978-1-933115-85-6 (pbk. : alk. paper)
1. Precautionary principle 2. Precautionary principle–United States. 3. Precautionary principle–European Union countries. I. Wiener, Jonathan Baert, 1962-
  K3585.R43 2010
  344.04'6–dc22   2010015414

A catalogue record for this book is available from the British Library

At Earthscan we strive to minimize our environmental impacts and carbon footprint through reducing waste, recycling and offsetting our CO_2 emissions, including those created through publication of this book.

ISBN 13: 978-1-933115-85-6 (pbk)

DOI: 10.4324/9781936331802

About Resources for the Future *and* RFF Press

Resources for the Future (RFF) improves environmental and natural resource policymaking worldwide through independent social science research of the highest caliber. Founded in 1952, RFF pioneered the application of economics as a tool for developing more effective policy about the use and conservation of natural resources. Its scholars continue to employ social science methods to analyze critical issues concerning pollution control, energy policy, land and water use, hazardous waste, climate change, biodiversity, and the environmental challenges of developing countries.

RFF Press supports the mission of RFF by publishing book-length works that present a broad range of approaches to the study of natural resources and the environment. Its authors and editors include RFF staff, researchers from the larger academic and policy communities, and journalists. Audiences for publications by RFF Press include all of the participants in the policymaking process—scholars, the media, advocacy groups, NGOs, professionals in business and government, and the public. RFF Press is an imprint of **Earthscan**, a global publisher of books and journals about the environment and sustainable development.

Contents

Preface

*T*his book began as an extended conversation with Michael Rogers—then at the Group of Policy Advisers of the European Commission in Brussels—when, to my great good fortune, he spent a year as a visiting fellow at Duke University. Michael and I were inspired to test the increasingly popular claim that Europe, having formally adopted the "precautionary principle," had now become "more precautionary" than the United States in the regulation of a host of important risks to health, safety, environment, and security. Michael and I then invited Jim Hammitt of the Harvard School of Public Health and Peter Sand of the University of Munich Faculty of Law to join us in organizing and editing this project. We consciously assembled an editorial team of two Europeans and two Americans, including a scientist and a legal scholar from each side of the Atlantic. We then sought contributions from top experts on key topics in both Europe and America, and we have been privileged to collaborate in this effort with more than 20 esteemed colleagues.

With support from numerous quarters, our initial conversation grew into a multiyear study project. The project featured a series of four conferences: the "Transatlantic Dialogues on Precaution," held in Bruges, Belgium, not far from Brussels (January 2002); at Airlie House in Warrenton, Virginia, not far from Washington, DC (June 2002); in Berlin, Germany (June 2003); and at Duke University in Durham, North Carolina (September 2004). We then undertook significant additional research, writing, discussion, presentations at conferences, and sabbatical visits. (In the Acknowledgments section at the end of this book, we express in detail our deep gratitude to those who supported the Dialogues and the book project, the numerous institutions that hosted conferences and presentations on the project, and the many colleagues who commented on earlier versions of the text.)

Compiling this volume took longer than we initially foresaw. In part, the duration was the normal result of holding several conferences and then organizing a large number of papers by different authors into one volume. In addition, it took several years to compile our dataset of thousands of risks and our quantitative measure of relative precaution over time. Moreover, we understood from the outset that this book needed to be a collaborative venture of both Americans and Europeans. And we each felt the obligation to spend some time viewing the world from the other side of the Atlantic—to gain a firsthand understanding of the risks, policies, institutions, politics, and cultures about which we would be writing. Goethe advised that one can never truly understand one's own language until one learns another; this insight applies as well to regulatory systems. So, after Michael Rogers's year visiting at Duke in 1999–2000, and the four Transatlantic Dialogues on Precaution that we held from 2002 to 2004, Jim Hammitt and I then both spent the year 2005–2006 on sabbatical in France— he in Toulouse and I in Paris. Meanwhile, Peter Sand visited at Duke and other U.S. universities, after an earlier post at the World Bank in Washington. In 2008 and 2010, I returned to teach in Paris, and in 2010, Jim returned to Toulouse. Each of us has made several return visits to these and other parts of America and Europe, speaking and learning about regulatory policies.

Our multinational project team and our several exchanges and sabbaticals have enabled us to gain, we hope, a more textured understanding of the reality of precaution and of evolving transatlantic relations. As Montaigne observed centuries ago, "Il se tire une merveilleuse clarté, pour le jugement humain, de la fréquentation du monde."[1] We hope our judgment has drawn clarity from seeing more of the world, its people, and its regulatory systems.

There also are benefits to a lengthy gestation. A good history can gain from some distance from its subject. Our perspective has ripened with time. And policies in Europe and America have unfolded, giving us new grist for insight and commentary. After the European Union's adoption of the "precautionary principle" in the 1990s, further events have set the stage for a new look at U.S.-European regulatory cooperation, notably new regulatory policies on both sides of the Atlantic, the development of Europe's "Better Regulation" initiative since 2001, and the inauguration of the new U.S. administration of Barack Obama in 2009. Now is thus a particularly apt time to synthesize and present our findings.

At the same time, we recognize that even this substantial volume is incomplete. Further research is needed on case studies of other risks we have not yet addressed; on policies within the Member States of the EU and the states of the U.S.; on policies in other countries around the world beyond the United States and Europe; on a longer historical timeline; on the causal factors accounting for the complex observed pattern of risk regulation; and on the consequences of precautionary policies. We look forward to this journey.

Jonathan B. Wiener, for the Editors
Durham, North Carolina, USA, and Paris, France

---

[1] In essence, "One gleans a marvelous clarity for human judgment by getting to know the world." Michel de Montaigne (1580), *Essays*, I 26 F 140; VS 157a, quoted in the Stanford Encyclopedia of Philosophy, http://plato.stanford.edu/entries/montaigne/, at n. 19, or directly at http://plato.stanford.edu/entries/montaigne/notes.html#19.

Contributors

John F. Ahearne is executive director emeritus of Sigma Xi, the Scientific Research Society, an adjunct professor of civil and environmental engineering at Duke University, and an adjunct scholar at Resources for the Future. Dr. Ahearne served as chair of the U.S. Nuclear Regulatory Commission from 1979 to 1981. He has also served as the principal deputy assistant secretary of defense and deputy assistant secretary of energy during the Nixon, Ford, and Carter administrations. He is a member of the U.S. National Academy of Engineering, a fellow of the American Academy of Arts and Sciences, the American Physical Society, the American Association for the Advancement of Science (AAAS), and the Society for Risk Analysis (SRA) (of which he served as president in 2001).

Jessica S. Ancker received her Ph.D. in the Department of Biomedical Informatics at Columbia University's College of Physicians and Surgeons, where her doctoral work included the study of cognitive science and decision theory with coauthor Elke U. Weber. She is currently an assistant professor of public health in the division of quality and medical informatics at Weill Cornell Medical College in New York City.

Lucas Bergkamp is a partner in the law firm of Hunton & Williams in Brussels, Belgium. He specializes in resources, regulatory, and environmental law and in international business transactions and trade law, including WTO law and the laws of the EU and its Member States. From 1998 through 2006, he was a professor of international environmental liability at Erasmus University Rotterdam.

Adolf Birkhofer is a member and former chairman of the International Nuclear Safety Advisory Group to the director general of the International Atomic Energy Agency. Dr. Birkhofer is the managing director of the ISaR Institute for Safety and Reliability GmbH and chief of reactor dynamics and reactor safety at the Technische Universitat München.

D. Douglas Blanke is the director of the Public Health Law Center at William Mitchell College of Law in Saint Paul, Minnesota, a legal resource center and think tank assisting advocates and public officials in using the law to improve public health. He also directs the Tobacco Control Legal Consortium, a national network of legal centers supporting the U.S. tobacco control community, and has advised the World Health Organization. As an assistant attorney general of Minnesota, he played a key role in the state's historic tobacco litigation of the 1990s.

Mark Cantley served as adviser to the Directorate for Life Sciences in the European Commission's Directorate-General for Research since 1999. He has headed the Biotechnology Unit within the Directorate for Science, Technology and Industry of the OECD and has been secretary of its Internal Coordination Group for Biotechnology.

Gail Charnley is the president of HealthRisk Strategies, a consultancy in Washington, DC, providing analysis of toxicology and risk issues related to chemical exposures and public health. She has previously served as executive director of the Presidential/Congressional Commission on Risk Assessment and Risk Management, president of the Society for Risk Analysis, and acting director of the Toxicology and Risk Assessment Program at the National Academy of Sciences/National Research Council.

E. Donald Elliott is an adjunct professor of law at Yale Law School and Georgetown University Law Center. He is also the global head of Willkie Farr & Gallagher's environmental law department and a partner in its DC office. Mr. Elliott was assistant administrator and general counsel at the U.S. Environmental Protection Agency (EPA) from 1989 to 1992. Before that, he was the Julien and Virginia Cornell Professor of Environmental Law and Litigation at Yale Law School.

David Freestone is the Lobingier Visiting Professor of Comparative Law and Jurisprudence at George Washington University School of Law. From 2004 to 2008, he served as deputy general counsel and senior adviser at the World Bank, before which he was the chief counsel and head of the Environmentally and Socially Sustainable Development (ESSD) and International Law Group in the Legal Vice Presidency of the World Bank. Prior to joining the bank in 1996, he was a professor of International Law at the University of Hull, England. He is the founding editor and now editor-in-chief of the International Journal of Marine and Coastal Law.

George Gray is a professor in the Department of Environmental and Occupational Health, and the director of the Center for Risk Science and Public Health, at the George Washington University School of Public Health. He served as assistant administrator heading the Office of Research and Development at EPA from 2005 to 2009. Prior to joining EPA, Dr. Gray was executive director of the Harvard Center for Risk Analysis and a lecturer in risk analysis at the Harvard School of Public Health.

James K. Hammitt is a professor of economics and decision sciences at Harvard School of Public Health and director of the Harvard Center for Risk Analysis. He has visited at the Toulouse School of Economics in 2005–2006 and again beginning in 2010. Before coming to Harvard in 1993, he was a senior mathematician at the RAND Corporation. He is a member of EPA's Science Advisory Board and chairs its Advisory Council on Clear Air Compliance Analysis.

Denise Kall is an assistant professor at St. Ambrose University, Iowa. She received her Ph.D. in the Department of Sociology at Duke University in 2008, focusing on environmental sociology and social stratification. From 2002 through 2008, she served as research associate at the Duke Center for Environmental Solutions working on the Reality of Precaution project.

Maurice Lex has been a member of the Directorate General for Research at the European Commission since 1990. At the commission, he was a member of the drafting team for the Commission's Communication on Life Sciences and Biotechnology, and he has served as project officer for the Eurobarometer surveys on biotechnology. He is the executive secretary of the EC/U.S. Task Force for biotechnology research and was elected a fellow of the UK's Royal Society of Arts and Sciences in 1986.

Giandomenico Majone is an emeritus professor of public policy at the European University Institute in Florence. Before joining the institute, he was a professor in the faculty of Economics and Social Sciences of the University of Calabria. He has also been a visiting professor at several institutions, including the Harvard Kennedy School of Government, Yale University, the University of Pittsburgh, and the Wissenschaftszentrum, Berlin.

Frances H. Miller is a professor of law emerita at Boston University School of Law and a visiting professor of law at the William S. Richardson School of Law, University of Hawaii at Manoa. She served on the White House Task Force on Health Care Reform in 1993 as a member of the working group on malpractice and tort reform, was a commissioner of the Massachusetts Rate Setting Commission, and has served as a member or chair of Massachusetts' Health Facilities Appeals Board for nearly two decades. She has been a Kellogg Foundation fellow, was twice appointed a Fulbright Scholar, and has studied at the London School of Economics.

Ortwin Renn is a professor and the chair of Environmental Sociology at the University of Stuttgart, Germany, and director of the nonprofit think tank DIALOGIK. He is a fellow of the American Association for the Advancement of Science (AAAS) as well as of the Society for Risk Analysis (SRA), and in 1997 served as president of SRA-Europe. He chaired the German Federal Committee on the Harmonization of Risk Standards, the Scientific Advisory Board of the Foundation "Precautionary Risk Management," and the State Scientific Committee for Environmental Research, as well as the White Paper project on risk governance of the International Risk Governance Council (IRGC).

Michael D. Rogers is an independent consultant focusing on subjects at the intersection of risk, ethics, and law. Dr. Rogers was a member of the Bureau of European Policy Advisers in the Office of the President of the European Commission, where he served for 13 years. In that capacity, he co-organized the Transatlantic Dialogues on Precaution that gave rise to this volume. He has been a visiting fellow at Duke University and a visiting professor in the School of Public Policy of the University of Tokyo. Previously, he also served as a science and technology counselor at the EC office in San Francisco and in the British Embassy in Tokyo.

Peter H. Sand is a lecturer in international environmental law at the Faculty of Law, University of Munich. Professor Sand has held a variety of international positions, including commissioner for environmental claims at the UN Compensation Commission, legal adviser for environmental affairs to the World Bank, principal programme officer at the UN Conference on Environment and Development, chief of the Environmental Law Unit at the UN Environment Programme, and assistant director-general of the International Union for Conservation of Nature and Natural Resources. He has also been an associate professor of law at McGill University and a visiting professor at Duke Law School, the University of Helsinki, and the University of Paris II.

Kathryn A. Saterson is the assistant laboratory director for Ecosystem Services and Global Change at the National Health and Environmental Effects Research Laboratory of EPA. As the executive director of the Duke Center for Environmental Solutions from 2001 to 2005, she was heavily involved in organizing the Transatlantic Dialogues on Precaution that gave rise to this volume. She remains an adjunct associate professor in the Division of Environmental Sciences and Policy at the Nicholas School at Duke University. Before coming to Duke, she was the director of the Environmental Management Center at the Brandywine Conservancy, and previously the executive director of the Biodiversity Support Program, a consortium of the World Wildlife Fund, the World Resources Institute, and The Nature Conservancy.

Turner T. Smith, Jr., is the head of Hunton & Williams' International Environmental Practice and the former resident managing partner of the Firm's Brussels office, where he has specialized in energy and environmental law for over 25 years. He has written extensively on the comparison of U.S. and European environmental law. He has taught environmental law at Washington & Lee, William & Mary, the University of Virginia, and George Mason Law Schools. He has also served as the chairman of the American Bar Association's Standing Committee on Environmental Law, the Board of Directors of the Environmental Law Institute, and the Virginia Chapter of The Nature Conservancy.

Jessica Stern is a member of the Hoover Institution Task Force on National Security and Law. She previously served as the director of the Program on Terrorism at Harvard Law School and a lecturer in public policy at the Harvard Kennedy School of Government. Before coming to Harvard, she served as the director for Russian,

Ukrainian, and Eurasian Affairs at the White House National Security Council (NSC) during the Clinton administration from 1994 to 1995. She has been the Superterrorism Fellow at the Council on Foreign Relations, as well as a national fellow at the Hoover Institution at Stanford University.

Cass R. Sunstein is the Felix Frankfurter Professor of Law at Harvard Law School (on leave), currently serving since 2009 as the administrator of the Office of Information and Regulatory Affairs (OIRA) within the U.S. Office of Management and Budget. (His chapter in this book was completed long before his appointment to OIRA, and he did not edit it further after his appointment to OIRA; a few copyedits were made by the publisher.) From 1981 to 2008, he was the Karl Llewellyn Distinguished Service Professor of Law and Political Science at the University of Chicago. Before joining the Chicago faculty, he was an attorney-adviser in the Office of Legal Counsel of the U.S. Department of Justice, and a law clerk for Justice Benjamin Kaplan of the Massachusetts Supreme Judicial Court and Justice Thurgood Marshall of the U.S. Supreme Court.

Brendon Swedlow is an associate professor in the Department of Political Science and a founding faculty associate of the Institute for the Study of the Environment, Sustainability and Energy at Northern Illinois University. Dr. Swedlow's research is directed toward developing theory, concepts, and methods that advance the study of American politics, public law, and public policy and includes comparative work on risk assessment and regulation. He is a research associate of the Centre for Analysis of Risk and Regulation at the London School of Economics, a fellow of the Center for Governance at the University of California, Los Angeles, and was a postdoctoral fellow at the Center for Environmental Solutions at Duke University, where he worked on the Reality of Precaution project.

Michael P. Walsh was the director of the motor vehicle pollution control programs for both the city of New York (1970–1974) and EPA (1974–1981). He was an adviser to the U.S. Senate on the 1990 Clean Air Act Amendments, served as chairman of the transportation subgroup of the IPCC Good Practices in Emissions Inventory Workgroup, and has been co-chair of EPA's Mobile Source Advisory Subcommittee. He has also helped advise the transportation air quality programs in Mexico and China. For his leadership in reducing automobile emissions around the world, he has received awards from EPA and the California Air Resources Board, and in 2005, he was named a MacArthur Fellow.

Elke U. Weber is the Jerome A. Chazen Professor of International Business in the Management Division of Columbia Business School and a professor of psychology at Columbia University, where she also co-directs the Center for Research on Environmental Decisions (CRED) and the Center for Decision Sciences (CDS). Over the past 25 years, she has held academic positions in the United States and Europe. She is past president of the Society for Mathematical Psychology, the Society for Judgment and Decision Making, and the Society for Neuroeconomics and has served on several National Academy of Sciences committees related to human dimensions in global change.

Jonathan B. Wiener is the William R. and Thomas L. Perkins Professor of Law in the Law School, a professor of environmental policy in the Nicholas School, and a professor of public policy in the Sanford School, at Duke University. From 2000 to 2005, he was the founding faculty director of the Duke Center for Environmental Solutions (since expanded into the Nicholas Institute for Environmental Policy Solutions), in which capacity he co-organized the Transatlantic Dialogues on Precaution that gave rise to this volume. He has been a university fellow of Resources for the Future (RFF) since 2002. He served as president of the Society for Risk Analysis (SRA) in 2008. He has been a visiting professor at Harvard, the University of Chicago, Paris-Dauphine, Sciences Po, and l'École des Hautes Études en Sciences Sociales. Before coming to Duke in 1994, he served at the White House Council of Economic Advisers (CEA) and at the U.S. Department of Justice, during both the first Bush and Clinton administrations. He was a law clerk to federal judges Stephen G. Breyer and Jack B. Weinstein.

Zheng (Jonathan) Zhou is an attorney with Cleary Gottlieb Steen & Hamilton, where he has worked in both its Beijing and New York offices. From 2002 to 2004, he served as a research assistant at the Duke Center for Environmental Solutions, working on climate change policy and the quantitative analysis of relative precaution between the United States and Europe.

PART I
INTRODUCTION

CHAPTER 1

The Rhetoric of Precaution

Jonathan B. Wiener

*H*uman beings have always faced risks. From prehistoric times to the modern era, successful risk assessment and risk management have been crucial to human survival and progress (Bernstein 1996). Those who manage risks successfully endure and prosper. Many risks have indeed been reduced over time; human life expectancies are now longer than ever before. But those gains may have come at the cost of, or concurrently with, new and emerging problems. New technologies may reduce some risks but also pose new risks; meanwhile, new science may enable detection of previously unseen risks. Longer lifespans, while they represent success against some risks, in turn draw our attention to the longer-term shadows of latent risks. Some say that today, despite our generally greater safety and security compared to our ancestors, we live in a "risk society" (Beck 1992; Peretti-Watel 2001).

Risk is now a global concern. Crises in credit markets, climate change, and international conflict over the past decade have demonstrated the increasing interconnectedness of risks across countries, which suggests the need for effective risk management at the local, national, and international scales. Policymakers confront a wide array of risks and associated demands for protective action on such diverse issues as chemicals, climate, disease, disasters, energy, environment, food, finance, tsunamis, terrorism, and more.

Increasing interconnectedness of risk has at least three implications. First, risks may spread more quickly across borders and populations, thus challenging us to develop earlier warning signals and more coordinated responses. Disease, pollution, financial crisis, and terrorism all illustrate this property of rapid transboundary spread. Second, in an interwoven web of increasingly interconnected risks, each intervention to reduce one risk may yield more trade-offs with other risks and social impacts, near and far, now and later. These side effects challenge us to think more comprehensively about systemic interactions, to make difficult choices among conflicting objectives, and to innovate better policies and institutions to reduce overall risks (Graham and Wiener 1995). Third, and more hopefully, potential solutions and accumulated experience can spread more readily in an increasingly interconnected marketplace of ideas, facilitating learning and borrowing of innovations in risk management, public policy, and law (Simmons et al. 2008; Slaughter 2004; Slaughter 2009; Wiener 2003; Wiener 2006; and Chapter 20, this volume).

Over the last five decades, enormous effort has been put into the construction and operation of risk regulation regimes around the world, particularly in the United States and in Europe. Since the late 1960s, Europe and America have adopted a plethora of new laws, agencies, and policies to protect our environment, health, safety, and security. Entire new government ministries have been created (for example, environmental and consumer regulatory bodies), while existing bureaucracies have been reorganized (for example, into new ministries on homeland security and on energy). Throughout this period, scholars, activists, businesses and regulators have debated how anticipatory and how stringent policies should be to prevent emerging uncertain risks.

The "precautionary principle" (PP), articulated as early as the 1960s, has been at the forefront of this debate since the 1990s. Controversial, it is variously viewed as salvation or blunder. Different summaries of what the PP means include "better safe than sorry," "uncertainty is no excuse for inaction," and "uncertainty requires action." Later in this chapter, we quote several prominent versions of the PP (for more detail on the terms of the PP and its elusive definition, see Sandin 1999; Stone 2001; Trouwborst 2002; Vander Zwaag 1999; Wiener and Rogers 2002; Wiener 2007; and Chapter 20 in this volume). Two decades ago, advocates forecast that the PP "could become *the* fundamental principle of environmental protection policy and law" (Cameron and Abouchar 1991, 2). Its advance was rapid: "The speed with which the precautionary principle has been brought on to the international agenda, and the range and variety of international forums which have explicitly accepted it within the recent past, are quite staggering" (Freestone 1991, 36). It soon reached the mountaintop: "If international environmental law were to develop Ten Commandments, the precautionary principle would be near the top of the list" (Bodansky 2004, 381). Yet its merits remain hotly contested: "The precautionary principle may well be the most innovative, pervasive, and significant new concept in environmental policy over the past quarter century. It may also be the most reckless, arbitrary, and ill-advised" (Marchant and Mossman 2004, 1).

In the last two decades, this debate over precaution and its ascent has been framed by many as a transatlantic contest for leadership. Who is "more precautionary," the United States or Europe? This book attempts to answer that question, and to unpack it and critique it. Within this comparative question lies a host of further debates, both descriptive and normative.

Today the oft-repeated claim is that Europe is, or has become, "more precautionary" than the United States in many kinds of risk regulation. In this book we examine that claim, testing the descriptive pattern of precaution in the United States and Europe from 1970 to the present. At least four basic accounts compete to characterize the history of regulatory precaution in Europe and America:

- convergence, driven by globalization and the pressure to harmonize standards;
- divergence, driven by different cultures and by regulatory competition;
- reversal, or "flip-flop," from greater U.S. precaution in the 1970s to greater European precaution since the 1990s, driven by broad shifts in internal politics and international rivalry; and
- "hybridization," the exchange of ideas and interweaving of diverse regulatory systems, driven by learning from experience in response to particular risks.

The first three of these accounts treat the United States and European Union (EU) as separate discrete entities, moving in large blocs, like tectonic plates, or "ships passing in the night" (Vogel 2001), or competitors "trading places" (Kelemen and Vogel 2010), or political movements rallying behind an iconic leader (think of Eugène Delacroix's painting *La Liberté guidant le peuple* (1830)). The fourth account treats the United States and EU as diverse and increasingly interconnected, more like complex interdependent communities in large ecosystems, or the myriad inhabitants of a landscape who are busy with their daily activities even as occasional momentous events punctuate their lives (think of the paintings of Pieter Bruegel the Elder, such as *The Numbering at Bethlehem* or *The Fall of Icarus*).

A Fresh Comparative Analysis

To move beyond claims based on just a few celebrated examples, in the present volume we assess a wide array of U.S. and European policies from 1970 to the present. We examine a dozen case studies in depth, including risks connected with food safety (genetically modified [GM] foods, beef hormones, and mad cow disease), air pollution, climate change, nuclear power, tobacco, chemicals, marine and terrestrial biodiversity, medical safety, and terrorism, as well as precaution embodied in risk information disclosure and risk assessment systems. In addition to these detailed case studies, we also conduct a broad quantitative analysis of relative precaution in a sample of 100 risks drawn from a dataset of nearly 3,000 risks over the period 1970 to the present. Our hope and expectation is that, taken together, these case studies and the quantitative analysis offer a more thorough and representative picture of the real pattern of precaution than has been captured by prior studies that focused more narrowly on selected risks. Looking across these descriptive inquiries, we then devote four chapters to investigating the causes of the observed pattern of precaution. In the final chapter, we synthesize our findings about the real pattern and consequences of precaution, and we offer recommendations for methods of comparing regulatory systems, for desirable regulatory policies, and for transatlantic relations and the exchange of ideas.

Our focus in this book is on the descriptive comparison and evolution of regulatory systems. Normatively, this book neither defends nor attacks precaution per se. Nonetheless, we do attempt to draw from the historical evidence some findings about the impacts of different policies, and we do offer some recommendations for future policy and future research. We recognize that the normative debate has been vigorous. Some laud the PP as essential to surviving dire risks (e.g., Raffensperger and Tickner 1999; Bourg and Schlegel 2001; Whiteside 2006; de Sadeleer 2007). Others condemn the PP as misguided and overregulatory or disabling (e.g., Cross 1996; Morris 2000; Goklany 2001; Sunstein 2005). The descriptive assertion or assumption that Europe is now more precautionary than the United States is often conflated with the normative debate over precaution. Some adopting this view see a civilized, precautionary Europe confronting a risky, reckless, and violent America (e.g., Richter 2000; Rifkin 2004), portraying the precautionary principle as an antidote to industrialization, globalization, and Americanization. Others also adopt the view of greater European precaution, but see a statist, technophobic, protectionist Europe trying to challenge a market-based, scientific, entrepreneurial America (e.g., Redwood 2001), portraying the precautionary principle as an obstacle to science, trade, and progress. U.S. and EU officials have publicly traded barbs over the PP. Our aim in this project has been to move beyond the acrimony over precaution as an abstract principle to see what can be learned from studying precaution as applied in real regulations.

We study the United States and Europe here, in part because we are responding to the comparisons between them that have been made by eminent scholars (e.g., Jasanoff 2005; Vogel 2003; Vogel, forthcoming), and in part because of their large impacts—both directly and through the examples they set for other countries (Hall and Soskice 2001; Pollack and Shaffer 2001). The United States and Europe are the world's two largest economies, and major trading partners. Together they comprise about a tenth of the world's population but contribute almost half of world economic output, along with more than a third of global greenhouse gas emissions (though declining shares of each). Both have seen strong public demands for protection against risks to environment, health, safety, and security. They have among the most extensive and well-developed systems of regulation. To be sure, other countries can and will play important roles. Other member states of the Organisation for Economic Co-operation and Development (OECD), such as Canada, Japan, and Australia (see, e.g., Fisher et al. 2006)—along with rising powers such as China, India, and Brazil—can and will influence debates over risk regulation. China and India have already played pivotal roles in global climate change negotiations, in part through their implicit influence on U.S. policymakers (Stewart and Wiener 2003). Indeed, one of the pitfalls in comparing U.S. and European risk regulation is the exaggeration of transatlantic differences that are small relative to the larger variation around the world. Moreover, significant variation exists within the United States and within Europe: for example, California and Sweden often adopt highly precautionary policies that influence their sister states and their federal or supranational regulators; and the United Kingdom (UK) often plays an intriguing intermediary role between the United States and continental Europe. Nonetheless, the EU and the United States play the most prominent roles in shaping the debate over precaution—some scholars even contend that these two giants are the only polities with the capacity for global leadership on environmental and regulatory issues (Kelemen and Vogel 2010; Vig and Faure 2004), although the criteria for being a "leader" are seldom specified. Staunch allies since World War II, they have sustained a spirited debate over when and how to regulate risks during at least the two decades since the end of the Cold War. The study of that debate can offer important insights for the future of risk regulation in the United States, Europe, and beyond.

We study the period from about 1970 to the present because it represents the modern regulatory era among wealthy democracies. On both sides of the Atlantic, the 1970s saw the first Earth Day, the first United Nations Conference on the Environment (in Stockholm in 1972), and an explosion of lawmaking on environment, health, and safety (Scruggs 2003, 20). Moreover, claims of shifting precaution posit that precautionary regulation began to arise around 1970 (e.g., Vogel 2003). Further research could extend our study further back into history, perhaps in a subsequent book.

The Claim of Greater European Precaution

The concept of precaution and the notion of rival cultural dispositions toward precaution on each side of the Atlantic are not new. But the codification of the PP as a legal doctrine, and the claim that Europe has become "more precautionary" than the United States by adopting the PP in formal laws and regulations, are modern constructs.

Cultural Roots?

Long-held cultural stereotypes depict Americans and Europeans as opposites. Robert Kagan says Americans are from Mars and Europeans are from Venus (Kagan 2003). Serge Sur suggests instead that Americans are the strong but doomed Achilles, whereas Europeans are the wily and surviving Odysseus (whom the French and the Irish call Ulysses) (Sur 2004). Richard Posner, however, argues that it is *Ulysses*, rather than Achilles, who is closest to American pragmatism, because "his dominant trait is skill in coping with his environment rather than ability to impose himself upon it by brute force" (Posner 2003, 27). Meanwhile, John Dryzek divides environmental discourses between the "Survivalists" (with most Europeans probably fitting that label) and the "First Americans") (Dryzek 1997, 23, 44; Dryzek 2006, 18; Dryzek 2007, 51). Others have described America and Europe as family members, variously as cousins (Patten 2006), as siblings with rivalries both mythical and empirical (Mock 2004), or as a mature European parent with an American offspring still in a rough adolescence (Markovits 2007).

According to prevalent stereotypes today, Americans are said to be individualistic, technologically optimistic, forward-looking, risk-taking, and antiregulatory, confident that new technology and the power of markets will solve every problem and that precaution is a waste of time and a hindrance to progress. Europeans are said to be more collectivist, technologically anxious, retrospective, risk-averse, afraid of the unknown, afraid of new technologies (especially American) and of global markets, and pro-regulatory, indeed eager to adopt precautionary regulations against remote and speculative risks (Kempton and Craig 1993, 16–20, 41–45; Levy and Newell 2000, 10). Even *The Economist* put it this way: "Tastes in risk vary across countries. Europe is considered fairly risk-averse. ... America, on the other hand, is often seen as having a strong risk-taking culture" (Economist 2004). Some might imagine that these cultural stereotypes derive from the history of self-selection over the last five centuries, as a result of which Americans (at least those who are descended from Europeans) may see themselves as the risk-takers who ventured across the ocean to the land of opportunity, while Europeans may see themselves as the risk-averse who stayed home to safeguard their culture and patrimony.

But these are all stereotypes, not empirical reality. The slightest serious inquiry makes plain that attitudes toward risks, technology, and regulation are not uniform or permanent on either side of the Atlantic, nor are views today dictated by early history. Studies of risk perception show significant variation by country and by type of risk, among other factors (Renn and Rohrmann 2000; Peretti-Watel 2000; Chapter 18, this volume). Weber and Hsee (1998) found "cross-cultural differences in risk perception, but cross-cultural similarities in attitudes towards perceived risks." And as we will see, the actual history of risk regulation does not match these fixed cultural stereotypes: the leading scholarly account is that the United States and Europe have switched places over the last five decades (Vogel 2003; Vogel, forthcoming), with America having been "more precautionary" and risk-averse than Europe in the 1970s (at odds with the stereotypes). Our own research, discussed below, finds even more variation on relative precaution among particular risks. Still, such stereotypes can frame public perception.

Long before the current debate over precaution in regulation, popular literature featured cultural stereotypes about precaution—sometimes in explicitly transatlantic terms. In 1773, Pierre-Augustin Caron de Beaumarchais penned *Le Barbier de Séville; ou, la Précaution Inutile* (*The Barber of Seville; or, the Futile Precaution*). There old Bartholo courts young Rosine and takes precautions to imprison and isolate her from her suitors, notably the Count. But the Count, with help from Figaro, deploys clever ruses to outwit Bartholo and marry Rosine. Beaumarchais was critiquing "futile precaution" as a reactionary stance against the coming of modernity; he has old Bartholo denounce the "follies" of "free-thinking, electricity, attraction, toleration, inoculation, ... the encyclopedia, and loads of nonsensical plays" (Act I, Scene III). Yet progress, symbolized by the marriage of the young lovers, could not be held back by the old guard's "futile precaution." Indeed, Beaumarchais's play was swiftly followed by the American and French revolutions (the latter, especially, unleashing its own populist upheaval against elite rule and thus championing its own form of precautionary empowerment of public governance). Some decades later, on the other side of the Atlantic—soon after Rossini adapted *The Barber of Seville* into an opera in 1816—a young American, finding contemporary English novels dull, declared that he could write a better one. His wife dared him to do it. And so James Fenimore Cooper produced his first novel, *Precaution*, in 1820. The book espoused precaution as sensible forethought. Cooper wrote that, "It is madness to defer; tomorrow's caution may arrive too late." But the book was not a commercial success. Cooper's later works—tales of risk and adventure—proved far more popular in America. By the late nineteenth century, in *The Canterville Ghost* (1887), Oscar Wilde lampooned British fear of unseen risks (ghosts haunting the English mansion, forcing the Britons to flee) and American technological hubris (a family from the United States brings a clever new invention to overcome every predicament, and the family's fearless daughter befriends the ghost). Wilde's point, of course, was to spoof these stereotypes of European caution and American innovation—to undo rather than to uphold these cultural caricatures.

After the Great Depression, two World Wars, and the era of the North Atlantic Treaty Organization (NATO) and nuclear weapons, in the last five decades America and Europe have been at peace, prosperous, and safeguarded by ever-growing regulatory systems to manage risks of all kinds. Today, travelers crossing the Atlantic may be struck by differences in cultural tolerances for risk—not a generic aversion to or appetite for risk, but idiosyncrasies and particular reactions to the specific risks that people face in everyday life. Europeans coming to America may be shocked, for example, by genetically modified foods, large sport utility vehicles, inexpensive gasoline and high greenhouse gas emissions, a thinner safety net of social insurance, the prevalence of guns, and high rates of obesity. At the same time, Americans coming to Europe may be shocked by high speeds on the major autoroutes and wild traffic in city centers, asbestos still being removed from public buildings, merry-go-rounds in parks, river quays without railings, metro (subway) doors that open while the train is still moving, motorcycles that drive on the sidewalk, choking hazards in food (like the prizes in Kinder Eggs and in Galettes des Rois), unpasteurized cheese (in the land of Pasteur!), medicine bottles that lack childproof caps, nuclear energy, heat waves with no air conditioning, and high rates of tobacco smoking (especially in public places).

These examples, and the stories by Beaumarchais, Cooper, and Wilde, offer an early clue to understanding precaution and its transatlantic incidence. Cultural stereotypes can be amusing, but in real life they quickly give way to a complex mixed bag of particular differences on particular risks.

The March of Precaution

The last five decades have seen the mounting codification of precaution as a formal legal principle. *Vorsorgeprinzip* in German law dates at least to the early 1970s (Boehmer-Christiansen 1994). At about that same time, similar doctrines of "precaution" were introduced in Swedish and Swiss law. In the United States, precautionary pre-market safety review of new drugs under the U.S. Federal Food, Drug and Cosmetic Act began before World War II, and the precautionary prohibition of carcinogens in food dates to the Delaney Clause in 1958, although neither of these laws used the term "precaution." Landmark court decisions expressly endorsed the notion of "precautionary" regulation: in *Ethyl Corp. v. EPA*, 541 F.2d 1 (D.C. Cir. 1976), the court held that the Clean Air Act was a "precautionary" statute authorizing anticipatory regulation of uncertain risks, and in *TVA v. Hill*, 437 U.S. 153 (1978), the court held that the Endangered Species Act embodied "institutionalized caution" by protecting species from extinction whatever the costs.

The march of precaution was arguably slowed by the U.S. Supreme Court's ruling in *Industrial Union Department, AFL-CIO v. American Petroleum Institute* et al., 448 U.S. 607 (1980) (commonly known as "the Benzene case"), along with the 1983 "Redbook" on risk assessment from the National Academy of Sciences (NAS/NRC 1983), both of which suggested that anticipatory precaution in U.S. federal regulation had to be based on a scientific risk assessment. Nonetheless, as we discuss in greater detail below, precaution is often invoked in recent U.S. law; for example, starting in 1999, the U.S. Food and Drug Administration (FDA) adopted explicitly "precautionary measures" to shield the U.S. blood supply from "mad cow disease"—bovine spongiform encephalopathy (BSE) and variant Creutzfeldt-Jakob disease (vCJD). Likewise, the U.S. Environmental Protection Agency (EPA) routinely labels its new and more stringent ambient air quality standards "precautionary." At the local level, the city of San Francisco adopted a version of the PP in 2003. Thus, while the United States has not officially adopted the PP as a general basis for regulation, precaution has been adopted in numerous specific U.S. laws (Applegate 2000; Whiteside 2006). And in 1999, Canada incorporated the PP in its revised Canadian Environmental Protection Act.

In international environmental law, the PP has been adopted in over 50 multilateral instruments, including several treaties on marine pollution adopted in the early 1980s, the Montreal Protocol on Substances That Deplete the Ozone Layer (1987), the Rio Declaration (1992, paragraph 15), the UN Framework Convention on Climate Change (UNFCCC) (1992), the Convention on Biological Diversity (1992), the Cartagena Protocol on Biosafety (2000), and the Stockholm Convention on Persistent Organic Pollutants (2002). Some scholars point to even earlier international environmental treaties that employed the logic, if not the terminology, of precaution, such as the Convention on the Prevention of Marine Pollution by Dumping of Wastes and Other Matter (London Convention) (1972) and the Convention on International Trade in Endangered Species of Wild Fauna and Flora (CITES) (1973), as well as the OECD Declaration of Anticipatory Environmental Policies (1979). For more detailed reviews of the PP in international agreements, see Trouwborst 2002, and de Sadeleer 2002.

The United States joined almost all of these treaties, but not, notably, the 1997 Kyoto Protocol on climate change nor the 2000 Cartagena Protocol on Biosafety. And disputes in the World Trade Organization (WTO) over precautionary restrictions on beef hormones, asbestos, and genetically modified foods—often brought by the United States against European precautionary restrictions—have raised the question whether international trade law, particularly the Agreement on the Application of Sanitary and Phytosanitary (SPS) Measures, precludes the precautionary principle by requiring regulation to be based on risk assessment (Alemanno 2007; Ansell and Vogel 2006). (Meanwhile, as discussed below, the European Commission's Communication on the PP, issued in February 2000, calls for risk assessment as part of the PP.)

Some have asserted that the PP may now be so widely adopted that it is ripening into an enforceable norm of customary international law (Sands 1995; Cameron and Abouchar 1996; McIntyre and Mosedale 1997). That could mean that the PP would be binding even on states that have not consented to it explicitly. However, others have argued that state practice on precaution is so diverse and inconsistent, and the formulations of the PP so varied, that no clear and binding norm of customary international law can yet be discerned (Wiener and Rogers 2002, 343; Marchant and Mossman 2004). U.S. courts have so far rejected claims that the PP or international environmental norms constitute enforceable customary international law, in *Beanal v. Freeport-McMoran, Inc.*, 197 F.3d 161, 167 (5th Cir. 1999), and *Flores v. Southern Peru Copper Co.*, 343 F.3d 140, 158–161 (2d Cir. 2003). And European courts have been adjudicating the PP under European law, not as a norm of customary international law (de Sadeleer 2009). The role of precaution and risk management in international law remains contested and awkward (Uruena 2008).

At the UN Earth Summit in 1992, the Rio Declaration (paragraph 15) adopted what has become a widely cited version of the PP:

> In order to protect the environment, the precautionary approach shall be widely applied by States according to their capabilities. Where there are threats of serious or irreversible damage, lack of full scientific certainty shall not be used as a reason for postponing cost-effective measures to prevent environmental degradation.

In Europe, the march of precaution continued. In its landmark Maastricht Treaty in 1992, the EU expressly provided that EU policy on the environment "shall be based on the precautionary principle" (Article 130R, then renumbered Article 174 of the 2000 Nice Treaty, and then Article 191 of the 2009 Lisbon Treaty on the Functioning of the EU). These treaties have "constitutional status" in EU law (Christoforou 2004, 40). But the article adopting the PP does not define the PP. And the very next subsection of that same article contains an instruction to consider "benefits and costs." In February 2000, the European Commission elaborated its interpretation of the PP in an important statement, giving detail and criteria to the PP, including the exhortations to consider benefits and costs and to keep precautions provisional as research continues (European Commission 2000); the Council of the EU agreed with this communication in December 2000. In 2002, the European Environment Agency published a major study advocating the PP as a corrective to the experience of past warnings not adequately heeded (Harremoes et al. 2002). European application of the PP, upheld by European courts, has extended its reach to public health and food safety as well as the environment (de Sadeleer 2002, 2009).

EU Member States have also adopted the PP. For example, in 2004 and 2006, Italy adopted major laws incorporating the PP (Butti 2007, 23–29). And in February 2005, France adopted the PP as part of its Charter on the Environment (Article 5) and in its national Constitution:

> *Lorsque la réalisation d'un dommage, bien qu'incertaine en l'état des connaissances scientifiques, pourrait affecter de manière grave et irréversible l'environnement, les autorités publiques veillent, par application du principe de précaution et dans leurs*

domaines d'attributions, à la mise en oeuvre de procédures d'évaluation des risques et à l'adoption de mesures provisoires et proportionnées afin de parer à la réalisation du dommage.[1]

It is worth noting that the French version, after invoking the premise of a serious and irreversible risk that is scientifically uncertain, calls for "evaluation procedures" as well as for measures to prevent the adverse impact, and provides that the preventive measures should be "provisional and proportionate." For further discussion of the French version of the PP, see Godard 2006.

The march of precaution in official legal texts has thus been widespread, but not uniform. In short, from the 1970s through the 1980s, both the United States and Europe adopted precaution in particular laws, and then in international agreements. In the 1990s, Europe—at both the level of the EU and in key Member States—then adopted the PP as its formal overarching basis for risk regulation, while the United States did not.

Flip-flop: Has Europe Become More Precautionary Than the United States?

Given this history, a leading contemporary view is that the United States was "more precautionary" than Europe in the 1970s, but that since about 1990 the positions have reversed—a "flip-flop." This view holds that, in general, Europe now endorses the PP and seeks proactively to regulate risks, while the United States opposes the PP and waits more circumspectly for evidence of actual harm before regulating (Lofstedt and Vogel 2001; Vogel 2003; Vogel, forthcoming).

The merit of the flip-flop or reversal claim is a central question of this book. It should immediately be recognized that this flip-flop account is itself at odds with the stereotypes noted above of fixed and conflicting American and European cultures regarding risk and precaution. The reversal account is also at odds with theories of persisting contrasts based on the origins of countries' legal systems (such as common law and civil law) (La Porta et al. 2008). If the degree of precaution in risk regulation were dictated by those (alleged) cultures of risk-taking and risk aversion, or legal origins, then the United States should not have been more precautionary than Europe in the 1970s. It seems clear that the fixed cultural accounts, like most stereotypes, are brittle and incomplete. Nor do early legal origins explain modern administrative regulation. The flip-flop account at least goes one large step better by recognizing the ebbs and flows of modern politics.

---

[1] As with any legal text, its interpretation and translation may be a close question. The French charter might be translated as follows: "When the occurrence of damages, even if scientific understanding is uncertain, could seriously and irreversibly affect the environment, public authorities oversee, by the application of the precautionary principle in their respective domains, the implementation of procedures to evaluate the risk and the adoption of provisional and proportionate measures in order to guard against the occurrence of the damages."

Nevertheless, as we discuss below and throughout this book, we find scant evidence for either the fixed cultural view or the flip-flop view. Both envision the body of risk regulation as a coherent entity moving roughly in sync within a bloc on each side of the Atlantic. We find that the reality of precaution is a much more complex pattern of overall parity, combined with detailed variation on particular risks. But because the view of a wholesale shift toward greater European precaution is so widespread and influential, and because it forms the main hypothesis that we test in our research, we present several accounts of this shift here.

Claims of a broad reversal in U.S. and EU precaution are legion and remarkably bold. In the mid-1980s, several comparative studies had found different procedural approaches but similar degrees of regulatory stringency in U.S. and European risk regulation (Brickman et al. 1985; Jasanoff 1986; Vogel 1986). By the 1990s, this view was being displaced by the reversal or flip-flop hypothesis, as European officials staked their claim to overtaking the United States. As early as 1992, a senior environmental official of the European Commission said that the United States "was definitely leading European policy back in the 1970s and early 1980s," but now "Europe has certainly managed to catch up" and on some issues Europe "has taken over the role as world leader" (Henningsen 1992, 25–26). In 1999, the trade commissioner of the European Union, Pascal Lamy (now head of the WTO), announced the sweeping assertion that "in the United States they believe that if no risks have been proven about a product, it should be allowed. In the EU it is believed something should not be authorized if there is a chance of risk" (quoted in Charnovitz 2000, 295 n. 181). (Note that this claim applies to all risks, contrasts two monolithic regional beliefs, and juxtaposes the term "proven"—a conclusory standard that no *ex ante* risk regulation ever truly requires—with "a chance of risk," a ubiquity that would require banning everything.) In 2004, a top trade and environment lawyer for the European Commission, Theofanis Christoforou, championed the flip-flop account: he wrote that in the 1970s, "regulation of risk on the basis of precaution in the United States was more rigorously applied" than in Europe, but by the 1990s, "the European Community accomplished tremendous progress in regulating risk to health and the environment and nearly closed the gap with the United States," and since the 1990s, "more stringent regulation of risk on the basis of precaution has become greater in the European Community than in the United States" (Christoforou 2004, 17). (Note his coupling of stringency and precaution.) Christoforou acknowledged that "precaution has long been well embedded in the regulation of risk in the United States," but argued that the PP does not have the "constitutional status" as a "binding" principle in the United States that it does in the EU. He attributed what he saw as the "current divergence in the regulatory approach of the two green giants" to "Europeans' desire to achieve and maintain a high level of health and environmental protection" and "Americans' greater reliance on economic cost-benefit and market-oriented values" (Christoforou 2004, 41). At the same time, his colleague in the European Commission's environment directorate, Ludwig Krämer, argued that Europe has a "stronger commitment … to environmental concerns than the United States" (Krämer 2004, 67), whereas the

United States in his view emphasizes economics and trade to such a degree that "Europeans [get] the impression that [in the United States] environmental policy is considered a fad, without much consequence for things that really matter in society. Notions of 'prevention' and 'precaution' ... do not seem to play an important role in current American political debate" (Krämer 2004, 70).

It is not only European officials who have proclaimed such wholesale assertions of transatlantic discord. The news media have echoed this view. The front page of the *New York Times* reported in 2000 that "More and More, Europeans Find Fault with US: Wide Range of Events Viewed as Menacing," asserting that Europeans feared the United States as violent, profit-driven, heartless, and imperialist (Daley 2000). Likewise, T.R. Reid wrote on the front page of the *Washington Post* in 2001:

> Americans seem to be pragmatic about new ideas and inventions. Europeans tend to worry. That leads to this concept of being always on the safe side—being against anything new until it is absolutely proven. It seems strange that this aversion to the new should break out in Europe, which gave the world the industrial revolution, quantum physics and modern genetics. Europe is the home of the Nobel Prize, the million-dollar award that celebrates scientific advances. Europeans cloned Dolly the sheep. They invented Viagra. The continent remains a formidable force in global technology. The world's fastest (the Concorde) and biggest (the forthcoming 550-seat Airbus A380) commercial jetliners are European products. Finland's Nokia and Sweden's Ericsson dominate global cellular phone markets, having passed the U.S. leader, Motorola, two years ago. And yet a pervasive technophobia throbs like background music beneath the rhythms of everyday life here, fueled by skeptical media, the political success of environmentally minded Green parties and a growing regulatory apparatus at European Union headquarters in Brussels. (Reid 2001)

Views like those just quoted on European precaution versus American risk tolerance were uttered both before and after the terrorist attacks of September 11, 2001. Daalder (2001) had already written of the prospect of a transatlantic "divorce" before those attacks. Even if those attacks temporarily brought the U.S. and Europe to rally closer together, the George W. Bush administration's 2003 invasion of Iraq (over objections by some European allies) appeared to widen the transatlantic divide (Ash 2003). Of course, enmity between the transatlantic allies, which ebbs and flows (Kohut and Stokes 2006), is neither new (Servan-Schreiber 1967) nor very deep-seated (Markovits 2007). In 2003, a *New York Times* analysis was headlined, "Precaution Is for Europeans"—although it concluded that the Bush administration's invasion of Iraq to prevent the uncertain risk of weapons of mass destruction amounted to "precaution, American-style" (Loewenberg 2003). (For more on precaution in counterterrorism policy, see Chapter 12).

The Nation took a similar view, observing a rising tide of European regulation of health risks based on the precautionary principle (Schapiro 2004). Even more moderate or conservative news outlets joined the chorus. *The Economist* magazine appeared to adopt—or at least observe—the simple culture conflict line when it posited in 2004 that "Europe is considered fairly risk-averse … America, on the other hand, is often seen as having a strong risk-taking culture." (*The Economist*'s use of the passive voice left unstated by whom these cultural predispositions are "considered" and "often seen." And as already noted, such characterizations of fixed cultures are at odds with the flip-flop claim.) Its longer statement, however, was a bit more nuanced:

> Over the past 20 years, the number of government regulations aimed at improving safety in both Europe and America has soared. … Tastes in risk vary across countries. Europe is considered fairly risk-averse, and has recently been fretting about greenhouse gases and genetically modified food. But even within Europe, says Ragnar Lofstedt, of the King's Centre for Risk Management in London, attitudes vary widely. Swedes are concerned about dangerous chemicals, and Danes worry a lot about Sweden's nuclear power stations. Italians, although addicted to their mobile phones, are bothered about radiation. America, on the other hand, is often seen as having a strong risk-taking culture, despite the draconian measures it has taken to snuff out smoking. (*Economist* 2004)

In 2005, the *Los Angeles Times* ran an extensive story on this debate, focusing on chemicals regulation but frequently encompassing all pollution or risk policies. The newspaper emphasized what it saw as a transatlantic reversal in regulatory initiative:

> Europe is setting environmental standards for international commerce. … Years ago, when rivers oozed poisons, eagle chicks were dying from DDT in their eggs and aerosol sprays were eating a hole in the Earth's ozone layer, the United States was the world's trailblazer when it came to regulating toxic substances. Regardless of whether Republicans or Democrats controlled the White House, the United States was the acknowledged global pioneer of tough new laws that aimed to safeguard the public from chemicals considered risky. Today, the United States is no longer the vanguard. Instead, the planet's most stringent chemical policies, with far-reaching impacts on global trade, are often born in Stockholm and codified in Brussels. "In the environment, generally, we were the ones who were always out in front," said Kal Raustiala, a professor of international law at UCLA. "Now we have tended to back off while the Europeans have become more aggressive regulators." (Cone 2005)

The article continued, highlighting the PP and exploring the political shifts behind its rise:

> Driving EU policy is a "better safe than sorry" philosophy called the precautionary principle. Following that guideline, which is codified into EU law, European regulators have taken action against chemicals even when their dangers remain largely uncertain. Across the Atlantic, by contrast, U.S. regulators are reluctant to move against a product already in use unless a clear danger can be shown. … In the 1970s and '80s, all the major chemical and pollution laws in the United States had a precautionary slant, said Frank Ackerman, an economist at Tufts University's Global Development and Environment Institute. Lengthy reviews of chemicals, which now dominate U.S. policy, began to evolve under President

Reagan and grew in the 1990s. Carl Cranor, an environmental philosophy professor at UC Riverside, said that a conservative groundswell in American politics and a backlash by industries set off "an ideological sea change." Part of the change stems from the much more vocal role of U.S. companies in battling chemical regulations, said Sheila Jasanoff, a professor of science and technology studies at Harvard University's John F. Kennedy School of Government. American attitudes toward averting environmental risks haven't changed since the 1970s, Jasanoff said. "What has changed is politics and political culture," she said. (Cone 2005)

But the *L.A. Times* article concluded on a more evenhanded note, recognizing the diversity of risks and offering some counterexamples:

It is ironic, says Richard Jensen, chairman of the University of Notre Dame's economics department, that Europeans "who embrace the precautionary principle should have such a high tolerance for risk from smoking and secondhand smoke." Americans are more fearful of cigarettes, nuclear power and car exhaust—and it shows in their laws. They also pasteurize foods to kill bacteria, while European children grow up drinking and eating raw milk and cheese. Said UCLA's Raustiala, "The United States is quite schizophrenic, as are Europeans, about when we decide" to be cautious. (Cone 2005)

In this book we examine just such a contest, not between the United States and Europe, but between claims of a general transatlantic shift or reversal, versus more detailed inquiries into the particular and varied choices about specific risks made on both sides. Further, we study a phenomenon essentially ignored by all of these claims of transatlantic divides, shifts, and reversals: the interconnected exchange or hybridization of ideas about risk and regulation between the United States and Europe.

In addition to those quoted in the news media accounts just cited, other scholars have also argued that Europe is now more precautionary, more regulatory, more environmentalist, and more risk-averse than the United States. Some speak in general cultural terms: Kempton and Craig (1993) maintained that Europeans are more concerned than are Americans about environmental impacts on future generations and on developing countries; thus, they said, Europeans are more likely to invoke caution regarding unforeseen risks, while Americans are more concerned about the economic costs of regulation and more optimistic about future technological solutions to environmental problems. Levy and Newell (2000, 10) called it the "conventional wisdom" that "Europeans demonstrate their considerable concern about environmental issues" while "people in the United States are more individualistic, more concerned about their lifestyles than about the environment, and more ideologically averse to regulation." Sunstein (2005, 13) reported that "it has become standard to say that with respect to risks, Europe and the United States can be distinguished along a single axis: Europe accepts the Precautionary Principle, and the United States does not." Wiener and Rogers (2002, 318) likewise characterized the view of greater European precaution since the 1990s as the "conventional wisdom," though they did so as the prelude to their rebuttal.

David Vogel has offered the most thorough articulation of what Lofstedt and Vogel (2001) called the "flip-flop" account (see Vogel 2001, 2002, 2003, and forthcoming). In his view, "[F]rom the 1960s through the mid 1980s, the regulation of health, safety, and environmental risks was generally stricter in the United States than Europe. Since the mid 1980s, the obverse has often been the case" (2001, 1). He emphasizes that these trends "have not produced policy convergence. On the contrary, European and American regulatory policies are now as divergent as they were three decades ago. What has changed is the direction of this divergence. In a number of areas, Europe has become more risk-averse, America less so" (2001, 31). In a new book, Vogel (forthcoming) undertakes four broad case studies—on food safety, air pollution, chemicals, and pharmaceuticals—to argue that since about 1990, the overall trend of regulatory precaution has shifted from the United States to Europe.

Similarly, focusing on chemicals regulation, Selin and VanDeveer (2006, 14) have argued that "[w]hereas U.S. chemical policy in the 1970s and the early 1980s often acted as an inspiration for European policymaking, the EU has taken over the role as leader in chemical policy development. The EU is increasingly replacing the United States as the de facto setter of global product standards and the center of much global regulatory standard setting is shifting from Washington, DC, to Brussels." (On the other hand, Sand (2000) finds variation in precaution within Europe, as does Zander (2010), who finds Sweden to be more precautionary about chemicals than the UK, while the UK is more precautionary about cell phone transmission systems than is Sweden.)

The transatlantic reversal in precaution is also alleged in U.S. and European enthusiasm for international regimes. In a recent paper titled "Trading Places," Kelemen and Vogel argue "that with respect to international environmental politics, a dramatic and systemic shift from U.S. to EU leadership has occurred since the early 1990s" (2010, 431). They explain:

> When environmental issues emerged on the international agenda in the late 1960s and early 1970s, the United States was of one of the strongest and most consistent supporters. ... The member states of the European Union subsequently ratified the international treaties created in this period, but U.S. leadership was crucial and European states were reluctant participants in many cases. Again in the 1980s, the United States played a leading role in the negotiations that led to the 1987 Montreal Protocol on Substances That Deplete the Ozone Layer, whereas EU member states (in particular the United Kingdom, France, and Italy) were reluctant supporters of this important international treaty.
>
> More recently, the political dynamics of international environmental policy have shifted. ... [D]uring the past two decades, the European Union has emerged as the strongest proponent of the expansion of international environmental law. The European Union has led efforts to "green" international trade institutions such as the World Trade Organization (WTO) and *to win worldwide acceptance for a "precautionary" approach to environmental regulation, whereas the United States has largely resisted these initiatives.* (Kelemen and Vogel 2010, 428; citations omitted; emphasis added)

Kelemen and Vogel sum up: "the European Union replaced the United States as the international environmental leader" (2010, 428), "[s]ince around 1990, the United States and European Union have traded places" (432), and "during the 1980s and early 1990s ... the US surrendered leadership on international environmental policy to the European Union" (434).

Kelemen and Vogel emphasize the reversal in international approaches, but they attribute this shift at the international level to a change in domestic politics within the United States and Europe, in which the influence of green parties and interests grew in Europe and declined in the United States over the period (437–444). Meanwhile, they argue that there was a change in the competitive effects of international treaties, which they contend had benefited U.S. business interests in the early years by extending strong U.S. domestic restrictions to apply to competitors internationally, but disadvantaged those interests in later years when U.S. businesses faced fewer prospects of strong new domestic restrictions (444–450). Thus, their account of an international reversal depends on a domestic policy reversal. "The shifting EU and U.S. positions on the international stage have their roots in dramatic changes in domestic environmental politics. ... Although U.S. domestic politics had stimulated ambitious environmental initiatives in the 1970s and 1980s, the development of major new domestic initiatives slowed significantly after 1990. By contrast, in the European Union domestic support for environmental policy increased in the 1990s, and the European Union's growing regulatory competence stimulated further advances in 'domestic' environmental policies" (444).

The story of the international extension of domestic regulatory politics told by Kelemen and Vogel tracks the "Baptists and Bootleggers" hypothesis, which holds that regulation often or even always results from an odd coalition: activists seeking public benefits who ally with businesses seeking private benefits by raising rivals' costs (Yandle 1989; see also Wiener 1999; Wiener and Richman 2010). Kelemen and Vogel rely for this view on Yandle and Buck (2002), which applies the Baptists and Bootleggers hypothesis to climate change policy. And Kelemen and Vogel point out that, although rising wealth and post-material values may explain greater support for environmental law in general (see Scruggs 2003; Esty and Porter 2005), this factor does not help distinguish the United States from Europe, because both are quite wealthy, and indeed wealth in the United States grew faster than in much of Europe during the 1980s and 1990s (Kelemen and Vogel 2010, 432–444). Thus, they urge, changing domestic regulatory politics, not aggregate wealth, better accounts for the flip-flop in environmental policy that they perceive. But Kelemen and Vogel do not explain the "Baptists" side of the domestic arena—why the underlying public attitudes shifted as they did—that is, why, as they assert, the American public became less interested in environmental protection in the 1990s at the same time that the European public kept wanting more (or why Europeans' demand for environmental law ramped up after Americans' had in the 1970s). They propose that in the 1990s, Americans became satisfied with past success at enacting stringent environmental measures adopted when the United States was "ahead" of Europe (though Lazarus 2004 emphasizes political polarization and gridlock), while Europeans still sought greater protection—perhaps to make up for their comparatively weaker standards in the past—and hence urged on both EU officials seeking to expand their regulatory power and proactive Member States seeking to impose equal standards on laggard Member States within the EU (Kelemen and Vogel 2010, 440–444). If so, this suggests that we might reach an equilibrium in which both American and European publics become satisfied at roughly equal levels—an equilibrium in which the rivalry over who is "more precautionary" becomes moot, or at least more moderate.

On the other hand, Kelemen and Vogel's institutional account could have pointed in the opposite direction. It seems equally plausible that the growing regulatory authority of the EU could have been deployed to restrain or preempt regulation by the Member States in order to protect the Single European Market (as the European Commission has indeed sought to do in several cases, notably the case of mad cow disease). And competition among the EU Member States to avoid uneven regulatory burdens could have produced pressure to relax standards (harmonizing downward rather than upward, or a race to the bottom).

Meanwhile, the contention that U.S. risk regulation significantly slowed after 1990 is substantially rebutted if not belied by the numerous significant regulatory measures adopted since then to address diverse risks. These and other cases are the subjects of several chapters in this book. They include U.S. policies to limit air pollution from both stationary and mobile sources, notably the acid rain regime adopted in 1990 and implemented by EPA beginning in 1995, the increasingly stringent restrictions on ozone and fine particulate matter from electric power plants and factories promulgated by EPA in 1997, 2005, and 2010, and from diesel engines promulgated by EPA in 1994, 1998, 2001, 2004, and 2008; the major drinking water pollution and food safety laws enacted in 1996; the relatively more stringent U.S. restrictions on nuclear power over the last three decades; increasingly stringent U.S. regulation of smoking in public places, as well as increasing state and federal taxes on cigarettes, and the landmark Family Smoking Prevention and Tobacco Control Act of 2009; the FDA's explicitly "precautionary" measures to prevent mad cow disease in the blood supply promulgated in 1999 and 2001; additional policies to protect biodiversity on land; the reauthorization of the major fisheries law in 2006; and the dramatic and historic expansion in the regulation of homeland security risks (to humans, property, and the environment) enacted in the years after September 11, 2001.[2] In terms of the seriousness of risk (a key predicate of most formulations of the precautionary principle), several of the most severe risks have been addressed by rising and greater U.S. (relative to EU) regulatory stringency since about 1990. For example, smoking

---

[2] Not to mention increasing U.S. financial risk regulation, such as the Sarbanes-Oxley law in 2002 and the further extensive financial regulations adopted after the severe 2008 recession, including the Dodd-Frank Act of 2010. In this book, we address a wide array of risks to human health, safety, environment, and security, but we do not address financial risks—a topic for further inquiry. Vogel (2001, 2003, and forthcoming) focuses on risks to environment and food safety, but says he is mainly interested in the politics of the regulation of business; if so, that ought to include tobacco, homeland security, and financial risk regulation.

tobacco arguably poses the largest public health burden of any of the risks considered here, killing several hundred thousand people each year in America and in Europe.[3] Particulate matter air pollution is not far behind, with about "350,000 premature deaths per year" in the 27 EU Member States (Kobe and Varenne 2010, 30) and about 25,000 to 50,000 such deaths per year in the United States (Mokdad et al. 2004). Terrorism with nuclear or biological weapons of mass destruction is viewed by many experts as a looming existential threat. On all three of these major risks, U.S. policies have been growing more precautionary than EU policies over the past two decades (though with significant complexity and variation, as described in our case study chapters on each of these risks). Yet Vogel (2001, 2003, and forthcoming) makes his claim of a reversal in relative precaution without addressing tobacco or homeland security, and treats particulate matter air pollution as just an exception. To be sure, other very serious risks, such as climate change (and chemicals and GM foods, depending on how serious one thinks they are), have been addressed by more precautionary policies in the EU than in the United States over the last two decades. The point here is simply that strong claims of a reversal in relative precaution and a slowdown or halt to U.S. regulation since 1990 are not supported by the evidence.

The degree of precaution can be distinguished from the style of regulatory decisionmaking. In earlier work, Vogel (1986) had emphasized contrasting "national styles" of regulation in the United States and Europe, but had found that these styles could yield comparable stringency. More recently, in Vogel (forthcoming), he finds U.S. and European regulatory systems to be less fixed by national styles and cultures and more open to change, as reflected in his account of shifting relative transatlantic precaution from the 1970s to the post-1990 period. And he dubs this shift "Trading Places" (Kelemen and Vogel 2010) and "Ships Passing in the Night" (Vogel 2001), metaphors that evoke the image of separate unconnected entities moving independently of one another—whereas we see increasingly interconnected systems exchanging ideas (see Wiener 2003, 2006; Chapter 20, this volume). Sheila Jasanoff had also emphasized the differences in procedure in the United States and Europe in the 1970s and 1980s, with American legal systems employing a greater degree of formal quantitative methods subject to public transparency and challenge, whereas European legal systems employed more informal, qualitative, consensus-building approaches; still, she found that the two styles could result in comparable stringency (Jasanoff 1986, 1998). Other scholars also found divergent styles of regulation across the Atlantic, with a more legalistic,

---

[3] The U.S. Centers for Disease Control website says that "[t]obacco use is the single most preventable cause of disease, disability, and death in the United States. Each year, an estimated 443,000 people die prematurely from smoking or exposure to secondhand smoke" (www.cdc.gov/chronicdisease/resources/publications/aag/osh.htm, accessed June 18, 2010); similarly, the European Commission website says that "[t]obacco is the single largest cause of avoidable death in the European Union accounting for over half a million deaths each year and over a million deaths in Europe as a whole. It is estimated that 25% of all cancer deaths and 15% of all deaths in the Union could be attributed to smoking" (http://ec.europa.eu/health/ph_determinants/life_style/Tobacco/tobacco_en.htm, accessed June 18, 2010).

formal, and adversarial approach on the American side (Rose-Ackerman 1995; Kagan and Axelrad 2000; Jasanoff 2005, 18; Kagan 2007). At the same time, though, the U.S. economy is often said to be more dynamic than the European economy, especially in starting new businesses and in labor markets (see the controversial World Bank "Doing Business" reports, available at www.doingbusiness.org; Kagan and Axelrad 2000, 25, 405; Kagan 2007, 101–102 and n. 5). These perspectives seem to cut against the view that American adversarial legalism is a major constraint on flexibility and initiative.

In recent work on biotechnology policy, Jasanoff (2005) also describes a reversal in positions after the 1980s that gave rise to a "distinctive European policy orientation" favoring greater precaution. In the 1970s and 1980s, she says, Americans were more risk-averse about food safety than were Europeans, citing "the American public's 'irrational' fear of chemicals such as the plant growth regulator Alar. Europeans at that time had seemed more complacent about risks related to food. How then did the shoe come to be on the other foot? ... [C]oncern about the safety and integrity of the food supply is not the prerogative of any single nation ..." (Jasanoff 2005, 120). By the 1990s, she writes, the situation had reversed:

> [T]he groundwork had been laid [in Europe] for a more precautionary, socially oriented biotechnology policy than that obtaining on the other side of the Atlantic. Later changes in the EU's founding treaties only strengthened the commitment to precaution in regulatory matters; by the turn of the century, this term stood for a distinctively European policy orientation, much as risk and sound science correspondingly did for US policy. (92–93)

By contrast, she sees the United States as turning away from precautionary regulation in the 1990s:

> A preference for market solutions as an alternative to state control grew during the 1980s. ... With the downfall of communism ... the ideology of the market gained additional political force. Promarket and antiregulatory tendencies manifested themselves across the entire range of governmental action, or more accurately inaction, on biotechnology. ... At the same time, a chronic aversion toward incurring opportunity costs, [was] expressed through a laissez-faire policy toward private initiative and risk-taking ... [this] both reflected and reinforced America's historical record of seeing technology as an instrument of progress ... (275–276)

Jasanoff is careful to point out that static characterizations of culture cannot be sustained: "terms like 'European' and 'American' are far more fluid and contested than is presumed by monolithic accounts of culture" (9–10), and to say that comparative study needs to employ a "dynamic concept of political culture" (15).

At the same time, however, Jasanoff observes that in another area of biotechnology policy—the regulation of embryonic stem cell research—the shift in relative transatlantic precaution has moved in the *opposite direction*: since the 1990s, Europeans have been more accepting of this new technology, while America has been more precautionary in restricting it (9). Overall, she contends, "Over the past thirty years, for example, industrial nations have often converged on which health, safety, and environmental problems merit legislative or regulatory attention, but there is much less uniformity in how the issues are characterized and which solutions are deemed most suitable for resolving perceived problems" (20). Thus, while making strong claims about a flip-flop in precaution regarding GM foods, she recognizes a more diverse pattern when a broader array of risks is considered.

The publications cited so far are largely based on case studies. Other work has looked at aggregate data, and found mixed results. Scruggs (1999, 2001, 2003) studied six pollution indicators—sulfur dioxide emissions, nitrogen oxide emissions, per capita municipal waste production, fertilizer use, recycling rates, and the percentage of the population connected to wastewater treatment facilities—in 17 OECD member countries during 1970–1995. He found that "neo-corporatist" systems experience better environmental outcomes than more pluralist systems, after controlling for income and manufacturing intensity. (Meanwhile, Europe and America have been borrowing each other's styles of regulation, with Europe becoming less neo-corporatist and more pluralist/adversarial over time, and the United States adopting more collaborative processes; see Wiener 2003, Kagan 2007.) Esty and Porter (2005) found that environmental performance—measured by levels of particulate matter (PM) and sulfur dioxide (SO_2) air pollution, and energy efficiency—generally improves with higher income; however, among countries of similar income, some perform better and have stronger environmental regulatory regimes than others. Among wealthy countries, Esty and Porter found that the United States performs worse (2005, 404–406, Tables 2–4) and has a weaker environmental regulatory regime (419, Table 9) than other wealthy countries. Their ranking, though, does not divide neatly between the United States and Europe: while Finland, Sweden, the Netherlands, France, Germany, Austria, and the UK rank above the median index value of environmental regulatory regime strength for wealthy countries, the United States, Ireland, Norway, Italy, Belgium, Japan, Australia, and Canada rank below the median. Esty and Porter (2005) only studied environmental quality (not other risks), and only studied three environmental indicators. Scruggs (2009) and Whitford and Wong (2009) found weak or no evidence that democracy (as opposed to prosperity) affects environmental outcomes.

The flip-flop account draws some support from the changing institutional structure over the past five decades. Several major federal laws and regulatory bodies in the United States were created in the 1970s, including the laws on clean air, clean water, pesticides, toxic substances, and endangered species, as well as the Environmental Protection Agency and the Occupational Safety and Health Administration (although the Food and Drug Administration was created in the early 1900s and the Department of Homeland Security after 2000). By contrast, the European Union's authority over risk regulation grew markedly after the Single European Act of 1987 and the Maastricht Treaty of 1992 (Krämer 2004; Kelemen and Vogel 2010). Thus, the creation of new authority and agencies at different times in the United States and EU might correspond to the growth in precaution at different times. Jasanoff's thesis is that governance institutions are not exogenous but are "coproduced" along with a society's understanding of science, nature, and democracy (2005, 19); she argues that the idea of Europe was evolving during this period, constructing the EU, and being coproduced through debates over biotechnology policy, so that the degree of precaution in EU biotechnology policy is intertwined with the simultaneous construction of EU institutions (65–69).

Along similar lines, Jordana et al. (2008) surveyed 48 countries in the OECD and Latin America from 1920 to 2007 and found that the addition of new regulatory agencies accelerated significantly in the 1980s and 1990s. In their estimation, this evidence supports a hypothesis of global diffusion of Weberian bureaucracy during this period (Jordana et al. 2008; Levi-Faur 2005). Especially relevant to the present discussion, Jordana et al. found that in most European countries, more than half of all regulatory agencies were created after 1989, whereas in the United States and Canada, almost all the regulatory agencies were already created before 1989 (2008, 38, Figure 4). Of course, this indicates the creation of new agencies, not the adoption of new regulations, nor the topic of these regulations, nor the degree of precaution embodied in them. (The survey by Jordana et al. covers all topics, including financial, competition, and other forms of economic regulation.) Existing agencies can also issue new regulations that are precautionary, and new agencies can issue regulations that are not precautionary.

The fact that EU institutions were gaining power since about 1990 does not necessarily mean that they would use that power to adopt more precautionary regulation; it is also plausible that EU institutions would use such power to *restrict* Member States' exercise of precaution where a patchwork of precaution would impede the free flow of goods and services in the Single European Market (as the European Commission sought to do in the case of mad cow disease and trade in beef). The power to harmonize does not by itself indicate whether the harmonization will be up or down. Moreover, focusing on the growth of U.S. institutions in the 1970s and of EU institutions since about 1990 could lead to biased sampling and skewed findings about precaution: if one looked only or primarily at new laws and agencies, rather than at actual regulatory policies, one would be more likely to find the flip-flop dynamic in action. Looking at the degree of precaution in actual regulatory policies, however, including those adopted by existing as well as by new institutions, would reveal a more accurate pattern of precaution.

Testing the Reality of Precaution

In the face of the widespread view that Europe has become "more precautionary" than the United States, and the associated debate (often acrimonious) between U.S. and European officials over the normatively desirable degree of precaution in domestic policies and international agreements, we undertook the present research project to test these claims. We had several objectives: improving the methods and accuracy of comparison by opening a wider scope onto a broader landscape of risks; overcoming the impasse in transatlantic debates over precaution as an abstract principle by looking at the reality of precaution as applied in actual policies; and furnishing a better basis for policymaking by illuminating the actual pattern, causal factors, consequences, and impacts of alternative approaches to precaution. To do so, we organized a series of four "Transatlantic Dialogues on Precaution"—two each in the United States and in Europe—and assembled a multidisciplinary team of leading experts to contribute to this book.

Prior Literature and Its Limitations

An extensive literature has been devoted to comparing U.S. and European risk regulation (e.g., Kelman 1981; Rehbinder and Stewart 1985; Brickman et al. 1985; Vogel 1986; Jasanoff 1986; Rose-Ackerman 1995; Baker 1997; Jasanoff 1998; Breyer and Heyvaert 2000; Kagan and Axelrad 2000; Lynch and Vogel 2000; Lofstedt and Vogel 2001; Vogel 2001; Schreurs 2002; Wiener and Rogers 2002; Vogel 2002; Vogel 2003; Bernauer and Meins 2003; Wiener 2003; Vig and Faure 2004; Harrington et al. 2004; Marchant and Mossman 2004; Hammitt et al. 2005; Jasanoff 2005; Wiener 2006; de Sadeleer 2007; Lindseth et al. 2008; Wiener 2008; Pollack and Shaffer 2009; Wiener and Alemanno 2010; Rose-Ackerman and Lindseth 2010; Zander 2010; Vogel, forthcoming).

Our book builds on and goes beyond this comparative literature in several ways. First, we study the degree of precaution in standard setting, rather than comparing choices in federalism (e.g., Rehbinder and Stewart 1985; Kelemen 2004), administrative agency procedure (e.g., Rose-Ackerman 1995; Breyer and Heyvaert 2000; Lindseth et al. 2008), judicial review (e.g., Marchant and Mossman 2004; Lindseth et al. 2008), executive oversight (Wiener 2008; Wiener and Alemanno 2010), or selection of policy instruments such as design standards or economic incentives (Harrington et al. 2004).

Second, we attempt to overcome limitations in the methods used by prior research to select cases and draw overall comparative assessments (see discussion in Wiener 2003). Flawed sample selection methods make broad inferences unsupportable. Many past studies have focused narrowly. Some studies have focused on just one product, such as GM foods (Lynch and Vogel 2000; Bernauer and Meins 2003; Pollack and Shaffer 2009) or biotechnology (Jasanoff 2005); one industrial sector, such as chemicals (Brickman et al. 1985; Selin and VanDeveer 2006); or one setting, such as workplace safety (Kelman 1981) or environmental law (Vig and Faure 2004; Kelemen and Vogel 2010). Studies like these can be highly informative about their focused domain, but they are on weak ground in attempting to draw broad comparative conclusions about overall national regulatory approaches to risks in general. Other studies have assembled cases of regulation of businesses and products (e.g., Kagan and Axelrad 2000; Vogel, forthcoming) but have not addressed the regulation of risks from other sources, such as disease and terrorism. Collections of case studies have typically relied on cases selected by convenience or selected in order to demonstrate particular insights. These methods did not select cases according to an unbiased representative sampling method, and thus they cannot support comparative conclusions about risk regulation overall (King et al. 1994). For example, Kagan and Axelrad (2000, 18) candidly declared: "This volume of case studies, therefore, cannot support unqualified generalizations about any of the national legal systems as a whole or about the across-the-board impact of national styles of law and regulation." Nonetheless, scholars forge ahead, as Kagan (2007, 100) forthrightly observed:

> This is a large topic. Generalizing about entire legal systems, each of which is pervaded by complexity and contradictory features, is a risky business. It is doubly risky when one subject is the USA, with its many different jurisdictions and administrative agencies, and the other subject is the "legal systems of Western European nations," each of which has its own distinctive traditions. The best available "data" on which to base comparisons are socio-legal case studies, which compare specific legal processes in the USA and one or two Western European countries. But these case studies provide an imperfect sample. Some are now 20 years old. Besides, there are not enough of them to provide a reliably representative picture of the entire legal landscape. Nevertheless, this article plunges incautiously ahead, using the readily available scholarly close-ups of particular clumps of trees to venture some wide-angle generalizations about the shape and dynamics of entire legal forests.

The same sample selection problem is well recognized in empirical studies of judicial decisions: published opinions are a visible but nonrepresentative and biased sample of all judicial decisions (Ashenfelter et al. 1995; Siegelman and Donohue 1990), and all judicial decisions are a nonrepresentative sample of all disputes (Priest and Klein 1984). Studying just the visible cases—or, worse still, only the highly celebrated cases—yields a misleading picture of the wider reality.

More empiricism in comparative policy studies would be helpful (Hinich and Munger 1998). Several studies have assembled aggregate data on regulation and environmental performance (e.g., Scruggs 1999, 2001, 2003; Esty and Porter 2005), but these did not study other types of risks to health, safety, and security. Also, they correlated environmental performance only to a general index of the national style of regulation rather than to particular regulatory policies. (Scruggs contrasts two styles—neo-corporatism versus adversarial pluralism; Esty and Porter develop an overall index of national regulatory quality.) A series of studies of aggregate data on business regulations prepared in part for the World Bank's "Doing Business" reports (La Porta et al. 2008) addressed only the rules for starting and managing businesses, not risk regulation.

Third, we attempt to avoid exaggerating transatlantic differences that are small in a global context. As Henri Tajfel (1970) found, group members tend to assert and exaggerate intergroup differences, even when the groups were randomly sorted. Sen (2006) counsels against lumping people into large groups by religion, nationality, or culture, which ignores enormous variations among group members. Perhaps commenters drawing sharp contrasts between U.S. and European regulatory systems are falling into this tendency. It may be a bit like the tendency to exaggerate the difference between New York and Los Angeles—which are more similar to each other than to anything else in between. Or, consider the supposed difference in relative chattiness between men and women. Brizendine (2006) asserted that women use 20,000 words per day while men use only 7,000 per day. Yet other studies (Mehl et al. 2007) find no difference: both use about 16,000 words per day, and variation among individuals within gender is far higher than the difference across genders, as men range from 700 per day to 47,000 per day. Nevertheless, the "chat gap" remains popular because people imbue it with their own normative biases—that women are chatterboxes while men are serious, or that women are more socially connected while men are loners (Goodman 2007). Likewise, the notion of the U.S.-EU precaution gap may persist because people imbue it with their own normative slants—even if it does not actually exist or the reality is far more textured.

Fourth, we look beyond large categorical groupings of legal systems, legal origins, families of law, and national styles of law or regulation. Scholars of comparative law have written at length on the alleged differences between legal systems (e.g., Zweigert and Kötz 1998; Kagan 2007; La Porta et al. 2008). Many of those comparatists take the English Channel, not the Atlantic, as their favorite great divide, drawing stark contrasts between civil law versus common law systems. Interestingly, the strong generalizations quoted above regarding precaution in U.S. and European regulation typically gloss over the civil law/common law divide; in that sense, they already reveal a more contemporary and fluid appreciation of the role of modern political institutions and popular attitudes (rather than civil law or common law origins) in shaping regulatory decisions.

Generalizations about national traits can serve as models that help distill insight from detail, but they can also become stereotypes that mislead. Max Weber's concept of an ideal type was an effort to abstract helpfully from excessive particularistic detail, but he did not assert that real groups or institutions actually instantiated the ideal type; he understood that the ideal type was a model and that details were crucial to accurate comparison. William Blake (1814, in Erdman 1988, 641) overstated the case: "To generalize is to be an idiot. To particularize is the alone distinction of merit." That itself is a hasty generalization. More astute was La Rochefoucauld (1665 [1946]): "*Pour bien savoir les choses, il en faut savoir le détail, et comme il est presque infini, nos connaissances sont toujours superficielles et imparfaites.*" (One must understand the details, but the nearly limitless array of details renders knowledge ever imperfect.) Alexis de Tocqueville generalized "Why the Americans Show More Aptitude and Taste for General Ideas Than Their Forefathers, the English" (1840, Vol. II, Section 1, Chapter 3) and "Why the Americans Have Never Been so Eager as the French for General Ideas in Political Affairs" (Chapter 4)—itself a generalization about each people, thereby showing that he fit his own characterization of the French. Yet on his travels in America, his eye was ever alert to detail.

Can we see both the general and the particular? In Isaiah Berlin's famous image, "There is a line among the fragments of the Greek poet Archilochus that says: 'The fox knows many things, but the hedgehog knows one big thing.' Scholars have differed about the correct interpretation of these dark words, which may mean no more than that the fox, for all his cunning, is defeated by the hedgehog's one defense. But, taken figuratively, the words can be made to yield a sense in which they mark one of the deepest differences which divide writers and thinkers, and, it may be, human beings in general" (Berlin 1953). Berlin was generalizing to a strong contrast between modes of thought and types of thinkers. His remark simultaneously embodies a twist: generalizers themselves, with their one big idea, are hedgehogs, which implies that a fox would view Berlin's contrasting generalization differently. Indeed, Berlin recognized the limits of broad generalizations: "Of course, like all over-simple classifications of this type, the dichotomy becomes, if pressed, artificial, scholastic, and ultimately absurd. But if it is not an aid to serious criticism, neither should it be rejected as being merely superficial or frivolous; like all distinctions which embody any degree of truth, it offers a point of view from which to look and compare, a starting-point for genuine investigation" (1953). A "starting point"—but not a definitive conclusion. It takes more detailed inquiry to test the difference.

The same concepts have been expressed in art. The mind's eye turns to Bruegel: rather than paint a central spiritual or military figure, instead he painted the utter variety and complexity of real life—hunters in the snow, skaters on the ice, children playing games, townspeople going about their business (even as Icarus falls into the sea, or Mary and Joseph arrive in Bethlehem). His paintings offer tributes to the quotidian, to the interconnected details of complex social systems not encapsulated in a simple generalization. The optimal observer sees both the trees and the forest.

The Organization of the Book

This chapter has merely introduced the debate over precaution. It is a debate about rhetoric and rivalry, one that we are trying in this book to overcome, or at least to inform. In Chapters 2 through 14, we present our in-depth case studies of precaution applied to specific risks and information systems (see Table 1.1). In each chapter, we ask: Over the period 1970 to the present, what has been the real pattern of relative precaution regarding this risk, in the United States and Europe? What explains this pattern? What have been the consequences of the observed policies?

Table 1.1 *Outline of the Cases*

Case study	Author(s)	Author home	Category
Genetically modified (GM) foods	Lex and Cantley	EU	Environment, health
Beef hormones and mad cow disease (BSE and vCJD)	Gray, Rogers, and Wiener	U.S. and EU	Health
Smoking tobacco	Blanke	U.S.	Health
Nuclear power	Ahearne and Birkhofer	U.S. and EU	Environment, health
Automobile emissions	Walsh	U.S.	Environment, health
Stratospheric ozone and climate change	Hammitt	U.S.	Environment, health
Marine environment	Freestone	EU	Environment
Biodiversity	Saterson	U.S.	Environment
Chemicals	Renn and Elliott	EU and U.S.	Environment, health
Medical care, new drugs, and patient safety	Miller	U.S.	Health, safety
Terrorism	Stern and Wiener	U.S.	Safety, security
Information disclosure	Sand	EU	All
Risk assessment methods	Rogers and Charnley	EU and U.S.	All

In Chapter 15, we present our quantitative analysis of a broad dataset. Here we conduct a broad quantitative analysis of relative precaution in a sample of 100 risks drawn from a dataset of nearly 3,000 risks over the period 1970 to the present. This inquiry is much broader than our case studies—and than the case studies selected by other researchers—and hence more representative of the full universe of risks, enabling us to draw findings that are more generalizable. But it is also less deep, as it focuses on the terms of enacted and adopted regulatory standards without looking into their implementation in practice (as the case studies do).

Neither the case study approach nor the large dataset approach is fully informative. But they may benefit from each other (see Blomquist 2007; Levi-Faur 2004; Lieberman 2005). Our combination of both an array of in-depth case studies addressing diverse risks, and a broad quantitative analysis of hundreds of risks, taken together, offers a better understanding of the reality of precaution than either approach taken alone.

To briefly preview our findings, our case studies and our quantitative analysis both indicate that, over the broad array of risks, neither the United States nor Europe can claim to be "more precautionary" across the board. The reality of precaution has not been principle, it has been *parity and particularity*. In the aggregate, we find little overall transatlantic difference over the past several decades. As to particular risks, Europe has been more precautionary than the United States about some risks, but the United States has been more precautionary about other risks. There is great diversity across risks and across policy domains on both sides of the Atlantic. This variation in precaution across risks has been true in recent years as well as in earlier decades. There is also considerable variation within each polity, both among the states of the United States and among the Member States of the European Union.

Then, Chapters 16 through 19 examine potential explanations for the observed pattern of relative precaution. We consider whether differences in political systems, legal systems, and perceptions and culture can explain the observed pattern. Because the pattern of precaution that we observe is one of complex diversity across risks and within polities, we find that the traditional comparative frames for contrasting "American" and "European" regulatory approaches are of limited explanatory value. Instead, we need more nuanced explanations that look to factors specific to the risk, context, and institutions involved.

Chapter 20 concludes with a synthesis of our findings on the real pattern of precaution, based on our diverse case studies and our large dataset study. In short, we find a complex pattern of parity and particularity, not a discrete reversal in U.S. and EU precaution. In this chapter, we collect and assess the preceding chapters' insights on the explanations for the observed pattern, and on the consequences of precautionary policies. We elaborate on the interconnected borrowing and hybridization of regulatory ideas across the Atlantic. We then offer recommendations on three major topics: policymaking, comparative research, and transatlantic relations.

References

Alemanno, Alberto. 2007. *Trade in Food: Regulatory and Judicial Approaches in the EC and the WTO.* London: Cameron May.

Ansell, Christopher, and David Vogel. 2006. *What's the Beef? The Contested Governance of European Food Safety.* Cambridge, MA: MIT Press.

Applegate, John. 2000. The Precautionary Preference: An American Perspective on the Precautionary Principle. *Human Ecological Risk Assessment* 6: 413–443.

Arnold, M. L. 1997. *Natural Hybridization and Evolution.* Oxford: Oxford University Press.

Ash, Timothy Garton. 2003. Anti-Europeanism in America. *New York Review of Books* (February 13): 32–34.

Ashenfelter, Orley, Theodore Eisenberg, and Stewart J. Schwab. 1995. Politics and the Judiciary: The Influence of Judicial Background on Case Outcomes. *Journal of Legal Studies* 24: 257–281.

Baker, Randall, eds. 1997. *Environmental Law and Policy in the EU and the US.* Westport, CT: Greenwood Publishing.

Beck, Ulrich. 1992. *Risk Society.* London: Sage.

Berlin, Isaiah. 1953. *The Hedgehog and the Fox: An Essay on Tolstoy's View of History.* New York: Simon and Schuster.

Bernauer, Thomas, and Erika Meins. 2003. Technological Revolution Meets Policy and the Market: Explaining Cross-National Differences in Agricultural Biotechnology Regulation. *European Journal of Political Research* 42: 643–684.

Bernstein, Peter L. 1996. *Against the Gods: The Remarkable Story of Risk.* New York: John Wiley and Sons.

Blake, William. 1814. Annotations to Sir Joshua Reynolds' *Discourses*. In *The Complete Poetry and Prose of William Blake* (rev. ed.; 1988), edited by David V. Erdman. New York: Anchor Books.

Blomquist, William. 2007. The Policy Process and Large-N Comparative Studies. In *Theories of the Policy Process.* 2nd ed., edited by Paul A. Sabatier. Boulder, CO: Westview Press, 261–291.

Bodansky, Daniel. 2004. Deconstructing the Precautionary Principle. In *Bringing New Law to Ocean Waters*, edited by D. D. Caron and H. N. Scheiber. Leiden, Netherlands: Koninklijke Brill NV.

Boehmer-Christiansen, S. 1994. The Precautionary Principle in Germany: Enabling Government. In *Interpreting the Precautionary Principle*, edited by Timothy O'Riordan and James Cameron. London: Cameron May, 31–60.

Bourg, Dominique, and Jean-Louis Schlegel. 2001. *Parer aux Risques de Demain: Le Principe de Précaution.* Paris: Seuil.

Brady, Henry E., and David Collier, eds. 2004. *Rethinking Social Inquiry: Diverse Tools, Shared Standards.* Berkeley, CA: Rowman and Littlefield and Berkeley Public Policy Press.

Breggin, Linda, Robert Falkner, Nico Jaspers, John Pendergrass, and Read Porter. 2009. *Securing the Promise of Nanotechnologies: Towards Transatlantic Regulatory Cooperation.* London: Chatham House.

Breyer, Stephen, and Veerle Heyvaert. 2000. Institutions for Regulating Risk. In *Environmental Law, the Economy, and Sustainable Development: The United States, the European Union, and the International Community*, edited by Richard L. Revesz, Phillipe Sands, and Richard B. Stewart. Cambridge: Cambridge University Press, 283–352.

Brickman, Ronald, Sheila Jasanoff, and Thomas Ilgen. 1985. *Controlling Chemicals: The Politics of Regulation in Europe and the United States.* Ithaca, NY: Cornell University Press.

Brizendine, Louann. 2006. *The Female Brain.* New York: Broadway/Morgan Road Books.

Butti, Luciano. 2007. *The Precautionary Principle in Environmental Law: Neither Arbitrary nor Capricious if Interpreted with Equilibrium.* Milan: Giuffré Editore.

Cameron, James, and Juli Abouchar. 1991. The Precautionary Principle: A Fundamental Principle of Law and Policy for the Protection of the Global Environment. *Boston College International and Comparative Law Review* 14: 1–27.

———. 1996. The Status of the Precautionary Principle in International Law. In *The Precautionary Principle and International Law*, edited by David Freestone and Ellen Hey. The Hague: Kluwer Law International, 29–52.

Charnovitz, Steven. 2000. The Supervision of Health and Biosafety Regulation by World Trade Rules. *Tulane Environmental Law Journal* 13: 271–302.

Christoforou, Theofanis. 2004. The Precautionary Principle, Risk Assessment, and the Comparative Role of Science in the European Community and the United States Legal Systems. In *Green Giants? Environmental Policies of the United States and the European Union*, edited by Norman J. Vig and Michael G. Faure. Cambridge, MA: MIT Press, 17–52.

Cone, Marla. 2005. Europe's Rules Forcing US Firms to Clean Up. *Los Angeles Times*, May 16.

Cross, Frank. 1996. Paradoxical Perils of the Precautionary Principle. *Washington and Lee Law Review* 53: 851–925.

Daalder, Ivo. 2001. Are the United States and Europe Headed for Divorce? *International Affairs* 77: 553–557.

Daley, Suzanne. 2000. Europe's Dim View of U.S. Is Evolving into Frank Hostility. *New York Times*, April 9, A1.

de Sadeleer, Nicholas. 2002. *Environmental Principles: From Political Slogans to Legal Rules*. Oxford: Oxford University Press.

———, ed. 2007. *Implementing Precaution: Approaches from Nordic Countries, the EU, and the USA*. London: Earthscan.

———. 2009. The Precautionary Principle as a Device for Greater Environmental Protection: Lessons from the EC Courts. *Review of European Community and International Environmental Law* 18 (April): 3–10.

Desai, Uday, ed. 2002. *Environmental Politics and Policy in Industrialized Countries*. Cambridge, MA: MIT Press.

de Tocqueville, Alexis. 1840. *Democracy in America*, Online version available from the University of Virginia at http://xroads.virginia.edu/~HYPER/DETOC/toc_indx.html (accessed October 19, 2010).

Dryzek, John S. 1997. *The Politics of the Earth: Environmental Discourses*. Oxford: Oxford University Press.

———. 2006. *Deliberative Global Politics: Discourse and Democracy in a Divided World*. Cambridge: Polity Press.

———. 2007. Paradigms and Discourses. In *Oxford Handbook of International Environmental Law*, edited by Daniel Bodansky, Jutta Brunnée, and Ellen Hey. Oxford: Oxford University Press, 44–62.

Dwyer, John P., Richard W. Brooks, and Alan C. Marco. 2000. The Air Pollution Permit Process for U.S. and German Automobile Assembly Plants. In *Regulatory Encounters: Multinational Corporations and American Adversarial Legalism*, edited by Robert A. Kagan and Lee Axelrad. Berkeley, CA: University of California Press, 173–224.

The Economist. 2004. The Price of Prudence. January 22. www.economist.com/surveys/displaystory.cfm?story_id=2347855 (accessed July 23, 2009).

Esty, Daniel, and Michael Porter. 2005. National Environmental Performance: An Empirical Analysis of Policy Results and Determinants. *Environment and Development Economics* 10: 391–434.

European Commission. 2000. Communication from the Commission on the Precautionary Principle. Doc. COM(2000)1. February 2. Brussels.

Fisher, Elizabeth, Judith Jones and René von Schomberg, eds. 2006. *Implementing the Precautionary Principle: Perspectives and Prospects*. Cheltenham, UK: Edward Elgar.

Freestone, David. 1991. The Precautionary Principle. In *International Law and Global Climate Change*, edited by Robin Churchill and David Freestone. London: Graham and Trotman.

Godard, Olivier. 2006. The Precautionary Principle and Catastrophism on Tenterhooks: Lessons from Constitutional Reform in France. In *Implementing the Precautionary Principle: Perspectives and Prospects*, edited by Elizabeth Fisher, Judith Jones, and René von Schomberg. Cheltenham, UK: Edward Elgar, 63–87.

Goklany, Indur. 2001. *The Precautionary Principle: A Critical Appraisal of Environmental Risk Assessment*. Washington, DC: Cato Institute.

Goodman, Ellen. 2007. The Mythical Chat Gap *Boston Globe*, July 20.

Graham, John D., and Jonathan Baert Wiener, eds. 1995. *Risk vs. Risk: Tradeoffs in Protecting Health and the Environment.* Cambridge, MA: Harvard University Press.

Hall, Peter A., and David Soskice, eds. 2001. *Varieties of Capitalism: The Institutional Foundations of Comparative Advantage.* Oxford: Oxford University Press.

Hammitt, James K., Jonathan B. Wiener, Brendon Swedlow, Denise Kall, and Zheng Zhou. 2005. Precautionary Regulation in Europe and the United States: A Quantitative Comparison. *Risk Analysis* 25: 1215–1228.

Harremoes, Poul, David Gee, Malcolm MacGarvin, Andy Stirling, Jane Keys, Brian Wynne, and Sofia Guedes Vaz, eds. 2002. *The Precautionary Principle in the Twentieth Century: Late Lessons from Early Warnings.* London: Earthscan.

Harrington, Winston, Richard D. Morgenstern, and Thomas Sterner, eds. 2004. *Choosing Environmental Policy: Comparing Instruments and Outcomes in the United States and Europe.* Washington, DC: Resources for the Future Press.

Henningsen, Jorgen. 1992. The Seven Principles of European Environmental Policies *Toward a Transatlantic Environmental Policy.* Washington DC: European Institute, 25–26.

Hinich, Melvin, and Michael Munger. 1998. Empirical Studies in Comparative Politics. *Public Choice* 97: 219–227.

Jasanoff, Sheila. 1986. *Risk Management and Political Culture.* New York: Russell Sage Foundation.

———. 1998. Contingent Knowledge: Implications for Implementation and Compliance. In *Engaging Countries: Strengthening Compliance with International Environmental Accords,* edited by E. Brown Weiss and H. Jacobson. Cambridge, MA: MIT Press.

———. 2005. *Designs on Nature: Science and Democracy in Europe and the United States.* Princeton, NJ: Princeton University Press.

Jordana, Jacint, David Levi-Faur, and Xavier Fernandez i Marin. 2008. The Global Diffusion of Regulatory Agencies and the Restructuring of the State. Draft. http://poli.haifa.ac.il/~levi/jlx.pdf (accessed January 11, 2009).

Kagan, Robert. 2003. *Of Paradise and Power: America and Europe in the New World Order.* New York: Knopf.

Kagan, Robert A. 2007. Globalization and Legal Change: The "Americanization" of European Law? *Regulation and Governance* 1: 99–120.

Kagan, Robert A., and Lee Axelrad, eds. 2000. *Regulatory Encounters: Multinational Corporations and American Adversarial Legalism.* Berkeley, CA: University of California Press.

Kelemen, R. Daniel. 2004. Environmental Federalism in the United States and the European Union. In *Green Giants: Environmental Policies of the United States and the European Union,* edited by Norman Vig and Michael Faure. Cambridge, MA: MIT Press, 113–134.

Kelemen, R. Daniel, and David Vogel. 2010. Trading Places: The Role of the US and EU in International Environmental Politics. *Comparative Political Studies* 43: 427–456.

Kelman, Steven. 1981. *Regulating America, Regulating Sweden: A Comparative Study of Occupational Safety and Health Policy.* Cambridge MA: MIT Press.

Kempton, Willett, and Paul P. Craig. 1993. European Perspectives on Global Climate Change. *Environment* (April) 16–20, 41–45.

King, Gary, Robert O. Keohane, and Sidney Verba. 1994. *Designing Social Inquiry: Scientific Inference in Qualitative Research.* Princeton, NJ: Princeton University Press.

Kobe, Andrej, and Katerina Varenne. 2010. Europe Fights Particle Pollution: Insight into Implementation of EU Law. *Natural Resources and Environment* 24 (4): 30–33, 63.

Kohut, Andrew, and Bruce Stokes. 2006. *America Against the World: How We Are Different and Why We Are Disliked.* New York: Times Books.

Krämer, Ludwig. 2004. The Roots of Divergence: A European Perspective. In *Green Giants? Environmental Policies of the United States and the European Union,* edited by Norman J. Vig and Michael G. Faure. Cambridge, MA: MIT Press, 53–72.

La Porta, Rafael, Florencio Lopez-de-Silanes, and Andrei Shleifer. 2008. The Economic Consequences of Legal Origins. *Journal of Economic Literature* 46: 285–332.

La Rochefoucauld, Francois. 1665 [1946]. Moral Maxim No. 106. *Maximes,* 61. Montreal: Les Editions Variétés.

Lazarus, Richard. 2004. *The Making of Environmental Law*. Chicago: University of Chicago Press.

Levi-Faur, David. 2004. Comparative Research Designs in the Study of Regulation: How to Increase the Number of Cases without Compromising the Strengths of Case-Oriented Analysis. In *The Politics of Regulation: Institutions and Regulatory Reforms for the Age of Governance*, edited by Jacint Jordana and David Levi-Faur. Cheltenham, UK: Edward Elgar, 177–199.

———. 2005. The Global Diffusion of Regulatory Capitalism. *Annals of the American Academy of Political and Social Science* 598: 12–32.

Levy, David L., and Peter Newell. 2000. Oceans Apart? Business Responses to Global Environmental Issues in Europe and the United States. *Environment* (November): 9–10.

Lieberman, Evan S. 2005. Nested Analysis as a Mixed-Method Strategy for Comparative Research. *American Political Science Review* 99: 435–452.

Lindseth, Peter L., Alfred C. Aman Jr., and Alan C. Raul. 2008. *Administrative Law of the European Union: Oversight*. Chicago: American Bar Association (ABA).

Loewenberg, Samuel. 2003. Precaution Is for Europeans. *New York Times*, May 18, 2003.

Lofstedt, Ragnar. 2004. The Swing of the Regulatory Pendulum in Europe: From Precautionary Principle to (Regulatory) Impact Analysis. *Journal of Risk and Uncertainty* 28: 237–260.

Lofstedt, Ragnar, and David Vogel. 2001. The Changing Character of Regulation: A Comparison of Europe and the United States. *Risk Analysis* 21: 399–405.

Lynch, Diahanna, and David Vogel. 2000. Apples and Oranges: Comparing the Regulation of Genetically Modified Food in Europe and the United States. Paper prepared for the American Political Science Association annual meeting. August 31–September 3.

———. 2001. *The Regulation of GMOs in Europe and the United States: A Case-Study of Contemporary European Regulatory Politics*. New York: Council on Foreign Relations.

Marchant, Gary E., and Kenneth L. Mossman. 2004. *Arbitrary and Capricious: The Precautionary Principle in the EU Courts*. Washington, DC: AEI Press.

Markovits, Andrei. 2007. *Uncouth Nation: Why Europe Dislikes America*. Princeton, NJ: Princeton University Press.

McIntyre, Owen, and Thomas Mosedale. 1997. The Precautionary Principle as a Norm of Customary International Law. *Journal of Environmental Law* 9: 221–241.

Mehl, M. R., S. Vazire, N. Ramirez-Esparza, R. B. Slatcher, and J. W. Pennebaker. 2007. Are Women Really More Talkative Than Men? *Science* 317 (July 6): 82.

Mock, Douglas W. 2004. *More Than Kin and Less Than Kind: The Evolution of Family Conflict*. Cambridge, MA: Belknap Press.

Mokdad, Ali H., James S. Marks, Donna F. Stroup, and Julie L. Gerberding. 2004. Actual Causes of Death in the United States, 2000. *Journal of the American Medical Association* 291: 1238–1245.

Morris, Julian, ed. 2000. *Rethinking Risk and the Precautionary Principle*. London: Butterworth-Heinemann.

NAS/NRC (National Academy of Sciences/National Research Council). 1983. *Risk Assessment in the Federal Government: Managing the Process*. Washington, DC: National Academy Press.

Patten, Chris. 2006. *Cousins and Strangers: America, Britain and Europe in a New Century*. New York: Times Books.

Peretti-Watel, Patrick. 2000. *Sociologie du Risque*. Paris: Armand-Colin.

———. 2001. *La Société du Risque*. Paris: Editions La Découverte.

Pollack, Mark A., and Gregory C. Shaffer, eds. 2001. *Transatlantic Governance in the Global Economy*. Lanham, MD: Rowman and Littlefield.

———. 2009. *When Cooperation Fails: The International Law and Politics of Genetically Modified Foods*. Oxford: Oxford University Press.

Posner, Richard A. 2003. *Law, Pragmatism, and Democracy*. Cambridge, MA: Harvard University Press.

———. 2004. *Catastrophe: Risk and Response*. Oxford: Oxford University Press.

Priest, George L. 1977. The Common Law Process and the Selection of Efficient Rules. *Journal of Legal Studies* 6: 65–82.

Priest, George, and Benjamin Klein. 1984. The Selection of Disputes for Litigation. *Journal of Legal Studies* 13: 1–55.

Raffensperger, Carolyn, and Joel Tickner, eds. 1999. *Protecting Public Health and the Environment: Implementing the Precautionary Principle.* Washington, DC: Island Press.

Redwood, John. 2001. *Stars and Strife: The Coming Conflicts between the USA and the European Union.* Basingstoke, Hampshire: Palgrave.

Rehbinder, Eckard, and Richard Stewart. 1985. *Environmental Protection Policy: Legal Integration in the United States and the European Community.* New York: De Gruyter.

Reid, T. R. 2001. In Europe, the Ordinary Takes a Frightening Turn: Health Scares Confound Continent. *Washington Post*, March 1, A01.

———. 2004. *The United States of Europe: The New Superpower and the End of American Supremacy.* New York: Penguin Press.

Renn, Ortwin, and Bernd Rohrmann, eds. 2000. *Cross-Cultural Risk Perception: A Survey of Empirical Studies.* Dordrecht, Netherlands: Kluwer.

Richter, Stephan-Götz. 2000. The U.S. Consumer's Friend. *New York Times* Sept. 21, A31.

Rifkin, Jeremy. 2004. *The European Dream.* New York: Tarcher/Penguin.

Rose-Ackerman, Susan. 1995. *Controlling Environmental Policy: The Limits of Public Law in Germany and the United States.* New Haven, CT: Yale University Press.

Rose-Ackerman, Susan, and Peter Lindseth, eds. 2010. *Comparative Administrative Law.* Cheltenham, UK: Edward Elgar.

Sand, Peter H. 2000. The Precautionary Principle: A European Perspective. *Human and Ecological Risk Assessment* 6: 445–458.

Sandin, Per. 1999. Dimensions of the Precautionary Principle. *Human and Ecological Risk Assessment* 5: 889–907.

Sands, Philippe. 1995. *Principles of International Environmental Law.* New York: Manchester University Press.

Schapiro, Mark. 2004. New Power for 'Old Europe.' *The Nation*, Dec. 27. www.thenation.com/doc/20041227/schapiro (accessed December 21, 2005).

Schreurs, Miranda. 2002. *Environmental Politics in Japan, Germany, and the United States.* Cambridge: Cambridge University Press.

Scruggs, Lyle. 1999. Institutions and Environmental Performance in Seventeen Western Democracies. *British Journal of Political Science* 29: 1–31.

———. 2001. Is There Really a Link between Neo-Corporatism and Environmental Performance? Updated Evidence and New Data for the 1980s and 1990s. *British Journal of Political Science* 31: 686–692.

———. 2003. *Sustaining Abundance: Environmental Performance in Industrialized Democracies.* New York: Cambridge University Press.

———. 2009. Democracy and Environmental Protection: An Empirical Analysis. Draft of April 2009. http://sp.uconn.edu/~scruggs/mpsa09e.pdf (accessed August 5, 2009).

Selin, Henrik, and Stacy VanDeveer. 2006. Raising Global Standards. *Environment* 48 (10): 6–17.

Sen, Amartya. 2006. *Identity and Violence: The Illusion of Destiny.* New York: Norton.

Servan-Schreiber, Jean-Jacques. 1967. *Le Défi Américain [The American Challenge].* Paris: Denoël.

Siegelman, Peter, and John J. Donohue III. 1990. Studying the Iceberg from Its Tip: A Comparison of Published and Unpublished Employment Discrimination Cases. *Law and Society Review* 24: 1133–1170.

Simmons, Beth A., Frank Dobbin, and Geoffrey Garrett, eds. 2008. *The Global Diffusion of Markets and Democracy.* New York: Cambridge University Press.

Slaughter, Anne-Marie. 2004. *A New World Order.* Princeton, NJ: Princeton University Press.

———. 2009. The Networked Century. *Foreign Affairs* 88 (January/February): 94.

Stewart, Richard B., and Jonathan B. Wiener. 2003. *Reconstructing Climate Policy: Beyond Kyoto.* Washington, DC: AEI Press.

Stone, Christopher D. 2001. Is There a Precautionary Principle? *Environmental Law Reporter* 31: 10790–10799.

Sunstein, Cass R. 2005. *The Laws of Fear: Beyond the Precautionary Principle.* Cambridge: Cambridge University Press.

———. 2007. *Worst Case Scenarios.* Cambridge, MA: Harvard University Press.

Sur, Serge. 2004. Ni Mars ni Vénus: Achille ou. *Documentation Française: Questions Internationales* 9 (September/October) www.afri-ct.org/membres/sergesur/spip.php?article104 (accessed July 13, 2010).

Susskind, Lawrence. 1994. *Environmental Diplomacy.* Oxford: Oxford University Press.

Tajfel, Henri. 1970. Experiments in Intergroup Discrimination. *Scientific American* 223: 96–102.

Trouwborst, Arie. 2002. *Evolution and Status of the Precautionary Principle in International Law.* The Hague: Kluwer Law International.

Uruena, René. 2008. Risk and Randomness in International Legal Argument. *Leiden Journal of International Law* 21: 782–822.

Vander Zwaag, David. 1999. The Precautionary Principle in Environmental Law and Policy: Elusive Rhetoric and First Embraces. *Journal of Environmental Law and Practice* 8: 355–375.

Vig, Norman, and Michael Faure, eds. 2004. *Green Giants: Environmental Policies of the United States and the European Union.* Cambridge, MA: MIT Press.

Vogel, David. 1986. *National Styles of Regulation: Environmental Policy in Great Britain and the United States.* Ithaca, NY: Cornell University Press.

———. 2001. Ships Passing in the Night: The Changing Politics of Risk Regulation in Europe and the United States. European University Institute Robert Schuman Centre for Advanced Studies. *Working Paper* 16: 1–137.

———. 2002. Risk Regulation in Europe and the United States *Yearbook of European Environmental Law.* Vol. 3. Oxford: Oxford University Press.

———. 2003. The Hare and the Tortoise Revisited: The New Politics of Consumer and Environmental Regulation in Europe. *British Journal of Political Science* 33: 557–580.

———. Forthcoming. *The Politics of Precaution: Regulating Health, Safety and Environmental Risks in the United States and Europe.* Princeton, NJ: Princeton University Press.

Weber, Elke U., and Christopher K. Hsee. 1998. Cross-Cultural Differences in Risk Perception, but Cross-Cultural Similarities in Attitudes towards Perceived Risks. *Management Science* 44: 1205–1217.

Whiteside, Kerry H. 2006. *Precautionary Politics: Principle and Practice in Confronting Environmental Risk.* Cambridge, MA: MIT Press.

Whitford, Andrew B., and Karen Wong. 2009. Political and Social Foundations for Environmental Sustainability. *Political Research Quarterly* 62: 190–204.

Wiener, Jonathan B. 1998. Managing the Iatrogenic Risks of Risk Management. *Risk: Health Safety and Environment* 9: 39–82.

———. 1999. On the Political Economy of Global Environmental Regulation. *Georgetown Law Journal* 87: 749–794.

———. 2001. Something Borrowed for Something Blue: Legal Transplants and the Evolution of Global Environmental Law. *Ecology Law Quarterly* 27: 1295–1371.

———. 2002. Precaution in a Multirisk World. In *Human and Ecological Risk Assessment: Theory and Practice,* edited by Dennis D. Paustenbach. New York: John Wiley and Sons, 1509–1531.

———. 2003. Whose Precaution after All? A Comment on the Comparison and Evolution of Risk Regulatory Systems. *Duke Journal of International and Comparative Law* 13: 207–262.

———. 2006. Better Regulation in Europe. *Current Legal Problems* 59: 447–518.

———. 2007. Precaution. In *Oxford Handbook of International Environmental Law,* edited by Daniel Bodansky, Jutta Brunnee, and Ellen Hey. Oxford: Oxford University Press, 597–612.

———. 2008. Issues in the Comparison of Regulatory Oversight Bodies. Paper prepared for the OECD Working Party on Regulation. October 21.

———. 2009. Toward a Global Policy Laboratory. Remarks at the SRA-RFF conference on New Ideas for Risk Regulation. June 22. www.rff.org/Events/Pages/New-Ideas-for-Risk-Regulation.aspx (accessed July 13, 2010).

Wiener, Jonathan B., and Alberto Alemanno. 2010. Comparing Regulatory Oversight Bodies across the Atlantic: The Office of Information and Regulatory Affairs in the U.S. and the Impact Assessment Board in the E.U. In *Comparative Administrative Law,* edited by Susan Rose-Ackerman and Peter Lindseth. Cheltenham, UK: Edward Elgar.

Wiener, Jonathan B., and Barak D. Richman. 2010. Mechanism Choice. In *Public Choice and Public Law*, edited by Daniel Farber and Anne Joseph O'Connell. Cheltenham, UK: Edward Elgar.

Wiener, Jonathan B., and Michael D. Rogers. 2002. Comparing Precaution in the U.S. and Europe. *Journal of Risk Research* 5: 317–349.

Wildavsky, Aaron. 1995. *But Is It True? A Citizen's Guide to Environmental Health and Safety Issues.* Cambridge, MA: Harvard University Press.

Yandle, Bruce. 1989. Bootleggers and Baptists in the Market for Regulation. In *The Political Economy of Government Regulation*, edited by Jason F. Shogren. Boston: Kluwer Academic Publishers, 29–54.

Yandle, Bruce, and Stuart Buck. 2002. Bootleggers, Baptists, and the Global Warming Battle. *Harvard Environmental Law Review* 26: 177–229.

Zander, Joakim. 2010. *The Application of the Precautionary Principle in Practice: Comparative Dimensions.* Cambridge: Cambridge University Press.

Zweigert, Konrad, and Hein Kötz. 1998. *An Introduction to Comparative Law.* Translated by Tony Weir. Oxford: Oxford University Press.

PART II
CASE STUDIES OF RELATIVE
PRECAUTION REGARDING
SPECIFIC RISKS

CHAPTER 2

Genetically Modified Foods and Crops

Mark Cantley and Maurice Lex

S ince biotechnology's birth in 1973, there has been continual and increasingly widespread debate around the world about whether and how to regulate modern biotechnology and its products, with significant recourse to the use of a precautionary approach. This chapter focuses primarily on debate and action in the European Union (EU) and the United States, while recognizing that the debates, actions, and impacts have been global. The debate has played in many theatres, of course, at both federal and state levels in the United States, and at both EU and national levels in Europe. It continues, too, at the global level: in many agencies of the United Nations; in the club of the "developed world," at the Organisation for Economic Co-operation and Development (OECD);[1] within federal countries, at state, and—in the United States—even at county levels. "Widespread" is an accurate adjective, because the debate also involves numerous supporting scientific disciplines, multiple sectors of a product's application, and the half dozen or more ministries or agencies involved within each national administration. The use of biotechnology in agriculture and food is thousands of years old, including breeding of crops and livestock as well as fermentation of alcoholic beverages and yogurt, but we focus our attention here on the use of the newer molecular methods of genetically modified (GM) foods and crops. We illustrate attempts to apply the precautionary principle (PP) in a specific area of new technology, and draw some lessons from three decades of experience. American usage prefers the phrase "precautionary approach," which more accurately conveys the concept, but

---

[1] The Paris-based Organisation for Economic Co-operation and Development, founded in the late 1940s, today includes the member countries of the North Atlantic Free Trade Agreement (NAFTA), almost all members of the EU, and Australia, Korea, Japan, and New Zealand.

"principle" has acquired widespread usage, especially in Europe. For simplicity, we use this term or the abbreviation PP.

Background: The PP and Potential Risks and Benefits

The development of modern biotechnology since its beginnings in research laboratories in the 1970s, and then its first applications in agriculture and the pharmaceutical industry in the 1980s, has been accompanied by a public policy debate whose dimensions have continually increased—especially to embrace wider societal impacts and even ethical implications. In this widespread and continuing global debate, now over 30 years old, risk assessment and management, perception and communication, have been major strands. Whether or not those specific terms were used, the development and application of the technology and the accompanying policy debates provide a rich context within which to consider the role of the PP. Regrettably, the story also illustrates in recent years how the PP may be misapplied or even cynically exploited to slow down the development and diffusion of a technology for reasons little related to objective assessment of risks.

From historical and scientific viewpoints, the development of biotechnology may be viewed on a continuum dating back to the earliest exploitation of living organisms by human beings. Food, health, and environment have always been on the agenda. One might note the contemporary echo of this 1906 statement from that great plant breeder Luther Burbank:

> We have recently advanced our knowledge of genetics to the point where we can manipulate life in a way never intended by nature. We must proceed with the utmost caution in the application of this new found knowledge. (Burbank 1906)

Classical breeding does indeed go far beyond what happens in nature without human intervention. While reasons exist to exercise some caution in the use of any genetic manipulation, until recent times this was rarely done. Indeed, the imperial powers in past centuries energetically experimented in shifting germplasm around the globe, to see what might profitably flourish in various regions. They did so unconstrained by any Convention on Biodiversity or environmental impact assessment. Some successes and innovations resulted, along with a few bio-disasters—but the impacts depend on the traits altered and the environment into which the organism was introduced, not on the method of its alteration. Classical breeding or introduction of exotic species can be far more damaging than modern molecular genetic modification, depending on the traits and the setting. Such a conclusion was drawn by the U.S. National Research Council in its study of "pest protected plants" (U.S. NRC 2000). Indeed, genetic solutions to breeding goals are often preferable to other forms of intervention—such as chemical or mechanical—because they use and work with the great biological principles of heredity, competition, and evolution. Genetic engineering is a truly "green" technology. The multidisciplinary spirit and practice of biotechnology explicitly erode or ignore any supposed frontier between "organic" and "inorganic"—or indeed, between "natural" and "unnatural." What could be more organic, after all, than DNA?

Pursuing this point, in the context of pest control, we might recall the indictment in Rachel Carson's 1962 *Silent Spring*, which looked at how chemical pesticides were used in the postwar years. Here is her plea for solutions based on greater biological understanding and selectivity:

> A truly extraordinary variety of alternatives to the chemical control of insects is available. Some are already in use and have achieved brilliant success. Others are in the stage of laboratory testing. Still others are little more than ideas in the minds of imaginative scientists, waiting for the opportunity to put them to the test. All have this in common: they are *biological solutions, based on understanding of the living organisms they seek to control, and of the whole fabric of life to which these organisms belong.* Specialists representing various areas of the vast field of biology are contributing—entomologists, pathologists, geneticists, physiologists, biochemists, ecologists all pouring their knowledge and their creative inspirations into the formation of a new science of biotic controls. (Carson 2002, 278; emphasis added)

Classical plant breeding and modern agricultural biotechnology have responded to that plea. But most of what we eat is not the object of safety regulations. Of course, performance-related field trials for new crops, general public health regulations, hygiene rules, and date limits for foods are all well established. Concerns about the safety of new crops and risk assessments for novel foods (as distinct from food additives), however, arose only with the advent of genetic engineering.

One very clear assessment of the comparative risks associated with human consumption of foods is illustrated in Table 2.1.

Comparing food-related risks in this way underlines a recurrent feature in the public policy debate on the risks of modern biotechnology: we are addressing fears, perceptions, and conjectures rather than objective risks. Similar gaps between objective evidence and public perceptions may also be found in the contexts of animal health or environmental damage: the policy debate—largely driven by perceptions and

Table 2.1 *Relative Costs to Society of Food Safety Issues*

Issue/risk	Approximate number of deaths in the UK
Cardiovascular disease*	73,000
Cancer*	34,000
Foodborne illness	50**
Food allergy (anaphylactic shock)	<20
VCJD	15
GMOs, pesticides, growth hormones	Nil
Choking to death	~200
Bed or chair accident	80

*Assumes one-third of cardiovascular disease deaths and one-quarter of cancer deaths are diet related
**The number may actually be much higher—up to 10 times this figure
Source: UK Advisory Committee on Research (2002)

conjectural assessment of risks—can result in political demands that cannot be ignored. We are trapped into a vocabulary chosen by modern biotechnology's opponents—"the GM debate"—when essentially all our food is genetically modified via classical breeding or mutagenesis and selection. Certain words and abbreviations are chosen to influence public debate through emotions and passions—e.g., "genetic pollution," "contamination," and "Frankenfoods." Natural scientists are at a disadvantage in a situation where subjective perceptions—which their whole training tells them to discount and distrust—become realities for the general public and consumer. This is familiar to any politician, or retailer, or even the insurance industry. Major economic loss can occur even in the absence of damage to health or environment whenever perceptions, and regulations based on perceptions, require the withdrawal and destruction, or ban the import and marketing, of products perceived or defined to be dangerous. Reconciling misconceptions with science-based risk assessment is difficult. The parties concerned speak different languages, use different logic and criteria, and question the validity of each other's reasoning. Hence the polarized debate that takes place in so many places.

European Commission Explication of the PP

The PP has become politically fashionable in recent years, but interpretations have been diverse. The European Commission, in its first communication of the new millennium (EC 2000a), sought to provide clarification. The communication draws upon the United Nations Conference on Environment and Development's 1992 Rio Declaration, paragraph 15, which stated, "[W]here there are threats of serious or irreversible damage, lack of full scientific certainty shall not be used as a reason for postponing cost-effective measures to prevent environmental degradation." The communication points out, however, that the scope of the PP is far wider than the environment; it can include human, animal, or plant health. The Commission communication was endorsed by the European Parliament (2000) and the European Council of Ministers (2000).

Recourse to the PP has become a central plank of EU policies relating to management of potential—or perceived!—risks to which the population and/or the environment are exposed.

Thus, the PP requires that decisions must wait until all the necessary scientific knowledge is available, until the reality and the seriousness of associated risks become fully apparent: "better safe than sorry." Delaying measures until the science is more certain would invite the political criticism that business and industry are being shielded from the costs of their responsibilities at the expense of public safety. But excessive precaution inhibits innovation, delays benefits, weakens competitiveness, and may introduce new risks. A balance must be found.

The EC communication provides in its opening summary a succinct specification of the desirable characteristics of measures under the PP—starting with an important conditional clause:

Where action is deemed necessary, measures based on the precautionary principle should be, *inter alia*:

- *proportional* to the chosen level of protection,
- *nondiscriminatory* in their application,
- *consistent* with similar measures already taken,
- *based on an examination of the potential benefits and costs* of action or lack of action (including, where appropriate and feasible, an economic cost/benefit analysis),
- *subject to review,* in the light of new scientific data, and
- *capable of assigning responsibility for producing the scientific evidence* necessary for a more comprehensive risk assessment.

These points underline the *dynamic* nature of the principle—especially arising from "review in the light of new scientific data"—and the commitment to more comprehensive risk assessment based on the production of scientific evidence. Scientific development has, of course, occurred with particular rapidity in the life sciences and biotechnology in recent decades. With the advent of high-speed, low-cost sequencing,[2] progress shows no sign of slowing.

The whole process starts with a scientific evaluation as complete as possible. But the triggering factor is very much a *political* decision on whether—to use the language of the communication—"action is deemed necessary." It is up to the risk managers to decide whether precautionary actions should be taken. Judging what is an "acceptable" level of risk is an eminently political responsibility. Decisionmakers faced with a high or unknown risk, scientific uncertainty, and public concerns have a duty to find practical answers. Once such a political decision has been taken, momentum and specific interests and investments of effort start to accumulate. These greatly constrain the possibility of making a later decision that action is no longer necessary, or that regulation can be reduced or eliminated in the light of fuller evidence. The concept of a "sunset clause"—automatic lapsing of a provisional measure after a prefixed period—is not familiar in European legislation.

The terms italicized in the above extract from the EC communication have been illuminated by specific cases in the courts—especially the European Court of Justice. They are central to the rational application of the PP and merit some further attention.

- *Proportionality* implies *appropriateness to a chosen level of protection.* This choice is political—and "zero risk" may be demanded, though it is rarely a realistic

---

[2] In February 2004, the U.S. National Institutes of Health issued requests for applications, for projects to reduce the cost of sequencing by two orders of magnitude within five years, and by at least four orders of magnitude within 10 years. Subsequent awards and announcements indicate the feasibility of these targets. For example, see 454 Life Sciences Corporation (www.454.com), for its October 14, 2004, press release, "454 Life Sciences Receives $5 million NIH Grant for Ultraminiaturized Technology to Sequence Whole Human Genomes." Likewise, on July 26, 2005, the company announced it had achieved all initial milestones under its exclusive worldwide agreement with Roche, bringing the total milestone payments received by 454 Life Sciences from Roche to $11.5 million.

objective in biological contexts. We would argue rather that appropriateness implies adjustment (in either sense) as experience and understanding of the risks increases, always seeking to ensure that the degree of oversight is commensurate with the degree of risk.

- *Nondiscriminatory* and *consistent* imply that like situations should not be treated differently but in a manner consistent with measures already adopted in similar circumstances in which fuller scientific data are available. Again, a dynamic and comparative approach is needed.

- The choice of action—or indeed, a decision not to take action—should be based on an *examination of costs and benefits*, economic and other. However, "other relevant factors" may lead into turbulent political waters, including not only efficacy, but social impacts, ethical dilemmas, and public perceptions.

- *Subject to review.* In the light of new scientific data, decisions are *provisional*. This again implies a continuing commitment to scientific research with corresponding regular review and re-examination of the measures previously taken. These measures may be modified in light of new evidence or practical experience.

- *Capable of assigning responsibility for producing the scientific evidence.* This may be unclear: is the burden of proof to be placed on the private interests involved—e.g., a producer or importer—or on publicly financed research, or on a general monitoring of global development of research and experience?

The PP and GM Pest-resistant Crops

How has the PP been applied to agricultural biotechnology in general and genetically modified foods and crops in particular? The resistance of crop plants to pests has been a primary objective of classical breeding for many years. Useful traits may be identified in wild plants or weeds, or they may be generated by chemical or radiation mutagenesis. Desired traits may then be selected and incorporated into cultivated varieties of crop plants by means of classical breeding. Such incorporation has required skill and time, as many years of crossing and selection may be needed to transfer the desired traits into the target cultivars, in the absence of tools or techniques to identify, characterize, and transfer the genetic elements specifically responsible for those traits. Genetic engineering is now capable of offering remarkable specificity and precision, along with acceleration of the classical processes. Dozens of crops are being engineered to have improved pest resistance. Such "insect-protected" crops took only 14 years of research and development to advance from initial concept to commercial reality. (Compare this with the progressive steps over multiple decades during which many of today's productive and disease-resistant crops have been created by scientists, breeders, and farmers.)

Specific protection is conveyed by a gene coding for a protein from the bacterium *Bacillus thuringiensis* (Bt) that is toxic to several sap-sucking insects—major plant pests—but not to man or other mammals. Forty percent of all U.S. corn[3] planted in

---

[3] U.S. usage of the term "corn" differs from European English, where "maize" is more common; as both are widely used, we retain both in this article, and the usage is determined by the context.

2006 was "Bt." In 2005, worldwide, 26.3 million hectares of Bt crops were grown, most of these Bt corn and cotton. Only in small areas were Bt crops grown in Europe.

Bt crops have distinct benefits but also some potential risks. Potential benefits include the following:

- significant reduction in chemical pesticide use; U.S., Chinese, and Australian experiences demonstrate the reduction in pesticide use on GM cotton (e.g., Crossan and Kennedy 2004; Brookes and Barfoot 2005);
- specificity to target pests—thus reducing "collateral damage" on non-target species, with benefit to biodiversity (Hellmich et al. 2001; Oberhauser et al. 2001; Pleasants et al. 2001; Sears et al. 2001; Stanley-Horn et al. 2001; and Zangerl et al. 2001, relating to earlier concerns about possible impacts of Bt corn on monarch butterfly larvae);
- health benefits to farm workers through greatly reduced spraying (Huang et al. 2002);
- enhanced management flexibility, in weed control by herbicides (Firbank et al. 2003);
- reduced aflatoxin contamination by improved control of corn borer (Williams et al. 2002).

On the other hand, potential risks of Bt crops include the following:

- development of Bt-resistant strains of pest insects—intelligent "management" is needed;
- effects on non-target organisms—see earlier references for an exploration of concerns (now resolved) about monarch butterfly larvae;
- accumulation of toxic molecules in soil, with impacts on soil ecology;
- outcrossing to non-GM crops, causing horizontal gene transfer to other species, with uncertain long-term consequences;
- alleged allergenic properties of molecules brought into established foods, e.g., the recall of products containing Starlink corn.

It is worth noting that—at least based on the experience to date—many of the benefits are now well-established; most of the risks, meanwhile remain conjectural. In some cases, these risks are not specific to GM plants.

Other GM crops might pose other benefits and risks. For example, crops engineered to be herbicide-tolerant—for example, GM crops designed by Monsanto to be tolerant of Roundup, the company's proprietary version of glyphosate—could enable use of a less toxic, more targeted herbicide. Or they could increase herbicide exposure and damage to non-crop species. But their risk assessment should include comparison with the alternatives offered by conventional products and practices.

The wide difference between the EU and the United States in the adoption of Bt maize might suggest that Europe endorses the PP and seeks to implement it proactively, whereas the United States opposes the PP and waits for evidence of actual harm before regulating. However, until the early 1990s, the North American and EU regulatory frameworks for biotechnology followed similar trajectories.

Both rested on the risk-analysis requirement, shared the intention of basing risk analysis on best available scientific advice, and incorporated a science-led precautionary approach. Much has been said about the Singer and Soll public letter of 1973 to the U.S. National Academy of Sciences, which first alerted the wider world to the developments that were taking place using recombinant DNA and the possible risks. The resulting committee report (Berg et al. 1974) was also published in *Science* (and *Nature*), and included the recommendation that there should be a voluntary moratorium on some types of experiments until the international scientific community could discuss the risks. The Asilomar Conference on Recombinant DNA took place in February 1975 (Rogers 1975; Berg et al. 1975). Such steps appear to be closely consistent with the emphasis of the PP on the gathering of further science-based information.

These events led to setting up the Recombinant DNA Advisory Committee (RAC) of the U.S. National Institutes of Health (NIH). In Europe, various national initiatives arose, such as the March 1975 establishment in France of the Commission Nationale de Classement des Recombinaisons Génétiques *in vitro* and the Genetic Manipulation Advisory Group (GMAG) in the UK. Guidelines for research were quite quickly established, against a background of widespread debate involving scientists, politicians, NGOs, and media. By 1982, the European Council's Recommendation 472 on national registration of rDNA work had been formed. Its text addressed the potential risks of rDNA work—but carefully included the word "conjectural" before each mention of "risks."

The debate on oversight of biotechnology was thus multinational from its earliest years. In more recent times, it may also be noted that the EU, the United States, and over 100 other countries are signatories of the world trade agreements, which include the Sanitary and Phytosanitary agreement (SPS). This agreement explicitly includes a paragraph (§ 7 of Article 5) which is tantamount to the PP:

> In cases where relevant scientific evidence is insufficient, a Member may provisionally adopt sanitary or phytosanitary measures on the basis of available pertinent information, including that from the relevant international organizations as well as from sanitary or phytosanitary measures applied by other Members. In such circumstances, Members shall seek to obtain the additional information necessary for a more objective assessment of risk and review the sanitary or phytosanitary measure accordingly within a reasonable period of time.

Article 5 concerns the assessment of risk, and requires members to take into account scientific evidence.

In the remainder of this chapter, we address four aspects of U.S. and European experience in the application of the PP in the area of GM foods and crops:

- the pattern of relative U.S. and European precaution over time;
- the explanatory factors behind the observed patterns of relative precaution;

- the consequences of the precautionary regulation; and
- the lessons for future debates over precaution.

The Pattern of Relative U.S. and European Precaution over Time

Modern biotechnology is usually defined as the ability to transfer pieces of DNA—the linear "data tape" molecule which carries genetic information—from one species to another, a technology that has advanced rapidly since its invention in 1973. Essentially the same DNA, with the same coding rules for reading it and "translating" it into proteins, applies in all living species—a fact that greatly facilitates such "recombination." The worldwide debates about biotechnology's conjectural risks, assessment of those risks, and the management of them by precautionary action or regulation provide a case study in how society in the last decades of the twentieth century coped with a sudden surge of new fundamental knowledge and techniques. These techniques are of broad relevance—at least potentially—in every area of the life sciences.

The 13 years from 1973 to 1986 were a period of very active international debate in the developed world, on both sides of the Atlantic and among OECD countries. This was a period of expert consensus and of the first significant precautionary actions, which can be summarized as follows:

- national activities of oversight, in various countries of Europe and in the United States;
- active debate in national and international fora, including also the establishment from July 1974 of a voluntary moratorium on certain types of recombinant DNA experiment;
- debates in the U.S. Congress and in EU institutions about possible legislative responses, leading in the United States to the "Coordinated Framework" being adopted in 1986 to apply existing agencies and statutes as necessary to the new activities, and in the EU to a Council recommendation being made (in 1984) concerning the desirability of national registration of such activities—"just in case"; and
- expert work at the OECD, leading to the publication in 1986 of the "Blue Book" on recombinant DNA safety considerations (OECD 1986).

The year 1986 may be described as a "hinge year," following which regulatory paths diverged between the two continents, despite continuing expert consensus. In that year, four events took place:

- The OECD Blue Book was published. In retrospect, this moment may be seen as a "high-water mark" of international consensus. Its conclusions were endorsed by an OECD Council Recommendation.
- The Danish government adopted and published the first national, technology-specific legislation, its "Gene Technology Act."

- The European Commission—partly to anticipate a likely proliferation of such national legislation—published a communication announcing its intention to create "A Regulatory Framework for Biotechnology."
- The U.S. government, having published for public comment the proposed "Coordinated Framework" in 1984, adopted that framework two years later as the continuing basis for its regulatory policy for the products of biotechnology. That step, in effect, endorsed the view that current statutes were adequate, and that no new legislation was necessary to address specifically the products of modern biotechnology.

Over the following years, the United States continued to base its policy on the Coordinated Framework, albeit taking various initiatives to clarify definitions and the regulatory scope and competence of the various interested federal agencies. The EU initiated the preparation of three horizontal legislative proposals for directives to cover all modern biotechnology products, which were finally adopted in 1990. For convenience, we cite them by the official numbers that they acquired after adoption.

- Directive 90/219, April 23, 1990, on the contained use of genetically modified microorganisms (GMMs). This directive, addressing the fermentation pharmaceutical industry, was intended to protect the environment against adverse effects either from the inadvertent spillage of GMMs or from unwanted side effects once they were placed on the market.
- Directive 90/220, April 23, 1990, concerned the deliberate release of GMOs into the environment. The directive addressed both research releases, which could be authorized at the national level, and the placing of GMOs on the market. The legal basis was thus related to the conditions for the creation of the common market, but it ensured that products authorized under the directive would meet the required high standard of safety for human health and the environment.
- Directive 90/679, November 26, 1990, concerned the safety of workers handling biological agents. This was part of a continuing development of legislation to ensure common high standards of protection of worker safety. The handling of GMOs was readily assimilated into the ongoing legislative provisions which categorized organisms—GM or other—into four risk categories in terms of the possible dangers which they presented, along with the available means of control, prophylaxis, and therapy.

To what extent have these laws been based on the PP? Although the PP is not mentioned specifically, the laws were clearly based on the precautionary approach of "case-by-case" and "step-by-step" that had been advocated by the OECD. The preamble sections of the directives mention that "the precise nature and scale of risks associated with genetically modified organisms are not fully known and the risk involved must be assessed case by case; whereas to evaluate risk for human health and the environment, it is necessary to lay down requirements for risk assessment."

However, on March 12, 2001, the European Parliament and the Council adopted a new, overriding directive. Titled "Directive 2001/18 of 12 March 2001 on the deliberate release into the environment of genetically modified organisms and repealing Directive 90/220," it repealed the 1990 directive. Significantly, Member States were required to implement this rule "in accordance with the Precautionary Principle." When finalizing the terms of the new directive, the EU Institutions in fact went far beyond the PP (as outlined by the Commission in its 2000 communication) and introduced many stringent additional demands. These include the following:

- respect for ethical principles;
- monitoring for cumulative long-term effects;
- common methodology for the environmental risk assessment;
- independent research on potential risks;
- phasing out use of antibiotic resistance marker genes which may have adverse effects on human health and the environment;
- GMO labeling and traceability (later put into effect by Regulation 1830/2003 of September 22, 2003, "concerning the traceability and labeling of GMOs and the traceability of food and feed products produced from GMOs and amending Directive 2001/18/EC");
- a unique identifier for each transformation event;
- a fixed 10-year maximum period for all consents; and
- the requirement for a report on socioeconomic advantages and disadvantages.

Notably, the member of the European Parliament who acted as "rapporteur" for the directive (i.e., having the drafting responsibility) described this legislation once it was adopted as the toughest GMO rules in the world. Such a tough step was justified by an asserted need to reassure a skeptical European public. It did not provide a reference to any evidence of actual risk.

It remains to be seen whether tough legislation will reassure a worried public or reinforce its unfounded risk perceptions. During all these legislative and broader public debates, knowledge and experience of GM crops was increasing worldwide. The recent legislation, although proclaiming its precautionary character, particularly in respect to monitoring, labeling, and traceability, has departed from such ideas as proportionality, nondiscrimination, consistency, and attention to scientific developments. It is in fact a strategy with high risks—for innovation, competitiveness, and environmental benefits.

Other regulatory burdens have followed: specifically, the EU has ratified the Cartagena Biosafety Protocol "in accordance with the precautionary approach." It introduced specific legislation—"Regulation 1946/2003 ... July 15, 2003, on transboundary movements of GMOs"—to convey these obligations on to EU-based exporters and researchers. A directive on environmental liability—"Directive 2004/35 ... of April 21, 2004, on environmental liability with regard to the prevention and remedying of environmental damage"—has added to these obligations. Similar initiatives are under consideration under the Cartagena Biosafety Protocol and at the national level. For example, in June 18, 2004, a German "Genetic Engineering" law holds farmers who use genetic engineering liable jointly and severally for "GMO pollution" in GMO-free farms, irrespective of fault.

Turning to the actual history of authorizations, the first GM crop to be given a marketing consent under the 1990 Deliberate Release Directive was a pest-resistant maize incorporating the gene for a Bt endotoxin. This was approved by the European Commission in 1996, on the basis of a strong endorsement from three scientific committees at the European level. The reasons that some Member States gave for rejecting this product typically went beyond immediate science-based risk assessment to broader uncertainties such as the consequences of using the ampicillin resistance gene as a marker, or the possibility of insects developing resistance.

The Sectoral Approach

Historically, foods have not in general been the objects of specific regulation. This leaves a vacuum for any comparative basis when regulations are introduced for some specific group of foods. In practice, that vacuum has been filled by the concept of substantial equivalence (SE). The concept of familiarity—that is, an extended history of safe use—was one of the criteria already suggested in the OECD (1986) report for rDNA Good Industrial Large-Scale Practice (GILSP) microorganisms, which warranted only minimal containment. SE may be viewed as a high degree of familiarity—a long history of safe use being typical of most established foodstuffs.

The safety discussions around modern biotechnology and its products were initially generic in character, focusing mainly on conjectural risks supposedly arising from application. The general conclusion was that the nature of the risks would depend upon the nature of the product, rather than on the technique used to produce it; these would not differ essentially from the risks already associated with the sector concerned. It followed that products of modern biotechnology might be assessed by the same methods, through the same regulatory procedures, that were already being applied in each sector. This has remained the case, for example, regarding pharmaceutical products, in both the EU and the United States.

In other areas, the debate considered technology-specific, cross-cutting regulation versus modified sectoral rules that would include the new products, where those rules already existed. In the EU, both routes were envisaged under the 1990 legislation, provided that sectoral legislation existed at the EU level and included environmental risk assessment at least equivalent to that required under the technical annexes to the Deliberate Release Directive. The prospect of regulating foods derived from GM crops raised the question as to why this technology should be the trigger for regulatory oversight. A partial answer was that novelty per se should trigger new regulations—a philosophy adopted by Canada, somewhat to the surprise and distress of the plant breeders who then encountered it.

At the OECD, following the earlier generic work, there was a shift towards sector-specific considerations of, for example, vaccines. In the food sector, this led to the 1993 publication of *Safety Evaluation of Foods Derived by Modern Biotechnology:*

Concepts and Principles—also known as "the Green Book." This strongly emphasized the value of SE as at least a starting point, based on the following principles:

- If the new or modified food or food component is determined to be substantially equivalent to an existing food, then further safety or nutritional concerns are expected to be insignificant;
- such foods, once substantial equivalence has been established, are treated in the same manner as their analogous conventional counterparts;
- where new foods or classes of new foods or food components are less well-known, the concept of substantial equivalence is more difficult to apply; such new foods or food components are evaluated taking into account the experience gained in the evaluations of similar materials (for example, whole foods or food components such as proteins, fats, or carbohydrates);
- where a product is determined not to be substantially equivalent, the identified differences should be the focus of further evaluations;
- where there is no basis for comparison of a new food or food component, that is, where no counterpart or similar materials have been previously consumed as food, then the new food or food component should be evaluated on the basis of its own composition and properties. (OECD 1993)

This report was undoubtedly influential in the drafting of the EU's Novel Foods Regulation, "Regulation 258/97 of January 27, 1997, concerning Novel Foods and Novel Food Ingredients." This regulation represented a means by which the food safety authorities would retain control over legislation specific to their products, subject to satisfying the environmental risk assessment as specified in Directive 90/220. It sets out rules for authorization and labeling of novel foods including food products containing, consisting, or produced from GMOs (thus covering, for example, products such as paste or ketchup from GM tomatoes or soya oil from GM soybeans). As a derogation from the full authorization procedure, the Novel Foods Regulation provides for a simplified procedure for foods derived from GMOs but no longer containing GMOs and which are "substantially equivalent" to existing foods with respect to composition, nutritional value, metabolism, intended use, and the level of undesirable substances. In such cases, the companies only have to notify the Commission when placing a product on the market, together with either scientific justification that the product is substantially equivalent or an opinion to the same effect, delivered by the competent authorities of a Member State.

The SE concept has been criticized because of its possible failure to pick up putative, unexpected, or long-term effects. However, in general it has been seen as a robust starting point, and the best available assessment paradigm. No alternative approaches have been proposed. It has been endorsed by other international bodies, such as the UN agencies. The concept of "substantial equivalence" is described in the report of the 2000 joint FAO/WHO expert consultations (FAO/WHO 2000).

A major thematic network, ENTRANSFOOD, was financed by the European Commission on the safety assessment of GM foods (Kuiper et al. 2004). Again, the leading paper summarized its work:

> The proposed approach to safety assessment starts with the comparison of the new GM crop with a traditional counterpart that is generally accepted as safe based on a history of human food use (the concept of substantial equivalence). This case-focused approach ensures that foods derived from GM crops that have passed this extensive test-regime are as safe and nutritious as currently consumed plant-derived foods. The approach is suitable for current and future GM crops with more complex modifications. (Kuiper et al. 2004)

The concept of SE is thus widely endorsed, not only in the EU and the United States, but globally. It has nonetheless suffered a reverse as part of the general precautionary approach in the September 22, 2003, EU legislation, "Regulation 1829/2003 ... on genetically modified food and feed." This law removed GM foods from the scope of the earlier regulation via the following language:

> Regulation (EC) No 258/97 also provides for a notification procedure for novel foods which are substantially equivalent to existing foods. Whilst substantial equivalence is a key step in the procedure for assessment of the safety of genetically modified foods, it is not a safety assessment in itself. In order to ensure clarity, transparency, and a harmonised framework for authorisation of genetically modified food, this notification procedure should be abandoned in respect of genetically modified foods.

As we can see, the situation thus continues to be marked by a tension between legislation underlining the *specific* character of GM foods versus pragmatic safety assessment procedures, which tend instead to assimilate GM foods to other comparable foods.

On the Value of a Comparative Approach

Innovation implies the successful introduction of a product or service which for at least some users or uses is superior to the existing one. In that sense it is "creative destruction," to borrow Schumpeter's phrase (1942 [1975], 82–85). It depends upon demonstrating superiority in a comparative test. This test may be left to market forces, or if the product is a regulated item (such as a pharmaceutical), a comparative assessment may be applied by the authorities. In such a case, even a quite dangerous product may be authorized, if the current alternative is either more dangerous or nonexistent, especially if the prognosis for the untreated patient is very negative.

In the context of health care, such comparative assessment is routine. In the context of new foods, however, we tend to be more conservative, since innovation is not strictly necessary. Food innovation is largely left to market forces in this traditionally unregulated sector. So the regulation of GM foods is in itself an innovation. Unfortunately, the EU legislation restricting GM foods focuses only on possible risks to human health and the environment. Thus, even products offering major environmental benefits—such as reduced use of chemicals or low till/no till agriculture, which have benefits for biodiversity in farmland soils—are restrained by a standard of appraisal that many established conventional products would fail. This is neither rational nor precautionary.

A striking example was provided by the UK Farm Scale Evaluation (FSE) of three crops, which were cultivated over three years in fields split between GM and non-GM versions. Various parameters were measured, but the results were essentially ambiguous. "Better weed control" was synonymous with "reduced farmland biodiversity." Indeed, the choice of crop had greater impact on insect abundance and biodiversity than did the difference between GM and non-GM variants. Squire et al. (2003) summarized the rationale and interpretation of the trials:

> The FSEs arguably constitute the most comprehensive and realistic experimental assessment yet undertaken of ecological impacts resulting from agricultural change. It is accepted, however, that *the choice of a comparable system as a benchmark may be enough to change a given ecological impact from being considered a hazard to being considered a benefit.* The analysis here identified that there was no logical benchmark or ideal system for the arable habitat. The FSEs were not primarily about attaining or setting such a standard, but the debate around the project and the data it generates will make a unique contribution. (emphasis added)

This ambiguity is a persistent problem in the appraisal of innovation. The same problem arose in the debate leading up to the adoption of the EU Directive on Environmental Liability. When the insurance industry was consulted, companies indicated that, while they were happy to expand their business, they could insure against only that damage that could be defined and measured. This did not appear to be the case for "damage to the environment." The uncertainty throws the risk manager back on choices which are essentially political in nature, and these political choices are rather vulnerable to the short-term orientation of high-profile media campaigns such as those currently mounted against GM crops and foods.

Causes of Precautionary Regulation in the United States and Europe

In the 1980s, industrial applications of biotechnology started to raise public concerns in several EU countries. A good example is the U.S. production in fermenters by GM microorganisms of detergent enzymes and high-value pharmaceuticals such as insulin. Undoubtedly, these early public pressures, as expressed by some nongovernmental organizations (NGOs), were influential in the decision to draw up a regulatory framework for Europe—all before any products were ready for marketing and before any clear picture of possible risks had emerged. The development in the early 1990s of horizontal and sectoral legislation as described above appeared to have calmed public concerns and restored some confidence in the ability of the regulatory authorities to safeguard against what risks there were likely to be. In February 1996, a GM tomato paste was successfully introduced and marketed in UK supermarkets with clear labeling stating, "This product is produced from genetically modified tomatoes." The tomatoes were grown in California; cultivation in Europe was subsequently requested but refused.

But then, in November 1996, the arrival of GM soybeans from the United States triggered a massive media and NGO response. The GM soybeans, imported as animal feed, had been engineered by Monsanto to resist their herbicide Roundup. Consent for their import had been given by the European Commission under a legal procedure that applied in the absence of a decision from the European Council. The environment commissioner, who had led the drive for that legislation, was forced to defend the decision before a hostile European Parliament. "When will the Commission learn the lesson of the mad-cow disease?" was a repeated cry from the European Parliament. Earlier, in March of that year, the UK minister of agriculture had had to announce in London that "mad-cow disease" had apparently jumped species to humans; it now accounted for a growing number of deaths from what became known as "new variant Creutzfeldt-Jakob disease (vCJD)." The outbreak of this terrible disease and other food and contaminated blood scandals, along with accompanying protracted, high-profile court cases, seemed to underline the message that "the experts got it wrong—they and the governments cannot be trusted." Such events that year helped create the political pressure in favor of highly precautionary regulatory action.

A European Parliament report of the time said it all: "The EU public no longer wants to bear the brunt of hazardous technological innovations which several years later prove to have entailed risks to public health or the environment. They are not prepared to be 'guinea pigs' for progress." The "hard sell" advertising campaign subsequently launched by Monsanto served only to exacerbate public concerns and raise the profile of the topic with the media. Headlines along the lines of "Europeans force-fed by profit-driven American chemical company" led to widespread media and public hysteria. As a result, some citizens went so far as to engage in civil disobedience by destroying field testing sites that were legally approved.

Many other complex social, ethical, cultural, and economic factors contributed to the European public's rejection of GM foods in the late 1990s. Public authorities inevitably responded with more stringent legislation, sometimes citing vaguely the PP. Other factors cited included consumer freedom of choice, GM-specific labeling and traceability, tolerance thresholds, coexistence with conventional agriculture, and environmental liability rules. These demands gained overwhelming political strength when a de facto alliance among a number of separate forces developed.

- The Environment Ministries, which were in general lead ministries, were happy to see their responsibilities and formal competence expanded.
- "Environmental" NGOs recognized a campaigning opportunity, especially where the most prominent opponent was an American multinational firm.
- Various agricultural and industrial interests were happy to seize an apparently respectable cloak to protect their interests, without being accused of simple anti-Americanism or trade protectionism.
- Consumer NGOs were happy to embrace the message of their being deprived of choice and "force-fed" unknown products with suspicious names.

- European print and television media saw opportunity in adopting a pious and sensational campaigning stance against the evil empire of profit-seeking multinationals.
- Organic farmers saw the opportunity to raise their profile and enhance their business opportunities. They could now market themselves as defenders of purity and enlightenment against contamination and the "industrialization" of agriculture.

In trying to understand the differences between the two continents, some might contrast the cultures of "food as fuel" (United States, Northern Europe) and "food as culture" (Southern Europe)—though these would be gross oversimplifications. Also significantly, Europeans live closer to their agriculture on a more densely settled continent, with generally smaller farms and shorter distances between cities. There is clearly a trend in Europe toward consumer demand for quality of locally sourced foods as opposed to mass produced factory farm foods, a movement reflected by the growth of the organic produce markets.

The longer-term consequences of this rejection of modern biotechnology in Europe were clearly perceived by the scientific community—but as Stalin once cynically remarked, "How many divisions has the Pope?"

The founding populations of the United States were not random samples from Europe (or Asia), but individuals either impatient and intolerant of the *anciens régimes* or actively persecuted and driven out by such old regimes. From the start, members of the New World culture were more likely to be pioneers and innovators, as illustrated by Mark Twain's story *A Connecticut Yankee in King Arthur's Court*. Our cultural roots, our histories, and our memories, are not identical.

Consequences of Precautionary Regulation in the United States and Europe

It is difficult to establish a precise causal relationship between a chosen level of precautionary regulation and the subsequent uptake, diffusion, and exploitation of a widely applied technology such as biotechnology. Much of the evidence is anecdotal or limited to a specific product: for example, the GM "Golden Rice" developed as a means of providing dietary supplementation of vitamin A addresses the very specific health problem of a vitamin deficiency, which leads to childhood blindness. The general scale of the problem is known, and massive.

Similarly, it is hard to link precautionary actions with any reduction in risk or benefit for the environment, or with enhanced human health—or, for that matter, with public confidence in the adequacy of regulation. Precautionary actions might even be seen as an implicit indication of danger, diminishing rather than increasing public confidence in the responsible authority. At present, press commentary and public attention tend to focus only the prevailing situation in Europe as compared with that in the United States, where a significant divergence is evident between which products are on the market or which technology is permitted. If this gap is to diminish as a result of changes on either side (or on both), it seems likely to result from longer-term experience. In particular, the monitoring of trends and developments as part of the EU regulatory framework may be a factor. Such worldwide monitoring of experience and scientific developments should be an intrinsic element of the precautionary approach. (On a shorter timescale, the monitoring now required of specific crops may also contribute some insights.) However, the Commission's paper on the PP did not specify the timespan within which review and adaptation might take place.

Clearly, if the PP is misapplied, abused, or misinterpreted (e.g., for trade protectionism), it could serve any country badly by blocking innovation, destroying competitiveness, and discouraging research. If intelligently applied, in the spirit of the Commission's communication, it ought to stimulate the innovation of safer products. These might include non-ozone-depleting refrigerants, catalytic converters for cars, and the use of GM crops to facilitate the transition to more sustainable agricultural practices. That has already begun with GM cotton, which allows for a huge reduction in pesticide use and consequent reduced risk of pollution from pesticide runoff.

However, a key trigger for the PP is "where there are threats of serious or irreversible damage," and that cannot be said for any of the products of modern biotechnology considered by the EU's scientific committees to date. On the contrary, in all the products they have so far considered, the scientists have been able to strongly endorse the lack of evidence for adverse effects.

Similarly, the biosafety research projects funded by the Commission since the start of its biotechnology research programs in the early 1980s have failed to find any compelling scientific arguments demonstrating that GM crops are innately different from non-GM crops. Their potential impacts—invasiveness, weediness, toxicity, or allergenicity— are very similar to those of non-GM crops. These effects can be understood and addressed by testing and good agricultural practices (Kessler and Economidis 2001).

The present situation is radically hurting innovation and investment in Europe. Moreover, it exports similar constraints to other countries, particularly in the developing world, where exporters to Europe fear causing any risk to this trade (James 2004).

In the summer of 2002, the governments of Zambia, Zimbabwe, and Mozambique, with widespread famine threatening the lives of 14 million of their people, rejected U.S. food aid because there was no certainty that it was not commingled with GM products. Their action was not necessarily out of fear for safety; they feared losing European markets in the future if their own agriculture became supposedly "contaminated" with GM traits.

While GM crops are being adopted at an increasing rate each year in some 21 countries worldwide, in Europe such developments have for many years been delayed or blocked. The adverse impact on research, both academic and industrial, is reflected in the number of field trials in Europe. GM crop field trials are down by more than 80% since their peak of 264 notifications in 1997—to 56 in 2002, 82 in 2003, 72 in 2004, 78 in 2005, and 93 in 2006. Meanwhile, in the United States, field trials have continued at some 1,000 per year, albeit with a significant decline in the number of crop species that are being tested. (Currently, four crops predominate: soya, corn, cotton, and oilseed rape.) There is no doubt that Monsanto's temporary withdrawal from GM wheat development and marketing reflects its apparent difficulty in obtaining regulatory approval in Europe, a major market for U.S. and Canadian wheat. Syngenta and BASF have stated outright their reasons for moving much of their field experimentation and research staff from Europe to the United States: its more favorable environment for innovation. Over 70% of European students who go to the United States to complete postgraduate training choose not to return to Europe. No scientist enjoys working in an area that is vilified publicly or where one's ability to carry out field experimentation is threatened.

The situation continues to evolve. Authorizations have now recommenced. The EU has in principle "completed" its legal framework, as the Commission energetically pointed out to the World Trade Organization (WTO) when defending itself against a complaint submitted by the United States (with Argentina and Canada) about the apparent GMO moratorium—a move that has cost U.S. farmers hundreds of millions of dollars' worth of lost exports. In September 2006, the WTO ruled (in a 1,148-page verdict) that European countries broke international trade regulations by preventing imports of 21 GM products, most of which were foods. National bans in six Member States, it determined, were illegal. The complainants urged the EU to immediately bring its GMO laws into WTO compliance. The Commission argued that, because the EU ended the moratorium in 2004, it had already done so. It also decided, in spite of reservations, not to appeal the decision. Instead, it asked for "reasonable time" to work with Member States to modify national measures. The WTO did not rule on whether the EU legislation was illegal and sidestepped the issue of whether biotech foods were safe. The United States has indicated its intention to continue with its WTO case until it is convinced that all applications for approval are being decided on scientific rather than political grounds.

The WTO can only authorize penalties for illegal trade restrictions still in force. But if the United States and the others prove that the EU has failed to act sufficiently on the national bans or the specific product barriers ruled illegal, the WTO may authorize retaliatory sanctions against Brussels. For a comprehensive analysis of the transatlantic dispute over GM foods and international trade law, see Pollack and Shaffer (2009).

The use of the PP is suboptimal if governments depart seriously from a rational balance between protection against risks of the unknown and protection which shuts down innovation and associated benefits. The dynamic dimension is ignored. Europe appears to be currently underestimating the latter risk, making a strategic error in maintaining the unjustified stringency of its regulatory framework for the products of modern biotechnology. This position contradicts its own earlier statements about the PP paying attention to scientific and technical developments. By that strategic error, it increases the overall risk. Its commitments acknowledge the need for improved regulatory practices (EC 2001, 2003), but steps have not yet been taken to effectively implement these improvements, nor to correct the errors of the past. These failures will constrain and frustrate implementation of the strategy for the life sciences and biotechnology. The tension between promoting its benefits and trying to reassure public opinion by means of the double-edged weapon of stringent regulation threatens to tear good science to pieces.

What Have We Learned and What Can We Do?

The experience recounted above describes a continuing dialogue between the EU and the United States, with various degrees of convergence or divergence and exchange of experience over the years. More significantly, it illustrates on both sides of the Atlantic an extended and continuing dialogue, with a rational, science-based approach to risk assessment and management under conditions of uncertainty one side, and various political forces on the other. Precautionary pragmatism and political push—sometimes aligned, sometimes in confrontation.

Some tension between science-based rationality and political necessity is inevitable. Politics will win in the short term, but the scientific method has a distinguished track record of long-term success. Irrational or excessive regulations impose a cost. They divert scientific, administrative, and political energies and resources from real problems to pseudo-problems. They set up barriers to innovation. Thus, it is in the public interest to facilitate the learning processes. The dynamic learning process envisaged by the PP should be allowed and encouraged to function. But the "irrationalities" of excessive precaution may in fact be quite rational viewed through the parochial lenses of various special interests—of environmental NGOs, environment ministries, industrial investments, organic farmers, or other players.

What lessons can be drawn for future regulatory policy? The consequences of initial adverse decisions may be underestimated. When investments—economic, psychological, political—are made or withheld, these choices are not easily reversed. Especially in the EU, we have seen a hysteresis effect—past errors leave scars, and laws, which constrain future choices. The practical and political difficulty of implementing a relaxation in the climate of public suspicion in Europe of the mid-1990s was evident. Yet in the United States, in the context of less public awareness, it has been possible for the U.S. National Institutes of Health Recombinant DNA Advisory Committee to achieve many revisions—mainly relaxations—in their guidelines for rDNA work. The U.S. Office of Management and Budget (OMB) gives procedural teeth to an administration demanding an economic justification to underpin regulatory proposals from federal agencies (Graham 2002). In Europe, the European Commission has at least made clear its commitment to "better regulation" (EC 2001, 2003), specifically including fuller impact assessments to precede regulatory proposals.

It has been difficult in Europe to avoid a process of politicization, or "instrumentalization," in which any proposal—on regulation of GM foods or anything else—risks becoming a political symbol. The details of scientific advice are of less interest than the possibilities for using any given dossier as an instrument in the continuing interinstitutional power play. Such continuing games operate in at least three arenas:

- relations between the Commission (with its sacred monopoly of political initiative) and the Parliament and Council;
- relations between the EU institutions and national administrations;

- relations between the many biotech-interested ministries and agencies within any national administration, and between the Directorates-General within the European Commission.

The rules by which these games are played are not those of science.

Over the past three decades, within national administrations and within the EU, various alliances have predominated at different times. For example, the rise of "Green" politics has paradoxically been bad news for the development and diffusion of products and services that scientific opinion generally sees as friendly to the environment. Successful propaganda campaigns against GM products contributed to persuading the Convention on Biological Diversity to divert much energy into the creation of a "Biosafety Protocol"—an agreement with marginal relevance to the protection of biological diversity. Once that diversion is translated into EU legislation, obligations are laid upon EU exporters of GM products. Only after the legislation had been adopted did the scientific community start to notice its adverse consequences. Failing to treat international research collaborations in GM crops separately had direct impacts on scientific research (De Greef 2004). Diverse interest groups competing in the media and the court of public opinion recognize the value of capturing, shifting, and maintaining control over public consensus. But "public opinion" is a slippery concept, and the surveys which seek to measure it are often of doubtful predictive value. "Deregulation" becomes a synonym, a slogan, an abbreviation for a whole package of assumed-to-be-correlated political attitudes favoring free trade, globalization, and the interests of multinational corporations. Such arguments may be simplistic and foolish, but they can be politically potent.

Transatlantic dialogues can contribute to improving the quality of debate, given steady leadership and an appropriate reticence about getting involved in current hot controversies. The track record of the EC-U.S. Task Force on Biotechnology Research over 15 years is a good model (EC 2000b). EU and U.S. differences in regulatory approaches to similar issues should be seen not only as a source of friction or an impediment to trade but also as an opportunity for learning, in both scientific and policy terms. In retrospect, we may appreciate the critical role that timing plays in regulatory developments. Is it really possible to debate rational, science-based regulations in a public climate of fear, merging on hysteria? Is there not a danger of short-term "knee-jerk" regulatory responses—in the name of precaution—to highly controversial issues? Do we not need a more balanced, long-term vision for our regulatory frameworks, one that ensures the protection of human health and the environment while allowing the safe development and diffusion of a new technology?

There are lessons for future use of precautionary regulation, and the experience with GM foods would certainly support the conclusions and recommendations of the European Policy Centre as summarized in Allio et al. (2004), presented here in Table 2.2. They note that since the early 1990s, a large number of reforms have been initiated to improve regulatory effectiveness in the EU. Nevertheless, the overall quality of EU regulatory activity remains suboptimal for a number of reasons, as articulated in the table. The case of GM crops and foods certainly confirms these conclusions.

Table 2.2 *Reasons for the Shortcomings of EC Regulatory Activity*

- No clear, well-articulated vision of the regulatory reform process as a whole
- No simple legal basis, and no legal requirement, to undertake comprehensive impact assessments (IAs) at EU level
- No single, consolidated, legally binding statement of "Regulatory Management Policy"
- Few (quantitative) targets and time scales for achieving improvements in the regulatory process
- No clear, mandatory guidelines that specify how and when assessments should be carried out; no single set of administrative procedures and tools for undertaking them; and no sanctions for failing to provide them
- Businesses are concerned that the IA process does not give sufficient emphasis to how regulatory changes will affect competitiveness, particularly among small and medium enterprises
- NGOs are concerned that the new IA process does not give sufficient weight to environmental and social factors
- No requirement for the Commission to undertake systematic *ex post* analyses of the actual impact of regulations
- The Commission secretariat-general has no power to reject legislative proposals that do not satisfy basic standards for IAs
- The institutions have not yet adequately addressed the issue of the resources and skills required for the effective planning and implementation of regulatory reforms, including IAs
- The initiative lacks external credibility because many stakeholders do not consider that the process is sufficiently independent

Source: Allio et al. (2004)

Specific steps could be taken to improve the process. One would be to facilitate the dynamic operation of the PP by formal review. That could mean several actions:

- Set defined-period sunset clauses.
- When a commitment to review is made, charge some independent entity with that review responsibility. Graham (2002) describes how this role is played in the United States by the OMB.
- Delegate technical decisions to appropriate expert committees and avoid letting them become heavyweight legislative issues. Take, for example, the thresholds and separation distances for coexistence of conventional and GM crops. The European Parliament has clamored for legislation, but the pragmatic solutions are straightforward familiar matters of good agricultural practice. Markets and legal system remedies can handle any residual risks.
- Pay more systematic and serious attention to the results of peer-reviewed research supported by the European Commission (Kessler and Economidis 2001). That includes not only the literature from around the world, but also on occasion reports from partially EC-sponsored international conferences on the biosafety results of field tests of GM plants and microorganisms, including 1990 in Kiawah Island, South Carolina; 1992 in Goslar, Germany; 1994 in Monterey, California; 1996 in Tsukuba, Japan; 1998 in Braunschweig, Germany; 2000 in Saskatoon, Canada; 2002 in Beijing, China; and 2004 in Montpellier, France.
- Note the evidence from practical experience. This is difficult to appraise objectively, but many relevant publications of good quality exist: Gianessi et al. (2002, 2003); Phipps and Park (2002); AFSSA (2004); and Huang et al. (2002).

A more basic structural problem is the need to improve interagency or interministerial coordination. This was well addressed in the U.S. federal context by the establishment of the interagency Biotechnology Science Coordinating Committee, which from 1985 to 1990 played a major role in ensuring coherence of policy—not least because it had strong backing from the president's office. All national administrations face this generic problem. The importance of coordination was recognized but inadequately addressed by the European Commission in its 1984 creation of the Biotechnology Steering Committee. Chaired by the Research Directorate-General (DG), it did not have the political muscle to impose itself when inter-DG controversies arose over regulation.

Similar failures of policy coordination at the national level gave EU environment ministries control over issues far beyond their normal competence. One might note here the importance of the pharma sector having retained control of its sectoral agenda. But maintaining this significant new EU environment ministry power depended upon sustaining the belief in the special environmental risks of biotech products as compared to similar conventionally produced products—in the face of growing evidence to the contrary. Efforts to strengthen interservice coordination were made within the European Commission, but they were repeatedly overthrown by the power of the one-dimensional "chef de file" dogma. That control was challenged several times over the years by attempts to create or impose a "strategy," coordinating the departmental activities of separate DGs. President Jacques Delors created such a "Biotechnology Coordinating Committee" in 1991 in the aftermath of complaints from scientific and industrial communities about the legislation agreed to by the EU environment ministers in April 1990. Following his departure, the effort faded. More recently, President Romano Prodi catalyzed the drafting of a high-profile "Strategy for the Life Sciences and Biotechnology" (EC 2002) with a 30-point Action Plan. Still, the questions remain:

- Will the strategy really overcome the individual powers of individual EU commissioners in concert with the corresponding national ministers?
- Will the strategy survive the departure of the president whose administration sought to impose it? *Verba volant, scripta manent*—that is, "spoken words fly away, written ones stay." In this context, the "scripta" are the adopted legislation.

Regarding possible lessons for future U.S.-European relations, one might hope for a more authoritative voice for scientific opinion. But by what means may "authority" be gained, maintained, and imposed? Intellectual authority plays by rules different from those of politics. Current attempts—however belatedly—seek to build a basis for the "voice of science" to be heard in the corridors of the meetings of international bodies discussing and imposing regulations and norms for trade in biotechnology. Within the United States, this role was played with success by the American Society of Microbiology in the post-Asilomar years (Cantley 1995). Europe, however, is more complicated. The merits of harmonization and common understanding for facilitating trade are evident, but such international machinery turns slowly and is not easily reversed. The impacts of the Cartagena Protocol on Biosafety are becoming restrictive for modern biotechnology. Meanwhile, the decision of the world's largest agricultural exporting country to remain outside this protocol may reflect a prudent skepticism.

These thoughts offer some ideas on how transatlantic and international debates over precaution might best be addressed. Learning from experiences such as the rather unhappy history of regulating GM crops and foods ought to inform that process. There remains a central problem: How do societies learn? Despite the many common elements among the problems, cultures, and attempted solutions, EU and U.S. societies are and will remain obstinately and distinctively different. That heterogeneity should be used as an asset in our ongoing policy and scientific learning processes—*vive la différence!*

References

AFSSA (Agence Française de Sécurité Sanitaire des Aliments). 2004. OGM et alimentation: peut-on identifier et évaluer des bénéfices pour la santé?. Agence Française de Sécurité Sanitaire des Aliments. August. www.afssa.fr/ftp/afssa/2004-SA-0246-Bénéfices-OGM.pdf (site now discontinued).

Allio, Lorenzo, Bruce Ballantine, and Dirk Hudig. 2004. *Achieving a New Regulatory Culture in the European Union: An Action Plan*, Working Paper No. 10. European Policy Centre. April. www.isn.ethz.ch/isn/Current-Affairs/Security-Watch/Detail/?fecvnodeid=110616&ord588=grp1&fecvid=33&ots591=0c54e3b3-1e9c-be1e-2c24-a6a8c7060233&lng=en&v33=110616&id=10825 (accessed April 13, 2010).

Berg, Paul, David Baltimore, Herbert W. Boyer, Stanley N. Cohen, Ronald W. Davis, David S. Hogness, Daniel Nathens, Richard Roblin, James D. Watson, Sherman Weissman, and Norton Zinder. 1974. Potential Biohazards of Recombinant DNA Molecules. July 26 Letter to *Science* 185: 303.

Berg, Paul, David Baltimore, Sydney Brenner, Richard O. Roblin III, and Maxine Singer. 1975. Asilomar Conference on Recombinant DNA Molecules: Summary Statement of the Report Submitted to the Assembly of Life Sciences of the National Academy of Sciences and approved by the Executive Committee on May 20, 1975. *Science* 188: 991.

Brookes, Graham, and Peter Barfoot. 2005. GM Crops: The Global Economic and Environmental Impact: The First Nine Years, 1996–2004. *AgBioForum* 8 (2–3): 187–196.

Burbank, Luther. 1906. *The Training of the Human Plant*. New York: The Century Co.

Cantley, Mark F. 1995. The Regulation of Modern Biotechnology: A Historical and European Perspective. A Case Study in How Societies Cope with New Knowledge in the Last Quarter of the Twentieth Century. In *Biotechnology: Legal, Economic and Ethical Dimensions*, edited by D. Brauer. Vol. 12: 505–681 of *Biotechnology: A Multi-Volume Comprehensive Treatise*. Weinheim: VCH.

Carson, Rachel. 2002. *Silent Spring*. New York: Houghton Mifflin Company, Mariner Books. (Orig. pub. 1962.).

Crossan, Angus, and Ivan Kennedy. 2004. *A Snapshot of Roundup Ready Cotton in Australia: Are There Environmental Benefits from Rapid Adoption of Roundup Ready Cotton in Australia?* Sydney University. www.agric.usyd.edu.au/research/p/2003.htm (site now discontinued).

De Greef, Willy. 2004. The Cartagena Protocol and the Future of Agbiotech. *Nature Biotechnology* 22: 811–812.

EC (European Commission). 2000a. Communication on the Precautionary Principle, COM(2000)1. Brussels: European Commission.

———. 2000b. *The EC-U.S. Task Force on Biotechnology Research: Mutual Understanding: A Decade of Collaboration (1990–2000)*. European Commission, EUR19407. Brussels: European Commission.

———. 2001. *Communication on Simplifying and Improving the Regulatory Environment*. COM(2001)726. Brussels: European Commission.

———. 2002. *Life Sciences and Biotechnology: A Strategy for Europe*. COM(2002)27. Brussels: European Commission.

———. 2003. *Report on Better Law-making 2003*. COM(2003)770. Brussels: European Commission.

European Council of Ministers. 2000. Resolution on the Precautionary Principle. Annex III of the Proceedings of the European Council. Nice, December 7–9. http://governance.jrc.it/pp/dec2000_en.pdf (accessed June 30, 2010).

European Parliament. 2000. Resolution on the Commission Communication on the Precautionary Principle (COM(2000) 1—C5-0143/2000—2000/2086(COS)). http://www3.europarl.eu.int/omk/omnsapir.so/pv2?PRG=DOCPV&APP=PV2&LANGUE=EN&SDOCTA=15&TXTLST=1&POS=1&Type_Doc=RESOL&TPV=DEF&DATE=141200&PrgPrev=TYPEF@A5|PRG@QUERY|APP@PV2|FILE@BIBLIO00|NUMERO@352|YEAR@00|PLAGE@1&TYPEF=A5&NUMB=1&DATEF=001214 (accessed June 30, 2010).

FAO/WHO (UN Food and Agriculture Organization/World Health Organization). 2000. Safety Aspects of Genetically Modified Foods of Plant Origin: Report of a Joint FAO/WHO Expert Consultation on Foods Derived from Biotechnology. Geneva, Switzerland: WHO and FAO. Available at www.fao.org/wairdocs/ae584e/ae584e00.htm (accessed July 19, 2010).

Firbank, L. G., et al. 2003. The Farm Scale Evaluations of Spring-sown Genetically Modified Crops. *Philosophical Transactions of the Royal Society of London, Series B: Biological Sciences* 358 (November 29): 1775–1913. www.pubs.royalsoc.ac.uk/phil_bio/news/fse_toc.html (site now discontinued).

Gianessi, Leonard P., Cressida S. Silvers, Sujatha Sankula, and Janet E. Carpenter. 2002. *Plant Biotechnology: Current and Potential Impact for Improving Pest Management in U.S. Agriculture: An Analysis of 40 Case Studies*. National Center for Food and Agricultural Policy.

Gianessi, Leonard P., Sujatha Sankula, and Nathan Reigner. 2003. *Plant Biotechnology: Potential Impact for Improving Pest Management in European Agriculture: A Summary of Three Case Studies*. National Center for Food and Agricultural Policy.

Graham, John D. 2002. Presidential Management of Regulatory Policy: A Stronger Role for Science, Engineering, and Economics. Remarks prepared for delivery to the National Academy of Engineering. February 20.

Hellmich, Richard L., Blair D. Siegfried, Mark K. Sears, Diane E. Stanley-Horn, Michael J. Daniels, Heather R. Mattila, Terrence Spencer, Keith G. Bidne, and Leslie C. Lewis. 2001. Monarch Larvae Sensitivity to *Bacillus thuringiensis*–Purified Proteins and Pollen. *Proceedings of the National Academy of Sciences of the United States of America* 98 (21): 11925–11930.

Huang, J., R. Hu, C. Fan, C. E. Pray, and S. Rozelle. 2002. Bt Cotton Benefits, Costs, and Impacts in China. *AgBioForum* 5 (4): 153–166. www.agbioforum.org (accessed June 10, 2010).

James, Clive. 2004. *Status of Commercialized Transgenic Crops: 2003*. ISAAA Brief 30. International Service for the Acquisition of Agri-biotech Applications (ISAAA). Executive summary available at www.biotech-info.net/global_status_2000.html (accessed June 10, 2010).

Kessler, Charles, and Ioannis Economidis, eds. 2001. *A Review of Results: EC-sponsored Research on Safety of Genetically Modified Organisms*. European Commission, EUR 19884. http://ec.europa.eu/research/quality-of-life/gmo/ (accessed June 10, 2010).

Kuiper, H. A., G. A. Kleter, A. König, W. P. Hammes, and I. Knudsen, eds. 2004 Safety Assessment, Detection and Traceability, and Societal Aspects of Genetically Modified Foods: European Network on Safety Assessment of Genetically Modified Food Crops (ENTRANSFOOD). Special Issue of *Food and Chemical Toxicology* 42 (7): 1043–1202.

Losey, John E., Linda S. Rayor, and Maureen E. Carter. 1999. Transgenic Pollen Harms Monarch Larvae. *Nature* 399 (May 20): 214.

Oberhauser, Karen S., Michelle D. Prysby, Heather R. Mattila, Diane E. Stanley-Horn, Mark K. Sears, Galen Dively, Eric Olson, John M. Pleasants, Wai-Ki F. Lam, and Richard L. Hellmich. 2001. Temporal and Spatial Overlap between Monarch Larvae and Corn Pollen. *Proceedings of the National Academy of Sciences of the United States of America* 98 (21): 11913–11918.

OECD (Organisation for Economic Co-operation and Development). 1986. *Recombinant DNA Safety Considerations: Safety Considerations for Industrial, Agricultural and Environmental Applications of Organisms Derived by Recombinant DNA Techniques* (the "Blue Book"). Paris: OECD. www.oecd.org/dataoecd/45/54/1943773.pdf (site now discontinued).

————. 1993. *Safety Evaluation of Foods Derived by Modern Biotechnology: Concepts and Principles* ("the Green Book"). Paris: OECD. www.oecd.org/dataoecd/57/3/1946129.pdf (site now discontinued).

Phipps, R. H., and J. R. Park. 2002. Environmental Benefits of Genetically Modified Crops: Global and European Perspectives on Their Ability to Reduce Pesticide Use. *Journal of Animal and Feed Sciences* 11: 1–18.

Pleasants, John M., Richard L. Hellmich, Galen P. Dively, Mark K. Sears, Diane E. Stanley-Horn, Heather R. Mattila, John E. Foster, Thomas L. Clark, and Gretchen D. Jones. 2001. Corn Pollen Deposition on Milkweeds in and near Cornfields. *Proceedings of the National Academy of Sciences of the United States of America* 98 (21): 11919–11924.

Pollack, Mark A., and Gregory C. Shaffer. 2009. *When Cooperation Fails: The International Law and Politics of Genetically Modified Foods.* Oxford: Oxford University Press.

Rogers, Michael D. 1975. The Pandora's Box Congress. *Rolling Stone* 189 (June 19): 36.

Schumpeter, Joseph. 1942 [1975]. *Capitalism, Socialism and Democracy.* New York: Harper.

Sears, Mark K., Richard L. Hellmich, Diane E. Stanley-Horn, Karen S. Oberhauser, John M. Pleasants, Heather R. Mattila, Blair D. Siegfried, and Galen P. Dively. 2001. Impact of Bt Corn Pollen on Monarch Butterfly Populations: A Risk Assessment. *Proceedings of the National Academy of Sciences of the United States of America* 98 (21): 11937–11942.

Singer, Maxine, and Dieter Soll. 1973. Guidelines for DNA Hybrid Molecules. Letter to *Science,* 181: 1114 September 21. Reproduced in Watson and Tooze, *op. cit.*

Squire, G. R., D. R. Brooks, D. A. Bohan, G. T. Champion, R. E. Daniels, A. J. Haughton, C. Hawes, S. Heard, M. O. Hill, M. J. May, J. L. Osborne, J. N. Perry, D. B. Roy, I. P. Woiwod, and L. G. Firbank. 2003. On the Rationale and Interpretation of the Farm Scale Evaluations of Genetically Modified Herbicide-Tolerant Crops. *Philosophical Transactions of the Royal Society of London, Series B: Biological Sciences* 358: 1779–1799.

Stanley-Horn, Diane E., Galen P. Dively, Richard L. Hellmich, Heather R. Mattila, Mark K. Sears, Robyn Rose, Laura C. H. Jesse, John E. Losey, John J. Obrycki, and Les Lewis. 2001. Assessing the Impact of Cry1Ab-expressing Corn Pollen on Monarch Butterfly Larvae in Field Studies. *Proceedings of the National Academy of Sciences of the United States of America* 98 (21): 11931–11936.

UK Advisory Committee on Research. 2002. Developing Tools for the Prioritisation and Assessment of Value for Money of Research. Discussion Paper ACR 010, Agenda Item 6. Annex A, Appendix 1: Consideration of Food Safety, Economics and Research Prioritisation, 16–17.

U.S. NRC (National Research Council). 2000. *Genetically Modified Plants: Science and Regulation.* Washington, DC: National Academy Press.

Watson, James D., and John Tooze. 1981. *The DNA Story: A Documentary History of Gene Cloning.* San Francisco: W.H. Freeman and Company.

Williams, W. P., G. L. Windham, P. M. Buckley, and C. A. Daves. 2002. Aflatoxin Accumulation in Conventional and Transgenic Corn Hybrids Infested with Southwestern Corn Borer (*Lepidoptera: Crambidae*). *Journal of Agricultural and Urban Entomology* 19 (4): 227–236.

Zangerl, R., D. McKenna, C. L. Wraight, M. Carroll, P. Ficarello, R. Warner, and M. R. Berenbaum. 2001. Effects of Exposure to Event 176 *Bacillus thuringiensis* Corn Pollen on Monarch and Black Swallowtail Caterpillars under Field Conditions. *Proceedings of the National Academy of Sciences of the United States of America* 98 (21): 11908–11912.

CHAPTER 3

Beef, Hormones, and Mad Cows

George Gray, Michael D. Rogers, and Jonathan B. Wiener

O ne of the sharpest transatlantic conflicts over relative precaution has been about beef. Here, we explore this example in some detail because it relates so closely to, and yet helps refute, the conventional wisdom of greater European precaution.

Recent headlines might suggest that Europe is more precautionary about beef than is the United States. But the reality is more complex: Europe has been more precautionary about *hormones* in beef, while the United States has been more precautionary about *mad cow disease* in beef, and especially in human blood donations. The trend over time is toward greater relative U.S. precaution, especially in the blood donor restrictions adopted since 1999; this is in the opposite direction of and casts doubt on the "flip-flop" hypothesis of increasing relative European precaution since 1990. The beef cases are telling because they illustrate the considerable variation in relative transatlantic precaution even within one field of regulation involving the same regulatory agencies.

This chapter examines specific actions taken by governments in Europe and the United States to address two distinct risks: the use of growth hormones in beef, such as bovine somatotropin (BST), and the outbreak of "mad cow disease," or bovine spongiform encephalopathy (BSE). Each risk was addressed with precautionary measures at a time when ultimate causes, scope, and effects were highly uncertain. We compare relative precaution in terms of the timing and stringency of the measures adopted (Wiener and Rogers 2002).

Beef Hormones

Bovine somatotropin (BST) is a hormone that occurs naturally in cows and controls their lactation. It is now commercially produced as an agricultural pharmaceutical, synthesized by genetically engineered bacteria that have had a bovine gene implanted to make the bacteria produce BST; this form of BST is called recombinant, or rBST. When rBST is injected into cows, their milk production can increase substantially. The U.S. Food and Drug Administration (FDA) approved the use of rBST in November 1993, finding that milk produced from cows that had been given the artificial hormone was indistinguishable from other milk. It is now widely used on U.S. farms. But it is banned in the European Union (EU).

Other hormones, both natural and synthetic, have also been used for some time as growth promoters in beef cattle. The use of such growth promoters has been the subject of a great deal of controversy in the EU and has for some time been totally banned in meat production there. Since growth promoters are widely used in the United States, Canada, and several other states that exported beef to the EU, those governments challenged the EU ban in an international trade dispute at the World Trade Organization (WTO).

Six hormones are involved in the WTO dispute. Three are naturally occurring: estradiol-17ß, testosterone and progesterone. Estradiol-17ß is a sex steroidal hormone with estrogenic action, responsible for female characteristics, while testosterone is a sex steroidal hormone with androgenic action, responsible for male characteristics. Progesterone is a sex steroidal hormone with gestagenic action, i.e., it is responsible for maintaining pregnancy. All three hormones are produced in animals and humans and are produced throughout life. They are required for normal physiological functioning of the body and for maturation. Their levels vary with age, sex, tissue, and species. The other three hormones are artificially produced: zeranol (which mimics the action of estradiol-17ß), trenbolone (which mimics the action of testosterone), and melengestrol acetate (or MGA, which mimics the action of progesterone).

In the United States, all six hormones are approved for growth promotion purposes. All except MGA are formulated as pellets that are implanted in the ear of the animal; MGA is administered as a feed additive.

These hormones are carcinogenic at high doses in animal experiments, and there are clear indications that these effects occur in humans as well. The essential uncertainty concerns the extrapolation to low doses, particularly because estradiol, testosterone, and progesterone already occur naturally in humans at levels that are arguably greater than those delivered in the meat from treated animals.

"Mad Cow Disease" (BSE)

Bovine spongiform encephalopathy (BSE), commonly called "mad cow disease," is a type of transmissible spongiform encephalopathy (TSE), a rare family of slowly progressive and uniformly fatal neurodegenerative disorders that can affect humans and other animals. All of these diseases have incubation periods of months to years between infection and the onset of clinical signs. The presumed infectious agent of BSE is the prion, an abnormal protein that somehow stimulates an array of TSEs including BSE, scrapie (a disease in sheep), chronic wasting disease (a disease in deer and elk), and kuru (a disease among cannibals) and Creutzfeldt-Jakob disease (CJD) among humans. Prions are highly resistant to traditional disinfection techniques and are not completely removed by digestion or high heat (Prusiner 1997). The discoveries that kuru is a TSE and that TSEs are transmitted by prions were each awarded the Nobel Prize in medicine.

BSE is not easily spread from cow to cow. There is no evidence that sharing quarters, food, or water sources, for example, can spread the disease from an infected animal to a healthy one. It appears that transmission primarily occurs if a healthy animal ingests high-infectivity tissues, principally from the central nervous system—brain, spinal cord, and other associated tissues—from a sick animal. This occurred in the United Kingdom (UK) and other countries when rendered animal protein that included infectious tissues from BSE-infected cattle and scrapie-infected sheep was used as a protein supplement in cattle feed (Anderson et al. 1996). The disease outbreak may have begun in Britain in the 1980s as the use of rendered protein in feed increased when alternatives like soy meal and fish meal became more expensive. Meanwhile, ironically, genetically modified (GM) soy—widely used in the United States to increase protein intake in cattle—had been restricted by ostensibly precautionary EU policies (O'Neill 2003). At the same time, the permitted methods for manufacturing cattle feed containing animal protein changed—for example, lower processing temperatures were permitted. This meant that greater numbers of cattle were consuming feed that may have contained the infectious prions that cause scrapie in sheep. Today, although the origin of the BSE epidemic remains controversial, there is little doubt that the outbreak was exacerbated by the recycling of bovine materials in the bovine feed chain (Wilesmith et al. 1991; Wilesmith et al. 1992; Kimberlin and Wilesmith 1994; Wilesmith 1994; Nathanson et al. 1997).

The first case of BSE was identified in the UK in 1985, followed by rapidly increasing numbers of BSE-infected cattle across England (over 2,000 cases by 1988). Mathematical modeling suggests that the epidemic probably started in the UK between 1981 and 1982 (Wilesmith et al. 1991; Wilesmith et al. 1992; Wilesmith 1994; Donnelly et al. 1997; Ferguson et al. 1997; Ferguson et al. 1999). The peak of the UK epidemic occurred in January 1993, with almost 1,000 new cases diagnosed per week (FDA 1997). As of late 2003, about 178,000 total cases of BSE had been confirmed in England on 35,275 farms (Cohen et al. 2003, 14); by 2005, the total was about 180,000 (OIE 2005). The disease has been detected in 24 countries, including the United States (USDA 2004a).

In addition to the affliction of cattle with BSE, there was growing concern that human consumption of BSE-infected cattle products might allow the disease to cross the "species barrier" and give rise to a human spongiform encephalopathy. For a long time the UK government insisted that there was *no* risk to humans from BSE, although the government did inaugurate a monitoring program for CJD, a TSE of humans, and similar afflictions (see UK 2000). Ruminants' brain and spinal tissues were not banned from entering the human food chain in the UK until late 1989. The "no-risk" assumption was based on experience with sheep—Britons had been eating sheep with scrapie for over 200 years with no evidence of a link to any human disease, let alone a TSE. At the same time, knowledge of cross-species transmission of other TSEs meant that scientists could not rule out a link between BSE and a CJD-like disease.

In 1990 a domestic cat in the UK was diagnosed as suffering from a "scrapie-like" spongiform encephalopathy. Later, TSEs were found in UK zoo animals, including large cats that had been fed cattle. These events generated concern that BSE might also be transmissible to other species, including humans. Although TSEs are most infective toward the same species, experimental evidence suggested that cross-species transmission might be possible. In 1994, the UK Spongiform Encephalopathy Advisory Committee (SEAC) judged the risk of transmissibility to humans to be remote, only because precautionary measures had been put into place, namely the removal of high infectivity tissues from the human food supply. Scientists theorized that if BSE were transmitted to humans, it would likely resemble CJD; they suggested that surveillance be put into place to identify atypical cases or changing patterns of the disease.

On March 20, 1996, the UK government reported the appearance of a new variant form of CJD (vCJD) afflicting young people. It raised the possibility that this vCJD may have come from humans eating BSE-infected beef (Goethals et al. 1998). As of March 2010, the total number of definite and probable cases of human vCJD deaths reported in the UK was 169 (UK National CJD Surveillance Unit 2010). Outside the UK, 25 vCJD cases have been reported in France, 4 in Ireland, and 18 in the rest of the world. Clinical, pathological, and molecular studies provide compelling evidence that the agent that causes vCJD is the same as that which causes BSE (Will et al. 1996; Collinge et al. 1996; Bruce et al. 1997; Hill et al. 1997; Scott et al. 1999). The number of human vCJD victims remains small—compare approximately 220 cases between 1996 and 2010 with over 180,000 cattle with BSE—but the appearance of CJD in young people is very rare; the type of brain damage is different from that of traditional CJD, suggesting that a new human disease might be arising associated with BSE in cattle. Its latency period for manifestation may be several years, suggesting that additional human cases of vCJD may appear over time as a result of earlier exposures to prions. (For a summary comparison, see FDA 2002, 2.) Currently, no test can diagnose CJD or vCJD while a patient is alive, though some symptoms are suggestive (see FDA 2002, 3); only autopsy inspection of the brain can identify the disease.

Relative Precaution in Europe and the United States

The EU approach to beef hormones was more precautionary than the U.S. approach. This finding is consistent with the conventional wisdom that Europe is more precautionary than the United States, particularly regarding products of genetic engineering, but also about new technological risks in general. Concerning BSE, however, the roles of relative precaution were reversed. The United States adopted its ban on imports of British beef earlier than did the EU, and maintained it far longer. While both the EU and United States introduced feed bans to reduce the potential for spread of BSE, only the United States put the feed ban in place before BSE was detected in its own herds. And the United States adopted much more precautionary measures to safeguard its blood donations against even remote risks of BSE and vCJD than did the EU.

Growth Hormones

Invoking the precautionary principle, the EU has banned the use of rBST and six beef growth hormones, along with imports of beef treated with these hormones. The United States permits the use of these hormones and objects to the EU precautionary restrictions.

The opposition to rBST in the EU was concerned with several impacts. The first was animal welfare. Cows given BST experienced an increased incidence of mastitis. Second came human health. When farmers used more antibiotics to counter the mastitis, these antibiotics could stay in the milk. They also could eventually reduce the effectiveness of antibiotics against bacteria that infect humans. The final concern was socioeconomic effects: potential harm could come to small farms that were unable to compete against the economies of scale offered by new technologies. So far, the available scientific evidence does not support the human health fears. Dr. Martin Bangemann, then EC commissioner responsible for Industrial Affairs, Information, and Telecommunication Technologies, stated:

> It is clear that neither from an ethics nor a health viewpoint, is there any argument against BST. The only decision that stands is one based on a political environment with its roots in agricultural beliefs and traditions. (Bangemann 1993)

It must be stressed that although this statement was very robust, the formal EU position at that time was that rBST was banned as a precautionary measure by the European Council Decision of April 25, 1990 (European Council 1990). By this decision, the EU prohibited the administration of rBST in any form to dairy cattle (Article 1) for a period of 10 years (up to December 31, 1999), except for the purposes of carrying out scientific and technical trials (Article 2).

At the end of 1999, the European Council made this prohibition permanent and removed the exception that had previously been available for scientific and technical trials (European Council 1999). This decision was based on research that had demonstrated that BST increased the risk of mastitis and increased the duration of necessary treatment for the affliction. Furthermore, increases in foot and leg disorders afflicted dairy cattle when BST was administered, together with severe reactions at the BST injection site. Thus, for animal welfare reasons—which were required under the European Convention for the Protection of Animals Kept for Farming Purposes (CoE 1976)—the prohibition was made permanent. Precautionary action under scientific and technical uncertainty (the time-limited European Council Prohibition of 1990) had been replaced by a risk management decision based on new knowledge. The question of possible human health effects was not addressed in these formal decisions.

EU concerns about the use of hormones for growth promotion purposes date from the 1970s. The illegal use of the hormone diethylstilbestrol (DES) in veal production had been implicated as a possible cause of hormonal irregularities observed in European adolescents (Vogel 1995). This had a significant negative effect on the veal market. Strong regulatory action was thought necessary to restore consumer confidence and to ensure the proper functioning of the European Single Market, i.e., to avoid market distortions arising from some Member States imposing bans when other Member States did not. The first directive banning the use of hormones for animal growth promotion purposes was adopted in 1981 (European Council 1981). DES was also banned in the United States (Vogel 1995). As a result of a July 1981 debate in the European Parliament, the Council of Ministers sponsored a scientific inquiry into the use of five hormones; this investigation found that three posed no health risk, while no data existed for two others, trenbolone and zeranol. Later studies in 1984 and 1985 found that neither poses significant risk to consumers (Vogel 1995; Vogel 1997). The U.S. FDA permits use of all five of these hormones (Vogel 1995).

In 1985 the Council of Ministers extended the 1981 directive to cover these five hormones. The EC's agricultural commissioner, Frans Andriessen, explained: "Scientific advice is important, but it is not decisive. In public opinion, this is a very delicate issue that has to be dealt with in political terms" (Vogel 1997, 16). The EU banned the import of beef that had been treated with these hormones as early as 1985. Sir Roy Denman, then EC head of delegation to the United States, compared the EU ban on hormone-treated beef products to U.S. restrictions on the sale of unpasteurized cheese from the EU because of "health reasons." He argued that the EU had never demanded a scientific inquiry for this restriction, but rather "accepted that Americans have expressed a democratic preference for hygiene over taste, however eccentric or unnecessary" (Vogel 1997, 18). Europeans also pointed to their restraint in declining to challenge the U.S. ban on Alar, despite its questionable scientific basis (Vogel 1995, 163). The EU readopted its "Hormone Directive" in 1988, effective January 1989.

In contrast to the EU ban on BST and growth hormones, the United States permits their use. The U.S. FDA began reviewing the use of BST as early as 1989 (FDA 1989). The FDA approved the first and only bovine growth hormone used in the United States, the Monsanto company's Posilac, on November 5, 1993. Controversy regarding rBST safety in the human food supply persists. In April 1998, the Canadian government issued a report that questioned the safety of rBST for humans based on results from a 90-day oral toxicity study conducted on rats, which tested the effect of the hormone on antibody responses. This test was conducted for European Union approval of rBST, and the FDA did not review it during the original approval process for Posilac. The Canadian study also found significantly higher levels of insulin-like growth factor 1 (IGF-1) in milk, thus raising concerns for human safety. The FDA then initiated a review of rBST. In February 1999, its report reviewing the current state of the science concluded that the use of rBST is safe for humans (FDA 1999a).

The next month, the European Commission Directorate General XXIV issued a "Report on Public Health Aspects of the Use of Bovine Somatotropin, March 15–16 1999." This report questioned the safety of IGF-1 in milk as a result of the use of rBST. The FDA then reviewed the available scientific data on the effect of rBST on IGF-1 in the spring of 1999 and reconfirmed that "the administration of rBST to dairy cows is safe for all consumers, including infants. Additional exposure data are not necessary." The FDA also cited two findings of the Joint Food and Agriculture Organization/World Health Organization Expert Committee on Food Additives (JECFA), which found in

1992 and again in 1998 that studies have shown that there is "an extremely large margin of safety for humans consuming products from rBST-treated cows" (FDA 1999b).

In response to the EU's "Hormone Directive" of 1988, the United States increased duties on selected EU products, but these duties were relaxed while negotiations on a settlement were undertaken. After entry into force of the WTO Agreement on the Application of Sanitary and Phytosanitary Measures (the SPS Agreement) on January 1, 1995, the United States and Canada initiated formal dispute resolution procedures against the EU under the WTO (Charnovitz 2000; Vogel 1997). The United States claimed that the EU ban adversely affected U.S. exports of meat and meat products, that the EU's measures were not based on an assessment of risk as required under the SPS Agreement, and that U.S. meat and animals were "like" EU meat and animals. The U.S. position was that the EU ban was

> not based on scientific principles and therefore ... violates the WTO Agreement on the Application of Sanitary and Phytosanitary measures. The United Nations Codex Alimentarius has recently confirmed the lack of a scientific basis for restricting the use of these growth hormones. (USTR 1996)

The United States maintained that these hormones pose no risk to human health, stating that

> decades of worldwide scientific studies have shown that consumption of beef from animals produced using the six approved growth promoting hormones—estradiol, melengestrol acetate, progesterone, testosterone, trenbolone acetate, and zeranol—does not present a risk to human health. U.S. beef is safe. (USTR 1999)

Further, the United States argued that the EU's official "Opinion" regarding the safety of hormones

> is not consistent with numerous scientific reviews conducted by reputable international organizations ... and represents a significant departure from the conclusions reached by all previous international review panels. (USTR 1999)

The USTR also pointed out that "hormones occur naturally in many foods. Consumers are exposed every day to foods with higher hormone levels than those found in any beef from animals treated with hormones"; for example, "hormone levels in beef are far less than those found in eggs," and "one bowl of split pea soup has more than nine times as much naturally-occurring estrogen as a five-ounce portion of meat from a steer raised using hormones" (USTR 1999).

In August 1997, the WTO Dispute Panel found that the EU's ban on U.S. beef and beef products violated the WTO regulations and resulted in an annual loss to the United States of $116.8 million (WTO 1997). This decision was upheld by the WTO Appellate Body in January 1998 (WTO 1998; Charnovitz 2000). The United States and Canada then imposed trade retaliation measures against the EU, and the parties sought to negotiate a resolution. The EU continues to defend its position that these growth hormones may be harmful to humans (Charnovitz 2000; Faull 2000); the United States continues to argue that they are not (USTR 1999).

BSE

Although the BSE outbreak began in the UK and has barely touched the United States, American policy has been more precautionary than EU policy regarding beef imports and especially regarding blood donations. It is difficult to classify precaution against BSE solely by U.S. and EU blocs, because EU Member States varied in their levels of precaution, with a particular distinction between Britain, where the disease outbreak originated, and other EU countries bent on protecting their own citizenry from the British threat (see Table 3.1).

During the first few years following the initial identification of BSE in Britain, the epidemic was primarily an animal health concern. That focus reflected the experience with scrapie. Despite its presence in the human food supply for hundreds of years, scrapie had never led to a known case of human illness. Very shortly after the beginning of the BSE outbreak, it became clear that the disease was being spread by cattle feed. In 1987, scientists suggested that BSE might be linked to feed containing the scrapie infectious agent. In 1988, the UK adopted a ban on feeding protein derived from ruminant animals to cattle, along with a slaughter policy for infected cattle. The rate of BSE began to drop after about four to six years—the average incubation period of BSE—after imposition of these feed controls (see Figure 3.1). The specifics of the feed ban were changed over the years to improve efficacy and implementation, but it is fairly clear that the feed ban was responsible for reversing the growth of the disease in the UK. During this initial period, the UK government continued to assert that there was no risk to humans from BSE, although the government did inaugurate a monitoring program for CJD (UK 2000).

Despite incomplete science, small precautionary measures were put in place to protect the human food supply, including a 1989 ban on the sale for human consumption of brain and spinal cord from cattle older than six months (material designated as specified bovine offal, or SBO). However, not until 1996—when the first cases of vCJD were found—were several additional measures taken to reduce human exposure to the infective agent. Foremost among these was a measure aimed specifically at protecting human health. Known as the "over 30 months scheme," it prohibited the sale of any beef from cattle over the age of 30 months for human consumption. Its

Table 3.1. *Summary of UK, EU, and U.S. Regulatory Actions on BSE*

Action	UK	EU	United States
Cases of BSE (see OIE 2005)	~ 180,000 (1986–)	~ 4,000 (1989–)	~ 2 (2003–)
Ban on UK beef	N/A	Temporary (1996–1999)	Yes (1989–)
Ban on meat and bone meal in feed	Yes (1988)	Yes (1994)	Yes (voluntary from 1990; mandatory from 1997)
Ban on eating specified risk material	Yes (1989)	Yes (1997)	Yes (2004)
Ban on beef > 30 months	Yes (1996)	No	No (partial 2004)
Testing at slaughter	No	Yes (2000)	No
Ban on UK, EU blood donors	No (leukodepletion)	Partial (2003)	Yes (1999–)

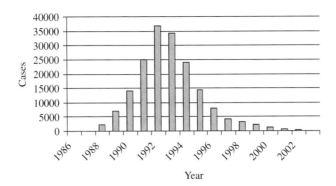

Figure 3.1. *Incidences of Confirmed BSE Cases in the UK*

Source: OIE (2005)

rationale was that cattle older than this could carry potentially substantial levels of infectivity in different tissues without having yet developed clinical signs of the disease.

Later, the official Phillips Inquiry delivered a stinging criticism of the slow response of the UK government to acknowledge and combat the risks of BSE and vCJD (UK 2000; Lyall 2000). A subsequent French parliamentary inquiry also denounced the British and EU policies—and even France's own comparatively aggressive stance—as inadequately precautionary (Daley 2001).

Other European countries attempted to shield themselves from British BSE. In the first half of 1990, at least seven countries, including France, West Germany, Italy, and Russia, banned the import of British beef. In June 1990, the EU agreed to tighten regulations to prevent the spread of BSE, and in response, France, West Germany, and Italy agreed to lift their bans. But in 1994, in light of the UK feed ban initially adopted in 1988, the EU decided to loosen its regulations on cattle born after January 1, 1992. On February 6, 1996, five German regional states banned the import of British beef.

In the few days after the UK announcement of vCJD found in humans in 1996, Germany, France, Belgium, the Netherlands, Portugal, and Sweden adopted temporary bans on British beef and in some cases on live cattle and beef products as well. On March 27, 1996, one week after the UK report of vCJD was issued, the European Commission banned all exports of beef, live cattle, and beef products from the UK in Decision 96/239 (European Commission 1996).

The UK challenged the Commission's export ban of March 27, 1996, in a case before the European Court of Justice. The British argued that the measures that had already been taken by the UK were adequate, effectively making the export ban disproportionate. Furthermore, they added, the Commission had exceeded its powers. The UK's additional measures included banning the sale for human consumption of meat from bovine animals over 30 months old and banning the use of mammalian-derived meat and bone meal in feed for any farm animal. Animal slaughter procedures were also made more stringent. The EU had adopted a feed ban in 1994.

The European Commission fully lifted its export ban on British beef two and a half years later, in Decision 98/692 of November 1998 (European Commission 1998). This decision also required EU Member States to lift their import bans, but France and Germany steadfastly maintained their import bans. Under pressure from the Commission, the German federal government reluctantly lifted its ban on March 17, 2000, but the French government maintained its ban, defending it with evidence from the French Food Safety Agency. France noted the increasing sensitivity of tests for prions, allowing for the detection of infectivity in tissues where none had previously been found. France also cited a possible slowdown in the rate of decrease of BSE cases in the UK. Other concerns related to the effectiveness of surveillance programs and meat traceability. After considering this evidence, the European Commission's Scientific Steering Committee (SSC) agreed unanimously that the French ban was unwarranted because "there are currently no grounds for revising the overall conclusions of the SSC Opinions directly related to the rationale of the Date-Based Export Scheme (DBES)," and because "the measures taken by the UK make any risk to human health from the UK DBES at least comparable to that in any other European Member State" (European Commission 1999a).

Following this finding, the European Commission again asked France to lift its ban; again France refused. In late 2000, despite the traditional reluctance of the European Court of Justice (ECJ) to grant injunctions against measures to protect public health, the European Commission decided to seek a court order to require France to adhere to Decision 98/692 and lift its ban on British beef (European Commission 1999b). On December 13, 2001, the ECJ ruled in the Commission's favor and ordered France to lift its ban (*CEC v. French Republic* 2001).

In late 2000, as small numbers of BSE cases continued to be reported, including in France, consumer demand for beef plummeted (Daley 2000a), several other European countries instituted bans on the import of French beef, and France undertook measures (as Britain had earlier) to restrict the use of animal protein in all animal feed and to prevent cattle over 30 months old from being marketed (Minder 2000). The EU decided to apply these precautions throughout the EU (Daley 2000b).

The UK government would later lurch toward use of the precautionary principle. A telling example is the decision to ban sale of "beef on the bone." As part of the investigations of BSE infectivity by the UK Ministry of Agriculture Fisheries and Food (MAFF), it was discovered that positive infectivity was present in nerve tissue connected to the spinal column, namely the dorsal root ganglia (DRG). This tissue was not removed with the spinal cord when the animal was slaughtered and was not covered by the UK regulations specifying those tissues that were banned from human consumption. The DRG were associated with the bones, creating a potential risk in the consumption of such beef products as T-bone steaks and rib joints. On the recommendation of SEAC, a regulation requiring the deboning of all beef from cattle over six months old was implemented in 1997. MAFF estimated that less than one gram of infected nerve tissue could induce BSE in 50% of an exposed population; that four cattle in two million might carry infected DRG tissue; and that about 5% of the DRG tissue would remain in cuts of beef on the bone. With these inputs, MAFF's probabilistic risk assessment predicted that the total beef consumption of the UK in 1997 would confer a risk equivalent to a 5% chance of one additional case of vCJD in the entire country per year, or an individual risk of around one in one billion per year (Comer 1998). There were large uncertainties in the analysis, and the results were highly dependent on the assumptions made (many of them tending to overstate the risk). Even so, the estimated risk amounted to much less than the chance of being struck by lightning. Nonetheless, the UK government opted for extreme precaution and banned all sales of beef on the bone until the BSE epidemic had been brought under control. The ban on retail sales of bone-in beef was eventually lifted in 1999, following a continued decline in the incidence of BSE and the implementation of other control measures to protect against the introduction of BSE into the human food supply.

In contrast to the meandering path of the UK and EU policy on the risk of BSE to humans described above, the United States acted early and resolutely—despite no cases of BSE having been observed yet in the United States.

First, the United States banned the import of UK (and later EU) beef far earlier than did the EU, and it kept that ban in place far longer. In 1988, the U.S. Department of Agriculture (USDA) established a BSE Working Group to evaluate the scientific evidence available on BSE and suggest appropriate responses. On July 21, 1989, the Animal and Plant Health Inspection Service (APHIS) of USDA implemented an import ban on all ruminants and certain cattle products from the UK. This was five years before the comparable EU export ban adopted in March of 1996. On December 6, 1991, APHIS further restricted the importation of ruminant meat, meat products, and by-products from all countries with confirmed cases of BSE (USDA 1991). APHIS broadened the import ban on December 12, 1997, to include all EU countries (USDA 2000). The U.S. ban on beef imports remains in effect, whereas the EU lifted its export ban and individual Member State import bans after only two and a half years, in November 1998.

Second, because rendered animal products used in animal feed may be the source of infection of TSEs, the FDA adopted a domestic feed ban prohibiting the feeding of ruminant and mink protein to ruminant animals (with a few exceptions such as milk and blood protein). That feed ban became effective August 4, 1997 (FDA 1998)—nine years after the UK prohibition on the use of mammalian protein in the manufacture of feed for ruminants and three years after a similar policy was adopted by the EU. A voluntary moratorium on mammalian protein in feed had been in effect in the United States for most of that period, however. Still, some argue that the U.S. policies, and especially its enforcement efforts on cattle feed restrictions and on tracking diseased animals, were less precautionary than those in the EU (McGarity 2005, 325, 346).

The USDA policies are avowedly precautionary:

> The USDA policy has been to be *proactive and preventative*. APHIS has taken measures in surveillance, prevention, education, and response. Import restrictions have been in place since 1989, and active surveillance efforts began in 1990. The USDA continually monitors and assesses all ongoing events and research findings regarding spongiform encephalopathies, as new information and knowledge may lead to revised conclusions and prevention measures. APHIS has also created a

Transmissible Spongiform Encephalopathy (TSE) Working Group to analyze risks of BSE to the United States, disseminate accurate information about the TSEs, and act as a reference source for responding to questions about TSEs. ... As of December 12, 1997, APHIS has prohibited the importation of live ruminants and most ruminant products from all of Europe *until a thorough assessment of the risks can be made*. ... This action was taken in the past year because the Netherlands, Belgium, and Luxembourg have reported their first cases of BSE in native-born cattle. There is evidence that European countries may have had high BSE risk factors for several years and less-than-adequate surveillance. Additionally, Belgium reported that a cow diagnosed with BSE was processed into the animal food chain. This science-based decision was made to protect human and animal health, to ensure the security of U.S. export markets, and to shield the safety and the integrity of our food supply. (USDA 2000; emphasis added)

Third, when the first BSE case was found in a U.S. cow in December 2003, the United States also acted extremely quickly in adopting BSE/vCJD control measures, including the following:

- a ban on slaughter for human consumption of all nonambulatory disabled cattle (*Federal Register* 2004a);
- the prohibition for human consumption of brain, skull, eyes, trigeminal ganglia, spinal cord, vertebral column, and dorsal root ganglia of cattle 30 months of age or older, as well as small intestines and tonsils of all cattle (*Federal Register* 2004a);
- the prohibition of production for human consumption of advanced meat recovery product from vertebrae or skulls of cattle 30 months of age or older along with prohibition for human consumption of mechanically separated beef derived from cattle of all ages (*Federal Register* 2004b);
- a ban on the use of ruminant blood in ruminant feed (*Federal Register* 2004c); and
- requiring dedicated lines for production of animal feeds containing prohibited (i.e., ruminant-derived) protein in facilities producing both prohibited and nonprohibited material (*Federal Register* 2004c).

Fourth, concern arose about possible human-to-human transmission of vCJD acquired from exposure to BSE through blood transfusions or other blood products. The United States therefore has also adopted restrictions on blood donors who have spent time in the UK or Europe during the BSE outbreak. It has been hypothesized that BSE might be transmitted not only by eating beef, but also by transfusions of blood from people who had eaten contaminated beef. It has long been known that spongiform encephalopathy diseases could be transmitted through dura mater (brain covering) grafts, contaminated supplies of human growth hormone, and cannibalism—when victims' brain tissue is eaten, which causes kuru. But the risk that TSE could be transmitted via ordinary blood transfusions from people who had eaten BSE-contaminated beef was a highly uncertain conjecture. Nonetheless, acting on that concern, pursuant to its authority under U.S. Public Health Service Act § 351, 42 U.S.C. § 262, in August 1999 the FDA instructed blood banks such as the American

Red Cross and independent blood banks to reject blood from any donor who had spent more than six months cumulative in the UK during the years 1980 to 1996, the period of the BSE epidemic (FDA 1999c). In June 2001, the FDA proposed to go further, rejecting any blood donor who had spent three months or more in the UK or five years or more anywhere in Europe since 1980 (Hernandez 2001). The FDA adopted this policy in January 2002 (FDA 2002), defining Europe as

> Albania, Austria, Belgium, Bosnia-Herzegovina, Bulgaria, Croatia, Czech Republic, Denmark, Finland, France, Germany, Greece, Hungary, Republic of Ireland, Italy, Liechtenstein, Luxembourg, Macedonia, Netherlands, Norway, Poland, Portugal, Romania, Slovak Republic, Slovenia, Spain, Sweden, Switzerland, United Kingdom, and Federal Republic of Yugoslavia. [For purposes of this guidance, the United Kingdom should be taken to include all of the following: England, Northern Ireland, Scotland, Wales, the Isle of Man, the Channel Islands, Gibraltar, and the Falkland Islands.]. (FDA 2002, 29)

The FDA officially titled this regulation a "Precautionary Measure" (FDA 1999c). It acted despite recognizing that in 1999, no studies had showed human blood transmission of CJD, animal data were conflicting, and no cases of vCJD had yet appeared in the United States. It even recognized that the "transmissibility of vCJD by blood or blood products is unknown," that the "transmissibility [of vCJD] cannot confidently be predicted from studies of CJD," and that "no transmission of CJD or vCJD by human blood components or plasma derivatives has been documented to date" (FDA 1999c). Similarly, in 2002, FDA recognized that

> to date, transmission of vCJD by human blood or plasma has not been demonstrated, and no laboratory or epidemiological studies have demonstrated infectivity of blood from vCJD donors. . . . However, blood from animals experimentally infected with transmissible spongiform encephalopathy (TSE) agents contains low levels of infectivity, and TSE infection, including BSE, has been transmitted by blood in some experiments. For this reason, the transmission of vCJD by blood components and plasma derivatives is considered a theoretical possibility. (FDA 2002, 8–9)

European Commission officials considered the risk "theoretical" and "very small" at the most (Tagliabue 2001). One commenter called the evidence "scanty . . . compared with [the evidence on] climate change"—which the U.S. government has not regulated so stringently (O'Neill 2003, 375). But the FDA said that

> until more is known about the possibility of vCJD transmission by blood components or plasma derivatives, a *precautionary policy* of withdrawal for all of these products is recommended for material from donors with vCJD. (FDA 1999c; emphasis added)

The FDA banned blood from all donors who had spent at least six (later, three) months in the UK, or five years in Europe, regardless of whether those people had eaten British beef; the FDA added no question to be asked of donors about their beef intake. This was a very contentious decision. Of the approximately 24 members of the TSE advisory committee, the ban passed by only a few votes. The Red Cross testified to the FDA that the 1999 policy would likely reduce the pool of eligible donors by about 2% (FDA 1999d), and the 2001 policy would reduce the pool of donors by 5% to 8% (Tagliabue 2001). FDA estimated a 5% loss of donors as a result of the newer policy, with higher losses in coastal cities where more donors travel to Europe (FDA 2002, 6). Blood shortages could be most severe in New York City, which imported 25% of its blood supply from European donors, all of whom would be banned (Tagliabue 2001). We assess these events further in the penultimate section of this chapter, on the consequences of precautionary regulation.

Like the United States, Canada also adopted a ban on blood donors who had spent six months or more in the UK between 1980 and 1996 (Blanchfield 2000; Stecklow 1999). Australia has adopted a similar ban.

By contrast, the EU Member States have not adopted such stringent restrictions on blood donations. The UK has undertaken leukodepletion—filtering out white blood cells from donated blood—on the theory that prions are more likely to be carried by white blood cells (Reaney 1998a). It also began importing plasma and blood for young children (Reaney 1998b). On February 23, 2000, France announced it would *not* ban blood donations from those who had traveled to Britain during the mad cow crisis, citing a shortage of blood supplies (Bilefsky 2000). This is especially noteworthy, because it was France that had suffered the most dramatic cases of HIV contamination in the blood supply. Later, France banned blood donations by people who had spent one year or more in Britain (Lee 2003). And by 2003, Austria, Finland, Germany, Ireland, Japan, New Zealand, Hong Kong, and Australia had also adopted restrictions on blood donated by people who had lived in the UK, although typically these are less stringent than the U.S. policy; for example, Ireland banned donations by anyone who had spent five years in the UK (O'Neill 2003).

Although no case of BSE or vCJD transmission via blood transfusion had been observed when the donor bans were adopted in 1999 and 2001, more recently some evidence of the possibility of such transmission has arisen (Bostock 2000; Llewelyn et al. 2004; Peden et al. 2004). Tests with animals suggested CJD could be transmitted via blood (Bostock 2000; BBC 2002). It was then discovered that seven people who had subsequently developed vCJD had donated blood, and that some of the blood from these donors had been mixed with the blood of other donors before distribution to hospitals (Leake 2000). These donations occurred before the beginning of leukodepletion procedures in 1998. Separately, a baby whose mother died of vCJD seemed to be showing symptoms of the same disease (Rumbelow 2000). Diagnosis of vCJD can only be certain after death, but since vertical transmission (from cow to calf) of BSE seems to occur in cattle, vertical transmission might also be found in humans. More recently, three human deaths from vCJD in Britain occurred in victims who appeared not to have eaten beef, but who did receive blood transfusions, although it is not definite that this was the source of the disease. The UK government warned the 100 donors who supplied the blood to these three victims that they may be carrying vCJD; they had to warn their own doctors and dentists (Cooke 2005).

Prion research has indicated that it is possible for prion replication to occur in laboratory animals without those animals manifesting disease symptoms (Hill et al.

2000). This opens the possibility of asymptomatic carriers of TSEs, and hence the risk of transmission from apparently healthy donors. Additional research suggests that prions might be transmitted—and also detected—in dried urine (Blakeslee 2001).

Explanations for Precautionary Regulation in the EU and the United States

European Commission officials offered two main reasons for the prohibition of hormones in beef. The first was plausible risk scenarios for animal health. Also, the various effects of substances like rBST and growth hormones were said to be insufficiently clear, so a period of time should be provided for in-depth studies—a reason that is precautionary in nature. The EC's Committee of Veterinary Medicinal Products had found that rBST was not a concern to humans. The second reason for banning hormones concerned the internal market, which could undergo distortions if different Member States made different decisions about their use. The ban on rBST, for example, "was based on the fear of Community officials that BST's introduction would undermine the competitive position of small-volume dairy farmers and thus hasten the long-term consolidation of the dairy farm sector" (Vogel 1995, 172; Vogel 1997, 24–25). In addition, when the EU had experienced an oversupply of dairy products, government subsidies had gone to dairy farms as dairy prices fell. These subsidies were being slowly decreased in the 1980s. Introduction of rBST might have exacerbated the dairy oversupply and thereby required more subsidies in the future (Vogel 1995).

As to BSE, the UK originally took the position that it posed no transferable risk to humans because scrapie-infected mutton, which had been eaten for over 200 years, had never been linked to CJD or any other human disease. Yet the science was uncertain. Scientists had always argued that a link between BSE and human TSE could not be ruled out. Adding to the scientific uncertainty was a practical matter—the protein of animal origin, including discarded brain and spinal tissue from previously rendered cattle and sheep, had increased from 1% to 12% of British cattle feed in the 1980s, in response to the increasing price of imported soy and fish meal (Rhodes 1997).

Once the first few cases of vCJD had occurred, the British went into damage control mode by implementing stricter slaughter procedures, the 30 months rule, and rules on the use of mammalian-derived meal in feed for any farm animal. Additionally, because it had lost so much public trust, from 1997 to 1999 the British government also began to employ the precautionary bans of "beef on the bone" described in detail above.

The public perception and fear associated with BSE cannot be underestimated. Print and television media warnings of "mad cow disease" conjured up scary images of creeping insanity. One hundred or even 10 cases of an insidious new brain-wasting disease with a long asymptomatic latency period, like vCJD, could elicit dread in the public and policymakers.

Economic considerations were also likely at play. Despite protective measures taken by the UK to prevent the spread of BSE to other countries, France defied the EU

Commission and maintained its ban on the import of British beef—potentially for public health reasons, but also potentially to serve national economic protectionism.

After the EU banned all exports of UK beef in Decision 96/239, the Commission defended its action on the ground that the precautionary principle empowered the Commission to take such action, which it said was proportional to the threat. The European Court of Justice agreed, holding that where there is uncertainty as to the existence or extent of risks to human health, institutions may take protective measures without having to wait until the reality and seriousness of those risks become fully apparent (*UK v. CEC* 1998). But the Commission soon lifted the export ban, relying on the feed ban and other measures taken in the UK. Undoubtedly, it was keen to resume open trade in beef products.

The story in the United States was different. Here the beef industry is economically significant. In 2003, U.S. beef production was 26.3 billion pounds from the slaughter of an estimated 36 million cattle, yielding a gross farm income of $44.1 billion in 2003 (USDA 2004b). U.S. export of 2.6 billion pounds of beef, veal, and variety meats in 2003 produced $3.8 billion in income (Otto and Lawrence 2005). The beef sector is considered the "largest single agricultural enterprise" in the United States, and it is the world's largest producer of beef for export markets (USDA 2004b).

On the view that protecting the beef industry strongly influenced government policy, one could infer that the United States did not precautionarily ban growth hormones and rBST because those pharmaceuticals are valuable for increased meat and milk production. Meanwhile, the United States *did* take precautionary action against BSE to save the industry from an outbreak that would reduce sales, it might seem. And banning imports of British beef served to protect the U.S. beef producers from some foreign competition.

On the other hand, the FDA policy on blood donations is not well explained by this theory of protection of the U.S. beef industry. The FDA may have been motivated by recent concern about AIDS in the United States and French blood supplies in the 1980 s. French officials were eventually convicted of crimes for inadequately screening HIV-contaminated blood. In a combination of the "availability" heuristic (overstatement of the risk of similar recent incidents) and the regulator's reputational incentive to avoid false negatives, this recent history may have encouraged the FDA to be especially precautionary about the next disease to threaten the blood supply, even if it were remote (Sunstein and Kuran 1999). O'Neill (2003) emphasizes the role of dread regarding a "vital fluid." Finally, the FDA could be more motivated to safeguard blood quality (for which it is accountable) than quantity (which is seen as a local issue for blood banks and hospitals).

The American Red Cross has both lobbied the FDA to impose blood donor restrictions regarding vCJD and adopted even more stringent restrictions itself—three months in the UK or six months anywhere in Europe (versus the FDA rule of five years). It is not clear why the Red Cross would favor exceedingly precautionary restrictions on blood quality, given the costs and countervailing risks. Its history does not suggest an obsession with blood quality: over the past two decades, the FDA has charged the American Red Cross with inadequately adhering to blood safety standards

(GAO 2002, 9), leading to a recent settlement with steep fines for further violations (*New York Times* 2003). Moreover, in most states, blood banks are immune from tort liability for contamination. But the blood banks might still favor tight restrictions in order to prevent loss of public trust in the blood supply after a case of blood-borne vCJD. Or the American Red Cross—which supplies about half of all U.S. blood—might favor government-mandated restrictions of the blood supply, a policy that would raise the price paid for blood by hospitals (the preference of a monopolist, were it not prohibited by antitrust law). One doctor noted, "It's difficult in this day and age to go down to administration and say, 'I need an extra half-million [dollars] for blood.' But right now, the Red Cross is the only supplier in town" (Kowalczyk 2001, A28). By contrast, a coalition of smaller blood banks, America's Blood Centers, has voiced concern about the restrictions on blood supply (Bianco 2002). Industry lobbying to obtain government policies that restrict supply as a monopolist would, or to remove antitrust law constraints, has been observed in other industries (e.g., Bartel and Thomas 1987; Adler 2004).

Meanwhile, these explanations fail to explain why France—where the worst AIDS blood scandal occurred—and other EU countries did *not* adopt similarly stringent measures against BSE in blood. The reluctance of France and the UK to restrict the blood supply probably derives from concern about the countervailing health risks of doing so, and because it would be difficult to exclude those who had eaten beef. Even in the United States, the FDA initially chose the "six months in Britain" criterion, rather than a shorter time period or a criterion of "ate British beef," because the FDA feared exacerbating the blood shortage by turning away too many donors.

Consequences of Precautionary Regulation in the EU and the United States

It is unclear whether the EU bans on rBST and growth hormones, or the United States permission of these products, have had any significant impact on animal or human health. The fundamental issue concerns the extrapolation to low doses, and this remains a major issue for toxicologists. Research continues to attempt to resolve the low-dose issue.

The stringent measures taken by the UK against BSE in the national cattle herd appear to have been successful in reversing the epidemic and reducing the incidence of BSE from over 30,000 cases in 1992 and 1993 to below 500 cases in 2004 (see Figure 3.1). Although the EU imposed a ban on exports of British beef in March 1996, within just months it began to lift its ban. On June 11, 1996, the ban on gelatin and semen was lifted, and on June 22, 1996, EU leaders signed the Florence Agreement outlining a progressive plan to lift the ban. Under this agreement, the export ban was not lifted until June 10, 1998, on the next category of beef product: deboned fresh British beef from BSE-free cattle aged 6 to 30 months and born after August 1, 1996. In November 1998, the export ban eventually was fully lifted by the European Commission in Decision 98/692 (European Commission 1998), which became effective August 1,

1999. Under the UK's Date-Based Export Scheme (DBES), deboned beef and beef products were subsequently exported from the UK.

While a return to normalcy did occur, the UK's initial failure to take precautionary action let the disease spread. The government was required to make payments of *ex post* compensation to vCJD victims and their families. Farmers were also compensated by the government for the loss of their cattle (Lyall 2000).

In the United States, the stringent measures taken earlier—the ban on imports of beef from the UK and other countries, the feed ban, and related policies—appear to have been successful so far in keeping BSE nearly absent from U.S. herds. But nearly is not zero; two cows have been identified with BSE in the United States, and critics argue that testing has not been widespread or sensitive enough (McGarity 2005). Japan has banned imports of U.S. beef since the first U.S. cow with BSE was identified in 2003. Still, two cases are hardly the 180,000 identified in the UK (see Table 3.1).

Both the European Commission in its Communication on the Precautionary Principle (European Commission 2000) and the UK Health and Safety Executive in its argument to the European Court of Justice argued that precautionary measures should be "proportionate" to the risk and to the required level of protection (UK-ILGRA 2004). However, neither actually defined how proportionality was to be determined. Similarly, in determining whether the EU export ban on British beef was lawful, the Court ruled that the export ban was not a disproportionate action by the Commission and furthermore reminded the litigants that the measures were temporary pending the results of further scientific studies and the analysis of the significance of new information on vCJD. The Court therefore dismissed the action brought by the UK (*UK v. CEC* 1998). However, the Court's statement did not address the real question of *what* measures to take in light of the inevitable uncertainty.

If "proportionate" means imposing costs proportionate to the expected benefits, a few actions stand out as possibly beyond proportional. One is the implementation of testing all slaughtered cattle over 30 months of age for BSE in the EU. On the other hand, because this scheme recognizes the risk of older animals while still allowing their use for human food, perhaps it should be thought of as an "over 30 months scheme lite." A second action that is possibly beyond proportional is the bone-in-beef bans implemented by the UK and EU. Although a theoretical chance exists for BSE infectivity to result from vertebral and other tissues being present in a T-bone steak, risk assessments done at the time suggested that, even with conservative assumptions, the risk is likely to be very small.

By taking such a precautionary approach, the UK government presumably reduced consumer intake of contaminated beef—although ironically, the regulations appear to have provoked some outbreaks of risky behavior: in some sections of the population, there seems to have been a willful desire to increase the consumption of beef on the bone. "Prohibition" dinners featuring beef on the bone were offered by one hotelier, oxtails were more in demand than before, and butchers flouted the law. Even Professor John Durant, whose specialty is the public understanding of science at Imperial College London, was moved to pronounce the ban farcical (Irwin 1997). Although the ban on the sale of beef on the bone has now been lifted in the UK, it is still the case that only deboned beef can be exported from the UK under European Commission Decision 98/692.

Another example of a precautionary measure against vCJD that was arguably taken too far by the UK government was its restriction on the reuse of surgical instruments for tonsil and adenoid surgery in the National Health Service (UKDH 2001a). Within the first year, there were reports of increased risk to patients from surgeons' use of these instruments, including excessive bleeding and one death. In December 2001, the decision was reversed and multiple use instruments were reintroduced (BBC 2001). In this case, a precautionary action resulted in greater public health risk than the threat it was meant to address.

Likewise, countervailing risks relate to the bans on blood from donors who have spent time in the UK or Europe (see listed countries above) (FDA 2002). As noted above, the benefit of this policy is to reduce what is already a very small risk of vCJD transmission; evidence of its theoretical possibility has strengthened since 1999, however. The boldness of this precautionary move is evident from the countervailing risk it creates: a shortage of blood for use in hospital operating rooms. The American blood supply is already very tight, and the FDA recognized that excluding donors could cause shortages (FDA 2001). The Red Cross testified to the FDA that the 1999 policy of excluding donors who had spent more than six months cumulatively in the UK since 1980 would likely reduce the pool of eligible blood donors by about 2% (FDA 1999d). It said the 2001 policy of excluding those who had spent more than three months in the UK or five years in Europe since 1980 would reduce the blood supply by 5% to 8% (Tagliabue 2001; FDA 2002, 6). The FDA noted that if the American Red Cross adopted nationally the even more stringent policy of excluding donors who had spent three months in the UK or just six months in Europe since 1980, such a policy would reduce the pool of donors by 8% to 9% (FDA 2002, 25–26). The FDA advised blood banks to follow this more stringent policy only if they undertook additional steps to ensure the supply of blood, including extra recruiting, contingency plans, and monitoring donors. As mentioned above, under the FDA or Red Cross policies, blood shortages could be most severe in New York City. In addition to losing 8% of its American donors, New York would lose the 25% of its blood supply that is imported from European donors, all of whom would be banned under the 2001 policy (Tagliabue 2001). These reductions in blood supply pose a high and fairly certain risk of death to those who need emergency blood during operations—in New York, a "disastrous … public health crisis" (Tagliabue 2001). America's Blood Centers, the coalition of smaller blood banks, voiced concern about the restrictions on blood supply and undertook surveys to demonstrate the shortages that may be looming (Bianco 2002).

In its decisions (FDA 1999c, 2002), the government recognized the potential for donor losses but did not weigh the health effects of reduced blood supply against the health benefits of reduced vCJD risk. Yet it did stop short of the more stringent Red Cross approach, citing the concern about blood shortages (FDA 2002, 26); it also allowed people who have lived in Europe for more than five years since 1980—now excluded from donating whole blood—to continue to donate "source plasma." This exception was made on the grounds that additional processing steps for source plasma reduce TSE transmission and make the balance of risks versus benefits more favorable (FDA 2002, 9).

In Canada, the ban on blood donors who had spent six months in the UK was expected to exclude 3% to 4% of donors. One employee of the Canadian Blood Supply predicted a 10% to 15% decline in blood supply (*Toronto Sun* 1999), presumably because the Canadian donors who visit the UK are especially significant donors. In August 2000, Canada extended the blood ban to include people who have spent six months or more in France (Blanchfield 2000).

Although not widely acknowledged, recruiting new donors to replace the donors who have lived in Europe could also increase the risk of other diseases contaminating the blood supply such as HIV and hepatitis C. Donated blood is tested for these diseases, but the tests are not perfect (false negatives occur), so contaminated blood is more likely to enter the blood supply from first-time donors than from oft-tested repeat donors. Balancing a theoretical or very low-probability risk (vCJD transmission in blood) with a well-known and significant risk (e.g., HIV) was not explicitly carried out. Thus, even apart from supply shortages, it could be argued that the "precautionary" ban on blood donors who have lived in Europe actually increased the risk of fatal disease being transmitted through donated blood.

It is difficult to tell whether the forecast blood shortages have actually occurred. The shortage was temporarily eased by the surge of blood donations just after the September 11, 2001, terrorist attacks, when about 500,000 units of blood were donated. The surviving victims needed only 260 units; at least 250,000 units had to be discarded after they expired unused. (GAO 2002, 18–25). By a year later, donations had dropped between 8% and 10% (Namiotka 2002). The price of blood charged by blood banks to hospitals escalated sharply, from about $80 per unit in 1998 to almost $130 per unit by 2001 (GAO 2002, 26–27; Kowalczyk 2001), suggesting a tightening supply. The price increase was due in part to the added safety measures adopted as precautions against BSE and vCJD, such as leukoreduction, which added about $30 per unit (GAO 2002, 25–27). Yet so far we still have not found data on increased emergency-room deaths due to lack of blood. It may be that this was an example of a claimed countervailing risk that did not come to pass. Blood supply had been rising before the restrictions were imposed (GAO 2002, 12–17). Perhaps collection efforts may have been augmented with other sources to keep the supply up. The Red Cross and others shifted supplies to the New York area, but the New York blood centers reported decreasing donations in the city after the 9/11 surge subsided (GAO 2002, 25). Demand may have been shifted from elective surgeries to emergency rooms to meet a decreasing supply. Or controls on restricted donors may have been relaxed, increasing the risk of other diseases like HIV. Or the shortages may in fact be occurring; a lack of publicly available information on this topic could be due to reluctance on the part of hospitals or blood banks to publicize the increased risk to the public. Moreover, shortages may still arise in the future. If supplies are tight—occasionally down to less than a day of O-negative supply in some areas—some other supply constraint, such as the flu or another illness making many donors ineligible, or demand surge, such as military need, could combine with the vCJD restrictions already in place to cause problems (Bianco 2002; O'Neill 2003, 364).

Ideally, this trade-off between quality (contamination) and quantity (shortages) could be overcome with a risk-superior solution. Efforts are under way to develop a synthetic blood substitute, but none is yet ready for use (ABC 2004). Conceivably, the invention of a blood or urine test for vCJD could enable effective screening so donors would not be unnecessarily excluded based on crude geographic criteria.

Lessons Learned from Precautionary Regulation of Beef

The case of beef illustrates the complex pattern of relative transatlantic precaution, even within one narrow domain of regulation. The EU was more precautionary than the United States regarding beef hormones and rBST. But the United States was more precautionary than the EU regarding BSE, in particular via the earlier and more stringent ban on imports of British beef and the ban on blood donations by people who have spent time in Europe. (The comparison of the U.S. and European Union feed bans reveals no clear edge.) The trend over time is toward greater relative U.S. precaution, especially in the blood donor restrictions adopted since 1999. The blood donor example here casts doubt on the "flip-flop" hypothesis that relative precaution has increased in the European Union since 1990, while the United States reversed that direction.

While Britain observed thousands of cases of BSE in the 1980s, it continued to export beef. The EU waited to adopt its ban on British beef until 1996, lifted that ban in phases between 1996 and 1999, and then pressed France to lift its remaining ban. Meanwhile, with zero domestic cases of BSE to that date, the United States imposed its ban on British beef in 1989, broadened it to cover several countries, and continues that ban in effect today. As to imports of beef, the United States acted more quickly in the face of uncertain risk, while the UK and EU spent more time conducting detailed risk assessments and ultimately imposed only temporary restrictions. Meanwhile, both the United States and UK banned mammalian protein in the feed for ruminants, with the United States doing so after Britain, but before BSE was identified in North America. And the United States adopted a much more stringent ban on blood donors who have lived in areas with BSE (regardless of what they have eaten), addressing a speculative risk while incurring the countervailing risk of blood shortages.

Both the EU beef hormones/rBST policies and the U.S. policies on BSE were expressly premised on the precautionary principle, at least in part. Yet both examples also suggest that other motivations may also have been at work, including protection of domestic economic concerns.

At this point there have been no formal cost–benefit analyses of measures to protect human health or animal health from BSE. Estimates of the economic costs to specific industries for implemented BSE control measures (Sparks Companies 1997) and proposed measures (Sparks Companies 1999) have been reported, but none addresses the benefits to be expected from such actions. New measures for the United States that were proposed after a BSE case was identified in the state of Washington in 2003 have not yet been subjected to cost–benefit analysis. It is likely that some of them will fall under Executive Order 12866, requiring cost–benefit analysis of all "major" rules and review by the Office of Management and Budget (OMB). (One wonders why the 1999 and 2001 blood donor bans adopted by the FDA did not.) As we have seen, questions remain about the relative costs and benefits of some of these actions, given the likely low prevalence of BSE in the United States and the efficacy of the different proposed steps.

The UK experience, with its short-lived precautionary ban on multiple-use surgical instruments for tonsillectomies, and the debate (or lack thereof) in the United States over precluding blood donations by people who have lived in Europe—both adopted to prevent the spread of vCJD—remind us of the importance of a full-portfolio analysis. Such a comprehensive approach would consider not only the target risk, but also the countervailing risks that may be induced by precautionary measures.

Acknowledgments

The authors thank Greg Andeck for very helpful research and editorial assistance.

References

ABC (America's Blood Centers). 2004. The Search for a Blood Substitute. *Blood Bulletin* 7 (1). June. www.americasblood.org/download/bulletin_v7_n1.pdf (accessed June 10, 2010).

Adler, J. H. 2004. Conservation through Collusion: Antitrust as an Obstacle to Marine Resource Conservation. *Washington and Lee Law Review* 61: 3–78.

Anderson, R. M., C. A. Donnelly, N. M. Ferguesen, M. E. J. Woolhouse, C. J. Watt, H. J. Udy, S. MaWhinney, S. P. Dunstan, T. R. E. Southwood, J. W. Wilesmith, J. B. M. Ryan, L. J. Hoinville, J. E. Hillerton, A. R. Austin, and G. A. H. Wells. 1996. Transmission Dynamics and Epidemiology of BSE in British Cattle. *Nature* 382: 779–788.

Bangemann, M. 1993. Key Note Address to the Bio-Europe '93 Conference. Brussels, June 1–6. *Proceedings*, 11–15. Brussels: SAGB.

Bartel, A. P., and L. G. Thomas. 1987. Predation through Regulation: The Wage and Profit Effects of the Occupational Safety and Health Administration and the Environmental Protection Agency. *Journal of Law and Economics* 30: 239.

BBC. 2001. U-Turn over Tonsil Operations. December 15. http://news.bbc.co.uk/hi/english/health/newsid_1711000/1711555.stm (accessed April 17, 2010).

———. 2002. Tests Suggest CJD Blood Risk. August 3. http://news.bbc.co.uk/2/hi/health/2169663.stm (accessed June 10, 2010).

Bianco, C. 2002. American's Blood Centers Statement before the Transmissible Spongiform Encephalopathies Advisory Committee, Food and Drug Administration. June 27. www.americasblood.org/index.cfm?fuseaction=display.showPage&pageID=139.

Bilefsky, D. 2000. French Reject Blood Ban. *News Digest, Financial Times* (London), Feb. 24. Available through LexisNexis Academic.

Blakeslee, S. 2001. A Marker for Mad Cow Disease May Be Found in Urine. *New York Times*, July 17, D5.

Blanchfield, M. 2000. Canada Widens Blood Ban: Mad Cow Precaution Bars Donors Who Spent Six Months in France. *Ottawa Citizen*, Sept. 1, A3. Available through LexisNexis Academic.

Bostock, C. 2000. VCJD Could Be Transmitted through Blood Transfusions. *Lancet* 356: 955–999.

Bruce, M. E., R. G. Will, J. W. Ironside, I. McConnell, D. Drummond, A. Suttie, L. McCardle, A. Chree, J. Hope, C. Birkett, S. Cousens, H. Fraser, and C. J. Bostock. 1997. Transmissions to Mice Indicate That "New Variant" CJD Is Caused by the BSE Agent. *Nature* 389 (6650): 498–501.

CEC (Commission of the European Communities) v. French Republic. 2001. European Court of Justice Case C-1/00 (Failure of a Member State to Fulfill Its Obligations—Refusal to End the Ban on British Beef and Veal), decided December 13. *European Court Reports 2001*, I–09989.

Charnovitz, S. 2000. The Supervision of Health and Biosafety Regulation by World Trade Rules. *Tulane Environmental Law Journal* 13: 271–302.

CoE (Council of Europe). 1976. European Convention for the Protection of Animals Kept for Farming Purposes, Strasbourg. 10.III.1976. http://conventions.coe.int/Treaty/en/Treaties/Html/087.htm (accessed June 11, 2010).

Cohen, Joshua, K. Duggar, G. Gray, S. Kreindel, H. Abdelrahman, T. HabteMariam, D. Oryang, and B. Tameru. 2003. Evaluation of the Potential for Bovine Spongiform Encephalopathy in the United States (October). www.hcra.harvard.edu/pdf/madcow.pdf (accessed April 3, 2005).

Collinge, J., K. C. Sidle, J. Meads, J. Ironside, and A. F. Hill. 1996. Molecular Analysis of Prion Strain Variation and the Aetiology of "New Variant" CJD. *Nature* 383 (6602): 685–690.

Comer, P. H. 1998. Assessing the Risk of Exposure to BSE from Beef on the Bone. Society for Risk Analysis, Europe. *Annual Conference Proceedings: Risk Analysis: Opening the Process.* October 11–14, Paris 605–614.

Cooke, J. 2005. Unseen Time Bomb. *Sydney Morning Herald,* Aug. 4. http://smh.com.au/articles/2005/08/04/1122748732720.html?oneclick=true (accessed April 17, 2010).

Daley, S. 2001. French Report Faults Response to Mad Cow Crisis. *New York Times,* May 18, A10.

———. 2000a. As Mad Cow Disease Spreads in Europe, Consumers Panic. *New York Times,* Dec. 1, A1.

———. 2000b. Europe Takes Toughest Steps to Fight Mad Cow Disease. *New York Times,* Dec. 5, A3.

Donnelly, C. A., N. M. Ferguson, A. C. Ghani, M. E. Woolhouse, C. J. Watt, and R. M. Anderson. 1997. The Epidemiology of BSE in Cattle Herds in Great Britain. I. Epidemiological Processes, Demography of Cattle and Approaches to Control by Culling. *Philosophical Transactions of the Royal Society of London, Series B: Biological Sciences* 352 (1355): 781–801.

European Commission. 1996. Decision of March 27, 1996, on Emergency Measures to Protect against Bovine Spongiform Encephalopathy. *Official Journal of the European Communities,* JOL 1996/78-18EN: 47–48.

———. 1998. Decision 98/692/EEC of November 25, 1998. *Official Journal of the European Communities,* JOL 1998/328EN: 28–35.

———. 1999a. Opinion of the Scientific Steering Committee, on the Scientific Grounds of the Advice of September 30, 1999, of the French Food Safety Agency (the Agence Française de Sécurité Sanitaire des Aliments, AFSSA), to the French Government on the Draft Decree Amending the Decree of October 28, 1998, Establishing Specific Measures Applicable to Certain Products of Bovine Origin Exported from the United Kingdom. Adopted at its meeting of October 28 and 29, 1999. Edited following a written procedure (October 30 to November 15, 1999) and re-edited at the SSC meeting of December 9 and 10, 1999. European Commission, Director General for Health and Consumer Protection.

———. 1999b. Seventeenth Annual Report on the Monitoring of Community Law (1999). COM/2000/0092. Case Number C-1/2000.

———. 2000. Communication from the Commission on the Precautionary Principle. February 2. http://europa.eu.int/comm/dgs/health_consumer/library/pub/pub07_en.pdf (accessed July 5, 2005).

European Council. 1981. Directive 81/602/EEC of July 31, 1981 Concerning the Prohibition of Certain Substances Having a Hormonal Action and of Any Substances Having a Thyrostatic Action (and Subsequent Amendments). JOL 222 07/08/1981: 32, 33.

———. 1990. Decision of April 25, 1990 Concerning the Administration of Bovine Somatotrophin. 90/21(and Subsequent Amendments). 8/EEC JOL 1990/116: 27.

———. 1999. Decision of December 17, 1999 Concerning the Placing on the Market and Administration of Bovine Somatotrophin (and repealing Decision 90/218/EEC), 99/879/EEC. JOL 1999/331: 71.

Faull, J. 2000. EU Ban on U.S. Beef Based on Firm Evidence. Letter. *The Financial Times.* July 6.

FDA (U.S. Food and Drug Administration). 1989. FDA Reviewing BST for Cows. August 4. www.fda.gov/bbs/topics/ANSWERS/ANS00140.html (accessed September 26, 2000).

———. 1997. Bovine Spongiform Encephalopathy and Creutzfeldt-Jakob Disease Fact Sheet, January 2. www.fda.gov/cvm/fda/infores/updates/bse/bsefact.html (accessed September 26, 2000).

———. 1998. Center for Veterinary Medicine. CVM Update, FDA Guidance on BSE Feed Regulation Available. July 14. www.fda.gov/cvm/fda/infores/updates/bse76up.htm (accessed September 27, 2000).

———. 1999a. Report on the FDA's Review of the Safety of Recombinant Bovine Somatotropin. February 10. www.fda.gov/cvm/fda/infores/other/rbrptfnLawhtm (accessed September 26, 2000).

———. 1999b. Center for Veterinary Medicine. FDA Analysis of DGXXIV Report on Public Health Aspects of BST. www.fda.gov/cvm/fda/infores/updates/dg24up.htm (accessed April 15, 1999).

———. 1999c. Guidance for Industry: Revised Precautionary Measures to Reduce the Possible Risk of Transmission of Creutzfeldt-Jakob Disease (CJD) and New Variant Creutzfeldt-Jakob Disease (vCJD) by Blood and Blood Products. August 17. *Federal Register* 64: 44739.

———. 1999d. Advisory Committee on Transmissible Spongiform Encephalopathies. In Minutes of 1999 Conferences/Meetings. Hearings of June 2, 1999. Statement of Dr. Williams. SAG Corp. p. 46. www.fda.gov/cber (accessed June 11, 2010).

———. 2001. Deferral of Blood Donors Potentially Exposed to the Agent of Variant Creutzfeldt-Jakob Disease (vCJD), June 28. www.fda.gov/ohrms/dockets/ac/01/briefing/3762b1_01.htm (accessed March 7, 2005).

———. 2002. Guidance for Industry: Revised Preventive Measures to Reduce the Possible Risk of Transmission of Creutzfeldt-Jakob Disease (CJD) and Variant Creutzfeldt-Jakob Disease (vCJD) by Blood and Blood Products. January 9. www.fda.gov/downloads/BiologicsBloodVaccines/GuidanceComplianceRegulatoryInformation/Guidances/Blood/UCM079761.pdf (accessed June 11, 2010).

Federal Register. 2004a. Prohibition of the Use of Specified Risk Materials for Human Food and Requirements for the Disposition of Non-Ambulatory Disabled Cattle. Vol.69 (7): 1861–1874.

———. 2004b. Meat Produced by Advanced Meat/Bone Separation Machinery and Meat Recovery (AMR) Systems. Vol.69 (7): 1874–1885.

———. 2004c. Federal Measures to Mitigate BSE Risks: Considerations for Further Action; Proposed Rule. Vol.69 (134): 42287–42300.

Ferguson, N. M., C. A. Donnelly, M. E. Woolhouse, and R. M. Anderson. 1997. The Epidemiology of BSE in Cattle Herds in Great Britain. II. Model Construction and Analysis of Transmission Dynamics. *Philosophical Transactions of the Royal Society of London, Series B: Biological Sciences* 352 (1355): 803–838.

———. 1999. Estimation of the Basic Reproduction Number of BSE: The Intensity of Transmission in British Cattle. *Proceedings of the Royal Society of London, Series B: Biological Sciences* 266 (1414): 23–32.

GAO (U.S. General Accounting Office). 2002. Blood Supply Generally Adequate despite New Donor Restrictions. U.S. General Accounting Office Report 02-754. July. www.gao.gov/new.items/d02754.pdf (accessed June 11, 2010).

Goethals, C., S. C. Ratzan, and V. Demko. 1998. Politics of BSE: Negotiating the Public's Health. In *The Mad Cow Crisis: Health and the Public Good*, edited by S. C. Ratzan. London: UCL Press.

Hernandez, R. 2001. Citing Mad Cow, FDA Panel Backs Blood Donor Curbs. *New York Times*, June 29, A23.

Hill, A. F., M. Desbruslais, S. Joiner, K. C. Sidle, I. Gowland, J. Collinge, L. J. Doey, and P. Lantos. 1997. The Same Prion Strain Causes vCJD and BSE. *Nature* 389 (6650): 448–450.

Hill, A. F., S. Joiner, J. Linehan, M. Desbruslais, P. L. Lantos, and J. Collinge. 2000. Species Barrier-Independent Prion Replication in Apparently Resistant Species. *Proceedings of the National Academy of Sciences* 97: 10248–10253.

Irwin, A. 1997. Risk-Assessment System Relies Too Much on Science. *Daily Telegraph*, Dec. 4.

Kimberlin, R. H., and J. W. Wilesmith. 1994. Bovine Spongiform Encephalopathy. Epidemiology, Low Dose Exposure and Risks. *Annals of the New York Academy of Sciences* 724: 210–220.

Kowalczyk, L. 2001. Hospitals Face Soaring Blood Prices: Red Cross Rates Hit Region Hard. *Boston Globe*, July 6, A28.

Leake, J. 2000. Blood Donors Feared to Have Spread CJD. *Sunday Times* (UK), Sept. 17. www.mad-cow.org/00/sep00_late_news.html (accessed June 30, 2010).

Lee, Kenneth. 2003. France Acts on Threat of BSE Transmission by Blood. *Scientist*, Jan. 23. www.biomedcentral.com/news/20010123/05/ (accessed June 11, 2010).

Llewelyn, C. A., P. E. Hewitt, R. S. Knight, K. Amur, S. Cousens, J. Mackenzie, and R. G. Will. 2004. Possible Transmission of Variant Creutzfeldt-Jakob Disease by Blood Transfusion. *Lancet* 263 (9407): 417–421.

Lyall, S. 2000. British Wrongly Lulled People on "Mad Cow," Report Finds. *New York Times*, Oct. 27, A8.

McGarity, T. O. 2005. Federal Regulation of Mad Cow Disease Risks. *Administrative Law Review* 57 (2): 289.

Minder, R. 2000. France Bans Beef on Bone and Suspect Feed. *Financial Times*, Nov. 15.

Namiotka, J. 2002. Donor Restrictions Lower Blood Supply. *Daily Record*, Dec. 12. http://dailyrecord.com/news/01/12/02/news5-blood.htm (site now discontinued).

Nathanson, N., J. W. Wilesmith, and C. Griot. 1997. Bovine Spongiform Encephalopathy (BSE): Causes and Consequences of a Common Source Epidemic. *American Journal of Epidemiology* 145 (11): 959–969.

New York Times. 2003. Red Cross Promises to Improve Blood Safety. April 13, A17.

OIE (World Organisation for Animal Health). 2005. Number of Cases of Bovine Spongiform Encephalopathy (BSE) Reported in the United Kingdom. World Organisation for Animal Health. www.oie.int/eng/info/en_esbru.htm (accessed July 15, 2005).

O'Neill, K. 2003. A Vital Fluid: Risk, Controversy, and the Politics of Blood Donation in the Era of "Mad Cow Disease." *Public Understanding of Science* 12: 359–380.

Otto, D., and J. D. Lawrence. 2005. Economic Impact of the United States Beef Industry. www.beef.org/dsp/dsp_locationContent.cfm?LocationID=42 (accessed Feb. 12, 2005).

Peden, A. H., M. W. Head, D. L. Ritchie, J. E. Bell, and J. W. Ironside. 2004. Preclinical vCJD after Blood Transfusion in a PRNP Codon 129 Heterozygous Patient. *Lancet* 364 (9433): 527–529.

Prusiner, S. 1997. Prion diseases and the BSE crisis. *Science* 278: 245–251.

Reaney, P. 1998a. Focus: Britain to Purify Blood to Remove CJD Risk. *Reuters*, July 17.

———. 1998b. UK to Import Blood Plasma as "Mad Cow" Move. *Reuters*, Feb. 26.

Rhodes, R. 1997. *Deadly Feasts*. New York: Simon and Schuster.

Rumbelow, H. 2000. CJD Victim May Have Infected Her Unborn Baby. *Times* (UK), Home News, Sept. 18. Available through LexisNexis Academic.

Scott, M. R., R. Will, J. Ironside, H. O. Nguyen, P. Tremblay, S. J. DeArmond, and S. B. Prusiner. 1999. Compelling Transgenetic Evidence for Transmission of Bovine Spongiform Encephalopathy Prions to Humans. *Proceedings of the National Academy of Sciences of the United States of America* 96 (26): 15137–15142.

Sparks Companies. 1997. *The Economic Impact of the Proposed Regulations Concerning Ruminant-Based Protein Products*. Alexandria, VA: National Renderers Association.

———. 1999. *Advanced Meat Recovery Systems: An Economic Analysis of the Proposed USDA Regulation*, www.fsis.usda.gov/OPPDE/rdad/FRPubs/98-027R/SparksCo_AMR_Economic_Analysis.pdf (accessed June 10, 2010).

Stecklow, S. 1999. "Mad Cow" Fears Lead to Blood Ban in U.S. *Wall Street Journals*, Aug. 18, B6.

Sunstein, C. R., and T. Kuran. 1999. Availability Cascades and Risk Regulation. *Stanford Law Review* 51: 683–768.

Tagliabue, J. 2001. U.S. Plan to Halt Blood Imports Worries Europe. *New York Times*, July 17, A1.

Toronto Sun. 1999. Blood Ban Fears Denied. July 16, 21.

UK (United Kingdom). 2000. Findings and Conclusions (Vol. 1). *In The BSE Enquiry Report* ("The Phillips Report," 16 vols.). Lord Phillips of Worth Matravers, J. Bridgeman, and M. Ferguson-Smith.

October 26. London: HM Stationery Office. http://collections.europarchive.org/tna/20090505194948/http://bseinquiry.gov.uk/report/volume1/execsum.htm (accessed June 15, 2010).

UK v. CEC. 1998. European Court of Justice. Case C-180/96. Judgment dated May 5. *In European Court Reports 1998,* I-02265.

UKDH (United Kingdom Department of Health). 2001a. £200 million for NHS Equipment to Protect Patients against Possible Variant CJD Risk. January 4. www.dh.gov.uk/PublicationsAndStatistics/PressReleases/PressReleasesNotices/fs/en?CONTENT_ID=4009912&chk=59R1/T (accessed March 5, 2005).

———. 2001b. Re-introduction of Re-usable Instruments for Tonsil Surgery, December 14. www.dh.gov.uk/PublicationsAndStatistics/PressReleases/PressReleasesNotices/fs/en?CONTENT_ID=4011629&chk=7VV%2BPw (accessed March 5, 2005).

UK-ILGRA (United Kingdom Interdepartmental Liaison Group on Risk Assessment). 2004. The Precautionary Principle: Policy and Application. January 13. www.hse.gov.uk/aboutus/meetings/ilgra/pppa.htm#7 (accessed March 5, 2005).

UK National CJD Surveillance Unit. 2010. http://www.cjd.ed.ac.uk/ (accessed October 19, 2010).

USDA (U.S. Department of Agriculture). 1991. Bovine Spongiform Encephalopathy. Animal and Plant Health Inspection Service. *Federal Register* 56: 63865–63870.

———. 2000. Bovine Spongiform Encephalopathy. Animal and Plant Health Inspection Service. www.aphis.usda.gov/oa/bse (accessed September 27, 2000).

———. 2004a. Prohibition of the Use of Specified Risk Materials for Human Food and Requirements for the Disposition of Non-ambulatory Disabled Cattle. January 12. *Federal Register* 69: 1862.

———. 2004b. Food Safety and Inspection Service. Preliminary Analysis of the Interim Final Rules and an Interpretive Rule to Prevent the BSE Agent from Entering the U.S. Food Supply. www.fsis.usda.gov/OPPDE/rdad/FRPubs/03-025N/BSE_Analysis.pdf (accessed June 11, 2010).

USTR (Office of the U.S. Trade Representative). 1996. Press Release: Statement of Mickey Kantor. January 11. www.ustr.gov/releases/1996/01/96-03.html (accessed September 27, 2000).

———. 1999. U.S. Response to EU Beef Import Ban. July. www.ustr.gov/releases/1999/07/fact.pdf (accessed September 27, 2000).

Vogel, David. 1995. *Trading Up: Consumer and Environmental Regulation in a Global Economy.* Cambridge, MA: Harvard University Press.

———. 1997. *Barriers or Benefits: Regulation in Transatlantic Trade.* Washington, DC: Brookings Institution Press.

Wiener, Jonathan B., and Michael D. Rogers. 2002. Comparing Precaution in the United States and Europe. *Journal of Risk Research* 5: 317–349.

Wilesmith, J. W. 1994. An Epidemiologist's View of Bovine Spongiform Encephalopathy. *Philosophical Transactions of the Royal Society of London, Series B: Biological Sciences* 343 (1306): 357–361.

Wilesmith, J. W., J. B. Ryan, and M. J. Atkinson. 1991. Bovine Spongiform Encephalopathy: Epidemiological Studies on the Origin. *Veterinary Record* 128 (9): 199–203.

Wilesmith, J. W., J. B. Ryan, W. D. Hueston, and L. J. Hoinville. 1992. Bovine Spongiform Encephalopathy: Epidemiological Features 1985 to 1990. *Veterinary Record* 130 (5): 90–94.

Will, R. G., J. W. Ironside, M. Zeidler, S. N. Cousens, K. Estibeiro, A. Alperovitch, S. Poser, M. Pocchiari, A. Hofman, and P. G. Smith. 1996. A New Variant of Creutzfeldt-Jakob Disease in the UK. *Lancet* 347 (9006): 921–925.

WTO (World Trade Organization). 1997. WTO Panel Report. EC Measures concerning Meat and Meat Products (Hormones)—Complaint by the United States. WT/DS26/R/USA. August 18, 1997. www.wto.org/english/tratop_e/dispu_e/cases_e/ds26_e.htm (accessed June 11, 2010).

———. 1998. WTO Appellate Body Report. EC Measures concerning Meat and Meat Products (Hormones). AB-1997-4, WT/DS26/AB/R, WT/DS48/AB/R. January 16, 1998. http://docsonline.wto.org/GEN_highLightParent.asp?qu=%28%40meta%5FSymbol+WT%FCDS26%FCAB%FCR%2A+and+not+RW%2A%29&doc=D%3A%2FDDFDOCUMENTS%2FT%2FWT%2FDS%2F26ABR%2EWPF%2EHTM&curdoc=3&popTitle=WT%2FDS26%2FAB%2FR%3Cbr%3EWT%2FDS48%2FAB%2FR (accessed June 11, 2010).

CHAPTER 4

Tobacco

D. Douglas Blanke

*N*o hazard of modern life would appear to have more urgent claim to the attention of regulators than the use of tobacco. Cigarettes kill about half of all regular smokers, making tobacco the leading preventable cause of death in both the United States and Europe (CDC 2005; EU 2003a). Every year, tobacco products kill more Americans than died on all the battlefields of World War II, along with more than a million Europeans (CDC 2005, 1; WHO 2002a, 1).

That tobacco products represent a profound threat to health has been known for 50 years. Science continues to expand our understanding of the breadth and gravity of the hazard, but experts had reached consensus in the 1950s that cigarettes cause lung cancer (Brandt 2004b, 67–78). That consensus received an official imprimatur in landmark reports of the Royal College of Physicians in the United Kingdom in 1962 and of the U.S. surgeon general in 1964. From that point forward, "the adverse health consequences of tobacco use were well known," according to the U.S. Supreme Court (*Food and Drug Administration v. Brown & Williamson Tobacco Corp.* 2000, 138). Today, the consensus language of the world's first public health treaty, the Framework Convention on Tobacco Control, declares that "scientific evidence has unequivocally established that tobacco consumption and exposure to tobacco smoke cause death, disease, and disability" (FCTC 2003), and a leading British medical journal has called for a complete ban on the sale and use of tobacco in the United Kingdom (*Lancet* 2003, 1865).

And yet tobacco products have long been among the least regulated of health risks. In half the countries of Western Europe, for example, there have long been no restrictions on the sale of tobacco to children (WHO 2002b, 17–20) (whereas such sales have long been illegal in the United States). In the United States, cigarettes kill more Americans than any other product, yet cigarettes had been almost untouched by regulation, having been deemed exempt from the authority of the Food and Drug Administration (FDA) and Consumer Product Safety Commission (CPSC), to take only two examples. This apparent paradox alone would make the treatment of tobacco products an inviting case study in regulation. (This chapter primarily examines the history of tobacco regulation during the period 1970–2004. Regulatory measures adopted since 2004, in both the United States and Europe, are addressed in the Epilogue at the end of this chapter.)

What makes this area particularly intriguing as a point of comparison, however, is the widely held perception on both sides of the Atlantic that tobacco products are regulated more aggressively in the United States than they are in Europe—a perceived difference that some would offer as a counterexample to claims that European regulation is more precautionary. While understandable, this perception is rooted almost entirely in the single aspect of tobacco regulation most salient to a casual observer: the treatment of smoking in public places. Admittedly, few cultural differences are more jarring to transatlantic travelers—in both directions—than the differences in public policies and social conventions surrounding public smoking. Americans return from Europe with tales of smoky German beer halls and French cafés, and of European smokers' blithe disregard for No Smoking signs. Europeans recount the indignity of being sent outside a New York restaurant for an after-dinner cigarette, or of being treated as pariahs for asking permission to smoke in a U.S. business meeting.

These differences in both laws and social norms are real enough, but they do not tell the whole story. Tobacco regulation involves a broad array of regulatory strategies, from taxation and advertising restrictions to warning labels, youth smoking prevention, smuggling controls, and product regulation. Expert consensus now recognizes that the most effective regulatory programs combine all of these strategies, and that regulation of public smoking—albeit perhaps the most visible facet of regulation—is only one piece of the puzzle. As will be seen, when other elements of regulation are examined, the patterns of relative precaution are neither uniform nor intuitive.

Moreover, tobacco control is not an exercise in risk regulation in the ordinary sense of the term. Policymakers seldom approach tobacco issues through the conceptual framework or terminology of quantitative risk analysis. The precautionary principle, per se, and the underlying concept of regulation in the face of scientific uncertainty are seldom invoked in the course of debates, even today. When they are cited, they rarely form the basis of decisions, but are cited instead as support for decisions driven by other considerations. Instead, decisions about tobacco regulation are inherently cultural and political, and they are made through the process of political power brokering and accommodation, with scientific evidence, estimates of risk and consequences, and objective analysis relegated to distinctly secondary roles (Brandt 2004a, 262–267).

This is not to minimize the political nature or intensity of debates in other areas of regulation, from nuclear power to genetically modified foods. Unlike novel technologies or emergent environmental threats, however, tobacco holds a centuries-old place in the culture, history, economies, and even psyches of both Europe and the United States. These roots are deep and powerful, and they assert themselves in unpredictable ways. Beyond the importance of tobacco in any objective economic or political sense, tobacco use has always had potent symbolic significance in different cultural contexts, in ways that are not obvious even within those cultures (Feldman and Bayer 2004, 292–297). Combined with the subtle psychological factors associated with chemical addiction, these considerations ensure that virtually every European and American has strong views on the subject, and that proposals for regulation invariably trigger emotional responses.

All this makes tobacco an unlikely candidate for dispassionate risk regulation. Were it not for these complex, interdependent factors, there can be little doubt that an objective regulatory response, based in science, would have resulted long ago in more stringent regulation in both Europe and the United States. As early as 1956, the medical director of the American Cancer Society observed wryly:

> If the degree of association which has been established between lung cancer and smoking were shown to exist between cancer of the lung and, say, eating spinach, no one would raise a hand against the proscription of spinach from the national diet. (quoted in Brandt 2004b, 68)

But tobacco is not spinach. And the regulation of tobacco is not like the regulation of chemical or dietary hazards devoid of cultural, symbolic, economic, and political meaning. These social dimensions of tobacco use have caused Congress to remove tobacco regulation from the purview of regulatory agencies and to reserve policymaking to the overtly political arena of Congress itself. In the words of the U.S. Supreme Court:

> Owing to its unique place in American history and society, tobacco has its own unique political history. Congress, for better or worse, has created a distinct regulatory scheme for tobacco products, squarely rejected proposals to give the Food and Drug Administration jurisdiction over tobacco, and repeatedly acted to preclude any agency from exercising significant policymaking authority in the area. (*Food and Drug Administration v. Brown & Williamson Tobacco Corp.* 2000, 160)

Identifying patterns of greater or lesser precaution in these political settings—where decisions are seldom made on the basis of risk assessments—is challenging at best. At some point, insisting on characterizing the outcomes of these political choices in the vocabulary of precaution runs the risk of becoming an artificial, and even misleading, exercise.

Further complicating the analysis is the wide variation in regulations among the nations of Europe and the states of the United States, and across the multiple dimensions of tobacco control. Norway's treatment of smoking in public places, for example, not only is far more stringent than that of Germany or Greece, but it is in fact more stringent than regulation in most of the United States. Tobacco taxes vary so greatly that premium cigarettes are twice as costly in the United Kingdom—where taxes are used to reduce tobacco consumption—as they are in Italy, the Netherlands, or the United States (WHO 2002b, 15–17; Corrao et al. 2000, 204, 300, 316, 352). Finally, policies are changing so rapidly in both regions, with a steady and accelerating trend toward stronger regulation (especially after the negotiation of the Framework Convention on Tobacco Control in 2003 and adoption of the landmark U.S. Family

Smoking Prevention and Tobacco Control Act in 2009), that categorizing either region's policies is precarious.

In this setting, rough generalizations are unavoidable. When those generalizations are extended across 50 states and dozens of countries, they risk becoming simplistic, if not wrong. On examination, the common preconception that U.S. tobacco regulations are stringent, comprehensive, and precautionary, while European policies are more lenient or nonexistent, proves to be such an oversimplification. While, on balance, policies in the United States may or may not be somewhat more stringent than a hypothetical European "average," European and U.S. policies are, at a minimum, converging. The clear trend, in both the United States and Europe, is toward more stringent regulation. Regulation is progressing, in fits and starts, toward a common set of policies generally recognized globally as best practices (Marmor and Lieberman 2004, 276). European policies were arguably changing more rapidly, driven in large measure by a process initiated by negotiation of the Framework Convention on Tobacco Control and by regulatory initiatives of the European Union; but the passage of U.S. legislation in 2009 giving the FDA authority to regulate tobacco reinvigorates American policies and builds on prior regulations at the federal, state, and local levels (Family Smoking Prevention and Tobacco Control Act 2009).

The Patterns of Regulation

Today, medical and policy experts have reached a broad global consensus that effective tobacco control requires a multifaceted regulatory program, integrating a wide variety of measures (FCTC 2003; CDC 1999). Europe and the United States entered the decade of the 1970s with few regulations in any of these areas. Over time, additional measures would accumulate, piecemeal, until both Europe and the United States would have at least some element of legislation in most of the key areas. To identify the patterns of regulation, it is useful to focus on four policy interventions recommended by the World Bank (2003) as "highly cost effective" in reducing tobacco use and identified by the European Network for Smoking Prevention as key indicators of the strength of national tobacco control programs (Joossens 2004): (a) large, direct warning labels; (b) comprehensive bans on advertising; (c) higher taxes to reduce consumption; and (d) restrictions on smoking in public places.

Warning Labels

Within six months after release of the U.S. surgeon general's landmark 1964 report, the Federal Trade Commission proposed that cigarette packages bear a mandatory warning that smoking "may cause death from cancer." At the instigation of tobacco manufacturers, Congress intervened, blocking the proposal and substituting less alarming language: "Caution: Cigarette Smoking May Be Hazardous to Your Health." Moreover, in doing so, Congress explicitly barred state and local authorities from regulating tobacco advertising or imposing their own warning requirements, citing a need to balance the public's right to know against the goal of "protecting commerce and the economy to the maximum extent."

Publicly, tobacco manufacturers fought the proposal while, behind the scenes, they followed the advice of their chief lobbyist: "Let's us write it." As Philip Morris's legal counsel, Abe Fortas, secretly informed the U.S. Department of Justice, tobacco companies welcomed the legislation, because "a requirement that packages be labeled would be helpful in civil litigation" (Kluger 1996, 284). (Perhaps the closest personal confidant of then-president Lyndon Johnson, Fortas would be appointed to the Supreme Court by Johnson the following year.) The industry had concluded that a "soft" warning that avoided the words "death" and "cancer" would not hurt sales, and that it might actually shelter tobacco manufacturers from legal accountability by allowing them to argue that smokers who developed cancer had been given notice of the hazard and had willingly assumed the risk of illness. That calculation successfully shielded them from liability for decades.

The labeling law was amended in 1969, strengthening the warning language marginally. In 1984, a series of rotating labels addressing specific health hazards was substituted for the previous warning, and the size of the text-only labels was enlarged slightly. In 1986, warnings were extended to smokeless tobacco containers. Through legal settlements with the Federal Trade Commission, warning labels were also required on most cigars. Notwithstanding these changes, warnings remained small and were placed on the less conspicuous side panels of cigarette packages, rather than on the face.

Europe was slower to require warning labels and did so with wide national variations. In some countries, the mandated warnings were weak, as in France— "Overuse Is Hazardous" in 1976—or in Denmark in 1986, where, by voluntary agreement, packages politely advised smokers, "The National Board of Health calls attention to the fact that tobacco smoking is injurious to health." Other countries required labels that were more prominent and stronger than those in the United States. Beginning in 1984, Iceland pioneered the use of graphic designs with large, rotating warning messages. Poland required different warnings on the front and back of each package, with each warning covering 30% of the surface area (1995). By 2002, 44 of the 51 countries in the World Health Organization's European Region required some form of warning label, although the strength of these warnings varied. Twenty-two countries required that the warnings appear not only on packages, but also in tobacco advertising (WHO 2002b, 21, 27).

These inconsistent approaches were superseded by the adoption of a European Union directive (EU 2001), effective in 2002, far exceeding the stringency of previous regulations in either the United States or most of Europe, and corresponding with the bold labels subsequently required under the new Framework Convention on Tobacco Control. Under the directive, 30% of the front surface of cigarette packages must be devoted to one of two stark general warnings: "Smoking Kills" and "Smoking Harms Those Around You." Fully 40% of the back of the package must be devoted to one of 14 specific health messages, which are far more directly worded—e.g., "Smoking Can Cause a Slow and Painful Death" and "Smokers Die Younger"—than those required in the United States. A 2003 decision of the European Commission set uniform guidelines for any country choosing to use photographic images in its warning labels, and the EU in 2004 tested and identified for potential use by Member States a set of photographs effective in encouraging smokers to reduce consumption. Belgium went even further than the EU directive, requiring some of the world's largest warning labels, occupying 55% of both the front and back of the pack.

Research shows that warning labels inform smokers of the hazards and encourage them to quit, but that to be effective, the warnings must use strong, direct language; must be prominent; and must use rotating messages. According to the research, Poland's bold warnings caused 3% of male smokers to quit smoking and another 16% to try to quit. Belgium's large warnings caused 8% of smokers to smoke less, and prominent Dutch warnings led 28% of teenage smokers to reduce their smoking (Joossens et al. 2004b, 150–153; Joossens 2004, 12–13; Zatonski 2003, 116). While the United States was first to require warnings, those warnings remain inconspicuous and relatively mild. Also, as we shall see in the next section, their value is sharply undercut by the accompanying legislative provision barring state regulation of advertising. The EU warning label requirements, although later in origin, are clearly far more stringent than the U.S. regulations.

Advertising Bans

A cornerstone of the approach favored by tobacco control advocates is a comprehensive ban on tobacco advertising. Endorsed not only by preeminent health experts, but also by such economic authorities as the World Bank, advertising restrictions are seen as a centerpiece of the Framework Convention on Tobacco Control, which obligates most parties to enact a comprehensive ban within five years (FCTC 2003). Countries where constitutional limitations prohibit advertising bans are exempted from this requirement but must regulate advertising within their constitutional ability.

These laws do not involve precaution in the ordinary sense. With isolated exceptions—tobacco advertising has been barred from Danish radio and television since their inception, for example—advertising bans gained currency only after the hazards of tobacco use were well established. An argument might nevertheless be made that advertising restrictions are "precautionary" in the sense that uncertainty remains as to whether advertising—as distinct from tobacco products themselves—endangers health. The empirical evidence on this point—persuasive but less than ironclad even today—was weak or nonexistent during early debates.

It would be an error, however, to impose precautionary constructs retroactively on decisions that were, in fact, made on other grounds. Most advertising laws are not rooted in evidence about advertising's impact as much as they are in a judgment about tobacco. As with alcohol, gambling, and other perceived vices, lawmakers have assumed that the harmful nature of the product provides ample basis to outlaw its promotion. On this basis alone, "Congress has the power to prohibit advertising of cigarettes in any media," declared a federal district court in 1971 (*Capital Broadcasting Co. v. Mitchell* 1971, 583). (Under subsequent First Amendment jurisprudence, the decision would almost surely be reversed.) This view has been reinforced by the advertising itself, much of which appeared calculated not only to associate cigarettes with vigor, energy, and health, but also to appeal to youth—impressions later confirmed by revelation of the industry's internal marketing strategies.

Further, the treatment of advertising is widely seen as sending a signal about the government's position on smoking. As a blue-ribbon Norwegian study committee explained in recommending a ban in 1967:

> Even if advertising may perhaps not strongly affect present consumption, it must be considered that the fact that advertising is permitted may, on a long-term basis, be interpreted as indicating that the harmful effects of smoking have not been proved. … The implicit effect could be that the public consciously or unconsciously believes that smoking cannot be so dangerous, since "responsible" authorities still permit tobacco advertising. (Bjartveit 2003, 4)

Today, these considerations are supported by substantial evidence that advertising bans do, in fact, reduce tobacco consumption. In 1989, the U.S. surgeon general concluded that it was "more likely than not" that advertising increased cigarette consumption (Surgeon General 1989). Subsequent influential research, comparing experiences in 22 countries over two decades, has concluded that comprehensive bans do reduce tobacco consumption, by more than 6%, and that a European ban would reduce consumption by 7% (Jha and Chaloupka 1999). Partial bans, in contrast, were found to have little effect, perhaps because advertising simply shifts to those communication channels that remain open. The evidence on this point is now sufficiently clear that the World Bank urges adoption of bans worldwide (World Bank 2003).

The U.S. response to this issue has been uneven. In 1967, advocates briefly persuaded the Federal Communications Commission, under its "fairness doctrine," to require television broadcasters for the first time to broadcast antismoking messages to balance the effects of ads. Again Congress intervened. Again with the covert acquiescence of tobacco manufacturers, Congress banned radio and television advertising, thereby ending the broadcast antismoking campaigns and simultaneously making it prohibitively expensive for potential new competitors to gain acceptance in the market. Within three years, per capita cigarette sales rose 18% (Kluger 1996, 332–335, 377).

Over the next 35 years, attempts to further restrict advertising at the national level failed. In the 1990s, a monumental effort by the FDA, focused on protecting children, sought to ban many billboards and magazine advertisements, along with most sponsorships and merchandise bearing cigarette brand names. This proposal was based on three years of investigation, a mammoth evidentiary record, and 700,000 public comments—the most in the agency's history. It came to an ignominious end in 2000 when a divided U.S. Supreme Court concluded that, although youth smoking was "perhaps the single most significant threat to public health in the United States," Congress had intentionally denied regulatory agencies the power to address the problem (*Food and Drug Administration v. Brown & Williamson Tobacco Corp.* 2000, 161). This situation changed with the enactment by Congress in 2009 of new legislation giving the FDA the authority to regulate tobacco that the court had not found in the prior statutes (Family Smoking Prevention and Tobacco Control Act 2009).

In the 1990s, several states, counties, and cities stepped in, adopting their own laws to restrict billboards or in-store advertising. These efforts were similarly undone when the Supreme Court ruled that Congress had barred them, too, from acting (*Lorillard Tobacco v. Reilly* 2001). Historic litigation by the U.S. states against major tobacco manufacturers was to provide a partial path around this roadblock when, in 1998 settlements, manufacturers agreed to end billboard and transit advertising, branded merchandise, most brand name sponsorships, and advertising that "targeted" youth. Still, the upshot was that, in the United States, tobacco manufacturers remained free to advertise inside stores; on the Internet; in newspapers, most magazines, and some outdoor settings; and through some sponsorships—as well as through the use of coupons, nonbranded giveaway merchandise, and other promotions. Despite the partial ban, advertising expenditures continued to increase dramatically; they were simply redirected to the remaining media.

The history of European regulation is more successful, though still checkered. While many European nations have been slow to act, a modern trend toward total advertising bans is illustrated by Norway. In 1973, with the support of 81% of the population, Norway enacted a total prohibition on advertising in any format. Smoking rates among young people, which had been rising for decades, began to fall immediately. In the years since, per capita tobacco consumption has fallen by over 40%. Although tax increases and smoking restrictions contributed to this result, experts credit the advertising ban with most of the reduction (Bjartveit 2003, 16–18). Broadly similar total bans have since been enacted in Belgium, Bulgaria, Croatia, Denmark, Estonia, Finland, France, Hungary, Iceland, Italy, Lithuania, Luxembourg, Poland, Portugal, and Sweden, although the level of enforcement varies greatly (WHO 2002a, 21).

Advertising regulation at the national level has now been largely overtaken by the efforts of the European Union (Joossens et al. 2004a, 116–120). The EU banned television advertising for cigarettes in 1989. For nearly a decade thereafter, proposals for a more comprehensive ban were blocked by Germany, long the most pro-tobacco of EU nations, with the intermittent support of the United Kingdom, the Netherlands, Greece, Denmark, and Austria (Gilmore and McKee 2002, 336–337; 2004, 234–239). As subsequent revelations show, this opposition was largely the result of an elaborate campaign of sabotage by tobacco companies, which included both influence at the highest political levels—including the apparent assistance of British cabinet minister Kenneth Clarke, later deputy chair of the British American Tobacco Company—and such "independent" allies as a coalition of 50 prominent Danes secretly organized by the industry to "defend freedom of expression." (Gilmore and McKee 2004, 238; Hastings and Angus 2004, 198–200). Nowhere was the industry's influence stronger than in Germany, "a constant and essential ally" (Gilmore and McKee 2004, 238) in the long-running campaign to defeat the advertising ban—to the extent that a 1995 "compromise" directive proposed by Germany was in fact written by the industry (Neuman et al. 2002). The industry's close relationship with German officials is reported to have included funding research by the president of the Federal

Health Office in the 1980s, and it may have involved the German commissioner heading the EU Directorate General responsible for the advertising proposal (Neuman et al. 2002).

Despite this powerful opposition, after years of contentious debate and maneuvering, a comprehensive advertising ban was adopted in 1998. The directive, immediately challenged by Germany and four British tobacco companies, was subsequently annulled by the European Court of Justice as beyond the jurisdictional competence of the EU, which does not extend to measures primarily for the protection of public health, but instead is limited to measures necessary to harmonize the internal market (*Federal Republic of Germany v. European Parliament and Council of the European Union* 2000). In response, the EU fashioned a new directive tailored to conform to the jurisdictional limits set by the court. The new directive (EU 2003b) prohibited radio advertising, advertising in the press, Internet advertising, cross-border sponsorships, and the distribution of free products. Another directive urged Member States to prohibit those forms of advertising that were beyond the reach of the EU itself (EU 2003a).

Even with these jurisdictional limits, the actions of the EU increased attention to the issue, energized civil society, and highlighted the weakness of some nations' policies, thereby helping to encourage enactment of additional comprehensive bans at the national level. As a result, advertisements in newspapers and magazines and on the Internet, which are permitted in the United States, are barred in the EU. In-store advertising—the focus of much U.S. advertising—is outlawed in many European countries, as are sponsorships and other forms of indirect advertising.

Moreover, the new Framework Convention on Tobacco Control obligated parties to implement comprehensive advertising bans within five years, subject only to any limitations imposed by their national constitutions. By mid-2005, some 18 European nations had ratified the treaty, and most EU members who had not yet ratified were expected to do so (Joossens et al. 2004a, 127). This was believed likely to end tobacco advertising in most of Western Europe, except in countries with constitutional impediments to a ban. In sum, although the U.S. was first to restrict advertising, European regulation was at this point far more stringent.

Taxation

Many authorities believe that the single most powerful regulatory tool for tobacco control is the use of tax policies to generate continual increases in the prices of tobacco products (World Bank 2003, 3). High prices discourage young people from using tobacco, reduce consumption among adults, and encourage quitting (Hopkins et al. 2001, 12). At the same time, they generate additional public revenues, some of which can be used to support tobacco prevention activities. Economists delight in elegant charts showing a near-perfect inverse correlation between price and consumption over time, in numerous countries (Jha and Chaloupka 1999). Their research suggests that a 10% increase in prices is likely to reduce consumption by about 4%, and that a 25% increase is likely to yield a 7% to 13% decrease, with the effect increasing over time

(WHO 2002a, 11–12; Joossens 2004, 14). The World Health Organization (WHO) has concluded that if every country were to raise tobacco prices by 10%, 10 million lives would be saved (Guindon et al. 2002).

Despite these recommendations, neither the United States nor Europe has made tobacco tax policy a primary tool for health improvement (although, as discussed in the Epilogue, the most recent trends may suggest new willingness to do so). Multiple attempts by the Clinton administration to increase the federal tax in the United States were rejected by Congress in the 1990s. In 2005, the tax stood at only $.39 per package of cigarettes.

Despite the unwillingness of Congress to act, tax increases have found increasing favor at the state and local levels in recent years. The 50 states impose their own excise taxes on tobacco products, in amounts ranging from $.03 a pack in the tobacco-growing state of Kentucky to $2.46 in Rhode Island. Between 2001 and 2004, a majority of the states, faced with fiscal crises, increased their tobacco taxes. These increases proved to be both a ready source of revenue and, unlike other taxes, popular with the public. Contributing to the proliferation of state taxes is the fact that, in some jurisdictions, tax increases can be triggered by ballot initiative, which has permitted the enactment of these measures even when the influence of tobacco companies or other factors make legislators unwilling to do so. Beginning in 1989, tobacco tax increases have been adopted by public vote in more than a dozen states.

In addition, more than 400 cities and counties collect their own tobacco taxes on top of federal and state levies. Notably, the city of New York in 2004 collected a municipal tax of $1.50 per pack, in addition to the $1.50 collected by the state of New York and the $.39 federal tax, bringing retail prices to as much as $7.50. When the local tax was implemented, a spokesperson for the city's mayor reported, "We sold half as many packs of cigarettes and revenues have gone up fivefold" (Cooper 2002).

As a result, while taxes remain controversial, state and local tax increases gained recognition as a health tool and have become a top priority of health advocates. Still, the historically low level of state taxes and the inaction of the federal government leave the United States with retail price levels substantially below those in the United Kingdom, France, or the Nordic countries. Most telling, perhaps, is the ratio of the taxes imposed to the final selling price, generally regarded as the measure of a government's commitment to using the tax for health benefits. In most of the United States, taxes account for less than 30% of the selling price—a figure less than half the level of taxation in other developed countries (Chaloupka et al. 2001).

Europe does not offer a single consistent pattern. Taxes and prices vary greatly (WHO 2002a, 15–17). In January 2004, the price of a pack of Marlboros ranged from €1.30 in Poland to €7.64 in Norway (Joossens 2004, 44–46). Taxes, too, vary widely, as does their role in a country's overall government revenues and the policy considerations that determine their levels. In general, taxes increased over the previous decade, but at irregular rates.

The EU is gradually reducing these differences among countries, albeit with great difficulty (Gilmore and McKee 2002, 338–330; 2004, 247–251). As part of the process of establishing and maintaining the single internal market, the EU continues to attempt to harmonize national rates of taxation across the different forms of tobacco taxes (*ad valorem* duties, fixed excise duties, and the value-added tax, or VAT). The Commission has expressed a desire to harmonize tax levels upward to serve public health, and a nonbinding Council recommendation of 2002 recommends that the Member States raise prices to discourage consumption. The Framework Convention on Tobacco Control, which is likely to have greater influence in Europe than in the United States, also calls for continual tax increases to reduce consumption.

Nevertheless, the opposing interests of different Member States have blocked progress and made tax harmonization a vexing undertaking. Directives adopted in 1992 set minimum levels of taxation, effectively requiring that combined taxes be at least 70% of the final selling price—roughly twice the combined rate of taxation in most of the United States. Largely through the intervention of the tobacco industry, however, this requirement was relaxed in 1999, and price differentials among countries persist. Still, the EU measures have resulted in price increases in countries where cigarettes were less expensive. Further, the accession process prompted many of the nations admitted to the EU in 2004 to raise their taxes toward the higher levels of the accumulated body of EU law, the "*acquis communautaire.*"

In summary, taxation and tax increases do not show a single clear pattern in either Europe or the United States. Europe has had higher levels of taxation (though U.S. federal and state taxes have increased markedly in recent years, now typically exceeding the EU level, as discussed in the Epilogue below). The EU harmonization process and the Framework Convention ensure that possible tax increases will receive continual discussion, and that health concerns will figure in the debates. In the United States, state and federal taxes are now increasing, and reducing tobacco use is a principal rationale for many of the increases. There is reason to believe that taxation is assuming a more central role in U.S. policy. Balancing these developments, it is fair to say that neither Europe nor the United States is obviously more precautionary than the other.

Controlling Secondhand Smoke

The common perception that the United States aggressively regulates tobacco products while Europe does not rests largely on a single dimension of the tobacco problem: the treatment of secondhand smoke. Here, for three decades, the United States demonstrated a greater willingness to regulate. Until recently, this sharp divergence in approaches even appeared to be increasing, as the United States moved toward ever more stringent policies. And yet impressions based on past policies—or even based on visits to today's smoky Paris bistros—obscure a dramatic rethinking of this issue in influential populations throughout Europe, as well as a convergence in policies.

The scientific basis for regulating secondhand smoke is now well established. The Framework Convention on Tobacco Control declares a global scientific consensus that "exposure to tobacco smoke causes death, disease, and disability" (FCTC 2003, Article 8). Exposure to tobacco smoke increases the risk of heart disease, lung cancer, and other illnesses (Sammet 2001). Secondhand smoke is thought to kill approximately 38,000 Americans annually—more than twice as many as die by homicide (National

Cancer Institute 1999)—with some estimates ranging as high as 65,000 deaths. In Europe, the WHO estimates that smoke causes 3,000 to 4,500 cancer deaths annually and an unknown but much larger number of deaths from cardiovascular disease (WHO 2000a); others have placed the European death toll as high as 100,000 (McNeill 2004, 57). And the evidence continues to mount. Strictly from the standpoint of protecting nonsmokers, therefore, there is a strong scientific basis for restricting public smoking.

Admittedly, uncertainty remains about specific aspects of the hazard. What is the level of risk associated with occasional or short-term exposure, for example? Is outdoor exposure a hazard, and if so, under what conditions? In practice, however, such lingering questions are not central to regulatory decisions about smoking, because those decisions are about more than the direct physical threat to nonsmokers.

Instead, smoking restrictions arise from a combination of concerns, including the social and aesthetic acceptability of smoking, the nuisance factor (the annoyance smoke causes most nonsmokers), concern that unrestricted public smoking undermines efforts to discourage youth smoking, and the symbolic value of policies in expressing society's views about smoking. In recent years, these policies have been supported by evidence that smoking restrictions are among the most effective tools for achieving other health goals, beyond protecting nonsmokers. Restrictions reduce tobacco consumption, reduce smoking rates, help smokers quit, and help keep those who quit from relapsing. Most important, these policies have now become central to the overarching goal of tobacco control advocates: to change the prevailing norms and make tobacco use socially unacceptable. These considerations have made smoking restrictions the central focus of advocacy in the United States and one of the highest priorities of tobacco prevention experts worldwide. It may explain why, as early as 1978, a secret tobacco industry poll identified smoking restrictions as "the most dangerous development to the viability of the tobacco industry that has yet occurred" (Roper Organization 1978, 6).

Against this backdrop, what have been the patterns of regulation? Beginning in the mid-1970s, as the public became more mindful of both environmental concerns and the hazards of smoking, American states and cities began to adopt "clean indoor air" laws designed to confine smoking to designated "smoking areas." Requiring the physical separation, however minimal, between smokers and nonsmokers was an approach adopted in some states and many cities as a logical "accommodation" of both smokers and nonsmokers. Premised only secondarily on health concerns, these laws rested first on the fact that smoke was annoying: the smell interfered with dining and lingered on clothing, ashes soiled clothing and furnishings, and smoke irritated eyes. To the extent health was a focus, the implicit assumption was that smoke was harmful to a limited number of people with asthma, allergies, or other conditions that made them unusually sensitive to its effects, so it was unfair to endanger this vulnerable population. With or without scientific evidence, this reasoning was supported by common experience.

From this beginning, smoking regulation expanded incrementally at different paces in different parts of the country. Through the 1980s and 1990s, specific venues identified with children or vulnerable adults were singled out as smoke-free zones, with many cities and states gradually eliminating smoking in government buildings, hospitals and medical clinics, public schools and childcare facilities, public transit, and similar settings. As the health consequences of smoking became better known, it became clear that separating smokers from nonsmokers within the same air space offered no meaningful health protections, and some cities and states moved to eliminate smoking completely.

Between 1975 and 2000, every state enacted some form of smoking regulation, ranging from very weak to very strong. By 1989, some 397 city and county ordinances further complicated this patchwork. By 1998, the number of municipal ordinances had risen to 859 (National Cancer Institute 2000; Jacobson and Zaawa 2001). Proliferation of local laws and the concerted efforts of health advocates, in turn, provided the impetus for adoption of a growing number of stronger statewide laws, beginning with California in the late 1990s. Although these laws enjoy broad public support, their enactment is always controversial. They are opposed fiercely by business owners, particularly the owners of restaurants, bars, and similar establishments. Once in place, however, these laws prove popular, and opponents' predictions of economic disaster and social unrest subside.

By 2005, more than a third of the U.S. population was covered by state or local laws eliminating smoking in workplaces, restaurants, or bars, and the adoption of new laws was accelerating. An estimated 70 million Americans were covered by laws requiring smoke-free bars—twice the population covered only three years earlier (ANR 2005). Some observers conclude that, with these sweeping changes, public attitudes in the United States have now reached a "tipping point," and that public smoking is becoming "de-normalized," as happened with smoking on airplanes in the 1990s. Some see the trend toward elimination of public smoking as irreversible.

The European experience does not present as clear a pattern, nor have smoking restrictions received comparable priority there, at least until recently (Gilmore and McKee 2004). Europe's pioneering legislation in this area was France's *Loi Veil* (1976), later strengthened by the *Loi Évin* (1991). Through these laws, France has followed an "intermediate" approach to regulation: strong legislation, ignored in practice. On its face, the broadly worded act of 1976 was years ahead of the rest of Europe; in practice, it was little more than a paper exercise. Enforcement was minimal, and despite strengthening amendments, a clarifying decree, and some enforcement through private litigation, the law remains openly disregarded (Évin 1993; Nathanson 2004, 142–150).

By 1990, regulations in other European nations followed a variety of approaches, from weak to strong (Roemer 1993, 97–128, 221–229), as illustrated by the contrasting cases of the United Kingdom and Norway. The UK, like Germany and Denmark, relied primarily on voluntary actions. Despite a 1988 government report recommending restrictions on public smoking and evidence of public support for regulation, smoking practices in most workplaces and places serving the public were left to their owners. Government policy was limited largely to encouraging the adoption of additional voluntary restrictions (Berredge 2004, 127–128). In contrast, Norway pursued a strict approach. There, 1988 legislation prohibited smoking in most public places, public transport, and work settings occupied by more than one worker.

Restaurants, bars, and other food and lodging establishments were required to introduce smoke-free areas within five years.

From the late 1980s, the emergence of the EU as a voice for regulating tobacco contributed strongly to the development of stronger national policies and a convergence of approaches, as did the encouragement of the WHO. In 1988, the European Commission and the WHO convened a Madrid Conference to promote European smoke-free policies (WHO 1988). In 1989, the Council of the European Communities urged Member States to prohibit smoking in public places and public transport—a development credited with helping to spur action in Austria, Sweden, Finland, and other Member States. Under its authority to regulate workplace safety, the EU also took modest steps to protect pregnant workers and require smoke free employee lounge rooms. In 1999, the WHO again convened European experts, this time in Lisbon, to discuss the medical evidence and recommended regulatory responses.

Perhaps as a result of such actions and increased public discussion of smoking regulation, a 1995 survey found 80% of EU citizens ready to support a general prohibition on smoking in all public places (Gilmore and McKee 2004, 246). Their governments were less enthusiastic. By 2001, most European nations had adopted legislation banning or seriously restricting smoking in hospitals, schools, government buildings, cinemas, public transport, or other designated public places, but many of these laws were poorly enforced. Fewer than half of the countries restricted smoking in restaurants or bars (WHO 2002a, 28–32).

Since 2001, however, a dramatic and probably transformative burst of regulation in this area has sparked debate across the continent and appears to have signaled a revolutionary change. The year 2001 saw the implementation of legislation requiring most Polish workplaces to limit smoking to enclosed smoking rooms, and a decision of the Norwegian Supreme Court awarding compensation to a bartender (herself a smoker) for cancer caused by smoke in her workplace. At the same time, debates in the course of negotiation of the Framework Convention on Tobacco Control were increasing awareness of the effects of smoke exposure, and the WHO devoted its annual World No Tobacco Day to the issue.

The watershed event was the enactment and March 2004 implementation of sweeping legislation in Ireland, eliminating smoking from public places, workplaces, restaurants, and—most visibly—the smoky pubs for which Ireland had long been known. The legislation was adopted with the support of trade unions representing pub workers, and implementation was relatively smooth. One year after introduction, the law was deemed a success by 96% of the Irish public (OTC 2005, 4). This unexpected transformation in a nation so strongly associated with smoking made Ireland the immediate point of comparison for other Europeans, redefining what was possible.

In June 2004, Norway's smoking regulations, long among the strongest in Europe, were extended to their logical conclusion, as Norway, too, eliminated all smoking in restaurants and bars. Within a year, similar prohibitions (with certain limited exceptions) were implemented in the restaurants and bars of Sweden, where opinion polls showed the support of 85% of the public. Perhaps more surprisingly, Italy was next. By mid-2005, smoking bans were under serious debate and winning popular support from Estonia and Geneva to Scotland, England, and Wales. Suddenly, it seemed, smoking was "on its way out" and "a significant cultural shift" was taking place, as the *Times* of London editorialized in June of that year (*Times* 2005).

With these developments, much of Europe appeared suddenly to be moving toward an aggressive new regulatory posture. The new legislation in Ireland, Norway, Italy, and Sweden—as stringent as any legislation in the United States—seemed to have set a new direction for European policy. Whether this foreshadowed similar regulations across the whole of Europe, and whether the United States would be overtaken by the new European trend, remained to be seen. At a minimum, it is apparent that U.S. and European approaches have been converging as both move toward more comprehensive smoke-free regulations.

Tracing the Trends

Are any patterns clear across the multiple dimensions of tobacco control? First, neither the United States nor Europe can be characterized as genuinely precautionary. Both have been reluctant regulators, and they remain so today. Such regulation as has been enacted has come many years after tobacco products were known to be carcinogenic. That contemporary regulation remains so disproportionate to the scale of the known harm is plainly the result not of scientific doubt, but of political and cultural explanations. When regulatory interventions are debated, they are routinely held to standards of scientific proof far beyond anything demanded of regulation in most other areas. In fact, stringent measures are now supported by a massive body of research. Yet, for reasons unrelated to risk, their adoption remains controversial and difficult.

Second, neither the United States nor Europe has shown a distinctly greater willingness to regulate. The reality of regulation is marked instead by cross-currents—crosscurrents complicated by the diversity of experience among U.S. states and the nations of Europe. With notable exceptions, it may be accurate to say that tobacco-related issues received greater attention earlier on in the United States, and that some U.S. measures were therefore adopted earlier. Regulation of public smoking clearly was of later concern in Europe. On the other hand, it is not clear which jurisdiction is more inclined to regulate today. It remains to be seen if the U.S. Family Smoking Prevention and Tobacco Control Act, enacted in 2009, will achieve policies that match the stringency of European measures to restrict advertising and the recent move to uniform strong health warnings.

Third, there appears to be a convergence of efforts, based on increased international collaboration and a shared understanding of the scientific evidence. Views among many of the expert elites who help shape policy have reached virtual consensus, so that international health organizations, medical societies, nongovernmental advocates, and to a large degree expert bodies within national ministries of health in both the United States and Europe are now pursuing a common agenda (Marmor and Lieberman 2004, 276).

Fourth, Europe appears to be changing more rapidly, driven perhaps by multinational factors, including the influences of the European Union, the WHO, and the Framework Convention on Tobacco Control. In the United States, where external developments play a lesser role, the primary source of movement toward greater regulation is the influence of state and local nongovernmental advocacy groups, whose ability to change policy in many areas—advertising, labeling, product regulation—is limited.

These conclusions suggest that Europe has closed, or is in the process of closing, some gaps between the relative stringency of its regulations and those of the United States, notably regarding restrictions on secondhand smoke in public places, for which U.S. restrictions had been more stringent since the late 1980s (as described above). Whether this represents a "catching up," or whether Europe is instead in the process of "leapfrogging" the United States, moving toward greater stringency, is not clear at this point. As described in the Epilogue below, recent U.S. policies may again be more stringent than those in Europe, including the U.S. federal legislation enacted in 2009, rising cigarette taxes imposed by states and the federal government over the past decade, and tougher enforcement of restrictions on smoking in public places.

Influences and Explanations

What accounts for the regulatory differences in Europe and the United States? Why has tobacco been treated so differently from many other health hazards? Several factors stand out.

A Powerful Industry

Tobacco-related public policies are determined to an unusual degree by the extraordinary influence of the tobacco industry. Most industries resist regulation, but the WHO has called tobacco "a case unto itself" because of the unprecedented scale, sophistication, and ferocity of the industry's activities (WHO 2000b, 244). The industry's strategies for avoiding regulation span decades and cover the globe. They involve mobilization of vast financial resources and natural business allies, from tobacco growers and retailers to media outlets dependent upon advertising (Hastings and Angus 2004).

Some elements of these campaigns are transparent. For example, in the mid-1990s, tobacco companies ran full-page newspaper advertisements across Europe that equated the cancer risk of secondhand smoke with the risk of eating cookies or drinking milk. They offered readers a reassuring scientific report by the industry-funded "European Working Group on Environmental Tobacco Smoke" (Gilmore and McKee 2004, 243). Similarly visible is the industry's hiring of powerful political figures as consultants—for example, former British prime minister Margaret Thatcher, at an annual fee of $250,000, and former U.S. Senate majority leader George Mitchell. In the main, however, tobacco companies are successful because they are invisible; they work through secret ties to ostensibly independent third parties in almost every sphere of public life. These groups are engaged with all the sophistication of a global war toward the common goal of minimizing the pressure for regulation (Blanke 2003, 133–142). Far beyond efforts to reach the public through advertising or public statements, or to influence lawmakers through direct lobbying, these strategies rely on the calculated funding of think tanks, universities, charities and cultural organizations, prominent scientists, economists, and others who are mobilized in concerted fashion to oppose regulation and dispute the science indicting tobacco products (Hirschhorn and Bialous 2001).

To take one audacious example, in the 1990s, the industry sought to escape regulation through no less than a rewriting of the very way in which science measures risk (Hirschhorn and Bialous 2001). This multipronged strategy apparently used such surrogates as a former president of the National Academy of Sciences and a former director of the U.S. Occupational Health and Safety Administration to dispute the science of risk assessment for low-dose toxin exposure. The strategy was designed to discredit the U.S. Environmental Protection Agency (EPA), which had identified secondhand smoke as a carcinogen, by assembling a broad coalition of industries to attack as "junk science" the evidence against asbestos, radon, diesel fumes, dioxin, agent orange, and other dangerous substances—thereby "concentrat[ing] all of EPA's enemies against it at one time" (Hirschhorn and Bialous 2001). These and similar efforts are calculated to minimize the perceived risks to health. At a minimum, they are meant to create the appearance of an active debate within the scientific community about the level of risk.

One explanation for the later emergence of strong regulations in Europe and for the greater European reluctance to regulate public smoking, at least until more recently, may be that these industry efforts have met less organized resistance in Europe. In the United States, a series of factors have helped to offset the industry's influence to some extent. First, a broad, community-based tobacco control advocacy movement focuses much of its energy on "delegitimizing" the tobacco industry by exposing its activities and influence. Second, the creation of large-scale media countermarketing campaigns, with a focus on exposing the industry's manipulation of youth and smokers, has helped raise awareness of the industry's role.

Third, highly visible litigation through much of the 1990s focused attention on the industry's behavior, as did the FDA's unsuccessful regulatory proposals and highly visible congressional hearings in which tobacco company executives famously insisted under oath that nicotine is not addictive and that cigarettes do not cause cancer. Internal documents exposing the industry's misconduct have received more attention in the United States. These documents now prove that most of the "scientific" objections to past regulatory initiatives were in fact orchestrated and paid for by tobacco manufacturers. These factors leave not only advocates but also much of the U.S. public highly suspicious of whatever opposition is presented to most tobacco regulation today.

Freedom and Choice

Debates about tobacco regulation often ignore risk assessment and turn on emotional arguments about "freedom," "liberty," and "personal choice." Indeed, tobacco companies work tirelessly to steer public debate away from troublesome issues of science and toward this arena of "rights," knowing that in both Europe and the United States, great power is invested in the idea that smokers have an inherent "right to smoke." While there is no legal basis for this idea, it is deeply rooted in fundamental beliefs about the role of the government and the prerogatives of the individual. In the United States, these ideas are often framed in terms of the American emphasis on individualism and fundamental political values of personal freedom and self-expression.

In Europe, similar ideas carry equal force. In many European countries, smoking has long been regarded as a private matter, existing within a zone of personal behavior. Despite general acceptance of an expansive role for the state in many aspects of life, this attitude is not extended to matters of personal lifestyle, with smoking seen as one of life's inviolable "small pleasures." From this perspective, European opponents have sometimes portrayed smoking restrictions as an offensive American export, and an example of narrow-minded moralizing—with French cartoons depicting them as the work of American Puritans and critics across Europe dismissing restrictions as "too American" or "a fundamentalist American approach" (Brandt 2004a, 262–267; Frankenberg 2004, 182; Nathanson 2004, 158–160). When Denmark's chain-smoking queen was criticized as a poor role model—dubbed "the Ashtray Queen"—Danes rallied to her defense, priding themselves on the tolerance that distinguished them from the rigid Americans and their neighbors in "Prohibition Sweden" (Albœk 2004, 193; Brandt 2004a, 265).

The U.S. tradition of individualism is no less strong and goes far to account for the weakness of smoking restrictions in much of the United States even today. Since the late 1980s, however, the idea that smoking is a matter of personal choice has been partially offset in the United States by three developments, each of which has been successfully exploited by health advocates to build support for regulation. First, beginning in the early 1990s, advocates focused the debate on children. In particular, FDA commissioner David Kessler, successfully characterizing tobacco use as "a pediatric epidemic," increased public understanding that almost all smokers develop the habit before reaching adulthood. As the debate was refocused on young people who were not regarded as legally capable of exercising mature judgment, "paternalistic" regulation became more acceptable.

Emphasis on youth reinforced a second development in the United States: increased attention to addiction. Advocates emphasized not only that most smokers become addicted before reaching adulthood, but also that a substantial majority of smokers say they would like to quit. Together, these developments undercut the argument that smoking is a free choice.

Finally, the emergence of solid evidence that secondhand smoke seriously threatens health altered the regulatory equation. As it became increasingly clear that smokers endanger not only themselves but also those around them, the argument that decisions about smoking should be left exclusively to smokers or business owners lost force.

This process differentiates the United States from Europe, at least with regard to the regulation of public smoking. Elements of the same process are no doubt under way in much of Europe, but a concerted, strategic effort to de-normalize tobacco use has not in the past been the guiding principle of regulatory efforts there. Nor have European campaigns been backed by the sustained efforts of a broad, community-based advocacy movement working to refute perceptions that tobacco use is the result of the free choice of well-informed adults. European attitudes and perceptions now appear to be changing, but the greater success of U.S. advocates in framing the debate to negate arguments about "freedom" and "choice" helps to explain why the United States has, until recently, shown greater readiness to regulate smoking.

Champions

Policy differences among nations or between Europe and the United States are attributable in part to the presence or absence of effective advocates. This factor is not to be underestimated. To a surprising degree, the course of regulation can often be traced to the influence of charismatic individuals and small but effective nongovernmental organizations (NGOs).

In some places, a single determined individual has been the catalyst for change. In Poland, Witold Zatonski, director of cancer prevention at Warsaw's leading cancer center, helped lead his country to a regulatory program that reduced smoking rates by a third—a program the WHO calls "a model for the world." Elsewhere, a small cadre of committed experts has made the difference. The decisive factor in the passage of France's effective advertising ban was the involvement of the *cinq sages*, an elite group of influential physicians and professors who used a deft combination of public pressure and inside connections to alter national policy.

The leadership of advocacy organizations is equally important. Aggressive advocacy groups emerged earlier in the United States than in Europe. Through creative use of existing regulatory mechanisms, individual gadflies helped trigger federal regulatory actions that mandated the free television broadcast of antismoking messages in the 1960s and then the phaseout of smoking on airplanes in the 1980s. The American Cancer Society, American Heart Association, and American Lung Association—voluntary health organizations with unimpeachable public reputations—brought not only credibility but also a nationwide grassroots structure to the debate. Significantly, the 1970s emergence of single-issue groups dedicated specifically to restricting smoking—notably, the national sparkplug Americans for Nonsmokers' Rights (ANR) and state-level Group Against Smoking Pollution (GASP) organizations—helps explain why smoking restrictions have gained greater acceptance in the United States. The sophistication of key strategists within these groups was central in the United States; in Europe, advocacy groups have generally appeared later and have not focused so intently on smoking restrictions.

In the 1990s, the foundations laid by pioneering advocates were strengthened with critical financial support from a leading charitable foundation and new resources derived from state tobacco litigation. As a result, the United States entered the twenty-first century with a well-developed infrastructure of professionals committed to stronger regulation; tobacco control conferences drew as many as 3,000 advocates. While European advocates were no less creative or assertive, no comparable base of grassroots and professional support backed their efforts.

International Influences

Europe's increasing willingness to regulate is explained in part by a series of international factors that are helping to reshape opinions in Europe. These factors, which have had no comparable impact in the United States, include the role of the European Union, activities of the WHO, the influence of the Framework Convention on Tobacco Control, and the increasing cohesion of advocacy efforts across national borders. In the United States, where attitudes are generally more insular and the public is less attuned to external events, these influences have been limited to nonexistent. In Europe, the situation is quite different.

The European Union obviously plays a role without parallel in the United States. Where the EU has competence to act, it is now "a key contributor to the action against tobacco in Europe" (Haglund 2000, 33; see generally Joossens et al. 2004a). The complex design of EU policymaking mechanisms opens multiple access points for regulatory initiatives, just as the fragmented structure of the federal system in the United States allows regulation to succeed at the local or state level even when stymied nationally. Moreover, because the EU is primarily a regulatory state, technical elites and health specialists—who, in both Europe and the United States, tend to support increased regulation—wield greater influence within the EU structure than do their counterparts in the United States, where Congress limits regulators' power and reserves policymaking to the legislative arena.

The WHO, while lacking the power to regulate, plays a parallel role in disseminating ideas, shaping expectations, and molding broad consensus about the evidentiary basis for action (Haglund 2000, 33). Through both its Geneva headquarters and its Copenhagen-based European Regional Office, the WHO encourages more stringent regulation across the spectrum of policy measures. This is achieved through policy statements, resolutions of the World Health Assembly, publications, and the convening of influential workshops, conferences, and other fora for mutual education, along with the development of a 1997 Action Plan for a Tobacco-Free Europe and a 2002 European Strategy for Tobacco Control.

No international development has had greater impact on Europe regulators' views than the Framework Convention on Tobacco Control. Within hours after assuming office as director general of the WHO in 1998, former Norwegian prime minister and Harvard-trained physician Gro Harlem Brundtland declared tobacco use reduction a top priority. Beginning in 1999, the WHO began a four-year negotiation process that led in 2003 to conclusion of the Framework Convention. The lengthy treaty negotiations served as an extended global seminar in the scientific evidence, encouraging consensus about the need for regulation, creating de facto global benchmarks of best practices, and highlighting the shortcomings of many nations' policies. This process greatly strengthened European support for regulation—even within countries that may never ratify the treaty. As of the end of 2004, the treaty process had no comparable impact in the United States.

Moreover, the treaty is becoming binding in much of Europe (see further discussion in the Epilogue, below). By mid-2005, the Framework Convention had been formally ratified by the European Union and 18 European nations. Another 19 European nations had signed the treaty, evincing their intention to become parties, and most EU nations were expected to become parties. In contrast, the United States had signed the treaty, but had not yet ratified it, and was not expected to become a party in the foreseeable future.

Finally, the increasing globalization of tobacco control efforts, driven largely by the Framework Convention negotiations, has increased the influence of European advocacy organizations. Four years of campaigning for a stronger treaty had the collateral effect of increasing coordination among European and global advocates, leading to the formation of a new global network of NGOs, the Framework Convention Alliance, and to a new unity in the agendas of these groups. Technology is reinforcing these developments. Through such mechanisms as a global listserv of 4,000 advocates and a daily electronic digest of European tobacco control news, advocates from Russia to Spain now collaborate daily, sharing scientific evidence and advocacy strategies and monitoring the tobacco industry and its allies. Such coordination enables advocates even in poor countries to play a more effective and sophisticated role in influencing policy.

Outcomes

A large body of evidence confirms that vigorous policies benefit health by reducing tobacco use and ultimately reducing the incidence of death and disease. Compiled by leading health authorities, such evidence continues to grow. One review estimates, for example, that using taxes to increase prices by 25% is likely to cut smoking prevalence by 7% to 13%, eliminating smoking in workplaces will cut smoking rates by 5% to 10%, a comprehensive advertising ban will cut rates by 6%, and an effective media campaign will cut rates by 5% to 10% (Joossens 2004, 14–18). The U.S. Centers for Disease Control and Prevention (CDC) estimates that the implementation of a comprehensive set of integrated policies can reduce tobacco use by half within 10 years (CDC 2001, 198).

Few jurisdictions have implemented all of the recommended approaches or sustained them for the time necessary to demonstrate clear reductions in disease. The state of California, however, has operated a comprehensive program since 1988. There, smoking rates—and, more recently, lung cancer rates—have fallen three times faster than in the rest of the United States, with youth smoking falling 43% between 1995 and 1999 (CDC 2001, 6). California's adult smoking rate now stands at 15%—one of the lowest in the world and a one-third reduction from levels when the tobacco control program began. Thirteen percent of California high school students are smokers, compared with 22% nationally (CDHS 2005). As a result, it is now possible to demonstrate that California's program has prevented tens of thousands of deaths from lung cancer and heart disease (CDC 2001, 6, 7). In Massachusetts, where a comprehensive program was conducted for 10 years before program funding was cut in 2003, smoking rates among sixth-grade students fell 70% in the late

1990s (CDC 2001, 16). Finally, smoking rates in New York City, which had not fallen in a decade, dropped by 15% in only two years after the city combined large tax increases with a near-complete prohibition on smoking in public places. With 188,000 fewer smokers, New York is expected to avert more than 60,000 premature deaths (NYCDH 2005).

Across the 51 countries of the WHO's European region, overall smoking prevalence has fallen from about 45% to about 30% over the last 30 years (WHO 2002a, 4, 5). Consistent with this decline, rates of lung cancer and related cancers in men began decreasing in Western Europe in 1985; by 1995, they had stabilized in Central and Eastern Europe. Cancer rates in women continued to increase, however, reflecting the fact that smoking became common among women later than it did among men.

Observations at a European level tell very little, however, because they obscure the great variation across the diverse region. In the 1990s, cigarette use decreased in some countries but increased in others (WHO 2002b). Smoking rates were significantly higher in Central and Eastern Europe than in the countries of the European Union, for example. Generalizations also obscured variations even within segments of a single country's population. For example, Belarus and the United Kingdom reported comparable overall smoking rates (26% and 27%, respectively), but this superficial similarity concealed the fact that British women were five times more likely to smoke than their Belarusian counterparts (WHO 2002b, 5–9).

Looking beneath European statistics to the evidence from particular countries is more instructive. Those nations with longer histories of regulation and with the most stringent approaches offer evidence that regulations do indeed reduce tobacco use and protect health (Joossens et al. 2004b). In Norway, where an advertising ban is combined with smoke-free spaces and tax increases in a comprehensive program, lung cancer mortality is now half that of the United Kingdom, which has fewer regulations and a history of longer and heavier smoking (Bjartveit 2003, 14–18). Norwegian tobacco sales fell 31% within four years after introduction of the advertising ban in 1975 (Joossens et al. 2004b, 153).

Similarly, within four years after France implemented its 1991 advertising ban, cigarette consumption fell by 9%, after having risen steadily for the preceding 15 years (WHO 1997, 15). Between 1999 and 2003, French smoking prevalence fell by another 12%, with tax-driven price increases cited by smokers as the top reason for quitting (Joossens et al. 2004b, 150). Tobacco consumption in the United Kingdom fell by 23% between 1976 and 1988, with half of this reduction attributable to the UK's policy of using taxation to raise prices (WHO 1997, 15).

In Sweden, multifaceted regulatory proposals were first developed in 1963. At that time, 36% of Swedes—40% of men and 25% of women—were smokers. By 1980, the rate had fallen to 33%; in 1998, Sweden became the first European nation to reduce smoking prevalence to 20%. As of 2005, its rate stood at 19%—among the lowest in Europe. This underestimated total tobacco consumption, however, because 20% of Swedish men used "snus," the Swedish form of moist snuff; nevertheless, the number of tobacco-related deaths fell by nearly 1,000 per year to an estimated 6,400 in 1999–2000 (National Institute of Public Health 2003).

In Poland, tobacco consumption rose steadily following World War II. By the late 1970s, 62% of men smoked, among the highest percentages in the world. By 1998, after implementation of comprehensive legislation—and despite aggressive marketing efforts by international tobacco companies in the newly opened economy—this rate had fallen to 40%. After rising continually since the 1950s, lung cancer rates leveled and began to fall. In contrast, rates in Hungary, a country with similar demographics but weak regulations, continued to climb. Oral, laryngeal, and pancreatic cancers show a similar trend in Poland. Cardiovascular disease decreased by 20%, and life expectancy has increased for both men and women. While other factors affect some of these outcomes, it was estimated in 2003 that reduced cigarette consumption was preventing 10,000 deaths per year (Zatonski 2003).

Trade-offs

Every regulation carries costs. The cost of implementation, the effect on businesses, and other direct consequences all contribute. In the case of tobacco regulations, these trade-offs are very modest. The cost of implementing and administering the regulations is inconsequential in relation to tobacco's health effects. Warning labels, advertising restrictions, and smoking controls all involve minimal costs of administration and enforcement. Rather than imposing costs, increased tobacco taxes generate additional government revenues.

Some other elements of comprehensive tobacco regulation not discussed here do involve ongoing costs. Large-scale marketing campaigns to educate the public and discourage youth smoking require substantial expenditures. Smoking cessation programs offering nicotine replacement products and counseling can be costly. Nevertheless, the cost of even the most comprehensive programs is small in relation to the medical and economic costs of tobacco use, even ignoring the human toll. The CDC has estimated that a comprehensive campaign costs approximately $5 to $20 annually per capita (CDC 1999, 3). The state of California calculates that every dollar spent on these programs saves $3.62 in direct medical expenditures (CDC 2001, 9).

Opponents often argue that tobacco regulation will cause economic harm. Reducing tobacco use will result in a loss of jobs, reduced economic activity, and a decline in government revenues, according to these arguments. After studying these claims, the World Bank has concluded that they have no basis. On the contrary, tobacco regulation produces economic benefits, its research concludes, because funds that would otherwise have been spent on tobacco products will be redirected to other productive activity, while the very substantial medical and economic costs of tobacco use will be reduced or avoided (Jha and Chaloupka 1999, 67–71).

More specific economic objections arise when smoking is restricted. Opponents invariably predict that eliminating smoking will drive restaurants and bars out of business. This issue has been the subject of nearly 100 studies. With the exception of studies commissioned or funded by tobacco manufacturers, research shows that smoke-free laws have no negative impact on overall employment or the overall profitability of food and beverage businesses in a community. This leaves open the possibility that a smoking regulation may hurt some individual businesses or even render them unprofitable. For each business that is affected negatively, however, another is benefited. In the aggregate, these regulations do not appear to impose an economic cost.

Finally, opponents argue that smoking restrictions carry another cost: the smokers' alleged loss of liberty. This claim is difficult to weigh. Whether the effect on smokers is characterized as harm or mere inconvenience, several things can be said about it. First, restrictions on smoking in public places do not outlaw smoking altogether; they only require smokers to step outside or defer a cigarette until they are in an unregulated location. Second, most smokers say they want to quit smoking, and a substantial percentage actually support smoking bans. Third, opposition to these laws tends to come from a surprisingly small group of smokers—typically less than 10% of the total population. An argument can be made that—even setting aside health issues—the inconvenience to this group is outweighed by the inconvenience, annoyance, and irritation that smoking causes the much larger nonsmoking population. When considerations of health are reintroduced to the equation, any cost to "liberty" would appear to pale in comparison to the benefits to the public as a whole.

Unintended Consequences

Because tobacco use involves such complex patterns of behavior, not to mention chemical addiction and subtle social and cultural issues, regulatory interventions have occasionally had unexpected results. As described above, some regulations have had the unintended effect of protecting tobacco manufacturers, as happened when U.S. labeling legislation created de facto protections against legal liability claims. Some jurisdictions have limited the tar content of cigarettes in the mistaken belief that low-tar cigarettes offer health benefits, only to learn that they are no safer than high-tar brands. Tax increases intended to reduce tobacco consumption may have the unintended effect in some cases of causing smokers to switch to less expensive brands with higher tar and nicotine levels (Warner 2001, 4). Research and experience continue to add to the understanding of such complexities and of what works and what does not.

Arguments about unintended consequences have figured most prominently in European discussions about appropriate levels of taxation (Gilmore and McKee 2002, 339; 2004, 249–250; Blanke 2003, 110–111). There, the tobacco industry has opposed tax increases by arguing that high taxes encourage the smuggling of cigarettes from low-tax jurisdictions to areas with higher taxes. By some estimates, the black market accounts for 7% of cigarette sales in Western Europe and twice that share of the Eastern European market. Research by the World Bank and others concludes, however, that smuggling is not the result of differences in taxation. It may, in fact, be more closely associated with the level of corruption in a given country than with tobacco prices. This conclusion is consistent with the European experience: smuggling is more common in low-tax countries of Southern and Eastern Europe than in high-tax, high-price areas such as the United Kingdom and the Nordic countries.

Implications and Conclusions

The case of tobacco regulation refutes the theory that clear differences in the level of precaution divide the United States and Europe. In dealing with tobacco, at least, neither has been consistently more precautionary than the other. Each has been first to regulate in some areas, and each is now more stringent than the other in some respects. Moreover, the patterns and agendas of regulation appear to be converging.

Moreover, it is inaccurate and misleading to speak of policies in this area as precautionary, if we mean that they require action in the face of uncertainty about the harm to be regulated. For decades, it has been well settled that tobacco products represent a profound threat to public health. Elements of uncertainty do remain, but regulatory decisions are seldom determined by lawmakers' level of precaution. Instead, decisions are guided by political, economic, social, and cultural considerations. The existing evidence and the symbolic significance of regulation play a part as well.

To the extent uncertainty does come into play, the evidence supports adherence to a high level of precaution. This conclusion is reinforced by the pattern of experience as science has increased the understanding of tobacco's health effects. For 50 years, without interruption, new research has expanded the list of harms attributable to tobacco use. Not until long after the original 1964 U.S. surgeon general's report, for example, did subsequent surgeons general identify tobacco as a cause of pancreatic cancer (1982), stroke (1989), and bladder cancer (1990). Scientists of earlier generations had no idea that smoking causes deafness, impotence, spontaneous abortions, or sudden infant death syndrome—all effects that are now well documented. Given this history, it is reasonable for policymakers to anticipate the future emergence of evidence about still more hazards by adopting a highly precautionary approach.

Precaution is also supported by the role of tobacco companies in distorting scientific understanding over the years. Irrefutable evidence now shows that many of the most outspoken "independent" critics of regulation over the years were in fact paid agents of tobacco manufacturers, hired to create the artificial perception of scientific "uncertainty." This long history makes it appropriate to maintain a degree of skepticism about the opposition to regulation in this area and, again, to err on the side of action.

Other case studies in this volume decry the occasional conflict between popular will and the dictates of the evidence—a conflict sometimes characterized as "politics versus science" or "emotion versus reason." Tobacco is not such a case. Here, public opinion and scientific knowledge are broadly aligned. On key elements of tobacco regulation—health warnings, advertising restrictions, taxation, smoking restrictions—both public sentiment and the scientific evidence tend to support regulation. Enacting regulations is difficult not because the evidence is insufficient or because public support is lacking. Rather, tobacco's unique historical and cultural status, along with the great influence wielded by tobacco companies and their allies, has effectively interposed a veto to most regulatory initiatives.

This argues for approaches that will strengthen both political accountability and regard for the evidence, both of which support increased regulation. Tobacco use stands as the leading preventable cause of death in both Europe and the United States; its harm to society dwarfs that of most other health risks. Proven regulatory interventions can reduce that harm; their effectiveness has been studied, measured, and confirmed. The costs of regulation are small. Many of the health effects of tobacco use and exposure to smoke are not visible until many years after exposure. In this context, where the scale of harm is so great, the cost is low, and many victims become ill many years after the fact, it is reasonable to resolve any doubts in favor of action. Indeed, in the final analysis, there can be few cases where precaution is more warranted.

Epilogue

The analysis presented above was prepared in 2004–2005. In the time since, the trends it describes have continued and accelerated. Medical science has continued to reveal chilling new information about the hazards of tobacco use. Recent studies in Ireland, Italy, Scotland, and the United States, for example, have demonstrated that heart attacks fall sharply and immediately wherever smoke-free policies are implemented (IOM 2010).

The global tobacco control treaty, the Framework Convention on Tobacco Control, has become one of the most rapidly adopted treaties in the history of the United Nations system. By mid-2010, the treaty had become law in 169 countries, representing 86% of the world's population. The United States remained the largest holdout nation. In Europe, only Andorra, the Czech Republic, Liechtenstein, Monaco, and Switzerland had yet to adopt the treaty.

In the United States, historic 2009 legislation, the Family Smoking Prevention and Tobacco Control Act, empowered the FDA to regulate tobacco products, opening the door to expansive new regulations that would end "light" cigarette brands, ban flavored cigarettes, restrict advertising formats, limit sales practices, and expand the regulatory authority of states and cities. Tobacco industry lawsuits challenging the legislation were pending in mid-2010.

By mid-2010, more than 30 European nations required cigarette packages to display large health warnings, but only four of these nations required the warnings to include pictures, despite compelling evidence that graphic imagery greatly increases warnings' effectiveness. In the United States, the new federal tobacco legislation included a requirement that cigarette packages display such large graphic health warnings, beginning in 2012.

Tobacco taxes continued to increase. In the United States, federal cigarette taxes were more than doubled in 2009, from $.39 per pack to $1.01. State cigarette taxes tripled between 2002 and 2010, with more than 100 tax increases raising the per-pack average from $.43 to $1.45. By 2010, combined state and city taxes in New York City were $5.85 per pack. In Europe, EU nations agreed in 2009 to increase the European floor for national cigarette taxes by nearly 50%, effective in 2014—to a minimum of €1.80 per 20-cigarette pack—and to require that national taxes constitute no less than 60% of the retail sales price. Many European nations imposed taxes substantially above these minimums.

Comprehensive smoke-free laws continued to proliferate. By the end of 2009, 17 European nations, including Italy (2005), the United Kingdom (2006, 2007), and France (2008), had adopted relatively strong laws (Global Smokefree Partnership 2009). In the United States, comprehensive smoke-free laws were in place in 22 states—including the leading tobacco-producing state, North Carolina—as well as 400 municipalities. Nearly 50% of the U.S. population was protected by laws prohibiting smoking in workplaces, restaurants, and bars.

With all these changes, it remains unclear whether Europe is more inclined to regulate than is the United States, or vice versa. What is clear is that regulatory standards in both regions continue to converge and that the pace of regulation is accelerating.

References

Albœk, Erik. 2004. Holy Smoke, No More? Tobacco Control in Denmark. In *Unfiltered: Conflicts over Tobacco Policy and Public Health*, edited by Eric A. Feldman and Ronald Bayer. Cambridge, MA: Harvard University Press, 190–218.

ANR (American Nonsmokers' Rights Foundation). 2005. U.S. Population Protected by Local and State 100% Smokefree Indoor Air Laws. www.no-smoke.org/pdf/EffectivePopulationGraph.pdf (accessed July 18, 2005).

Berredge, Virginia. 2004. Militants, Manufacturers, and Governments: Postwar Smoking Policy in the United Kingdom. In *Unfiltered: Conflicts over Tobacco Policy and Public Health*, edited by Eric A. Feldman and Ronald Bayer. Cambridge, MA: Harvard University Press, 114–137.

Bjartveit, Kjell. 2003. Norway: Ban on Advertising and Promotion. In *Tools for Advancing Tobacco Control in the XXIst Century: Success Stories and Lessons Learned*. Geneva: World Health Organization.

Blanke, D. Douglas. ed. 2003. *Tobacco Control Legislation: An Introductory Guide*. Geneva: World Health Organization.

Brandt, Allan M. 2004a. Differences and Diffusion: Cross-Cultural Perspectives on the Rise of Anti-Tobacco Policies. In *Unfiltered: Conflicts over Tobacco Policy and Public Health*, edited by Eric A. Feldman and Ronald Bayer. Cambridge, MA: Harvard University Press, 255–274.

———. 2004b. Written Direct Examination in *United States v. Philip Morris, et al.* (Dist. D.C., 99-CV-2496-GK). September. www.usdoj.gov/civil/cases/tobacco2/20040920%20Allan%20M.%20Brandt,%20Ph.D.,%20Written%20Direct.pdf (accessed July 18, 2005).

Capital Broadcasting Co. v. Mitchell. 1971. 333 F. Supp. 582 (D.D.C.).

CDC (Centers for Disease Control and Prevention). 1999. *Best Practices for Comprehensive Tobacco Control Programs*. Atlanta: U.S. Department of Health and Human Services, Centers for Disease Control and Prevention.

———. 2001. *Investment in Tobacco Control, State Highlights, 2001*. Atlanta: U.S. Department of Health and Human Services, Centers for Disease Control and Prevention.

———. 2005. Targeting Tobacco Use: The Nation's Leading Cause of Death at a Glance. Atlanta: U.S. Department of Health and Human Services Centers for Disease Control and Prevention. www.cdc.gov/nccdphp/aag/pdf/aag_osh2005.pdf (accessed July 18, 2005).

CDHS (California Department of Health Services). 2005. California Smoking Rates Drop 33 Percent since State's Anti-Tobacco Program Began. Press Release No. 05-16. April 5. Sacramento, CA: CDHS. www.applications.dhs.ca.gov/pressreleases/store/pressreleases/05-16.html (accessed July 18, 2005).

Chaloupka, Frank, Melanie Wakefield, and Christina Czart. 2001. Taxing Tobacco: The Impact of Tobacco Taxes on Cigarette Smoking and Other Tobacco Use. In *Regulating Tobacco*, edited by Robert Rabin and Stephen Sugarman. Oxford: Oxford University Press, 39–71.

Cooper, Michael. 2002. Cigarette Tax, Highest in Nation, Cuts Sales by Half. *New York Times*, Aug. 6, B1.

Corrao, Marlo A., G. Emmanuel Guindon, Namita Sharma, and Dorna F. Shokoohi. 2000. *Tobacco Country Profiles*. Atlanta: American Cancer Society.

EU (European Union). 2001. Directive on the Approximation of the Laws, Regulations and Administrative Provisions of the Member States concerning the Manufacture, Presentation and Sale of Tobacco Products, European Parliament and Council of the European Communities (2001/37/EC, June 5, 2001). *Official Journal of the European Communities* [2001] L 194:26–35.

———. 2003a. Recommendation on the Prevention of Smoking and on Initiatives to Improve Tobacco Control, Council of the European Communities (2003/54/EC, December 2, 2002). *Official Journal of the European Communities* [2003] L 22: 31–34.

———. 2003b. Directive on the Approximation of the Laws, Regulations and Administrative Provisions of the Member States relating to the Advertising and Sponsorship of Tobacco Products, European Parliament and Council of the European Communities (2003/33/EC, May 26, 2003). *Official Journal of the European Communities* [2003] L 152: 16.

Évin, Claude. 1993. Foreword. In *Legislative Action to Combat the World Tobacco Epidemic*, by Ruth Roemer. 2nd ed. Geneva: World Health Organization, vii–ix.

Family Smoking Prevention and Tobacco Control Act. 2009. Public Law 111-31 (signed June 22, 2009). www.fda.gov/TobaccoProducts/ (accessed August 1, 2010).

FCTC (Framework Convention on Tobacco Control). 2003. Adopted by Resolution 56.1 of the World Health Assembly. May 21. Geneva: World Health Organization.

Federal Republic of Germany v. European Parliament and Council of the European Union European Court of Justice. 2000. Judgment of the European Court of Justice of October 5, 2000, Case C-376/98, European Court Reports [2000] I, 8419.

Feldman, Eric A., and Ronald Bayer. 2004. Conclusion: Lessons from the Comparative Study of Tobacco Control. In *Unfiltered: Conflicts over Tobacco Policy and Public Health*, edited by Eric A. Feldman and Ronald Bayer. Cambridge, MA: Harvard University Press, 292–307.

Food and Drug Administration v. Brown & Williamson Tobacco Corp. 2000. 529 U.S. 120.

Frankenberg, Günter. 2004. Between Paternalism and Voluntarism: Tobacco Consumption and Tobacco Control in Germany. In *Unfiltered: Conflicts over Tobacco Policy and Public Health*, edited by Eric A. Feldman and Ronald Bayer. Cambridge, MA: Harvard University Press, 161–189.

Gilmore, Anna, and Martin McKee. 2002. Tobacco Control Policy: The European Dimension. *Clinical Medicine* 2 (4): 335–342.

———. 2004. Tobacco Control Policy in the European Union. In *Unfiltered: Conflicts over Tobacco Policy and Public Health*, edited by Eric A. Feldman and Ronald Bayer. Cambridge, MA: Harvard University Press, 219–254.

Global Smokefree Partnership. 2009. Global Voices Status Report 2009: Rebutting the Tobacco Industry; Winning Smokefree Air. www.globalsmokefreepartnership.org/ficheiro/GV_report_09.pdf (accessed July 30, 2010).

Guindon, G. Emmanuel, S. Tobin, and Derek Yach. 2002. Trends and Affordability of Cigarette Prices: Ample Room for Tax Increases and Related Health Gains. *Tobacco Control* 11: 35–43.

Haglund, Margaretha. 2000. Regional Summary for the European Region. In *Tobacco Country Profiles*, edited by Marlo A. Corrao, G. Emmanuel Guindon, Namita Sharma, Dorna F. Shokoohi. Atlanta: American Cancer Society, 32–35.

Hastings, Gerard, and Kathryn Angus. 2004. The Influence of the Tobacco Industry on European Tobacco-Control Policy. In *Tobacco or Health in the European Union: Past, Present and Future*. ASPECT Consortium. Luxembourg: European Commission, 195–225.

Hirschhorn, Norbert, and Aguinaga Stella Bialous. 2001. Second Hand Smoke and Risk Assessment: What Was in It for the Tobacco Industry? *Tobacco Control* 10: 375–382.

Hopkins, David P., Jonathan E. Fielding, and the Task Force on Community Preventive Services, eds. 2001. The Guide to Community Preventive Services: Tobacco Use Prevention and Control; Reviews, Recommendations and Expert Commentary. *American Journal of Preventive Medicine* 20 (2S): 1–88.

IOM (Institute of Medicine). 2010. Secondhand Smoke Exposure and Cardiovascular Effects: Making Sense of the Evidence. IOM Board on Population Health and Public Health Practice. http://books.nap.edu/openbook.php?record_id=12649 (accessed July 30, 2010).

Jacobson, Peter, and Lisa Zaawa. 2001. Clean Indoor Air Act Restrictions: Progress and Promise. In *Regulating Tobacco*, edited by Robert Rabin and Stephen Sugarman. Oxford: Oxford University Press, 207–244.

Jha, Prabat, and Frank Chaloupka. 1999. *Curbing the Epidemic: Governments and the Economics of Tobacco Control*. Washington, DC: World Bank.

Joossens, Luk. 2004. *Effective Tobacco Control Policies in 28 European Countries*. Brussels: European Network for Smoking Prevention.

Joossens, Luk, Martin Raw, and Fiona Godfrey. 2004a. The Development of European Union Tobacco-Control Policy. In *Tobacco or Health in the European Union: Past, Present and Future*. Analysis of the Science and Policy for European Control of Tobacco (ASPECT) Consortium. Luxembourg: European Commission, 99–138.

———. 2004b. The Impact of Tobacco-Control Policy on Smoking in the European Union. In *Tobacco or Health in the European Union: Past, Present and Future*. Analysis of the Science and Policy for European Control of Tobacco (ASPECT) Consortium. Luxembourg: European Commission, 139–166.

Kluger, Richard. 1996. *Ashes to Ashes: America's Hundred-Year Cigarette War, the Public Health, and the Unabashed Triumph of Philip Morris*. New York: Alfred A. Knopf.

Lancet. 2003. How Do You Sleep at Night, Mr. Blair? *Lancet* 362: 1865.

Loi Évin. 1991. *Loi no 91-32 du 10 Janvier 1991 relative à la lutte contre le tabagisme et l'alcoolisme. Journal Officiel*, Jan. 12, 615.

Loi Veil. 1976. *Loi no 76-616 du 9 Juillet 1976 relative à la lutte contre le tabagisme. Journal Officiel*, July 10, 4148.

Lorillard Tobacco v. Reilly. 2001. 533 U.S. 525.

Marmor, Theodore R., and Evan S. Lieberman. 2004. Tobacco Control in Comparative Perspective: Eight Nations in Search of an Explanation. In *Unfiltered: Conflicts over Tobacco Policy and Public Health*, edited by Eric A. Feldman and Ronald Bayer. Cambridge, MA: Harvard University Press, 275–291.

McNeill, Ann. 2004. Tobacco Use and Effects on Health. In *Tobacco or Health in the European Union: Past, Present and Future*. Analysis of the Science and Policy for European Control of Tobacco (ASPECT) Consortium. Luxembourg: European Commission, 25–68.

Nathanson, Constance A. 2004. *Liberté, Egalité, Fumée*: Smoking and Tobacco Control in France. In *Unfiltered: Conflicts over Tobacco Policy and Public Health*, edited by Eric A. Feldman and Ronald Bayer. Cambridge, MA: Harvard University Press, 138–160.

National Cancer Institute. 1999. *Health Effects of Exposure to Environmental Tobacco Smoke: The Report of the California Environmental Protection Agency*. Smoking and Tobacco Control Monograph No. 10. NIH Pub. No. 99-4645. Bethesda, MD: U.S. Department of Health and Human Services, National Institutes of Health, National Cancer Institute.

———. 2000. *State and Local Legislative Action to Reduce Tobacco Use*. Smoking and Tobacco Monograph No. 11. NIH Pub. No. 00-4804. Bethesda, MD: U.S. Department of Health and Human Services, National Institutes of Health, National Cancer Institute.

National Institute of Public Health. 2003. *Progress and Challenge, Tobacco Control, Swedish Style, Disarming a Deadly Weapon*. Stockholm: National Institute of Public Health.

Neuman, Mark, Asaf Bitton, and Stanton Glantz. 2002. Tobacco Industry Strategies for Influencing European Community Advertising Legislation. *Lancet* 359: 1323–1330.

NYCDH (New York City Department of Health and Mental Hygiene). 2005. Nearly 200,000 Fewer Smokers in New York City since 2002, at Least 60,000 Early Deaths Prevented. Press Release No. 062-05. June 9. www.nyc.gov/html/doh/html/pr/pr062-05.shtml (accessed July 18, 2005).

OTC (Office of Tobacco Control). 2005. Smoke-Free Workplaces in Ireland: A One Year Review. Clane, County Kildare, Ireland: Office of Tobacco Control. www.otc.ie/Uploads/1_Year_Report_FA.pdf (accessed July 18, 2005).

Roemer, Ruth. 1993. *Legislative Action to Combat the World Tobacco Epidemic.* 2nd ed. Geneva: World Health Organization.

Roper Organization. 1978. A Study of Public Attitudes toward Cigarette Smoking and the Tobacco Industry in 1978. Vol. 1. Bates No. 680042929-680042981. www.bwdocs.com/rjrtdocs/image_downloader.wmt?MODE=PDF&SEARCH=4&ROW=1&DOC_RANGE=001413011-3063&CAMEFROM=1&tab=search (accessed July 18, 2005).

Sammet, Jonathan. 2001. The Risks of Active and Passive Smoking. In *Smoking: Risk, Perception, and Policy,* edited by Paul Slovic. Thousand Oaks, CA: Sage Publications, 25–26.

Surgeon General. 1989. *Reducing the Health Consequences of Smoking—25 Years of Progress: A Report of the Surgeon General.* Washington, DC: U.S. Department of Health and Human Services.

Times (of London). 2005. How to Ban Smoking—And How Not To. An Unnecessarily Complicated Government Plan. June 21. www.timesonline.co.uk/article/0,542-1662520,00.html (accessed July 18, 2005).

Warner, Kenneth. 2001. Tobacco Control Policy: From Action to Evidence and Back Again. *American Journal of Preventive Medicine* 20 (2S): 2–5.

WHO (World Health Organization). 1988. *It Can Be Done: A Smoke-Free Europe, Report of the First European Conference on Tobacco Policy, Madrid, November 7–11, 1988.* Copenhagen: WHO Regional Office for Europe.

———. 1997. *Third Action Plan for a Tobacco-Free Europe, 1997–2001.* Copenhagen: WHO Regional Office for Europe.

———. 1999. *International Consultation on Environmental Tobacco Smoke (ETS) and Child Health: Consultation Report.* Geneva: WHO.

———. 2000a. *Air Quality Guidelines for Europe.* 2nd ed. Copenhagen: WHO Regional Office for Europe.

———. 2000b. *Tobacco Companies Strategies to Undermine Tobacco Control Activities at the World Health Organization: Report of the Committee of Experts on Tobacco Industry Documents.* Geneva: WHO.

———. 2002a. *European Strategy for Tobacco Control.* Copenhagen: WHO Regional Office for Europe.

———. 2002b. *The European Report on Tobacco Control Policy: Review of Implementation of the Third Action Plan for a Tobacco-Free Europe, 1997–2001.* Copenhagen: WHO Regional Office for Europe.

World Bank. 2003. Tobacco Control at a Glance. Washington, DC. http://wbln0018.worldbank.org/HDNet/hddocs.nsf/c840b59b6982d2498525670c004def60/88db854ff9b86b9a85256a3b0055aabf?OpenDocument (accessed July 18, 2005).

Zatonski, Witold. 2003. Democracy and Health: Tobacco Control in Poland. In *Tobacco Control Strategies, Successes and Setbacks,* edited by Joy de Beyer and Linda Waverly Brigden. Washington, DC: World Bank and Research for International Tobacco Control, 97–120.

CHAPTER 5

Nuclear Power

John F. Ahearne and Adolf Birkhofer

*T*his chapter addresses the meaning and application of the precautionary principle (PP) in the case of nuclear power generation in the United States and the EU. As noted elsewhere in this volume, there are many formulations of the PP. In fact the PP's "greatest problem, as a policy tool, is its extreme variability in interpretation. One legal analysis identified 14 different formulations of the principle in treaties and nontreaty declarations" (Foster et al. 2000). A French study included the comment that "the precautionary principle is neither understood nor interpreted in a single way" (Kourilsky and Viney 1999). A U.S. report noted that "[i]n the case of EMFs [electromagnetic fields], a variant of the PP called 'prudent avoidance' (defined as 'undertaking only those avoidance activities which carry modest costs') has been adopted by some states in the United States and several countries" (Graham 1999).

These multiple formulations of the PP complicate its application to a technology such as nuclear power. And even if a precautionary stance were warranted for nuclear power in its early days, some would now argue that nuclear power is sufficiently well understood to obviate highly precautionary measures. For example, a report to the prime minister of France (Kourilsky and Viney 1999) distinguishes between precaution and prevention:

> Precaution and prevention are two aspects of prudence, which is required in all situations where harm may occur. ... Precaution relates to potential risks and prevention to established risks. ... [I]n the case of precaution, we are concerned with the probability that the hypothesis is correct; in the case of prevention, the danger is established and we are concerned with the probability of the occurrence.

That report identifies nuclear facilities as particularly appropriate for prevention as opposed to precaution because, according to its authors, "the risks associated with nuclear facilities are established" (Kourilsky and Viney 1999). Others would argue that the risks of nuclear power remain uncertain and warrant precaution. Still others would emphasize the need to weigh trade-offs among the risks associated with different energy options.

This chapter considers the history of precautionary policies applied to nuclear power in both the United States and Europe. It compares these policy histories, finding important connections and contrasts across the Atlantic. And it comments on the explanations, impacts, and merits of applying precaution to nuclear power. Overall, the basic approach to the safety of nuclear power generation has been similar in the United States and the EU.

Current Status of U.S. and EU Nuclear Power Generation

Nuclear power generation grew rapidly in both the United States and the EU in the second half of the twentieth century. Although the first commercial nuclear power station was built in Europe—Calder Hall in the UK in 1956 (see IAEA 2009)—initially the growth was most rapid in the United States. Eventually hundreds of nuclear power plants (NPPs) were built in both Europe and the United States, as well as in Japan, Canada, and numerous other countries. Worldwide, some 440 civilian nuclear power stations are operating today (Guinnessy 2006; NEA 2006). The growth phase continued for longer in Europe than in the United States, resulting in a greater reliance on nuclear power in Europe.

The pattern is not uniform within Europe. Seven Member States have a total of 140 reactors supplying 850 terawatts of electricity, or about a third of the EU's electricity; about half of this total is in France. Others have none: Denmark, Greece, Ireland, Luxembourg, Portugal, and Norway have no nuclear power plants. Austria voted against nuclear power production by a 1978 referendum confirmed by Parliament in 1997. Italy closed down its last nuclear plant in 1990. In some countries, new plants are being planned: Finland has four nuclear power stations generating about 30% of its electricity, and in 2002 the Finnish Parliament approved the construction of a fifth for operation in 2009[1]. France recently sited a new nuclear power station to start operating by 2012, and in 2006, President Chirac proposed adding new stations by 2020. And in Switzerland, a moratorium on the construction of new nuclear power plants was terminated by referendum in 2003. Elsewhere, Canada, Japan, and South Korea are also planning new facilities (Guinnessy 2006). In other European countries, however, existing nuclear plants are being phased out. Germany announced in June 2000 its intention to phase out its nuclear power plants by about 2020[2]. Spain has enacted legislation prohibiting the construction of additional nuclear power plants; Poland has stopped construction of a new reactor. Slovenia announced a phaseout by 2023. Belgium plans to phase out its current seven reactors by 2025. In the Netherlands, a phaseout initially planned by 2003

---

[1] Construction problems have pushed operation back to 2012.
[2] The German government has now proposed extending the life of all nuclear plants beyond 2020.

Table 5.1 *Percentages of Electrical Power Generation in the United States, the EU, and France, 2003*

	Nuclear	Conventional	Other	Total TWh
United States (1)	19.7	71	9.3	3,883
EU25 (2)	31.2	54.9	13.9	3,121
France (3)	77.8	9.8	12.4	567

Note: TWh = terawatt-hours
Sources: 1. EIA (2006); 2. European Commission (2005); 3. IEA (2003)

has been postponed to 2033; Sweden's phaseout, planned for 2010, may also be postponed (see European Commission 2004; Guinnessy 2006).

Table 5.1 shows clearly that the EU in general, and France in particular, is much more dependent on nuclear power generation than is the United States. Overall, the EU produces about a third of its electricity from its approximately 150 nuclear power stations, whereas the United States produces only about a fifth of its electricity from just over 100 civilian nuclear power stations. Within Europe, as noted above, some countries produce no nuclear power, while France produces over three-quarters of its electricity from its 59 civilian nuclear power stations. Belgium's seven stations produce over half of its electricity, and the UK's 23 stations produce one-fifth of its electricity (NEA 2006). Table 5.1 also highlights that nuclear power generation makes a proportionately greater contribution to the reduction in greenhouse gas emissions reduction in Europe than does nuclear power in the United States.

Studies of public opinion have suggested that perceptions of the risks of nuclear power are roughly similar across countries, while perceptions of its benefits differ. For example, a 1996 study found that the percentage of French and American respondents perceiving nuclear power as posing moderate or high risks was roughly the same (about 70% in both countries), but the French public perceived both a greater need for nuclear power (about 70% compared with about 50%) and greater trust in the institutions and experts managing nuclear power (about 70% compared with about 40%) than Americans did (Slovic et al. 1996). (However, public perceptions change over time, so care must be taken when using studies of a decade ago.) This pattern may be the converse of the situation for genetically modified foods (see Chapter 2), where Americans perceive greater benefits and have greater trust in institutions than do Europeans.

Concerns about climate change associated with fossil fuel power plant emissions (see Chapter 7) may also influence choices about nuclear power—both the deferral or reversal of planned phaseouts of nuclear power in some European countries mentioned above and the potential for new construction in the United States. Almost 9 out of 10 of the EU respondents to a Eurobarometer questionnaire on energy issues considered that global warming was a "serious problem requiring immediate action" (Eurobarometer 2002). This in turn seems to produce a greater willingness to accept nuclear power. In a UK survey, 55% endorse the statement "I am willing to accept the building of new nuclear power stations if it would help to tackle climate change"

(Poortinga et al. 2006). Some surveys have been even more optimistic. Recent polling indicates growing support for nuclear power among the American public. The 2009 Gallup Environment Poll found 59% of the public supporting the use of nuclear power, up from a low of 46% in 2001. A 2010 poll taken on behalf of the Nuclear Energy Institute found 74% of the public favoring nuclear power (Bisconti Research 2010).

By contrast, climate change has been less of a public policy concern in the United States (see Chapter 7; Sunstein 2007). Thus, in the precautionary risks versus risk trade-offs discussion comparing greenhouse gas emissions contribution to climate change with nuclear power expansion, for Americans nuclear power may seem to pose the greater risk. However, both the EU and the United States are participating in the development of safer nuclear power systems through the Generation IV International Forum program. Further, Joskow (2006) argues the likelihood of new nuclear power plants in the United States has increased because of support and subsidies from the Energy Policy Act of 2005. However, the estimated costs of building new nuclear reactors will remain higher than that of building new coal plants unless the United States adopts a cap-and-trade program for CO_2 emissions.

U.S. Nuclear Safety Regulation

In the United States, safety regulation (as opposed to economic regulation) of civilian nuclear power is the responsibility of the Nuclear Regulatory Commission (NRC) and its predecessor, the Atomic Energy Commission (AEC). The NRC's duties are spelled out in statutes such as the Atomic Energy Act of 1954, as amended, and the Energy Reorganization Act of 1974, as amended. These acts authorize the NRC to regulate so as to ensure adequate protection of the public health and safety. This charge—both broad and ambiguous—has led to many court cases in which the NRC has prevailed against critics who argue that the NRC has not been aggressive in protecting the public. Whereas local jurisdictions, including states, have regulatory roles in many areas, in the U.S. nuclear reactor safety regulation is a federal, not a state, responsibility.

Substantial debate remains about how to measure the extent to which the NRC's responsibility for safe operation extends. The NRC's position is that maintaining safety is the responsibility of the operator of the nuclear facility, not the regulator's.

> Inherent in the Atomic Energy Act, as amended, and in the licensing process for utilities is the idea that the primary responsibility for the safety of commercial nuclear power plants rests with the operator (the licensee). The important role of federal regulation must not be allowed to detract from or undermine the accountability of utilities and their line management organizations for the safety of their plants. (NRC 1992, 62)

The regulator provides the legal requirements in the form of regulations and advisory material, but the operator is responsible for meeting these requirements. These roles were in contention following the Three Mile Island (TMI) accident in 1979, with the operator arguing that the NRC was at fault. The federal courts accepted the government's position that responsibility lay with the owning utility.

However, this does not mean that the NRC takes a neutral or "hands-off" approach to reviewing safety performance. On the contrary, the NRC can be seen as an aggressive regulator. It has resident inspectors stationed at each nuclear reactor, a large headquarters staff of technical experts who perform incident-specific analyses and broader safety analyses, a long-range safety research program, and inspection teams that are sent out whenever a serious issue arises at a reactor. As will be mentioned, this aggressive characteristic can be seen when the NRC shuts down a reactor.

Several approaches are used in developing regulations for reactor safety:

- defense in depth;
- risk-informed, performance-based regulations; and
- ALARA (as low as reasonably achievable).

Defense in depth requires redundant, diverse, reliable safety systems with two or more safety systems performing key functions independently. If one system fails, another always backs it up, providing continuous protection. The essential problem for nuclear power risk management is that despite the low probability of occurrence of harm—from, says, a loss of coolant accident (LOCA)—the consequence or harm is potentially high (see, e.g., Ropeik and Gray 2002, 254). Renn and Klinke (2001, 16) term such risks "Sword of Damocles risks."

Defense in depth has been a foundation of U.S. nuclear regulation for nearly 40 years.

> In overall perspective, the purpose of the combined elements in this system of protection is to insure that reactor facilities are designed, built, and operated to high standards, with specific emphasis placed on reducing to the lowest feasible level the likelihood of serious accident, and with provisions made to confine or minimize the escape of radioactivity to the environment if a serious accident should occur. (Walker 2004, 52)

Not unlike the PP, "there is no official or preferred definition" of defense in depth (Sorensen et al. 1999).

> The history ... indicates that defense in depth is considered to be a concept, an approach, a principle, or a philosophy, as opposed to being a regulatory requirement per se. ... We have identified two different schools of thought (models) on the scope and nature of defense in depth. ... The structuralist model asserts that defense in depth is embodied in structure of the regulations and in the design of the facilities built to comply with those regulations. ... The rationalist model asserts that defense in depth is the aggregate of provisions made to compensate for uncertainty and incompleteness in our knowledge of accident initiation and progression. (Sorensen et al. 1999)

The quotation above reflects the view of knowledgeable members of the NRC's main advisory group. For most people in the nuclear industry, defense in depth is used to mean multiple layers of protection against release of radioactive materials. Such layers are

- well-designed plants,
- well-trained operators,
- reactor vessels that are many inches thick, and
- containment buildings, coupled with
- redundancy in the safety systems.

A more formal summary was presented by a long-time member of the NRC's advisory committee (Apostolakis 2003):

> Defense in depth is an element of the Nuclear Regulatory Commission's safety philosophy that employs successive compensatory measures to prevent accidents or mitigate damage if a malfunction, accident, or naturally caused event occurs at a nuclear facility. (NRC 1999)

However, faced with increased demands on its staff, criticism of what were seen as overly prescriptive regulations, and pressures on operators to improve economic efficiency, in the late 1990s the NRC introduced the concept of risk-informed, performance-based regulation. This approach incorporates two concepts. First, the assessment of the operation of a nuclear facility should be based on overall performance, not on its compliance with many detailed regulations. Second, the NRC should concentrate on what is determined to be most important as identified by risk analysis.

The second of these concepts reflects the growth in the application to nuclear reactor safety of probabilistic risk analysis (PRA)—also called probabilistic safety analysis (PSA). PRA began in earnest with the publication in 1975 of WASH 1400, the Reactor Safety Study (NRC 1975). "[I]t is generally agreed that the study made a very important contribution to pioneering the application of methods of probabilistic risk assessment (PRA) to the analysis of nuclear reactor safety" (Bodansky 1996, 196). For at least a decade after this study, many NRC staffers and some commissioners resisted application of PRA, preferring instead to rely on engineering deterministic analyses (analyses using engineering calculations that do not include probabilities for actions of the equipment). Eventually risk analysis became an accepted approach, but only after several industry-based PRAs had been completed, methodological improvements had been accepted, enough data had been collected, computer codes were improved, and—notably—a new generation of analysts joined the NRC. (As physics giant Max Planck wrote in 1936 in *The Philosophy of Physics*, "A new scientific truth does not triumph by convincing its opponents and making them see the light, but rather because its opponents eventually die, and a new generation grows up that is familiar with it" (Kuhn 1962, 151).) A major advantage of PRA is the ability to examine the integrated plant and identify weak points in a plant's design or operations that may not show up in the engineering design approach.

Gradually the NRC moved to use PRA in regulatory matters, as seen in the following 1995 policy statement:

> The use of PRA technology should be increased in all regulatory matters to the extent supported by the state-of-the-art in PRA methods and data and in a manner that

complements the NRC's deterministic approach and supports the NRC's traditional defense-in-depth philosophy. (NRC 1995)

This approach developed into the current risk-informed, performance-based approach.

ALARA is a risk minimization approach used *after* the regulations have been met to address whether further reduction in either plant vulnerability or worker exposure is economically justified. The premise is that when the plant already meets the regulatory requirements and the workers are protected, if the cost of a further safety improvement is low, then that improvement should be made. Ambiguity arises when determining what is achievable at low or acceptable cost.

Application of the PP to Reactor Safety Standards

The NRC has been developing a regulatory approach for a quarter of a century with no mention of the PP. In response to a request for how the PP was applied in the NRC, an NRC director of nuclear regulatory research replied:

> There is no indication that the "precautionary principle" as such has played any role whatsoever in the development of NRC regulations. It does not appear explicitly in that regard in any documents that can be accessed via the NRC internal and eternal websites (approximately 60,000 possible sources). (Thadani 2004)

Furthermore, the former chair of the NRC, Dr. Richard Meserve, was asked whether he was aware of any attempts to invoke the PP in the area of nuclear regulation. He replied:

> In a nutshell, the precautionary principle is frequently invoked by EPA in rulemakings on the theory that is always better to err on the side of caution. The problem with it, of course, is that there never is a real limit on how much caution is enough. The NRC has a considerably more sophisticated approach that reflects that balancing is ultimately necessary. We call it ALARA (as low as reasonably achievable). In practice, the ALARA principle serves the same purpose but is much more intellectually sound. Whether you can find some literature that sets out the issue in this way is not clear to me. (Levin 2004)

However, if NRC practices are examined, aspects of the PP can be seen in PRA and in ALARA.

In a briefing at the White House, a representative of a nongovernmental organization (NGO) described the precautionary principle as having five components (Raffensperger 1999). Below we compare each of these five components to the NRC application of safety standards to nuclear reactors.

The first component is "taking precautionary action before scientific certainty of cause and effect." As discussed above, by its inherent nature, PRA is designed to address such uncertainty and to target risk reduction measures before certainty of cause and effect is established. Moreover, defense in depth and ALARA lead to the adoption of safety measures where they are low-cost and enhance redundancy—even when the degree of risk reduction is not estimated.

The second component is "setting goals." The NRC's charge to provide adequate protection for the health and safety of the public is an explicit goal. The NRC also has promulgated explicit safety goals. For example, "the risk of an immediate fatality to an average individual in the vicinity of a nuclear power plant that might result from reactor accidents should not exceed 0.1% of the sum of immediate fatality risks that result from other accidents to which the U.S. population is generally exposed." (NRC 1986).

The third characteristic of the PP listed in Raffensperger is "seeking out and evaluating alternatives to harmful practices." Even when specific practices may be considered acceptable, ALARA guides the operator to examine alternatives to reduce exposure and hence to reduce risk even further.

Fourth, "shifting burdens of proof" influence "the licensees' duty to monitor, understand, investigate, inform, and act." As noted above, the NRC position is that the operators are responsible for reactor safety. In addition, this approach can be seen as a description of the practices of the NRC headquarters regulatory staff and the NRC inspectors, some of whom are stationed at operating facilities.

Last comes "developing more democratic and thorough decisionmaking criteria and methods." Although many of its critics would disagree, the NRC's hearing process, under the Administrative Procedures Act, does provide considerable openness and public participation, although the relevance and standing requirements are limiting.

A former NRC official and longtime practitioner in the field of reactor safety wrote:

> The NRC has never used the PP words, but the concept has been part of their thinking right along. They call it "conservatism in the deterministic regulations." "[C]onservatism" is actually embedded in "deterministic" regulation, inserted in several conceptually different ways, sometimes down in the bowels of specific design regulations, and other times up at the top after a more-realistic design analysis has been done. Conservatism is embedded in many different ways in NRC's reactor safety regulations, and most of them are, frankly, an embodiment of the precautionary principle, even though it is never called that. (Budnitz 2004)

Wiener and Rogers (2002, 320–21) describe three main versions of the PP:

> **Version One: Uncertainty does not justify inaction**. ... This version rebuts the contention that uncertainty precludes regulation but does not answer the real question: *what* action to take, given the inevitable uncertainty.

> **Version Two: Uncertainty justifies action**. ... Again, the real question is what action to take, given the uncertainty.

> **Version Three: Uncertainty requires shifting the burden and standard of proof**.

The NRC approach to using PRA provides a methodology to quantify the uncertainty, enabling both the operator and the regulator to address those elements that pose the most significant risks. Examining options to reduce these risks and applying PRA to those options will identify what actions to take. Thus, the NRC's practices can be interpreted as meeting both versions one and two above. Defense in depth and ALARA also fit version two. The NRC approach once an operator has been penalized can be seen as an application of version three (see below).

While in principle the NRC approach can be seen as meeting the philosophy of the PP, some complications arise in the execution of this precautionary policy.

NRC enforcement following a safety breach can be seen as "PP after the fact." When the NRC shuts down a reactor because of a problem, the utility has a significantly difficult task to convince the NRC to allow the plant to restart. This could be seen as application of Wiener and Rogers' version three.

The most serious nuclear reactor "near-miss" in recent years was the discovery in March 2002 of a pineapple-size hole in the 8-inch-thick reactor vessel lid of the Davis-Besse nuclear plant near Toledo, Ohio. Corrosion had eaten away the lid material, and only a thin stainless steel liner separated the high-temperature fluid inside the reactor from the containment. The operator was instructed to shut down the reactor. The reactor lid was replaced and operational practices scrutinized. Among the problems identified were lax maintenance, a poor "safety culture," and weaknesses in the NRC's oversight. As the utility attempted to recover, the NRC continued criticizing during the succeeding reviews: "The errors that crews made while operating the reactor during heat-ups, and the results of a recent employee survey led the NRC and others to question whether the plant's 'safety culture' had been adequately restored" (Funk and Mangels 2004).

The utility and the NRC had several meetings to address restart. In a meeting in mid-January, Jack Grobe, chair of the NRC panel overseeing Davis-Bessse's recovery, said, "What's important is why, why did these things happen. ... That's a question we'll continue to ask ourselves as we do our inspections. The challenge this panel faces [is] whether or not your performance will be continuing. ... You need to show us" (Funk and Mangels 2004). Finally, after two years and a cost to the utility of over $500 million, the plant received approval from the NRC to restart in March 2004.

As mentioned earlier, the NRC's mandate to provide "adequate protection" is not a clear instruction. A 1999 congressionally encouraged study identified this as one of the key issues that needed to be addressed to improve nuclear regulation.

> Because no human activity is absolutely safe, it is important and entirely appropriate to establish a clear, consistent, and well-understood statement of safety philosophy and the meaning of adequate protection. In a prescriptive, deterministic framework this may be impossible. A risk-informed framework that makes use of risk insights together with engineering judgment and operational data can narrow the difference and provide greater clarity. There is little controversy between advocates and adversaries of nuclear power that is not rooted somehow in differences of opinion as to what adequate protection really means. ... The existing safety philosophy, which rests largely on the legal presumption that substantial compliance with the regulations provides adequate protection, does not provide a clearly defined safety philosophy that is consistently applied for all nuclear power plants. (CSIS 1999, 9, 12)

Reviews such as this one supported the move to performance-based, risk-informed regulation.

At the same time, PRA can reduce costs. As in other areas of regulation, a common theme in regulatory discussions between Congress and presidential administrations for the last several decades has been the desire to reduce what is described as "regulatory burden." According to Dr. George Apostolakis, one of the lessons learned from the introduction of PRA was that some regulations were not well targeted to reducing risks. "In some instances, unnecessary regulatory burden is imposed, wasting valuable resources" (Apostolakis 2003).

Regulatory burden is a somewhat pejorative term conveying the message of unneeded, costly bureaucratic government intervention. In that context, the basic concepts of the PP immediately produce objections. From the NRC's viewpoint, however, its regulations are designed to meet the necessary goal of protection, achieving defense in depth and going further to achieve ALARA. In debates between the NRC and operators or the NRC and Congress, relying on the PP would weaken the NRC's case, because the NRC's opponents in industry would argue that the NRC had no basis other than being overly cautious. The use of PRA helps NRC regulation reduce risk both more effectively and at a lower cost.

After the terrorist airplane attacks on September 11, 2001, in the United States, the NRC substantially increased the requirements for protection of nuclear plants against terrorism. This has led to a new focus on emergency planning.

> The Nuclear Regulatory Commission, citing new security concerns raised by the September 2001 terrorist attacks, announced this week it is creating an Emergency Preparedness Project Office to highlight its increased focus on improving emergency planning at commercial nuclear plants. (*Energy Daily* 2004, 3)

Although the NRC has moved toward application of PRA, terrorism analysis and related threat estimates might be hampered by the lack of data on which to base probabilistic analysis. Evaluating the NRC's approach in this area is difficult because the data and its analyses are classified. Richard Croteau, a staff member of the NRC chairman, said, "Our approach in this area includes 'risk insights.' We address equipment reliability and survivability as well as human reliability. We do not attempt to develop initiating event frequency, but judgment is used to determine if an event is reasonable versus remote" (Croteau 2004). The PP and terrorism are discussed further in Chapter 12.

Meanwhile, the notion of formally applying the PP to nuclear power has its detractors. One of those is Chauncey Starr, one of the founders of risk analysis, who has been a significant voice in support of nuclear power for nearly 40 years. Starr's 1969 article laid the groundwork for including benefit analysis in risk analyses (1232–1238). In 2003, he wrote:

> In recent decades, some major governments have officially responded to the unfamiliar consequences of new options by defensively foreclosing the entry of such intrusions, particularly in area of health, food, and environment. Such negative responses have been publicly justified by reference to a vague "precautionary principle" as the basis for action. There is no such principle. An analytic basis to support its verification and predictability as a "principle" does not exist. It is a

rhetorical statement that provides government a public welfare masquerade for indefinite deferment of a long-term policy response, or allows the deferment of disclosure of near-term actions motivated by political pressures. ... The horserace scenario is analogous to circumstances faced by governments and regulators when they turn to the precautionary principle to avoid risk taking decisions. A horserace provides an example of decisionmaking with an extremely inadequate risk analysis base, a situation faced by governments when new intrusive options appear that significantly relate to public health and safety. ... Governments asked to regulate public exposure to risks from manmade sources (food, water, air, radiation, pollutants, electromagnetic fields, etc.) face a tortuous decision process because of the ... uncertainties of risk analysis. The use of the precautionary principle as a politically defensible umbrella is not cost-less, as a protection from a risk that may be nonexistent or trivial may deprive the public of attractive and valuable lifetime choices. The only defensible approach is a comparative risk analysis of alternative pathways, taking into account our most credible projections of the lifetime economic, environmental, and health values of these alternatives. (Starr 2003, 1–3)

These are the well-developed views of an expert in risk analysis. Many in the risk analysis profession, including those in the nuclear industry, will agree with him.

However, there is an alternative view, expressed in 1998 in the "Wingspread Statement of the Precautionary Principle" developed in a conference at Wingspread, Wisconsin:

The release and use of toxic substances, the exploitation of resources, and physical alterations of the environment have had substantial unintended consequences affecting human health and the environment. Some of these concerns are high rates of learning deficiencies, asthma, cancer, birth defects, and species extinction. Along with global climate change, stratospheric ozone depletion and worldwide contamination with toxic substances and nuclear materials. ... While we realize that human activities may involve hazards, people must proceed more carefully than has been the case in recent history. Corporations, government entities, organizations, communities, scientists and other individuals must adopt a precautionary approach to all human endeavors. ... Therefore, it is necessary to implement the Precautionary Principle: When an activity raises threats of harm to human health or the environment, precautionary measures should be taken even if some cause and effect relationships are not fully established scientifically. (Raffensperger and Tickner 1999, 353)

Most technologically educated professionals, such as those in the nuclear industry and regulatory communities, will relate to the Starr view rather than the Wingspread position.

Safety Standards beyond the Reactor

The NRC also has a role in regulating transportation of radioactive materials, such as spent fuel from nuclear reactors. The planned opening of a geologic repository for such fuel would lead to thousands of shipments. These potential shipments have already been criticized by opponents, who have labeled them "mobile Chernobyls." In the transportation debate, the NRC possesses data on which to base PRAs, including results from tests conducted at Sandia National Laboratories on the transportation containers. To what extent precaution will dominate the route structure for transporting the fuel has not been decided. Local community concerns may not be alleviated by risk analysis. Moving the routes—an application of the precautionary principle—may be necessary.

A geological repository for high-level radioactive waste (spent fuel from reactors and certain waste from nuclear weapons production) was planned in Yucca Mountain, Nevada. In setting the standards for Yucca Mountain, the U.S. Environmental Protection Agency (EPA) used a regulatory time frame of 10,000 years. However, in July 2004, the U.S. Court of Appeals ruled that EPA's use of 10,000 years was inconsistent with the U.S. National Academy of Sciences' recommendations concerning peak dose. Peak dose is the point in time, perhaps long in the future, when an individual would be at highest risk from radiation deriving from the nuclear waste depository. EPA has responded to this ruling by preparing an amended standard that will address the first *million* years after the facility is closed (EPA 2005). As EPA admits, "Extending the Yucca Mountain standard out to one million years is an unprecedented scientific challenge" (EPA 2005, 2). Obviously, large uncertainties exist in projecting forward over such a long period of time. Here is a case where strong application of the precautionary principle to prevent any risk over a 10,000-year or one-million-year time horizon could preclude licensing Yucca Mountain. Using such a long time horizon, coupled with a strongly precautionary approach—such as Wiener and Rogers' (2002, 320–321) version 3—could preclude any and all decisions. Any choice—be it building the repository at Yucca Mountain, not building it, or shifting to other energy sources—may pose some long-term risks. Whether that approach would be sound public policy will be debated over the next decade. The current U.S. administration has canceled funding for developing the Yucca Mountain repository and has requested the NRC to stop work on the license application. The administration formed a commission to explore alternatives for handling the spent fuel from nuclear reactors and U.S. defense waste.

One area where the EPA may be using the PP is in basing its risk assessment of potential health effects on the linear no-threshold model of cancer caused by radiation. This model assumes first that there is no level of radiation that does not lead to cancer, and second that the dose-response relationship at very low levels of exposure can be determined by a linear extrapolation from observed effects at very high doses. However, the exposure standard that the EPA adopted was that the average exposure to residents living close to Yucca Mountain should be no greater than the exposure to natural radiation experienced by residents of Colorado (EPA 2005). Although the Yucca Mountain proposal has been canceled, the approach[3] taken by EPA most likely will be

---

[3] As of summer 2010, the NRC Licensing Board has rejected the attempt by the Department of Energy (DOE) to withdraw the licensing application for Yucca Mountain. Congress is not funding more work at Yucca Mountain.

used by the NRC to license whatever is constructed following recommendations made by the presidential commission that lead to long-term storage.

European Nuclear Safety Regulation

The use of nuclear power in Europe began more than 40 years ago with the construction of light water reactors imported from the United States into Belgium, Germany, Italy, the Netherlands, Spain, Sweden, and Switzerland. Only the UK and France constructed reactors of different types, such as gas cooled and pressurized water reactors. Along with the reactor designs, these European countries also imported the basic safety concept and approaches that had been adopted in the United States. These had been refined over the years to take into account operating experience and research. A typical example is the defense in depth concept.

European regulators have generally followed the International Atomic Energy Agency's International Nuclear Safety Advisory Group (INSAG) definition of defense in depth (which is broadly in line with the U.S. approach to defense in depth discussed earlier):

> All safety activities, whether organizational, behavioral or equipment related, are subject to layers of overlapping provisions, so that if a failure should occur it would be compensated for or corrected without causing harm to individuals or the public at large. This idea of multiple levels of protection is the central feature of defense in depth. (INSAG 1988)

The strategy of defense in depth is explained as follows.

> The strategy for defense in depth is twofold: first, to prevent accidents and, second, if prevention fails, to limit their potential consequences and prevent any evolution to more serious conditions. Accident prevention is the first priority. ... The general objective of defense in depth is to ensure that a single failure, whether equipment failure or human failure, at one level of defense, and even combinations of failures at more than one level of defense, would not propagate to jeopardize defense in depth at subsequent levels. The independence of different levels of defense is a key element in meeting this objective. (INSAG 1996)

Thus, there has been a generally similar initial approach to the risk management of nuclear power plants in the United States and Europe based on defense in depth. Both the United States and Europe also adopted ALARA. Subsequently, both the United States and Europe adopted PRA procedures, but the ways in which the PRA is applied do result in some risk regulation differences The levels of defense in depth as applied today can be seen in Table 5.2.

The defense in depth concept—together with large safety margins in the design of NPPs—indicates a precautionary attitude in nuclear safety. If we consider the Graham (2003) definition of the PP—"The precautionary principle deals with what we don't

Table 5.2 *Levels of Defense in Depth*

Levels of defense in depth	Objective	Essential means
Level 1	Prevention of abnormal operation and failures	Conservative design and high quality in construction and operation
Level 2	Control of abnormal operation and detection of failures	Control, limiting and protection systems, and other surveillance features
Level 3	Control of accidents within the design basis	Engineered safety features and accident procedures
Level 4	Control of severe plant conditions, including prevention of accident progression and mitigation of the consequences of severe accidents	Complementary measures and accident management
Level 5	Mitigation of radiological consequences of significant releases of radioactive materials	Off-site emergency response

know or are uncertain about scientifically"—then the PP has only been applied partly in the implementation of the nuclear safety concept.

PRAs are used to estimate the probability and consequences of very improbable events occurring in complex systems such as nuclear power plants. Starting from event trees and comprehensive databases, an event's probabilities can be derived. This ability to evaluate the safety margins embedded in design and operation through PRA has become an extremely important tool for risk estimation. In modern PRA, the nuclear power plant is analyzed as a sociotechnical system. However, regulatory responses to the actual PRA-determined failure probabilities are not uniform. The question still remains: How safe is safe enough?

Determining how safe is safe enough has been handled through safety goals or probabilistic safety criteria formulated by INSAG as well by some individual European countries. In fact PRA or PSA are now widely used in European states, as in the United States, for design and safety evaluations of nuclear power plants, event analysis, and risk management (Magne and Shepherd 2003). The regulatory use of PRA varies across countries as described below.

INSAG's 1999 report, "Basic Safety Principles for Nuclear Power plants," described a quantitative technical safety objective.

> The target for existing nuclear power plants consistent with the technical safety objective is a frequency of occurrence of severe core damage that is below about 10^{-4} events per plant operating year. Severe accident management and mitigation measures could reduce by a factor of at least ten the probability of large off-site releases requiring short term off-site response. Application of all safety principles and the objectives of para. 25 to future plants could lead to the achievement of an improved goal of not more than 10^{-5} severe core damage events per plant operating year. Another objective for these future plants is the practical elimination of accident sequences that could lead to large early radioactive releases, whereas severe accidents that could imply late containment failure would be considered in

the design process with realistic assumptions and best estimate analyses so that their consequences would necessitate only protective measures limited in area and in time.

In the framework of the Sizewell B enquiry, the UK Health and Safety Executive (HSE) published a document regarding the level of risk for workers and members of the public. These criteria specified three regions: unacceptable, tolerable, and broadly acceptable regions of risk. In addition, numerical criteria for the risk of death for workers and members of the public were given.

> We propose to maintain our existing position that a risk of 1 in 10^4 per annum to any member of the public is the maximum that should be tolerated from any large industrial plant in any industry with, of course, the ALARP [as low as reasonably practicable] principle applying to ensure that the risk from most plants is in fact lower or much lower. But in accordance with Barnes' findings we propose to adopt a risk of 1 in 10^5 per annum as the benchmark for new nuclear stations in the UK. (HSE 1992)

In 1977, the French nuclear safety authority (now DGSNR) set an overall probabilistic objective so that for a pressurized water reactor (PWR), the probability that the plant could be the source of unacceptable consequences should not exceed 10^{-6} per year. In addition, a subsidiary target (10^{-7} per year) has been set for several sequences "beyond basis design." However, these probabilistic objectives have been considered only as general guidance; they have never been considered as regulatory criteria. The term "unacceptable consequence" was quite vague. Therefore, DGSNR did not expect probabilistic objectives to be used in any safety demonstration.

In the Netherlands, the concept of environmental risk management has been developed so that criteria and objectives have been set which relate to individual and societal risk. The requirement is that the risk of death of an individual should be $< 10^{-5}$ per year from all sources of radioactivity and $< 10^{-6}$ per year from a single source. The societal risk—defined as the death of 10 people within a few weeks with no credit being taken from countermeasures—should be $< 10^{-5}$ per year, with more restrictive criteria being defined if greater numbers of people are affected. As a result of this, an intermediate level of PSA is required as part of the licensing process for nuclear installations.

Germany did not establish probabilistic safety goals. However, since the publication of a 1979 German risk study (GSRS 1979), PSA has been used to check if specific accident sequences—according to the estimated frequency of occurrence—needed improved protection.

All construction permits and operational licenses of German nuclear power plants have been brought to court by NGOs or communities. The question of how safe is safe enough has played a very important role in the legal process. Nevertheless, the degree of protection in design and operation could not be communicated to the public in probabilistic terms.

However, the Federal constitutional court (*Bundesverfassungsgericht*) ruling in the case of the SNR (fast breeder reactor) established that (*inter alia*)

Table 5.3 *Risk-Informed Applications in Different OECD Countries*

	Design evaluation PSR	Modification management	Technical specifications at power maintenance	Risk-informed in-service testing	Risk-informed in-service inspections	PSA-based event analysis precursors	Configuration risk management risk monitors	Training
Belgium	X		O			X		X
Canada	X		O			O	O	O
Czech Republic	X	X	X	O	O	X	X	O
Finland	X		X	O	O	X	X	
France	X	X	X/O	O	O	X	O	
Germany	X	X				X		
Hungary	X		X			X	X	X
Japan	X		X					
South Korea	X	X	X	X	X			
Mexico	X	X	X	O	O			X
Netherlands	X	O	O	O	O		O	
Spain	X		X	X	X	X		
Sweden	X	X	X	X			X	
Switzerland	X	X	X			X	X	
United Kingdom	X		X				X	

Notes: X means that the country has currently implemented the considered application; O means that the country is experimenting with the considered application
Source: Magne and Shepherd (2003)

- absolute safety (zero risk) is unattainable; and,
- demanding that legislators produce regulations that aim at such absolute safety is illogical (*Bundesverfassungsgericht Karlsruhe* 1978).

Furthermore, this decision settled two important elements:

- The Atomic Law (1976) entitles the government to license installations with performances and safety characteristics that are very controversial, such as fast breeder reactors; and
- there is a limit beyond which further protection against harms is not warranted, and the residual risk uncertainty has to be accepted by all citizens.

In 2003, Magne and Shepherd summarized the most developed risk-informed applications in some Organisation for Economic Co-operation and Development (OECD) countries (see Table 5.3). Also evident in Table 5.3 is the importance of PSA in nuclear power plant safety evaluation.

The INSAG approach is to limit the probability of severe core damage events. The UK approach is to reduce the probability of death to below 1 in 10^5. France follows the INSAG approach but with a lower probability. They are all precautionary in nature, though some more than others. The United States, on the other hand takes a risk comparison approach, making the rule that "the risk of an immediate fatality to an average individual in the vicinity of a nuclear power plant that might result from reactor accidents should not exceed 0.1% of the sum of immediate fatality risks that result from other accidents to which the U.S. population is generally exposed" (see the discussion of U.S. nuclear safety in the section above) (NRC 1986). While a detailed analysis might suggest that one regulatory system is more precautionary in nature than another, the philosophy followed is very similar, with regulatory objectives broadly in the same ballpark. Nevertheless, countries differ in their dependencies on nuclear power, and we will take up the question of the differences in current rationales between the EU and the United States in the concluding section of this chapter.

EU Safety Standards beyond the Reactor

In contrast to the risk regulation of nuclear power plants, regulation concerning radiation exposure to workers and the general public is laid down by the European Union. This responsibility derives from Article 30 of the Euratom Treaty, which states, "Basic standards shall be laid down within the Community for the protection of the health of workers and the general public against the dangers arising from ionizing radiation" (European Union 1987). Council Directive 96/29/Euratom sets out these basic standards (European Commission 1996). This directive uses the International Commission on Radiological Protection (ICRP) standards given in its Report 60 (ICRP 1991). The ICRP recommended exposure-dose levels are set at a point where the costs of further reduction are not justified by the benefit achieved and at an exposure limit above which the consequences would be "widely regarded as unacceptable" (ICRP 1991). However, they go further by calling for the application of the ALARA principle. These limits and this principle are transposed into the directive in its preamble.

> Whereas, the development of scientific knowledge concerning radiation protection, as expressed in particular in Recommendation No. 60 of the International Commission on Radiological Protection, makes it convenient to revise the basic standards and to lay them down in a new legal instrument. (ICRP 1991)

Its articles concur, and Article 6 in particular stresses that "in the context of optimization, all exposures shall be kept as low as reasonably achievable, economic and social factors being taken into account" (ICRP 1991).

Neither the ICRP nor the Council directive uses the word *precaution*. However, as argued previously, extrapolating from known high-dose effects to determine low-dose effects is certainly precautionary in nature. The EPA uses a linear extrapolation, while the ICRP uses a quadratic linear extrapolation for some forms of radiation (which may be marginally less precautionary). Certainly the EU requirement to use ALARA is precautionary in nature.

Conclusions

Neither the United States nor Europe uses the term "the precautionary principle" in nuclear energy regulation. However, in both the United States and Europe, nuclear power plant regulations and safety reviews rely more and more on the application of probabilistic risk analysis (PRA, or probabilistic safety analysis, PSA), along with the principle of defense in depth. While not explicitly adopting the PP, in practice these approaches can be seen as consistent with it, particularly when combined with "as low as reasonably achievable" (ALARA).

The degree of direct regulatory precaution is broadly similar. However, differences appear when one considers the varying degrees of dependence on nuclear power. Europe is much more dependent on nuclear energy than the United States. Europe continued building a greater number of nuclear power stations over a longer time period than did the United States, and some European countries are now planning to build new reactors. Meanwhile, the United States stopped ordering new nuclear power stations after 1980. Although no new nuclear power plant was ordered (and finished) in the United States after 1978, more than 20 notices have been filed with the NRC of intent to request a combined construction and operating license.

Some say the halt to new civilian U.S. nuclear reactor orders after 1979 was due to regulatory restrictions adopted or enforced after the Three Mile Island incident. A better view is that in the 1980s and 1990s, nuclear energy was just too costly relative to less expensive fossil fuels for new electricity generation capacity. These costs may in turn have been raised by regulatory hurdles and by obstacles to siting facilities that were imposed out of an excess of caution. Still, the high costs of nuclear reactor construction and operation stem at least as much from poor management in the nuclear industry itself (MIT 2003). Whether well-managed construction can hold costs down to competitive levels will be a challenge as new plants enter construction in the United States.

For radiation protection regulation, large precautionary differences appear. American authorities do not follow the ICRP recommendations (Sunstein 2002). Furthermore, wide differences exist among United States agencies, with EPA being the most precautionary. In fact, the EPA regulatory response to Yucca Mountain, detailed above, is extremely precautionary and takes no apparent cognizance of the cost–benefit balance for the repository. By contrast, the EU explicitly requires such a cost–benefit analysis, both when considering precautionary action and explicitly in the nuclear safety regulations.

Acknowledgments

The authors are grateful for advice from Robert Budnitz and George Apostolakis, and for research assistance from Mark Marvelli.

References

Apostolakis, George E. 2003. The Precautionary Principle and Defense in Depth. Paper presented at the Second ILK Symposium. October 28, Munich.
———. 2004. Personal communication with the authors.
Atomic Law. 1976. German Nuclear Energy Act [Atomgesetz] of 23 December 1959, as revised in 1976. *Bundesgesetzblatt* [Federal Legislation Gazette] 1976 (I): 3053.
Bisconti Research. 2010. Public Support for Nuclear Energy at Record High. www.nei.org/resourcesandstats/documentlibrary/protectingtheenvironment/reports/march-2010-public-opinion-memo (accessed June 2, 2010).
Bodansky, David. 1996. *Nuclear Energy: Principles, Practices, and Prospects.* New York: American Institute of Physics Press.
Budnitz, Robert. 2004. Personal communication with the authors from Dr. Robert Budnitz, former NRC director of regulatory research.
Bundesverfassungsgericht Karlsruhe. 1978. German Federal Constitutional Court, Judgment of August 8, 1978 (Kalkar Case). *Entscheidungen des Bundesverfassungsgerichts* 49: 89.
Croteau, Richard. 2004. Personal communication with the authors from NRC staff member Richard Croteau.
CSIS (Center for Strategic and International Studies). 1999. The Regulatory Process for Nuclear Power Reactors: A Review. Report of the CSIS Nuclear Regulatory Process Review Steering Committee. Washington, DC: CSIS Press.
EIA (Energy Information Administration). 2006. Net Generation by Energy Source by Type of Producer. www.eia.doe.gov/cneaf/electricity/epa/epat1p1.html (accessed June 2, 2006).
Energy Daily. 2004. NRC Creates Emergency Planning Office. King Publishing Group., January 23.
EPA (U.S. Environmental Protection Agency). 2005. EPA's Proposed Public Health and Environmental Standards for Yucca Mountain. EPA 402-F-05-026. October. www.epa.gov/radiation/yucca (accessed June 30, 2010).
Eurobarometer. 2002. Energy: Issues, Options, and Technologies—Science and Society EUR 20624. December. Luxembourg: Office for Official Publications of the European Communities. http://ec.europa.eu/public_opinion/archives/ebs/ebs_169.pdf (site now discontinued).

European Commission. 1996. Council Directive 96/29/Euratom of May 13, 1996, Laying Down Basic Safety Standards for the Protection of the Health of Workers and the General Public against the Dangers Arising from Ionizing Radiation. *Official Journal L* 159, 29/06/1996: 1–114.

———. 2000. *Communication from the Commission on the Precautionary Principle.* COM(2000) 1, Brussels. February 2. http://europa.eu.int/comm/dgs/health_consumer/library/pub/pub07_en.pdf (site now discontinued).

———. 2004. DG Research. Nuclear Energy. *RTD Info: Magazine on European Research* 40. February. http://ec.europa.eu/research/rtdinfo/40/01/article_493_en.html (accessed June 30, 2010).

———. 2005. European Union: Energy and Transport in Figures 2005, Part 2, Energy. Table 2.4.3. http://ec.europa.eu/dgs/energy_transport/figures/pocketbook/doc/2005/etif_2005_energy_en.pdf (accessed June 2, 2006; site now discontinued).

European Union. 1987. Article 30 of the *Treaty Establishing the European Atomic Energy Community.* In *Treaties Establishing the European Communities.* Vol. I: 644. Luxembourg: Office for Official Publications of the European Communities.

Foster, K. R., P. Vecchia, and M. H. Rapacholi. 2000. Science and the Precautionary Principle. *Science* 288: 979–981.

Funk, J. and J. Mangels. 2004. Another Test Run at Davis-Besse. *Plain Dealer* (Cleveland), Jan. 22.

Gallup. 2009. Support for Nuclear Energy Inches Up to New High. www.gallup.com, search Nuclear (accessed June 2, 2010).

Graham, John D. 1999. Making Sense of the Precautionary Principle. *Risk in Perspective* 7: 1–6.

Graham, Peter. 2003. Harmonisation of Risk-Based Regulatory Regimes. Paper presented at the Second International ILK Symposium, Harmonisation of Nuclear Safety Approaches: A Chance for Achieving More Transparency and Effectiveness? Munich, Germany. www.ilk-online.org/public/en/symposium.htm (accessed June 30, 2010).

GSRS (German Society for Reactor Safety). 1979. *Deutsche Risikostudie Kernkraftwerke* [German Risk Study for Nuclear Power Plants]. Deutsche Gesellschaft für Reaktorsicherheit (GSRS). Cologne: Verlag TÜV Rheinland.

Guinnessy, Paul. 2006. Stronger Future for Nuclear Power. *Physics Today* 59 (February): 19.

HSE (UK Health and Safety Executive). 1992. *The Tolerability of Risks from Nuclear Power Stations.* 2nd ed. London: HMSO.

IAEA (International Atomic Energy Agency). 2009. *Nuclear Power Reactors in the World.* Reference Data Series No. 2. Vienna: IAEA.

ICRP (International Commission on Radiological Protection). 1991. *1990 Recommendations of the International Commission on Radiological Protection.* ICRP Publication 60. Ottawa, Canada: Pergamon Press.

IEA (International Energy Agency). 2003. IEA Statistics for Electricity Generation in France in 2003. www.iea.org/Textbase/stats/electricityoecd.asp?oecd=France&COUNTRY_LONG_NAME=France (accessed June 2, 2006; site now discontinued).

INSAG (International Nuclear Safety Advisory Group of the International Atomic Energy Association). 1988. INSAG-3: Basic Safety Principles for Nuclear Power Plants. Vienna: INSAG.

———. 1996. INSAG-10: Defence in Depth in Nuclear Safety. Vienna: INSAG.

———. 1999. INSAG-12: 75-INSAG-3 Rev.1: A Report by the International Nuclear Safety Advisory Group. Vienna: INSAG.

Joskow, Paul L. 2006. The Future of Nuclear Power in the United States: Economic and Regulatory Challenges. Working Paper 06-25. http://web.mit.edu/ceepr/www/2006-019.pdf (site now discontinued).

Kourilsky, P. and G. Viney. 1999. *Le Principe de Précaution: Rapport au Premier Ministre* [The Precautionary Principle: Report to the Prime Minister of France]. Paris: Odile Jacob. *Documentation française* October 15.

Kuhn, Thomas. 1962. *The Structure of Scientific Revolutions.* Chicago: University of Chicago Press.

Levin, Alan. 2004. Personal communication by email with the authors. January 7.

Magne, L. and C. Shepherd. 2003. Status of Probabilistic Safety Assessment: Methodology and Applications in Europe. Paper presented at the Second International ILK Symposium,

Harmonisation of Nuclear Safety Approaches: A Chance for Achieving More Transparency and Effectiveness? Munich, Germany. www.ilk-online.org/public/en/symposium.htm (accessed June 30, 2010).

MIT (Massachusetts Institute of Technology). 2003. The Future of Nuclear Power. http://web.mit.edu/nuclearpower/ (accessed June 30, 2010).

NEA (Nuclear Energy Agency). 2006. Nuclear Energy Agency, OECD, Facts and Figures. www.nea.fr/html/general/facts.html (site now discontinued).

NRC (U.S. Nuclear Regulatory Commission). 1975. Reactor Safety Study: An Assessment of Accident Risks in U.S. Commercial Nuclear Power Plants. Report WASH-1400 (NUREG 75/014) Washington, DC: NRC.

———. 1986. Safety Goals for the Operation of Nuclear Power Plants. Policy Statement 10 CFR Part 50. August 4, 1986.

———. 1992. *Nuclear Power: Technical and Institutional Options for the Future.* Washington, DC: National Academy Press.

———. 1995. An Approach for Using Probabilistic Risk Assessment in Nuclear Regulatory Activities; Final Policy Statement. In *On the Role of Defense in Depth in Risk-Informed Regulation*, edited by J. M. Sorensen, G. E. Apostolakis, T. S. Kress, and D. A. Powers, 1999. *Federal Register* 60 FR 42622.

———. 1999. U.S. Nuclear Regulatory Commission White Paper. March 16.

Planck, Max. 1936. *The Philosophy of Physics.* New York: W.W. Norton.

Poortinga W., N. F. Pidgeon, and I. Lorenzoni. 2006. Public Perceptions of Nuclear Power, Climate Change, and Energy Options in Britain: Summary Findings of a Survey Conducted during October and November 2005. Technical Report. Understanding Risk Working Paper 06-02. Norwich: Centre for Environmental Risk.

Raffensperger, Carolyn. 1999. The Precautionary Principle. Paper presented at NGO Biotechnology Briefing for White House Officials. June 30.

Raffensperger, Carolyn, and Joel Tickner, eds. 1999. *Protecting Public Health and the Environment: Implementing the Precautionary Principle.* Washington, DC: Island Press.

Renn, O. and A. Klinke. 2001. On Science and Precaution in the Management of Risk: Case Studies, Vol. 2, edited by A. Stirling. EUR 19056. Luxembourg: Office for Official Publications of the European Communities. ftp://ftp.jrc.es/pub/EURdoc/eur19056IIen.pdf (accessed June 30, 2010).

Ropeik, D. and G. Gray. 2002. *Risk: A Practical Guide for Deciding What's Really Safe and What's Really Dangerous in the World Around You.* New York: Houghton Mifflin.

Slovic, P., J. Flynn, C. K. Mertz, C. Mays, and M. Poumadere. 1996. Nuclear Power and the Public: A Comparative Study of the Risk Perception in France and the United States. Report number 96-6. Eugene, OR: Decision Research. In *Cross-cultural Risk Perception: A Survey of Empirical Studies*, edited by O. Renn and B. Rohrmann. Dordrecht, the Netherlands: Kluwer Academic, 55–102.

Sorensen, J. M., G. E. Apostolakis, T. S. Kress, and D. A. Powers. 1999. On the Role of Defense in Depth in Risk-Informed Regulation. Presentation at August PSA. Washington, DC.

Starr, C. 1969. Social Benefit versus Technological Risk. *Science* 165: 1232–1238.

———. 2003. The Precautionary Principle versus Risk Analysis. *Risk Analysis* 23: 1–3.

Sunstein, Cass R. 2002. *Risk and Reason.* Cambridge: Cambridge University Press.

———. 2007. On the Divergent American Reactions to Terrorism and Climate Change. *Columbia Law Review* 107 (2): 503–557.

Thadani, Ashok. 2004. Personal communication by email with the authors. January 6.

Walker, J. Samuel. 2004. *A Nuclear Crisis in Historical Perspective: Three Mile Island.* Berkeley, CA: University of California Press.

Wiener, J. B. and M. D. Rogers. 2002. Comparing Precaution in the United States and Europe. *Journal of Risk Research* 5 (4): 317–349.

CHAPTER 6

Automobile Emissions

Michael P. Walsh

*T*his chapter compares the evolution of the motor vehicle pollution control efforts in the United States and Europe. It highlights the different patterns and points of focus and describes significant transatlantic differences. It shows that with regard to the public health risks of motor vehicle pollution (especially from diesel), the United States has been more precautionary than Europe, including since 1990. But simultaneously, with regard to the risks of global warming from motor vehicle emissions, Europe has been more precautionary than the United States (although the United States is closing this gap in recent years). This divergence is most stark in the use of diesel engines and fuels: while diesel vehicles represent only about 1% of new car sales in the United States, they have grown from 28% to over 52% of sales in Europe in the last 10 years (EIA 2009). The case of automobile emissions thus illustrates simultaneous precaution by the United States and Europe against risks pointing in conflicting directions.

Background

During the 1950s, motor-vehicle-related air pollution began to emerge as a serious issue in both the United States and Europe. Much of that decade and the next were directed toward fact-finding and initial studies. Emphasis was placed on defining the problem, establishing the motor vehicle role, developing test procedures and emissions measurement techniques, as well as assessing public health and environmental damages. In addition, some initial but modest control efforts were initiated. But by the end of the 1960s and into the early 1970s, it became clear that the approaches of the United States and Europe would fundamentally diverge.

Many factors contributed to this difference. The different internal political structures of the United States and Europe played one role. In the United States, federal authority over motor vehicle regulation enabled Congress to enact the Clean Air Act (CAA) of 1970 and subsequent amendments, which delegated power to the U.S. Environmental Protection Agency (EPA) to set national standards. Moreover, California received a special opportunity in the CAA, one not granted to any other state, to set its own more aggressive standards on motor vehicle emissions; other states could opt to follow them, provided EPA granted California's request, which it typically did. By contrast, Europe functioned, at least with respect to motor vehicle standards, as a multination coalition of independent states that varied substantially in economic development, industrial structure, and public opinion. When the European Community was established to foster free trade, initial efforts to set motor vehicle emissions standards by Member States such as Germany and France were seen by some other Member States as potential impediments to free trade—and emissions standards were therefore resisted.

Another important factor was a difference in public concerns. The emergence of the environmental movement in the United States, culminating in the first Earth Day in 1970, became closely linked to public health concerns. The year 1970 was also the one in which Senator Edmund Muskie—who at the time was expected to become the Democratic candidate for president in 1972—spearheaded adoption of the landmark 1970 Clean Air Act Amendments. Simultaneously, in an effort to politically neutralize the environmental issue, President Nixon created the Environmental Protection Agency. In Europe, air pollution control was also gaining advocates, but with a stronger emphasis on ecological impacts such as forest degradation (and later, climate change); less emphasis was placed on local public health and epidemiologic evidence. (Other differences included the amount of driving, or vehicle miles traveled, in the United States versus in Europe, and the use of alternative transportation modes; this chapter, however, will focus on policies to reduce pollution from vehicles and fuels.)

Development of the U.S. Program

In 1960, California adopted legislation that called for the installation of pollution control devices as soon as three workable control devices were developed (Krier and Ursin 1977). In 1964, the state was able to certify that three independent manufacturers had successfully developed such devices, which triggered the legal requirement that new automobiles must comply with California's standards beginning with the 1966 model year. Soon afterward, the major U.S. domestic manufacturers announced that they too could and would clean up their cars with technology they had developed, thus eliminating the need for the independently developed devices.

Subsequent to California's pioneering efforts, and as a result of recognition of the national nature of the automobile pollution problem, in 1964 Congress initiated federal motor vehicle pollution control legislation. As a result of the 1965 Clean Air Act Amendments, the 1966 California auto emissions standards were applied nationally in 1968.

In December 1970, the Clean Air Act was amended by Congress "to protect and enhance the quality of the nation's air resources." Congress took particular notice of the significant role of the automobile in the nation's effort to reduce ambient pollution levels by requiring a 90% reduction in emissions from the level previously prescribed in emissions standards first for 1970 models for carbon monoxide (CO) and hydrocarbons (HC), and then for 1971 models for nitrogen oxides (NO_x). Congress clearly intended to aid the cause of clean air by mandating levels of automotive emissions that it hoped would essentially remove the automobile from the pollution picture.

In many ways, the serious effort to control motor vehicle pollution can be considered to have begun with the passage of the landmark 1970 law. By including the stringent "technology forcing" requirements in the law and providing only very limited flexibility to EPA in implementing these requirements, it forced the manufacturers to work aggressively toward compliance, because only Congress itself could provide relief. In addition, the law provided EPA with broad authority to implement the requirements, including provisions to mandate a recall of vehicles whenever "a substantial number of properly maintained and used" vehicles failed to meet standards in use over their useful lives, and to modify fuel quality—including the level of lead (Pb) in gasoline—if necessary to enable compliance. This latter authority was especially critical, because the principal technology that emerged to enable compliance with the emissions standards was the catalytic converter—a technology that could not withstand lead additives. (Lead had been added to gasoline since the 1920s to smooth combustion.) Finally, the 1970 law grandfathered in the California motor vehicle pollution control program and left that state with the unique authority (subject to EPA approval) to set its own standards and regulations for vehicle emissions. This proved critical over the years that followed, as California—suffering from the most serious vehicle-related air pollution problem in the country—consistently pushed the technology envelope over the next three decades, something it continues to do to this day. In 1977, the CAA was "fine-tuned" by Congress, which delayed and slightly relaxed the auto standards under pressure from the vehicle industry. In doing so, though, Congress authorized the states to adopt either the federal EPA motor vehicle emissions standards or the California standards (thereby yielding two car designs that the manufacturers would have to produce), but Congress prohibited the states from setting any other standards that would require the creation of a so-called "third car." The 1977 amendments also expanded the law by imposing similarly stringent emissions requirements on heavy-duty trucks. More recently, Congress passed the 1990 Clean Air Act Amendments, further expanding EPA's authority to regulate off-road vehicles and fuels. Also, EPA has issued a series of increasingly stringent regulations under both Democratic and Republican administrations.

As a result of these requirements, substantial and rapid improvements in vehicle emissions have occurred over the past 40 years, as illustrated in Figure 6.1.

Shortly after the 1970 law went into effect, a gradual phaseout of the use of lead in gasoline was initiated, which allowed auto manufacturers to introduce lead-intolerant catalysts on most 1975 model-year cars. Further tightening of the NO_x standards, first in California and then across the country in the early 1980s, accelerated the

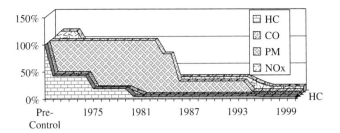

Figure 6.1 *New Car Emissions Standards in the United States*

introduction of advanced electronic controls, which also enabled improvements in fuel economy during this same period. By the mid-1980s, stringent particulate matter (PM) standards were also introduced for diesel cars. Following the 1990 Clean Air Act Amendments, as illustrated in Figure 6.1, a further reduction in all of the pollutants was phased in throughout the 1990s.

While Congress was in the late stages of the debate regarding what became the 1990 Clean Air Act Amendments, two significant events occurred:

In September 1990, California adopted the Low Emissions Vehicle (LEV) Program, which was distinctive in several important respects:

- It provided flexibility to manufacturers by allowing them to certify vehicles meeting several distinct categories or sets of emissions standards (called "bins") as long as their fleet sales on average complied with an overall standard for nonmethane organic gases (NMOGs), which declined year by year throughout the 1990s.
- It created a new category of vehicles, zero-emitting vehicles (ZEVs), in an effort to force the vehicle industry to devote significant resources to developing and introducing into the marketplace vehicles that effectively did not rely on the internal combustion engine. This arguably resulted in the introduction first of electric cars, then of hybrid electric cars, and may eventually lead to commercially available fuel-cell-powered vehicles.
- It also specifically linked vehicles and fuels, and it forced the introduction of "reformulated" gasoline with reduced sulfur levels, lower volatility, and other changes in composition.

Just as California was adopting the LEV program, New York became the first state that used Section 177 of the 1977 Clean Air Act Amendments to adopt California's vehicle emissions standards. Subsequently, a number of other states have also adopted the California requirements.

As a backdrop to all these developments, the air pollution problem in the United States, although improved, remained widespread and serious. A growing body of public health studies—especially epidemiologic evidence of thousands of fatalities per year in areas with higher air pollution levels—impelled EPA to tighten health-based air quality requirements for both ozone (or photochemical smog) and PM.

Thus the broader authority provided to EPA under the 1990 Clean Air Act Amendments, the surge in California to push the air pollution technology envelope even further, and the healthy cooperation and occasional competition between EPA and California to mandate clean vehicles and fuels have all combined to bring several additional important elements into the U.S. program. These include the following:

- Unexpectedly, a new class of vehicles called sport utility vehicles (SUVs) emerged, soon representing almost half the U.S. light-duty vehicle market. SUVs were legally classified as light trucks, which were traditionally covered by more lenient emissions standards. Today's latest emissions standards will now require light trucks to meet the same requirements as cars.
- Light-duty diesel vehicles had been allowed to meet a more lenient NO_x standard than their gasoline counterparts; both California and EPA now require diesel and gasoline vehicles to meet the same standards.
- The close linkage between vehicle emissions requirements and fuel quality is now recognized and established, with the result that very low levels of sulfur in both gasoline and diesel fuel are being mandated not only in California, but across the entire country.
- Heavy-duty trucks, which traditionally had more lenient emissions requirements, have been forced to introduce very advanced after-treatment technologies by 2010.
- Nonroad vehicles, especially diesel-fueled farm and construction equipment, as well as ships and locomotives, will be required to meet stringent emissions standards similar to the limits covering on-road heavy-duty vehicles, with a lag of only a few years. Tier I standards adopted in 1991 have now been tightened by Tier II standards adopted in 2004.

Development of the European Program

Automobile emissions regulations in Europe have been developed in least three arenas: the individual Member States, the European Community (now the EU), and the United Nations Economic Commission for Europe (UNECE).

As noted earlier, during the 1950s and 1960s, efforts were under way in Europe as well as in the United States to deal with motor vehicle air pollution. France and Germany were especially active during this period, working independently toward emissions test procedures and emissions standards. The French organization Union Technique de l'Automobile du Motocycle et du Cycle (UTAC) was, for example, working on a driving cycle based on city driving in Paris. Similarly, the German Auto Manufacturers Association, Verband der Automobilindustrie (VDA), requested that Professor Luther at the University of Clausthal be given a research assignment to develop a driving cycle for emissions testing.

One of the primary purposes of the European Economic Community (EEC), since the Treaty of Rome in 1957, was the elimination of trade barriers among the Member

States. For many years, Directorate General III of the European Commission was responsible for harmonization within the internal market. It could develop directives on motor vehicle standards and, with the unanimous agreement of the other Directorates General, could send them forward to the Council of Ministers and the Parliament for approval. Once a directive was adopted and transposed into the national laws of each Member State, a Member State was obliged to accept an approved vehicle from another Member State and must issue a harmonized certificate for that vehicle.

The UNECE deals with economic issues as well as transportation and traffic questions, pursuant to the 1958 Geneva Agreement concerning the adoption of uniform conditions of approval and reciprocal recognition of approval for motor vehicle equipment and parts (335 United Nations Treaty Series 211, as amended). Transportation matters are handled by the Inland Transportation Committee, with Subcommittee One dealing with road traffic. Under this subcommittee, Working Party 29 (WP 29) is responsible for motor vehicle regulations, with the Groupe des Rapporteurs pour la Pollution et l'Energie (GRPE) responsible for the development and evolution of all emissions control legislation and related subjects.

As France and Germany developed their motor vehicle standards, officials at the European level recognized the potential for individual countries proceeding unilaterally to create a patchwork of regulations that would act as a barrier to trade. In late 1965, WP 29 of the UNECE began an effort to define a European driving cycle. To lead that and other efforts in this emerging field, WP 29 created an expert working group on automobile pollution, GRPA (subsequently renamed GRPE). After investigations and negotiations, especially among the French, Germans, and British, in January 1967 the European Driving Cycle was accepted by the GRPA, and it was sent forward to WP 29 in March of that year.

While discussions continued in Geneva (UNECE) and Brussels (EEC), pressure was building in the Member States to take action. A German draft regulation announced on January 1, 1968, called for idle CO controls and crankcase controls in 1969 and emissions controls under driving conditions in 1970. Other countries became increasingly concerned regarding the potential for these regulations to effectively become barriers to trade within Europe. Other factors confounded this concern. Some European manufacturers were active in the U.S. market, but those that were not expected that having to adopt U.S. procedures or standards could place them at a competitive disadvantage. And European manufacturers and markets were quite diverse, with some focused almost exclusively on small cars and others only on large cars; the form of the standard could have differential effects by size of car.

A race against time ensued because of the German plans. If a UNECE regulation on vehicle emissions were adopted and an EEC directive based on it were subsequently issued before the German requirements went into effect, the German regulators agreed that their requirements would be made moot. If not, the German regulation would become national law, and each country would be free to develop its own requirements. In fact, with less than two months to spare, UNECE Regulation 15, or ECE R 15, was published (ECE 1970). It went into effect on August 1, 1970, following the adoption of the EEC Directive on March 20, 1970, Directive 70/220/EEC. Thus, the German regulation, which would have become effective on October 1, 1970, was superseded.

Following the initial development of the ECE R 15 requirements, a series of gradual steps to lower emissions was introduced. The second step, calling for a 20% reduction in CO and a 15% reduction in HC, entered into force on October 1, 1975 (ECE R 15, series 1). Next, restrictions were imposed for the first time on nitrogen oxides on October 1, 1977 (ECE R 15, series 2). A further modest step went into effect on October 1, 1979, when ECE R 15, series 3, called for a 12% to 19% reduction.

This trail of events set the process in place that effectively constrained the pace and stringency of European motor vehicle emissions regulation for the next 20 years. Two critically important features characterized the development of European regulations during this period. First, for the "Common Market" countries of the EEC, the development of emissions directives focused much more on ensuring that barriers to free trade did not occur than it did on protecting the environment and public health. Second, because unanimous agreement was required by all Member States of the EEC, the pace of regulation was in effect set by the least aggressive Member State rather than by the limits of technological feasibility or environmental need.

The Important Role Played by Lead in Gasoline

To illustrate these transatlantic institutional differences, consider the issue of lead (Pb) in gasoline. In the United States in early 1971, it was already apparent that catalytic converters requiring lead-free gasoline were likely to be the dominant technology of choice to comply with the 1975 emissions standards. EPA initiated steps to phase out the use of leaded gasoline and to ensure that lead-free fuel would be widely available before 1975 model-year cars entered the marketplace. Several European (including German) vehicle manufacturers that were active in the U.S. market were also working on catalyst technology. In 1971, Germany adopted its "Lead in Petrol Law," which reduced the lead content to 0.4 grams/liter (g/l) from January 1, 1972, and to 0.15 g/l from January 1, 1976. Because of concerns that Germany would mandate lead-free fuel and create a barrier to trade, the EEC then issued a Directive that prohibited any member of the European Common Market from mandating fuel with less than 0.15 grams of lead per liter. In other words, the result in Europe was no lead-free fuel, and hence no catalytic converters were allowed. This prohibition on lead-free fuel clearly delayed progress in Europe for at least another decade. By contrast, the United States phased out lead in gasoline during the 1970s and 1980s—a more precautionary approach against the risks posed by lead exposure such as cognitive impairment in children (see Walsh 1999).

Breaking the European Logjam

Public concern about motor vehicle air pollution in Europe continued to build throughout the 1980s, and individual Member States began to consider ways to get around the restrictions and weak standards of the EEC and ECE. Several European manufacturers were producing much cleaner vehicles for the U.S. market than for their home market, and the European public began demanding these cleaner technologies. The issues came to a head with the growing evidence showing serious damage to the Black Forest in Germany and Austria and other signs of ecological deterioration. As knowledge of these technological improvements in cars spread, and as the adverse effects of motor vehicle pollution became more widely recognized, more and more people across Europe began demanding the use of these systems in their countries. During the mid-1980s, Austria, the Netherlands, and the Federal Republic of Germany adopted innovative economic incentive approaches to encourage purchase of low-pollution vehicles. Sweden and Switzerland—not members of the Common Market at that time and therefore not legally constrained by its Directives—decided to adopt mandatory requirements based on the use of lead-free fuel and catalytic converters.

A key breakthrough occurred on May 16, 1984, when the European Commission proposed that Member States be allowed to mandate the availability of unleaded gasoline by January 1986; it also mandated that unleaded gasoline *must* be available in every Member State by 1989. Thus widespread availability of unleaded fuel; mandatory requirements for U.S.-type emissions standards in some countries outside the Common Market such as Austria, Sweden, and Switzerland; and economic incentives encouraging U.S.-type control technology in Germany and the Netherlands resulted in large numbers of catalyst-equipped cars emerging across Europe as the decade came to a close.

In 1990, the European Council of Environmental Ministers, in what became known as the Consolidated Directive, reached unanimous agreement to require all new models of light-duty vehicles by 1992/1993 to meet emissions standards roughly equivalent to U.S. 1987 levels. Specifically, the ministers decided to do the following:

- require all light-duty vehicles to meet emissions standards of 2.72 grams per kilometer (g/km) CO, 0.97 g/km of HC plus NO_x, 0.14 g/km of particulates for type approval, and 3.16 g/km CO, 1.13 g/km for HC plus NO_x, and 0.18 g/km particulates for conformity of production;
- require the Commission to develop a proposal before December 31, 1992, that, taking account of technical progress, required a further reduction in limit values;
- have the Council decide before December 31, 1993, on the standards proposed by the Commission; and
- allow Member States, prior to 1996, to encourage introduction of vehicles meeting the proposed requirements through "tax systems" that include pollutants and other substances in the basis for calculating motor vehicle circulation taxes (European Commission 1990).

Where We Stand Today

The dominant regulatory programs for motor vehicle emissions around the world today are those of the United States (including California) and the EU. Emissions regulations

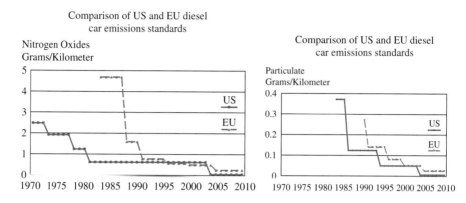

Figure 6.2 *NOₓ and PM Standards for Automobiles in the United States and EU*

in every other country of the world, except Japan, are derivatives of one of these two programs, especially the EU program. The United States and EU are each currently in the process of phasing in tighter standards applicable to both light- and heavy-duty vehicles. In recent years, as noted above, EPA, led by the California Air Resources Board, has moved toward progressively more stringent emissions standards for all categories of vehicles, while plugging loopholes such as the weaker requirements for SUVs.

While the EU has tightened its overall standards substantially, its standards for diesel cars currently remain much weaker than those for gasoline cars. The U.S. standards for diesel vehicles are much tighter than those in Europe and have been sharply tightened under U.S. administrations of both political parties. This contrast between the U.S. and EU standards for diesel cars is illustrated in Figure 6.2. (More precise comparisons between the U.S. and EU vehicle emissions standards are impossible due to differences in test procedures, in-use durability requirements, and other factors.)

As Figure 6.2 illustrates, the EU requirements for diesel vehicles—while substantially more stringent than in the past—continue to lag those of the United States. The United States has adopted even more stringent diesel emissions standards since 2004, including on heavy-duty vehicles and off-road vehicles, and not only cars. Because diesels represent over 50% of new light-duty vehicle sales in the EU but only about 1% in the United States (EIA 2009), this difference in emissions standards results in significantly higher overall PM and NO_x emissions in the EU than in the United States.

EU Leadership on Greenhouse Gas Emissions Reductions

The EU's much larger market share of diesel vehicles and its associated more lax emissions standards result from several factors. These include not only less stringent NO_x and PM standards, but also higher European fuel taxes and differential vehicle taxes in Europe favoring purchase of diesels (EIA 2009). Europe's adoption of policies favoring diesel vehicles is due in part to efforts to reduce petroleum consumption through fuel taxes and tax benefits for more fuel-efficient diesel vehicles. In part it may also reflect the influence of lobbying by corporations and labor unions manufacturing diesel engines in France, Germany, and other Member States. Unlike in the United States (especially California), environmental advocacy groups in Europe seem not to have made the public health and epidemiologic case for tighter PM and NO_x standards on diesels.

Since about 1990, another reason has played a role: the EU has taken a leadership role in addressing emissions of greenhouse gases, notably from the transportation sector. CO_2 from passenger cars accounts for about half of CO_2 emissions from transport, and about 12% of total CO_2 emissions in the EU (see European Commission 1995). The share of total CO_2 emissions coming from passenger cars is even higher in countries like France that rely on non-fossil-fuel sources of energy such as nuclear power to generate electricity. Under a "business as usual" scenario, CO_2 emissions from cars in Europe were expected to increase by about 36% by the year 2010 from 1990 levels. In one year, an average medium-size car in the EU emits some 3 tons of CO_2 (assuming 12,600 km/year and average on-road fuel consumption of 9.6 liters/100 km). The road transport sector has stood out in recent years as one of the few sectors in the EU to experience CO_2 emissions growth. And diesel vehicles emit less CO_2 per kilometer driven than do gasoline vehicles.

In the face of these concerns, the European Automobile Manufacturers Association (ACEA) entered into a voluntary agreement with the European Commission to reduce the CO_2 emissions from new light-duty passenger vehicles, with firm fleetwide targets of 140 g CO_2/km ($\sim$41 mpg for gasoline) by 2008, measured under the new European test cycle (Directive 93/116/EU). This represents about a 25% reduction from the 1995 average of 187 g/km ($\sim$30 mpg) on this cycle. Increased penetration of diesel cars with their lower tailpipe CO_2 emissions per kilometer driven can obviously play a key role in achieving these commitments.

Note that the 140 g CO_2/km goal is a collective target, not a target for each individual company. The participants in the agreement—BMW, Fiat, Ford of Europe, GM Europe, DaimlerChrysler, Porsche, PSA Peugeot Citroen, Renault, Rolls-Royce, Volkswagen, and Volvo—did not publicly define individual objectives, but before signing the agreement, they discussed among themselves the likely trade-offs that would have to be made to achieve the goal.

The agreement applied to light passenger vehicles classified as M1 in European Council Directive 93/116/EEC, which includes vehicles with no more than eight seats in addition to the driver. The agreement included a promise to introduce some models emitting 120 g/km ($\sim$48 mpg) or less by 2000, and a nonbinding 2003 target range of 165–170 g/km ($\sim$34–35 mpg). In addition, the commitment was to be reviewed periodically, with the aim of moving toward a fleetwide goal of 120 g/km by 2012. Finally, ACEA agreed to monitor compliance with the agreement jointly with the Commission.

In exchange for its commitment to meeting the 2008 CO_2 emissions goal, the European automobile manufacturing industry asked that a number of conditions be met:

- *Clean fuels availability.* Because the industry believed that direct injected engines would play a key role in achieving the targets, the agreement asked for the "full market availability" of clean fuels needed for this technology by 2005—gasoline with 30 parts per million (ppm) sulfur content and less than 30% aromatics, diesel fuel at 30 ppm sulfur, and cetane number greater than or equal to 58. (In fact, as noted above, the Commission mandated the widespread availability of both gasoline and diesel fuel with a maximum of 10 ppm sulfur.)
- *Protection against unfair competition.* Non-ACEA members had to commit to similar goals, and the European Community would agree to try to persuade other car manufacturing countries to embrace equivalent efforts. The latter was designed to protect ACEA members from suffering in world market competition for their European efforts. Both the Japanese Automobile Manufacturers Association (JAMA) and the Korean Automobile Manufacturers Association (KAMA) agreed to a revised version of the ACEA targets—achievement of the 2008 target levels in 2009.
- *Regulatory ceasefire.* No new regulatory measures to limit fuel consumption or CO_2 emissions.
- *Unhampered diffusion of technologies.* The companies assumed that the Commission would take no action that would hamper the diffusion of efficiency technologies, particularly direct injected gasoline and diesel engines. (Presumably, this could preclude tighter emissions standards on NO_x and particulates.)

In spite of these constraints, the European Union moved ahead to develop so-called "Euro 5" standards for light-duty vehicles and "Euro VI" standards for heavy-duty engines. These new standards require PM filters on all new diesel vehicles. As the Euro 5 standards were moving toward adoption, several Member States encouraged early introduction through tax incentives. So-called "pseudo" Euro 5 PM standards were put in place by the Commission to serve as a common benchmark for tax incentives.

The voluntary agreement broke down in early 2007 as it became clear that the target of 140 g/km by 2008 would not be met. As a result, the EU imposed a mandatory limit of 130 g/km to be phased in between 2012 and 2015 and will likely further tighten limits to 95 g/km in approximately 2020, subject to a review in 2013.

The United States continues to have more stringent standards than the EU for the conventional pollutants PM and NO_x, emitted from motor vehicles and from diesels in particular. These standards were tightened further since 2000 under the George W. Bush administration, with additional restrictions imposed on heavy-duty vehicles, off-road vehicles, snowmobiles, ships, and locomotives.

But the United States has historically lagged with regard to greenhouse gases from the transport sector. The United States has had a mandatory fuel efficiency program called Corporate Average Fuel Economy (CAFE) since 1975. The Energy Policy and Conservation Act, passed that year (to come into effect in model year 1978), amended the Motor Vehicle Information and Cost Saving Act to require new passenger cars to get at least 27.5 miles per U.S. gallon (8.55 liters/100 km) by model year 1985, as measured by EPA test procedures. The Act required the Department of Transportation to establish standards for light-duty trucks, including jeeps, mini-vans, and SUVs. The National Highway Traffic Safety Administration established corporate fuel economy standards of 20.0 mpg (11.76 liters/100 km) for the 1984 model year and 20.5 (11.48) for 1987.

In the 1990s, fuel prices dropped. The CAFE pressures to improve fuel efficiency were not tightened, and U.S. new-car fuel efficiency slipped steadily, as illustrated in Figure 6.3.

Significantly, U.S. efficiency improvements began with the industrialized world's least-efficient car fleet. Only after the dramatic improvements observed to date are typical U.S. cars as generally efficient as those in the same weight class in other countries. But because vehicles tend to be bigger and heavier in the United States—where light trucks and SUVs account for approximately half of new light-duty vehicles sales—the fuel consumption and CO_2 emissions per mile driven tend to be the highest in the world (on early U.S. efforts and difficulties in reducing greenhouse emissions from motor vehicles, see Walsh and MacKenzie 1990).

As it has in the past with "conventional" air pollutants, California has taken the lead in the United States in addressing greenhouse gas emissions from vehicles. In 2003, the California legislature adopted the Pavley bill, directing the California Air Resources Board (CARB) to achieve the maximum feasible and cost-effective reduction of greenhouse gases from California's motor vehicles. In response, CARB adopted near-term standards to be phased in from 2009 through 2012, and midterm standards to be phased in from 2013 through 2016. California also sought a waiver from EPA to impose CO_2 emissions standards on cars, which was initially denied by the George W. Bush administration but later granted by the Obama administration in 2009.

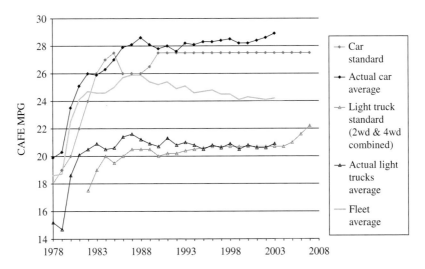

Figure 6.3 *CAFE Standards versus Actual Averages for Cars and Light Trucks*

Source: Adapted from An and Sauer (2004), 27, Fig. 1

To compare the relative fuel economies of cars in the EU, United States, and California, An and Sauer (2004) compared the data summarized in Figure 6.4. This figure shows that cars in the EU, by being much more fuel-efficient than cars in the United States, will have much lower CO_2 emissions per kilometer driven. California's program will narrow the gap, though it is important to note that it regulates only greenhouse gas emissions, not fuel efficiency. (For comparison purposes, An and Sauer converted the California greenhouse gas standards to equivalent fuel economy requirements.) A more recent comparison by the ICCT (2010) is discussed below.

In the last three years, American regulators have taken significant steps to improve fuel economy and reduce greenhouse gas emissions from motor vehicles. The federal Energy Independence and Security Act of 2007, signed by President George W. Bush, raised the U.S. fuel economy standard for passenger vehicles and light trucks to 35 mpg by the year 2020. On May 19, 2009, President Barack Obama announced a policy that called for a standard of 35.5 mpg by 2016, essentially requiring federal light-duty vehicles to meet the same requirements as California. President Obama called for a joint rulemaking by EPA and the National Highway Transportation Safety Administration, which was issued in September 2009 (*Federal Register* 2009).

To compare the fuel economy and greenhouse gas emissions standards adopted by key countries, updated through early 2010, the International Council on Clean Transportation (ICCT) developed a normalized comparison metric (ICCT 2010). As indicated in Figures 6.5 and 6.6, the ICCT analysis shows further progress by the

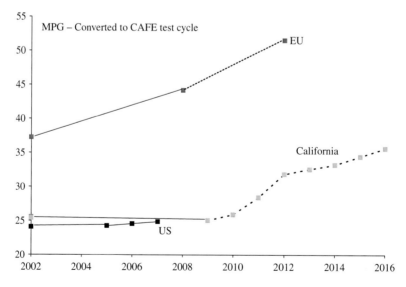

Figure 6.4 *Miles per Gallon Standards (Converted to CAFE Test Cycle)*

Source: Adapted from An and Sauer (2004, 25, Fig. 9)

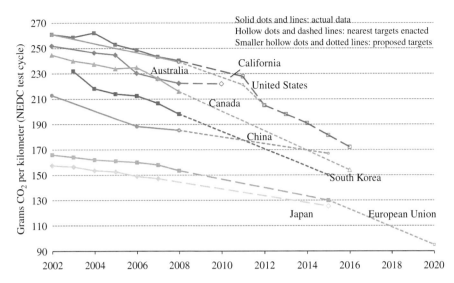

Figure 6.5 *Passenger Vehicle GHG Emissions Fleet Average Performance and Standards by Region*

Source: ICCT (2010)

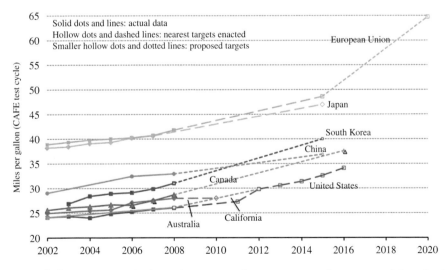

Figure 6.6 *Passenger Vehicle Fuel Economy Fleet Average Performance and Standards by Region*

Source: ICCT (2010)

United States (beyond the levels found by An and Sauer 2004, above). But it still indicates more stringent policies in effect in Europe and Japan—and even in China.

On May 21, 2010, President Obama took the initial step toward developing first-ever standards for fuel economy and greenhouse gas emissions from medium- and heavy-duty trucks. Obama directed EPA and the Department of Transportation to begin a rulemaking for the truck standards for model years 2014–2018. He also told the agencies to develop new fuel economy and greenhouse gas emissions standards for cars and light trucks for model year 2017 and beyond, standards that would take effect after current rules for those vehicles expire in model year 2016. Obama also directed EPA to reduce emissions of conventional pollutants, such as nitrogen oxides, from motor vehicles. (For more information on these standards as they become promulgated and implemented, see EPA 2010.)

Conclusions

The case of automobile emissions illustrates simultaneous precaution in the United States and Europe, but regarding conflicting risks: the United States has been more precautionary regarding the local public health risks from pollutants such as lead, PM, and NO_x, while Europe has been more precautionary regarding the global climate risks of greenhouse gases such as CO_2. And, contrary to the flip-flop hypothesis of rising relative European precaution since 1990, the case of automobile emissions illustrates consistently greater U.S. precaution toward public health risks over the last four decades, and even rising relative U.S. precaution toward the global climate risks in the last few years.

Over the course of the past 50 years, substantial progress has been made in both Europe and the United States in reducing emissions from vehicles. The United States—often led by California, but nationally as well—has been the clear leader in pushing the development and commercialization of technologies for reducing emissions of lead (Pb), CO, HC, NO_x, and PM from both gasoline- and diesel-fueled vehicles, and thereby the leader in proactively reducing serious risks to public health. The risks posed to public health by such pollutants have been serious. For a variety of reasons, including its apparent inability to mandate lead-free gasoline until 1989, Europe has lagged the U.S. control program by as much as almost 20 years. Since the 1990s, Europe has moved aggressively toward clean vehicles and fuels and has narrowed the gap considerably. But especially with regard to diesel vehicles, which have been promoted in Europe but tightly restricted in the United States, a significant difference remains: U.S. standards continue to be more precautionary regarding the public health risks of diesel emissions (based on substantial epidemiologic evidence, and even in the face of uncertainties about precise hazard-harm mechanisms). The standards on diesel engines and low-sulfur diesel fuels adopted by the United States since 1990, notably under Presidents Bill Clinton and George W. Bush, addressed the uncertain risks of fine PM from diesel in a decidedly more precautionary stance than that taken in Europe.

Conversely, Europe has recognized the threat of global warming earlier and to a much greater extent than the United States, as evidenced by its ratification of the Kyoto Protocol and adoption of EU climate policies. One result has been a strong effort in Europe to reduce CO_2 emissions from light-duty vehicles. European CO_2 emissions per kilometer are much lower than U.S. CO_2 vehicle emissions as a result—although other factors contribute, such as high European fuel prices, which predate climate policy. The greater prevalence of diesel vehicles in Europe helps explain this transatlantic difference in vehicle CO_2 emissions rates. This gap even increased as the fuel consumption and CO_2 emissions of the U.S. light-duty fleet deteriorated. But this gap may be closed by the greenhouse gas regulations recently adopted in California and more aggressive CAFE standards adopted at the U.S. federal level in 2007 and 2009, along with potential new federal greenhouse gas standards for motor vehicles under the Clean Air Act. Thus, even regarding fuel economy and CO_2 emissions, the trend since 2007 has been toward rising relative U.S. precaution compared with Europe.

An important question for the future will be how major developing countries decide to address these issues, and whether they borrow regulatory approaches from the United States or Europe, or both (see Walsh 2003). In these countries, the size of their vehicle fleets and their emissions of conventional air pollutants and of greenhouse gases are growing rapidly. Both local public health and global climate will be strongly influenced by the choices made in developing countries.

References

An, Feng, and Amanda Sauer. 2004. Comparison of Automobile Fuel Efficiency and GHG Emission Standards around the World. Pew Center on Global Climate Change. December. www.pewclimate.org/docUploads/Fuel%20Economy%20and%20GHG%20Standards_010605_110719.pdf (accessed July 27, 2010).

ECE (United Nations Economic Commission for Europe). 1970. Uniform Provisions concerning the Approval of Vehicles Equipped with a Positive-Ignition Engine with Regard to the Emission of Gaseous Pollutants by the Engine, Annexed to the Agreement of March 20, 1958, concerning the Adoption of Uniform Conditions of Approval and Reciprocal Recognition of Approval for Motor Vehicle Equipment and Parts. 740 United Nations Treaty Series 364, as Revised/Consolidated in 1078 United Nations Treaty Series 351. August 1.

EIA (U.S. Energy Information Administration). 2009. Light-Duty Diesel Vehicles: Efficiency and Emissions Attributes and Market Issues. Report # SR/OIAF(2009)02. Executive Summary. February. www.eia.doe.gov/oiaf/servicerpt/lightduty/execsummary.html (accessed July 27, 2010).

EPA (U.S. Environmental Protection Agency). 2010. Transportation and Climate: Regulations and Standards. http://epa.gov/otaq/climate/regulations.htm (accessed July 24, 2010).

European Commission. 1990. Commission of the European Communities, COM (89) 662. Proposal for a Council Directive Amending Directive 70/220/EEC on the Approximation of the Laws of the Member States Relating to Measures to Be Taken against Air Pollution by Emissions from Motor Vehicles, Brussels, February 2.

———. 1995. A Community Strategy to Reduce CO_2 Emissions from Passenger Cars and Improve Fuel Economy. COM (95) 689. Communication from the Commission to the Council and the European Parliament. December 20.

Federal Register. 2009. Notice of Proposed Rulemaking. September 28. http://yosemite.epa.gov/opei/RuleGate.nsf/byRIN/2060-AP58 (accessed July 27, 2010).

ICCT (International Council on Clean Transportation). 2010. Updated Comparison Charts of Global Passenger Vehicle Fuel Economy/GHG Regulations. April. www.theicct.org/information/reports/passenger_vehicle_greenhouse_gas_and_fuel_economy_standards_a_global_update (accessed August 3, 2010).

Krier, James E., and Edmund Ursin. 1977. *Pollution and Policy: A Case Essay on California and Federal Experience with Motor Vehicle Air Pollution, 1940–1975.* Berkeley, CA: University of California Press.

Walsh, Michael P. 1999. Phasing Lead out of Gasoline: An Examination of Policy Approaches in Different Countries. United Nations Environment Programme/Organisation for Economic Co-operation and Development. www.airimpacts.org/documents/local/LeadinGasoline.pdf (accessed August 2, 2010).

———. 2003. Vehicle Emissions and Health in Developing Countries. In *Air Pollution and Health in Rapidly Developing Countries,* edited by Gordon McGranahan and Frank Murray. Stockholm: Stockholm Environment Institute, 146–175.

Walsh, Michael P., and James MacKenzie. 1990. Driving Forces: Motor Vehicle Trends and Their Implications for Global Warming, Energy Strategies, and Transportation Planning. Washington, DC: World Resources Institute.

CHAPTER 7

Stratospheric Ozone Depletion and Global Climate Change

James K. Hammitt

*R*esponses to the threats of stratospheric ozone depletion and global climate change differ markedly between the United States and Europe. In the case of stratospheric ozone depletion, caused by release to the atmosphere of chlorofluor-ocarbons (CFCs) and other ozone-depleting substances (ODSs), the United States acted earlier and more aggressively to reduce the threat. While the policy response to global climate change remains a story in process, Europe is clearly leading the United States in taking actions to reduce the threat.

The contrast between these issues is intriguing because the issues share many similarities. In both cases, the problems can be characterized as global externalities, with long time lags between the human activities that cause the threat (release of gases to the atmosphere) and the ensuing environmental changes and consequences for humans and ecosystems. Both effects are caused by the release of chemically stable gases into the atmosphere. Because of their stability, these gases remain in the atmosphere for decades to centuries, so they are well mixed in the atmosphere. This global mixing has two important consequences for policy. First, the effect of a unit emission does not depend on the location from which it is released, so emissions reductions by one country or region will be ineffectual if they are offset by comparable emissions increases by another. Second, unlike environmental releases having only local or regional effects, it is impossible to learn from regional variation in emissions and environmental response about the effects of these gases on stratospheric ozone or climate. Any experimentation on the overall response is necessarily global in scale. Finally, because the gases persist for decades in the atmosphere, actions to prevent or minimize the threat must be taken well before the ultimate consequences of current emissions are observed; they must be based on theoretical predictions of harm rather than reactions to observed adverse consequences. (The climatic response is further retarded by other factors, notably the thermal inertia of the oceans.) In this sense, actions to prevent or minimize these threats are by definition precautionary rather than reactionary.

The following section provides background on the two issues and describes some of the similarities and differences between these threats that may influence the differences in policy between the United States and Europe. The two subsequent sections provide brief histories of the policy responses in each polity to stratospheric ozone depletion and to global climate change, respectively. The concluding section speculates on some potential explanations for the differences in response to these issues on the two sides of the North Atlantic.

Background and Comparison of the Two Issues

The threat that synthetic chemicals—specifically, CFCs—could reduce the concentration of ozone in the stratosphere was first identified in the early 1970s. The seminal paper, Molina and Rowland (1974), identified the geochemical pathway. Because CFCs are chemically stable, they do not break down in the atmosphere until they are wafted into the stratosphere, where they are broken down by the intense ultraviolet radiation. Upon photodissociation, CFCs release their chlorine in the stratosphere. The chlorine catalyzes a reaction that converts ozone (O_3) to molecular oxygen (O_2). By accelerating the ozone-destruction reaction, the increased presence of stratospheric chlorine leads to a reduction in the concentration of stratospheric ozone. This reduction could be important because ozone absorbs much of the ultraviolet light from the sun. With less ozone, more ultraviolet light penetrates to ground level, where it causes damage to human health (e.g., skin cancer and cataracts), ecosystems (e.g., destruction of phytoplankton), certain crops, and some materials (e.g., plastics). Because CFCs are so stable, their atmospheric lifetimes are on the order of decades. Atmospheric lifetimes of the two most important ODSs, CFC-11 and CFC-12, are approximately 70 years and 100 years, respectively. These imply that CFCs will continue to deplete stratospheric ozone for a century or more after they are released to the atmosphere.

The first commercially important CFCs were developed in the 1930s for use as the fluid in refrigeration systems. These compounds are chemically stable, nonflammable, and nontoxic. By the 1970s, CFCs were widely used in a variety of industrial and consumer applications. In addition to their use in building, home, and automobile air-conditioning and refrigeration systems, CFCs were used as aerosol propellants for personal care and other products, as blowing agents in manufacturing rigid foams (for insulation and packaging) and flexible foams (for cushioning), and as solvents in the manufacture of electronic and other components. Closely related compounds were also used as solvents (e.g., methyl chloroform) and in fire-extinguishing systems (e.g., halons). CFCs and other ODSs were released to the environment either during use (e.g., aerosols, manufacture of open-cell foams) or through leakage or product disposal (e.g., refrigeration, closed-cell foams).

In contrast to the relatively recent discovery that CFCs could deplete stratospheric ozone, the possibility that release of carbon dioxide to the atmosphere would lead to global climate change through an enhanced greenhouse effect was recognized by the end of the nineteenth century. In addition to its primary constituents, nitrogen and oxygen, the atmosphere contains a number of gases that are present in only tiny proportions. Among these minor and trace gases, water vapor, carbon dioxide (CO_2), and ozone are important in shaping the Earth's climate. These gases allow the sun's visible, ultraviolet, and near-infrared radiant energy to penetrate to the Earth's surface but absorb the outgoing infrared radiation emitted by land and ocean, thus containing this energy within the Earth system. Without an atmosphere, the temperature at the Earth's surface would average 32°C lower than its current 15°C. At this temperature, water would be frozen and life as we know it could not exist.

While there is no doubt that carbon dioxide, water vapor, and other trace gases keep the Earth's surface warmer than it would otherwise be, there is debate about the extent to which this natural "greenhouse" effect has been and will be enhanced by increasing atmospheric concentrations of greenhouse gases (GHGs) released through human activities. The major anthropogenic GHG is carbon dioxide, which is released primarily through combustion of fossil fuels, with additional amounts released through deforestation and cement production. Significant additional contributions to the greenhouse effect are due to methane, produced by sheep, cattle, and other ruminant (cud-chewing) animals; termites; rice paddies; landfills; leaking natural-gas pipelines; coal mining; and other sources. Nitrous oxide from agriculture and combustion and various CFCs and other industrial compounds contribute as well.

Greenhouse warming and ozone depletion interact in several ways. The direct greenhouse effect of CFCs is largely offset by their destruction of stratospheric ozone, itself a greenhouse gas. In contrast, hydrofluorocarbons and some other CFC substitutes contribute to the greenhouse effect without providing this offsetting "benefit." Moreover, greenhouse warming reduces ozone depletion by cooling the stratosphere and slowing the ozone-loss reactions.

Scientific understanding and policy attention to the possibility of global climate change have developed over many decades. The possibility that carbon dioxide from combustion of fossil fuels could alter global climate was identified by Arrhenius as early as 1896. (For an extensive history of the science of global climate change, see Weart (2003).) By the 1930s, a warming trend had been observed in the United States and Europe, and G. S. Callendar argued that carbon dioxide emissions from fossil fuel combustion could be an explanatory factor (Weart 2003). At the time, however, the general scientific opinion was that the observed warming was due to natural factors and that human activities were too insignificant to alter global climate (though local climatic effects were recognized, e.g., from deforestation). Important contributions to understanding the potential for human-caused emissions of carbon dioxide to alter global climate include the recognition by Revelle and Suess (1957) that the oceans would not remove carbon dioxide from the atmosphere sufficiently rapidly to prevent a substantial increase in atmospheric concentrations, especially if fossil fuel emissions continued to grow rapidly (as they have), and the continuing series of measurements of atmospheric carbon dioxide made by Charles Keeling at Mauna Loa in Hawaii beginning in 1957 (Weart 2003).

By the 1960s and 1970s, the possibility that fossil fuel combustion would alter global climate was widely cited and began to attract policy concern. During this period, the most likely direction of the effect was ambiguous, because it was argued that smoke and other particulate matter might reflect more solar energy than the enhanced carbon dioxide concentrations would trap, leading to global cooling and potentially triggering an ice age. The possibility of rapid change, whether cooling (discussed by Bryson) or warming (discussed by Broecker), also arose in the 1970s (Weart 2003). The issue attracted serious policy attention in the mid- to late 1980s, leading to the creation of the Intergovernmental Panel on Climate Change, a body established to provide regular reports describing the scientific understanding of the issue.

The worldwide policy responses to stratospheric ozone depletion and global climate change differ significantly in the speed and efficacy with which each has been addressed. The response to the possibility that ODSs would deplete stratospheric ozone was impressively swift and effective. In 1987, less than 15 years after the threat was identified, an international agreement to limit production and use of the major chemicals was reached; within an additional 10 years, production and use of these chemicals were nearly eliminated in the industrialized countries and on a path toward elimination in the rest of the world.

By contrast, the global response to the possibility that carbon dioxide and other GHGs would affect climate has been much slower and less effective, reflecting the much greater difficulties in mitigating this threat. Concern about the need to limit GHG emissions began to develop in the 1970s, about the same time as the concern about CFCs. An international agreement to control GHG emissions was signed in 1997, but it requires only modest emissions reductions in the industrialized countries and no reductions in the developing countries (which account for a much larger share of GHG emissions than they did of ODS emissions). Moreover, the largest emitter of GHGs at the time, the United States, never ratified and has subsequently withdrawn from the agreement. Despite reductions in some countries, global GHG emissions continue to grow.

Although both stratospheric ozone depletion and global climate change can be characterized as global externalities with long response times and persistent consequences, there are significant differences between the issues that may help to explain the apparent differences in worldwide policy response and perhaps also between the American and European responses. First, although CFCs and other ODSs were used in a wide range of industrial applications and consumer products, the number of sources of these substances was quite modest. Ozone-depleting substances, which are synthetic chemicals, were produced by only a dozen or so chemical manufacturers worldwide; probably more than three-quarters of the world's production occurred in the industrialized countries of North America and Europe (Hammitt et al. 1986). Moreover, these firms had at least the potential to benefit from regulations that provided an opportunity to develop and commercialize alternative chemicals that might be sold at greater profit.

In contrast, the sources of carbon dioxide and other greenhouse gases (GHGs) that cause global climate change are virtually limitless. They include not only combustion of all fossil fuels (coal, oil, natural gas), but also release of methane from coal mining, landfills, agricultural production and livestock, and other gases and sources. The United States and European Union, while accounting for relatively large GHG emissions per capita, contribute only 35% to global carbon dioxide emissions from fossil fuels (EIA 2006). Both are likely to contribute substantially smaller shares over time as lower- and middle-income countries develop economically and increase their use of fossil fuels. Because fossil fuels are extracted rather than synthesized, policy actions that discourage use of fossil fuels are likely to harm those who own fossil fuel stocks, and there seems to be less possibility that these owners would benefit from regulation than was true for the firms that synthesized ODSs. Moreover, the two issues rose to prominence in slightly different time periods, so any secular changes in proclivity toward precautionary regulation that may have occurred might contribute to the difference in response.

Response to the Threat of Stratospheric Ozone Depletion

The policy response to possible depletion of stratospheric ozone can be divided into several periods. (Much of the following discussion of stratospheric ozone depletion is taken from Hammitt (2004); the history of CFC regulation is described by Andersen and Sarma (2002), Benedick (1998), Cagin and Dray (1993), Cogan (1988), Dotto and Schiff (1978), Hammitt and Thompson (1997), Maxwell and Weiner (1993), Parson (2003), and Roan (1989).)

Soon after the issue was identified, countries in both North America and Europe imposed unilateral restrictions to reduce CFC consumption and emissions. These included the United States, Canada, Norway, Sweden, Denmark, Germany, Switzerland, and the Netherlands. By 1980, these measures were in place and policy action stalled: the initial controls had significantly reduced CFC emissions, an economic recession suppressed the rate of growth of CFC production, and scientific developments suggested that the effect of CFCs on stratospheric ozone might be less severe than initially proposed. In the mid-1980s, however, economic growth and further scientific research shifted the balance toward greater concern, culminating in the signing of the Montreal Protocol in September 1987. The protocol provides an international framework to restrict both production and consumption of CFCs and other ozone-depleting substances. Since 1987, the protocol has been amended several times, in each case to tighten the controls or expand the set of chemicals subject to its jurisdiction. Production of the primary CFCs (11, 12, and 113) was eliminated in the advanced countries by 1996, as was consumption, except for small quantities in narrowly defined "essential uses."

In recent years, attention has shifted to controlling emissions of some chemicals developed as substitutes for CFCs as well as other compounds that were not initially regulated, such as methyl bromide (a grain fumigant). Although the Montreal Protocol and its amendments provide a framework and limits on ODS production and consumption, implementation of these restrictions is the responsibility of the parties that have signed and ratified the protocol. Both the United States and the European Union (together with its Member States) are signatories to the protocol and its amendments, and each has imposed regulations to ensure compliance with it. The details of these regulations are described below.

Early Regulations: 1974–1987

In the United States, there was a strong public reaction to the discovery that CFCs might deplete stratospheric ozone. Attention focused on the use of CFCs as a propellant in personal-care aerosol products, such as deodorants and hair sprays, and included consumer boycotts and regulation in several states (e.g., Oregon prohibited CFCs in aerosols and New York required that they be labeled). Industry responded quickly. For example, Johnson Wax announced in June 1975 that it would eliminate CFCs from its products. Removal of CFCs from aerosol products was accomplished relatively easily, in large part by substituting hydrocarbon propellants, which are flammable and less expensive, or by replacing aerosol dispensers with pump sprays that require no propellant. The federal government determined that under existing legislation, it had authority to regulate only aerosol uses of CFCs, with different agencies having authority over different products. In 1978, the relevant agencies—the Consumer Product Safety Commission, the Environmental Protection Agency (EPA), and the Food and Drug Administration—issued a rule prohibiting use of CFCs as aerosol propellants effective in 1979.

The reaction in Europe differed significantly among countries. Sweden and Norway, which had little or no production, adopted aerosol bans at about the same time as the United States. Germany, which was a major producer, concluded a voluntary agreement with industry to reduce CFC use in aerosols by 30% from its 1976 level by 1979, and Denmark and Switzerland achieved similar voluntary reductions. The Netherlands imposed a labeling requirement. In contrast, there was little response in the United Kingdom, France, and Italy, which were also major producers.

The difference in response between the United Kingdom and France, on the one hand, and the United States, on the other, may have been colored by the earlier debate about the effect of supersonic transport (SST) aircraft on stratospheric ozone. The first concerns about ozone depletion, which arose in the 1960s, involved the possibility that water vapor in SST exhaust, released in the stratosphere, would catalyze and accelerate the ozone-loss reaction. This concern was cited by the United States as one factor in its decision to halt its SST development program, although economic factors were seen as more important. In contrast, a consortium of the United Kingdom and France developed and eventually manufactured the Concorde supersonic passenger aircraft. The possibility of ozone depletion continued to be raised in disputes about landing rights for the Concorde in the United States. In addition, most of the scientists working on stratospheric ozone issues worked in the United States, so the British and French governments did not have as much input from their own scientists on the CFC issue.

Because aerosol uses of CFCs accounted for about half of consumption, the aerosol bans and other responses in the United States and Europe led to significant reductions in CFC releases to the atmosphere. Growth in other uses was small in the early 1980s, due to slow economic growth associated with the oil price shock of 1979 and other factors. As scientific developments suggested that the effects of CFCs on ozone would not be as great as initially forecast, it appeared that the issue had been adequately addressed, at least for the moment.

By the mid-1980s, however, economic growth had resumed and CFC production began to increase. The science also began to point toward larger effects on stratospheric ozone, culminating in the 1988 Ozone Trends Panel Report (NASA 1988), which identified a statistically significant reduction in globally averaged stratospheric ozone. The 1985 discovery of the Antarctic "ozone hole" (Farman et al. 1985) attracted much scientific and policy attention. The "hole" is a large but geographically and temporally limited reduction in stratospheric ozone that occurs in the austral spring. It was discovered by observations at the British Antarctic research station and was neither predicted nor explained by current theories of ozone depletion. For this reason, its connection with CFCs was speculative.

In this climate, international negotiations led first to the 1985 Vienna Convention, an agreement to conduct research and monitor the situation, and subsequently to the 1987 Montreal Protocol. These negotiations were encouraged by Canada, some of the Nordic countries, and the United States. The CFC-producing and CFC-consuming industries were skeptical of the need for additional regulation, but U.S. industry eventually supported the international effort—in part because it feared that in the absence of international rules, additional domestic rules might be imposed that would weaken its international competitive position.

The Montreal Protocol and Its Amendments

The Montreal Protocol limits both production and consumption of CFCs, halons, and other ODSs. Consumption is not measured but is defined as production plus imports minus exports. The limits apply at the national level, with the exception of the European Union, where production and consumption of the Member States are not individually limited so long as the union as a whole complies with EU-wide limits.

Initially, the protocol limited CFC and halon production and consumption to their 1986 levels, with 20% and 50% reductions in CFCs scheduled for 1993 and 1998, respectively. These limits were strengthened by the 1990 London amendment and the 1992 Copenhagen amendment, which, with limited "essential use" exemptions, eliminated CFC production and consumption in 1996 and halon production and consumption in 1994. These and subsequent amendments have also enlarged the set of substances controlled under the Montreal Protocol, perhaps most significantly by including hydrochlorofluorocarbons (HCFCs), which have proved to be important substitutes for CFCs in refrigeration, foam-blowing, and other applications, and methyl chloroform, an industrial solvent.

The Montreal Protocol provides some flexibility in the particular ODSs that are controlled. Production and consumption limits apply not to individual compounds, but to the total quantities of ODS within a defined group, weighted by their relative ozone-depletion potentials. Ozone-depletion potential is a measure of the relative efficacy with which a unit emission of each ODS can deplete stratospheric ozone. It depends partly on the number of chlorine and bromine atoms the ODS releases in the stratosphere and also on the time it spends in the atmosphere.

The 1987 protocol included the three primary CFCs (11, 12, and 113) and two potential substitutes (CFCs 114 and 115) in the first group; it placed the halons (1211, 1301, and 2402) in a second group. The HCFCs, added under the London amendment, form a third group. Emission limitations of the Montreal Protocol and subsequent amendments are summarized in Table 7.1. Implementation of the limits established under the Montreal Protocol is the responsibility of the parties. The following sections describe the rules implementing the protocol in the United States and in the European Union and its Member States.

Implementation in the United States

Implementing rules for the Montreal Protocol in the United States were adopted in 1988 (53 FR 30566), and current authority is contained in Title VI of the 1990 Clean Air Act Amendments. U.S. implementation relies on a system of tradable production and consumption permits, supplemented by excise taxes and end-use controls.

The EPA issues annual permits for production and consumption to firms that manufacture ODSs or import them to the United States. Allocation is based on historical production or import shares. The permits correspond to the ODS groups established under the Montreal Protocol and were initially denominated in ozone-depletion-potential-weighted pounds per group; thus firms may allocate their production and importation among the ODSs in a group in response to market conditions. Under the

Table 7.1. *Allowable Production and Consumption of Primary CFCs in the United States and European Union*

Authority	Reduction from 1986 consumption (%)
Montreal Protocol, September 1987	1989: 00
	1993: 20
	1998: 50
London amendment, June 1990	1995: 50
	1997: 85
	2000: 100
Copenhagen amendment, November 1992	1994: 75
	1996: 100

Note: Primary CFCs are 11, 12, 113, 114, and 115. Under the Montreal Protocol, restrictions apply to years beginning July 1. Under the London and Copenhagen amendments, restrictions apply to years beginning January 1.
Source: Hammitt (2004)

1990 Clean Air Act Amendments, the permit system was altered so that permits are defined for *each* ODS, but intercompound trades based on relative ozone-depletion potential are still allowed (Lee 1996). To introduce a quantity of an ODS into commerce, a firm must present the corresponding number of both production and consumption permits. The permits are tradable among firms without restriction and can be banked (i.e., saved for later use). By controlling the quantities of ODSs introduced into commerce, this system has ensured U.S. compliance with the Montreal Protocol.

Taxes were not included in the initial implementation policy, at least in part because EPA does not have authority to impose them. (EPA was also uncertain about its authority to sell or auction the tradable permits.) Congress subsequently introduced ODS taxes, in part to capture some of the rents that producers and importers gain by receipt of tradable permits (Barthold 1994). Two types of taxes were imposed: an excise tax on new ODSs produced or imported, and a floor tax on ODSs held in stock. The excise tax was initially set at $1.37 per ozone-depletion-potential-weighted pound for 1990 through 1992 and subsequently increased to $3.35 in 1993, $4.35 in 1994, and $5.35 in 1995. Some commentators credit the tax with holding U.S. consumption of CFCs below the limits required by the protocol (Barthold 1994; Hoerner 1995).

The economic-incentive mechanisms were supplemented by a variety of command-and-control measures. These include specific prohibitions on ODS use in certain applications, such as nonpropellant aerosol uses not included in the 1978 rule (e.g., horns) and use as blowing agents in flexible and packaging foams. Other rules require specific equipment and training for refrigeration and air-conditioning service personnel, and sales of small quantities of ODSs were prohibited to prevent amateur mechanics without proper recycling equipment from recharging automobile air conditioners. Perhaps the most important of the command-and-control mechanisms is the significant new alternatives policy (SNAP), which prohibits the replacement of an ODS with certain substitutes if alternative choices would better reduce overall environmental or health risk. Under this policy, EPA provides lists of acceptable and unacceptable alternatives to ODSs in a range of applications. In addition, the United States has adopted rules requiring labeling of products containing ODSs and has revised federal purchasing guidelines to eliminate requirements for ODSs and encourage substitutes. The influence of government purchasing specifications (e.g., MilSpec) extends beyond government purchasing, since these guidelines are often incorporated into private contracts (Wexler 1996).

Implementation in the European Union

In the EU, implementation of the Montreal Protocol is organized through European Commission regulations that are binding on and enforced by the Member States, some of which have supplemented the EU rules with additional regulations or voluntary agreements with industry. The negotiation of the Montreal Protocol coincided with the development of centralized authority for the environment at the EU level, which also affected its implementation.

The initial EU regulation (EC 3322/88) imposed a system of tradable production or import permits. Similar to the system in the United States, these permits apply to total quantities of ODS within a group, weighted by ozone-depletion potential. These permits are tradable between firms within and among Member States. EC Regulation 3322/88 also required labeling CFCs and halons with a warning about their danger to stratospheric ozone.

Regulation EC 3093/94, adopted after the London amendments, extended the tradable permit system to the additional ODSs added to the protocol. The permit limits were somewhat more stringent than required by the London amendments, creating a faster phaseout of CFCs in the EU than in the U.S. This regulation also prohibited import of ODSs and products containing ODSs from countries that are not party to the Montreal Protocol. In addition, EC 3093/94 included a large number of end-use restrictions. It prohibited CFC uses except as solvents, refrigerants, or in rigid foam used for insulation or safety applications, and it prohibited CFC use in open solvent applications, domestic refrigeration, automobile and public bus air-conditioning after 1995; public rail air-conditioning after 1996; and large refrigerators (e.g., cold-storage warehouses) after 2000.

EC regulations are implemented and enforced by the Member States. Oberthür and Pfahl (2000) describe substantial variation in implementation among Member States, several of which impose additional restrictions while others appear to lack the capacity or legal tools to enforce even the EC regulations. Member States can be divided into three classes. One group has adopted national legislation encompassing comprehensive use controls and often including more stringent reductions in ODS use. This group includes Austria, Denmark, Finland, Germany, Italy, Luxembourg, the Netherlands, and Sweden. A second group, including Belgium, France, Spain, and the United Kingdom, has no comprehensive legislation. Some of these countries have adopted end-use controls; for example, Belgium has controls on aerosol use and refrigeration, and France has controls on refrigeration. The third group, which includes Greece, Ireland, and Portugal, has not legislated sanctions and so may be unable to prosecute violations of the EC regulations.

Member States that supplemented the EC regulations chose a variety of restrictions. Germany, for example, has rules restricting use of any ODS in a variety of specified products, whereas other countries prohibit use of specified substances in certain applications. Germany also requires producers to take back ODS for destruction and requires labels on ODS-containing products. The Netherlands prohibits stocking of used refrigeration systems for commercial purposes—a rule intended to discourage export of ODS-containing refrigeration systems that might otherwise travel through Dutch ports to developing countries. The United Kingdom has adopted a system of information provision and codes of practice for maintenance and servicing of ODS-containing products.

A few EU Member States have also adopted economic incentives. Austria created a deposit-refund system for refrigerants to encourage the recovery of ODSs from systems at maintenance and disposal. In 1989, Denmark introduced a tax of DKK 30 (€3.7) per kilogram on ODS when produced or used in certain products (Oberthür and

Pfahl 2000). From 1993 to 1997, Sweden imposed a fee on successful applications for exemptions from end-use controls. The fee was proportional to the quantity of ODS use exempted, at a rate of approximately $10 per kilogram in 1993, increasing to about $75 per kilogram in 1997.

As one indication of the extent to which the United States and Europe took action to prevent stratospheric ozone depletion, Figure 7.1 illustrates consumption of the two major ODSs, CFCs 11 and 12, over the period after the Montreal Protocol took effect in 1989. For the period 1989–1993, permitted CFC consumption in the two regions was about equal. European consumption was significantly below the limit in 1989, and U.S. emissions rapidly fell to near the European level. Both regions continued to reduce their consumption and hold it below the limits, even as these were strengthened in succeeding years. Europe virtually eliminated CFC consumption in 1995, two years earlier than the United States. Although data on CFC consumption for Europe prior to 1989 are not publicly available, it is clear that consumption of CFCs fell much more sharply in the United States than in Europe. Between 1974 and 1985, U.S. consumption of CFCs 11 and 12 declined about 45%, from about 375 to 210 thousand metric tons. In contrast, consumption of these chemicals in Europe, Japan, and other countries outside the communist bloc increased by about 10% from 435 to 480 thousand metric tons (Hammitt et al. 1986).

Response to the Threat of Global Climate Change

Global climate change reached the policy agenda in the mid- to late 1980s. In 1985, an international group of scientists met at Villach, Austria, and produced scenarios of future emissions of the major GHGs in addition to carbon dioxide. This led to a scientific consensus that the issue was serious (Franz 1997; Jaeger and O'Riordan

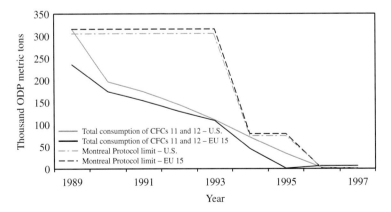

Figure 7.1 *CFC Consumption*

Source: Hammitt (2004)

1996). In 1988, participants at the Toronto Conference called for a 20% reduction in global carbon dioxide emissions by 2005 (Franz 1997). The Intergovernmental Panel on Climate Change was created by the United Nations Environment Programme and the World Meteorological Organization in the same year and published its first assessment report in 1990. Also in 1990, a joint meeting of EU environment and energy ministers agreed that EU carbon dioxide emissions in 2000 should not exceed their 1990 level.

The Framework Convention on Climate Change was signed at the 1992 Earth Summit in Rio de Janeiro. It called for "stabilization of greenhouse-gas concentrations . . . at a level that would prevent dangerous anthropogenic interference with the climate system." While European nations were enthusiastic, the United States was a reluctant signatory and exacted certain concessions for its participation, such as the language amending or qualifying the statement of the precautionary principle by stating that "policies should be cost-effective so as to ensure global benefits at the lowest possible cost."

While the 1992 Framework Convention established principles for responding to climate change, it did not require actual changes in emissions. In contrast, the 1997 Kyoto Protocol required the United States, EU, and other industrialized nations to hold their average GHG emissions in the 2008–2012 period to a level below their emissions in 1990. The agreed emission reductions are 7% in the United States and 8% in the EU. Internally, the EU agreed on a system of Member State emission targets under which some Member States—for example, those with lower average incomes and more rapid growth—are permitted to increase their emissions relative to 1990 while others decrease their emissions by more than the EU-wide average. The Kyoto targets for the United States, EU, and the Member States are listed in Table 7.2.

The United States was a reluctant partner to the Kyoto Protocol, as it was to the Framework Convention. The United States signed the protocol, but the Clinton administration never submitted it to the Senate for ratification, knowing that ratification would fail. Indeed, prior to the signing of the protocol, the Senate adopted the 1997 Byrd-Hagel resolution (S. Res. 98) by a vote of 95 to 0. The resolution expressed the "sense of the Senate" that the United States should not be a party to any agreement that would limit U.S. GHG emissions without also limiting emissions from developing countries. Similarly, the Clinton administration's 1993 effort to increase energy taxes, in part to reduce GHG emissions, had received little support, and ultimately only a small increase in the gasoline tax had been imposed. The subsequent Bush administration, even less supportive of the Kyoto Protocol than the Clinton administration, officially withdrew the United States from the protocol.

In contrast, the EU and its then 15 Member States ratified the protocol by May 2001 and have adopted policies to limit emissions. As in the case of the Montreal Protocol for ODSs, compliance with the Kyoto Protocol is achieved if the EU-wide emission limit is satisfied, even if individual Member States exceed their agreed-upon limits. The centerpiece of these policies is a far-reaching emissions trading system, which covers the current 25 members of the EU and began operation in January 2005.

Table 7.2. *Kyoto Protocol Emission Targets for the United States and EU*

Region/country	Change from 1990 emissions (%)
United States	−7
EU 15	−8
Austria	−13
Belgium	−7.5
Denmark	−21
Finland	0
France	0
Germany	−21
Greece	+25
Ireland	+13
Italy	−6.5
Luxembourg	−28
Netherlands	−6
Portugal	+27
Spain	+15
Sweden	+4
United Kingdom	−12.5
EU accession states	
Estonia	−8
Cyprus	No target
Czech Republic	−8
Hungary	−6
Latvia	−8
Lithuania	−8
Malta	No target
Poland	−6
Slovakia	−8
Slovenia	−8

Note: The EU-15 targets are not part of the protocol but are determined by the June 1998 burden-sharing agreement of the EU Council of Ministers

The EU emissions trading system was established by legislation adopted by the European Parliament and the Member States. In its initial form, the trading system applies to carbon dioxide emissions from designated facilities (allowing for future extensions to include other facilities and other GHGs). These facilities include large installations in energy-intensive sectors such as electric power and heat generation, combustion plants, oil refineries, coke ovens, and production of iron and steel, cement, lime, bricks, ceramics, and pulp and paper. The approximately 11,500 covered facilities account for 6.5 billion metric tons of carbon dioxide emissions per year, about 45% of EU carbon dioxide and 30% of EU GHG emissions. Emissions allowances were allocated to facilities (generally at no cost) by their respective national governments in accordance with national action plans prepared by each Member State. The national action plans were reviewed by the European Commission to ensure the total number of allowances granted by each Member State was consistent with that state's emissions target for compliance with the Kyoto Protocol, taking into account its other policies to control emissions (including projects to reduce emissions in developing countries through the Joint Implementation and Clean Development Mechanism provisions of the protocol).

Emissions allowances can be banked within the 2005–2007 warm-up period, the 2008–2012 initial compliance period, and from the initial compliance period to a subsequent compliance period that may be established by a successor agreement to the Kyoto Protocol. Facilities are required to report their emissions of carbon dioxide and other GHGs annually. Penalties for noncompliance are significant. Carbon dioxide emissions in excess of a facility's allowances must be offset in the following year by acquiring sufficient allowances; they also incur a penalty of €40 per metric ton during the warm-up period and €100 per metric ton during the first compliance period. These penalties are substantially larger than the anticipated market price of emissions allowances (Kruger and Pizer 2004)—on the order of €20 per metric ton in 2010. After their introduction in January 2005, market prices rose from a few euros in the winter to about €20 per metric ton in the summer of 2005. The quantity of allowances traded was on the order of 20 million metric tons per month in the spring and summer of 2005, about one-third of a percent of the total annual allocation (EC 2005a).

The adoption of an emissions trading program marks a significant shift from the European nations' skepticism of the use of market mechanisms as advocated by the United States during the Kyoto Protocol negotiations. Some Member States have made large reductions in GHG emissions, notably through the shift away from coal in the UK and through modernizing or closing older industrial capacity in the former East Germany. In some of the 10 accession states that joined in EU in 2004, however, increases in energy use—particularly in transportation—make the Kyoto targets challenging both for them and for the EU as a whole (EC 2005b; Kruger and Pizer 2004). As of 2008, the EU was anticipating compliance with the Kyoto limits for the 2008–2012 period, in part by adopting additional measures such as those affecting land use and forestry (EEA 2008).

In the United States, policies to slow or prevent climate change have largely taken the form of encouraging voluntary efforts augmented by tax incentives (e.g., for gasoline-electric hybrid automobiles) and government spending on research on advanced energy technologies such as hydrogen fuel cells for transportation, zero-emission coal plants for generating electricity, and nuclear fusion (White House 2004). Several proposals for national emissions-trading systems have been discussed in Congress (Pizer 2007). In June 2009, the House of Representatives passed the Waxman-Markey Bill (HR 2454), which calls for the establishment of a tradable permit system for carbon dioxide and other GHGs that would reduce emissions from 2005 levels 3% by 2012, 17% by 2020, 42% by 2030, and 83% by 2050. In contrast to the limited federal action, a variety of efforts to limit GHG emissions have been undertaken at the state and regional levels, such as the Regional Greenhouse Gas Initiative trading program in the Northeast, designed to limit carbon dioxide emissions from electric power plants in the region to the 1990 level in 2009–2015 and to reduce them by 10% beginning in 2019 (RGGI 2010), and the California GHG emissions standards for new motor vehicles beginning with the 1990 model year (CARB 2010). However, such policies are unlikely to have significant effects on U.S. emissions unless they spur national policies.

Current U.S. emissions are well above their 1990 level, and there is little chance that the U.S. will meet its Kyoto target (which is not binding because the United States did not ratify and ultimately withdrew from the protocol). Although it has taken little action to reduce GHG emissions, the United States has for many years supported an active research program to better understand the effects of GHGs on climate, human activities, and ecosystems, and to evaluate potential responses.

To provide an indication of the degree to which the United States and EU have undertaken actions to prevent or reduce global climate change, Figure 7.2 presents carbon dioxide emissions from fossil fuel consumption and flaring for the period 1980–2006 (EIA 2008). Separate estimates are provided for the sets of countries comprising the EU-27 and the EU-15. Over the entire period, U.S. emissions have exceeded those from the countries that comprise the EU-27. During the economic recession of the early 1980s, carbon dioxide emissions declined in the United States and Europe. Beginning about 1983, U.S. emissions have grown steadily, at an average rate of about 1.4% per year for the period 1983–2006. In contrast, European emissions remained relatively constant for the next decade before beginning to increase. For the period 1993–2006, the average annual rate of increase in the United States (1.0%) exceeded that in both the EU-15 (0.8%) and the EU-27 (0.4%). In part, the difference in emissions trends reflects stronger economic growth in the United States than in Europe over this period. In addition, it should be noted that recent carbon dioxide emissions are not necessarily the best measure of actions taken to reduce global climate change. First, emissions of methane, nitrous oxide, and other GHGs are also important. More significant, because halting the continuous increase in the greenhouse effect by stabilizing GHG concentrations in the atmosphere will require major reductions in

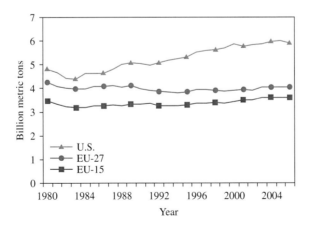

Figure 7.2 *CO_2 Emissions from Fossil Fuel Consumption and Flaring, 1980–2006*

Source: Data based on EIA (2008)

global emissions—by 50% or more—policies that lead to development of massive changes in energy supply and other technologies may be much more beneficial than policies to reduce current emissions.

Explaining the Difference in Response

The cases of stratospheric ozone depletion and global climate change present a stark difference in relative precautionary action between the United States and Europe. What factors might account for the difference?

One factor that has drawn much attention is the secular change in the two regions, with the United States becoming more reluctant to regulate on environmental and economic grounds, and in many cases deregulating formerly regulated industries. Beyond this overall change, however, factors specific to the two issues may be suggested.

In the case of stratospheric ozone depletion, there appear to have been important differences in the markets for CFCs and other ODSs between the United States and Europe. In part because of the earlier bans on use in aerosols in the United States, by the mid-1980s aerosol applications of CFCs accounted for less than half of U.S. production but about three-quarters of European production. For example, Johnson Wax used CFCs in about 5% of its U.S. products but 20% of its UK products. It is not clear why this difference would favor stronger U.S. action, as aerosols appear to have been one of the easier and lower-cost opportunities for reducing CFC use. Perhaps more important was the greater reliance of the European CFC producers on exports. As the U.S. producers had a comparatively small export share, they might have benefited from a cap on production that would have forced the European producers to give up part of their export market in order to satisfy domestic demand. (Ironically, Europeans had proposed a production cap while the United States proposed an aerosol ban.) Because the sources of GHG emissions are numerous and diffuse, these industry-strategy factors appear less relevant to the climate issue.

A second factor that may have contributed to the difference is the stronger tort system in the United States. CFC producers were concerned about the potential for lawsuits alleging that CFCs were defective products because of their environmental harm. The early tobacco lawsuits, seeking to hold tobacco firms liable for lung cancer and other ailments in smokers, were beginning during the period when ODS regulations were developed. Potential tort liability for emissions of carbon dioxide and other GHGs seems much less plausible at present, in part because of the ubiquity of sources.

A third factor is that the American public appears to have been more concerned about the threat of ozone depletion, and more willing to alter their purchasing behavior to reduce the threat, than the European publics. Whether this difference was simply an accident of history or reflects some more deep-seated cause is unclear. With respect to the major health risk—skin cancer—exposure to ultraviolet radiation is likely to be higher in the United States than in Europe because of its more southerly latitude, so perhaps the U.S. population was at greater risk than the European population.

In the response to global climate change, there are significant differences in energy use, geography, and other factors that may help to explain why Europe has adopted the more precautionary path. First, European economies are less carbon-intensive than the United States. In part, this reflects a smaller transportation share due to shorter distances and higher population density, and also a better-developed rail infrastructure (rail travel is often more energy efficient than road and air travel). However, growth in carbon dioxide emissions from the transportation sector is proving to be an obstacle to European compliance with the Kyoto targets. The United States has large reserves of coal that can be mined using relatively low-cost strip mines, while European coal tends to be less accessible and more expensive to mine. Hence reducing coal use would impose higher marginal costs on the United States than on the European economy. Overall, there is greater reliance on nuclear power in Europe than the United States. Coincident with this, there may be less public opposition to nuclear power, so the possibility of even greater reliance on nuclear power to reduce GHG emissions may be less feared in Europe than in the United States.

Political factors are surely important in explaining the difference in response to the threat of global climate change. The European parliamentary systems allow smaller parties greater influence in governments, and Green parties may obtain the environmental ministry. In the United States' winner-take-all system, environmental parties have little influence. In addition, the United States has seen a shift in population and political power to the South and Southwest—regions that are more conservative and more opposed to federal environmental regulation than the Northeast.

References

Andersen, S. O., and K. M. Sarma. 2002. *Protecting the Ozone Layer: The United Nations History*. London: Earthscan.

Barthold, T. A. 1994. Issues in the Design of Environmental Excise Taxes. *Journal of Economic Perspectives* 8:133–151.

Benedick, R. E. 1998. *Ozone Diplomacy: New Directions in Safeguarding the Planet*. enlarged ed. Cambridge, MA: Harvard University Press.

Cagin, S., and P. Dray. 1993. *Between Earth and Sky: How CFCs Changed Our World and Endangered the Ozone Layer*. New York: Pantheon Books.

CARB (California Air Resources Board). 2010. www.arb.ca.gov/cc/cc.htm (accessed April 27, 2010).

Cogan, D. G. 1988. *Stones in a Glass House*. Washington, DC: Investor Responsibility Research Center.

Dotto, L., and H. Schiff. 1978. *The Ozone War*. Garden City, NY: Doubleday and Company.

EEA (European Environmental Agency). 2008. Greenhouse Gas Emission Trends and Projections in Europe 2008: Tracking Progress towards Kyoto Targets. EEA Report No. 5/2008. Copenhagen: EEA.

EIA (U.S. Energy Information Administration). 2006. *International Energy Annual 2006*. Washington, DC: EIA.

———. 2008. http://tonto.eia.doe.gov/cfapps/ipdbproject/iedindex3.cfm?tid=90&pid=44&aid=8&cid=&syid=1980&eyid=2006&unit=MMTCD (accessed July 10, 2010).

European Commission. 2005a. *EU Action against Climate Change: EU Emissions Trading—An Open Scheme Promoting Global Innovation*. KH-70-05-116-EN-C. Brussels: European Commission.

————. 2005b. *Report of the Commission: Progress toward Achieving the Community's Kyoto Target.* COM(2005). Brussels: European Commission.

Farman, J. C., Gardiner B. G., and J. D. Shanklin. 1985. Large Losses of Total Ozone in Antarctica Reveal Seasonal ClO_x/NO_x Interaction. *Nature* 315: 207–210.

Franz, W. E. 1997. The Development of an International Agenda for Climate Change: Connecting Science to Policy. ENRP Discussion Paper E-97-07. Cambridge, MA: Kennedy School of Government, Harvard University.

Hammitt, J. K. 2004. CFCs: A Look across Two Continents. In *Choosing Environmental Policy: Comparing Instruments and Outcomes in the United States and Europe*, edited by W. Harrington, R. D. Morgenstern, and T. Sterner. Washington, DC: Resources for the Future Press, 158–174.

Hammitt, J. K., and Thompson K. M.. 1997. Protecting the Ozone Layer. In *The Greening of Industry: A Risk Management Approach*, edited by J. D. Graham and J. K. Hartwell. Cambridge, MA: Harvard University Press, 43–92.

Hammitt, J. K., K. Wolf, Camm F., W. F. Mooz, Quinn T. H., and A. Bamezai. 1986. *Product Uses and Market Trends for Potential Ozone-Depleting Substances: 1985–2000.* R-3386-EPA. Santa Monica, CA: RAND.

Hoerner, J. A. 1995. Tax Tools for Protecting the Atmosphere: The U.S. Ozone-Depleting Chemicals Tax. In *Green Budget Reform*, edited by R. Gale, S. Barg, and A. Gillies. London: Earthscan, 185–199.

Jaeger, J., and T. O'Riordan. 1996. The History of Climate Change Science and Politics. In *Politics of Climate Change: A European Perspective*, edited by J. Jaeger and T. O'Riordan. London: Routledge.

Kruger, J. A., and W. A. Pizer. 2004. Greenhouse Gas Trading in Europe: The New Grand Policy Experiment. *Environment* 46 (8): 8–23.

Lee, D. 1996. Trading Pollution. In *Ozone Protection in the United States: Elements of Success*, edited by Elizabeth Cook. Washington, DC: World Resources Institute, 31–38.

Maxwell, J. H., and S. L. Weiner. 1993. Green Consciousness or Dollar Diplomacy? The British Response to the Threat of Ozone Depletion. *International Environmental Affairs* 5: 19–41.

Molina, M. J., and F. S. Rowland. 1974. Stratospheric Sink for Chlorofluoromethanes: Chlorine Atom-Catalysed Destruction of Ozone. *Nature* 249: 810–812.

NASA (National Aeronautics and Space Administration). 1988. *Executive Summary: Ozone Trends Panel.* Washington, DC: NASA.

Oberthür, S., and S. Pfahl. 2000. *The Implementation of the Montreal Protocol on Substances That Deplete the Ozone Layer in the European Union.* Final Report to the European Commission, Environment DG and the UK Department of the Environment, Transport, and the Regions. Berlin: Ecologic.

Parson, E. A. 2003. *Protecting the Ozone Layer: Science and Strategy.* New York: Oxford University Press.

Pizer, W. A. 2007. Practical Global Climate Policy. In *Architectures for Agreement: Addressing Global Climate Change in the Post-Kyoto World*, edited by Joseph E. Aldy and Robert N. Stavins. Cambridge: Cambridge University Press.

Revelle, R., and H. E. Suess. 1957. Carbon Dioxide Exchange between Atmosphere and Ocean and the Question of an Increase of Atmospheric CO_2 During the Past Decades. *Tellus* 9:18–27.

RGGI (Regional Greenhouse Gas Initiative). 2010. www.rggi.org (accessed April 27, 2010).

Roan, S. 1989. *Ozone Crisis: The 15-Year Evolution of a Sudden Global Emergency.* New York: John Wiley and Sons.

Weart, S. 2003. *The Discovery of Global Warming.* Cambridge, MA: Harvard University Press. www.aip.org/history/climate (accessed April 25, 2010).

Wexler, P. 1996. New Marching Orders. In *Ozone Protection in the United States: Elements of Success*, edited by E. Cook. Washington, DC: World Resources Institute, 77–86.

White House Office of the Press Secretary. 2004. U.S. Climate Change Policy. Fact Sheet. Washington, DC. November 19. www.state.gov/g/oes/rls/fs/2004/38641.htm (site now discontinued).

CHAPTER 8

The Marine Environment

David Freestone

*T*his chapter will discuss the extent to which the precautionary principle or precaution has been incorporated into legal and policy discussions with regard to the marine environment. Neither space nor time permits a systematic review of all legislative and policy actions relating to the marine environment on both sides of the Atlantic. What is attempted here is, of necessity, a brief description of the evolution of the place of precaution in the marine sphere and an assessment of the extent to which it has taken root within the policy debate globally and in Europe and the United States. The chapter starts by tracing the emergence of precaution, initially in Europe in the debates about the quality of the North Sea, and its rapid spread into other marine environmental sectors including fishery regulation. If there is a uniting theme for the variety of instruments covered, it will be broadly the conservation of marine ecosystems.

What emerges from the evidence seems to be the following: although the United States had taken a number of proactive, arguably precautionary steps itself in relation to the protection of the marine environment, it was taken aback by the rapid emergence of precaution within the context of first European and then global marine environment debates, which were aggressively pressed by the nongovernmental organization (NGO) community. Within the International Maritime Organization (IMO) and at other international fora at which questions were raised in the late 1980s and early 1990s, the United States seemed far less comfortable than the Europeans with the legal and political implications of adopting precaution. A symbolic symptom of this suspicion was the fact that the U.S. State Department resisted—and continues to resist—the use of the term "precautionary principle," preferring the term "precautionary approach." At the IMO, the United States seemed to be happier endorsing specific actions that could be seen to be precautionary—rather than endorsing the principle per se. At the IMO and a number of other marine environmental fora, such as the Wider Caribbean Cartagena Convention, the United States pressed for further details of what was meant by the precautionary principle before agreeing to it in a muted form. In 1996, the IMO parties finalized a protocol to the 1972 London Convention (London Protocol 1996) that gives precaution a much more central role (see its General Obligations, Article 3.1). Although the United States signed the protocol, 14 years later it has still to ratify.

The year 1992 seems to have been something of a turning point. In the same year that the precautionary principle became a principle of European Community environmental law through its incorporation in the Maastricht Treaty on European Union, the United States had argued strongly for the qualifications that are included in the final version of Principle 15 in the Rio Declaration, including the use of the word "approach" rather than "principle." It did, however, sign the declaration without making a formal reservation to Principle 15, as it had to other provisions (UN 1992, paragraph 16).[1]

However, after the conclusion of the 1992 UNCED Declaration and the adoption of Agenda 21, Chapter 17, on the Protection of the Oceans,[2] which called for "approaches that are integrated in content and are precautionary and anticipatory in ambit," an interesting reversal in the respective positions of the EU and the United States took place. Chapter 17 (paragraph 50) also called for "an intergovernmental conference ... to promote the effective implementation of the UN Convention on the Law of the Sea on straddling fish stocks and highly migratory fish stocks." Acting in response to this mandate in Agenda 21, the UN Food and Agriculture Organization (FAO) convened a "technical consultation" in Rome in September 1992 (FAO 1992a, 1992b). From the record of the 1992 Technical Consultation, it seems that strong political divisions emerged between coastal states led by Canada and New Zealand with the strong backing of the Latin American states and the distant water fishing nations, notably Japan and the EU. The United States was much more comfortable espousing a precautionary approach to fisheries conservation and management, and this time it was the EU and some of its members that had reservations about the extension of this approach to the management of capture fisheries.

The precautionary approach and the ecosystem approach to the conservation and management of straddling fish stocks and highly migratory fish stocks were both reflected in the 1995 UN Fish Stocks Agreement, which also contains in Annex II the very first guidelines for the application of a precautionary methodology for capture fisheries management. FAO invested considerable resources in fleshing out this approach (see FAO 1996a, 1996b; and Garcia 1994, 99).[3] The United States has been a much more enthusiastic supporter of the precautionary approach to the

---

[1] For example, Principles 3,7,12, and 23.

[2] The full title is Protection of the Ocean, All Kinds of Seas, Including Enclosed and Semi-Enclosed Seas, and Coastal Areas, and the Protection, Rational Use, and Development of their Living Resources.

[3] That is also contained in its 1995 Code of Conduct for Responsible Fisheries.

conservation and management of capture fisheries than the EU—despite the fact that fisheries is an area of exclusive competence under the EC Treaty, with the precautionary principle a guiding principle of the Maastricht Treaty (Article 130(r), which also requires that environmental protection be integrated into the implementation of other Community policies). The 1996 U.S. Sustainable Fisheries Act adopted precautionary methodology as "the core of the solution to reverse the current state of U.S. fisheries" (Matlock 1998). This approach is continued by the Magnuson-Stevens Reauthorization Act (MSRA) of 2006. It is more difficult to argue that the European Common Fisheries Policy—which has many of the same tools available—has in the past actually been conducted in a precautionary way (Howarth 2008).

Another important dimension to this situation is that not all aspects of marine environmental protection are within the central legislative competence of the EC or the federal authorities of the United States. Hence there are often differences of opinion and approach among the EU, the U.S. federal authorities, and their respective Member States. This will be discussed further below.

History and Evolution of Precaution in Relation to the Marine Environment

It is well known that the origins of the precautionary principle, or the principle of precautionary action, appear to lie in concepts of national law, notably the German law *Vorsorgeprinzip*, which some regard as the most important principle of German environmental law (von Moltke 1988; Gündling 1990, 23; Nollkaemper 1991, 107). The origins and development of the precautionary principle have been well documented and analyzed elsewhere (Ehlers 1990, 3; Gündling 1990, 23; Freestone 1991, 21; Freestone and Hey 1996, 3; Trouwborst 2002). It seems first to have come to some prominence in the international arena some three decades ago, when concern was gathering over the state of the shallow Wadden Sea bordering the North Sea coast of the Netherlands, Germany, and Denmark. In 1980, the influential German Council of Experts on Environmental Matters (*Rat von Sachverständigen für Umweltfragen*), in its report on environmental problems in the North Sea (*Umweltprobleme der Nordsee*), described a precautionary approach as follows:

> A successful environmental policy has to be guided by the principle of precautionary action. ... Mechanisms which determine the limits of environmental capacity are still largely unknown. Environmental policy therefore has to prevent adverse ecological developments, without having the opportunity to be guided only by already established impacts on the marine environment when specific measures have to be taken. ... Three levels of measures are conceivable:
>
> - by developing a preventive defence to protect the marine ecological system against ecological dangers;
> - by taking emission-related measures;

- by prohibiting operations seriously affecting the natural environment especially the introduction of substances alien to the environment. (reproduced in Freestone 1991, 21)

This innovative formulation of the principle of precautionary action goes beyond simple preventive action, encompassing positive actions to prevent damage to natural systems (Gündling 1990, 26).[4]

The first explicit appearance of the principle in an international instrument is in the Declarations of the International Conferences on the Protection of the North Sea. As a result of the cooperative work done by Denmark, Germany, and the Netherlands in the Wadden Sea, the German government invited ministers from the North Sea coastal states to the First International Conference on the Protection of the North Sea, which it convened and hosted in Bremen in 1984. Ehlers reports that the German government took the following view:

> One should not wait until large scale harmful effects had been proved. On the contrary, with the application of the precautionary principle, all measures should be taken as early as possible within the framework of the co-operation of all the neighbouring states in order to avoid irreversible damage.[5] (Ehlers 1990, 5)

The London Declaration issued after the Second International North Sea Conference (INSC) in November 1987 contains the first explicit reference to the precautionary approach and the principle of precautionary action. The participating states declared that they accepted that

> VII … in order to protect the North Sea from possible damaging effects of the most dangerous substances, a precautionary approach is necessary which may require action to control inputs of such substances even before a causal link has been established by absolutely clear scientific evidence. (full text reproduced in Freestone and IJlstra 1991, 41)

Putting this principle into effect in relation to inputs via rivers and estuaries of "dangerous substances" and also in relation to dumping and incineration at sea, the participants then agreed to

---

[4] Gündling offers the following understanding of precautionary action: "… a more stringent form of preventive environmental policy. It is more than repair of damage or prevention of risks. Precautionary action requires reduction and prevention of environmental impacts irrespective of the existence of risks. This must not be understood in the sense that aspects of risks are not relevant; the crucial point is that environmental impacts are reduced or prevented before the threshold of risks is reached. This means that precautionary action must be taken to ensure that the loading capacity of the environment is not exhausted, and it also requires action if risks are not yet certain but only probable, or, even less, not excluded."

[5] Gündling says that the adoption of the precautionary principle was a major German negotiating goal at the Bremen meeting, and that the importance the German delegation attached to this may account for the fact that although the term *Vorsorgemassnahmen* appears in the German text, the English text talks only of "timely preventive measures" (1990, 61–89).

XVI ... 1. accept the principle of safeguarding the marine ecosystem of the North Sea by reducing polluting emissions of substances that are persistent, toxic and liable to bioaccumulate at source by the use of the best available technology and other appropriate measures. This applies especially when there is reason to assume that certain damage or harmful effects on the living resources of the sea are likely to be caused by such substances, even where there is no scientific evidence to prove a causal link between emissions and effects ("the principle of precautionary action"). (Freestone and IJlstra 1991, 44)

In implementation of these policy objectives agreed by the London Conference, the contracting states to the Paris Convention for the Prevention of Marine Pollution from Land-Based Sources, the relevant competent regional organization, passed a Recommendation on June 22, 1989, on the Principle of Precautionary Action (Freestone 1991, 152), which, after making preambular reference to paragraph XVI.1 of the 1987 London Declaration, reproduced the text of that paragraph virtually verbatim.

At that same meeting, the Paris Convention parties also passed another Recommendation (89/2) on the use of the best available technology, by which they gave more obvious effect to the general principle when they agreed that

the programmes and measures adopted under Article 4 and 5 of the Convention and especially the application of the best available technology should be applied in such a way as to prevent pollution in Convention waters, any increase in pollution in other sea areas or in other parts of the environment, or any increased risk to the health of industrial workers or the general population. (Freestone and IJlstra 1991, 153)

The Recommendation goes on to require that

[i]n determining whether a set of processes, facilities and methods of operation constitute the best available technology in general or individual cases, special consideration is given to ... the precautionary principle. (Freestone and IJlstra 1991, 153)

By contrast, the undertakings of the London Declaration relating to dumping and incineration of waste were implemented most rigorously by the competent regional body, the Oslo Commission, which at its Fifteenth Meeting in Dublin adopted on June 14, 1989, a binding Decision 89/1 on the reduction and cessation of dumping industrial wastes at sea (Freestone 1991, 119). The contracting parties agreed that "the dumping of industrial wastes in the North Sea shall cease by December 31, 1989, and in other parts of the Convention waters by December 31, 1995, except for inert materials of natural origin, and except for those industrial wastes for which it can be shown to the Commission through the Prior Justification Procedure (PJP) both that there are no practical alternatives on land and that the materials cause no harm in the marine environment." The Prior Justification Procedure is a most rigorous application of the precautionary principle, in that it places the burden of proof on the applicant to demonstrate that no harm will be caused to the marine environment.

At its meeting in The Hague in March 1990, the Third International Conference on the North Sea was even more explicit in its endorsement of the precautionary principle. In the Preamble to The Hague Declaration, the participants record that they adopted a number of premises for their future work, including a declaration that they will continue to apply the precautionary principle, that is to take action to avoid potentially damaging impacts of substances that are persistent, toxic, and liable to bioaccumulate even where there is no scientific evidence to prove a causal link between emissions and effects. (Freestone and IJlstra 1991, 5)

Because this acceptance of the principle constitutes part of the general chapeau of the Preamble, it applies to all areas of the work of the INSC. This is clearly a much wider acceptance of the general principle than in the London Declaration, in which it was explicitly accepted only in relation to inputs of such substances through rivers and estuaries. Although it still applies to such inputs—indeed, the requirements are further strengthened—as well as to dumping, the participants have in addition explicitly applied it to reduction of nutrient inputs (Freestone and IJlstra 1991, 8) and to pollution from ships, under which head the participants "agree that the application of the precautionary principle requires the application of the Best Available Technology in order to minimise discharges of waste residues" (Freestone and IJlstra 1991, 12).

The significance of the adoption of this approach to marine dumping by the littoral States of the North Sea and subsequently by the parties to the regional Oslo Convention was not ignored by the parties to the global 1972 London Convention on the Prevention of Marine Pollution by Dumping of Wastes and Other Matter (the London Convention), to which the United States is a party. It has been observed that the way that the Convention has been implemented reflects a "precautionary approach" (London Convention 1990, 22–30).

At the Thirteenth Consultative Meeting of the Parties to that Convention held at IMO headquarters in London in October/November 1990, a discussion of the precautionary approach took place within the context of a report from the Scientific Group of Experts on the Annexes to the Convention and New Assessment Procedures (London Convention 1990, 9–17). The group took the view that a precautionary approach had several informal meanings—ranging from waste management strategies to prohibition of disposal at sea of most waste materials (London Convention 1990, 15). Papers were submitted to the meeting on this issue, and although some delegations considered that the London Convention already reflected a precautionary approach, other delegations felt that a clear definition of the precautionary approach was necessary and should become part of the legal framework of the Convention. The secretariat was mandated to prepare a detailed working paper on all aspects of the precautionary approach for discussion at the Fourteenth Meeting in November/December 1991 (London Convention 1990, 16, paragraph 3.31). It was further pointed out that if a definition of a precautionary approach were developed, it would be important to understand both how it would be used and what its status would be with regard to the Articles, Annexes, and Guidelines of the London Convention. Nevertheless, the meeting went on to adopt by consensus a resolution to present to the March 1991 Preparatory Committee Meeting in Geneva for the forthcoming 1992 United Nations Conference on the Environment and Development (UNCED). The parties questioned the adequacy of traditional scientific approaches to assessing the impact of ocean dumping—the so-called "assimilative capacity" concept—and, using terminology that has been regarded as an endorsement of the principle, called for intensified efforts to adopt a precautionary approach to disposal of wastes in the ocean (Freestone 1991, 26).

Eventually, Resolution LDC 44/14, On the Application of the Precautionary Approach to Environmental Protection within the Framework of the London Dumping Convention, was adopted in December 1991 (see Hey 1991a, 244–254, and 1991b, 14). Although the United States did not oppose it, it had argued against the resolution on the basis that "[i]t is largely because the Convention employs such an approach that it is unclear how the express adoption of a precautionary approach would change decisionmaking under the LDC" (see FAO 1996a, 1996b; and Garcia 1994, 99).[6]

Within the United Nations Environment Programme (UNEP), the principle was explicitly accepted at the Fifteenth Session of the Governing Council on May 25, 1989. By Decision 15/27 on the precautionary approach to marine pollution, including waste-dumping at sea, the Governing Council declared itself to be aware of the threat to the marine environment from a variety of polluting sources and of the need to protect marine biological diversity. It recognized that "waiting for scientific proof regarding the impact of pollutants discharged into the marine environment may result in irreversible damage to the marine environment and in human suffering" and was "aware that policies allowing uncontrolled discharges of pollutants continue to pose unknown risks." The Council then took note of the decision of the 1987 London Conference on the Protection of the North Sea to adopt the precautionary principle; it recommended

> 1. ... that all governments adopt the "principle of precautionary action" as the basis for their policy with regard to the prevention and elimination of marine pollution ...

and further urged

> 3. ... the international community to work actively towards the complete elimination of the practice of dumping of pollutants liable to endanger the marine environment. (Freestone 1991, 27)

Following on from this decision, at the Sixth Meeting of the Contracting Parties to the Barcelona Convention for the Protection of the Mediterranean Sea against Pollution, held in Athens in October 1989, the parties, when considering the implementation of the Barcelona Convention and its Protocol on dumping, recommended the following:

> 6. Recalling the decision of the Governing Council of UNEP 15/27 on [the] precautionary approach, agree to fully adopt the principle of precautionary approach regarding the prevention and elimination of contamination in the Mediterranean Sea area and request the secretariat to review the Dumping Protocol in the light of the

---

[6] A further example is the role of the United States in the IMO debates over Particularly Sensitive Sea Areas. For reports of three Expert Meetings, see Gjerde and Freestone (1994, 431–577).

principle of precautionary approach in order to identify any necessary amendments to the protocol. (Barcelona Convention, 1995)[7]

In addition, the participants at the October 1989 Nordic Council Conference on Pollution of the Seas in Copenhagen agreed on

the need for an effective precautionary approach, with that important principle intended to safeguard the marine ecosystem by, among other things, eliminating and preventing pollution emissions where there is reason to believe that damage or harmful effects are likely to be caused, even where there is inadequate or inconclusive scientific evidence to prove a causal link between emissions and effects ...

and recommended

that all states accept the Precautionary Principle and assume responsibility for their own waste disposal. (Freestone 1991, 27)

In January 1990, at the Second Meeting of the Parties to the 1983 Cartagena Convention for the Protection and Development of the Marine Environment of the Wider Caribbean Region, held in Kingston, Jamaica, Mexico proposed that the precautionary principle be adopted as an operational principle for all the decisions of the parties. The proposal was not adopted after opposition by the United States, but the meeting did instruct the secretariat to produce a paper detailing the principle for consideration at the following meeting of the parties scheduled for 1992 (UNEP 1990, 6). This was prepared and the resolution was agreed at that next meeting (UNEP 1992, 5, 20).

In his November 1990 Report on the Law of the Sea, the UN secretary general expressly recognized the "considerable significance" of the precautionary principle for future approaches to marine environmental protection and resource conservation, reporting that the principle had been endorsed "by virtually all recent international forums" (UN 1990 20, paragraph 60).[8]

So, within IMO and at other new fora at which the precautionary principle was raised in the late 1980s and early 1990s, the United States seems to have been far less comfortable with the legal as well as political implications of adopting precaution than the Europeans. As noted in the introductory paragraphs of this chapter, the U.S. State Department continues to prefer the term "precautionary approach" to the term "precautionary principle." When the United States has endorsed actions that some might label precautionary, it did not endorse the principle per se but pressed for details about the meaning of the phrase before agreeing to it in a muted form.

---

[7] The revised text of the Barcelona Convention amended in 1995 now explicitly endorses the precautionary principle in its General Obligations, Article 3.1.

[8] Examples of such documents include the Odessa Declaration 1993, 235–236 (Hey and Mee 1994, 215–220, 72ff); UNFCCC 1992, 848; CBD 1992, 818; Helsinki Convention 1992a, 215 (with commentary by Ehlers 1993, 191); Helsinki Convention 1992b, 1312; Maastricht Treaty 1992, 247; and Paris Convention 1992, 50–76. For further information, see Hey et al. 1993, 1–49, and of course, the 1995 UN Fish Stocks Agreement itself.

Precaution and the Fisheries Sector

In relation to the application of precaution to capture fisheries, however, the position seems to have been rather different. It can be argued that the United States has been a much more enthusiastic supporter of the precautionary approach to the conservation and management of capture fisheries than the EU—despite the fact that fisheries is an area of exclusive competence under the EC Treaty, and the precautionary principle is a guiding principle of that treaty.

The evolution of the 200-nautical-mile Exclusive Economic Zone (EEZ), as now recognized in the 1982 UN Law of the Sea Convention (LOSC), has shifted the balance of fisheries conservation and management to coastal states. The majority of marine living resources now come within EEZs. Because of the commensurate shrinking of high seas resources, it is difficult to draw too many detailed parallels from the treaty practice relating to high seas fisheries that preceded the Third UN Conference on the Law of the Sea (UNCLOS III, 1973–1982)—much of which reflected disputes between coastal and distant water fishing states. Nevertheless, a number of such treaties give a significant place to conservation of high seas living resources.

Of particular interest is the *abstention principle*—a creature of the 1952 International Convention for High Seas Fisheries of the North Pacific Ocean (205 UNTS 80). The Convention has been much criticized as a vehicle for perpetuating the notion that "first comers had a special claim to fishery resources already being harvested at Maximum Sustainable Yield (MSY)" (Scheiber 1989, 23), but at the same time, it did establish a system ostensibly based on conservation criteria. The North Pacific Commission, established by the treaty, was one of the few international fisheries bodies given the power to monitor designated stocks, to decide on conservation measures, and to allocate total allowable catches (TACs) for them (Koers 1973, 97). Underpinning the regime was the concept that one or two of the parties would abstain from fishing stocks of designated species[9] for as long as the Commission was able to determine on a yearly basis, that the following three conditions were fulfilled:

(i) Evidence based on scientific research indicates that more extensive exploitation of the stock will not provide a substantial increase in yield which can be sustained year after year;

(ii) That the exploitation of the stock is limited or otherwise regulated through legal measures by each Party which is substantially engaged in its exploitation, for the purpose of maintaining or increasing its maximum sustained productivity; such limitations and regulations being in accordance with conservation programmes based upon scientific research; and

---

[9] The Annex provided in paragraph 1 that the Japanese would abstain from fishing for halibut, herring, and salmon in designated high seas areas in return for Canada and the United States "continu[ing] to carry out necessary conservation measures." In paragraph 2, Japan and Canada agreed to abstain from fishing for salmon in designated waters, also in return for the United States continuing necessary conservation measures.

(ii) The stock is the subject of extensive scientific study designed to discover whether the stock is being fully utilised and the conditions necessary for maintaining its maximum sustained productivity. (North Pacific Treaty 1952, Article IV(1))

According to these same criteria, the Commission was also empowered to determine whether or not new stocks qualified for abstention (North Pacific Treaty 1952, Article III(1)(b)).

The wider significance of the abstention doctrine—for which the United States sought, for a time, to gain support from the world community to elevate it to the status of general law—is that its implementation purported to be science-driven. In order for stocks to be released from abstention, evidence "based on scientific research" had to be available (North Pacific Treaty 1952, Article IV(1)(b)(i)).[10] Hence the burden of proof was on the party seeking to enter the fishery and thus in favor of conservation; in the absence of such scientific evidence, no further exploitation was possible.

Virtually all high seas fishery treaties promote conservation as an objective, but no others appear to elevate the status of scientific evidence to the position it was given in the 1952 North Pacific Treaty. For example, the 1966 International Convention for the Conservation of Atlantic Tunas (ICCAT 1966) simply empowers the Commission "on the basis of scientific evidence" to make recommendations designed to maintain populations at levels that will permit maximum sustainable catches (Article VIII(1)(a)).[11] The Inter-American Tropical Tuna Commission (IATTC) only had power to recommend TACs on the basis of scientific research (IATTC 1949; see also Koers 1973, 95).

The International Whaling Commission (IWC), established by the 1946 International Convention for the Regulation of Whaling (Whaling Convention 1946; see Birnie 1985, 689), has developed a system of classification of whale stocks based on scientific findings and the advice of the Scientific Committee (Birnie 1985, 713). However, the 1982 decision of the Commission to impose an indefinite "moratorium" on commercial whaling (Lyster 1985, 19)[12] has made conservation the primary objective of the IWC. In fact, although there was evidence of population decline verging on endangered status for some larger cetacean species, for some smaller species—including, arguably, the minke—the moratorium may be seen as an operational precautionary measure. In the early 1990s, the IWC devised new procedures that incorporate precautionary catch limits for some species (see Cooke and Earle 1993, 252).

There is also evidence that in the interpretation of the general obligation to conserve and manage high seas living resources, precautionary thinking is being more widely

---

[10] To maintain the abstention system in place, the beneficiary had to maintain a conservation program "based on scientific research" (North Pacific Treaty 1952, Article IV(1)(b)(ii)).

[11] In 1999, ICCAT parties explicitly adopted the precautionary approach in decision ICCAT COMSCRS/99/11 (Cooney 2004, 23).

[12] This was done by amending the schedule under Article V of the Convention so that "catch limits for the killing for commercial purposes of whales from all stocks for the 1986 coastal and 1985–1986 pelagic seasons and thereafter shall be zero."

accepted as the proper course to adopt in the absence of adequate scientific evidence. For example, the Commission for the Conservation of Antarctic Marine Living Resources (CCAMLR), established under the 1980 Convention (Canberra Convention 1980, 837) to coordinate research on Antarctic marine living resources and to adopt appropriate conservation and management measures,[13] has developed "precautionary" catch limits on fish stocks within its jurisdiction.[14]

Obvious precautionary thinking can also be seen in the 1989 General Assembly Resolution on Driftnet Fishing. Resolution 44/225, entitled Large Scale Pelagic Driftnet Fishing and Its Impact on the Living Marine Resources of the World's Oceans and Seas,[15] calls on "all those involved in large scale pelagic driftnetting to cooperate in the enhanced collection and sharing of statistically sound scientific data" (FAO 1991, Annex 2). The Resolution recommends a number of measures to eliminate the practice, including moratoria on all large scale driftnet fishing on the high seas by June 30, 1992. That measure, however, is on the understanding that it

> will not be imposed on a region or, if implemented can be lifted, should effective conservation and management measures be taken based upon statistically sound analysis … to prevent the unacceptable impact of such fishing practices on that region and to ensure the conservation of the living marine resources of that region.

This measure is precautionary in the sense that it proposes action to address a serious threat to the environment. While there may have been some scientific uncertainty as to the impacts of driftnet fishing (see, e.g., the arguments adduced by Professor Kazuo Sumi 1991), the Resolution can also be seen to be precautionary because it shifts the burden of proof onto those who seek to continue the practice to demonstrate—using "statistically sound analysis"—that measures have been taken "to prevent the unacceptable impact" of driftnet fishing and to "ensure conservation of the living marine resources." In this sense, its effect is not dissimilar from the abstention principle discussed above, in that it shifts the burden of proof, and also the standards of proof (i.e., "using statistically sound analysis"), in favor of conservation.

---

[13] According to Churchill (1987, 188), this has been one of the most advanced environmental management conventions because of its ecosystem approach. Its powers include the establishment of quantities to be harvested, designation of protected species, and closed seasons, as well as regulation of gear.

[14] In 1991, it established a precautionary catch limitation on *Euphausia superba* (CCAMLR 1991), and a working group of the Scientific Committee was established to develop "precautionary measures on krill fishing" in order to prevent the "unregulated expansion of the fishery at a time when the information available for predicting potential yield [was] very limited" (CCAMLR 1991). The impetus for that work was the Statement at the Ninth Meeting of the Commission by the USSR, Japan, and Korea that they were not in principle opposed to the idea of a precautionary limit of krill fishing, but that "the quantitative basis for such a precautionary limit on fishing should have scientific justification based on assessments performed by the Scientific Committee" (CCAMLR 1991).

[15] This also reproduces the text of other UNGA resolutions and regional action against driftnets, including the Wellington Convention.

Of particular relevance to the issue is the 1994 Convention on the Conservation and Management of Pollock Resources in the Central Bering Sea (CCMPR 1994, 127).[16] This highly innovative convention provides that the States party will meet annually to decide allowable harvest levels and to establish catch quotas. It also endorses a precautionary approach to fishery conservation in that no fishing will be allowed unless Aleutian Basin pollock biomass is determined to exceed 1.67 million metric tons (Dunlap 1995, 114; CCMPR 1994, 134). This determination is to be made by parties jointly or, failing this, by the United States and Russian Federation jointly and, failing this, by the United States unilaterally.

At UNCED in 1992, the provisions relating to straddling fish stocks and highly migratory fish stocks in paragraph 17.50 of Agenda 21 were among the last provisions to be agreed. This committed parties to convening, as soon as possible, an intergovernmental conference on straddling fish stocks and highly migratory fish stocks.[17] The FAO Technical Consultation was to prepare technical papers for the conference (FAO 1992a, 1992b), and this initiated discussions on the role of precaution in high seas fisheries management. After vigorous debate (Hewison 1996, 301–332),[18] and despite the FAO's position that the precautionary approach to fisheries management was compatible with the UN Law of the Sea Convention, the Draft Report of the Technical Consultation (FAO 1992b) advocated a more modest interpretation of the precautionary approach, reflecting the concerns of fishing states. Some were clearly concerned that a wholesale endorsement of the precautionary principle might entail the suspension of many fishing operations until they could be shown to be sustainable—something that had been advocated by NGOs (Hewison 1996, 310).[19] Although hedged by caveats, the report did show that the Consultation had agreed that fisheries should be managed in a cautious manner, that overharvesting of renewable resources can have serious consequences on fisheries populations and on ocean ecosystems, and that precautionary management might include, but does not necessarily require, a moratorium on fishing. It also accepted that management decisions should be based on the best scientific information, as provided for in the 1982

---

[16] The Convention was signed in Washington, DC, on June 16, 1994, by China, Korea, Russia, and the United States; Japan and Poland signed on August 4 and 25, respectively. For background and commentary, see also Dunlap (1995, 114–126).

[17] The objective set was that the conference, "drawing *inter alia* on scientific and technical studies by FAO, should identify and assess existing problems relating to the conservation and management of such fish stocks, and consider means of improving cooperation on fisheries among States, and formulate appropriate recommendations." This was then implemented by UN General Assembly Resolution 47/192 on the UN Conference on Straddling Fish Stocks and Highly Migratory Fish Stocks (UNGA 1992). For a general discussion of the issues involved, see Kwiatkowska (1993, 327–358).

[18] For example, Japan, Korea, Norway, and the Russian Federation expressed "grave reservations over the use of … precaution … as a tool for fisheries management"; Sweden, on the contrary, pointed out it had been endorsed and adopted at UNCED.

[19] For example, Hewison reports that Greenpeace recommended rejecting the Draft Report because it did not reflect evolving state practice.

Convention, and that precautionary management measures taken in the absence of sufficient scientific data should be revised or revoked as appropriate when new information becomes available (FAO 1992b, 65–67).

It seems that strong political divisions emerged between, on the one hand, coastal states, led by Canada and New Zealand with strong backing from Latin American states, and, on the other hand, distant water fishing nations, notably Japan and the EU. It also seems that the United States was much more comfortable espousing a precautionary approach to fisheries conservation and management; this time it was the EU and some of its members that had reservations about extending this approach to the management of capture fisheries.

The Intergovernmental Conference, at which both the United States and the EU were very active, resulted in the Agreement for the Implementation of the Provisions of the United Nations Convention on the Law of the Sea of December 10, 1982, Relating to the Conservation and Management of Straddling Fish Stocks and Highly Migratory Fish Stocks (UN Fish Stocks Agreement 1995). Preambular recital number seven lists the first and most significant statement of the environmental importance of international fisheries issues. It declares an aspiration to improve upon previous fisheries management treaties by recognizing the independent need to protect the marine environment through the protection of its biodiversity, maintenance of the integrity of marine ecosystems, and the minimization of the risk of long-term or irreversible effects of fishing operations. This statement, albeit preambular, means that the 1995 Agreement is the first global fisheries agreement[20] to recognize at a primary level the environmental significance of fishing activities: not simply as an issue to take into account when, for example, calculating total allowable catch (TAC), but as an *independent* issue in its own right (Freestone and Makuch 1997, 24). The implications of the recognition of this key concept are worked out in the detail of the Agreement in Article 6, which expressly espouses a "precautionary approach"—note the United States influence on the terminology—and in Annex II, which sets out an innovative precautionary methodology.[21] The agreement also reflects international concerns—led by the United States—against environmentally harmful bycatch, which can also be characterized as precautionary. These concerns—directed primarily at the use of nonselective gear—were manifested in the international and regional action against

---

[20] One could note that the 1980 Canberra Convention on the Conservation of Antarctic Marine Living Resources (Canberra Convention 1982, 841) envisages "rational use" and has been described as a "model of the ecological approach" per Kiss and Shelton (2004, 645). However, it is not strictly a fisheries agreement.

[21] Guidelines for Application of Precautionary Reference Points in Conservation and Management of Straddling Fish Stocks and Highly Migratory Fish Stocks are set out in Annex II of the Agreement. These feature strategies that prescribe biological limits on harvesting; allow only a limited risk of exceeding harvesting limits; and address situations where there is insufficient information on specific species by permitting provisional reference points. In the event that precautionary reference points are approached, they must not be exceeded. If they are exceeded, then States must take immediate remedial action pursuant to Annex II of the Agreement.

driftnetting[22] and in a number of national initiatives. The best known of the national initiatives are the U.S. actions against turtle and dolphin bycatch.[23] These concerns are also reflected in the 1995 Agreement (UN Fish Stocks Agreement 1995, Article 5f). The conclusion of the 1995 FAO Code of Conduct,[24] which of course covers a much wider spread of issues than simply the regulation of straddling and high migratory fish stocks, was delayed until the 1995 Agreement had itself been finalized and signed. This mandates the use of the precautionary approach, the theoretical bases for and methodology for implementation of which the FAO has also developed (see, e.g., Garcia 1994, 99; FAO 1996a, 1996b).

Since the finalization of the UN Fish Stocks Agreement, several developments are worth noting. The newly established Regional Fisheries Management Organizations (RFMOs)—the Commissions set up by the 2000 Convention for the Conservation and Management of Highly Migratory Fish Stocks in the Western and Central Pacific Ocean (WCPFC 2000) and the 2001 South-East Atlantic Fisheries Organization (SEAFO 2001)—have constituent instruments that oblige them to address the new ecosystem maintenance and conservation of biological diversity concerns introduced by the 1992 UNCED, including precaution. Some preexisting RFMOs have enacted new treaties or have incorporated these concerns retrospectively by other means. These include the International Commission for the Conservation of Atlantic Tunas (by decision COMSCRS/99/11), the North Atlantic Fisheries Organization, and the International Pacific Halibut Commission (IPHC 1999 Catch Recommendations) (Cooney 2004, 23). In 2005, for example, the parties to the North East Atlantic Fisheries Commission (NEAFC) adopted the London Declaration on the "Interpretation and Implementation of the Convention," whose paragraph 2(b) requires the Commission to *inter alia* "apply the precautionary principle."

---

[22] See *supra*.

[23] Subject to litigation in the WTO. An enormous literature on this exists, including the famous tuna/dolphin cases discussed by Benedict Kingsbury (1994, 1–40). For a discussion of the wider implications of bycatch, see Cullet and Kameri-Mbote (1996, 333–348).

[24] The Open-Ended Technical Committee established by FAO to conclude the Code finalized its work in September; after linguistic harmonization the text was finalized as FAO Doc C95/20 (Rev. 1) and submitted to the 28th session of the FAO Conference in October for adoption. The final text is dated November 1 (Edeson 1996, 233–238). The Code covers all fishery operations—not simply high seas fisheries—and draws on the provisions of the Compliance Agreement (above) as well as the 1995 UN Fish Stocks Agreement. It is also designed to be consistent with the 1982 LOSC, but also to take into account the 1992 Cancun Declaration, the 1992 Rio Declaration, Chapter 17 of Agenda 21, the conclusions and recommendations of the 1992 FAO Technical Consultation on High Sea Fishing, as well as other relevant instruments. Key articles cover General Principles, followed by Fisheries Management, Fisheries Operations, Aquaculture Development, Integration of Fisheries into Coastal Area Management, Post-harvest Practices and Trade, and Fisheries Research.

CBD Jakarta Mandate on Marine Biological Diversity

Parallel developments took place in the context of the Convention on Biological Diversity (CBD), signed at the Rio de Janeiro UNCED.[25] Although the United States is not a party to the Convention, it habitually sends large delegations that are very active lobbyists in the halls. Article 2 of the Convention defines "biological diversity" to include the "variability among living organisms from all sources including ... marine and other aquatic ecosystems and the ecological complexes of which they are a part." However, it goes on to specify that "this includes diversity within species, between species, and of ecosystems." Nowhere else in the Convention is specific reference made to the protection of marine biodiversity[26]—although Article 22 (2) does specifically provide that contracting States "shall implement the Convention with respect to the marine environment consistently with the rights and obligations of States under the law of the sea."[27] (On the State Department view on this issue, see Chandler 1993, 141.) In fact, the whole approach of the Convention—directed as it is to finance and biotechnology issues—presumes a concept of national ownership of biological resources based on assumptions about endemic species that many argue (e.g., Scully 1992, 22–25) bypasses some of the key issues of marine biodiversity conservation.

It seemed paradoxical that, although the particular problems of conservation of many marine creatures, particularly pelagic creatures, make them particularly suitable to regulation at an international level under a treaty on biological diversity, in fact the most important discussions concerning conservation of marine biological diversity took place in the context of other fora such as the straddling fish stocks negotiations (Freestone and Hey 1996). This issue was in fact taken up within the context of the CBD by the Subsidiary Body on Scientific, Technical, and Technological Advice (SBSTTA), established pursuant to Article 25 of the Convention, which in September 1995 adopted a recommendation on the issue of conservation of coastal and marine biodiversity.[28] The Second Conference of the Parties to the CBD meeting in Jakarta in November 1995 endorsed, with some modifications, the SBSTTA recommendation as its Decision II/10. That decision, together with the SBSTTA Recommendation on which it is based, has been called the "Jakarta Mandate."

---

[25] The CBD, designed to address the threat of extinction of species throughout the world, has three principal objectives: conservation of biological diversity, the sustainable use of its components, and fair and equitable sharing of the benefits arising out of the utilization of genetic resources.

[26] This was one of the reasons why the United States initially refused to become a party; see Scully (1992, 22–25). Scully suggests that in relation to marine biodiversity the Convention is "poorly drafted and a weak instrument" and that "one could read its obligations as a setback" (1992, 148).

[27] Although it is apparent from this paper by a U.S. State Department legal adviser that U.S. concerns in introducing Article 22(2) were primarily related to issues such a freedom of navigation, it can be argued that this provision incorporates the environmental principles of customary international law of the sea (codified in the 1982 Convention) into the 1992 Treaty.

[28] For a further discussion see Hey (1996, 485) and also Goote (1997, 377–389), which reproduces the text of the Annex to the SBSTTA Recommendation as an appendix.

Decision II/10 of the Conference of the Parties recognizes the importance of regional and subregional fisheries conservation measures and emphasizes the importance of ensuring that fisheries management decisions are based upon, *inter alia*, the precautionary principle (Paragraph 12(a)).

Regulation of Coastal and Fisheries Resources in the EU and United States

As the introduction to this volume points out, there is a tendency for us to restrict our comparisons between the European Union and the United States to Union or federal level, rather than looking also at the regulatory polices of their respective Member States. For the marine environment, this is a particularly important distinction. Not all aspects of marine environmental protection are within the central legislative competence of the EU or the federal authorities of the United States. Hence there are often differences of opinion and approach among the EU, the U.S. federal authorities, and their respective Member States.

On the EU side, Article 2B of the new Treaty of Lisbon, which entered into force on December 1, 2009 (C306/42 OJEU) recognizes the "exclusive competence" of the Union for "the conservation of marine biological resources under the common fisheries policy." This continues earlier EU practice. The degree of quasi-federal "exclusivity" in this field emerged step by step over time and does not completely "federalize" Europe's marine environment, for Article 2C recognizes that the environment as a whole is an area of shared competence (between the Union and its Member States).

The Common Fisheries Policy (CFP) dates back to EEC Council Regulations 2141/70 and 2142/70, passed in 1970 just as the UK, Ireland, Denmark, and Norway began negotiations to join the Community. It was largely responsible for the "no" vote on a referendum in Norway. Amended in 1983 (EEC Council Reg. 170/83) and regularly thereafter, it is based on the presumption that the common fisheries policy is part of the *acquis communautaire*—an area of exclusive EC competence. The 1992 Treaty of Maastricht introduced the precautionary principle as a principle of community environmental law. Nevertheless, the implementation of the CFP has been anything but precautionary, even if the European Court of Justice (ECJ), in the 1993 *Mondiet* case (Case C–404/92 [1993] ECR–I 6133), upheld a strict interpretation of precaution in relation to the Community regulation banning driftnets. As Bergkamp and Smith comment in Chapter 17 of this volume, "Real precaution is a matter of enforced result, not mere 'hortatory law.'" Overcapacity and failure to follow scientific advice, resulting in overfishing and unsustainable bycatches, have all been hallmarks of the CFP implementation. In 2001, the European Commission itself, prior to proposals for more effective use of precaution, acknowledged that "many stocks are ... outside safe biological limits. ... If current trends continue, many stocks will collapse" (European Commission 2001, 6). Howarth comments, "The failures of the Community effectively to address the ecological challenges inherent in fisheries management may be seen as an extreme case of sectoral mismanagement" (2008, 14).

The fact that the CFP is an area of undisputed Union competence does not mean, however, that the EU has competence over all marine environmental issues, or that

Member States are agreeable to surrendering their own powers in this sphere. For example, the initial establishment of a 200-mile EC Fisheries Zone in the North Sea—put in place in September 1992 by The Hague Declaration—was a collective decision of the EU states, not of the EU (Freestone 1993). Similarly, as Saterson points out in Chapter 9 of this volume, the reactions of the Member States—particularly Germany and the UK—to two decisions of the ECJ greatly restricting the discretion of Member States in the establishment of Specially Protected Areas under the 1979 Wild Birds Directive 79/409 (the *Leybucht Dykes* case and its follow-up, *Commission vs. Germany*, 1991) demonstrate that they were considerably less "precautionary" than the Commission. Indeed, the EU Member States succeeded in retaining their "shared" competences for coastal development by simply rewording Article 4(4) of the 1979 Birds Directive to make it *Leybucht*-proof in the 1992 Habitats Directive Article 6(4) (Freestone 1997). Besides, even though the avocet bird species—central to the *Leybucht* case—inhabits the marine environment, that does not make it a "marine biological resource." Hence, *national* policies of the Member States, precautionary or not—and often the latter—continue to predominate in practice when it comes to real environment versus development conflicts in this sector. Interestingly, in this instance it was Germany (and the UK, as intervening party) that turned out to be on the "other" side of the precautionary debate.

On the U.S. side, too, it may not be enough to look at federal regulation only. While it may be true, as Dan Bodansky (1994) points out, that "U.S. [federal] domestic law has in many respects been precautionary" in the marine sector, the same is not necessarily true for state laws. It is true to say that a precautionary approach has been used at the federal level in the fisheries sector, particularly in relation to the impact on endangered species under the 1973 Endangered Species Act and the 1972 Marine Mammals Act.[29]

Although the United States has yet to ratify the 1982 Law of the Sea Convention, it has, as Turnipseed et al. (2009, 30) point out, tended to follow its norms. In 1983, the United States claimed an Exclusive Economic Zone (EEZ) in accord with the 1982 Convention (1983 Proclamation). In 1988, it extended its territorial sea from 3 to 12 nautical miles (1988 Proclamation, published January 1989). However, the U.S. coastal states retain their 3 nautical miles of seaward state jurisdiction, except for Texas and Florida, which claim 9 miles in the Gulf of Mexico (Turnipseed et al., 2009, 31). As to coastal environment and development, the U.S. counterpart to the EU *Leybucht* problem is the 1972 Coastal Zone Management Act and the states' own CZMAs, which give the coastal states significant authority to adopt their own policies. The act authorizes the federal government to make grants available to states to administer their coastal zone management plans. Grants are conditioned on compliance with minimal federal requirements set forth in Section 1455(d). Once a state's plan is approved by the

---

[29] Although in *Winter v. Natural Res. Def. Council, Inc.* (2008), the NRDC had argued for a precautionary approach to the use of sonar in light of the risks of serious injuries to marine mammals. The Supreme Court held that the Navy's need to conduct realistic training with active sonar plainly outweighed the interests advanced by the plaintiffs. I am grateful to LCDR Jeanine Womble, JAGC US for bringing this decision to my attention.

Commerce Department, federal agency actions must be consistent with such a plan "to the maximum extent practicable" under Section 1456(c)(1)(A). States need not participate in the program at all, but the act creates financial incentives to do so. Although the states have considerable discretion to shape their policies and plans, the federal government has retained some authority, at least through the carrot of federal funds, to determine the fate of activities within state coastal zones. The situation is not unlike that under the Clean Air Act, where state policies are allowed to be, and often are, more stringent than federal policy. It also resembles the kind of "cooperative federalism" practiced under some other U.S. statutes, with federal agencies setting the standards and the states implementing them.

The 1976 Magnuson-Stevens Fishery and Conservation and Management Act did not "federalize" state marine fisheries governance; indeed, it empowered regional (state-based) fisheries management councils. Because the act predated the establishment of the U.S. EEZ, it envisaged an "economic hardship" exemption from some of its management requirements to allow "American" fishing to continue. The regional councils were often beholden to the fishing industry, and these exemptions tended to become the norm, resulting in overfishing and collapse of several key fisheries (Kass and McCarroll 2007, 1).

The 1976 Magnuson-Stevens Act was amended and reenacted in 1996 as the Sustainable Fisheries Act (16 U.S.C. § 1801 *et seq.*). The amended act eliminated the "economic hardship" loophole and set a 10-year target to rebuild depleted stocks. Unfortunately, stocks continued to decline (Kass and McCarroll 2007). In response to evidence produced by the 2004 President's Commission on Ocean Policy, supplemented by work financed by the Pew Foundation, the National Marine Fisheries Service (NMFS) of the National Oceanic and Atmospheric Administration (now known as NOAA Fisheries) sought congressional approval for legislative authority to end overfishing. In 2006, the act was reauthorized as the Magnuson-Stevens Fishery Conservation and Management Reauthorization Act (U.S. Public Law No. 109-479, 120 § 3575 2007), or MSRA.

The responsibility for implementing this act is delegated by the U.S. secretary of commerce to NOAA Fisheries. While the 1976 Act did not expressly refer to precaution, the former director of sustainable fisheries of the NMFS has claimed with some justification that "the precautionary approach forms the core of the solution to reverse the current state of U.S. fisheries" (Matlock 1998, 13). This approach is pursued by the 2006 MSRA. Indeed, the September 2009 Interim Report of the Interagency Ocean Policy Task Force appointed by President Obama specifically provides: "Decisions affecting the ocean, our coasts, and the Great Lakes should be informed by and consistent with the best available science. Decisionmaking will also be guided by a precautionary approach as reflected in the Rio Declaration of 1992" (IOPTF 2009, 14).[30]

---

[30] Note that the U.S. Commission on Ocean Policy found that "because scientific information can never fully explain and predict all impacts, strict adoption of the precautionary principle would prevent most, if not all, activities from proceeding." It proposed a "more balanced precautionary approach that weighs the level of scientific uncertainty and the potential damage as part of every management decision" (USCOP 2004, 65).

While application of precaution may be somewhat patchy, a 2002 independent study of the Bering Sea and Gulf of Alaska Walleye Pollock Fishery (WWF 2002)[31] found that the Management Plan for that fishery—managed by the North Pacific Fishery Management Council with oversight from the NMFS—did reflect a precautionary approach. The study highlighted the fact that the 1996 Act had changed the definition of optimum yield—a concept used in the 1982 Convention—from "maximum sustainable yield as modified by relevant factors [including environmental factors]" to "[maximum sustainable yield] as *reduced* by relevant factors" (Section 3, Definitions 104-297 28(B)). The result has been a much more conservative standard for determining catch levels. Notably in assessing catch levels in the Eastern Bering Sea (the U.S. zone), the management regime has no control over, or independent verification of, the catches in the Western (Russian) zone. The management plan, operating under the assumption that there is significant underreporting of Russian catches, reduces Eastern zone fisheries accordingly.

Another recent example is the precautionary decision by Gary Locke, the secretary of commerce, to approve a plan that would prohibit commercial fishing in a huge swath of American waters in the Arctic that have never been actively fished (*NYT* 2009). These waters are believed to be rich in cod and snow crab, among other species. In time, they could well provide a new home for cold-water species like pollock and salmon that are already moving north as global warming increases water temperatures in their normal habitats. Conservationists and harvesters agreed not to take any at all—until it seems safe to do so. The prohibition covers nearly 200,000 square miles north of the Bering Strait.

Conclusions

It is not an exaggeration to say that precaution is now an established principle of international marine environmental law. It is to be found not only in the pollution conventions but also in the coastal wildlife and fishery management regimes. Both the United States and the EU have participated in the development of the legal and policy instruments which have brought this situation about. While the United States seemed to have had initial reservations about the use of precaution in relation to pollution prevention, it did not exhibit the same reservations in relation to fisheries regulation. Indeed the United States, while not yet party to the 1982 Law of the Sea Convention, is a party to the 1995 UN Fish Stocks Agreement (UNFSA), which explicitly endorses precaution. The United States has been a strong supporter of its implementation—the UNFSA informal meetings of parties and its Review Conferences have been chaired by the United States. Precaution has now become an accepted part of the armory of national fisheries management—maybe even marine decisionmaking

---

[31] This report was prepared by a World Wildlife Fund team to identify issues important for the certification of this fishery under the Marine Stewardship Council Principles.

(IOPTF 2009)—and certainly at the federal level. Not all U.S. states may share this view, but even if it is not always practiced, some good examples such as the Bering Sea Walleye Pollock Fishery nevertheless exist on record.

By contrast, the EU and its Member States seemed much more comfortable with the use of the precautionary principle in relation to pollution control—perhaps because of its European origins—but less enthusiastic about its extension to wildlife conservation, development, and fisheries decisionmaking. Although the precautionary principle is an overarching principle of European environmental law, its application has not been unproblematic. There is no evidence that the CFP has effectively utilized a precautionary approach—indeed the European Commission itself accepts that the evidence is to the contrary, although it is seeking to strengthen its application. One of the Regional Fisheries Management Bodies (RFMBs) to which a number of its members belong is the International Commission for the Conservation of Atlantic Tunas (ICCAT). ICCAT, like other RFMBs, may have endorsed precaution (Cooney and Dickson 2005, 11), but a 2008 performance review of ICCAT commented that, "ICCAT [Contracting Parties'] performance in managing fisheries on Bluefin Tuna particularly in the eastern Atlantic and Mediterranean Sea is widely regarded as an international disgrace." (ICCAT 2009, 2).

It seems clear from this, albeit brief, examination of the evolution and use of precaution in relation to the marine environment that, just as there is dissonance between the rhetoric and the reality in the positions of both the United States and the EU, there is also dissonance between the official views of the U.S. federal authorities, the EU, and the practice of their respective Member States.

Acknowledgments

I am extremely grateful to Peter Sand for very helpful suggestions and to my colleagues Dinah Shelton and Robert Glicksman for reviewing and commenting on the final draft.

References

Barcelona Convention. 1976. Convention for the Protection of the Mediterranean Sea against Pollution. Adopted February 16, 1976; in force February 12, 1978. *International Legal Materials* 15: 290.
———. 1995. Convention for the Protection of the Marine Environment and the Coastal Region of the Mediterranean Sea. Adopted June 10, 1995; in force July 9, 2004. *International Legal Materials* 976: 13.
Birnie, Patricia. 1985. *The International Regulation of Whaling.* Vol. 2. New York: Oceana.
Bodansky, Daniel. 1994. The Precautionary Principle in U.S. Environmental Law. In *Interpreting the Precautionary Principle,* edited by T. O'Riordan and J. Cameron. London: Earthscan, 203–224.
Canberra Convention. 1980. Convention on the Conservation of Antarctic Marine Living Resources. Adopted May 20, 1980; in force April 7, 1982. *International Legal Materials* 19: 837.
CBD (Convention on Biological Diversity). 1992. Convention on Biological Diversity. Adopted June 5, 1992; in force December 29, 1993. *International Legal Materials* 31: 818.

CCAMLR (Commission for the Conservation of Antarctic Marine Living Resources). 1991. Conservation Measures in Force. www.ccamlr.org/pu/E/quick_links.htm (accessed April 27, 2010).

CCMPR (Convention on the Conservation and Management of Pollock Resources in the Central Bering Sea). 1994. Adopted February 11 by Russia and U.S. (other states signed later). *International Journal of Marine and Coastal Law* 10: 127.

Chandler, Melinda. 1993. The Biodiversity Conventions: Selected Issues of Interest to the International Lawyer. *Colorado Journal of International Environmental Law and Policy* 4: 141–175.

Churchill, R. R. 1987. *EEC Fisheries Law.* Dordrecht, Netherlands: Martinus Nijhoff.

Cooke, J., and M. Earle. 1993. Towards a Precautionary Approach to Fisheries Management. *Review of European Community and International Environmental Law* 2: 252–259.

Cooney, Rosie. 2004. *The Precautionary Principle in Biodiversity Conservation and Natural Resource Management: An Issues Paper for Policymakers, Researchers and Practitioners.* IUCN Policy and Global Change Series No. 2. Gland, Switzerland: International Union for Conservation of Nature (IUCN).

Cooney, Rosie, and B. Dickson. 2005. *Biodiversity and the Precautionary Principle: Risk and Uncertainty in Conservation and Sustainable Use.* London: Earthscan.

Cullet, Philippe, and Patricia Kameri-Mbote. 1996. Dolphin Bycatches in Tuna Fisheries: A Smokescreen Hiding the Real Issues? *Ocean Development and International Law* 27: 333–348.

Dunlap, W. V. 1995. Bering Sea: The Donut Hole Agreement. *International Journal of Marine and Coastal Law* 10: 114–126.

Edeson, W. M. 1996. The Code of Conduct for Responsible Fisheries: An Introduction. *International Journal of Marine and Coastal Law* 11: 233–238.

Ehlers, P. 1990. The History of the International North Sea Conferences. In *The North Sea: Perspectives on Regional Environmental Cooperation,* edited by David Freestone and Ton IJlstra. London/Dordrecht: Graham and Trotman/Martinus Nijhoff, 3–14.

———. 1993. Commentary on Helsinki Convention. *International Journal of Marine and Coastal Law* 8: 191–243.

Endangered Species Act. 1973. 16 U.S.C. § 1531 *et seq.*

European Commission. 2001. The Future of the Common Fisheries Policy. Green Paper COM(2001) 135. March 20.

FAO (Food and Agriculture Organization of the United Nations). 1991. Legislative Study No. 47, Annex 2. Rome.

———. 1992a. Legal Issues Concerning High Seas Fishing. FI/HSF/TC/92/8.

———. 1992b. Draft Report II: Technical Consultations of High Seas Fishing. Rome, September 7–15.

———. 1996a. *Precautionary Approach to Capture Fisheries and Species Introductions.* FAO Technical Guidelines for Responsible Fisheries.

———. 1996b. *Precautionary Approach to Fisheries.* Part 2, *Scientific Papers.* Prepared for the Technical Consultation on the Precautionary Approach to Capture Fisheries (Including Species Introductions). Lysekil, Sweden, June 6–13, 1995. FAO Fisheries Technical Paper No. 350. Rome.

Freestone, David. 1991. The Precautionary Principle. In *International Law and Climate Change,* edited by R. Churchill and D. Freestone. London: Graham and Trotman/Nijhoff, 21–40.

———. 1993. The North Sea Declaration on the Coordinated Extension of Jurisdiction. *International Journal of Marine and Coastal Law* 8: 172–175.

———. 1997. The Enforcement of the Wild Birds Directive: A Case Study. In *Protecting the European Environment: Enforcing EC Environment Law,* edited by Han Somsen. London: Blackstone Press, 229–250.

———. 2000. Caution or Precaution: "A Rose by Any Other Name … ?" In Symposium on the Southern Bluefin Tuna Cases. *Yearbook of International Environmental Law* 12: 25–32.

Freestone, David, and Ellen Hey, eds. 1996. *The Precautionary Principle and International Law: The Challenge of Implementation.* London: Kluwer Law International, 3–15.

Freestone, David, and Ton IJlstra, eds. 1991. *The North Sea: Basic Legal Documents on Regional Environmental Cooperation*. Dordrecht, Netherlands: Martinus Nijhoff.

Freestone, David, and Zen Makuch. 1997. The New International Environmental Law of Fisheries: The 1995 Straddling Stocks Agreement. *Yearbook of International Environmental Law* 7: 3–49.

Garcia, Serge. 1994. The Precautionary Principle: Its Implications in Capture Fisheries Management. *Ocean and Coastal Management* 22: 99.

Gjerde, Kristina, and David Freestone. 1994. PSSAs: An Important Environment Concept at a Turning Point. *International Journal of Marine and Coastal Law Special* 9: 431–577.

Goote, Maas. 1997. The Jakarta Mandate on Marine and Coastal Biological Diversity. *International Journal of Marine and Coastal Law* 12: 377–389.

Gündling, L. 1990. The Status in International Law of the Precautionary Principle. In *The North Sea: Perspectives on Regional Environmental Cooperation*, edited by David Freestone and Ton IJlstra. London/Dordrecht: Graham and Trotman/Martinus Nijhoff, 23–30.

Helsinki Convention. 1992a. Helsinki Convention on the Protection of the Baltic Sea Area. *Yearbook of International Environmental Law 3* and *International Legal Materials* 8: 215.

———. 1992b. Helsinki Convention on the Protection and Use of Transboundary Watercourses and Lakes. *International Legal Materials* 31: 1312.

Hewison, G. 1996. The Precautionary Approach to Fisheries Management: An Environmental Perspective. *International Journal of Marine and Coastal Law* 11: 301–332.

Hey, Ellen. 1991a. The Precautionary Approach: Implications of the Revision of the Oslo and Paris Conventions. *Marine Policy* 15: 244–254.

———. 1991b. *The Precautionary Approach and the London Dumping Convention*. LDC 14/4. September 4.

———. 1996. Global Fisheries Regulations in the First Half of the 1990s. *International Journal of Marine and Coastal Law* 11: 459–490.

Hey, Ellen, Ton IJlstra, and André Nollkaemper. 1993. The 1992 Paris Convention for the Protection of the Marine Environment of the North-East Atlantic: A Critical Analysis. *International Journal of Marine and Coastal Law* 8: 1–49.

Hey, Ellen, and Laurence D. Mee. 1994. Black Sea, The Ministerial Declaration: An Important Step. *Environmental Policy and Law* 23: 215–220; also in *International Journal of Marine and Coastal Law* 9: 72ff.

Howarth, William. 2008. The Interpretation of "Precaution" in the European Community Common Fisheries Policy. *Journal of Environmental Law* 20: 213–244.

IATTC (Inter-American Tropical Tuna Convention). 1949. Washington, DC. Adopted May 31, 1949; in force March 3, 1950. 80 UNTS 4.

ICCAT (International Commission for the Conservation of Atlantic Tunas). 1966. Adopted May 14, 1966; in force March 21, 1969. 37 UNTS 63.

———. 2009. *Report of the Independent Performance Review of ICCAT*. Madrid. www.iccat.int/Documents/Other/PERFORM_%20REV_TRI_LINGUAL.pdf (accessed July 30, 2009).

IOPTF (Interagency Ocean Policy Task Force). 2009. *Interim Report of the Interagency Ocean Policy Task Force*. White House Council on Environmental Quality Washington, DC: Executive Office of the President.

Kass, Stephen L., and Jean McCarroll. 2007. Saving the Oceans: Magnuson-Stevens Act Amendments. *New York Law Journal*, August 24.

Kingsbury, Benedict. 1994. The Tuna-Dolphin Controversy, the World Trade Organization, and the Liberal Project to Reconceptualize International Law. *Yearbook of International Environmental Law* 5: 1–40.

Kiss, A.-C., and D. Shelton. 2004. *International Environmental Law*, 3rd ed. Ardseley, NY: Transnational.

Koers, A. W. 1973. *International Regulation of Marine Fisheries*. London: Fishing News Books.

Kwiatkowska, B. 1993. The High Seas Fisheries Regime: At a Point of No Return? *International Journal of Marine and Coastal Law* 8: 327–358.

London Convention, 1990. London Dumping Convention. Report of the Thirteenth Consultative Meeting of the Parties, October 29–November 2, LDC 13/15, 22–30.

London Protocol. 1996. Protocol to the Convention on the Prevention of Marine Pollution by Dumping of Wastes and Other Matter. Adopted November 7, 1996; in force March 24, 2006 *International Legal Materials* 36: 1462.

Lyster, S. 1985. *International Wildlife Law.* Cambridge: Grotius.

Maastricht Treaty on European Union. 1992. *International Legal Materials* 31: 247; *International Legal Materials* 32: 1693, 1993.

Magnuson-Stevens Fishery Conservation and Management Reauthorization Act. 2007. Pub. L, No. 109-479, 120 § 3575.

Marine Mammals Act. 1972. 16 U.S.C. § 1361 *et seq.*

Matlock, Gary. 1998. Management History, Management Future. In *Sustainable Fisheries for the Twenty-First Century*, edited by J. Speir. New Orleans: Tulane Institute for Environmental Law and Policy, 9–16.

NYT (*New York Times*). 2009. A Real Fish Story. Editorial. Aug. 23, A18.

Nollkaemper, A. 1991. The Precautionary Principle in International Environmental Law: What's New under the Sun? *Marine Pollution Bulletin* 22 (3): 107–110.

North Pacific Treaty. 1952. International Convention for the High Seas Fisheries of the North Pacific Ocean. Tokyo. Adopted May 9, 1952; in force June 12, 1953. 205 UNTS 80.

Odessa Declaration. 1993. Ministerial Declaration on the Protection of the Black Sea. Adopted April 7, 1993. *Environmental Policy and Law* 23: 235–236.

Oude Elferink, Alex. 1995. Fisheries in the Sea of Okhotsk High Seas Enclave: The Russian Federation's Attempts at Coastal State Control. *International Journal of Marine and Coastal Law* 10: 1–18.

Paris Convention. 1992. Convention on the Protection of the Marine Environment of the North-East Atlantic. *International Journal of Marine and Coastal Law* 8: 50–76.

Scheiber, H. N. 1989. Origins of the Abstention Doctrine in Ocean Law: Japanese-U.S. Relations and Pacific Fisheries, 1937–1958. *Ecology Law Quarterly* 16: 23.

Scully, Tucker. 1992. The Protection of the Marine Environment and the UN Conference on Environment and Development. In The Law of the Sea: New Worlds, New Discoveries, *Proceedings of the 26th Annual Conference of the Law of the Sea Institute.* June 22–25, Genoa.

SEAFO (South-East Atlantic Fisheries Organization). 2001. Convention on the Conservation and Management of the Fisheries Resources in the South-East Atlantic Ocean. Adopted April 20, 2001; in force April 13, 2003 *International Legal Materials* 41: 257.

Sumi, Kazuo. 1991. *International Legal Issues Concerning the Use of Driftnets with Special Emphasis on Japanese Practices and Responses.* In FAO Legislative Study No. 47.

Sustainable Fisheries Act. 1996. 16 U.S.C. § 1801 *et seq.*

Trouwborst, Arie. 2002. *Evolution and Status of the Precautionary Principle in International Law.* Dordrecht, Netherlands: Kluwer.

Turnipseed, Mary, Stephen E. Roady, Raphael Sagarin, and Larry B. Crowder. 2009. The Silver Anniversary of the United States' Exclusive Economic Zone: Twenty-Five Years of Ocean Use and Abuse, and the Possibility of a Blue Water Public Trust Doctrine. *Ecology Law Quarterly* 36: 1–70.

UN (United Nations). 1990. Doc A/45/721. November 19.

———. 1992. Report of the United Nations Conference on Environment and Development. A/CONF.151/26, Vol. IV.

UNEP (United Nations Environment Programme). 1990. Report of the Fifth Intergovernmental Meeting on the Action Plan for the Caribbean Environment Programme and Second Meeting of the Contracting Parties to the Convention for the Protection and Development of the Marine Environment of the Wider Caribbean Region. January. UNP(OCA)/CAR IG 6.

———. 1992. Relevance and Application of the Principle of Precautionary Action to the Caribbean Environment Programme. Secretariat paper prepared for the CEP Meeting of Experts and the Third Meeting of the Parties to the Cartagena Convention. UN OCA/CAR WG.10/INF. November 4.

UNFCCC. 1992. UN Framework Convention on Climate Change. Adopted May 9, 1992; in force March 21, 1994. *International Legal Materials* 31: 848.

UN Fish Stocks Agreement. 1995. Agreement for the Implementation of the Provisions of the United Nations Convention on the Law of the Sea of December 10, 1982, Relating to the Conservation and Management of Straddling Fish Stocks and Highly Migratory Fish Stocks. Adopted by the negotiating parties without a vote (i.e., by consensus) on August 4, 1995; in force November 11, 2001. *International Legal Materials* 34: 1542.

UNGA (United Nations General Assembly). 1989. Resolution on Driftnet Fishing. Resolution 44/225.

UNGA (United Nations General Assembly). 1992. Resolution 47/192 Adopted by the General Assembly on Straddling Fish Stocks and Highly Migratory Fish Stocks. December 22. www.un.org/documents/ga/res/47/a47r192.htm (accessed May 4, 2010).

USCOP (U.S. Commission on Ocean Policy). 2004. *An Ocean Blueprint for the Twenty-First Century*. Washington, DC. www.oceancommission.gov (accessed October 1, 2009).

U.S. Presidential Proclamation. 1983. Proclamation No. 5030, 3 C F R. 22, 23.

———. 1988. Proclamation No. 5928, 54 *Federal Register* 777. December 27.

von Moltke, K. 1988. The *Vorsorgeprinzip* in West German Policy. Appendix 3. Royal Commission on the Environment, Twelfth Report.

WCPFC (Convention on the Conservation and Management of Highly Migratory Fish Stocks in the Western and Central Pacific Ocean). 2000. Adopted September 5, 2000; in force June 19, 2004. *International Legal Materials* 40: 277.

Whaling Convention. 1946. Washington International Convention for the Regulation of Whaling. Washington, DC. Adopted December 2, 1946; in force November 10, 1948. 161 UNTS 72.

Winter v. Natural Res. Def. Council, Inc. 2008. 129 S. Ct. 365.

WWF (World Wildlife Fund). 2002. *Report: Issues to Be Considered by the Evaluation Team for the Bering Sea and Gulf of Alaska Walleye Pollock Fishery*. Washington, DC: WWF.

CHAPTER 9

Biodiversity Conservation

Kathryn A. Saterson[1]

*H*umans have developed formal and informal regulations for the conservation and use of nature for hundreds—even thousands—of years, but the focus until recently has been primarily on protecting species of direct value to humans. In the 1960s and 1970s, scientists began to accumulate enough data on species extinction, deforestation, and tropical biology to become aware of a global problem (Wilson 1988). At the same time, awareness was growing about the links between conservation of biodiversity and economic development (Prescott-Allen and Prescott-Allen 1982). Global interest increased in the conservation of species and ecosystems more for their intrinsic value, and for their direct contribution to ecosystem services and the balance of nature. One of the first uses of the term "biological diversity" was in the 1980 U.S. Council on Environmental Quality and State Department annual report to the president (CEQ 1980).

Biological diversity—shortened to biodiversity—refers to the variety of genes, species, and ecosystems on the Earth. Simpler definitions refer simply to living things (IUCN 1980) or the web of life. Biodiversity is continually evolving, so conservation efforts must conserve the dynamic processes of evolution. Currently the greatest threats to biodiversity are habitat destruction and land use change; single species exploitation; exotic species; pollution; and climate change. Conservation regulations are essential because biodiversity is central to maintaining human life support systems, extinction is irreversible, and human population levels continue to increase. Conservation of biodiversity is central to the concept of sustainable development; the

---

[1] The views expressed in this chapter are those of the author and do not necessarily reflect the views or policies of the U.S. Environmental Protection Agency.

current generation's use of biodiversity must not compromise the ability of future generations to benefit from biodiversity.

Conservation is challenging for many reasons, including the current uncertainties about ways that human activities impact biological systems. It is estimated that there are 10 million to 100 million species on the Earth, with only about 1.4 million yet named by science. There is certainty that the rate of species extinctions due to human activity is well above the estimated natural rate of extinction. There is certainty about the value of biodiversity to human subsistence, and the role of biodiversity in ecosystem processes becomes clearer all the time. As our use of technology becomes more sophisticated, we obtain more certainty about some issues, such as remote sensing of the quantity of different habitats remaining. But at the same time, we have increased uncertainty about human impacts on thresholds and tipping points for change in habitat quality due to cumulative impacts, feedback loops, and nonlinearities in the resistance and resilience of species and systems. Precaution is warranted because humans are altering the physical, chemical, and biological world faster than we are increasing our ability to understand our impacts and how they interact in complex and cumulative ways.

It is a challenge to separate many aspects of natural variation from human-induced variation, particularly related to climate change and the biological, physical, and chemical balance of nature. As a result, it is very difficult to measure and monitor the impacts of projects and policies to determine which changes are natural and which result from regulation (Saterson et al. 2004). In addition, there are problems of scale; local patterns not necessarily global, and vice versa.

Although the term "precautionary principle" was not formally adopted until the mid-1980s (in international treaties such as those protecting the North Sea in Europe), some earlier legislation was precautionary in nature. This analysis attempts to evaluate the precautionary nature of biodiversity legislation in the United States and Europe— even when the terms "precautionary principle" or "precautionary approach" are not literally used.

This chapter attempts to address four questions:

(1) **What has been the pattern of precaution in biodiversity regulation in the United States and Europe over the three decades from 1970 to 2000?** A "greater degree of precaution" is defined primarily as a combination of both the timing (earliness, anticipatory character) and the stringency of regulatory standards. Precautionary timing is reflected in regulations passed in advance of scientific proof of biodiversity loss and of the potentially significant risks resulting from loss of genetic, species, and ecosystem diversity.

(2) **What explains the observed pattern of precaution in the United States and Europe?** Why does biodiversity conservation evoke the policy responses it does in the United States, the EU, and within individual European countries? What generic factors and what factors specific to conserving biodiversity might help explain the observed pattern of transatlantic precautionary regulation?

(3) **What have been the impacts of precautionary approaches to biodiversity conservation in practice?** Do we see a slowing of loss of biodiversity, the appearance of countervailing risks, costs, innovations, public confidence, or other outcomes?

(4) **Considering the answers to the first three questions, when and to what degree is precaution in regulation of biodiversity use and conservation desirable?** What lessons can be drawn for future regulatory conservation policy?

This chapter focuses primarily on regulations with a direct focus on biodiversity through conservation and use of terrestrial species, habitats, and ecosystems. Chapter 2, by Mark Cantley and Maurice Lex, addressed regulation of genetically modified organisms. Chapter 8, by David Freestone, focused on regulation of the marine environment. Space precludes addressing the many important regulations in the United States and Europe that do not focus primarily on conservation of biodiversity but which still have potentially significant positive impacts on conservation. Future analysis should include, for example, the Common Agricultural Policy in the EU; the 1985 U.S. farm bill "swampbuster and sodbuster" provisions that provided incentives to protect wetlands and erodable land; and the EU 2000 Water Framework Directive. Extensive discussion of the evolution of the precautionary principle and its many definitions can be found in other chapters of this book and in Wiener and Rogers (2002).

Relative Precaution in Regulation of Biodiversity in the United States and Europe

This section compares the relative pattern of transatlantic precaution in biodiversity regulation in the United States and Europe over two time periods: 1970–1985 and 1986–2000. European regulations can include both the European Union/European Community policies and those of individual EU Member States.

United States: 1970–1985

Prior to 1970, much of the U.S. nature conservation legislation focused on protecting charismatic species such as eagles or bison, because doing so provided economic benefit (primarily though hunting) and evoked emotional responses from legislators and the American public (Burton 2002, 201–202). The 1900 Lacey Act and 1913 Migratory Bird Treaty Act are important laws that are still enforced today, and they supplement the 1973 Endangered Species Act. U.S. conservation law prior to 1970 is well described in Bean and Rowland (1997).

President Nixon noted in 1972 that existing law did not provide the tools to "act early enough to save a vanishing species" (Bean and Rowland 1997, 198). The 1973 Endangered Species Act (ESA) replaced the 1966 Endangered Species Preservation Act and the 1969 Endangered Species Conservation Act (USFWS 1996), both of which were considered to offer weak protection by only listing species (1966) and only barring import of species threatened with global extinction (1969). The ESA improves on prior legislation by including lists of threatened and endangered species, critical habitat protection, development of recovery plans, delisting of species, and reintroduction of species that have already been extirpated (USFWS 2003). Under the ESA, the U.S. Fish and Wildlife Service (USFWS) and the National Marine Fisheries Service are charged with listing species as either threatened or endangered, depending upon the severity of the threat to the population as well as the health of the remaining population (USFWS 2003). This listing process includes substantial scientific research to determine whether the species is truly in need of federal protection. Upon determination of a species' need for protection, a recommendation is made to the secretary of the interior to list the species under the ESA.

Section 4 of the ESA authorizes the secretary of the U.S. Department of Interior (or Commerce for marine species) to declare a species endangered or threatened after review of the best scientific data available on the species, and to designate critical habitat for protection of the species. Section 7 specifies that all "Federal departments and agencies shall ... carry out programs for the conservation of endangered species ... and ... insure that actions authorized, funded, or carried out by them do not jeopardize the continued existence of such endangered species or threatened species or result in the destruction or modification of habitat of such species which is determined by the Secretary ... to be critical" (ESA 1973, 1536 § 7A2). The ESA also prohibits individuals, government, and private sector entities from importing, exporting, taking, possessing, selling, or transporting any endangered species (ESA 1973, 1538).

Shortly after the ESA was passed, the secretary of interior was petitioned to list the snail darter fish as an endangered species under the ESA. The snail darter lived only in a portion of the Little Tennessee River that would be completely inundated by the reservoir created as a consequence of the completion of the Tellico Dam. The secretary declared that area as the endangered snail darter's "critical habitat." In the 1978 U.S. Supreme Court case *Tennessee Valley Authority v. Hill*, the court supported halting construction of the Tellico Dam to prevent the extinction of the endemic snail darter fish. The court noted that it was in mankind's best interest to minimize loss of genetic diversity in order to protect biological resources that can be useful in the future. It wrote, "The institutionalization of caution lies at the heart of the act. ... It is clear from the Act's legislative history that Congress intended to halt and reverse the trend toward species extinction—whatever the cost." The pointed omission of the type of qualified language previously included in endangered species legislation reveals a conscious congressional design to give endangered species priority over the "primary missions" of federal agencies. Congress, moreover, foresaw that Section 7 would on occasion require agencies to alter ongoing projects in order to fulfill the act's goals. Shortly after this landmark court decision, Congress amended the act to specify that USFWS could take economic considerations into account when determining critical habitat designation (USFWS 1996). However, the species listing process is still void of these requirements. Listing of a species is to be conducted solely on scientific evidence and the biological needs of a species in decline. Congress amended the ESA again in 1982 to add Section 10(a), allowing the Department of Interior to permit "incidental" private takings of endangered/threatened species as part of an approved Habitat Conservation Plan (HCP) that would minimize the risk to the species in the wild.

Determining how precautionary the ESA is depends on one's view of earliness, anticipation/uncertainty, and stringency. Global and U.S. concern about the risk of biodiversity loss began in earnest in the early 1970s, so passing the ESA in 1973 can be seen as early and precautionary in a chronological sense. However, the law can be viewed as acting too late biologically, because species are not listed and protected until they are already threatened or endangered—a point in time often too late for recovery. In addition, the requirement of significant scientific data to support requests for listing as endangered or threatened weakens the precautionary nature of the ESA in terms of earliness.

The ESA can be viewed as precautionary from a stringency standpoint in terms of protecting threatened and endangered species. While the science required does not make listing of species particularly precautionary from an earliness standpoint, the "no jeopardy" clause could be considered strongly precautionary in its stringency by shifting the burden of proof to federal agencies to demonstrate that their proposed actions will not jeopardize listed species. The 1978 *TVA v. Hill* case stressed the precautionary understanding that agencies need to protect the entire habitat of threatened species regardless of cost. The 1982 amendments adding HCPs can be viewed as making the ESA more anticipatory—but less stringent—by allowing incidental taking. Later, the 1995 Supreme Court *Babbitt v. Sweet Home* ruling reinforced the precautionary nature of the ESA. The prohibition of any public or private taking of endangered or threatened species by Section 7 is also stringent, as is the requirement to protect critical habitat for listed species. The ESA would be more firmly precautionary if it protected more than threatened and endangered species—but it would also need a new name!

In 1974, the United States ratified the 1973 Convention on International Trade in Endangered Species of Wild Fauna and Flora (CITES), which restricts international trade in endangered species and assigns protected species to one of three appendix lists. Appendix I species are threatened by extinction and could be affected by trade, thus requiring import and export permits certifying that trade will not harm species survival, among other provisions. Appendix II species may not be currently threatened, but trade could jeopardize survival. Two-thirds of parties to the convention must approve addition or removal of a species from Appendix I or II. The precautionary principle was explicitly endorsed at the Ninth Conference of Parties to CITES in 1994 (Dickson 1999).

The 1980 Alaska National Interest Lands Conservation Act (ANILCA) added over 53 million acres to the U.S. National Wildlife Refuge System, with a general purpose of conserving fish and wildlife populations and habitats "in their natural diversity."

In 1979, the U.S. Foreign Assistance Act (FAA) was amended to require that the U.S. Agency for International Development (USAID) conduct environmental impact assessments on major overseas projects to minimize impacts on tropical forests and biodiversity (Saterson 2001). In 1983, Congress amended the FAA (Section 119b) to direct USAID to work with counterparts in developing countries receiving development assistance. These countries were to protect and maintain wildlife habitats and develop sound wildlife management and plant conservation programs; establish and maintain wildlife sanctuaries, reserves, and parks; enact and enforce anti-poaching measures; and identify, study, and catalog animal and plant species. This amendment grew out of both the awareness that terrestrial biodiversity is often highest in tropical developing countries and increased understanding of the links between biological resources and economic development.

The 1970s to mid-1980s also saw the creation of a number of U.S. laws whose primary goals were not biodiversity conservation but which nonetheless continue to significantly affect biodiversity. These include the 1969 National Environmental Policy Act, the 1970 Clean Air Act, and the 1977 Clean Water Act.

United States: 1986–2000

While the years since 1986 have not seen the rapid addition of new conservation legislation witnessed from 1970 to 1985, all of those laws remain in effect and have been enforced. In 1987, the United States ratified the Ramsar Convention for Conservation of Wetlands. Its goal is "the conservation and wise use of all wetlands through local, regional and national actions and international cooperation, as a contribution towards achieving sustainable development throughout the world" (Ramsar 2002). As a contracting party, the United States had designated 19 wetlands of international importance in 2002.

In 1988, Public Law 100-478 amended the ESA to require the secretary of interior to develop and implement recovery plans for the conservation and survival of endangered species and threatened species, and to implement a system in cooperation with the states to monitor the status of recovered species. In 1995, the U.S. Supreme Court upheld Department of Interior regulations that defined ESA "taking" as including "significant habitat modification or degradation" and ruled that ESA prohibition of species taking is not equivalent to a taking of property from landowners (*Babbitt v. Sweet Home 1995*).

U.S. President George H. W. Bush refused to sign the international Convention on Biodiversity (CBD) at the 1992 Earth Summit in Rio de Janeiro, Brazil. After the CBD was signed by the Clinton administration, the 103rd Congress did not ratify it. Among the reasons for U.S. refusal to ratify the CBD in 1994 was the view that strong conservation laws in the United States were already sufficient, so even with ratification, the United States would not have required specific new implementing legislation. U.S. industry was initially concerned about protection of intellectual property, terms of technology transfer, and a potential biosafety protocol. While those concerns were largely eased prior to the vote (DOS 1994), ratification was not approved. While the U.S. reluctance to ratify the CBD is in part a discomfort with explicit acceptance of the precautionary principle, it is also important to acknowledge that implicit acceptance of precautionary action exists in many U.S. environmental regulations (Kormos et al. 2001).

Since 2004, a range of proposals before Congress and others have sought either to strengthen or weaken biodiversity conservation regulations. The U.S. administration's 2005 support for drilling for oil in the Alaska National Wildlife Refuge is viewed by many scientists as insufficiently precautionary about potential impacts on biodiversity. The Clinton administration banned snowmobiles in Yellowstone National Park to help prevent adverse impacts on wildlife. The George W. Bush administration proposed allowing snowmobiles in Yellowstone in the belief that conservation objectives should be given equal weight with recreational objectives. Concerns in 2004 over U.S. national security had prompted proposals to exempt U.S. Department of Defense lands from the ESA and the National Environmental Policy Act, thus risking adverse impacts on biodiversity during military training.

European Union: 1970–1985

The 1979 EU Council Directive on Conservation of Wild Birds (EU Council Directive 79/409/EEC) enabled EU Member States to meet their obligations under the 1979 Bern Convention, which was adopted under the auspices of the Council of Europe. The Birds Directive directs EU Member States to maintain the population of all "species of naturally occurring birds in the wild state" in the European territory "at a level which corresponds in particular to ecological, scientific, and cultural requirements, while taking account of economic and recreational requirements." This is accomplished by Member States establishing protected areas, maintaining habitats both inside and outside protected areas, restoring destroyed habitats, and creating new habitat. All species of wild birds are protected—although exceptions are made for hunting and some other reasons. Prohibitions include deliberate killing or capture of birds, destroying or damaging nests and eggs, disturbing birds during breeding and rearing, and keeping birds whose hunting and capture is prohibited.

Annex I to the Birds Directive lists 181 vulnerable bird species (Haigh 2000), which are subject to special habitat conservation measures as outlined originally in Article 4, and later in the 1992 Habitats Directive (see below). Member States are required to create both terrestrial and marine special protection areas (SPAs) needed to conserve the species in Annex I as well as common migratory species not listed in Annex I. Wetlands are to receive special attention. Member States are to avoid pollution or deterioration of all SPA habitats and take specific measures to conserve SPAs as outlined in the Habitats Directive. If Member States do not enforce the directive, they risk not receiving regional development funding.

The Birds Directive can be considered strongly precautionary in both earliness and stringency by protecting all migratory birds and their habitats before there is evidence of their decline, and by protecting habitats for vulnerable species.

European Union: 1986–2000

The 1992 Habitats Directive (EU Council Directive 92/43/EEC) replaced Article 4 of the 1979 Birds Directive. This directive is the means by which the European

Community meets its obligations as a 1982 signatory of the Convention on the Conservation of European Wildlife and Natural Habitats (Bern Convention). While it does not contain explicit references to the precautionary principle, the directive requires Member States to protect species listed in the Annexes, to monitor habitats and species, and to report every six years on the implementation of the directive. The 189 habitats listed in Annex I of the Habitats Directive and the 788 species listed in Annex II are to be protected by means of a network of sites. Each Member State is required to prepare and propose a national list of sites; these sites are then evaluated during formation of a European network of Sites of Community Importance (SCIs). Selected sites are next designated by Member States as Special Areas of Conservation (SACs). Along with Special Protection Areas (SPAs) from the Birds Directive, they form a network of protected areas across Europe known as Natura 2000. The EC notes that this is one of the first applications of the precautionary principle to protected areas.

While this formal link between the Birds and Habitats Directives provides the framework for European nature conservation, some provisions of the Habitats Directive weaken its precautionary nature, likely in response to the Leybucht Dykes case discussed below (Freestone 1996, 231). Under the provisions of Article 6(2-4) of the Habitats Directive, SPAs can be damaged or destroyed if it can be shown that a project must be carried out for "imperative reasons of overriding public interest, including those of a social or economic nature" (Haigh 2000), but Member States must balance that authority with the directive's obligation to prevent irreversible damage to biodiversity (de Sadeleer 2002, 271). Freestone (1996, 247) also notes that the European Court of Justice (ECJ) interprets this increased discretion very strictly. The Habitats Directive is precautionary in putting the burden of proof with proponents, noting, "competent authorities shall agree to the plan or project only after having ascertained that it will not adversely affect the integrity of the site concerned, and, if appropriate, after having obtained the opinion of the general public."

A number of ECJ judgments have reinforced the precautionary nature of the 1979 Birds Directive. In February 1989, the European Commission charged Germany with failing to prevent deterioration of an SPA called the Leybucht Bay when it proceeded with a project installing dikes. While the February 1991 judgment from the ECJ allowed the dikes to be built because of their importance in preventing flooding damage—and possibly increasing the area of wetland—the judgment indicated that Member States have very limited discretion in reducing the size and quality of specially protected areas (European Court Reports 1991). The decision caused such concern in the United Kingdom, which had intervened in support of the German government, that the UK led a campaign to add amendments to the draft Habitats Directive to give Member States more discretion in approving projects with adverse effects on SPAs (Freestone 1996, 237).

In 1990, the European Commission charged the kingdom of Spain with failing to classify the Santona Marshes as an SPA and with failing to prevent degradation and pollution of the marshes by allowing road construction, aquaculture facilities, and discharge of untreated wastewater. This wetland of international importance was regularly visited by 19 species listed on Annex I of the Birds Directive and more than 14 species of migratory birds. The Spanish government argued that destruction of habitat did not violate the directive because a reduction in bird numbers had not been reported. The ECJ ruled against Spain in 1993, noting that "[t]he obligations on Member States under Articles 3 and 4 of the directive therefore exist even before any reduction is observed in the number of birds or any risk of a protected species becoming extinct has materialized" (European Court Reports 1993, paragraph 15). In addition to this support for precaution in the face of uncertainty, the ECJ also ruled in this case that economic and social considerations could not be considered as more important than ecological objectives (paragraph 18). Spain was required to pay the costs of the case.

In 1992, the Administrative Court of Nantes, France, asked the European Court for rulings on interpretation of the Birds Directive in relation to dates for ending the hunting season set in prefects in France. In 1994, the ECJ replied that in order to protect all species during pre-breeding migration, and given the uncertainty of predicting when species will migrate, the Member States should not set closing dates for the hunting season that are based on when an average number of species migrate; instead, end dates for hunting should protect the species that migrates earliest (European Court Reports 1994, paragraph 21). The ECJ indicated that staggering hunting end dates for individual species is acceptable where there is scientific evidence for that species (paragraph 22). In 1996, a criminal case was brought against an individual in the Netherlands who imported a subspecies of goldfinch that only occurred outside Member States, although the species it belonged to occurred naturally in the Netherlands. The ECJ ruled in 1996 that the Habitats Directive applies not only to species and subspecies found within Member States but also to subspecies of European species that are found outside Europe. The ruling was intended to "safeguard biological balances" from accidental release of exotic subspecies (European Court Reports 1996, paragraph 17). While not directly using the term "precaution" in the above cases, the ECJ clearly supported a strongly precautionary approach to the actions covered by the Birds Directive.

In 1993, the EU approved the CBD that had been adopted at the 1992 Rio Earth Summit. The CBD's primary goals are to call on each nation to take domestic action to conserve biological diversity, encourage sustainable use of biodiversity, and promote equitable sharing of benefits and access to genetic resources among those nations that conserve biodiversity in natural habitats and those nations that use biological diversity for commercial purposes. The CBD encourages environmental impact assessments for proposed projects likely to have significant impact on biodiversity. Preamble paragraph 9 states that "where there is a threat of significant reduction or loss of biological diversity lack of full scientific certainty should not be used as a reason for postponing measures to avoid or minimize such a threat." Although this is a weak definition of precaution, the Convention's overall goals are strongly precautionary. The CBD is not particularly stringent, however. The CBD calls on developed nations to provide financial support for conservation in developing nations, currently through the Global Environment Facility (GEF).

Country eligibility for financial support is supposed to be linked to progress on conservation, including preparation of national conservation plans.

The 2000 Cartagena Protocol on Biosafety, adopted under the CBD, is extremely precautionary in authorizing parties to the convention to refuse to import genetically (called living) modified organisms (GMOs) if there is uncertainty about impacts of GMOs on conservation and sustainable use of biodiversity in the importing country. The EU approved the protocol on November 9, 2003, and it has subsequently been approved by many Member States including Germany, the United Kingdom, Norway, France, Spain, and the Netherlands. A summary of the specific protocol provisions and their precautionary nature is provided in Mackenzie et al. (2003).

EU Member State Biodiversity Regulation

A limited review of European Member State regulation of biodiversity conservation reveals no consistent pattern of precaution that could contribute to conclusions about whether Europe is more or less precautionary than the United States in any given time period. De Sadeleer (2002, 124, 134) notes that while the precautionary principle is increasingly part of national environmental laws in Europe (e.g., in Germany, France, Belgium, and Sweden), it is most in evidence in litigation in Member States. He notes that while there is a great deal of variation across Member State litigation, precautionary rulings "are not exceptional in litigation under Belgian law."

The UK was considered to have some of the strongest bird protection legislation prior to passage of the Birds Directive (Haigh 2000). While Germany formally endorsed the precautionary principle in the 1980s, the UK endorsed a weak version of it in 1990, with an emphasis on prevention using cost–benefit analysis and sound science (Jordan 2001, 146). The British Wildlife and Countryside Act of 1981 was passed to implement the obligations of the Birds Directive, while the 1994 Conservation Regulations were passed to implement the Habitats Directive (Haigh 2000). Freestone (1996, 248) questioned whether the UK strategy for voluntary compliance with designation of Sites of Special Scientific Interest (SSSIs) complies with the Habitats and Birds Directive requirement to designate SPAs and SACs. This strategy likely contributes to the slow designation of SPAs in the UK (Haigh 2000). Water withdrawal licenses in the UK are required to properly safeguard wetlands designated as SPAs (O'Riordan et al. 2001, 19).

Another scenario took place in the Netherlands. The Dutch Nature Conservancy Act of 1967 was unclear about when licensing of development activity should be precautionary (Backes and Verschuuren 1998). The revised Nature Conservation Act (NCA) of 1998 implements the 1992 EU Habitats Directive and conforms to obligations from the 1992 CBD. Although the NCA expresses the intent of the precautionary principle in Article 16(3), it does not use the word "precaution." Dutch courts have been reluctant to apply the precautionary principle in a number of instances (Douma 2001, 165, 181). The act gives authorities discretion to give priority to economic concerns over conservation concerns (Douma 2001, 169).

Comparing Relative Precaution

Comparison of the precautionary nature of conservation regulations in the United States and EU defies simple conclusions about one side of the Atlantic being more precautionary than the other. Characterizations of regulations are influenced by the relative value one places on regulations being early, anticipatory, and stringent. Depending on how one defines precaution, one can conclude that the United States was equally precautionary to the EU or more precautionary than the EU with regard to regulation of biodiversity conservation from 1970 to 1985. From 1986 to 2000, the EU and United States have both addressed biodiversity conservation with precautionary regulations, but they have addressed different aspects and scales of conservation. This conclusion might change if the examination also included regulations with indirect impacts on biodiversity.

Some European environmental NGOs might argue that the 2000 EC Communication on Precaution reflects movement toward the U.S. view, with its emphasis on cost–benefit and risk assessment (Jordan 2001, 158). Individual EU Member States exhibit a wide range in degree of precaution in implementing EU directives, and additional analysis is needed to track Member State biodiversity regulations over time.

One of the main differences in approach is the U.S. primary focus on all endangered species compared with the European focus on all species of birds and important habitats for other endangered species that occur in Europe (before there is evidence of population decline). While some contrast the EU approval of the CBD with nonratification by the United States as evidence of stronger EU precaution, this conclusion is not strongly supported given the lack of stringency of the CBD. As will be discussed below, legislation may not necessarily reflect actual increased conservation of species and habitats. As has been noted by others (Wiener and Rogers 2002), it is likely that both the United States *and* the EU are at the more precautionary end of a spectrum compared with much of the rest of the world. Some of the major illustrative U.S. and EU regulations, treaties, and judicial decisions directly related to terrestrial biodiversity conservation are listed in Table 9.1.

Causes of Precautionary Regulation of Biodiversity in the United States and Europe

As noted above, a number of considerations make it difficult to discern clear differences in relative precaution in the United States and in Europe. It is also equally challenging to identify the specific factors that might actually account for the differences in regulation of biodiversity conservation. Still, a number of hypotheses can be considered.

Table 9.1 *Illustrative U.S. and EU Biodiversity Regulations, Treaties, and Major Judicial Decisions*

	United States		European Union		
	FEDERAL	INTERNATIONAL TREATIES	EU-WIDE	INTERNATIONAL TREATIES	NATIONAL
1971	Wild Horses Act				1967 Dutch Nature Conservancy Act
1972	Clean Water Act (indirect) Marine Mammal Protection Act				
1973	Endangered Species Act (ESA)				
1974		CITES ratified			
1975					
1976	National Forest Management Act				
1977					
1978	Supreme Court Decision *TVA v. Hill* (Protect critical habitat regardless of cost)				
1979	Alaska National Interest Lands Conservation Act (ANILCA)		Wild Birds Directive		
1980					
1981					British Wildlife and Countryside Act (Birds Directive)
1982	ESA amended to add Habitat Conservation Plans and incidental taking.			CITES regulation adopted Bern convention approved	
1983	Foreign Assistance Act Amendments for Biodiversity		Ban on import of seal pups and products	Bonn Convention on Migratory Species approved	
1984					
1985					
1986					
1987		Ramsar Convention ratified			
1988	Endangered Species Act recovery plans				
1989					
1990					

Table 9.1 (continued)

	United States		European Union		
	FEDERAL	INTERNATIONAL TREATIES	EU-WIDE	INTERNATIONAL TREATIES	NATIONAL
1991			ECJ Leybucht Dykes case		
1992			Habitats Directive		
1993			ECJ Spain case	Convention on Biological Diversity approved	
1994			ECJ Préfet de Main et Loire case		UK Conservation Regulations (Habitat Directive)
1995	U.S. Supreme Court Decision *Babbitt v. Sweet Home*				
1996			ECJ van der Feesten case		
1997	National Wildlife Refuge System Improvement Act				
1998					Netherlands Nature Conservation Act (Habitats Directive)
2001					
2002					
2003				Cartagena Biosafety Protocol approved	

An obvious place to start is the fact that most of the landscape in Europe has been used and altered by humans for thousands of years, while in comparison, the U.S. landscape has been much less changed by Native American and then European settlement. One hypothesis might suggest that U.S. regulation could therefore be less precautionary about biodiversity conservation because more "natural" habitat remains, whereas European regulation reflects the importance of conserving what little "natural" habitat is left. Another view might hold that it is easier to regulate nature when it is already disturbed. In explaining European concern over genetically modified food, O'Riordan et al. (2001, 29) note that most natural and scenic landscapes in Europe have been modified by agriculture, and those landscapes now include sustainable agriculture that also protects species and habitats. They note that most of the Natura 2000 protected sites include some farm management.

One can also examine whether cultural factors in the United States influence how the risk of biodiversity loss is perceived and then regulated. With a few exceptions—say, noticing changes in birds or amphibians in backyards, or seeing media headlines on the loss of snail darters or spotted owls—loss of species is not a particularly salient risk to most Europeans and Americans. Changes in habitats and ecosystems at the landscape level are more salient. Jordan (2001, 155) hypothesizes that the EU is more like the "egalitarian-hierarchists" who "regard human impact on nature as unpredictable and potentially calamitous," whereas the United States more resembles an "individualist" who regards the environment as robust and resilient to human impacts. However, Rohrmann (2000) noted insignificant differences between national perceptions of risk in Western countries, and one would expect this to hold true for views of biodiversity as well.

Political and economic factors are usually considered to play a major role in explaining biodiversity conservation regulations. The increase in public awareness of environmental risks in the early 1960s and the political and cultural environment in the United States in the late 1960s and early 1970s opened the policy window for a large number of groundbreaking environmental laws in the United States in which the environmental objectives were more important than economic concerns (Kingdon 1995, 165).

Wiener and Rogers (2002) hypothesize that the United States might be more likely to enforce regulatory measures, and therefore more reluctant to pass strongly precautionary regulations. When the European Commission receives complaints from individuals about management of Natura 2000 sites, it has discretion in deciding whether to bring the case to the ECJ. De Sadeleer (2002, 138, 139) notes that the precautionary principle is not found in statutory law in the UK and United States in part because the Anglo-Saxon based legal system resists use of legal principles. The idea of precautionary *action*, however, can be found in law and legal rulings.

Consequences of Precautionary Regulation of Biodiversity

As difficult as it might be to pass precautionary regulation, it can be even more difficult for institutions to implement the regulations and then to determine the impact of the regulations on biodiversity and other outcomes. While it is difficult to link most conservation outcomes directly to a single policy, it is also difficult to determine what might have happened without the policy. Most regulations lack specific guidance for evaluating positive and negative impacts. When should a species be declared "recovered"? When is a protected area considered protected? Often impacts are viewed as remaining primarily rhetorical.

A number of successes have been attributed to conservation legislation—saving the piping plover and bald eagle from extinction in the United States, and increasing wetland area and reintroducing the red kite in England. However, for the most part, the risk of loss of species, habitats, and ecosystems is still extreme. As policymakers consider ways to improve regulation, consideration needs to be given not only to assessment of the intended impacts of current regulations, but also to the unintended, countervailing risks in order to move toward "risk superior" regulations for biodiversity conservation (Graham and Wiener 1995). Systems and methods for assessing all consequences of biodiversity regulations are still needed.

Impacts of U.S. Regulations on Biodiversity Loss

Bean and Rowland (1997, 276) point out that although the ESA was intended to serve as "a sort of emergency room … it has more often served as an intensive care unit or even a hospice." They note that while the "threatened" category was intended to prompt early attention to declining species, it is used sparingly, and often for species that are in reality already endangered. Many argue that the ESA would be far less costly and more successful if action were taken *before* species were faced with pending extinction (Ecological Society of America 1996, 11; Cole 1992, 358). Others point out that the ESA's focus on the species level misses attention to the more critical aspects of biodiversity loss at the habitat and ecosystem level.

In 2004, over 1,200 native species and 558 foreign species were listed as threatened or endangered in the United States. There were 280 "candidate" species waiting for consideration for listing (USFWS 2004). Only 16 species had been delisted due to species recovery since the passage of the ESA in 1973, while 9 species had been delisted due to extinction (USFWS 2004). There were 108 species known to have gone extinct in the first 21 years after the passage of the ESA (Suckling et al. 2004, 1). To many critics, these figures illustrate failure of the ESA to achieve its goals. If the purpose of the act is to bring species to the point where they can recover healthy population levels, then a greater number of species should have been delisted (Suckling et al. 2004, 9). However, the political controversy associated with delisting may allow some species that have recovered sufficiently to remain on the list and others to come off the list before populations have recovered in a range of locations. At the same time, the ESA is also considered a great success in protecting species that might have been even worse off without it.

Additional constraints to effective implementation of the ESA include challenges with funding and enforcement. Bean and Rowland (1997, 276) point out that ESA has the greatest gap of any conservation program between its goals and the funds Congress makes available to meet those goals. Some critics point to the lack of designation of critical habitat for over 80% of listed species (Smith 1999, 343) as a failure of the ESA. Others note that USFWS may view designation of critical habitat as a lower priority than listing given limited budgets, because destruction of habitat that threatens a listed species can be prosecuted as a taking, even without the critical habitat designation. However, when USFWS attempts to prosecute takings of listed species, there is a very high burden of proof, and the penalties may not be deterrents.

In response to the 1982 amendments allowing the Department of Interior to permit "incidental" private takings of listed species as part of an approved HCP, by late 1999 over 250 HCPs had been negotiated, with several of them covering areas greater than 100,000 acres; 200 more were in negotiation (Johnston 2001, 274). The ESA could potentially lead to tens of millions of acres being protected in HCPs, which has the potential to reduce loss of threatened and endangered species, as well as other species. However, many HCPs have shown greater interest in protecting open space for scenic and recreational purposes than for protecting endangered species.

Impacts of EU Regulations on Biodiversity Loss

Implementation and enforcement of the Birds and Habitats Directives in EU Member States have faced a number of problems (Wils 1994; Haigh 2000). A number of Member States still need to make progress on creating and protecting the required network of specially protected areas. A Birdlife International study in 2000 listed 3600 important sites for birds covering 7% of Europe. They found that 50% of these Important Bird Areas were seriously threatened by development—intensive agriculture in particular—and 60% remain unprotected (Haigh 2000).

The Habitats and Birds Directives, combined with the doctrine of direct effect, are unclear about whether citizens have the right to bring suit in national courts. It can be difficult for NGOs to obtain standing in judicial review applications (Faulks and Rose 1996, 197, 202). Use of the "complaints procedure" to bring an issue directly to the attention of the European Commission or the ECJ has limited ability to help with enforcement or to immediately help avoid adverse impacts to biodiversity. While NGOs in Europe find the complaints procedure cheap and easy to invoke, it also has many disadvantages, including that the complainant is "a whistle blower rather than a litigant" (Faulks and Rose 1996, 197–201). Other disadvantages are a lack of transparency and the political nature of attention to complaints. NGOs have limited rights before the ECJ (Faulks and Rose 1996, 204). High UK legal costs may be considered an obstacle to enforcement of the directives in national courts. Lower legal costs in France, Belgium, and the Netherlands make it easier for environmental organizations to engage in litigation in those countries (Wils 1994).

How Conservation Regulations Affect Other Risks

One of the most debated aspects of the U.S. Endangered Species Act is the restrictions that the federal government can place on the use of both public and private property once a listed species is discovered there. Since the "taking" of a listed species is illegal, modification of habitat that the species depends upon can be limited in order to protect the threatened or endangered species. Species proposed or listed could be put at greater risk from harm by individuals who either fear economic loss due to limits on development of their land (Meltz 1993) or simply fear government intervention on their rights and intrusions on their freedom to manage personal property. Some landowners have been known to purposely destroy individuals from a proposed listed species or to ruin the habitat of such a species to win exemption from regulation once the listing is approved (Pombo 2004; Sugg 1994, 45). Landowners concerned about potential economic loss have also vehemently resisted reintroduction of endangered species such as the gray wolf in the northern Rocky Mountains.

The fact that the United States has not ratified the CBD is seen by some as having a high political cost in terms of how the United States is perceived by other governments and NGOs on environmental issues. Those who lobbied hard for the United States not to ratify obviously have a different view. Many indigenous peoples' organizations and local communities have questioned whether the objectives of the CBD could be interpreted as conflicting with their rights to use biological resources. The International Union for the Conservation of Nature (IUCN) passed a resolution at the November 2004 World Conservation Congress calling on members to consider how the precautionary principle can help strengthen efforts to conserve biodiversity while also being sensitive to public participation and intergenerational equity (IUCN 2004). The U.S. delegation to this meeting did not deliberate on the resolution.

U.S. regulations prohibiting use of foreign assistance for projects that can adversely impact biodiversity and tropical forest habitat resulted in less U.S. support for large dams and other infrastructure projects in developing countries, beginning in the 1980s. Ministries of economic development in developing nations often still found donors from other nations to fund these projects—at times resulting in fewer environmental impact controls than the United States requires in projects funded with foreign assistance.

Success in protecting species and habitats can lead to additional countervailing risks. In highly fragmented landscapes, federal and state protected areas can often become the only contiguous "open space." They then become targeted as right-of-way opportunities for power and other utility lines, cell phone towers, and roads—all of which can increase adverse impacts on biodiversity. Successful protection of species in protected areas can lead to increases in poaching. The nature tourism that helps sustain many protected landscapes can lead to habitat degradation due to too many visitors. Much has been written about the CITES elephant ivory control policies leading to elephant population levels in some reserves that damage farms outside the reserves (Young 2003).

Other Effects on Public Health, Economic Growth, and Innovation

The economic benefits and costs of conserving biodiversity have been estimated from a wide range of perspectives, including the provision of ecosystem services, mitigating climate change, and ecological tourism. There is potentially enormous future value in the undiscovered chemical properties in plants and animals. An estimated 25% of pharmaceutical drugs sold in the United States in 2004—with an annual market value over $10 billion—have active ingredients derived from plants.

The economics of the ESA are a politically controversial subject as well (Swanson 1994). Some question whether the millions spent on recovering individual species could have had greater impact if habitat had been purchased for permanent protection. A species with high economic costs of recovery and possibly low economic benefits to humans has the same merit in consideration of listing as a species with potentially large economic benefits and lower costs of recovery (Brown and Shogren 1998, 6). The highly public and heated controversy over protection of the spotted owl in the Pacific Northwest led to the unconstructive view that conserving biodiversity is counter to economic growth ("jobs versus owls").

A number of innovative approaches to conservation on private lands have been stimulated by the ESA, including conservation agreements (Frank 1997) and tradable permits (Wilcove 2004). Conservation agreements with landowners are also an approach taken in implementing the EU Habitats Directive (European Commission 2000).

Conclusions and Lessons Learned

This analysis indicates that regulation of terrestrial biodiversity conservation from 1970 to 2000 does not support claims that the EU is universally more precautionary than the United States, nor hypotheses that the "flip-flop" metaphor described in Chapter 1 applies to biodiversity conservation. It appears that from 1970 to 1985, the United States was equally precautionary to the EU or more precautionary. From 1986 to 2000, the United States and the EU applied precaution to regulation of different aspects and scales of biodiversity. A detailed analysis resists simple characterization.

Given that extinction of species and destruction of most habitats are irreversible, policymakers should be encouraged to adopt the strongest possible version of the precautionary principle, defined to mean that uncertainty requires prohibiting actions potentially destructive of biodiversity until the proponent proves an activity has either no risk or some acceptable level of risk. The irreversible nature of biodiversity loss and the difficulty in determining the thresholds for various types of human-induced change that can lead to that loss suggest taking a "guilty until proven innocent" precautionary approach to regulation of human activity. Many have pointed out that when the "precautionary principle" remains as a general guiding principle instead of a hard law, short-term human interests are likely to continue to receive priority over longer-term, uncertain conservation concerns (de Sadeleer 2002, 372; Cooney 2004).

Traditional cost–benefit analysis of regulatory impacts is difficult and often inappropriate to use in deciding whether precautionary regulation is appropriate for biodiversity conservation. The negative impacts of biodiversity loss—and the positive impacts of conservation—are difficult to quantify and will be realized over very long time horizons.

Future analysis should include the role of U.S. state and EU Member State regulations in implementing and reinforcing U.S. federal and EU directives. In the United States, at least 12 state constitutions declare that citizens have rights to conservation of natural resources, thus creating a basis for increasing state level precaution and for shifting the burden of proof to proponents of activities potentially harmful to biodiversity (Saterson 2001). Additional analysis should be conducted on the many regulations that address biodiversity indirectly—regulation of habitat alteration, forest management, exotic species introduction, pollution, and climate change to name only a few.

Use of precaution in regulating biodiversity conservation demands monitoring, assessment, and adaptation. To protect biodiversity, we must not only improve the degree of certainty about impacts we already understand, but also increase understanding of unintended impacts we cannot imagine now. Just as biodiversity is dynamic and continually evolving in response to natural disturbances and changing conditions, so should regulations be. The CBD requires regular monitoring and reporting in order to respond to emerging increased risks.

Interdisciplinary, multiple stakeholder input to the range of regulations impacting biodiversity might help with the challenge of determining how to integrate laws from different sectors, how to determine which laws take precedence, and how to balance economic, ecological, social, and other objectives. Article 6 of the EC treaty specifies that environmental protection needs to be integrated with other EC policies (de Sadeleer 2002, 272).

The poet T. S. Eliot asked, "Where is the wisdom we have lost in knowledge, and the knowledge we have lost in information?" We need to act wisely on both the uncertainty and the information we have available now, while continuing research to reduce uncertainty. While there are numerous examples of "late lessons from early warnings" (EEA 2001) with respect to individual species losses, we are just beginning to learn about the ways that cumulative loss of genes, species, and ecosystems can have potentially catastrophic effects on human and environmental health and well-being.

Wider application and stronger implementation of precaution in biodiversity regulation should help stimulate innovation and provide opportunities to improve knowledge about how to decrease the impacts of human activities on the Earth's biological systems.

Acknowledgements

I thank Deserai Anderson-Utley for her excellent research assistance and for her specific contributions to analyses of the U.S. Endangered Species Act. I also thank Mark Axelrod and Zheng Zhou for research assistance. For comments on an earlier draft, I thank Peter Sand, Jonathan Wiener, and participants in the Fourth Transatlantic Dialogue on Precaution held September 2004 at Duke University.

References

Babbitt v. Sweet Home Chapter of Communities for a Great Oregon. 1995. U.S. Supreme Court Decision 115 Supreme Ct. 2407. June 29.

Backes, Chris W. and Jonathan M. Verschuuren. 1998. The Precautionary Principle in International, European and Dutch Wildlife Law. *Colorado Journal of International Law and Policy* 9: 43.

Bean, Michael J., and Melanie J. Rowland. 1997. *The Evolution of National Wildlife Law.* 3rd ed. Westport, CT: Praeger.

Bern Convention on the Conservation of European Wildlife and Natural Habitat. 1979. *European Treaty Series (ETS)* No. 104.

Brown Jr., Gardner M., and Jason F. Shogren. 1998. Economics of the Endangered Species Act. *Journal of Economic Perspectives* 12 (3): 3–20.

Burton, Lloyd. 2002. *Worship and Wilderness: Culture, Religion and Law in Public Lands Management.* Madison, WI: University of Wisconsin Press.

CEQ (U.S. Council for Environmental Quality). 1980. *Global 2000 Report to the President. Entering the Twenty-first Century,* edited by Gerald O. Barney. Vol. 3. Washington, DC: Government Printing Office.

Cole, Christopher A. 1992. Note. Species Conservation in the United States: The Ultimate Failure of the Endangered Species Act and Other Land Use Laws. *Boston University Law Review* 72: 343.

Convention on Biological Diversity. 1992. *International Legal Materials* 31 (June 5): 818.

Cooney, Rosie. 2004. *The Precautionary Principle in Biodiversity Conservation and Natural Resource Management: An Issues Paper for Policy-makers, Researchers and Practitioners.* Gland, Switzerland: International Union for Conservation of Nature (IUCN).

de Sadeleer, Nicolas. 2002. *Environmental Principles: From Political Slogans to Legal Rules.* Translated by Susan Leubusher. Oxford: Oxford University Press.

Dickson, B. 1999. The Precautionary Principle in CITES: A Critical Assessment. *Natural Resources Journal* 39 (2): 211–228.

DOS (U.S. Department of State). 1994. Dispatch: Ratification Sought for the Convention on Biological Diversity. Counselor of the State Department Timothy E. Wirth Speech. Transcript of Statement before the Senate Foreign Relations Committee. April 12, Washington, DC.

Douma, Wybe. 2001. The Precautionary Principle in the Netherlands. In *Reinterpreting the Precautionary Principle,* edited by Tim O'Riordan, James Cameron, and Andrew Jordan. London: Cameron May Publishers, 163–181.

Ecological Society of America. 1996. Strengthening the Use of Science in Achieving the Goals of the Endangered Species Act: An Assessment by the Ecological Society of America. *Ecological Applications* 6 (1): 1–11.

EEA (European Environment Agency). 2001. *Late Lessons from Early Warnings: The Precautionary Principle, 1896–2000.* Environmental Issue Report No. 22. Luxembourg.

ESA (U.S. Endangered Species Act). 1973. 16 U.S.C. §§ 1531–1542.

EU Council. 1979. Directive 79/409/EEC, Directive on the Conservation of Wild Birds. April 2.

———. 1992. Directive 92/43/EEC, Directive on the Conservation of Habitats. May 21.

European Commission. 2000. Managing Natura 2000 Sites: The Provisions of Article 6 of the Habitats Directive 92/43/EEC. Luxembourg, Belgium.

European Court Reports. 1991. Case C-57/89. *Commission of the European Communities v. Germany. The Leybucht Dykes Case.* February 28. I–883.

———. 1993. Case C-355/90 *Commission of the European Communities v. Kingdom of Spain.* August 2, I–4221.

———. 1994. Case C-435/92. *Association pour la Protection des Animaux Sauvages et al. v. Préfet de Main-et-Loire et Préfet de Loire-Atlantique.* January 19, I–67.

———. 1996. Case C-202/94. *Criminal Proceedings against Godefridus van der Feesten.* February 8. I–355.

Faulks, John, and Laurence Rose. 1996. Common Interest Groups and the Enforcement of European Environmental Law. In *Protecting the European Environment: Enforcing EC Environmental Law,* edited by Han Somsen. London: Blackstone Press Limited, 195–207.

Frank, Andrew G. 1997. Note. Reforming the Endangered Species Act: Voluntary Conservation Agreements, Government Compensation, and Incentives for Private Action. *Columbia Journal of Environmental Law* 22: 137.

Freestone, David. 1996. Enforcement of the Wild Birds Directive: A Case Study. In *Protecting the European Environment: Enforcing EC Environmental Law*, edited by Han Somsen. London: Blackstone Press Limited, 229–250.

Graham, John D. and Jonathan B. Wiener, eds. 1995. *Risk Versus Risk: Tradeoffs in Protecting Health and the Environment*. Cambridge, MA: Harvard University Press.

Haigh, Nigel, ed. 2000. Birds and Their Habitats. In *Manual of Environmental Policy: The EC and Britain*. Institute for European Environmental Policy (IEEP). London: Longman Press. www.environmentalpolicy.net/ep-net/sample.html (accessed July 26, 2004).

IUCN (International Union for Conservation of Nature). 1980. *World Conservation Strategy: Living Resource Conservation for Sustainable Development*. Gland, Switzerland: IUCN.

———. 2004. Resolution RESWCC 3.075. Applying the Precautionary Principle in Environmental Decisionmaking and Management. Passed November 25 by the 3rd session of the IUCN World Conservation Congress. November 16–25, Bangkok.

Johnston, Jason S. 2001. The Law and Economics of Environmental Contracts. In *Environmental Contracts: Comparative Approaches to Regulatory Innovation in the United States and Europe*, edited by Eric W. Orts and Kurt Deketelaere. London: Kluwer Law International.

Jordan, Andrew. 2001. The Precautionary Principle in the European Union. In *Reinterpreting the Precautionary Principle*, edited by Tim O'Riordan, James Cameron, and Andrew Jordan. London: Cameron May Publishers, 143–161.

Kingdon, John W. 1995. *Agendas, Alternatives, and Public Policies*. Reading, MA: Addison-Wesley Educational Publishers.

Kormos, Cyril, Brett Grosko, and Russell Mittermeier. 2001. U.S. Participation in International Law and Policy. *Georgetown International Environmental Law Review* 13: 661.

Mackenzie, Ruth, Françoise Burhenne-Guilmin, Antonio G. M. La Viña, and Jacob D. Werksman in cooperation with Alfonso Ascencio, Julian Kinderlerer, Katharina Kummer, and Richard Tapper 2003. *An Explanatory Guide to the Cartagena Protocol on Biosafety*. IUCN Environmental Policy and Law Paper No. 46. Gland, Switzerland: IUCN Publications.

Meltz, Robert. 1993. *The Endangered Species Act and Private Property: A Legal Primer*. Congressional Research Service Report for Congress.

O'Riordan, Tim, James Cameron, and Andrew Jordan, eds. 2001. *Reinterpreting the Precautionary Principle*. London: Cameron May Publishers.

Pombo, Richard W. 2004. *The ESA at 30: A Mandate for Modernization*. Committee on Resources, U.S. House of Representatives.

Prescott-Allen, R., and C. Prescott-Allen. 1982. *What's Wildlife Worth? Economic Contributions of Plants and Animals to Developing Countries*. London: International Institute for Environment and Development.

Ramsar (Ramsar Convention). 2002. Eighth Meeting of the Conference of the Contracting Parties to the Ramsar Convention. www.ramsar.org/cda/en/ramsar-documents-cops-cop8/main/ramsar/1-31-58-128_4000_0__ (accessed on May 5, 2010).

Rohrmann, Bernd. 2000. Cross-national Studies on the Perception and Evaluation of Hazards. In *Cross-Cultural Risk Perception Research*, edited by O. Renn and B. Rohrmann. Dordrecht, Netherlands: Kluwer Academic Publishers.

Saterson, Kathryn A. 2001. Government Legislation and Regulation. In *Encyclopedia of Biodiversity*, Vol. 3. Durham, NC: Academic Press, 233–245.

Saterson, K. A., N. L. Christensen, R. B. Jackson, R. A. Kramer, S. L. Pimm, M. D. Smith, and J. B. Wiener. 2004. Disconnects in Evaluating the Relative Effectiveness of Conservation Strategies. Editorial in *Conservation Biology* 18 (3): 1–3.

Smith, Shawn E. 1999. Comment. How "Critical" Is a Critical Habitat? The United States Fish and Wildlife Service's Duty under the Endangered Species Act. *Dickinson Journal of Environmental Law and Policy* 8: 343.

Suckling, Kieran, Rhiwena Slack, and Brian Nowicki. 2004. *Extinction and the Endangered Species Act.* Tucson, AZ: Center for Biological Diversity.

Sugg, Ike C. 1994. Caught in the Act: Evaluating the Endangered Species Act, Its Effects on Man and Prospects for Reform. *Cumberland Law Review* 24: 1.

Swanson, Timothy M. 1994. The Economics of Extinction Revisited and Revised: A Generalised Framework for the Analysis of the Problems of Endangered Species and Biodiversity Losses. *Oxford Economic Papers*, n.s., 46 (Special Issue on Environmental Economics): 800–821.

Tennessee Valley Authority (TVA) v. Hill et al. 1978. U.S. Supreme Court Decision. 437 U.S. Supreme Court 153, 180, 184. June 15.

USFWS (U.S. Fish and Wildlife Service). 1996. *History and Evolution of the Endangered Species Act of 1973, Including Its Relationship to CITES*, October. www.fws.gov (accessed July 2004).

———. 2003. *ESA Basics: 30 Years of Protecting Endangered Species.* www.endangered.fws.gov (accessed July 2004).

———. 2004. *Summary of Listed Species; Candidate Species List;* and *Delisted Species Report*, www.fws.gov (accessed July 2004).

Wiener, Jonathan B. and Michael D. Rogers. 2002. Comparing Precaution in the United States and Europe. *Journal of Risk Research* 5 (4): 317–349.

Wilcove, David. 2004. Using Economic and Regulatory Incentives to Restore Endangered Species: Lessons Learned from Three New Programs. *Conservation Biology* 18 (3): 639–645.

Wils, Wouter P. J. 1994. The Birds Directive 15 Years Later: A Survey of the Case Law and a Comparison with the Habitats Directive. *Journal of Environmental Law* 6 (2): 219–242.

Wilson, Edward O., ed. 1988. *Biodiversity.* Washington, DC: National Academy Press.

Young, Saskia. 2003. Notes & Comments: Contemporary Issues of the Convention in International Trade in Endangered Species of Wild Fauna and Flora (CITES) and the Debate Over Sustainable Use. *Colorado Journal of International Law and Policy* 14: 167.

CHAPTER 10

Chemicals

Ortwin Renn and E. Donald Elliott

*P*rotest against the manifestations of technology has been present since the time of the industrial revolution (Sieferle 1985; Renn 1987). The introduction of trains, steamboats, motorcars, and electric lights was met with skepticism and public discomfort (von Winterfeldt and Edwards 1984). The history books are full of accounts of people's rejections of technological changes. Just to cite one example, in 1824, the daily newspaper of the German city of Augsburg purchased a printing machine driven by a steam engine (Mittelstraß 1999, 3). Subsequently, the editor proclaimed that he would write all his editorials in the park rather than ever enter the print shop again, and another employee terminated his contract with the company and declared his life was endangered. Even pedestrians decided to avoid the street on which the building was located. Although history has recorded numerous examples of unwarranted anxieties, there have been equally worrisome accounts of overconfidence in allegedly foolproof safety measures and human abilities to cope with disasters (Harremoës et al. 2001). The responses to the change of technology over time seem to oscillate between courage and caution, between overconfidence in the human ability to manage risks and the paralysis of immobility in the light of pending opportunities and threatening hazards.

Most former critics of technological changes have learned over time that cultural evolution rests on innovation and that innovation implies risk-taking. Opportunities rise out of uncertainties. American political scientist Aaron Wildavsky called the drive toward zero risk the highest risk of all (Wildavsky 1990). Most technical experts, on the other side, have learned that good models of risk analysis and stringent methodology in designing technologies can serve only as approximations toward a safer society. Strategies of resilience and flexibility need to accompany safety improvements and to ensure control, monitoring, and public communication (Kolluru 1995). The debate on how to evaluate and manage risks focuses on three major strategies (Stirling 1998; Klinke and Renn 2001):

- risk-based approaches, including numerical thresholds (no observable effect level, or NOEL, standards; performance standards; and so on);
- reduction activities derived from the application of the precautionary principle (examples are ALARA, as low as reasonably achievable, and BACT, best available control technology, as well as containment in time and space and constant monitoring of potential side effects); and
- standards derived from discursive processes such as roundtables, deliberative rulemaking, mediation, or citizen panels.

This chapter focuses in particular on the second strategy of precaution in the realm of regulation of chemicals in the United States and the EU. In focusing on the particular case of regulating chemicals as an illustration of these general challenges, the present chapter will engage with a series of intractable questions. First, what does the precautionary principle mean in different regulatory contexts? More specifically, what was the actual pattern of precaution in the United States and Europe during the period from 1970 to 2004? Second, how can we understand the different practical applications of the precautionary principle in the United States and Europe? More specifically, what were the factors that evoked precautionary regulation and that accounted for the difference in degree of precaution in the United States and Europe? Third, what are the consequences of precaution in terms of how precaution relates to parallel (and sometimes contending) principles of good governance, such as proportionality and nondiscrimination, transparency and public reason, accountability and effectiveness (Fisher 2001)? Finally, the chapter will address some normative conclusions on the basis of the comparison.

The Different Meanings of Precaution

The precautionary principle has been adopted in a variety of forms at international, EU, and national levels (see Fisher 2002; the following discussion draws on Stirling et al. 2006). It is applied across an increasing number of national jurisdictions, economic sectors, and environmental areas (Trouwborst 2002; de Sadeleer 2002). It has moved from the regulation of industry, technology, and health risk to the wider governance of science, innovation, and trade (O'Riordan and Cameron 1994; Raffensberger and Tickner 1999; Harding and Fisher 1999; O'Riordan et al. 2001). As it has expanded in scope, so it has grown in profile and authority. In particular, as Article 174(2) in the EC Treaty of 2002, precaution now constitutes a key underlying principle in European Community policymaking (European Commission 2002). In the aftermath of a series of formative public health controversies, economic calamities, and political conflicts—for example, those involving BSE ("mad cow disease") and genetically modified (GM) crops—precaution is of great salience or importance in many fields, including the regulation of chemicals.

Despite the intensity of the policy attention, however, there remain a number of serious ambiguities and queries concerning the nature and appropriate role of the precautionary principle in governance (Cross 1996, 1998; Morris 2000; Majone 2002; Marchant and Mossman 2004; Löfstedt 2004). These are addressed—if not resolved— in a burgeoning literature both academic (Sand 2000; Fisher 2001; Klinke and Renn 2001; Stirling 2003; van Zwanenberg and Stirling 2004) and more policy-oriented (Stirling 1999; Harremoës et al. 2001). Although the precautionary approach has been formulated in many different ways in many different places (one root may be the "foresight principle" in Germany in the 1970s), the formulation in the Rio Declaration is the most popular (Paterson 2005):

> In order to protect the environment, the precautionary approach shall be widely applied by States according to their capabilities. Where there are threats of serious of irreversible damage, lack of full scientific certainty shall not be used as a reason for postponing cost-effective measures to prevent environmental degradation. (Rio Declaration 1992, Principle 15)

The meaning of this principle is highly debated among analysts and policymakers. To understand the debate, it is helpful to distinguish three positions toward risk analysis (see also Resnik 2003):

- *Classic risk assessment approach.* Within the first frame of scientific risk analysis, risk management relies on the best scientific estimates of probabilities and potential damages and uses expected values as the main input to judge the tolerability of risk as well as to design risk reduction measures that are cost-effective, proportional to the threat, and fair to the affected population. In this frame, precaution may best be interpreted as being conservative in making risk judgments and choosing cautious assumptions when calculating exposure or determining safety factors (of 10, 100, or more) to cover variability.
- *"Precaution" approach.* Within the frame of "precaution," the concept of risk is seen from the perspective of pervasive uncertainty—and even ignorance. Precautious risk management means ensuring prudent handling of decision options in situations of high uncertainty about causes and effects and where high vulnerability of the population under risk is present. Instruments of precaution include minimization requirements such as ALARA (as low as reasonably achievable) or ALARP (as low as reasonably practicable), diversification of risk agents, containment in time and space, and close monitoring.
- *Deliberative approach.* The third frame of deliberation has been advocated as an alternative or an addition to purely analytical procedures of both assessing and managing risks. The task of risk management here is to organize in a structured and effective manner the involvement of stakeholders and interested public for designing risk management strategies based on each stakeholder's knowledge (epistemic community) and value system. This strategy can go along with both the risk analysis and the precautionary approach, but it has been

advocated either as an independent path to risk management or, more often, as a policy-oriented implementation of the precautionary approach.

Over the last few years, advocates of the classic risk assessment, precaution-based, and deliberative approaches have launched fierce debates over the legitimacy of each method. This debate has been particularly strong between the classic and the precautionary camp. One side argues that precautionary strategies ignore scientific results and lead to arbitrary regulatory decisions (Cross 1996). On the other hand, the precautionary statement "one should be on the safe side" could be interpreted as a mandate to ban everything that might result in negative side effects. Such a rule would logically apply to any substance or human activity and would lead to total arbitrariness (Stone 2001; Majone 2002, 101). The principle has been labeled as ill defined or even incoherent (Sunstein 2005), absolutist, a path to increased risk-taking, a value judgment or an ideology, and an unscientific choice that marginalizes the role of science (Sandin et al. 2002, 288; Paterson 2005). Some analysts claim that using the precautionary principle risks holding science "hostage to interest group politics" (Charnley and Elliott 2002, 103, 66). In addition, policymakers could abuse the precautionary principle as a policy strategy to protect their economic interests and to impede world trade (Majone 2002).

On the other side of the fence, the advocates of the precautionary approach have argued that precaution does not automatically mean banning substances or activities; it is a step-by-step diffusion of risky activities or technologies until more knowledge and experience are accumulated (Fisher 2001, Stirling 2003). These advocates have accused their critics of ignoring the complexity and uncertainty of most hazardous situations and of relying on data that often turns out to be insufficient for making prudent judgments. Because the application of the precautionary principle has been associated with stricter and more rigid regulations, environmental groups have usually rallied around the precautionary approach, while most industrial and commercial groups have been fighting for the assessment-based approach. Again, the issue is not resolved, and the debate became even more pronounced with the defeat of the European Community in the World Trade Organization (WTO) settlement of hormones in beef. The European Community failed to provide sufficient evidence that the precautionary approach could justify the restriction of imported beef treated with hormones.

It is interesting to note that the first data-driven approach has been widely adopted by the official U.S. regulatory bodies, while the precautionary approach has been widely advocated by the EU regulatory bodies. There are, however, also numerous elements of precautionary approaches interspersed into the actual practices of U.S. regulatory agencies, just as there are judgments about magnitudes of risk in the actual practices of regulators in the EU (Löfstedt 2004). A strict dichotomy between "precautionary" in Europe and "risk-based" in the United States is therefore too simple to describe actual practice (Charnley and Elliott 2002).

The third approach—deliberation among stakeholders—has found wide acceptance among social scientists and risk analysts from academia. Yet so far, it has had little impact on the institutional design of risk analysis (Renn 2004). There are, however, isolated examples of community participation in risk decisions, such as in selecting the remedy under the Superfund cleanup program or negotiated rulemaking in the United States (Harter 1982; Coglianese 1997). In recent years, however, risk policymakers have acknowledged that participation in risk analysis provides many practical advantages (Charnley and Elliott 2003). Among others, community participation transforms difficult issues of resolving epistemic uncertainty to topics that can be dealt with at the negotiation table. "If society participates in the production of policy-relevant scientific knowledge, such 'socially robust' knowledge is less likely to be contested than that which is merely reliable" (Funtowicz et al. 2000, 333–334). Accordingly, the EU communication on good governance (2001) has highlighted the need for more stakeholder involvement and participation in risk management, as have the recommendations of many authoritative bodies in the United States (Presidential/Congressional Commission on Risk Management and Risk Assessment 1997). How to implement this requirement in day-to-day risk management decisions is still under dispute. Many scholars have also questioned the value of deliberative approaches in some settings, arguing that "when there is trust in the regulator, a top-down form of risk communication (information transfer) may be better than dialogue" (Löfstedt 2005, 3; Rose-Ackerman 1994; Coglianese 1997).

Application of the Precautionary Principle in Europe

First, we examine European approaches to applying precaution. The 2000 Communication on Precaution of the European Commission (European Commission 2000, 1) highlights the general relevance of the precautionary principle for EU policy areas such as environmental, consumer, and health protection. The significance of the principle is highlighted in the first section of the document: "Applying the precautionary principle is a key tenet of its policy, and the choices it makes to this end will continue to affect the views it defends internationally, on how this principle should be applied" (European Commission 2000, 3).

The communication specifies some of the major conditions and requirements for applying the principle. Two conditions are mentioned: "The measures, although provisional, shall be maintained as long as the scientific data remain incomplete, imprecise, or inconclusive and as long as the risk is considered too high to be imposed on society" (European Commission 2000, 21). In addition to the presence of remaining uncertainty, the EU communication lists the condition that the risk must be too high to be imposed on society. This relates to the requirement of proportionality mentioned as one of the major requirements of applying the principle.

The Commission's communication highlights three important issues in developing the precautionary principle (Fisher 2009). Each of these constitutes a means to ensure that decisionmaking pursuant to the precautionary principle is not arbitrary (Article 13, 16, 22). First, the precautionary principle "should be compatible with the classic division of risk analysis: risk assessment, risk management, risk communication." In the communication, the precautionary principle is largely understood as belonging to the stage of risk management, but it should also inform the risk assessment process. The "implementation of an approach based on the precautionary principle should start with a scientific evaluation, as complete as possible, and where possible, identifying at each stage the degree of scientific uncertainty." Second, the Commission's communication highlights the need for "proportionate, nondiscriminatory, and transparent actions." It further stresses the benefit of using cost–benefit analysis, based on the best scientific data. The communication also points out the need to "involve as early as possible and to the extent reasonably possible all interested parties." Third and finally, the communication allows for a wide range of risk management initiatives (Article 16). In particular, such measures need not be of a legally binding nature and, as noted above, should be revisable (Fisher 2009).

U.S. Approaches to Applying Precaution to Chemicals

One distinctive precautionary feature of the U.S. approach to regulation is redundancy. Americans are deeply suspicious that any government program can be designed to work perfectly, so they typically deploy multiple, overlapping approaches to deal with any problem—a strategy sometimes called "defense in depth." A sage European observer of the American legal system, Walter Bagehot, wrote of this feature of the American legal system long ago: "The English constitution, in a word, is framed on the principle of choosing a single sovereign authority, and making it good; the American, upon the principle of having many sovereign authorities, and hoping that their multitude will atone for their inferiority" (Bagehot 1901, 296).

A chemical company contemplating bringing a new material to market must consider regulation emanating from multiple sources. Regulation by the federal Environmental Protection Agency (EPA) under the Toxic Substances Control Act (TSCA), 15 U.S.C. §§ 2601–2692, is certainly one. But others include the threat of product liability lawsuits, state bans or regulations such as labeling requirements for particular substances, and specialized federal requirements for transportation, handling, environmental release, and cleanup. Moreover, separate regulatory systems govern particular uses or types of products such as drugs or consumer products. Added to these "hard law" systems of official state-sponsored regulation are important "soft law" systems such as the Responsible Care System of life-cycle requirements sponsored by the American Chemistry Council. Private requirements by customers to reduce or eliminate certain substances must be taken into consideration. Producing a chemical in the United States means considering multiple sources of regulation (see Elliott and Thomas 1993).

The same philosophy of multiple, overlapping sources of authority tends to characterize U.S. regulatory statutes. Rather than the well-organized and logical code of Europe, many U.S. statutes are a "toolbox" that gives a regulatory agency a variety of different tools to attack a particular problem. Table 10.1 summarizes the main sections of TSCA that EPA uses to regulate chemicals.

In addition, EPA has a number of other important tools, including the High Production Volume testing program and the Toxic Release Inventory, which are not

Table 10.1 *TSCA's Major Sections for Chemical Data Collection and Control*

Section	Purpose
4	Chemical testing
5	New chemical review and control and significant new use rules
6	Chemical regulation
8	Industry reporting of chemical data
9	TSCA's relationship to other laws
14	Disclosure of chemical data

Source: GAO (2005, 7)

codified as part of TSCA but are relevant to controls of chemicals. For brevity's sake, this analysis will focus first on EPA's ability to make precautionary decisions under one of the most successful sections of TSCA—the "pre-manufacture notification" requirements of Section 5—and then on one of the less effective sections, Section 6, regulation of unreasonable risks. These two sections illustrate both the best and the worst of the U.S. style of legal regulation of chemicals. For a more comprehensive evaluation of TSCA with suggestions for improvement, see GAO (2005).

Regulation of Chemicals in the United States

The following discussion will focus on the pre-manufacture notification (PMN) procedures for new chemicals under Section 5 of TSCA. But first it is important to bear in mind that in practice, TSCA PMN procedures are only one hurdle that a company would have to consider before placing a new chemical substance on the market. Even if EPA signs off on a substance, the company would still have to consider multiple other sources of regulation, including the not insubstantial possibilities of civil liability if any harm were caused by its product. In its recent modest expansions to its own system of environmental liability, the European Union recognized that the threat of civil liability can be an important additional source of precautionary regulation by creating incentives for preventing harm. Directive 2004/35/CE of the European Parliament and of the Council of April 21, 2004, on environmental liability with regard to the prevention and remedying of environmental damage says, "The fundamental principle of this directive should therefore be that an operator whose activity has caused the environmental damage or the imminent threat of such damage is to be held financially liable, *in order to induce operators to adopt measures and develop practices to minimise the risks of environmental damage* so that their exposure to financial liabilities is reduced" (emphasis added). The potent civil liability system in the United States is at least as important a regulatory system for chemicals as EPA regulation under TSCA; the effects of both must be taken into account in evaluating the system.

Moreover, in the specific case of pre-market clearance of new chemicals, we are comparing almost 30 years of practical implementation in the United States under the 1976 TSCA with the aspirations of a 2006 EU regulation called Registration,

Evaluation and Authorisation of Chemicals (REACH). As of mid-2010, REACH is only in the early stages of implementation.

In the United States, a central purpose for the adoption of TSCA in 1976 was to adopt a more precautionary approach toward the regulation of new chemicals. Reacting to then-recent incidents such as concerns about the effects of polychlorinated biphenyls (PCBs) on nature and contamination of the James River in Virginia by the pesticide Kepone, Congress determined to shift the burden of proof of safety to the manufacturers of new chemical substances. TSCA specifically legislates that "[i]t is the policy of the United States that ... adequate data should be developed with respect to the effect of chemical substances and mixtures on health and the environment and that the development of such data should be the responsibility of those who manufacture and those who process such chemical substances and mixtures" (15 U.S.C. § 2601(b)(1)). The legislative decision to shift the burden of producing information to manufacturers to prove the safety of substances before they went onto the market was accompanied by legislative rhetoric very similar to what we heard recently in Europe during the legislatives debates leading up to the enactment of REACH. For example, the 1976 Senate Committee report on TSCA stated the following:

> More than 200,000 infants are born with physical or mental damage each year, a staggering seven percent of all births. ... A total of 15 million Americans have birth defects serious enough to drastically affect their daily lives. ... It is with alarm that our attention is drawn to some aspects of modern technology which work counterproductive to our aims. Each year billions of pounds of chemicals which are virtually untested and unregulated are produced in industrial processes and used in commercial products. Experience with vinylchloride has shown it to be a highly toxic substance which experimentally can cause cancer and birth defects; but this experience came only with its burden of proof on the public. *We look now to preventative testing of toxic substances in industrial production prior to manufacture or distribution as one critical means to reduce exogenous causes of birth defects.* ... In order to protect against these dangers, the proposed Toxic Substances Control Act would close a number of major regulatory gaps, for while certain statutes ... may be used to protect health and the environment from chemical substances, none of these statutes *provides the means for discovering adverse effects on health and environment before manufacture of new chemical substances.* ... *The most effective and efficient time to prevent unreasonable risks to public health or the environment is prior to first manufacture.* (S. Rep. No. 94-698, 1976, 5; emphasis added)

In retrospect, perhaps Congress erred by focusing too much attention on "new" chemical substances and not enough on existing chemicals that were already on the market. As enacted, TSCA (like REACH) contemplates that prior to placing a new chemical on the market, the manufacturer will be responsible for conducting testing and other analysis to develop information adequate to convince the regulators that a new substance is safe. In a subsection titled "Submission of Test Data," the law specifically provides that the manufacturer will submit data to "show that ... the manufacture, processing, distribution in commerce, use, and disposal of the chemical substance or any combination of such activities will not present an unreasonable risk of injury to health or the environment" (15 U.S.C. § 2604(b)(2)(B)).

Under the pressure of actual implementation, however, EPA has developed simplified screening techniques for assessing which of the many applications received are most likely to present risks to health or the environment:

> The PMN review process is designed to accommodate the large number of PMNs received (approximately 1,500 annually), while adequately assessing the risks posed by each substance within the 90-day timeframe prescribed by TSCA. The information included in PMNs is limited: 67% of PMNs include no test data and 85% include no health data. Consequently, OPPT (EPA's Office of Pollution Prevention and Toxics, which administers TSCA) uses several general approaches to address data gaps to rapidly evaluate potential risks and make risk management decisions for new chemicals. For example, OPPT has developed and relies on Structure-Activity Relationship (SAR) analyses to estimate or predict physical-chemical properties, environmental fate, and human and environmental effects. A SAR is the relationship between the chemical structure of a molecule and its properties, including any possible interaction with the environment or organisms. EPA's New Chemicals Program has established 55 chemical categories to facilitate the PMN review process. (Battelle 2003, 8)

A recent GAO report criticizes EPA for relying too heavily on SARs as a screening tool rather than "actual testing"—by which GAO presumably means principally toxicological testing involving dosing animal species with the chemicals. EPA responds that it "believes the models are generally useful as screening tools for identifying potentially harmful chemicals and, in conjunction with other information, such as the anticipated potential uses and exposures of the new chemicals, provide a reasonable basis for reviewing new chemicals" (GAO 2005, front matter).

In addition to the use of SARs rather than more animal testing, EPA has also developed a number of other techniques for setting priorities for using its limited resources to produce the greatest benefit. Over almost 30 years of administrative interpretations, EPA has developed a number of administrative exemptions that have the effect of giving lesser scrutiny to some categories of substances and greater scrutiny to others. One illustration is the so-called "low-release, low-exposure" (LoREX) exemption, under which a substance that is shown to have low potential for dermal, inhalation, water-borne, or air releases to workers and the general population may receive expedited review and is subject to reduced requirements for production of data (*Federal Register* 1995). A similar philosophy underlies EPA's standard consent decree, which allows limited production and use of substances in specified uses with limited potential to cause harm while further information is developed:

> Under a § 5(e) consent order, the manufacturer is usually permitted to proceed with commercial manufacture, and in return agrees to certain restrictions on the production, distribution, and disposal of the new chemical, pending development of information that EPA considers necessary to evaluate the potential hazards. (Landfair 1997, 243)

In sum, through administrative construction and interpretation, EPA has gradually converted a statute that originally contemplated comprehensive testing and safety analysis before any new chemical went on the market into one that now often permits limited use of chemicals judged to present low risks in controlled and limited situations while additional data is developed. This approach is a good example of the risk reduction strategy that Aaron Wildavsky called "resilience": designing a system that minimizes harm and provides an increased ability to "rebound" out of a recognition that despite our best efforts, we are not wise enough to anticipate and prevent all harm in advance (Wildavsky 1988). It is also reminiscent of the 2000 European Commission communication on the precautionary principle, which also urges the balancing of the risk of harm with other factors and assigns responsibility for developing additional data.

Finally, EPA's transformation of TSCA Section 5 by administrative interpretation illustrates the broad powers of administrative agencies in the United States under the *Chevron* doctrine (1984's *Chevron v. NRDC*, 467 U.S. 837) to reinterpret and update statutes in light of experience. Unless Congress is deemed to have spoken to the exact question at issue in the statute, the agency is deemed to have been delegated very broad discretionary powers of interpretation. This broad power to reinterpret statutes without explicit legislative amendment makes frequent revisions to implementing legislation less necessary in the United States, where agencies are able to adapt generally worded statutes quickly to deal with new issues—say, biotechnology or nanotechnology (Elliott 2005a, 2005b).

However, Congress is now considering proposed legislative changes to TSCA, such as the so-called Kid Safe Chemical Act (Lautenberg 2010). The main reform being considered would shift the burden of proof to industry, as was done previously in California's Proposition 65 (Roe 1988) and more recently in REACH. The Obama administration recently announced principles for legislative reform that include support for shifting a greater burden of proof to industry to "provide sufficient hazard, exposure, and use data for a chemical to support a determination by the Agency that the chemical meets the safety standard" (EPA 2009). Even the leading U.S. chemical industry trade association is now supporting "modernizing" TSCA (American Chemistry Council 2009). However, the timing and nature of eventual TSCA reform by legislative amendment in the United States remains uncertain at the time of this writing.

EPA generally receives good marks for reaching precautionary results under the PMN program for reviewing new chemicals. As of October 2003, EPA had reviewed about 36,600 PMNs. About 4% of chemicals (1,552) were withdrawn during the review process, generally when it becomes clear that EPA would not sign off on the substance without additional testing. In many of these instances, EPA probably could not have proven in court that the substance was definitely harmful, but rather was able to keep the substance off the market by pointing out that the manufacturer had not produced enough information to convince EPA that it was safe. In another 5% of cases (1984), EPA took some other form of regulatory action, such as imposing requirements for additional testing or restricting the permitted uses of the chemical. And about half of the new chemicals for which review was sought were never commercialized, which could include market factors as well as concerns about possible liability (Battelle 2003, 11). In fact, it is possible that EPA may have been overly precautionary in some instances, and that at least some harmless but useful "orphan chemicals" may have been prevented from coming onto the market. No human system is perfect, and both "false positives" and "false negatives" may occur. The challenge is to optimize a system that effectively prevents harm while at the same time does not unnecessarily impede progress.

Despite EPA's best efforts to strike the appropriate balance, a chemical does occasionally slip through the system and cause harm. For example, EPA not only allowed the gasoline additive methyl *tert*-butyl ether (MTBE) onto the market, but also promoted it for its air pollution prevention benefits—only to discover later that it had substantial potential to migrate and contaminate groundwater. As a fuel additive regulated under another statute administered by EPA, the Clean Air Act, MTBE was presumptively exempted from review under TSCA § 9(b), 15 U.S.C. § 2609(b).

Such occasional failures to prevent unsafe chemicals from coming onto the market, or unsafe new uses of existing substances, have not resulted from any lack of moral purity or absence of high aspirations for precautionary decisions to prevent harm by legislators and regulators in the United States. Nor have they resulted from an overreliance on quantitative approaches to risk assessment. Rather, they have generally resulted from two factors: (1) a lack of foresight, i.e., "bounded rationality" (Simon 1983), the pervasive inability of human beings with their limited cognitive capacities to predict a complex future and to envision all potential scenarios by which chemicals may cause harm through advance screening and "testing"; and (2) the requirements of the U.S. system of administrative law that an agency must build a factual record to support its regulatory decisions in court (Charnley and Elliott 2002; Martonik et al. 2001).

It will be interesting to observe to what extent developments in Europe will follow a course similar to the evolution of TSCA. The European Council adopted REACH in 2006, and all of its regulations were formally enacted by mid-2007 (see the section titled "The European Approach to Chemical Regulation: REACH," below). The chemical industry has from 2007 to 2012 to provide all the information necessary to be licensed under REACH. Highly toxic or hazardous material must be registered by 2010. There is still much discussion whether it will be feasible to process large volumes of information and to devise adequate testing protocols for the thousands of substances that need to be tested. Over 143,800 substances have been registered, versus a pre-enactment estimate of only 29,000. This total undoubtedly includes many duplicates that will eventually be weeded out. Nonetheless, former European Commission official Thomas Hartung and a coauthor have recently projected that REACH implementation may require the deaths of 54 million animals, at a financial cost of approximately €9.5 billion (roughly $12 billion) (Hartung and Rovida 2009). These estimates have been strongly disputed by the European Chemicals Agency (ECHA), however, which projects that "only" 9 million animals will be required (ECHA 2009). Several EU research projects (such as OSIRIS) have been launched to simplify testing methods, avoid an excessive use of lab animals, and produce routine operations for classes of chemicals. In addition, a 2007 report by the National Research Council of the U.S.

National Academy of Sciences outlines a "vision" for decreased reliance on whole body animal testing and increased use of *in vitro* methods for "pathway-based" toxicity testing in human cells lines (NRC 2007). EPA is developing similar methods in its TOXCast program, but it does not use these advanced techniques yet in implementing TSCA. These practical differences suggest that ambitious precautionary goals may eventually be tempered by practical realities in implementation.

Unreasonable Risk Regulation under TSCA Section 6

EPA's record in taking precautionary action against chemicals that are already on the market and are later found to pose an unreasonable risk to human health or the environment is not as good as under the PMN process (Lautenberg 2010; GAO 2005). In theory, Section 6 of TSCA gives EPA broad powers to "prohibit" or "limit the amount" or "otherwise regulat[e] any manner or method of commercial use of such substance or mixture" (15 U.S.C. § 2605(a)). The substantive standard for taking action to prevent harm would appear to be very low and to encourage precautionary action; EPA need only find there is "a reasonable basis to conclude that the manufacture, processing, distribution in commerce, use, or disposal of a chemical substance or mixture, or that any combination of such activities, presents, or will present an unreasonable risk of injury to health or the environment" (15 U.S.C. § 2605(a)). However, as this seemingly precautionary language has actually been interpreted and applied by the courts, it is very difficult for EPA to take effective action against a chemical that is already on the market without solid proof of demonstrated harm.

An important lesson here is that one cannot determine how precautionary a regulatory system actually is from the words of substantive law alone; rather, one must also consider the procedural and institutional structures within which the substantive law is embedded. As the great English legal historian Sir Henry Maine put it, substantive law is "secreted in the interstices of procedure" (Maine 1883, 245).

Throughout its 40-year history, EPA has attempted to use its TSCA Section 6 authority on only a few occasions. But when it has done so, its principal attempts to use Section 6 for precautionary regulation to prevent harm have been set aside in court. As a result of this experience, EPA has generally drawn the lesson that Section 6 of TSCA is not a useful "tool" for precautionary regulation. Section 6 presents two separate problems. First, as the price of removing its opposition to the enactment of TSCA in 1976, the chemical industry negotiated virtually unique procedural provisions that require EPA to hold cumbersome oral hearings—including cross-examination of witnesses—before issuing a Section 6 rule (15 U.S.C. § 2605(c)). These so-called "hybrid rulemaking proceedings" are much slower, more cumbersome, and more expensive for EPA to conduct than the notice-and-comment rulemaking proceedings under 5 U.S.C. § 553 of the Administrative Procedure Act that are typical of most other statutes administered by EPA.

Even where EPA has shouldered the burden of mounting the extensive procedural hearings required by Section 6 of TSCA, its rules have been set aside in court for lack of sufficient support in the record. The key case is *Corrosion Proof Fittings v. EPA*, 947 F.2d 1201 (5th Cir. 1991), which invalidated EPA's 1989 TSCA rule to ban virtually all uses of asbestos (54 *Federal Register* 29,460 (1989)). Asbestos was identified by the ancient Greek physician Galen as constituting a risk to health; thousands of American workers have suffered from asbestos-related disease, hundreds of thousands of civil lawsuits for damages now clog our courts, and over 70 companies have been forced into bankruptcy. In 1989, in an attempt to deal with this major public health problem, EPA attempted to ban all uses of asbestos for which there were readily available substitutes. EPA's rule was supported by 10 years of hearings and over 100,000 pages of record, including several hundred scientific studies. This was a clear and self-conscious attempt by EPA to use Section 6 of TSCA on a precautionary basis, arguing that since asbestos had been shown to be harmful in many uses, it should be banned in other contexts as well, at least where substitutes were readily available. The court disagreed, striking down EPA's precautionary asbestos ban on the grounds that sufficient proof of actual harm from each and every use of asbestos was lacking. In one (in)famous footnote, the court even opined (based on a numerical risk assessment cited by industry) that more people die from accidentally aspirating toothpicks than from some of the uses of asbestos that EPA wanted to ban.

Unfortunately, the *Corrosion Proof Fittings* case is not an outlier. Unlike regulators in Europe, who may act on a precautionary basis in advance of hard and fast scientific proof by relying on consensus expert judgments, regulators in the United States must generally build a factual "record" to support their decisions to regulate or to take a product off the market. For example, *AFL v. OSHA*, 965F.2d 962 (11th Cir. 1992) invalidated permissible exposure limits for 428 toxic substances in the workplace that had been based on expert consensus standards. U.S. administrative law requirements to assemble a comprehensive factual record and for adversarial and "searching" judicial review of the factual basis of expert decisions tend to discourage U.S. agencies from promulgating risk-based regulations on a "precautionary" (i.e., weak or preliminary scientific) basis; instead, agencies wait until a risk assessment can be conducted to provide the necessary "record" for judicial review (Martonik et al. 2001). We have argued that this unfortunate situation results because in recent years most U.S. courts have mistakenly assimilated questions of scientific support for precautionary regulations to questions of fact, rather than recognizing their true nature as questions of "policy." See *Ethyl Corp. v. EPA*, 541F.2d 1 (D.C. Cir.)(en banc), *cert. denied*, 426 U.S. 941 (1976), and Charnley and Elliott (2002).

The European Approach to Chemical Regulation: REACH

Prior to the present REACH regime, EU legislation distinguished between so-called "existing" and "new" chemicals using 1981 as a cutoff date. "Existing" substances are those that had been introduced before 1981; "new" chemicals are those that have been introduced since 1981. Of the roughly 30,000 substances that were produced annually at a volume of more than 1 metric ton, only 140 had been sufficiently tested for their effects. The requirement to provide risk assessments was followed by public authorities in the Member States (ISI/Oekopol 2004). Until 2006, new chemicals had to be notified and tested in production volumes as low as 10 kilograms (kg) per year, while there were no such provisions for existing chemicals. This policy had encouraged the continued use of "existing"—untested—substances, and it inhibited research and development and innovation. The number of new chemicals put on the market from 1981 to 2006 reached only around 3,000 while the number of "existing" chemicals in 1981 was 100,106. When testing new chemicals, each country pursued its own path to determine whether any of them needed to be examined and then to do so. Procedures were lengthy and cumbersome. For example, from 1993 to 2003, only 140 high-volume chemicals were singled out for risk assessment. Only a few were actually assessed before the new REACH regime took effect in 2007.

Dissatisfied by the chemical risk regulation in the EU, the Commission began to work on a major overhaul of the existing regulations in 1999. In early 2001, the Commission published a White Paper on the Strategy for a Future Chemicals Policy (European Commission 2001). In this report, the Commission outlined its strategy for ensuring a high level of chemical safety and a competitive chemical industry through a system for the Registration, Evaluation and Authorisation of Chemicals—the so-called REACH system. After more than three years of negotiation and modification of the proposed regulation, the European Parliament reached an agreement for a final version in December 2006. The European Council representing all Member State governments formally adopted the new regulation at the Environment Council Meeting on December 18, 2006. The REACH regime, formally adopted in the summer of 2007, replaces over 40 existing directives and regulations. Under the REACH system, companies that manufacture or import more than 1 ton of a chemical substance per year are required to register these substances in a central database, whether they are old or new. This process must be completed by 2012. So companies were given five years to provide data, design testing protocols, and report about the results of risk assessments. For highly toxic or hazardous substances, this grace period was much shorter—it ended in 2010. The EU expects from the new regulation an improvement in protecting human health and the environment while maintaining the competitiveness and enhancing the innovative capability of the EU chemical industry (European Commission 2003b). More specifically, the EU expects the following advantages once the REACH regime is fully implemented:

- protection of human health and the environment;
- maintenance and enhancement of the competitiveness of the EU chemical industry;
- prevention of fragmentation of the internal market;
- increased transparency;
- integration with international efforts;
- promotion of non-animal testing to avoid harming animals; and
- conformity with EU international obligations under the WTO.

A brief look into the legislative history of the proposal (Williams et al. 2009) is warranted. On October 29, 2003, the European Commission adopted the REACH proposal for a new EU regulatory framework for chemicals (European Commission 2003a, 644). The proposal was then forwarded to the European Parliament and the EU's Council of Ministers for approval under the so-called Co-Decision (CoD) procedure. The first reading in the European Parliament took place on November 17, 2005 (provisional amendments (2005) 0434 and (2005) 0435). Following its political agreement on December 13, 2005, the Council adopted its Common Position on June 27, 2006 (7524/06 and 7525/06). The Commission communication stating the Commission's opinion on the Common Position was adopted on July 12, 2006 (COM (2006) 375), and on December 13, the Parliament adopted in second reading the compromise package it had agreed to with the Council on November 30. Finally, the European Council approved the package at the Environment Council Meeting on December 18, so that REACH could be formally enacted by mid-2007.

Former environment commissioner Margot Wallström has characterized REACH as follows:

> REACH is a groundbreaking proposal. Once adopted, it will allow us to take advantage of the benefits of chemicals without exposing ourselves and the environment to risks. Thus it will create a win-win situation for industry, workers and citizens, and our ecosystem. It will give Europe's citizens the high level of protection that they have the right to expect. The EU will have one of the most progressive chemicals management systems in the world. (European Commission 2003a)

REACH requires companies that produce and import chemicals to assess the risks arising from their use and to take the necessary measures to manage any risk they identify. The objective is to reverse the burden of proof from public authorities to industry for ensuring the safety of chemicals on the market. REACH treats existing and new chemicals in the same way and will streamline bureaucratic procedures by simplifying the registration process. The proposed new system focuses on the following:

- identifying substances of high concern, including those that are carcinogenic, mutagenic, or toxic to reproduction (known as CMRs), those that are persistent, bioaccumulative, and toxic (known as PBTs), or very persistent and very bioaccumulative (vPvBs);
- streamlining the licensing and authorization process by requiring only essential safety and use information for chemicals manufactured or imported in volumes of 1–10 tons per year;
- encouraging research and innovation by lengthening the trial period, raising the threshold for the registration of research substances (from 10 kg currently to 1 ton), and simplifying the regulation for downstream users; and
- preventing increased bureaucracy for downstream enterprises by utilizing existing systems for the exchange of safety information, i.e., Safety Data Sheets.

Table 10.2 *Comparison between the Previous Regulatory System and REACH*

Prior system	REACH
The "burden of proof" is on the authorities: they need to prove that the use of a chemical substance is unsafe before they may impose restrictions.	The "burden of proof" will be on industry. It has to be able to demonstrate how the chemical can be used safely. All actors in the supply chain will be obliged to ensure the safety of the chemical substances they handle.
Notification requirements for "new substances" start at a production level of 10 kg. Already at this level, one animal test is needed. At 1 ton, a series of tests including other animal tests must be undertaken.	Registration will be required when production or import reaches 1 ton. As far as possible, animal testing will be minimized.
It is relatively costly to introduce a new substance on the market. This encourages the continued use of "existing" untested chemicals and inhibits innovation.	Innovation of safer substances will be encouraged under REACH through more exemptions for research and development; lower registration costs for new substances; and the need to consider substitute substances for decisions on authorization and restrictions.
Public authorities are obliged to perform comprehensive risk assessments that are slow and cumbersome.	Industry will be responsible for assessing the safety of identified uses prior to production and marketing. Authorities will be able to focus on issues of serious concern.

Source: European Commission (2003a)

Table 10.2 lists the main differences between the previous EU regulations and the REACH regime.

Registration and Authorization of Chemicals

REACH obliges all companies to register chemicals that were manufactured or imported in quantities of more than 1 ton per year and per manufacturer/importer in a central database. Some groups of substances do not have to be registered, such as certain intermediates, polymers, and some chemicals managed under other EU legislation. The registration process requires industry to provide several kinds of information:

- The intrinsic properties and hazards of each substance—its physicochemical, toxicological, and ecotoxicological properties—must be described. This information—if not already available—can be found through a variety of means, such as computer modeling and epidemiological studies, or through testing.
- The use(s) of the substance must be identified by the importer or manufacturer or by its customers. A report of an assessment of risks for human health and the environment, as well as how those risks will be adequately controlled, must be given for the identified uses for substances produced or imported in volumes of 10 tons or more per year per manufacturer or importer. These are known as chemical safety reports. For lower volumes, safety information produced for the safety data sheets will be submitted as part of the technical dossiers.

The information required is proportional to production volumes and the risks that a substance poses. The safety information will be passed down the supply chain. To cope with the large number of "existing" substances, a phased approach is proposed. The deadlines for registration are set according to either the volume of the substance on the market or the hazard. The shortest deadlines apply to very high-volume substances (those above 1,000 tons) and carcinogenic, mutagenic, or reproductive-toxic substances above 1 ton. These had to be registered within three years. For all other substances, a timeline of five years was specified.

The European Chemicals Agency (ECHA), an agency of the European Union, started operation in mid-2007. The agency has the mandate to manage the database, receive the registration dossiers, and be responsible for providing nonconfidential information to the public. Within the REACH regime, the ECHA checks the validity of the dossiers provided by the companies—in particular, their data from animal tests. The main purpose of this compulsory evaluation is to minimize animal testing. Second, the agency and the respective Member State risk management authorities have the right reevaluate any substance where they have justified reasons to suspect that a risk to human health or the environment went unreported by the respective companies. For both types of evaluation, the outcome could be a request for further information or clarification. The agency can demand further information from companies for specific chemicals if all Member States agree. In the case of disagreement, the European Commission would make a decision.

In the new EU-wide Impact Assessment, the direct costs of REACH to the chemical industry are estimated at a total of some €2.3 billion over an 11-year period—representing a saving of 82% costs from the 2003 Internet-published draft (see the following section). The costs to downstream users of chemicals are estimated at €2.8 billion to €3.6 billion over a period of 11 and 15 years, respectively—if the market reacts as expected, with 12% of substances being withdrawn when continued production becomes unprofitable. Costs could rise to €4.0 billion to €5.2 billion if industry faced higher supply chain adaptation costs. These estimates include the direct costs passed on from the chemical sector to downstream users. The total costs for the chemical industry and the downstream users are thus estimated at somewhere between €2.3 billion and €5.2 billion. The anticipated benefits to environment and human health are expected to be significant. An illustrative scenario put the health benefits in the order of magnitude of €50 billion over a 30-year period.

More recent estimates of the burden that REACH will impose in chemical manufactures are less optimistic. Thomas Hartung and Costanza Rovida (2009) estimate that 68,000 chemicals will need to be registered, up from the European Commission's estimate of 29,342 in 2003. As noted above, testing them may require 54 million research animals and cost $13.5 billion over the next 10 years (Hartung and Rovida 2009). Hartung and Rovida assert that a temporary solution is to substitute a one-generation reproductive toxicity test for the current two-generation test that REACH presently requires. Also, they suggest that regulators focus only on chemicals that appear to pose the greatest threat. Whether or not this particular suggestion is adopted, the sheer volume of chemicals to be examined makes it likely that there will be continuing calls for screening and priority-setting to target limited resources where they are most likely to produce the greatest benefit.

Public Consultation

In May 2003, the Commission presented a draft of the proposed regulation on the Internet to gather further comments on the workability of REACH. Some 6,000 replies were sent in. The main contributors were industry associations and individual companies, as well as environmental and animal rights NGOs. A number of Member States also provided comments, alongside several countries outside the EU. In addition, many individuals, including workers, expressed their opinions. Commenters raised a range of issues:

- concern that the inclusion of polymers in the system would overburden it and add costs;
- calls for protection of the commercial confidentiality of data;
- calls for publicly accessible data about risks of chemicals, and the right to access information about chemicals used in products;
- a desire for a clearer and more effective role for the proposed ECHA, particularly with regard to handling registrations and in ensuring uniformity and consistency in evaluation decisions taken by Member States;
- calls to include the principle of substitution of dangerous substances by safer alternatives in the proposal;
- a desire to ensure a level playing field for articles produced inside the EU and in countries outside of the EU.

For more detail on public responses to the draft, see European Commission 2003b; RPA/BRE 2003; BDI, VCH, and VDI 2004; BUND 2004; and KPMG 2005.

The comments resulted in several changes designed to make the proposed new system less costly, less bureaucratic, and more workable, while reinforcing the guarantees for health and environmental protection. In addition, a high-level expert group was established to investigate the impacts of the proposed REACH regulation. The report (European Commission 2005) lists the following conclusions:

- There is limited evidence that higher-volume substances are vulnerable to withdrawal following the REACH registration requirements. However, lower-volume substances under 100 tons are most vulnerable to being made less profitable or unprofitable by the REACH requirements.
- There is limited evidence that downstream users will be faced with a withdrawal of substances of greatest technical importance to them.
- Small and medium-size companies (SMEs) can be particularly affected by REACH with regard to their more limited financial capacity and lower market power in terms of passing on costs.
- Companies have recognized some business benefits from REACH.

EU Commissioner for the Environment Stavros Dimas also commented on the report:

> All the parties concerned will recognise that we have gone to great lengths to explore and assess the practical impact of REACH. The results of these studies are reassuring—the costs and impacts of REACH are manageable. There is, however, no reason to become complacent. We need to continue putting all efforts in development of specific guidance and tools to facilitate implementation, which will be helpful for all companies, in particular SMEs, and alleviate most of their concerns. (Dimas 2005)

Many national agencies and stakeholder groups voiced their concerns in numerous papers and statements. A synthesis study by the Fraunhofer Institute and Oekopol (ISI/Oekopol 2004) arrived at the conclusion that "REACH will improve the knowledge about properties of existing chemical substances related to environment and health. However, to a large extent, the interviewed companies do not expect these REACH mechanisms to result in business benefits. More concretely, none of the companies expects that customers will be willing to pay a higher price for 'safe products' with paper documentation according to the REACH standard" (ISI/Oekopol 2004). The report lists several proposals for improvement, in particular related to the establishment of one consolidated database and the assessment of exposure data. Environmental groups such as the German BUND, which welcomed the REACH regime, saw a major need for improvement in transparency and openness of information, strengthening of the authorization process, and exclusion of imported products from the REACH regime (BUND 2004).

During the deliberations in 2005 and 2006, the original REACH proposal was changed in order to accommodate major concerns from industrial and commercial interests. The main difference between the proposal and the adopted version of REACH centers on the treatment of substances that are carcinogenic, mutagenic, or toxic to the reproductive system (CMR substances). The proposal included a mandate for all chemical companies to phase out such substances and replace them if substitutes were available—irrespective of costs or other considerations. The new version softened this requirement and introduced two sets of CMRs: those with a threshold of toxicity and those without a threshold or with other problematic properties (such as persistence). For the first group of substances, an authorization will be granted if the producer or importer can show that risks from the use in question can be adequately controlled. This means that scientists can agree on a "safe threshold" below which a substance does not create negative effects to the human body or the environment. For other CMR substances and substances with persistent, bioaccumulative, or genotoxic properties (PBT and vPvB substances), where adequate control is not possible, an authorization will only be granted if no safer alternative exists and/or if the socioeconomic benefits of the use of the substance outweigh by far the risks. More specifically, three options are now given to a producer or importer of these chemicals: (a) replacement if substitutes are available and economically feasible; (b) strict containment within the chemical production process, connected with the guarantee that consumers or upstream handlers are not exposed to the substance; or (c) slower phaseout or even continuation for substances with a high benefit when both a and b do not apply (European Commission 2006).

Link to Precaution

The REACH regime is explicitly linked to the precautionary principle of the EU. It is based on Article 95 of the EC Treaty in keeping with the objective of safeguarding the internal market, while ensuring a high level of health, safety, and consumer and environmental protection. The precautionary principle (Article 174.2 of the treaty in combination with Article 6 and Article 95.3) has been cited as a guidance for drafting the REACH provisions.

The provisions within REACH, however, do not directly relate to any of the commonly used definitions of precaution. There is only reference to the issue of burden of proof. The document states that the burden of proof is reversed so that the chemical companies have to provide relevant information and assessments. This documentation requirement, however, is not a reversal of proof in the strict sense. The proposal does not oblige companies to prove that their chemicals are safe; rather, it obliges companies to provide the data and information that will allow regulators to form a balanced judgment about the tolerability or acceptability of the respective risk. It is not the burden of *proof* that is reversed, but the burden of *cost*.

It is also worth noting that the terms *uncertainty, characterization*, and *management* are not explicitly mentioned in the document (only in the technical annex). The main thrust is to include the existing chemicals in the regulatory regime, provide traceability, and build up a database for the vast amount of new and existing chemicals (WWF/EEB 2003). The actual assessment and evaluation process underlying the authorization process is not further specified in the document. However, from the data that is required, one can make some implicit assumptions. Much of the required information relates to hazards, not to risks. The underlying rationale here is that because of the uncertainties with respect to exposure, it is assumed that all chemicals above 1 ton will expose some individuals or ecosystems during their lifetime. The exclusion of small quantities and commodity chemicals that are tightly kept within the chemical facilities demonstrated the reasoning behind the regulation. Rather than relying on exposure data, authorization may concentrate only on hazards. The language of the legislation, however, remains vague about the underlying criteria and decision rules when it comes to explaining the process by which a substance is authorized or not.

Given the vagueness of the REACH proposal with respect to the tolerability criteria, the EU commissioned a report by a consortium of scholars to define the criteria and procedures that could be used for the authorization process based on the precautionary principle. The report, called "Precaupri," was completed in 2003 (Renn et al. 2003). The "Precaupri" report includes a preassessment phase for assessing and managing chemical risks (Mueller-Herold et al. 2009; Mueller-Herold et al. 2005). This phase provides for a screening stage (see Figure 10.1) in order to identify chemicals deserving special attention or even to eliminate substances of high concern at an early stage. For

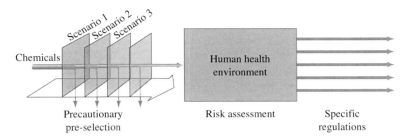

Figure 10.1 *Extended Assessment Scheme for Chemicals Recommended by the "Precaupri" Report*

Source: Renn et al. (2003)

the screening stage, a filter series approach was developed and applied. Each filter is designed to screen for a particular threat scenario.

Precautionary filters can be conceptualized as classification schemes with three outcomes: green ("may pass"), yellow ("needs further consideration"), and red ("will be stopped"). For filters based on two assessment parameters—with each parameter having the grades high, medium, or low—the outcomes are defined using these grades of the two parameters (Figure 10.2):

- green (white in Figure 10.2): medium/low, low/low, low/medium
- yellow (gray in Figure 10.2): high/low, medium/medium, low/high
- red (black in Figure 10.2): high/medium, high/high, medium/high

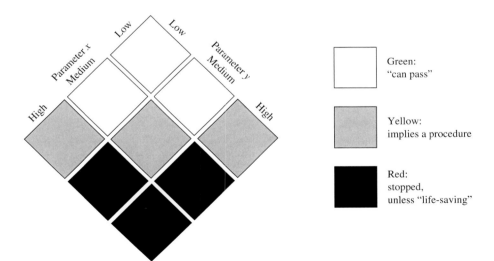

Figure 10.2 *Two-Parameter Filter with Three Grades*

Source: Renn et al. (2003)

If a substance is classified as red by at least one filter, it triggers preventive measures: such a chemical should be eliminated—with the possible exemption of "lifesaving" pharmaceuticals or some intermediates in industrial synthesis, if they can be contained under extreme safety standards. Chemicals not classified as red enter the normal chemical risk assessment process.

This proposal was introduced as an addition to the REACH framework for finding a fast, nonbureaucratic, and inexpensive way to include precautionary measures in the REACH regime. The filters that were tested in the report were based on assessment parameters such as potential to long-range transport, persistence, and bioaccumulation. The parameters applied to three types of substances: persistent organic chemicals, high production volume chemicals, and a group of nonreferential test chemicals. So far, the EU Commission has not adopted this amendment to the REACH regime; however, more research is under way to test more specific guidelines for registration and risk evaluation.

Using the Precautionary Approach in Risk Management

Risk management has the task of reducing identified undesirable effects of human activities or natural events through appropriate modification of their causes or through mitigation of their consequences. Since there are more risks in the world than anyone could handle at one time, risk management always implies the task of setting priorities. The conventional solution to this problem has been to design risk reduction policies in proportion to the severity of the potential effects (Crouch and Wilson 1982). Severity has been operationalized as a linear combination of magnitude of harm and probability of occurrence. Risk-risk comparisons constitute the most appropriate instrument in this perspective for setting risk management priorities (Merkhofer 1987; Cohen 1991).

The underlying rationale of this approach is based on the assumption that risk should be reduced in proportion to the expected or modeled harm to humans or ecosystems. This assumption is highly contested in the wider risk community: social actions to cope with risk are not confined to the single goal of risk minimization but include other objectives such as equity, fairness, flexibility, or resilience (Vlek 1996). The most significant argument against the proportional risk management approach comes from the analysis of uncertainty (Cooke 1991; van Asselt 2000). Most risk data constitute aggregate results over large segments of the population and long time duration (Funtowicz and Ravetz 1987).

It is essential to acknowledge in this context that human knowledge is always incomplete and selective and thus contingent on uncertain assumptions, assertions, and predictions (Funtowicz and Ravetz 1992; Laudan 1996; Bruijn and ten Heuvelhof 1999). It is obvious that the modeled probability distributions within a numerical relational system can only represent an approximation of the empirical relational system with which to understand and predict uncertain events (Cooke 1991). It therefore seems prudent to include other, additional aspects of uncertainty (Morgan and Henrion 1992; van Asselt 2000, 93–138; RIVM/MNP 2003). Although there is no consensus in the literature on the best means of disaggregating uncertainties, the following categories appear to be an appropriate means of distinguishing the key components of uncertainty:

- *target variability* (based on different vulnerability of targets);
- *systematic and random error in modeling* (based on extrapolations from animals to humans or from large doses to small doses, statistical inferential applications, etc.);
- *indeterminacy or genuine stochastic effects* (variation of effects due to random events, in special cases congruent with statistical handling of random errors);
- *system boundaries* (uncertainties stemming from restricted models and the need for focusing on a limited amount of variables and parameters); and
- *ignorance or nonknowledge* (uncertainties derived from lack or absence of knowledge).

In this respect, risk analysts have introduced a crucial distinction between *aleatory* and *epistemic* uncertainty (Rosa 2008, 109ff):

- *Aleatory uncertainty.* Decision and risk analysts refer to aleatory uncertainties as "those that stem from variability in known (or observable) populations and, therefore, represent randomness in samples" (Paté-Cornell 1996; Aven and Vinnem 2007, 39ff). A simple example of this type of variability is represented by the distribution of possible values from the roll of a fair set of dice. A random process gives rise to any possible value at any point in time; but in the long run, with a large enough sample (or rolls of the dice, in our example), the distribution of possible values can be well characterized. Collecting additional information or increasing the sample sizes can help to characterize this distribution more precisely; but neither option can reduce its fundamental parameters.
- *Epistemic uncertainty.* Epistemic uncertainty arises from "basic lack of knowledge about fundamental phenomena" (Paté-Cornell 1996). The impacts of global warming have been considered to be very uncertain for precisely these reasons. Epistemic uncertainty can, in principle, be reduced by the generation of additional knowledge, the collection of samples, or other forms of research appropriate to the particular issue. As scientists have begun to better understand some of the fundamental science underlying climate change, many have become less uncertain about its potential impacts (Rosa 2008).

In reality, what is often loosely referred to as "uncertainty" is some combination of the contribution of aleatory and epistemic uncertainty. What is their relevance regarding risk assessment? For the risk assessor, these distinctions between types of uncertainty can be helpful in developing an approach to characterizing uncertainty (Renn and Walker 2008). If the assessor knows that some fundamental random process gives rise to an outcome—as in the case of the roll of a pair of dice or in the combinatorics that predict genetic variability in some trait—this may be a starting and ending point for characterizing uncertainty (but only when the assessor is certain that aleatory uncertainty or variability tells the whole story). If the assessor does not know whether such a random process is actually responsible, or is otherwise unsure about the actual parameters of the process, epistemic uncertainty exists. The analyst may need to collect more data or use expert judgment to characterize the extent of epistemic uncertainty. Bayesian analysis, in which probabilities are defined as degrees of belief, can be used for this purpose. Degrees of belief—also known as subjective probabilities—are grounded in all available evidence, as well as in judgments about how good or relevant that evidence is, and thus can combine both aleatory and epistemic uncertainties (Paté-Cornell 1996).

In the end, epistemic uncertainty may not be reducible. In this case, risk analysts have to face the trade-offs implicit in taking actions that have uncertain outcomes. Because different stakeholders might value those outcomes differently, or have different tolerance for risks, they may argue for alternative decisions. Based on the distinction between epistemic and aleatory uncertainty, it is possible to design generic strategies of risk management to be applied to classes of risks, thus simplifying the risk management process as outlined above. One can distinguish four such classes (Renn 2008, 178–181):

- *Simple risk problems.* This class of risk problems requires hardly any deviation from traditional decisionmaking. Data are provided by statistical analysis, goals are determined by law or statutory requirements, and the role of risk management is to ensure that all risk reduction measures are implemented and enforced. Traditional risk-risk comparisons (or risk-risk trade-offs), risk–benefit analysis, and cost-effectiveness studies are the instruments of choice for finding the most appropriate risk reduction measures. Additionally, risk managers can rely on best practice and, in cases of low impact, on trial and error. It should be noted, however, that simple risks should not be equated with small or negligible risks. The major issues here are that the potential negative consequences are obvious, the values that are applied are noncontroversial, and the remaining uncertainties low. Examples include well-known chemicals with toxic but not carcinogenic or mutagenic properties.
- *Risk problems related to aleatory and statistically calculable uncertainty.* For this risk class, major input for risk management is provided by the scientific characterization of the risk. These risk problems are often associated with major scientific dissent about complex dose-effect relationships or the alleged effectiveness of measures to decrease vulnerabilities (for complexity refers to both the risk agent and its causal connections and the risk absorbing system and its vulnerabilities). Epistemic risk problems are in strong contrast to risk managers' expectation to receive a complete and balanced set of risk assessment results that fall within the legitimate range of plural truth claims. In a situation where there is no complete data, the major challenge is to define the factual base for making risk management or risk regulatory decisions. So the main emphasis is on improving the reliability and validity of the results that are produced in the risk appraisal phase. Risk assessors as well as risk managers need to make sure that all relevant knowledge claims are selected, processed, and evaluated. They may not get a single

answer, but they might be able to get a better overview on the issues of scientific controversy. If these efforts lead to an acknowledgment of wide margins of uncertainty, the management tools of the next category (remaining epistemic uncertainty) should be applied. If input variables to decisionmaking can be properly defined and affirmed, evaluation can be done on the basis of risk–benefit balancing and normative standard setting (risk-based/risk-informed regulation). Examples for chemicals include carcinogenic substances that are well researched and where the probability function over outcome has been empirically tested and verified. For evaluating the tolerability of these risks, traditional methods such as risk-risk comparison, cost-effectiveness, and cost–benefit analysis are also well suited to evaluate the acceptability or tolerability of the chemical substance under review.

- *Risk problems due to remaining epistemic uncertainty.* If there is a high degree of remaining uncertainties, the *precautionary approach* can and should be applied. Risk management needs to incorporate hazard criteria (which are comparatively easy to determine), including aspects such as reversibility, persistence, and ubiquity, and select management options empowering society to deal even with worst-case scenarios (such as containment of hazardous activities, close monitoring of risk-bearing activities, and securing reversibility of decisions in case risks turn out to be higher than expected). Since high unresolved uncertainty implies that the (true) dimensions of the risks are not (yet) known, one should pursue a cautious strategy that allows learning by restricted errors. The main management philosophy for this risk class is to allow small steps in implementation (containment approach) that enable risk managers to stop or even reverse the process as new knowledge is produced or the negative side effects become visible. The primary thrust of precaution is to avoid irreversibility (Klinke and Renn 2001). With respect to the risk target, the main objective is to make these systems resilient so they can withstand or tolerate even surprises. Resilience is a protective strategy against unknown or highly uncertain hazards. Instruments for resilience include the strengthening of the immune system, diversification of the means for approaching identical or similar ends, reduction of the overall catastrophic potential or vulnerability even in the absence of a concrete threat, design of systems with flexible response options, and the improvement of conditions for emergency management and system adaptation. Examples include genotoxic substances with high uncertainty over low dose exposure and hormone disrupting chemicals with uncertain consequences on human fertility.

- *Risk problems due to interpretative and normative ambiguity.* Whereas uncertainty refers to a lack of clarity over the scientific or technical basis for decisionmaking, (interpretative and normative) ambiguity is a result of divergent or contested perspectives on the justification, severity, or wider "meanings" associated with a given threat (Stirling 2003). The term *ambiguity* may be misleading, because it has different connotations. In risk and decisionmaking, some analysts define ambiguity as the conflicting goals of participants in the process (Skinner 1999); others mean the inability to estimate probabilities of an event occurring (Ho et al.

2002; Stirling 2003). Here, ambiguity denotes the variability in interpretation and normative implications with respect to accepted evidence. In relation to risk, it is understood as "giving rise to several meaningful and legitimate interpretations of accepted risk assessments results." It can be divided into interpretative ambiguity (different interpretations of an identical assessment result; e.g., as an adverse or non-adverse effect) and normative ambiguity (different concepts of what can be regarded as tolerable, referring to ethics, quality-of-life parameters, distribution of risks and benefits, to list but a few examples). If risk information is interpreted differently by different stakeholders in society—i.e., different viewpoints exist about the relevance, meaning, and implications of factual explanations and predictions for deciding about the tolerability of a risk as well as management actions—and if the values and priorities of what should be protected or reduced are subject to intense controversy, risk management needs to address the causes for these conflicting views (von Winterfeldt and Edwards 1984). Risk managers should thus initiate a broader societal discourse to enable participative decisionmaking. These discursive measures are aimed at finding appropriate conflict resolution mechanisms capable of reducing the ambiguity to a manageable number of options that can be further assessed and evaluated. The main effort of risk management is hence the organization of a suitable discourse combined with the assurance that all stakeholders and public groups can question and critique the framing of the issue as well as each element of the entire risk chain. The most prominent examples here are genetically modified organisms in food or drugs.

Table 10.3 provides a summary of these four risk strategies and lists the instruments and tools that are most appropriate for risk management once the risks are assessed and the complexities, uncertainties, and ambiguities characterized. Again, it should be emphasized that the list of strategies and instruments is not exhaustive and can be amended if the case requires it.

Conclusions

Taking a closer look at the risk regulation about chemicals in the United States and Europe, this chapter demonstrates that the differences are not so pronounced as may appear on first glance. The underlying assumption that Europe is governed by the notion of precaution and the United States solely by evidence based on risk assessments is misleading. Charnley and Elliott (2002) have also argued convincingly that a simplistic opposition between the precautionary principle in Europe and quantitative risk assessment in the United States is actually a "false dichotomy." Even the new REACH by the European Union does not substitute risk assessments with a pure "better safe than sorry" attitude. On the contrary, the REACH regime puts most emphasis on a scientific assessment of hazards and risks for both existing and new chemicals and places the burden of providing these assessments on industry.

Table 10.3 *Risk Characteristics and Their Implications for Risk Management*

Knowledge characterization	Management strategy	Appropriate instruments	Stakeholder participation
"Simple" risk problems	*Routine-based:* (tolerability/acceptability judgment)	→ Applying "traditional" decisionmaking Risk–benefit analysis Risk-risk trade-offs	Instrumental discourse
	(risk reduction)	Trial and error Technical standards Economic incentives Education, labeling, information Voluntary agreements	
Aleatory Uncertainty-induced risk problems	*Risk-informed:* (risk agent and causal chain)	→ Characterizing the available evidence Expert consensus seeking tools: Delphi or consensus conferencing Meta analysis Scenario construction, etc. Results fed into routine operation	Methodological discourse
	Robustness-focused: (risk absorbing system)	→ Improving buffer capacity of risk target through: Additional safety factors Redundancy and diversity in designing safety devices Improving coping capacity Establishing high-reliability organizations	
Epistemic Uncertainty-induced risk problems	*Precaution-based:* (risk agent)	→ Using hazard characteristics such as persistence, ubiquity, etc., as proxies for risk estimates Tools include: Containment ALARA (as low as reasonably achievable) and ALARP (as low as reasonably possible) BACT (best available control technology)	Reflective discourse
	Resilience-focused: (risk absorbing system)	→ Improving capability to cope with surprises Diversity of means to accomplish desired benefits Avoiding high vulnerability Allowing for flexible responses Preparedness for adaptation	
Ambiguity-induced risk problems	*Discourse-based:*	→ Application of conflict resolution methods for reaching consensus or tolerance for risk evaluation results and management option selection Integration of stakeholder involvement in reaching closure Emphasis on communication and social discourse	Participative discourse

Source: Modified from Renn (2008, 182f)

REACH is more concerned with traceability than looking for precautionary methods for dealing with uncertainty.

Both the U.S. and the European regulatory regimes are faced with the question of how to make regulatory decisions under uncertainty or even ignorance. It may be helpful in this respect to resort to a differentiation that Resnik (2003, 332) has proposed:

- *decisions under certainty*: the outcomes of different choices are known.
- *decisions under risk*: probabilities can be assigned to the outcomes of different choices.
- *decisions under ignorance*: it is not possible to assign probabilities to the outcomes of different choices.

A similar distinction has been made by Stirling (2003). One of the main conclusions of our analysis in this chapter has been that using precaution for the first two cases is neither necessary nor prudent, given that regulations need to meet both objectives—namely, protection of public health and the environment and securing economic welfare. The legitimate realm of using precaution is in the case of ignorance or other forms of remaining uncertainties (such as system boundaries or truly stochastic events). In order to avoid misunderstanding, some analysts have proposed to avoid the term *precaution* and replace it with the more adequate term *principle of insufficient reason* (see Peterson 2003, 71). This is the place where precaution is required. The main purpose of precaution in this respect is to avoid irreversible decisions. Although highly critical about the use of the precautionary principle, policy analyst Giandomenico Majone conceded that the precautionary principle does have a role, namely, where "losses (or utilities) are unbounded" and where it is "clearly impossible to calculate expected values"—for example, where there is a threat of "serious and irreversible damage" (Majone 2002, 104). In this chapter, we make a strong plea first for screening chemical risks according to the degree of remaining uncertainties, and then for using those risk reduction methods that are most suited for the type of risk under scrutiny.

Charnley and Elliott (2002) have argued that regulatory decisions both in the United States and the EU involve on the one hand a factual component ("How great do we think the risk of harm is?") and on the other a value or policy component ("Are we willing to accept the risks, including the unknown risks?"). What changes from decision to decision is the relative weight assigned to each component. A widespread perception on both sides of the Atlantic suggests that Europe tends to place more weight on the second component (acceptability), whereas many U.S. agencies, under the pressure to build a record for judicial review, tend to place more emphasis on the first component (extent of demonstrated risk). One should note, however, that there is little actual empirical evidence supporting these stereotypes. Wide variations exist within and among agencies in the United States and Europe. For example, the now-repealed Delaney clause banning any carcinogens in U.S. food safety regulation was certainly inspired by a strong link to the value component and precaution, while traffic safety regulation in most European countries is clearly guided by risk assessments.

With regard to chemical regulation, there are definitely some elements of "precaution" in the existing U.S. system. For example, EPA has successfully kept some new chemicals from coming onto the market—not because they were proven to be hazardous, but because the evidence proving their safety was inadequate and they resembled other chemicals known to be hazardous. On the other hand, some notable failures to act in a precautionary manner in the United States have occurred, principally where a dangerous substance was already on the market and the burden was on a government agency such as EPA to build a factual case that would stand up in court to ban or regulate the substance. But other structural features of the U.S. lawmaking system tend to encourage precautionary action, such as the threat of tort liability and the expansive authority of U.S. agencies to interpret existing statutes to deal with new problems. Some observers have suggested this broad authority to reinterpret statutes enables U.S. regulators to be more "agile" than their colleagues in Europe in responding to emerging technologies; hence, U.S. regulators may be able to be more "precautionary" in the sense of regulating earlier in some circumstances that would require new legislation in Europe (Elliott 2005b).

Once the REACH regime is fully implemented in Europe, it will greatly expand the obligations of manufacturers to provide test data for certain chemicals, especially existing chemicals that are already on the market. As pointed out above, however, it remains to be seen whether requiring more test data will necessarily translate into regulatory decisions that are more precautionary. Ironically, the strong emphasis in REACH on increasing the amount of scientific data about chemicals available to future regulatory decisionmakers seems to belie the stereotype mentioned above that Europeans are "more precautionary" because they are more comfortable than Americans with making regulatory decisions based on values alone with relatively little factual data.

The issue of whether Europe or the United States is really "more precautionary" is ultimately less important than how regulatory decisionmakers in both systems can strike the most appropriate balance in particular areas of regulation between the components of facts (risk) and values (precaution). One of us (Elliott 1992) has suggested that this problem becomes more tractable when viewed diachronically (over time) rather than analytically assessing what relative weights should properly be given to facts (risk) and values (precaution) synchronically and in the abstract. Thus, the practical question that every regulator must ask is, "Shall I act to address this particular problem now, basing my decision on what is currently known (or, more accurately, *believed* to be known)? Or shall I instead defer action until a later date, when more may be known, but at the cost of what occurs in the meantime?" Viewed from this practical, diachronic perspective—which is the situation that a regulator actually faces in trying to decide on concrete actions—the problem of the relative weights to be assigned to fact (risk) and to value (precaution) may become much more tractable. As a matter of common sense, a regulator may be well advised to wait until later to act if, but only if, (a) it seems unlikely that much preventable harm will occur in the meantime, but (b) it also seems likely that enough useful information will be developed in the meantime so that making a better decision in the future will be substantially less difficult than it is today. Because these quantities are incommensurable (i.e., they exist in different realms and implicate different values), and because they involve predictions about the future, they cannot be reduced to a precise formula. But it may be helpful to frame the issues in this way nonetheless, because there are many "easy cases" in which it is clear that the harm that may occur in the meantime is far greater than any likely benefit that may result from waiting for more information, and vice versa.

References

American Chemistry Council. 2009. ACC Releases Roadmap to Next Generation of Chemical Safety. www.americanchemistry.com/s_acc/sec_news_article.asp?CID=206&DID=9941 (accessed May 31, 2010).

Aven, Terje, and Jon E. Vinnem. 2007. *Risk Management: With Applications from the Offshore Petroleum Industry*. Heidelberg: Springer.

Bagehot, Walter. 1901. *The English Constitution and Other Political Essays*. New York: D. Appleton & Co.

Battelle. 2003. *Overview: Office of Pollution Prevention and Toxics Programs*. Columbus, OH: Battelle Memorial Institute.

BDI, VCH, and VCI (Federation of German Industries, German Association of Chemical Distributors, and German Chemical Industry Association). 2004. Comments of the Stakeholders to the Research Project *Analysis of the Costs and Benefits of the New EU Chemicals Policy*. Commissioned by the Federal Environmental Agency to ISI (Institute for Systems and Innovation Research) and Oekopol (Institute for Environmental Strategies). Berlin: Environmental Protection Agency of Germany.

Bruijn, Hans, J. A., and Ernst F. ten Heuvelhof. 1999. Scientific Expertise in Complex Decisionmaking Processes. *Science and Public Policy* 26 (3): 151–161.

BUND (Bund für Umwelt und Naturschutz Deutschland). 2004. Comments of the Stakeholders to the Research Project *Analysis of the Costs and Benefits of the New EU Chemicals Policy*. Commissioned by the Federal Environmental Agency to ISI (Institute for Systems and Innovation Research) and Oekopol (Institute for Environmental Strategies). Berlin: Environmental Protection Agency of Germany.

Charnley, Gail, and E. Donald Elliott. 2002. Risk versus Precaution: Environmental Law and Public Health Protection. *Environmental Law Reporter* 32 (2): 10363–10366.

———. 2003. Democratization of Risk Analysis. In *Human and Ecological Risk Assessment: Theory and Practice*, edited by Dennis J. Paustenbach. Boston, MA: Wiley–Interscience.

Coglianese, Cary. 1997. Assessing Consensus: The Promise and Performance of Negotiated Rulemaking. *Duke Law Journal* 46: 1255.

Cohen, Bernhard L. 1991. Catalog of Risks Extended and Updated. *Health Physics* 61: 317.

Cooke, Roger M. 1991. *Experts in Uncertainty: Opinion and Subjective Probability in Science*. New York: Oxford University Press.

Cross, Frank B. 1996. Paradoxical Perils of the Precautionary Principle. *Washington and Lee Law Review* 53: 851–925.

———. 1998. Facts and Values in Risk Assessment. *Reliability Engineering and Systems Safety* 59: 27–45.

Crouch, Edmund A. C., and Richard R. Wilson. 1982. *Risk Benefit Analysis*. Cambridge, MA: Ballinger.

de Sadeleer, Nicolas. 2002. *Environmental Principles: From Political Slogans to Legal Rules*. Oxford: Oxford University Press.

Dimas, Stavros. 2005. Press release. http://europa.eu/rapid/pressReleasesAction.do?reference=IP/05/495&format=HTML&aged=0&language=EN&guiLanguage=en (accessed May 31, 2010).

ECHA (European Chemicals Agency). 2009. New Study Inaccurate on the Number of Test Animals for REACH (ECHA/PR/09/11). http://apps.echa.europa.eu/registered/registered-sub.aspx (accessed May 31, 2010).

Elliott, E. Donald. 1992. Global Climate Change and Regulatory Uncertainty. *Arizona Journal of International and Comparative Law* 9: 259.

———. 2005a. *Chevron* Matters: How the *Chevron* Doctrine Redefined the Roles of Congress, Courts, and Agencies in Environmental Law. *Villanova Environmental Law Journal* 16: 1–18.

———. 2005b. Regulate Nano Now. *Environmental Forum* 22: 43. Washington, DC: Environmental Law Institute.

Elliott, E. Donald, and Michael Thomas. 1993. Chemicals. In *Sustainable Environmental Law*, edited by Celia Campbell-Mohn, J. William Futrell, and Barry Breen. St. Paul, MN: West Publishing Co, 1257–1354.

EPA (U.S. Environmental Protection Agency). 2009. Essential Principles for Reform of Chemicals Management Legislation. www.epa.gov/oppt/existingchemicals/pubs/principles.html (accessed May 31, 2010).

European Commission. 2000. *Communication from the Commission on the Precautionary Principle.* COM(2000) Final: 1. Brussels: EU.

———. 2001. *White Paper: Strategy for a Future Chemicals Policy.* COM (2001), 88. Brussels: EU.

———. 2002. Treaty Establishing the European Community. *Official Journal of the European Commission* C 325:33–184. December 24. Brussels: EU. http://eur-lex.europa.eu/en/treaties/dat/11997D/htm/11997D.html (accessed May 31, 2010).

———. 2003a. *Proposal for a Regulation of the European Parliament and of the Council concerning the Registration, Evaluation, Authorisation and Restriction of Chemicals (REACH).* COM (2003), 644. Brussels: EU. http://eur-lex.europa.eu/en/dossier/dossier_44.htm (accessed May 31, 2010).

———. 2003b. *Extended Impact Assessment concerning the EU Communication COM 2003, 644.* SEC 2003. 1171/3. Brussels: EU. http://trade.ec.europa.eu/doclib/html/121479.htm (accessed May 31, 2010).

———. 2005. *High Level Expert Report on Impacts of REACH.* EU document (2005) 2. Brussels: EU.

———. 2006. *Legislative Acts and Other Instruments. Common Position Adopted by the Council.* No. 7524/06. Council of the European Union. Interinstitutional File: 2003/0256. Brussels: EU.

Federal Register. 1995. 40 C.F.R. § 723.50(c)(2), *Federal Register* 60: 16,336.

Fisher, Elizabeth. 2001. Is the Precautionary Principle Justiciable? *Journal of Environmental Law* 3: 315–334.

———. 2002. Precaution, Precaution Everywhere: Developing a "Common Understanding" of the Precautionary Principle in the European Community. *Maastricht Journal of European and Comparative Law* 9 (1): 7–46.

———. 2009. The Legal Dimension of Developing a General Model for Precautionary Risk Regulation. In *The Application of the Precautionary Principle in the European Union*, edited by O. Renn, P.-J. Schweizer, U. Mueller-Herold, and A. Stirling. Bremen, Germany: Europäischer Hochschulverlag, 62–75.

Funtowicz, Silvio O., and Jerry R. Ravetz. 1987. The Arithmetics of Uncertainty. *Physics Bulletin* 38: 412–414.

———. 1992. Three Types of Risk Assessment and the Emergence of Post-Normal Science. In *Social Theories of Risk*, edited by S. Krimsky, and D. Golding. Westport, CT: Praeger, 251–273.

Funtowicz, Silvio O., Iain Shepherd, David Wilkinson, and Jerry Ravetz. 2000. Science and Governance in the European Union: A Contribution to the Debate. *Science and Public Policy* 5 (27): 327–336.

GAO (U.S. Government Accountability Office). 2005. *Chemical Regulation: Options Exist to Improve EPA's Ability to Assess Health Risks and Manage Its Chemical Review Program.* Washington, DC: Government Printing Office.

Harding, Richard, and Elizabeth Fisher, eds. 1999. *Perspectives on the Precautionary Principle.* Sydney: Federation Press.

Harremoës, Paul, David Gee, Malcolm MacGarvin, Andrew Stirling, Jane Keys, Brian Wynne, and Sofia Guedes Vaz, eds. 2001. *Late Lesson from Early Warnings: The Precautionary Principle, 1898–2000.* Environmental Issue Report No. 22. Copenhagen: European Environment Agency.

Harter, Phillip J. 1982. Negotiating Regulations: A Cure for Malaise. *Georgetown University Law Journal* 71: 1.

Hartung, Thomas, and Costanza Rovida. 2009. Chemical Regulators Have Overreached. *Nature* 460 (August 27): 1080–1081.

Ho, Joanna L. Y., Robin L. Keller, and Pamela Keltyka. 2002. Effects of Probabilistic and Outcome Ambiguity on Managerial Choices. *Journal of Risk and Uncertainty* 24 (1): 47–74.

ISI/Oekopol (Institute for Systems and Innovation Research/Institute for Environmental Strategies). 2004. *Analysis of the Costs and Benefits of the New EU Chemicals Policy.* Report Commissioned by the German Federal Environmental Agency. FKZ 203 65 423. Berlin: Environmental Protection Agency of Germany.

Klinke, Andreas, and Ortwin Renn. 2001. Precautionary Principle and Discursive Strategies: Classifying and Managing Risks. *Journal of Risk Research* 4 (2): 159–173.

———. 2002. A New Approach to Risk Evaluation and Management: Risk-Based, Precaution-Based and Discourse-Based Management. *Risk Analysis* 22 (6): 1071–1994.

Kolluru, Rao V. 1995. Risk Assessment and Management: A Unified Approach. In *Risk Assessment and Management Handbook for Environmental, Health, and Safety Professionals,* edited by R. Kolluru, S. Bartell, R. Pitblade, and S. Stricoff. New York: McGraw-Hill, 1.3–1.41.

KPMG (KPMG International Cooperative). 2005. REACH—Further Work on Impact Assessment. A Case Study Approach. Report for the EU Commission. REACEI/RR/mh. July.

Landfair, Stanley W. 1997. Toxic Substances Control Act. In *Environmental Law Handbook,* 14th ed., edited by Thomas F. P. Sullivan. Rockville, MD: Government Institutes.

Laudan, Larry. 1996. The Pseudo-Science of Science? The Demise of the Demarcation Problem. In *Beyond Positivism and Relativism: Theory, Method, and Evidence,* edited by L. Laudan. Boulder, CO: Westview Press, 166–192.

Lautenberg, Frank. 2010. "Kid Safe Chemical Act" Would Ensure All Chemicals Used in Everyday Products, Including Those Used in Baby Bottles and Children's Toys, Are Proven Safe. http://lautenberg.senate.gov/newsroom/record.cfm?id=298072 (accessed May 31, 2010).

Löfstedt, Ragnar E. 2004. The Swing of the Pendulum in Europe: From Precautionary Principle to (Regulatory) Impact Assessment. AEI-Brookings Joint Center for Regulatory Studies Working Paper 04–07. London: Kings College.

———. 2005. *Risk Management in Post-Trust Societies.* New York: Palgrave MacMillan.

Maine, Henry. 1883. *Dissertations on Early Law and Custom.* London: John Murray.

Majone, Giandomenico. 2002. What Price Safety? The Precautionary Principle and Its Policy Implications. *Journal of Common Market Studies* 40 (1): 89–109.

Marchant, Gary E., and Kenneth L. Mossman. 2004. *Arbitrary and Capricious: The Precautionary Principle in the European Union Courts.* Washington, DC: AEI Press.

Martonik, John F., Edith Nash, and Elizabeth Grossman. 2001. The History of OSHA's Asbestos Rulemakings and Some Distinctive Approaches That They Introduced for Regulating Occupational Exposure to Toxic Substances. *American Industrial Hygiene Association Journal* 62: 208, 215.

Merkhofer, Lee W. 1987. The Use of Risk Comparison to Aid the Communication and Interpretation of the Risk Analyses for Regulatory Decision Making. In *Risk Assessment and Management,* edited by L. B. Lave. New York: Plenum, 581–607.

Mittelstraß, Juergen. 1999. *Zwischen Prometheus und Kassandra. Licht und Dunkel in der Welt des technischen Verstandes.* In *Technologie und Gesellschaft an der Jahrtausendwende,* edited by D. Ruloff. Zürich: Rügger.

Morgan, Granger, and Max Henrion. 1992. *Uncertainty: A Guide to Dealing with Uncertainty in Quantitative Risk and Policy Analysis.* Cambridge: Cambridge University Press.

Morris, Julian, ed. 2000. *Rethinking Risk and the Precautionary Principle.* London: Butterworth Heinemann.

Mueller-Herold, Ulrich, Marco Morosini, and Olivier Schucht. 2005. Choosing Chemicals for Precautionary Regulation: A Filter Series Approach. *Environmental Science and Technology* 39: 683–691.

Mueller-Herold, Ulrich, Marco Morosini, Olivier Schucht, and Martin Scheringer. 2009. Precautionary Pre-Selection of New Organic Chemicals: A Case Study on the Application of the Precautionary Principle in the European Union. In *The Application of the Precautionary Principle in the European Union*, edited by O. Renn, P.-J. Schweizer, U. Mueller-Herold, and A. Stirling. Bremen: Europäischer Hochschulverlag, 76–102.

NRC (National Research Council). 2007. *Toxicity Testing in the Twenty-First Century: A Vision and a Strategy*. Washington, DC: National Academy Press.

O'Riordan, Timothy, and James C. Cameron. 1994. *Interpreting the Precautionary Principle*. London: Earthscan.

O'Riordan, Timothy, James C. Cameron, and Andrew Jordan, eds. 2001. *Reinterpreting the Precautionary Principle*. London: Cameron May.

Paté-Cornell, Elisabeth M. 1996. Uncertainties in Risk Analysis: Six Levels of Treatment. *Reliability Engineering and Systems Safety* 54: 95–111.

Paterson, John. 2005. *Sustainable Development, Sustainable Decisions, and the Precautionary Principle*. Aberdeen: University of Aberdeen. www.springerlink.com/index/N2XU545621643TH5.pdf (accessed May 31, 2010).

Peterson, Martin. 2003. Transformative Decision Rules. *Erkenntnis* 58: 71–85.

Presidential/Congressional Commission on Risk Management and Risk Assessment. 1997. *Risk Assessment and Risk Management in Regulatory Decisionmaking*. Available at http://cfpub.epa.gov/ncea/cfm/recordisplay.cfm?deid=55006 (accessed July 28, 2010).

Raffensberger, Carolyn, and Joel Tickner. 1999. *Protecting Public Health and the Environment: Implementing the Precautionary Principle*. Washington, DC: Island Press.

Renn, Ortwin. 1987. *Eine kulturhistorische Betrachtung des technischen Fortschritts*. In *Fortschritt der Technik—gesellschaftliche und ökonomische Auswirkungen*, edited by H. Lübbe. Heidelberg: R. von Deckers Verlag, 65–100.

———. 2004. The Challenge of Integrating Deliberation and Expertise: Participation and Discourse in Risk Management. In *Risk Analysis and Society: An Interdisciplinary Characterization of the Field*, edited by T. L. MacDaniels and M. J. Small. Cambridge: Cambridge University Press, 289–366.

———. 2008. *Risk Governance*. London: Earthscan.

Renn, Ortwin, Andrew Stirling, Ulrich Müller-Herold, Elizabeth Fisher, Marion Dreyer, Christine Losert, Andreas Klinke, Marco Morisini, and Patrick van Zwanenberg. 2003. *The Application of the Precautionary Principle in the European Union* ("Precaupri"). Final Report to the EU Commission. Stuttgart: University of Stuttgart.

Renn, Ortwin, and Katharine D. Walker. 2008. Lessons Learned. A Re-Assessment of the IRGC Framework on Risk Governance. In *Global Risk Governance: Concept and Practice Using the IRGC Framework*, edited by O. Renn and K. Walker. International Risk Governance Council Bookseries 1. Berlin: Springer, 331–360.

Resnik, David. 2003. Is the Precautionary Principle Unscientific? *Studies in History and Philosophy of Biological and Biomedical Sciences* 34: 329–344.

RIVM/MNP (Netherlands National Institute for Public Health and the Environment/Netherlands Environmental Assessment Agency). 2003. RIVM/MNP Guidance for Uncertainty Assessment and Communication. Report No. NWS-E-2003-163. Utrecht and Bilthoven, Netherlands: Copernicus Institute for Sustainable Development and Innovation and Netherlands Environmental Assessment Agency.

Roe, David. 1988. Barking up the Right Tree: Recent Progress in Focusing the Toxics Issue. *Columbia Journal of Environmental Law* 13: 275.

Rosa, Eugene A. 2008. White, Black, and Grey: Critical Dialogue with the IRGC's Framework for Risk Governance. In *The IRGC Risk Governance Framework: Concepts and Practice*, edited by O. Renn and K. Walker. Heidelberg: Springer, 112–165.

Rose-Ackerman, Susan. 1994. Consensus versus Incentives: A Skeptical Look at Regulatory Negotiation. *Duke Law Journal* 43 (6): 1206–1220.

RPA/BRE (Risk & Policy Analysts Ltd. and BRE Environment). 2003. The Impact of the New Chemicals Policy on Health and the Environment. Final Report to the EU Commission. London: RPA/BRE.

Sand, Peter. 2000. Precautionary Principle: A European Perspective. *Human and Ecological Risk Assessment* 6:3, 445–458.

Sandin, Per, Martin Peterson, Sven Ove Hansson, Christina Rudén, and André Juthé. 2002. Five Charges against the Precautionary Principle. *Journal of Risk Research* 5 (4): 287–299.

Sieferle, Rolf P. 1985. *Fortschrittsfeinde? Opposition gegen Technik und Industrie von der Romantik bis zur Gegenwart.* Munich: Beck.

Simon, Herbert A. 1983. *Reason in Human Affair.* Stanford, CA: Stanford University Press.

Skinner, David C. 1999. *Introduction to Decision Analysis.* 2nd ed. London: Probabilistic Publishers.

Stirling, Andrew. 1998. Risk at a Turning Point? *Journal of Risk Research* 1 (2): 97–109.

———. 1999. *On "Science" and "Precaution" in the Management of Technological Risk.* Vol. 1, *Synthesis Study.* Report to the EU Forward Studies Unit by European Science and Technology Observatory (ESTO). EUR19056 EN. Seville: IPTS. ftp://ftp.jrc.es/pub/EURdoc/eur19056 IIen.pdf (accessed May 31, 2010).

———. 2003. Risk, Uncertainty, and Precaution: Some Instrumental Implications from the Social Sciences. In *Negotiating Change*, edited by F. Berkhout, M. Leach, and I. Scoones. London: Edward Elgar, 33–76.

Stirling, Andrew, Ortwin Renn, and Patrick van Zwanenberg. 2006. Framework for the Precautionary Governance of Food Safety: Integrating Science and Participation in the Social Appraisal of Risk. In *Implementing the Precautionary Principle: Perspectives and Prospects*, edited by E. Fisher, J. Jones, and R. von Schomberg. London: Edward Elgar, 284–315.

Stone, Christopher. 2001. Is There a Precautionary Principle? *Environmental Law Reporter* 31: 10790.

Sunstein, Cass. 2005. *Laws of Fear. Beyond the Precautionary Principle.* Cambridge: Cambridge University Press.

Trouwborst, Arie. 2002. *Evolution and Status of the Precautionary Principle in International Law.* The Hague: Kluwer.

van Asselt, Marjolein B. A. 2000. *Perspectives on Uncertainty and Risk.* Dordrecht, Netherlands: Kluwer.

van Zwanenberg, Patrick, and Andrew Stirling. 2004. Risk and Precaution in the U.S. and Europe. *Yearbook of European Environmental Law* 3: 43–57.

Vlek, Charles A. 1996. A Multi-Level, Multi-Stage and Multi-Attribute Perspective on Risk Assessment, Decision-Making, and Risk Control. *Risk, Decision, and Policy* 1: 1, 9–31.

von Winterfeldt, Detlof, and Ward Edwards. 1984. Patterns of Conflict about Risk Debates. *Risk Analysis* 4: 55–68.

Wildavsky, Aaron. 1988. *Searching for Safety.* New Brunswick, NJ: Transaction Books.

———. 1990. No Risk Is the Highest Risk of All. In *Readings in Risk*, edited by T. S. Glickman, and M. Gough. Washington, DC: Resources for the Future Press, 120–127.

Williams, E. Spencer, Julie Panko, and Dennis J. Paustenbach. 2009. The European Union's REACH Regulation: A Review of Its History and Requirements. *Critical Review in Toxicology* 39 (7): 553–575.

WWF/EEB (World Wildlife Fund European Toxics Programme/European Environmental Bureau). 2003. *A New Chemicals Policy in Europe. New Opportunities for Industry.* Discussion paper. London: WWF/EEB.

CHAPTER 11

Medical Errors, New Drug Approval, and Patient Safety

Frances H. Miller

*H*ippocrates enunciated the precautionary principle for medicine in 400 B.C. when he said, "*Primum, non nocere*" ("First, do no harm"). All physicians are taught that precautionary rule in medical school. Hippocrates' advice might have worked well to safeguard patient safety in his time, when doctors could not do much for (or to) patients, but medical treatment is very different now. Much has changed over the past five decades in particular, driven by technological advance, and health care has become far more sophisticated, complex, and potentially dangerous to patients than it ever was before. At roughly the same time, health sector oversight has been evolving away from the professional self-regulation and laissez-faire regulatory mindset of much of the past, when the precautionary principle seemed superfluous because the risks of medical intervention were all but invisible outside the profession.

Over the past half century of dramatic medical progress, accompanied by increasing medical risks, physicians have ruefully come to acknowledge that sometimes they have to bury their own mistakes. Heightened public and professional awareness of iatrogenic (treatment-caused) injury and concern for patient safety are helping to drive health system improvements today (Starr 1982). Four of these changes deserve special attention for the light they shed on the mounting governmental and public perception of medical risk, and on the regulatory and private sector responses to it.

First, computerization has been a boon to medical research and treatment, but it has also facilitated data collection revealing a high prevalence of medical accident that went unnoticed previously (Leape 2001). Leape notes, "If a hospital has a real commitment to safety, it is going to get so much information that you don't need an [expensive] reporting system. I can talk to any three nurses in a unit for an hour about what bothers them, and come out with a safety agenda that will keep me busy for a year" (2004).

The worrisome patient safety implications of these data have been impossible to ignore, and that fact alone has spurred precautionary reforms.

Second, while technological advances have prolonged both the length and the quality of human life, many of them involve more invasive and risk-laden methods of treatment than those they replaced. In addition, modern technology often calls for more technical sophistication from caregivers than used to be required (HEW 1973, 3). Medical injuries thus have more opportunities to surface in the modern era, and they are often more serious when they do.

Third, patient awareness of medical risk has increased in tandem with the civil rights, women's liberation, gay rights, and other social movements of the latter half of the twentieth century. The patients' rights movement (*Wyatt v. Stickney* 1971; Annas 2004) generated a more skeptical and risk-conscious patient culture, particularly in the United States—a fact not lost on payers, providers, and regulators. They have responded in ways varying from outright hostility (Sprecher 1978), to cooperation,[1] to voluntary proactive measures,[2] to increased governmental oversight designed to forestall medical accidents (Hallinan 2004, 1).[3]

Finally, U.S. congressional enactment of Medicare and Medicaid in 1965 brought a massive infusion of government funding into the U.S. health sector and enabled many Americans to afford medical care who had previously gone without. More patients were thus exposed to the possibility of medical accident than ever before. Medicare and Medicaid funding also sharply increased government attention to the risks—and the value—of the health services it now underwrites (MedPAC 2004).

The open-ended nature of Medicare and Medicaid funding in the United States has made increased governmental oversight of the health sector partly an exercise in fiscal self-preservation. Most European Union (EU) countries, on the other hand, exert tighter control over total health care spending through budgetary processes, so they do not experience as intense fiscal pressures to implement quality improvement measures.

---

[1] For example, PhRMA, the pharmaceutical industry's trade association, has adopted principles by which "the PhRMA companies commit to the timely communication of all meaningful results of clinical trials, whether those results are positive or negative" (PhRMA 2004).

[2] For example, the Joint Commission on the Accreditation of Healthcare Organizations instituted a sentinel Events Policy in 1995, which requires accredited institutions to report "unexpected occurrence[s] involving death or serious physical or psychological injury" and issues periodic Sentinel Event Alerts to its members (JCAHO 2005).

[3] For example, Congress established the National Practitioner Data Bank pursuant to the Health Care Quality Improvements Act of 1986, 42 U.S.C. § 11131–11137 (1995) to create a central repository of actions taken against physicians indicating quality of care problems. The legislation requires state licensing and disciplinary agencies to report sanctions against physicians to the Data Bank, and hospitals and other entities taking adverse action against doctors must do so as well. Moreover, medical malpractice awards must be reported to the Data Bank as well. See Hallinan (2004, 1) on a "corporate shield" protecting a negligent physician whose name never technically appears on a malpractice settlement or judgment from being reported to the Data Bank; U.S. Dept. of Health and Human Services Office of Inspector General (HHS 2001) raises red flags about the Data Bank's effectiveness in safeguarding the public from substandard practitioners.

On both sides of the Atlantic, however, payer oversight also attempts to improve patient safety and welfare. The regulatory response to medical risks has nonetheless been relatively low-key and cautious everywhere. Apart from a few subject areas—U.S. drug and device regulation, and EU regulation of genetically modified food (see Chapter 2), for example—the precautionary principle has not found robust expression in regulatory policy focused on health care itself. In both the United States and the EU, the reasons for this range from the difficulty of identifying iatrogenic risk, to the traditional deference accorded to self-regulation in the medical profession, to the paucity of enforcement resources.

Adverse Drug Reactions

Adverse reactions to drugs can be both dangerous for patients and extremely costly to society (Classen et al. 1997). They materialize in more than 6% of all hospitalizations and constitute almost 20% of all adverse medical events taking place in that setting (Lesar et al. 1997). One 2000 study estimated that the yearly costs associated with drug-related adverse events in the United States amount to $177.4 billion (Ernst and Grizzle 2001). Those costs were almost double the $91.8 billion in direct medical expenditures for diabetes care in 2002 (ADA 2003). Estimates posit that anywhere from 28% to 95% of all adverse drug events are preventable (AHRQ 2001).

Some adverse drug reactions are the undesired but not wholly unexpected side effects of the risk–benefit balancing doctors must engage in whenever they prescribe drugs (Wiener 1998). Drugs are defined as "articles . . . intended to affect the structure or any function of the body" (Federal Food, Drug, and Cosmetic Act, 21 U.S.C. § 321(g)(1)), and the body reacts to them in both positive and negative ways. Other adverse drug events, however, are simply the result of prescribing errors, and those can be deadly. One relatively recent study determined that hospitalized patients suffering an adverse drug event almost double their risk of death (Classen et al. 1997). The highly publicized demise of the *Boston Globe*'s health reporter Betsy Lehman after being administered inadvertent overdoses of experimental chemotherapy for metastatic breast cancer at Harvard's Dana-Farber Cancer Institute brought that point home with a vengeance (Knox 1995; Mohl 1998). The Lehman case also proved a powerful stimulus for broad patient safety reform efforts, locally, nationally, and even internationally (Romano 1999).

Safety and Efficacy Evaluation

In 1962, efficacy requirements were added to the newly strengthened safety requirements of the Federal Food, Drug, and Cosmetic Act of 1938 (21 U.S.C. § 355), a law passed after more than 100 people died from ingesting a product named elixir sulfanilamide, a sulfa drug (Pina and Pinds 2002). Ever since, the U.S. Food and Drug Administration (FDA) has generally been considered the international gold standard for rigorous pre-marketing safety and efficacy evaluation of pharmaceutical products

(Pina and Pinds 2002). That golden reputation became tarnished in the wake of several FDA safety and conflict-of-interest controversies over the past few years, and it has yet to recover (Thomas 2006).

The precautionary principle had theoretically been paramount in FDA policy until the 1990s (Olson 1995),[4] unlike the retroactive focus of most medical practice oversight. The FDA's 1999 precautionary measure instructing blood banks not to accept blood from donors who had spent more than six months in the UK between 1980 and 1996, for fear of their transmitting bovine spongiform encephalopathy virus, serves as a relatively recent example of the agency's historically guarded approach toward low-probability medical risk (Goodman 2004; FDA 1999a; Wiener and Rogers 2002; Chapter 3 of this volume).

Precaution was the FDA's official watchword in part because congressional oversight committees habitually announce hearings to rake the agency over the coals whenever the media accuses it of failing to protect the public from unsafe drugs and devices (Hutt 1996). A recent case in point is Merck's "voluntary" withdrawal of its blockbuster COX-2 inhibitor pain medication Vioxx in 2004. Studies showing significant cardiovascular risk associated with its use (Oberholzer-Gee and Inmader 2004) immediately hit the front pages of the popular and medical presses, and the negative publicity was not lost on politicians. Other studies soon raised similar questions about the safety of all COX-2 type pain medications. That COX-2 inhibitor controversy roughly coincided with contemporaneous and highly publicized debates over the safety of prescribing selective serotonin reuptake inhibitors (SSRIs) for depressed adolescents (Brent 2004; EG-SSRI 2004; FDA 2004b). Predictably, publicity triggered high-profile congressional investigations of allegedly lax standards and conflicts of interest associated with the FDA's recent drug regulatory activities (Davis 2005).

In response, the FDA hurriedly announced that it was asking the Institute of Medicine to evaluate independently the way the agency assesses and monitors adverse events associated with drugs currently on the market (FDA 2004a). Even more recent revelations—about the integrity of the clinical studies on which the FDA based its approval of Vioxx, about conflicts of interest on FDA advisory committees, and most recently about the safety of cardiac devices—have generated further calls for FDA safety reform (Strom 2006; Ray and Stein 2006). A similar legislative reaction took place in Great Britain in 2005 when the House of Commons Health Committee held a series of hearings on the influence of the pharmaceutical industry, including the unsafe use of SSRIs and COX-2 inhibitor drugs.

The Institute of Medicine (IOM) issued *The Future of Drug Safety: Promoting and Protecting the Health of the Public* (Baciu et al. 2007) in response to the FDA's request to evaluate its adverse event reporting program. The IOM's comprehensive report critiques the entire drug regulatory process and recommends a broad range of reforms: (1) increased drug safety funding, (2) expanded FDA authority, (3) better post-market pharmacovigilance, and (4) upgraded management practices (McClellan 2007).

---

[4] Meaning, consumer safety trumps other interests in FDA new drug approvals.

In essence, the IOM advocates a shift in the FDA's regulatory oversight from a relatively hands-off posture after new product approval (barring significant problems) toward more stringent continuing responsibility for monitoring drug safety throughout all approved products' marketing life cycles (Psaty and Burke 2006). The FDA's unusually detailed 2007 response (FDA 2007b) accepted many of the IOM's recommendations, but the FDA stopped short of fully embracing the IOM's far-reaching proposals for significantly enhanced drug safety, transparency, independence, and proactivity (Psaty and Charo 2007, 1917).

In the fall of 2007, the U.S. Congress responded to mounting public concern over drug safety by passing the Food and Drug Administration Revitalization Act (FDA 2007a). The legislation basically accepts the IOM's recommendation for a philosophical shift in direction toward a more dynamic post-approval safety role for the FDA. It gives the FDA responsibility for actively overseeing safety throughout the life cycle of a drug and provides funding for the job. The statute also gives the FDA explicit post-marketing authority to order manufacturers to conduct additional studies and make labeling changes including warnings. FDA may also limit drug distribution when the agency believes that to be warranted.

Much U.S. food and drug legislation prior to 1962 was enacted in reaction to widespread public health disasters (Hutt 1996). Likewise, Congress passed the 1962 safety and efficacy amendments to the drug approval process largely in reaction to the rash of thalidomide-caused birth defects in Europe (Hutt 1996). The United States had fortuitously avoided experiencing a parallel rise in birth defects, because by the time neonatal deformities began surfacing in Europe, the FDA still had awarded thalidomide only investigational new drug status. The problematic drug was thus not then widely available in America (House of Commons Health Committee 2005).

While the United States remains more stringent than the EU with respect to general safety and efficacy standards—notwithstanding the recent safety controversies—it has relaxed its more rigorous precautionary approach over the past 10 or 15 years (Olson 2002). Knowledgeable providers and their sick patients have been able since the 1980s to work their way around regulatory barriers keeping them from access to experimental therapy in certain circumstances. They could end-run formal approval processes and obtain investigational drugs without enrolling in clinical trials by securing "treatment INDs" (Investigational New Drug Applications), which permit experimental drugs to be shipped in interstate commerce prior to FDA approval. Before these treatment INDs became available, sick patients could obtain access to experimental drugs only by enrolling in formal clinical trial protocols and risking assignment to placebo or "standard therapy" arms of the studies. Those receiving placebo or standard care were obviously precluded from access to the experimental medication, although since most studies are blinded, they would not know for sure to which arm of the study they had been assigned.[5] Alternatively, patients suffering from certain serious diseases—AIDS, for example—

---

[5] Treatment INDs were permitted by FDA regulation in 1987 and incorporated into statute by the Food and Drug Administration Modernization Act of 1997 (FDAMA).

could secure experimental drugs through the FDA's "parallel track" policy, which permits seriously ill patients to take investigational drugs for treatment purposes.

Congress passed the Prescription Drug User Fee Act (PDUFA) in 1992 in response to mounting criticism—especially from AIDS activists—that the FDA's process for approving new drugs had become unduly lengthy and burdensome in comparison with faster European regulatory schemes (Andersson 1992; GAO 1980; see Federal Food, Drug, and Cosmetic Act, 21 U.S.C. § 379 (2002)). The FDA had been devoting much of its limited personnel and resources to generic drug approvals at that time, which meant that staff dedicated to evaluating new drug applications was stretched thin. PDUFA introduced substantial user fees for new drug applications, earmarked for hiring more FDA reviewers for clinical studies (Carpenter et al. 2003). In return for this increased funding, the agency promised to expedite review processes (Pina and Pinds 2002). The review cycle did indeed speed up in the aftermath of PDUFA and its follow-up legislative companion, the Food and Drug Administration Modernization Act of 1997 (FDAMA) (21 U.S.C. § 353a (1998)). According to at least one analysis, the review cycle accelerated by 50% (Kaitin 1997; Shulman and Kaitin 1996), but the number of adverse drug reactions reported to the FDA also tripled within the ensuing five years (FDA 1998).

At least a third of those reported adverse events were deemed "serious," and 10 drugs receiving FDA approval after PDUFA's 1992 passage were removed from the market for safety reasons in the 4 years between September 1997 and August 2001. This compares with the *20* years (between 1974 and 1993) it took for the same number of drugs to be withdrawn from the market pre-PDUFA (Olson 2002). This indicates that the accelerated review processes seem to have added not-insignificant safety costs.

In addition, troublesome conflict-of-interest questions have increasingly been raised in connection with FDA approval (Harris and Berenson 2005). Many members of the expert advisory panels that recommend to the FDA whether new drugs should be approved turned out to have direct or indirect financial interests in the drug or category of drugs they were asked to evaluate (Cauchon 2000). Even more pointed conflict-of-interest questions have now been raised concerning British, French, and European Medicines Agency (EMEA) pharmaceutical approval processes, because those authorities have historically invited direct industry participation in the decision of whether to grant licensing approval (Mossialos et al. 2004). The European agencies are also funded far more substantially than the FDA is by fees paid by the pharmaceutical companies they regulate. In 2001, for example, 70% of the EMEA's budget was projected to come from industry fees, whereas only 10% of the FDA's budget was dependent on industry sources (Garattini and Bertele 2004).

Some of the increase in adverse drug reactions leading to U.S. withdrawals post-PDUFA can be accounted for by the fact that more (and more novel) drug products were being marketed in the 1990s than during the 1970s and 1980s (Olson 2004). Nonetheless, an FDA policy switch that altered the cost–benefit ratio for drug approvals to weight considerations other than unalloyed patient safety—stemming in part from a desire to compete with faster (and more drug industry-involved) European approval policies—had to bear some responsibility as well.

Health care professionals, the pharmaceutical industry, and consumer groups lobbied for five years after PDUFA was passed to persuade Congress to enact additional reform via FDAMA. FDAMA further streamlined and accelerated the whole U.S. review process for new pharmaceutical products, and it codified the statutory fast-track approval process for those drugs and biologics targeted for serious or life-threatening diseases that had achieved surrogate endpoints.[6] The average time for fast-track drugs to progress from development through approval was in fact reduced by two to two and a half years soon after FDAMA was enacted (TCSDD 2003; FDA 2003). Congress explicitly lowered the regulatory barrier imposed by the FDA's historically precautionary approval policies in response to pressure to "get innovative drugs to critically ill patients faster" and to harmonize global approval processes. By doing so, it moved the U.S. regulatory approach officially closer in spirit to that of its less precautionary and more approval-friendly European counterparts (Wiktorowicz 2003). This has not, however, proved an unmixed blessing for patients, as witness the increased number of recalls (Olson 2004).

The thalidomide tragedy of the early 1960s had illustrated the need for more stringent drug regulatory schemes throughout Europe as well as in the United States. Great Britain implemented its own "modern" drug regulatory processes in 1963,[7] and its regulatory agencies have generally been influenced more by the demands of industry through a "corporatist tradition of negotiation and accommodation" (Wiktorowicz 2003) than has been seen in the United States. British drug and device regulation have recently been merged to create the current Medicines and Health Care Products Regulatory Agency (MHRA).

The MHRA's approach toward pharmaceutical companies has been perceived as more precautionary than that of other European countries, notwithstanding the historically corporatist British tradition (Wiktorowicz 2003). This stems in part from a complex relationship between government and drug manufacturers wherein the UK Department of Health (DH) sets the level of profits that the pharmaceutical industry is allowed to make from drug sales within the country as a whole and evaluates the cost-effectiveness of drugs (Harris 2008), but does not overtly limit the drugs available for National Health Service (NHS) patients (Mossialos et al. 2004). As the by-product of a cooperative initiative between industry and a newly safety-conscious British government, the MHRA now has enough influence and resources to enforce heightened safety standards. Although the agency has the capacity to generate stricter standards, it nonetheless still allows the industry to wield critical influence to soften regulatory policy (House of Commons Health Committee 2005). Some believe this may be inevitable given that drug companies provide the largest percentage of MHRA funding through user fees, as is also the case in other European countries (Abraham 2002).

---

[6] According to the Tufts Center for the Study of Drug Development (TCSDD 2000), between 1995 and 1999, biotech drugs had faster approval times going through the European Medicines Evaluation Agency (EMEA) than they did being evaluated by the FDA.

[7] The Committee on the Safety of Medicines (CMS) consisted of a group of experts responsible for reviewing product applications before sending them to the Medicines Division of the Department of Health and Social Security with their recommendations, which issued the actual drug licenses.

France instituted a formal system of drug regulation in 1945, much earlier than did the British, albeit a system with more limited powers. The legislation required "the pharmacy profession to conduct its activities in the public interest and assume legal responsibility for them" (Wiktorowicz 2003), but the government's role in this decentralized system was merely to police the self-regulatory activities of professional and trade associations. These controls have developed into an extensive set of formal rules, which cover most manufacture and marketing processes. Since one of the pharmaceutical industry's goals was to gain increased access to international markets, both government and industry have worked cooperatively to enhance the rigor of the regulatory system—but not too much. When France introduced mandatory review of products marketed prior to 1990, the change failed to provoke any significant industry protest (Wiktorowicz 2003).

In the 1990s, the European Union, attempting to bring a measure of uniformity to European drug approvals, established the European Medicines Evaluation Agency (it was renamed the European Medicines Agency in 2004 but retained the EMEA acronym) (European Parliament 2004). It functions as a centralized regulatory body to evaluate drugs, devices, and veterinary products for all member countries (Garattini and Bertele 2004).

All pharmaceuticals manufactured using certain biotechnological methodologies or utilizing gene therapy must be approved by the EMEA before they can be marketed throughout the EU. In addition, orphan drugs and "any medicinal product containing an entirely new active substance ... for which the therapeutic indication is the treatment of acquired immune deficiency syndrome, cancer, neurodegenerative disease, or diabetes" must now also go through the centralized licensure process (European Parliament 2004). Moreover, by May 2008, all medicinal products intended for treatment of viral diseases, autoimmune diseases, and other immune dysfunctions also had to be approved by the EMEA. A high degree of scientific expertise and sophistication are necessary to evaluate these treatments, and the requirement for central approval is designed to "preserve the confidence of patients and the medical profession in the evaluation" (European Parliament 2004). It also prevents unnecessary duplication of expensive scientific and regulatory expertise throughout the 25 European member countries.

Manufacturers of other drugs can seek EMEA marketing approval as well, and EMEA approval permits the subject pharmaceuticals to be marketed directly in all Member States (Mossialos et al. 2004). Manufacturers can still seek local approval through a decentralized process using the Member States' own regulatory mechanisms if they choose, relying on mutual recognition procedures to provide marketing access thereafter in other Member States. The expanding scope of mandatory EMEA jurisdiction presages the eventual withering away of most Member States' own evaluative and licensing processes. However, notwithstanding recent constitutional uncertainties, differences in regulatory standards among Member States still continue to be relevant. Individual nations tend to compete for licensing fees on the basis of whose approval cycle is the fastest and most likely to result in a favorable outcome. This indicates a less-than-meticulous regard for scientific processes of evaluation in some countries (Abraham and Lewis 1999), although they have begun to converge toward a more uniform model since issuance of harmonizing directives and regulations governing the EMEA. In truth, very few applications for approval are actually denied at either the EMEA or the Member State level. Most manufacturers prefer to withdraw individual applications if they sense disapproval in the offing rather than having to face an outright central agency rejection. That way they can keep dossier information confidential—and perhaps thereafter apply for approval in a more lenient venue (Garattini and Bertele 2004).

Post-marketing Surveillance

The efficacy of post-marketing surveillance leaves much to be desired in both the United States and the EU. Theoretically, the trade-off for relaxing safety and efficacy requirements pursuant to PDUFA and FDAMA was to increase U.S. pharmacovigilance in the post-marketing period (Noah 2000; FDA 1999b), but the Vioxx controversy and other recent events have underscored the woeful inadequacy of current post-market safety screening. FDA has had the power to require Phase IV (post-approval) studies when new drug approvals (NDAs) are granted for years, and in fact has conditioned one-third to one-half of its approvals on the manufacturers' agreements to conduct Phase IV trials (21 CFR § 310.303(a); Mattison and Richard 1987). Those agreements have been honored more in the breach than in the performance, however, with one study finding that only 13% of those drug companies required between 1990 and 1994 to conduct post-marketing studies had completed them by the year 2000 (Sasich et al. 2000). A more recent congressional review determined that the FDA required 91 further studies on 42 products approved between 1993 and 2004, but as of mid-2005, only 46 had been completed, while half of the unfinished studies had not even begun (Markey 2005).

Manufacturers learn about adverse drug events (ADEs) primarily from adverse drug reports (ADRs) from the physicians and institutions that first detect problems, and then take sufficient interest and the time to notify them and the FDA. In 1993, the FDA introduced the MedWatch Medical Products Reporting Program, designed to encourage doctors to report suspected problems with medical products to the agency voluntarily, as well as to the manufacturer. Although the quantity of ADRs has increased dramatically over the years (Noah 2000), and in fact went up by 14% between 2003 and 2004 (FDA 2004d), underreporting by professionals is still perceived to be the norm rather than the exception.

The FDA has issued several Guidances to Industry designed to support and reinforce timely ADE/ADR reporting, but the promptness and effectiveness of the FDA's post-marketing surveillance still depends on voluntary reporting (even if technically mandatory for manufacturers). According to informed observers, reporting still leaves much to be desired (Struve 2005). Moreover, many have been pessimistic about FDA's willingness and ability to take action on the basis of what it does learn through a flood of often incomplete and sometimes inaccurate ADRs, ADEs, and other reports, absent the external pressure generated primarily by media scrutiny following well-publicized patient injuries. Critics point out that chronic understaffing hampers the agency's capacity to do thorough analyses and take appropriate action in all but high-profile or very serious cases (Noah 2000).

The thalidomide disaster of the early 1960s spurred the development of systematic adverse drug reaction reporting throughout Europe as well as in America. Widespread misconceptions about the damaging potential of medications had prevented the medical community from identifying the now-apparent causal relationship between phocomelia and thalidomide when those birth defects first began appearing. In 1963, the Sixteenth World Health Conference passed a resolution reaffirming the "need for early action in regard to rapid dissemination of information on adverse drug reactions" (WHO 1973). The project's goal was to devise a transnational system that would detect "previously unknown or poorly understood adverse effects of medicines" (WHO 1972). The effort produced the WHO Programme for International Drug Monitoring, which maintains the world's largest medicine database and is located in the Uppsala Monitoring Centre in Sweden. This database contains nearly three million recorded instances of adverse drug reactions, but once again a paucity of sufficient analysts to make sense of these data hampers their effective utilization.

In 1971, WHO organized a conference on international drug monitoring, advocating creation of national centers for drug monitoring within its Member States (WHO 1972). Shortly thereafter, European nations began to introduce adverse drug reporting systems, largely modeled after Britain's 1964 voluntary patient reporting program, commonly referred to as the "Yellow Card Scheme" (Otero and Domínguez-Gil 2000). Today most European nations employ similar yellow card schemes, and medications have been altered or removed from the market pursuant to these early warning signals.[8] However, the systems are often overburdened and understaffed, as has been the case nearly worldwide, which impedes the ability to analyze data and then react appropriately.

The furor over allegedly lax post-marketing pharmacovigilance stirred up by the COX-2 inhibitor and SSRI controversies of 2004, along with allegations of conflicts of interest infecting FDA drug approval processes in the United States, prompted the secretary of Health and Human Services to establish an independent Drug Safety Oversight Board to monitor pharmaceuticals in early 2005 (FDA 2004c). The board, composed of government medical experts and FDA employees, confers with outside medical experts along with consumer and patient groups in carrying out its monitoring function. Pointedly omitted from those to be consulted are representatives from the pharmaceutical industry. The board's primary task is to gather information about drug safety from a broad range of sources (including the public), to analyze it, and to devise

---

[8] The Yellow Card Scheme linked remoxipride to spontaneous reports of aplastic anemia, causing the medication be withdrawn from the market after it had been used by 10,000 patients; the nonsteroidal anti-inflammatory drug tiaprofenic acid was linked to acute cystitis; and high lipase pancreatins for cystic fibrosis were linked to colonic strictures in children, a condition that disappeared after the Committee on Safety of Medicines (CSM) recommended against the use of high-strength enzymes in 1995.

ways to minimize suspected risks and improve drug safety. Whether it will have adequate staff and expertise to process this information, let alone recommend appropriate remedial action, has not been determined. Critics contend that this initiative is structurally flawed and inadequate to cope with the important safety task (Ray and Stein 2006).

Computerization has somewhat eased the burden on reporting centers on both sides of the Atlantic, and the 2004 EC regulation reorganizing and streamlining EMEA procedures now requires electronic transmission of adverse reaction reports, which helps simplify their analysis (European Parliament 2004). Britain's MHRA currently operates an Adverse Drug Reactions On-Line Information Tracking (ADROIT) database as well. ADROIT has increased the incidence and effectiveness of reporting, analysis, and hazard detection, but its effectiveness is hampered, as elsewhere, by lack of sufficient staffing to do sophisticated analysis of causation and other issues (Stricker and Psaty 2004). Although one could argue that the precautionary principle is now at work with respect to post-marketing surveillance, pharmacovigilance in its present form functions as only a weakly protective mechanism against adverse drug reactions, and a retroactive one at that.

Drug Advertisements

Direct-to-consumer advertising (DTCA) of prescription-only pharmaceuticals is prohibited in the EU by Article 3 of Directive 92/28/EEC (European Parliament 1992). Although no mention of precaution is made in any of the EU regulatory instruments related to DTCA, banning DTCA is clearly a precautionary measure based on the uncertain risks—to economic interests, to patient–doctor communications, to health care outcomes, and so on. However, little research has been conducted in the EU on this issue.

By contrast, DTCA is allowed in the United States. Research on it has been carried out by the FDA's Center for Drug Evaluation and Research (CDER). CDER has investigated the impact on the physician–patient relationship with broadly positive conclusions (Aikin 2003). However, harms have been identified, and the evidence of benefits seems weak, such as an increased uptake of new drugs with significant benefits to patients. Statins, drugs used to lower cholesterol, are one example. Steven Findlay, however, has criticized increased statin use (2001), noting that while the number of people taking these medicines has mushroomed in the last two decades, "it is entirely possible that the cost of having every American with elevated cholesterol levels take a drug for extended periods (years to decades) would exceed the benefit derived (in reduced fatal and nonfatal cardiovascular events) compared with other interventions, such as insurance-paid dietary counseling programs" (quoted in Meek 2001).

So with regard to DTCA, the United States seems less precautionary than the EU. However, in the aftermath of the Vioxx controversy, both the pharmaceutical industry and Congress have been toying with the idea of banning DTCA for the first two or three years after a new drug has gained approval (Vastag 2005, 1807). The hiatus would provide time for more safety data to accumulate before advertising campaigns stimulate widespread patient demand.

Medical Accidents and Patient Safety

Medical accidents, defined for the purposes of this chapter as treatment-caused patient injuries or "near misses," tended historically to be viewed as isolated, rare, and relatively unpredictable events (Leape 1994). Licensing authorities in all countries have usually made sure that physicians met basic standards of education and training before they were permitted to practice medicine, but beyond that, they did little historically to regulate the quality of care their licensees actually delivered (Jost 1997). The public usually learned about medical accidents anecdotally, if at all, and then often only after a mass disaster or an injured patient had initiated a medical malpractice lawsuit. Although individual hospitals had a somewhat better sense of the prevalence of iatrogenic injury, and payers had a more informed sense of the societal costs of medical accidents, neither tried very hard to prevent patient injury until relatively recently.[9] These institutional players were reluctant to intervene because physicians had traditionally dominated the health sector (Starr 1982), and legislation prohibiting corporations from practicing medicine reinforced that dominance by raising legal obstacles to many of their ameliorative efforts (Chase-Lubitz 1987).

External oversight for medical accidents was thus relatively sparse and basically reactive in both the United States and Europe until the mid-1980s. Precautionary measures apart from those of the FDA were sporadic. Oversight after the fact of medical injury consisted primarily of institutional and professional licensure sanctions (Kusserow et al. 1987; Relman 1985), occasional reimbursement penalties (42 U.S.C. § 1320c-2 (1982)), and malpractice litigation (Studdert et al. 2004; Mohr 2000; see Weiler et al. 1993 for a comprehensive survey of the medical malpractice liability system and the Harvard Medical Practice Study on New York hospitals). These measures were neither effectively proactive nor sharply focused on anticipating future medical accidents and safeguarding patient welfare (Miller 1997), apart from the odd safety regulation directed at such issues as radiation exposure (21 CFR § 1020.31) or the blood supply (Goodman 2004; Zou et al. 2004). To the extent that providers failed to improve medical safety on their own (Bosk 2003), the public had little choice but to rely on these *ex post* quality control mechanisms. Whatever deterrent effect was generated by retroactive punitive measures and the relatively few instances of direct governmental safety regulation focused on medical treatment was difficult to quantify (Danzon 1985).[10]

---

[9] The Leapfrog Group Consortium of large employer-purchasers of employee health insurance issued Purchasing Principles in 2005 that include standards for providers designed to improve patient safety. These standards include 24/7 coverage of intensive care units by intensive medicine specialists, computerized order entry of medication orders, and referral of patients needing high-risk procedures to medical centers meeting volume criteria (see Freudenheim 2000).

[10] One economist (Danzon 1985) examining the deterrent effect of malpractice litigation estimated that "only a 4% reduction in the rate of negligent injury is required to justify the costs of the tort system" (using 1974 estimates of claims frequency and patient compensation). See also Bovbjerg (1986) for a general discussion of malpractice litigation's deterrent effects.

Since little reliable information about the widespread extent and increasingly systemic origin of medical accidents existed, few believed that much of great significance could be done to prevent them (Leatherman and McCarthy 2002). Accordingly, little pressure for precautionary reforms existed until the U.S. medical malpractice insurance crisis of the mid-1970s stimulated comprehensive fact gathering about the extent and severity of medical accidents (GAO 1986). Similar pressure was not felt in Europe, because medical malpractice lawsuits were relatively rare, and thus their signaling effect was weak. To the surprise of many interested parties, the American studies showed that a great deal more medical negligence actually took place—in hospitals, at least—than ever culminated in litigation, notwithstanding a more litigious legal culture in the United States (Bok 1983).

Rates of Medical Errors in the United States and the EU

Collecting data on iatrogenic injury was especially difficult in the era before computerization, not least because medical care is delivered in fragmented settings ranging from large teaching hospital centers, to doctors' offices, to patients' own homes. The California Medical Society and the California Hospital Association underwrote the first large-scale (27,000 hospital admissions) investigation of the extent and impact of medical error in California hospitals in the 1970s. The study (Mills 1977), designed to collect data providing the foundation for medical malpractice reform legislation in that state, found that although 1 in 126 California hospital admissions produced injuries due to negligence, fewer than one-tenth of those injuries resulted in a malpractice claim. The cost and personnel requirements required for such comprehensive research undertakings deterred further wide-ranging studies until the New York state legislature funded the now-famous 1990 Harvard School of Public Health report analyzing adverse medical events in 31,000 New York hospitalizations during 1984 (Harvard Medical Practice Study 1990). Once again, this research was undertaken to provide the factual underpinnings for malpractice reform legislation in the wake of yet another U.S. medical malpractice insurance crisis, this time in the mid-1980s.

Both the landmark California and New York investigations revealed a surprisingly high incidence of adverse medical events related to hospitalization (4.6% of all hospital admissions in California and 3.7% in New York). Both studies found a relatively low incidence of malpractice claims related to those adverse events the reviewers determined were caused by negligence. The Harvard study found that in 1984, eight times more negligent adverse events occurred than the number of malpractice claims eventually filed (Localio et al. 1991). A similar large-scale Harvard School of Public Health investigation carried out toward the end of the 1990s in Colorado and Utah produced comparable statistical results both for inpatient injury (Thomas et al. 2000) and for malpractice claims related to those injuries (Studdert et al. 2000a, 2000b). Numerous other studies on smaller patient bases have produced additional evidence of widespread patient harm caused by medical treatment (Classen et al. 1997; Steel et al. 1981).

The Harvard analyses, comparing medically adverse events with malpractice claims filed within the relevant limitations period (as well as the resolution of those claims), concluded that the tort system was an inefficient means of compensating injured patients (Brennan et al. 1996). These and the many other smaller studies reinforced the insight that far more iatrogenic injury occurs in hospitals than the public perceived (Romano et al. 2003). In the words of three respected researchers of adverse medical events writing about the Colorado and Utah findings, "the burden of iatrogenic injury is large, enduring, and an innate feature of hospital care in the United States" (Studdert et al. 2000a, 1643, 1662; Zahn and Miller 2003).

A large-scale analysis of adverse medical events in the United States was released in mid-2004 (HealthGrades Quality Study 2004). That investigation applied the Agency for Healthcare Quality and Research's Patient Safety Indicators (AHRQ 2004) to approximately 37 million Medicare discharges between 2000 and 2002, and then used other peer-validated research techniques (Zahn and Miller 2003) to assess the morbidity, mortality, and costs of the adverse events uncovered. HealthGrades, Inc., "a health care ratings and services company," conducted the study, which excluded obstetric patients. Its extrapolated findings were that "an extra $19 billion was spent, and over 575,000 preventable deaths occurred as a result of the 2.5 million patient safety incidents that occurred in U.S. hospitals" in those three years. The study was well publicized, again capturing public attention (*Wall Street Journal* 2004).

As patient care has increasingly migrated to outpatient settings over the past two decades, it has carried the burden of medical accident with it. In the case of ambulatory surgery, for example, an investigation of adverse incident reports to the Florida Board of Medicine between 2000 and 2002 documented a startling tenfold increased risk of iatrogenic injury—including death—for procedures performed in doctors' offices instead of in ambulatory surgical centers (Vila et al. 2003; Organ 2004).

On the other side of the Atlantic, a four-part television documentary in 2000 titled *Why Doctors Make Mistakes* (BBC 2000) exposed a similarly high incidence of medical errors in Britain (Martyn 2000). According to this documentary, 40,000 of the estimated 320,000 adverse medical events occurring there each year kill patients. This equals 10 times the number of people who die yearly in automobile accidents on British roads. The *British Medical Journal* (*BMJ*) also published a special issue that year (*BMJ* 2000) devoted entirely to medical errors and patient safety, "calling for a rethink of health care systems and training to cut the number of mistakes made by doctors to the low levels observed among pilots or nuclear plant workers." The editor of the *BMJ* attributed many of these problems to Britain's faulty "culture in medicine which doesn't quite acknowledge that all these errors happen" (BBC News 2000).

In 2001, a retrospective pilot study conducted by the clinical risk unit of University College, London, examined 1,000 randomly drawn case records from two hospitals in the London area. Their analysis showed that "10.8% of patients had experienced an adverse event; half of these events were preventable; and a third of adverse events led to either serious complications or death" (Vincent et al. 2001, 517). While this investigation was small and limited to two hospitals, it indicated that adverse medical events appear to be as pervasive in England as they are in the United States—perhaps even more so.

These medical mistakes are costly in terms of both the unnecessary suffering and deaths they cause and the resources they drain. They cost Great Britain "approximately £2 billion a year in hospital stay alone, over £400 million in clinical negligence settlements, and £1 billion in hospital-acquired infections a year" (Emslie et al. 2002, 5). Despite increased patient safety awareness in recent years, 1 in 10 hospitalized British patients will still contract a staph infection, 40% of which are resistant to antibiotics. Moreover, within Europe, only Greece has a higher incidence of hospital-acquired methicillin-resistant *Staphylococcus aureus* than Britain (Alvarez 2004).

European doctors fail to report medical error adequately, whether for fear of economic consequences, licensure sanctions, or public humiliation, a failing shared by their American counterparts. The voluntary reporting schemes for medical accident almost all countries use, compounded by a lack of sufficient computerization to pinpoint and analyze the causes of iatrogenic injury, are partly to blame. Britain's original 1955 guidelines for reporting medical errors merely required that adverse events—later expanded to include "near-miss" incidents (Shaw and Coles 2001)—be reported to a hospital "as soon as possible" (Ministry of Health 1955); that injured parties and witnesses be named; that "the full facts" (Ministry of Health 1955), be provided; and that appropriate action be taken to remedy the situation (Shaw and Coles 2001). But apparently little follow-up took place, and the underreporting persists.

A 1999 survey conducted by Britain's National Health Service (NHS) demonstrated significant inconsistencies in the frequency and procedures used in incident reporting at local levels (Dineen and Walsh 1999). Similar inconsistencies and communications failures were brought to light during the 1994 Allitt Inquiry into a hospital's failure to uncover a serial-killer nurse (Dyer 1994; NHS 1994). They also surfaced in the *Kent and Canterbury Screening Report* of 1997, revealing that cervical screening services failed to detect cancers in hundreds of women (Wells 1997).

Policy Response in the United States and EU

All of these factors and many other investigations have formed the statistical backdrop against which the patient safety movement began to achieve both prominence and momentum in both the United States and Europe as the millennium arrived. As evidence about suboptimal care causing medical accidents was accumulating, medical researchers were simultaneously detecting substantial variations in medical practice that could not be accounted for by demographics or other "rational" scientific explanation. For example, in the United States, Dartmouth's Dr. John Wennberg found a 50% variation in the rates of hysterectomy in one geographic market, a 45% variation in the rates of prostatectomy in another one, and a 62% variation in the rates of tonsillectomy in yet another (Wennberg 1984; Wennberg et al. 1982). Lynn Payer's 1996 book, *Medicine and Culture*, explored dramatic differences in treatment modalities among countries as well. Other researchers soon found other evidence of excess and inappropriate and invalid medical treatment, indicating that the overall quality of both U.S. and European medical care left much to be desired (Chassin et al. 1986; Kemper 1988; Schroeder et al. 1973).

The stage was thus set for government and health insurers to begin "managing" care, using evidence-based practice guidelines (Field and Lohr 1990; Rosoff 1995). These guidelines are standardized specifications for managing clinical problems, ideally developed by the medical profession. They are designed to improve the quality (and presumably the safety) of the medical care that government, health insurers, and employers underwrite. Guidelines are also intended to reduce the cost of care, so that government can offer broader benefits for its covered citizens, insurers can stem the rate of increase in subscriber premiums, and employers will continue to subsidize health insurance for their employees.[11]

Britain's National Institute for Clinical Excellence (NICE) was established in the past decade to produce evidence-based guidance for Britain's NHS in three areas: clinical guidelines, technology assessment, and diagnostic or therapeutic interventions. Although NICE was set up to reduce unwarranted variations and improve the quality of British health care, in part by assessing the cost-effectiveness of medical options (Harris 2008), critics contend that it has failed to fulfill its original mandate to identify the most effective, and presumably safe, treatments for medical problems (Maynard et al. 2004; Rao 2004). Some argue that NICE clinical guidelines not only should take cost-effectiveness for individual patients into consideration, but also should take the most efficient and equitable use of limited health care resources for all patients into account, since NICE guidelines function as de facto requirements for NHS purchasing decisions (Wailoo, et al. 2004; Devlin et al. 2003).

Differing national ideologies have dictated the way different European countries attempt to prevent and remedy medical errors. England and Scotland, for example, sanction deterring negligence by suing for malpractice, notwithstanding a generally less litigation-prone patient population than can be found in the United States. A lawsuit after the fact of medical accident falls short of achieving the theoretical tort objectives of deterrence and compensation in Britain, however, because "less than 1% of people suffering preventable harm receive compensation through the tort system, and there is little relationship between successful litigation and the degree to which negligent practice has contributed to harm" (Runciman et al. 2003, 974).

Tort law's perceived shortcomings persuaded policymakers in several other European nations to enact no-fault compensation schemes for medical accident many years ago. No-fault regimes, whereby a party suffering iatrogenic injury theoretically need only establish a causal relation between medical treatment and subsequent injury in order to recover, have been available for the past 30 years in Sweden, for almost 20 years in Norway, and for lesser periods of time in both Denmark and Finland as well (Gaine 2003). In the words of one commentator, the "socialist legal ideology" of Scandinavia opts for insurance rather than litigation to provide compensation when

---

[11] The U.S. consumer backlash against managed care in the late 1990s dampened private insurers' enthusiasm for managing care, however, so in the United States, private payers are for the moment less likely to continue being a strong driving force for quality improvement and therefore patient safety (see Robinson 2001; Swartz 1999).

dealing with medical error (Gaine 2003, 997–998). Several other countries, including England and Scotland, have considered enacting no-fault as well.

These no-fault systems have hardly proved a panacea for injured patients, however, since nearly half of all Scandinavians who seek no-fault redress for medical accident fail to meet the eligibility criteria (Gaine 2003). While Scandinavian doctors do not have to face being hauled into court when they are implicated in iatrogenic injury cases, provider behavior still matters within the system. Although physicians do not incur monetary penalties for their medical negligence, they report experiencing painful losses of personal and professional integrity when named as parties to medical accident claims (Raef 2002). By way of contrast, "[i]n France, medical negligence claims against the state are handled under an administrative law scheme, separate from the civil justice system, and patient compensation for hospital mistakes is automatic" (Gaine 2003, 997–998).

While post hoc inquiries into systems failures have increased in frequency and scope since the UK's first "modern inquiry" was commissioned in 1967, their conclusions about medical accident causality have remained remarkably consistent. A *BMJ* study identified 2 inquiries in the 1970s, 5 in the 1980s, and 52 from 1990 through 2002 (Walsh and Higgins 2002). By equating errors with blame, health systems sometimes reprimanded individuals for statistically unavoidable mistakes, yet they failed to uncover and prevent often rampant, pervasive, and persistent failures within the systems themselves.

Findings of the public inquiry into pediatric cardiac surgery at the Bristol Royal Infirmary (Kennedy 2001), for example, bore a striking resemblance to those reported by the inquiry into "allegations of abuse and ill treatment of vulnerable long stay patients" in Ely Hospital, Cardiff, more than 30 years before. Both investigations described problems of "poor clinical leadership, an isolated and inward looking culture, inadequate management structures and systems, and inadequate recourses" (DHSS 1969). A 2002 article in the *BMJ* concluded that the "consistency with which inquiries highlight similar causes suggests that their recommendations are either misdirected or not properly implemented" (Walsh and Higgins 2002, 894). These reports not only have been influential in shaping more recent British policy, but also have led to calls for improvement in patient safety throughout much of Europe as well.

In 1998, after almost a decade of little-heeded hand-wringing and escalating pleas for reform from expert analysts of medical error, the U.S. patient safety movement finally took off with the IOM's landmark publication *To Err Is Human: Building a Safer Health System* (Kohn et al. 1999). The Executive Summary's flat statement that the 98,000 yearly "deaths due to medical errors exceed the number attributable to the eighth leading cause of death" was a riveting showstopper, which the media immediately picked up and publicized. (In fact, the HealthGrades study six years later estimated that the annual number of iatrogenic deaths was almost double that number; see above.) The book's next statement that "[m]ore people die in a given year as a result of medical errors than from motor vehicle accidents (43,458), breast cancer (42,297), or AIDS (16,516)" (Kohn et al. 1999, 1) put the problem sharply in context for a lay audience. Almost immediately, a sizable segment of the public grasped the magnitude of the medical error problem, and public attention became focused for the first time on serious efforts to avert it (Leape 2001). The IOM report was more than just a compendium of adverse medical events and their consequences—it went on to offer "something new" in the way of attacking the prevalence of iatrogenic injury: systems reform designed to forestall it completely.

To Err Is Human changed the dynamics of reform rhetoric by downplaying the traditional fault-finding approaches to curing medical error that had achieved only limited success and by showing that defective and inefficient health care delivery systems—as distinguished from mere personal error—could be a large contributing factor to medical injury. The report sought to refocus reform efforts away from concentrating on fault-finding, blaming, and punishment. Instead, it advocated devising new systems and incentives for *preventing* errors before they have a chance to materialize (see Latham 2001 for a provocative philosophical discussion of the IOM report's recommendations). If the systems approach could increase accountability and avert errors, there would be less need for the relatively ineffective blaming mechanisms of punishment after the fact of medical injury.

In 2001, the IOM followed up public acceptance of that first comprehensive foray into patient safety with a second book, *Crossing the Quality Chasm: A New Health System for the Twenty-First Century*. This second publication sought to capitalize on the spotlight *To Err Is Human* had focused on medical error by making 13 specific recommendations for systems improvement (IOM 2001) and articulating "Ten Simple Rules for the Twenty-First Century Health System" (IOM 2001). These rules and recommendations are designed to shift provider and payer behavior toward performance predicted to improve patient and population health outcomes.

For example, the IOM stated that "[d]ecisionmaking is based on training and experience" under the current approach, but under the proposed treatment rules, decisions would be evidence-based. Few would contest the basic wisdom of utilizing what evidence-based medicine has to offer, but a rule shift from "professionals control care" to the IOM's proposed ideal that "the patient is the source of control" requires the kind of 24-hours-a-day, seven-days-a-week continuous patient access to care providers that many commentators believe would be impossible to provide. Notwithstanding varying degrees of agreement with its proposed rules and recommendations, the IOM Committee professed that implementing them could help "close the quality gap and save lives" (IOM 2001). Most of the IOM's recommendations remain aspirational at this stage, and few have yet found expression in formal practice or governmental regulation. The dialogue has, however, shifted from skepticism about the extent of the medical accident problem—e.g., Millenson (2003) blaming the medical profession for "failing to take corrective actions ... and failing to discuss openly the consequences of that inertia"—to a cooperative search for solutions to acknowledged shortcomings in patient safety. In other words, precautionary measures have gained credibility as feasible strategies.

Whether the precautionary principle will gain momentum and the patient safety movement will accomplish a significant reduction in iatrogenic injury across the board still remains to be seen (Leape and Berwick 2005). As safety expert Dr. Donald Berwick

observes, "all improvement is change, and human systems resist change...
improvement requires a source of tension, discomfort with the status quo, sufficient
to overcome this inertia" (Berwick 2002, 1523). A few early bright spots—like the
near-universal adoption of the Harvard Anesthesia Standards, which have appreciably
reduced the incidence of anesthesia morbidity and mortality worldwide—show what
can be achieved to improve the safety of narrowly targeted high-risk procedures on a
systems-wide basis (Eichhorn et al. 1986).

That example bears repeating for the lessons it teaches. When the Harvard teaching
hospitals began self-insuring for medical malpractice at the end of the 1970s,
they analyzed where their losses were greatest and what could be done to reduce them.
Once they pinpointed that approximately 35% of their malpractice payouts were going
to the 5% of their claims related to anesthesia accidents, the motivation to improve
that ratio was strong. The stimulus to improve safety arose from a genuine desire
to protect surgical patients from the devastating consequences of anesthesia mishaps,
but an equally strong spur was economic self-interest. In essence, the Harvard teaching
hospitals now had to pay for their own mistakes directly because they were
underwriting their own liability insurance.

Harvard Medical School's Anesthesia Department accordingly analyzed every
anesthesia accident occurring in recent years, and then devised eight "minimal
standards" for patient monitoring during anesthesia designed to improve safety in all
Harvard surgical suites. The first two standards were hardly revolutionary. They merely
required that (1) an anesthesia specialist remain in the operating room with an
anesthetized patient at all times during surgery, and (2) there be continuous monitoring
of patients' respiratory and cardiac functions as long as they remain anesthetized. Those
unfamiliar with surgical suite procedures were startled to realize that those two simple
safety rules had not been observed routinely before. The Harvard hospitals then
mandated implementation of these eight standards in all of their operating rooms.
Almost immediately, the anesthesia accident rate dropped so significantly that the
system's costs for insuring anesthesiologists for malpractice plummeted. Little more
than two months after Harvard's implementation experience was published in the
Journal of the American Medical Association, the American College of Anesthesiology
adopted the standards as recommended procedures for all operating rooms (ACS 2004).

The Joint Commission on the Accreditation of Healthcare Organizations (JCAHO)
now all but forces hospitals to implement similar anesthesia standards as a condition
for accreditation. JCAHO accreditation is in turn all but required for a facility to
be certified for reimbursement under the federal Medicare program (see 42 U.S.C.
§§ 1395x(e), 1395 bb), and most states have built JCAHO standards into their
requirements for facility licensure as well (e.g., Texas Health and Safety Code
§ 222.024). The Harvard anesthesia standards are thus de facto, if not *de jure*,
governmental regulatory requirements. The evidence supporting the dramatic
difference their implementation makes is so strong that they have also been adopted
as ideal patient safety precautions for operating rooms worldwide.

Recent attention to patient safety in the EU can be largely attributed to the release of
To Err Is Human in the United States, which prompted the international news media to

focus on the extent of medical accident all over the globe. Soon afterward, a group of experts on adverse events from Britain's NHS produced the widely celebrated report *Organisation with a Memory* (DH 2000), calling for a mandatory patient safety reporting system. Health Minister Lord Hunt introduced the National Patient Safety Agency shortly thereafter, advocating a fundamental change in organizational culture within the NHS "from one of individual blame to one of organizational accountability" (Emslie et al. 2002, 5). Articulating the parallel between the airlines and the health industry, Health Minister Lord Norman Warner later asserted that "most problems affecting patient safety occur as a result of weaknesses in systems and processes, rather than the acts of individuals" (Emslie et al. 2002, 5). In aviation maintenance, which also relies on individuals to perform high-risk activities, "some 90% of quality lapses were judged as blameless" (Reason 2000, 768–770).

In February 2004, the British National Patient Safety Agency initiated the first countrywide patient safety reporting program (NPSA 2004), the National Reporting and Learning System (NRLS). Frankly modeled after the aviation industry practices advocated by the IOM, the program is founded on the principle that human error is inevitable and systems can be designed to prevent it (Reason 2000). The NRLS coordinates the activities of local risk management systems to identify and analyze national trends. More important, it functions anonymously and is divorced from disciplinary procedures in order to encourage reporting (Reason 2000). Again, the model is aviation's nonpunitive reporting systems; as these have proliferated, the number of serious airplane accidents has markedly declined.

This shift toward preventing error by reforming systems has thus resonated throughout Europe as policymakers have become increasingly aware of medical error's prevalence, echoing the similar movement in the United States. That politicians are at last publicly focusing on this issue marks a dramatic change in approach, because professional self-regulation and after-the-fact legal remedies rather than precautionary policies were previously thought sufficient to protect patients (Leape and Berwick 2005). The patient safety movement is still in its infancy, however, and cannot yet be considered an example of precautionary activity in the true regulatory sense.

Conclusions

The precautionary principle has not been a widely adopted health sector concept on either side of the Atlantic. Until fairly recently, most medical accidents were not thought to be foreseeable and therefore were not considered responsive to precautionary measures. Empirical research over the past several decades has revealed the pervasive, predictable, and often systemic nature of iatrogenic patient injury, however, and attempts to improve patient safety are now being undertaken in both the United States and Europe. Since most patient safety initiatives are still voluntary, they are not currently being addressed in precautionary principle terminology.

Neither the United States nor the EU can accurately be considered more rigorous in its current approach to safety improvement, because the movement is relatively new. Both are keenly interested in observing each other's improvement efforts, not least because medical accidents have substantial financial costs. One can predict that U.S. and EU regulatory approaches will be more likely to converge than to diverge in the future, whether or not they are officially articulated in terms of the precautionary principle.

With respect to drug regulation, the situation is somewhat different. The U.S. FDA has traditionally taken a more cautious stance when licensing pharmaceuticals than have its European counterparts, and thus precautionary principle terminology carries more resonance with respect to drug and medical device licensing in America. In recent years, however, under pressures from medical activists for faster access to experimental drugs and from the pharmaceutical industry for accelerated approval policies as the drug industry globalizes, the FDA has relaxed its comparatively rigorous regulatory barriers. At the same time, the EU has increasingly centralized its drug approval processes, tightening the standards in use by some of the less safety-focused Member States, but it has not appreciably raised the level of rigor already in effect in others.

Current highly publicized controversies concerning widely used pain medications, antidepressants, and medical devices have recently precipitated a reassessment of drug approval and oversight policies on both sides of the Atlantic. As additional data accumulates, U.S. and EU drug approval policies—as well their patient safety initiatives—are more likely to converge toward increased rigor than to grow any further apart.

References

Abraham, J. 2002. Making Regulation Responsive to Commercial Interests: Streamlining Drug Industry Watchdogs. *British Medical Journal* 325: 1163.

Abraham, J., and G. Lewis. 1999. Harmonising and Competing for Medicines Regulation: How Healthy Are the European Union's Systems of Drug Approval? *Social Science and Medicine* 48: 1655.

ACS (American College of Surgeons). 2004. Patient Safety Principles for Office-Based Surgery Utilizing Moderate Sedation/Analgesia, Deep Sedation Analgesia, or General Anesthesia. *Archives of Surgery* 139: 240.

ADA (American Diabetes Association). 2003. Economic Costs of Diabetes in the U.S. in 2002. *Diabetes Care* 26: 917–932.

AHRQ (Agency for Healthcare Research and Quality). 2001. Reducing and Preventing Adverse Drug Events to Decrease Hospital Costs. www.ahcpr.gov/qual/aderia/aderia.htm (accessed June 5, 2006).

———. 2004. Patient Safety Quality Indicators, Version 2.1, Revision 1. March. Rockville, MD.

Aikin, Kathryn. 2003. Direct-to-Consumer Advertising of Prescription Drugs: Physician Survey Preliminary Results. Presentation to Society of Women's Health Research. October 25, 2005.

Alvarez, Lizette. 2004. British Hospitals Struggle to Limit "Superbug" Infections. *New York Times*, August 14.

Andersson, F. 1992. The Drug Lag Issue: The Debate Seen from an International Perspective. *International Journal of Health Services* 22 (1): 53.

Annas, George J. 2004. *The Rights of Patients*. New York: New York University Press.

Baciu, Alina, Kathleen Stratton, and Sheila P. Burke, eds. 2007. *The Future of Drug Safety: Promoting and Protecting the Health of the Public*. Washington, DC: Committee on the Assessment of the U.S. Drug Safety Program, National Academies Press.

BBC (British Broadcasting Service). 2000. *Why Doctors Make Mistakes.* Television series. October 2–17.

BBC News. 2000. *Medical Errors Kill Thousands.* http://news.bbc.co.uk/l/hi/uk/682000.stm (site now discontinued).

Berwick, Donald M. 2002. Public Performance Reports and the Will for Change. *Journal of the American Medical Association* 299: 1523.

BMJ (*British Medical Journal* special issue). 2000. *British Medical Journal* 320 (7237), March 18.

Bok, Derek. 1983. A Flawed System. *Harvard Magazine* (May–June): 38.

Bosk, Charles L. 2003. *Forgive and Remember: Managing Medical Failure.* 2nd ed. Chicago: University of Chicago Press.

Bovbjerg, Randall R. 1986. Medical Malpractice on Trial: Quality of Care Is the Important Standard. *Law and Contemporary Problems* 49: 321.

Brennan, Troyen A., Colin M. Sox, and Helen R. Burstin. 1996. Relation between Negligent Adverse Events and the Outcomes of Medical Malpractice Litigation. *New England Journal of Medicine* 335: 1963.

Brent, D. A. 2004. Treating Depression in Children: Antidepressants and Pediatric Depression—The Risk of Doing Nothing. *New England Journal of Medicine* 351: 1598–1601.

Carpenter, Daniel, Michael Chernew, Dean G. Smith, and A. Mark Fendrick. 2003. Approval Times for New Drugs: Does the Funding for FDA Staff Matter? *Health Affairs*, December 17. 10.1377/hlthaff.w3.618.

Cauchon, D. 2000. FDA Advisers Tied to Industry. *USA Today*, September 25, A1.

Chase-Lubitz, Jeffrey F. 1987. The Corporate Practice of Medicine Doctrine: An Anachronism in the Modern Health Care Industry. *Vanderbilt Law Review* 40: 445.

Chassin, Mark L., R. H. Brook, R. E. Park, J. Keesey, A. Fink, J. Kosecoff, K. Kahn, N. Merrick, and D. H. Solomon. 1986. Variations in the Use of Medical and Surgical Services by the Medicare Population. *New England Journal of Medicine* 314: 285–290.

Classen, David C., Stanley L. Pestotnik, R. Scott Evans, James F. Lloyd, and John P. Burke. 1997. Adverse Drug Events in Hospitalized Patients: Excess Length of Stay, Extra Costs and Attributable Mortality. *Journal of the American Medical Association* 277 (4): 301–306.

Danzon, Patricia. 1985. *Medical Malpractice: Theory, Practice, and Public Policy.* Cambridge, MA: Harvard University Press.

Davis, Tom. 2005. Risk and Responsibility: The Roles of FDA and Pharmaceutical Companies in Ensuring the Safety of Approved Drugs like Vioxx. http://reform.house.gov/GovReform/Hearings/EventSingle.aspx?EventID=26298 (accessed July 10, 2005).

Devlin, N., David Parkin, and Marthe Gold. 2003. WHO evaluates NICE. *British Medical Journal* 327: 1061.

DH (UK Department of Health). 2000. *An Organisation with a Memory: Report of an Expert Group on Learning from Adverse Events in the NHS.* London: Department of Health.

DHSS (UK Department of Health and Social Security). 1969. *The Report of the Committee of Inquiry into Allegations of Ill-Treatment of Patients and Other Irregularities at the Ely Hospital, Cardiff.* London: HMSO.

Dineen, M., and K. Walsh. 1999. Incident Reporting in the NHS. *Health Care Risk Report* 5 (March): 20–22.

Dyer, C. 1994. Inquiry into Serial Killer Criticises Hospital's Response. *British Medical Journal* 308: 491.

EG-SSRI (Expert Group on Safety of Selective Serotonin Reuptake Inhibitor Antidepressants). 2004. Report of the Committee on Safety of Medicines Expert Working Group on Safety of Selective Serotonin Reuptake Inhibitor Antidepressants. www.mhra.gov.uk/news/2004/SSRIfinal.pdf (accessed July 10, 2005).

Eichhorn, J. H., J. B. Cooper, D. J. Cullen, W. R. Maier, J. H. Philip, and R. G. Seeman. 1986. Standards for Patient Monitoring during Anesthesia at Harvard Medical School. *Journal of the American Medical Association* 256: 1017–1020.

Emslie, Stuart, Kirstine Knox, and Martin Pickstone, eds. 2002. *Improving Patient Safety: Insights from American, Australian, and British Healthcare.* London: ECRI and Department of Health.

Ernst, Frank R., and Amy J. Grizzle. 2001. Drug-Related Morbidity and Mortality: Updating the Cost-of-Illness Model. *Journal of the American Pharmaceutical Association* 41: 192–199.

European Parliament. 1992. European Parliament and the Council of March 31, 1992. Directive on Advertising of Medicinal Products for Human Use. 92/28/EEC. http://eur-lex.europa.eu/LexUriServ/LexUriServ.do?uri=CELEX:31992L0028:EN:HTML (accessed June 30, 2010).

———. 2004. European Parliament and the Council of March 31, 2004. Regulation (EC) No. 176/2004.

FDA (U.S. Food and Drug Administration). 1998. *Report to the Nation: Improving Public Health through Human Drugs.* Center for Drug Evaluation and Research (CDER).

———. 1999a. FDA Guidance for Industry: Revised Precautionary Measures to Reduce the Possible Risk of Transmission of New Variant Creutzfeld-Jakob Disease (vCJD) by Blood and Blood Products. 64 *Federal Register* 44739. August 17.

———. 1999b. *Managing the Risks from Medical Products Use: Creating a Risk Management Framework.* Silver Spring, MD: FDA.

———. 2003. Prescription Drug User Fee Act (PDUFA). www.fda.gov/oc/pdufa/report2002/2003-onpa.html (accessed December 30, 2004).

———. 2004a. FDA Acts to Strengthen the Safety Program for Marketed Drugs. www.fda.gov/bbs/topics/news/2004/NEW01131.html (accessed July 10, 2005).

———. 2004b. FDA Public Health Advisory: Suicidality in Children and Adolescents Being Treated with Antidepressant Medications. www.fda.gov/cder/drug/antidepressants/SSRIPHA200410.html (accessed July 10, 2005).

———. 2004c. FDA Press Release (November 18). www.fda.gov.cdr/fedreg/fr19921211.txt (site now discontinued).

———. 2004d. FDA Adverse Event Data. www.fda.gov/cder/aers/extract.htm (accessed May 9, 2010).

———. 2007a. Food and Drug Administration Amendments Act of 2007. Pub. L, No. 110-85, 121 Stat. 823.

———. 2007b. *The Future of Drug Safety: Promoting and Protecting the Health of the Public: FDA's Response to the Institute of Medicine's 2006 Report.* Washington, DC: U.S. Department of Health and Human Services.

Field, Marilyn J., and Kathleen N. Lohr, eds. 1990. *Institute of Medicine, Clinical Practice Guidelines: Directions for a New Program.* Washington, DC: National Academy Press.

Findlay, Steven D. 2001. Direct-to-Consumer Promotion of Prescription Drugs: Economic Implications for Patients, Payers, and Providers. *Pharmacoeconomics* 19: 109–119.

Freudenheim, M. 2000. Big Companies Lead Efforts to Reduce Medical Errors. *New York Times,* November: 16.

Gaine, William J. 2003. No-Fault Systems of Compensation. *British Medical Journal* 326 (May): 997–998.

GAO (U.S. General Accounting Office; now Government Accountability Office). 1980. *FDA Drug Approval: A Lengthy Process That Delays the Availability of Important New Drugs.* Washington, DC: GAO.

———. 1986. *Medical Malpractice: No Agreement on the Problems or Solutions.* Washington, DC: GAO.

———. 2004. *Medicare: CMS Needs Additional Authority to Adequately Oversee Patient Safety in Hospitals.* GAO-04-850. Washington, DC: GAO.

Garattini, Silvio, and Vittorio Bertele. 2004. The Role of the EMEA in Regulating Pharmaceutical Products. In *Regulating Pharmaceuticals in Europe: Striving for Efficiency, Equity, and Quality,* edited by Elias Mossialos, Monique Mrazek, and Tom Walley. Berkshire: Open University Press, 80–96.

Goodman, Jesse L. 2004. The Safety and Availability of Blood and Tissues: Progress and Challenges. *New England Journal of Medicine* 351: 819.

Hallinan, Joseph T. 2004. Attempt to Track Malpractice Cases Is Often Thwarted. *Wall Street Journal,* Aug. 27, 1.

Harris, Gardner. 2008. British Balance Benefit vs. Cost of Latest Drugs. *New York Times*, Dec. 2, A1. www.nytimes.com/2008/12/03/health/03nice.html (accessed May 9, 2010).

Harris, Gardner, and Alex Berenson. 2005. 10 Voters on Panel Backing Pain Pills Had Industry Ties. *New York Times*, Feb. 25.

Harvard Medical Practice Study. 1990. *Patients, Doctors and Lawyers: Medical Injury, Malpractice Litigation, and Patient Compensation in New York: The Report of the Harvard Medical Practice Study to the State of New York*. Albany, NY: New York State Department of Health.

HealthGrades Quality Study. 2004. Patient Safety in American Hospitals. July. www.healthgrades. com/media/english/pdf/hg_patient_safety_study_final.pdf (accessed June 30, 2010).

HEW (U.S. Department of Health, Education, and Welfare). 1973. *Medical Malpractice: Report of the Secretary's Commission on Medical Malpractice*. Washington, DC: GPO.

HHS (U.S. Department of Health and Human Services). 1999. *The External Review of Hospital Quality: A Call for Greater Accountability*. OEI-01-97-00050. Washington, DC: HHS Office of the Inspector General (OIG).

———. 2001. *Managed Care Organization Nonreporting to the National Practitioner Data Bank*. OEI-01-99-00690. Washington, DC: HHS OIG.

Hippocrates. 400 B.C. *Of the Epidemics*. Book I, § XI.

House of Commons Health Committee. 2005. *The Influence of the Pharmaceutical Industry*. Fourth Report of Session 2004–05. London: Stationery Office Limited.

Hutt, Peter Barton. 1996. The Transformation of U.S. Food and Drug Law. *Journal of the Association of Food and Drug Officials* 60 (September): 1.

IOM (Institute of Medicine). 2001. *Crossing the Quality Chasm: A New Health System for the Twenty-First Century*. Washington, DC: National Academy Press.

JCAHO (Joint Commission on the Accreditation of Heathcare Organizations). 2005. Revised Guidance to Help Prevent Kernicterus, Revised Sentinel Event 31. www.jcaho.org/about+us/ news+letters/sentinel+event+alert/sea_31.htm (site now discontinued).

Jost, Timothy Stoltzfus. ed. 1997. *Regulation of the Health Care Professions*. Chicago: Health Administration Press.

Kaitin, K. I. 1997. The Prescription Drug User Fee Act of 1992b and the New Drug Development Process. *American Journal of Therapeutics* 4: 167.

Kemper, Kathi J. 1988. Medically Inappropriate Hospital Use in a Pediatric Population. *New England Journal of Medicine* 318: 1033.

Kennedy, Ian. 2001. *Learning from Bristol: The Report of the Public Inquiry into Children's Heart Surgery at the Bristol Royal Infirmary, 1984–1995*. London: HMSO.

Knox, R. 1995. Doctor's Orders Killed Cancer Patient: Dana-Farber Admits Overdose Causes Death of Globe Columnist. *Boston Globe*, March 23, 1.

Kohn, Linda T., Janet M. Corrigan, and Molla S. Donaldson, eds. 1999. *To Err Is Human: Building a Safer Health System*. Washington, DC: National Academy Press.

Kusserow, Richard P., Elisabeth A. Handley, and Mark R. Yessian. 1987. An Overview of State Medical Discipline. *Journal of the American Medical Association* 257 (6): 820–824.

Latham, Stephen R. 2001. System and Responsibility: Three Readings of the IOM Report on Medical Error. *American Journal of Law and Medicine* 27: 163.

Leape, Lucian L. 1994. Error in Medicine. *Journal of the American Medical Association* 272: 1851.

———. 2001. Foreword: Preventing Medical Accidents: Is "Systems Analysis" the Answer? *American Journal of Law and Medicine* 27: 145.

Leape, Lucian L., and Donald M. Berwick. 2005. Five Years after *To Err Is Human*: What Have We Learned? *Journal of the American Medical Association* 293: 2384.

Leatherman, Sheila, and Douglas McCarthy. 2002. *Quality of Health Care in the United States: A Chartbook*. New York: Commonwealth Fund.

Lesar, Timothy, Laurie Briceland, and Daniel S. Stein. 1997. Factors Related to Errors in Medication Prescribing. *Journal of the American Medical Association* 277 (4): 312–317.

Localio, A. R., A. G. Lawthers, T. A. Brennan, N. M. Laird, L. E. Hebert, L. M. Peterson, J. P. Newhouse, and P. C. Weiler, and H. H. Hiatt 1991. Relation between Malpractice Claims and

Adverse Events Relating to Negligence: Results of the Harvard Medical Practice Study III. *New England Journal of Medicine* 325: 245.

Markey, Edward D. 2005. *Conspiracy of Silence: How the FDA Allows Drug Companies to Abuse the Accelerated Approval Process*. Staff Summary, Rep. Edward D. Markey, Energy and Commerce Committee, U.S. House of Representatives. June.

Martyn, Christopher. 2000. Uncomfortable Viewing. *British Medical Journal* 321: 904.

Mattison, Nancy, and Barbara W. Richard. 1987. Postapproval Research Requested by the FDA at the Time of NCE Approval. *Drug Information Journal* 21: 309–323.

Maynard, Alan, Karen Bloor, and Nick Freemantle. 2004. Challenges for the National Institute for Clinical Effectiveness. *British Medical Journal* 329: 227.

McClellan, Mark. 2007. Drug Safety Reform at the FDA: Pendulum Swing or Systematic Improvement? *New England Journal of Medicine* 356: 17.

MedPAC (Medicare Payment Advisory Commission). 2004. *Quality of Care for Medicare Beneficiaries. Report to the Congress: Medicare Payment Policy*, March.

Meek, Colin. 2001. Direct-to-Consumer Advertising of Prescription Medicines: A Review of International Policy and Evidence. Royal Pharmaceutical Society of Great Britain. November. www.rpsgb.org.uk/pdfs/dtcarep.pdf (accessed June 30, 2010).

Millenson, Michael L. 2003. The Silence. *Health Affairs* 22 (2): 103.

Miller, Frances H. 1997. Medical Discipline in the Twenty-First Century: Are Purchasers the Answer? *Law and Contemporary Problems* 60: 31.

Mills, D., ed. 1977. *Report on the Medical Insurance Feasibility Study*, California Medical Association and California Hospital Association. San Francisco: Sutter Publications.

Ministry of Health. 1955. *NHS Reporting of Accidents in Hospitals*. HM(55)66. London: Ministry of Health.

Mohl, B. 1998. Doctor Penalized for Error in Dosage. *Boston Globe*, Nov. 10, B3.

Mohr, J. C. 2000. American Medical Malpractice in Historical Perspective. *Journal of the American Medical Association* 283: 1731.

Mossialos, Elias, Monique Mrazek, and Tom Walley. 2004. Regulating Pharmaceuticals in Europe: An Overview. In *Regulating Pharmaceuticals in Europe: Striving for Efficiency, Equity, and Quality*, edited by Elias Mossialos, Monique Mrazek, and Tom Walley. Berkshire: Open University Press, 1.

NHS (UK National Health Service). 1994. Report of the Independent Inquiry Relating to Deaths and Injuries on the Children's Ward at Grantham and Kesteven General Hospital during the Period February to April 1991. EL(94)16. Leeds: NHS Management Executive.

Noah, Barbara A. 2000. Adverse Drug Reactions: Harnessing Experiential Data to Promote Patient Welfare. *Catholic Law Review* 49: 449.

NPSA (UK National Patient Safety Agency). 2004. World's First National Patient Safety Reporting System Launched in England and Wales. *NPSA News*, Feb. 24. www.nelm.nhsuk/en/NeLM-Area/News/478796/479006/479013/ (accessed June 30, 2010).

Oberholzer-Gee, Felix, and S. Noorein Inmader. 2004. Merck's Recall of Rofecoxib: A Strategic Perspective. *New England Journal of Medicine* 351: 2147.

Olson, Mary K. 1995. Regulatory Agency Discretion among Competing Industries: Inside the FDA. *Journal of Law, Economics, and Organization* 11: 379.

———. 2002. Pharmaceutical Policy Change and the Safety of New Drugs. *Journal of Law and Economics* 45: 615–616.

———. 2004. Are Novel Drugs More Risky for Patients Than Less Novel Drugs? *Journal of Health Economics* 23: 1135.

Organ, Claude H. 2004. Letter. Comment on the Ambulatory Surgery Controversy and Reprinting the American College of Surgeons' Evolving "Patient Safety Principles for Office-Based Surgery Utilizing Moderate Sedation/Analgesia, Deep Sedation Analgesia, or General Anesthesia." *Archives of Surgery* 139: 240.

Otero, M. J., and A. Domínguez-Gil. 2000. Acontecimientos Adversos por Medicamentos: Una Patología Emergente [Adverse Drug Events: An Emerging Pathology]. *Farmacia Hospitalaria* [*Hospital Pharmacy*] 24 (4): 258–259.

Payer, Lynn. 1996. *Medicine and Culture: Varieties of Treatment in the United States, England, West Germany and France.* New York: Holt.

Pear, Robert. 2007. Senate Approves Tighter Policing of Drug Makers. *New York Times,* May 10.

PhRMA (Pharmaceutical Research and Manufacturers of America). 2004. Principles on Conduct of Clinical Trials and Communication of Clinical Trial Results. www.phrma.org/files/attachments/Clinical%20Trials.pdf (accessed June 30, 2010).

Pina, Kenneth R., and Wayne L. Pinds. 2002. *A Practical Guide to Food and Drug Law and Regulation.* Washington, DC: Food and Drug Law Institute.

Psaty, Bruce M., and Sheila P. Burke. 2006. Protecting the Health of the Public: Institute of Medicine Recommendations on Drug Safety. *New England Journal of Medicine* 355 (17): 1753–1755.

Psaty, Bruce M., and Alta Charo. 2007. FDA Responds to Institute of Medicine Drug Safety Recommendations—In Part. *Journal of the American Medical Association* 297 (17): 1917.

Raef, Susan. 2002. Denmark Launches Patient Safety Initiative. *National Patient Safety Foundation* 5 (1): 1–2.

Rao, Jammi N. 2004. NICE and Its Value Judgements: Favourable Appraisal Amounts to Compulsory Purchase. *British Medical Journal* 329: 740.

Ray, Wayne A., and C. Michael Stein. 2006. Reform of Drug Regulation: Beyond an Independent Drug-Safety Board. *New England Journal of Medicine* 354 (2): 194–201.

Reason, James. 2000. Human Error: Models and Management. *British Medical Journal* 320: 768–770.

Relman, Arnold S. 1985. Professional Regulation and State Medical Boards. *New England Journal of Medicine* 312: 784.

Robinson, James C. 2001. The End of Managed Care. *Journal of the American Medical Association* 285: 2622.

Romano, Patrick S., Jeffrey J. Geppert, Sheryl Davies, Marlene R. Miller, Anne Elixhauser, and Kathryn M. McDonald. 2003. A National Profile of Patient Safety in U.S. Hospitals. *Health Affairs* 22: 154–166.

Romano, R. 1999. Fatal Error Becomes Catalyst for Reform. *Boston Globe,* March 15.

Rosoff, Arnold J. 1995. The Role of Practice Guidelines in Health Care Reform. *Health Matrix* 5: 369.

Runciman, William, Alan F. Merry, and Fiona Tito. 2003. Error, Blame and the Law in Health Care: An Antipodean Perspective. *Annals of Internal Medicine* 138 (12): 974–979.

Sasich, Larry D., Peter Lurie, and Sidney M. Wolfe. 2000. *The Drug Industry's Performance in Finishing Postmarketing Research (Phase IV) Studies.* www.citizen.org/Page.aspx?pid=2362 (accessed on May 9, 2010).

Schroeder, Steven A., Kathryn Kenders, James K. Cooper, and Thomas E. Piemme. 1973. Use of Laboratory Tests and Pharmaceutical Variation among Physicians and Effect of Cost Audit on Subsequent Use. *Journal of the American Medical Association* 225: 969.

Shaw, Charles, and James Coles. 2001. The Reporting of Adverse Clinical Incidents: International Views and Experience. CASPE Research. www.healthcarewebs.net/medsafe/incidentreportdoc3.pdf (site now discontinued).

Shulman, Sheila, and Kenneth I. Kaitin. 1996. The Prescription Drug User Fee Act of 1992: A 5-Year Experiment for Industry and the FDA. *Pharmacoeconomics* 9: 121.

Sprecher, Sue. 1978. Psychosurgery Policy Soon to Be Set. *Real Paper,* Jan. 21.

Starr, Paul. 1982. *The Social Transformation of American Medicine.* New York: Basic Books.

Steel, Knight, P. M. Gertman, C. Crescenzi, and J. Anderson. 1981. Iatrogenic Illness on a General Medical Service at a University Hospital. *New England Journal of Medicine* 304: 638.

Stricker, Bruno, and Bruce M. Psaty. 2004. Detection, Verification and Quantification of Adverse Drug Reactions. *British Medical Journal* 329: 44–45.

Strom, Brian L. 2006. How the U.S. Drug Safety System Should Be Changed. *Journal of the American Medical Association* 295 (17): 2072.

Struve, Catherine. 2005. The FDA and the Tort System: Postmarketing Surveillance, Compensation, and the Role of Litigation. *Yale Journal of Health Policy, Law, and Ethics* 2: 587.

Studdert, David M., Troyen A. Brennan, and Eric J. Thomas. 2000a. Beyond Dead Reckoning: Measures of Medical Injury Burden, Malpractice Litigation and Alternative Compensation Models from Utah and Colorado. *Independent Law Review* 33: 1643–1686.

Studdert, D. M., E. J. Thomas, H. R. Burstin, B. I. Zbar, E. J. Orav, and T. A. Brennan. 2000b. Negligent Care and Malpractice Claiming Behavior in Utah and Colorado. *Medical Care* 38: 250.

Studdert, David M., Michelle M. Mello, and Troyen M. Brennan. 2004. Medical Malpractice. *New England Journal of Medicine* 350: 283.

Swartz, Katherine. 1999. The Death of Managed Care as We Know It. *Journal of Health Politics, Policy, and Law* 24: 1204.

TCSDD (Tufts Center for the Study of Drug Development). 2000. *European Approval of New Biotech Drugs Outpaces U.S. Approval.* Tufts CSDD Impact Report. Boston: TCSDD.

———. 2003. FDA's Fast Track Initiative Cut Total Drug Development Time by Three Years, According to Tufts Center for the Study of Drug Development. November 13. http://155.212.10.127/NewsEvents/RecentNews.asp?newsid=34 (accessed December 30, 2004; site now discontinued).

Thomas, E. J., D. M. Studdert, and H. R. Burstin. 2000. Incidence and Types of Adverse Events and Negligent Care in Utah and Colorado. *Medical Care* 38: 261.

Thomas, John. 2006. The Vioxx Story: Would It Have Ended Differently in the European Union? *American Journal of Law and Medicine* 21: 381.

Vastag, Brian. 2005. Congress Considers Tightening Regulations to Direct-to-Consumer Advertising. *Journal of the National Cancer Institute* 97 (24): 1807.

Vila, Hector, Roy Soto, Alan B. Cantor, and David Mackey. 2003. Comparative Outcomes Analysis of Procedures Performed in Physician Offices and Ambulatory Surgery Centers. *Archives of Surgery* 138: 991.

Vincent, C., Graham Neale, and Maria Woloshynowych. 2001. Adverse Events in British Hospitals: Preliminary Retrospective Record Review. *British Medical Journal* 332: 517.

Wailoo, A., Jennifer Roberts, John Brazier, and Chris McCabe. 2004. Efficiency, Equity and NICE Clinical Guidelines. *British Medical Journal* 328: 536.

Wall Street Journal. 2004. Medical Errors Cause 195,000 Patient Deaths Annually, Health Grades Study Finds. July 27.

Walsh, Kieran, and Higgins Joan. 2002. The Use and Impact of Inquiries in the NHS. *British Medical Journal* 325: 894–895.

Weiler, Paul C., Howard Hiatt, Joseph P. Newhouse, William G. Johnson, Troyen Brennan, and Lucian Leape. 1993. *A Measure of Malpractice.* Cambridge, MA: Harvard University Press.

Wells, W. 1997. *Kent and Canterbury Screening Report.* Leeds, UK: NHS Executive.

Wennberg, John E. 1984. Dealing with Medical Practice Variations: A Proposal for Action. *Health Affairs* 3: 6.

Wennberg, John E., Benjamin A. Barnes, and Michael Zubkoff. 1982. Professional Uncertainty and the Problem of Supplier-Induced Demand. *Social Science and Medicine* 16 (7): 811.

WHO (World Health Organization). 1972. *International Drug Monitoring: The Role of National Centers.* WHO Technical Report Series No. 498. Geneva: WHO.

———. 1973. *Handbook of Resolutions and Decisions of the World Health Assembly and Executive Board.* Vol. 11948–1972 WHA 16.36 Clinical and Pharmacological Evaluation of Drugs. Geneva: WHO.

———. 2002. *The Importance of Pharmacovigilance: Safety Monitoring of Medicinal Products.* Geneva: WHO.

Wiener, Jonathan B. 1998. Managing the Iatrogenic Risks of Risk Management. *Risk: Health, Safety, Environment* 9 (Winter): 39–82.

Wiener, Jonathan B., and Michael D. Rogers. 2002. Comparing Precaution in the U.S. and Europe. *Journal of Risk Research* 5 (4): 317–334.

Wiktorowicz, Mary E. 2003. Emergent Patterns in the Regulation of Pharmaceuticals: Institutions and Interests in the United States, Canada, Britain and France. *Journal of Health Policy, Politics, and Law* 28: 615.

Wyatt v. Stickney. 1971. 325 F. Supp. 781 (1971).

Zahn, C., and M. R. Miller. 2003. Excess Length of Stay, Charges, and Mortality Attributable to Medical Injuries during Hospitalization. *Journal of the American Medical Association* 290: 1868.

Zou, Shimian, Roger Y. Dodd, Susan L. Stramer, and D. Michael Strong. 2004. Probability of Viremia with HBV, HCV, HIV, and HTLV among Tissue Donors in the United States. *New England Journal of Medicine* 351: 751.

CHAPTER 12

Terrorism and Weapons of Mass Destruction

Jessica Stern and Jonathan B. Wiener

*T*errorism poses a serious risk to health, safety, and the environment. Using either conventional methods, such as bombs or aircraft, or weapons of mass destruction (WMD)—whether chemical, biological, or nuclear—terrorism can cause dozens to thousands to millions of human fatalities, spread toxic plumes of smoke, trigger widespread fear and restrictions on civil liberties, and lead to irreparable ecological devastation. As U.S. and European societies have become more prosperous and more focused on reducing risk (Beck 1992), and in response to dramatic events such as the attacks of September 11, 2001, concerns about the Cold War have been succeeded by fears of terrorism. Managing the risk of terrorism has become the paramount concern of many governments, especially those of the United States and the UK. The risk of terrorism was the reason for the creation of the Department of Homeland Security and the position of national intelligence director—the most sweeping reorganization of the U.S. government bureaucracy since the overhaul to address health and environmental risks that created the Environmental Protection Agency (EPA), Council on Environmental Quality (CEQ), and other agencies in the 1970s. The risk of terrorism was arguably the leading issue in the 2004 U.S. presidential election campaign. And the terrorist bombings of Madrid on March 11, 2004, played a significant role in the national election held days later.

In short, terrorism has become one of the great risk problems of the current era—a risk that may come, in time, to define the era. The sources of terrorism risks are highly uncertain, very difficult to assess and manage, and intent on evading preventive measures. Governments have many options for managing risks to national security, including reactive measures to recover from emergencies, strategies to deter and retaliate against attacks, measures to harden prospective targets, diplomatic and assistance programs to foster prosperity and improved relations, and anticipatory actions (including military force) to curtail terrorist capabilities before they are used. This chapter compares the degree of precaution exhibited by counterterrorism policies in the United States and Europe from 1970 to 2005. (A companion paper, Stern and Wiener 2008, examines the normative merits of precautionary policies against terrorism.) In general, the degree of precaution is measured in terms of timing (earliness) and stringency. The sooner such measures are adopted (anticipating earlier, but hence with greater uncertainty, the future manifestation of the risk), and the more stringently they attempt to control the risk, the more "precautionary" such measures are deemed to be (Wiener and Rogers 2002). This approach enables us to compare relative precaution in the basic terms of the precautionary principle, which typically holds that uncertainty is no excuse for inaction against serious or irreversible risks, and that rather than waiting for evidence of harm to be demonstrated before acting, the burden of proof should be shifted to require sponsors of a risky product or activity to demonstrate that it is safe or else be subject to risk reduction measures (see, e.g., Raffensberger and Tickner 1999; Sandin 1999; Wiener and Rogers 2002). For example, the Rio Declaration proclaimed:

> Where there are threats of serious or irreversible damage, lack of full scientific certainty shall not be used as a reason for postponing cost-effective measures to prevent environmental degradation. (Rio Declaration 1992, Principle 15)

And the European Environment Agency advised in January 2002:

> Forestalling disasters usually requires acting before there is strong proof of harm. (EEA 2002, 13)

The second section of this chapter compares the relative precaution of U.S. and European counterterrorism policies over the last three decades. It finds that Europe was generally more precautionary about terrorism in the 1970s, but the United States has become more precautionary about terrorism since 2001 (as has the UK).

The most striking development is that the U.S. and UK governments' new counterterrorism strategy since 9/11 adopts the logic and the language of the precautionary principle—almost verbatim. Other key European countries, which generally favor precaution as applied to health and environmental risks, have opposed this strategy as applied to terrorism and the war in Iraq.

This reversal over time—toward greater relative U.S. precaution against terrorism—is analogous to the "flip-flop" hypothesis of greater U.S. precaution in the 1970s followed by increasing relative European precaution by the 1990s (Vogel 2003; see Chapter 1 of this volume)—*but in the opposite direction*. And it reveals divergence within Europe and within the United States. The pattern indicates that neither the United States nor Europe can claim to be precautionary or antiprecautionary across the board; rather, the reality is of precautionary particularity, not broad principle—of selective use of precaution against selected risks at different times, on both sides of the Atlantic.

The next section, "Explanations for the Observed Pattern," seeks to explain why the United States and Europe have adopted the policies they have. It examines strategic needs, risk assessment errors, and psychological heuristics. The subsequent section,

"Consequences of Precaution against Terrorism and WMD," then evaluates the results of precautionary counterterrorism policies, including attention to the countervailing risk increases and the ancillary benefits that may be induced. It finds that some precaution against terrorism may be necessary, but that aggressive precaution through "preventive war" can spawn new risks of terrorism and often make the world less safe. This highlights a general problem with aggressive precaution in all domains: that precaution itself creates new risks, and hence that a strict application of the precautionary principle would swallow itself.

Finally, this chapter concludes with lessons from the historical evidence. The complex pattern and its consequences should help both Americans and Europeans see that precaution is not an all-or-nothing proposition, to be favored or rejected on principle, but rather that its merits and its actual adoption in practice depend crucially on the specific risk and context being addressed. A highly precautionary approach to terrorism, driven by narrow focus on the target risk, is likely to entail larger, more expensive interventions, with greater opportunity costs and countervailing risks. A better approach to managing risk involves an assessment of the full portfolio of risks—those reduced by the proposed intervention, as well as those increased.

Comparing U.S. and European Precaution against Terrorism

A wide variety of counterterrorism measures have been undertaken by the United States, the European Union, and individual Member States of the EU over the past three decades. We attempt to collect some of the main examples here, though we expect that experts in the field will call to our attention others we have omitted to mention. Table 12.1 summarizes the comparison of U.S. and European measures. Tables 12.2 and 12.3 give more detail on the policy history within the United States and Europe, respectively.

Comparing Policies in the Period 1970–2001

Overall, Europe appears to have been more precautionary against terrorism in the 1970s. The UK, Italy, and Spain enacted tough antiterror legislation in the mid-1970s, long before the United States did. In the name of fighting terrorism, European countries accepted more significant restrictions on civil liberties long before Americans did (or perhaps ever will). For example, the UK has long had a domestic spy agency, MI-5, in addition to its foreign spy agency (MI-6) and its domestic law enforcement agency (Scotland Yard); the United States has counterparts to the latter two agencies—the Central Intelligence Agency (CIA) and Federal Bureau of Investigation (FBI)—but no domestic spy agency. European countries have long had national identification card requirements, a precautionary policy that the United States has never adopted. European countries had far more border patrol officers and were more proactive in screening arriving passengers (Koslowski 2004). EU countries shared information on travelers and other individuals across national borders and agencies beginning in the

Table 12.1 *Summary Comparison of U.S. and European Counterterrorism Measures, 1970–2004*

Year	United States	Europe
1970	Sky Marshal Program	Switch from public to private security in airports
1971		
1972		
1973	FAA Emergency Rule	
1974		(UK) Prevention of Terrorism Act
1975		
1976		(EU) TREVI System
1977	International Emergency Rule	(IT) Intelligence Systems Reform Act; (SP) Government negotiation with terrorists
1978		(IT) Emergency legislation
1979	Export Administrative Act	(EU) Dublin Agreement; (SP) AT legislation suspends civil liberties
1980		(SP) Centralized AT apparatus created
1981		
1982		(FR) Target bombed in Lebanon
1983		(SP) Spain sponsors attacks on terrorists
1984	Act to Combat International Terrorism	
1985	International Trade and Security Act	(UK) Anglo-Irish Agreement
1986		
1987		
1988	Antiterrorism Assistance Program	
1989		
1990		
1991	Gulf War	Gulf War
1992		(EU) Maastricht Treaty: Europol
1993	U.S. bombs Iraq	
1994		
1995		
1996	Nunn-Lugar-Domenici Act; Antiterrorism and Effective Death Penalty Act	
1997		
1998	Presidential Directives 62 and 63; United States bombs Afghanistan, Sudan	(UK) Good Friday Agreement; (EU) Europol Convention
1999		(UK) Power sharing agreement
2000		
2001	Aviation and Transportation Security Act; USA PATRIOT Act; Executive Order 13224; war in Afghanistan	(EU) Council Common Position; (EU) Money Laundering Directive; war in Afghanistan
2002	Homeland Security Act; Enhanced Border Security and Visa Entry Reform Act; new National Security Strategy calls for preventive war	(EU) Schengen Information System
2003	National Defense Authorization Act; war in Iraq	UK, Spain, Italy, Poland, and others join United States in war in Iraq
2004	US-VISIT Program; Executive Order against Syria	(EU) Passenger Name Record Data Arrangement; (UK) Civil Contingencies Bill

Notes: EU = European Union; UK = United Kingdom; SP = Spain; FR = France; IT = Italy

Table 12.2 *Chronology of U.S. Counterterrorism Measures, 1970–2004*

Date	Name and description of measure	Type
1970	Sky Marshal Program begins (changed to the Federal Air Marshal Program in 1985)	AV
1973	FAA Emergency Rule makes inspection of passengers and carry-on baggage mandatory (1974 anti-hijacking bill sanctions universal screening)	AV
1977	International Emergency Economic Powers Act grants the president expanded authority	
1979	Export Administration Act limits exports to state sponsors of terrorism of controlled items and technology	$
1984	Act to Combat International Terrorism establishes the Rewards for Justice program, which rewards up to $5 million for information relating to the capture of terrorists (USA PATRIOT Act increases this to $25 million)	INT
1985	International Trade and Security Act authorizes trade embargo of Libya and other countries that support terrorists	$
1986	Money laundering made a separate criminal offense; U.S. bombs Libya	$, UF
1988	Antiterrorism Assistance Program gives aid to foreign countries working to fight terrorism within those countries	DEV
1991	Gulf War	UF
1993	U.S. bombs Iraq in response to assassination attempt on President George H. W. Bush	UF
1996	• Nunn-Lugar-Domenici Act passes to prepare U.S. for unconventional attacks • Antiterrorism and Effective Death Penalty Act makes it a crime to provide material support to foreign terrorist organizations • Sale of arms prohibited to any country not cooperating with U.S. counterterrorism efforts; requires withholding of foreign assistance to countries helping those on the list of state sponsors of terrorism	$, TH
1998	• Presidential Directives 62 and 63 establish a working group whose focus is exclusively preparedness for WMD attacks • Executive Order freezes the assets of Osama bin Laden and prohibits U.S. firms from doing business with him • CAPPS II program: information collected, and passengers screened for danger on the basis of this information	TH, $ AV
2001	• Aviation and Transportation Security Act makes federal government responsible for airport security, and changes rules regarding allowable items on airplanes • Transportation Security Administration created (2002 budget: $1.35 billion) • Requires Passenger Name Record data to be collected for all flights landing inside U.S. • USA PATRIOT Act • Executive Order 13224 designates 350 terrorist entities and freezes their assets • U.S. invades Afghanistan and implements regime change	AV, TH, INT, $, UF
2002	• Homeland Security Act creates a single department responsible for domestic defenses against terrorism; $31 billion appropriated to the department. • National Security Strategy and speeches by President Bush articulate the preventive war doctrine • Enhanced Border Security and Visa Entry Reform Act requires airlines to submit passenger lists before arrival • Container Security Initiative	TH, UF
2003	• National Defense Authorization Act authorizes $9.1 billion for a ballistic missile defense program • U.S. invades Iraq and deposes Saddam Hussein	TH, UF
2004	• US-VISIT Program and the biometrics initiative pass to increase border security • Executive Order imposes military and economic sanctions on Syria as a state sponsor of terrorism • Passenger Name Record Data Arrangement with the EU shares passenger data for all flights originating in or going to the U.S.	BC, $, AV

Notes: AV = aviation security; BC = border controls; UF = use of force to attack terrorist groups; TH = target hardening; INT = intelligence; $ = targeting funding of terrorists; DEV = development aid, trade, and assistance

Table 12.3 *Chronology of European Counterterrorism Measures, 1970–2004*

Date	Name and description of measure	Type
1970s	Europe changes from public to private system of baggage screening	AV
1974	(UK) Prevention of Terrorism Act excludes Irish designated as terrorists from Great Britain (extended in 1989)	BC
1976	(EU) TREVI System formed to facilitate counterterrorism cooperation among nations	INT
1977	(IT) Intelligence Systems Reform Act	INT
	(SP) The government negotiates with terrorists to release prisoners from prison if they renounce violence	
1978	(IT) Emergency legislation	
1979	(EU) Dublin Agreement eliminates the political offense exception from international extradition treaties (implementing the 1977 European Convention for the Suppression of Terrorism)	INT
	(SP) Antiterrorism legislation passes that allows civil rights to be suspended: preventive detention allowed	
1980	(SP) Centralized apparatus created to fight terrorism	INT, TH
1982	(FR) France bombs target in Lebanon in response to bombing of French embassy	UF
1983–1987	(SP) Spain sponsors attacks on members of a domestic terrorist group	UF
1985	(UK) Anglo-Irish Agreement signed	
1991	Gulf War	UF
1992	Maastricht Treaty establishes Europol	INT
	(EU) Eurodac implemented (an EU-wide fingerprint database intended to counter asylum shopping)	INT, BC
1998	(UK) Good Friday Agreement reached	
	(EU) Europol Convention ratified	
1999	(UK) Power-sharing government set up in Northern Ireland	
2001	(EU) Council Common Position designates certain individuals and groups as terrorists (EU) Money Laundering Directive, and an EU-wide asset freezing order	BC, $
2002	• Measures taken to improve the early detection of nonconventional weapons	TH,
	• Stocking up on vaccines and antibiotics	BC
	• (EU) Schengen Information System implemented (database accessible at border crossings within the EU with information about member-citizens)	
2003	UK, Spain, Italy, Poland, and others join the U.S. in invasion of Iraq (UK volunteers > 40,000 troops)	UF
2004	(EU) Passenger Name Record Data Arrangement with the United States shares passenger data for all flights originating in or going to the U.S.	AV, BC
	(UK) Civil Contingencies Bill (called UK's Patriot Act)	

Notes: EU = European Union; UK = United Kingdom; SP = Spain; FR = France; IT = Italy; AV = aviation security; BC = border controls; UF = use of force to attack terrorist groups; TH = target hardening; INT = intelligence; $ = targeting funding of terrorists

1990s, through Europol and the Schengen Information System (SIS)—earlier than did the counterpart U.S. agencies (DiPaolo and Stanislawski 2004).

In the 1970s, in response to airline hijackings, Europe stiffened its passenger and baggage screening systems. U.S. policy on aircraft hijackings was aimed at preventing hostage-taking. "The FAA-approved 'Common Strategy' had been elaborated over decades of experience with scores of hijackings, beginning in the 1960s. It taught flight crews that the best way to deal with hijackers was to accommodate their demands, get the plane to land safely, and then let law enforcement or the military handle the situation" (9/11 Commission Report 2004, 85). Later, in the 1980s, U.S. policy did not make aviation risks a priority, largely because there had been no hijackings of U.S. airplanes since 1986 (Posner 2004b, 9).

On the military front, the United States was not aggressively precautionary in the 1970s. European countries had effective commando strike forces to rescue hostages from hijacked airplanes in the mid-1970s (such as the Israeli raid at Entebbe in 1976 and the West German raid at Mogadishu in 1977), but the United States did not. The United States then created the Delta Force to serve this function, but it famously failed in its attempt (dubbed "Desert One") to rescue the American hostages in Iran in 1980 (9/11 Commission Report 2004, 96).

After the 1983 attack in Beirut that killed 200 U.S. marines, President Reagan withdrew U.S. forces from Lebanon, an act apparently seen by jihadists as a sign of weakness (9/11 Commission Report 2004, 96). He also signed National Security Directive 138, "calling for a 'shift ... from passive to active defense measures'" (9/11 Commission Report 2004, 98), but its practical effect was largely to exhort cooperation among the intelligence agencies, not to engage in precautionary counterterrorism policies. Meanwhile, in response to a different attack, France bombed Lebanon in 1982.

The United States did lead the Gulf War in 1991 to oust Iraq from Kuwait, with broad participation by Europe and other allies, but that was a response to a traditional use of military force by a state against another state, not a response to an attack on the United States by a nonstate terrorist group. The Gulf War was limited to pushing Iraqi forces back out of Kuwait and curtailing their future activities; it was not a precautionary effort to prevent future terrorist attacks. The United States bombed Iraq in 1993 in response to an assassination attempt on former President George H. W. Bush, and at other times thereafter to enforce the no-fly zones and other restrictions imposed on Iraq after the Gulf War.

But the United States did not take strong precautionary measures against al Qaeda even after the 1993 bombing of the World Trade Center buildings (9/11 Commission Report 2004, 108–109). In the 1990s, the United States was more focused on humanitarian interventions in Somalia, Haiti, Bosnia, and Kosovo, and on domestic terrorism such as the Oklahoma City bombing.

After the bombings of the U.S. embassies in Kenya and Tanzania in 1998 by al Qaeda, the United States did strike Osama bin Laden's camp in Afghanistan (and a target in Sudan) with cruise missiles on August 20, 1998, but the missiles did not hit bin Laden (9/11 Commission Report 2004, 117). And on several occasions, the United States considered but decided not to strike at bin Laden with cruise missiles—in particular in December 1998, February 1999, May 1999, and December 2000. The reasons for holding fire included fear of hitting civilians (collateral damage), fear of inciting reprisals, fear of hitting delegates from the United Arab Emirates (evidently visiting bin Laden in February 1999), fear of Pakistan mistaking the U.S. missiles for missiles from India and sparking a Pakistan-India war, embarrassment regarding the May 1999 mistaken bombing of the Chinese embassy in Belgrade based on erroneous intelligence, and uncertainty about bin Laden's actual location and his actual culpability for attacks such as the bombing of the USS *Cole* in October 2000 (9/11 Commission Report 2004, 134–41, 195–97).

Domestic Measures after 2001

After the 9/11 attacks in 2001, several categories of domestic measures were taken by the U.S. government. These include stepped-up law enforcement and surveillance, hardened vulnerable sites, increased aviation security, and others.

Law Enforcement and Surveillance. Soon after the attacks of September 11, 2001, the Bush administration proposed the Uniting and Strengthening America by Providing Appropriate Tools Required to Intercept and Obstruct Terrorism Act (the "USA PATRIOT Act"), which Congress enacted as Public Law 107-56. The act's significant provisions seek to do the following:

- Cut off funding of terrorist organizations.
- Enable more vigorous prosecution of suspected terrorists.
- Give law enforcement agencies greater powers of search and surveillance. For example, Section 201 added crimes of terrorism or production/dissemination of chemical weapons as predicate offenses under Title III, suspicion of which enable the government to obtain a wiretap of a party's communications. Section 213 eliminated a prior requirement to inform a person subject to a search warrant with contemporaneous notice of the search. The new "secret search" provision applies where the court finds that notification of the search warrant may compromise the search. Section 216 of the act significantly expanded law enforcement authority to use trap and trace and pen register devices, and expanded pen register capacities to the Internet, covering electronic mail, Web surfing, and all other forms of electronic communications. The act also gave the government new powers to seize library and bookstore records.

Part of the USA PATRIOT Act was declared unconstitutional: U.S. District Judge Aubrey Collins held that the act's ban on providing "expert advice or assistance" to terrorist groups was impermissibly vague (*Humanitarian Law Project v. Ashcroft* 309 F.Supp.2d 1185 (C.D.Cal. 2004)).

Related but distinct from the USA PATRIOT Act was the administration's creation of the Terrorist Information Awareness program—originally called the Total Information Awareness program until it was met by public criticism that it amounted to Big Brother collecting personal information on every American. Because the likelihood is very low that most of the people being monitored are terrorists, this strategy is highly precautionary; the damage to innocent subjects of false positive identifications could be high.

The George W. Bush administration also apparently authorized the National Security Agency (NSA) to undertake domestic surveillance of electronic communications. This occurred from 2002 on—perhaps even earlier—but it was not disclosed publicly until late 2005. This surveillance took place without search warrants obtained under the Fourth Amendment to the U.S. Constitution, and without the approval of the special court required under the Foreign Intelligence Surveillance Act (FISA). Congress subsequently enacted legislation attempting to authorize these activities.

On the other hand, the United States has done less than some European countries have in recent years to deploy video surveillance of public places. The United Kingdom has made widespread use of video monitoring cameras to record ordinary daily life in public places—intersections, shopping malls, parks—as a precautionary strategy to detect and deter crime and terrorism. The installation of closed circuit television (CCTV) systems in public places in the UK increased after the bombing at the 1984 Conservative Party conference (aimed at Prime Minister Margaret Thatcher), and it accelerated after the 1993 abduction of a toddler was caught on videotape and the national government then began funding installation of cameras across the country (Norris et al. 2004, 111). By 2004, there were over 40,000 cameras monitoring public spaces in Britain, compared with fewer than 1,000 in the rest of Europe (Norris et al. 2004, 113). Such a policy had not been adopted in the United States, and though it might be held unconstitutional, it may now become increasingly practiced and accepted in the United States since the terrorist attacks of September 11, 2001; the Madrid bombings in 2004; and the London subway bombings in 2005. By 2002, Washington, DC, had installed a comprehensive network of centrally monitored cameras, and in 2004, Chicago announced plans to deploy 2,000 cameras (Norris et al. 2004, 114–115, 119–120).

This history suggests that precautionary video surveillance was often adopted in response to notorious crisis events (the availability heuristic), yielding substantial diversity in relative precaution across the Atlantic and within both the United States and Europe. Some countries have not yet suffered crises spurring the adoption of cameras, and some countries (such as Norway, Denmark, and Canada) have legal rules on privacy rights that restrict surveillance without probable cause (Norris et al. 2004, 121–122).

Meanwhile, whether the precautionary use of surveillance videos is actually effective in preventing violence or catching perpetrators is largely unstudied and unknown. There has been little rigorous evaluation of such systems, and the few studies that have been done indicate small or inconclusive effects on crime rates (Norris et al. 2004, 123–125). The "appeal of CCTV had less to do with CCTV's proven effectiveness in reducing crime and far more to do with its symbolic value that something was being done about the problem of crime" (Norris et al. 2004, 123).

Hardening Vulnerable Sites. Since September 11, 2001, the United States has reinforced defenses at government buildings (e.g., cordoning off Pennsylvania Avenue and other streets around the White House and the adjacent Old Executive Office Building (OEOB)), and at tall buildings (e.g., Citicorp Center in Manhattan). The United States had hardened federal buildings after attacks in the past, such as closing off West Executive Drive (between the White House and the OEOB) after the assassination of President Kennedy in 1963, and putting cement planters in front of federal courthouses after the truck bombing of U.S. marines in Lebanon in 1983. Since

9/11, some have urged even greater attention to hardening, especially at dams, chemical factories, and nuclear power plants. The bombings in London subways on July 7, 2005, raised calls to harden U.S. mass transit systems.

The hardening of specific targets may be circumvented by terrorists who shift to other targets (Lakdawalla and Zanjani 2002; Keohane and Zeckhauser 2003). Still, some targets, such as the White House, are so valuable that hardening them may be worthwhile even if it displaces terrorist attacks toward more vulnerable but less valuable targets.

Aviation Security.   After terrorists used aircraft as projectiles on September 11, 2001, the United States sought to strengthen its system for screening out terrorists from airline passengers lists. It also took other steps such as requiring cockpit doors to be fortified and locked and posting federal air marshals on some flights (Kaplan 2006). Congress enacted the Aviation and Transportation Security Act in November 2001. Building on its Computer Assisted Passenger Prescreening System (CAPPS), which had been adopted in 1997 to assist in passenger screening in response to the 1996 crash of TWA 800 and the Atlanta Olympics bombing, the Transportation Security Agency (TSA) (itself a new agency created after 9/11 to undertake the security role of FAA) developed the CAPPS II system in 2003. CAPPS II assesses the identity of every passenger and performs a risk assessment to detect potentially risky passengers based on identity and assumptions about how terrorists travel; it flags passengers for additional screening if they fit the profile (DHS 2003; Alberto and Bogatz 2004). CAPPS II is designed to reduce the time needed for security checks by better pinpointing those in need of screening and thereby reducing the number of passengers to go through extensive screening. Civil liberties advocates have worried that CAPPS II may permit excessive data-mining, erroneous screenings, and intrusions on privacy (Alberto and Bogatz 2004; but see DHS 2003).

Europe already collected more identity information than did the United States under the Schengen Information System (SIS), which was to be updated to SIS II (DiPaolo and Stanislawski 2004). Nonetheless, the EU was hesitant to share additional passenger information with the United States after 2001 because of concerns about data privacy. The U.S. Department of Homeland Security (DHS) sought more types of information, for broader purposes, and for longer durations than the EU was initially willing to provide. The United States sought the transfer of passenger data from the Customs and Border Protection agency to the TSA, which the EU—in particular the European Parliament—resisted (Koslowski 2004). In December 2003, after being assured that the data would be secure (though transferable to TSA) and obtaining U.S. compromises on types and duration, the European Commission agreed to the Passenger Name Record (PNR) Data Arrangement, in which the EU will share passenger data with the United States for all flights originating in or going to the United States. This agreement was signed in May 2004 (USEU 2003, 2004), but tensions between Washington and Brussels remain, because of the lower level of data protection in the United States. The United States pressed the EU to adopt encoded biometric markers in passports or else discontinue visa-free travel from Europe to the United States (Koslowski 2004).

Additional aviation safety measures were adopted in the years after 9/11:

- U.S. baggage screeners were made federal employees of the TSA (P.L. 107-71), and every bag must now be X-rayed; if a passenger whose bags are checked does not board the flight, the flight is held while his or her bags are removed.
- Prohibitions were placed on certain carry-on items, including larger containers of liquids or gels.
- Air marshals have been put on some flights, both in the United States and Europe. Some critics argue the number is too few, while others argue that the program is expensive and useless. Some point out that U.S. air marshals stand out from other passengers due to formal dress requirements and preboarding procedures, which may reduce their effectiveness, shift terrorist attention to flights without marshals, and make marshals targets.
- Arming pilots was authorized by U.S. legislation in 2002 but not significantly implemented; pilots must first be trained and rules promulgated (Levin 2002). Experts debate whether arming pilots will deter or stop terrorists from seizing aircraft or instead will increase the risk of accidental discharge or theft of the weapon in flight (e.g., Lott 2003).
- Passenger movement in the aircraft cabin was prohibited within 30 minutes' flight time of Reagan Washington National Airport; in light of improvements in cockpit security and air marshals on flights, this restriction was deemed no longer necessary and removed in July 2005 (TSA 2005).

Other Measures. The United States spends significantly more on defense and homeland security than the members of the European Union combined. Nonetheless, there are some conceivable precautionary measures that were *not* taken after September 11. For example, internment of Arab-Americans—a highly precautionary move, given high uncertainty about which if any members of the ethnic group pose any threat, but one that was made in past conflicts, such as the internment of Japanese-Americans in World War II—has not been undertaken despite calls for such action (e.g., Malkin 2004). There has also been concern that too little has been done to screen shipping containers coming into U.S. ports.

Since 9/11, the United States has also imposed additional sanctions on countries thought to support terrorist groups. For example, on May 11, 2004, President Bush signed an executive order imposing military and economic sanctions on Syria. President Obama extended these sanctions in 2010. The European policy toward Syria has been to attempt political and cultural engagement (Berman 2004).

Precautionary Use of Military Force after 2001

A year after the terrorist attacks of September 11, 2001, the Bush administration adopted a new National Security Strategy in September 2002 (Bush 2002b). This new strategy called for anticipatory attacks against potential enemies with uncertain capacities and intentions even before their threat is imminent. Rather than wait for proof of WMD, it shifts the burden of proof, obliging states to show that they do not harbor WMD or terrorist cells or else face the preventive use of force. It invites international cooperation, but it does not oblige unilateral action to wait for UN authorization. The new U.S. National Security Strategy stated:

> We cannot let our enemies strike first ... [but must take] anticipatory action to defend ourselves, even if uncertainty remains as to the time and place of the enemy's attack. To forestall or prevent such hostile acts by our adversaries, the United States, will, if necessary, act preemptively. ... America will act against such emerging threats before they are fully formed. ... The greater the threat, the greater is the risk of inaction and the more compelling the case for taking anticipatory action to defend ourselves, even if uncertainty remains as to the time and place of the enemy's attack. (Bush 2002b)

The Bush administration argued that the highly uncertain, serious, and irreversible risks of terrorism with WMD required the option of preventive war: destroying the adversaries' weapons even if there is little or no evidence that an attack is imminent. President Bush put the issue in terms almost identical to the precautionary language from the European Environment Agency:

> Facing clear evidence of peril, we cannot wait for the final proof, the smoking gun that could come in the form of a mushroom cloud. (Bush 2002c)

> Forestalling disasters usually requires acting before there is strong proof of harm. (EEA 2002, 13)

Or compare the following two statements, the first by President Bush justifying the new National Security Strategy, the second by the EU's Environment Commissioner Margot Wallstrom justifying the precautionary principle:

> If we wait for threats to fully materialize, we will have waited too long. (Bush 2002a)

> If you smell smoke, you don't wait until your house is burning down before you tackle the cause. (Wallstrom 2002)

Likewise, nongovernmental advocates of the precautionary principle say:

> Sometimes if we wait for proof it is too late. ... If we always wait for scientific certainty, people may suffer and die, and damage to the natural world may be irreversible. (SEHN 2002)

And former vice president Al Gore has written regarding global warming:

> We need to act now on the basis of what we know. ... The insistence on complete certainty about the full details of global warming—the most serious threat that we have ever faced—is actually an effort to avoid facing the awful, uncomfortable truth: that we must act boldly, decisively, comprehensively, and quickly, even before we know every last detail about the crisis. (Gore 1992, 37, 40)

The justifications for precaution use virtually the same language employed by President Bush and UK prime minister Tony Blair for preventive intervention to fight the uncertain risk of terrorism. "President Bush argued that the risk of WMD was great enough to warrant an attack, without absolute proof that Iraq was hiding such weapons. That's the PP [precautionary principle], American style" (Loewenberg 2003). The British government took a similar stance (Runciman 2004).

Thus, the new strategy amounted to the adoption of the precautionary principle against the risk of terrorism. Although the U.S. government has often criticized the precautionary principle when applied to risks such as beef hormones, genetically modified foods, and climate change, the Bush administration made precisely the precautionary case for its decisions to undertake anticipatory counterterrorism measures—from domestic security (as discussed above), to detaining prisoners (such as the preventive detentions without trial at Guantanamo Bay), to the use of military force in Afghanistan and then in Iraq.

Moreover, the Bush administration also adopted the precautionary strategy of shifting the burden of proof. The traditional basis for the use of force in national self-defense is that the country has been attacked, or that an attack is imminent. The burden of proof is on the country exercising preemptive self-defense to show that its enemy is about to attack, just as often the burden of proof is on regulatory agencies to demonstrate evidence of risk before they may act. The precautionary principle shifts that burden: it authorizes or requires action unless the *absence* of risk is demonstrated. With respect to Iraq, there was no evidence that Iraq was about to attack the United States or Britain, but the administration brought forth intelligence claims that Iraq had capabilities—WMD—to attack without warning and with catastrophic consequences. Iraq had admitted it possessed biological and chemical-weapons programs (UN 1999). Still, during the 1990s, the burden of proof was on the United States and the UN Security Council to find evidence of Iraqi WMD before authorizing further sanctions or intervention. Hence, the team of UN inspectors searched for WMD in Iraq (until they left in 1998); but even after 9/11/2001, the United States and Britain had a hard time convincing other countries that invading Iraq was warranted. Then the Bush and Blair administrations made the argument that, instead, it was Saddam who bore the burden of proof—to show that Iraq had no WMD by cooperating with inspectors, disclosing any WMD or precursor materiel, and disarming. Shifting the burden of proof was a centerpiece of Secretary of State Colin Powell's landmark speech to the UN on February 5, 2003, presenting the case for war (Robbins 2003; Saletan 2003; Zengerle 2003). Canadian foreign minister Bill Graham commented that the speech "amounts to a transfer of the burden of proof from the United States to Saddam Hussein" (Murphy 2003). Secretary Powell reiterated the burden-shifting point to the UN Security Council a month later (Powell 2003). Back in December 2002, White House Press Secretary Ari Fleischer had said, "The burden of proof lies with Saddam Hussein" (Fleischer 2002). Madeleine Albright, secretary of state in the Clinton administration, had agreed: "There's no question that the burden of proof is on Iraq. I mean we've all said that; everybody believes that" (Albright 2002).

This is precisely the same type of shift in the burden of proof advocated under the precautionary principle: instead of the government regulatory agency having to prove that a substance or activity is dangerous, the applicant or proponent of an activity or process or chemical needs to demonstrate that the environment and public health will be safe. The proof must shift to the party or entity that will benefit from the activity and that is most likely to have the information. (Raffensberger and Tickner 1999, 345–346)

Like Secretary Powell, Prime Minister Blair made the same move:

Blair's position can just as well be expressed in the more neutral language of precaution. What lawyers, bureaucrats, and even some philosophers like to call the precautionary principle states that when faced with risks with uncertain and potentially catastrophic downsides, it's always better to err on the side of caution. In such circumstances, the burden of proof is said to lie with those who downplay the risk of disaster, rather than with those who argue that the risks are real, even if they might be quite small. This appears to be Blair's current position on the war in Iraq. (Runciman 2004)

Further indication of the shift to precaution comes from the kind of criticism leveled against the new strategy. The criticisms of precaution against terrorism are virtually identical to the criticisms of precaution against environmental risks—but on the opposite political feet. When the United States announced its new doctrine of anticipatory war in September 2002, German foreign minister (and Green Party vice chairman) Joschka Fischer worried aloud to the UN General Assembly:

To what consequences would military intervention lead? . . . Are there new and definite findings and facts? Does the threat assessment justify taking a very high risk? . . . [W]e are full of deep skepticism regarding military action. (Fischer 2002)

While the U.S. government wanted fast and forceful action to prevent the next terrorist attack despite the uncertainty of the threat, its detractors in Europe wanted more evidence—"findings of fact" and a "threat assessment," in Fischer's words—and deliberation before acting (ironically, precisely the stance that European Greens oppose as an obstacle to precautionary regulations on food safety and the environment). After the war in Iraq and the failure to find compelling evidence that Iraq was creating or deploying WMD (Duelfer 2004), critics questioned whether the United States and Britain had acted prematurely (e.g., Krugman 2003)—in effect, whether the United States and Britain "cried wolf" and undertook precaution based on a false positive (in other words, the same critique leveled by skeptics of precaution in the environmental arena (e.g., Wildavsky 1995)). UN weapons inspector Hans Blix said:

It is clear that the critical thinking we applied led us less astray than did the assertive thinking of the U.S. administration. . . . We never said there were weapons of mass destruction. What we said was that the Iraqis could not answer all our questions regarding their arsenal. But, for the Bush administration, "unaccounted for" equalled "existing." (Blix 2003)

The Bush position described by Blix is the same as that of advocates of precautionary environmental regulation, who say that "absence of evidence" of harmfulness "is not evidence of absence" of harmfulness, and therefore that regulation should go forward to address the potential risk even without clear evidence. Blix would have preferred action based on evidence, not on uncertainty. Likewise, the *New York Times* (2003) editorialized: "If intelligence and risk assessment are sketchy—and when are they not?—using them as the basis for preemptive war poses enormous dangers." Replace "preemptive war" with "precautionary regulation," and one has the standard industry line against precaution in health and environmental policy.

Meanwhile, the Bush administration has made this same critique of precaution against food and environmental risks, emphasizing uncertainty as a reason not to act. "Mr. Bush, explaining to senators why he opposed the Kyoto Protocol on global warming, spoke of the 'incomplete state of scientific knowledge of the causes of, and solutions to, global climate change'" (Lewis 2001). The Bush administration official in charge of regulatory policy called the precautionary principle "a mythical concept, perhaps like a unicorn" (Loewenberg 2003, quoting John D. Graham, Remarks at the First Transatlantic Dialogue on Precaution, Bruges, Belgium, January 2002).

The war in Afghanistan was precautionary in the sense of anticipating and attempting to prevent al Qaeda's next attack, but it was also in direct response to clear evidence of threat, namely the attacks of 9/11. The war in Iraq was far more precautionary. In justifying the war in Iraq, both the U.S. and British governments cited uncertain risks of serious or irreversible damage requiring prompt precautionary action. The British government highlighted the threat of surprise attack with WMD, mentioning that Iraqi forces could deploy WMD within 45 minutes (Butler et al. 2004, 125–127). The U.S. government also cited several indicia of WMD in Iraq to justify its military action, such as chemical and biological weapons activities in Iraq and a purported attempt to obtain nuclear weapons materials from Niger (Commission on the Intelligence Capabilities of the U.S. Regarding WMD 2005; Shane and Sanger 2005; Select Committee on Intelligence 2004). This evidence was highly uncertain before the war and later proved to be unfounded. Still, *ex ante*, the small and uncertain probability of a catastrophic outcome was cognizable and is precisely the situation to which the precautionary principle speaks (Runciman 2004). Now, with several extensive reports in both the United States and Britain (Duelfer 2004; Commission on the Intelligence Capabilities of the U.S. Regarding WMD 2005; Select Committee on Intelligence 2004; Butler et al. 2004) finding that no WMD threat existed in Iraq before the war, and with the U.S. search for WMD in Iraq having officially ended on January 11, 2005, the invasion of Iraq appears to have been premised on a serious false positive. This simply underscores the degree to which the war itself was a highly precautionary move: undertaken in anticipation of a serious threat but under enormous uncertainty about the risk, with very little good evidence to back it up, and with far greater concern about false negatives (WMD unknown but existing) than about false positives (WMD claimed but not existing).

To be sure, it is possible that WMD did exist in Iraq but were moved or hidden someplace else. And even if the WMD did not exist, the *ex ante* risk assessment may have been sufficiently worrisome to warrant precaution despite the high chance of error (Runciman 2004; Weeks 2003, postscript). These possibilities are part and parcel of precaution against an uncertain risk with a high damage worst-case scenario.

Alternatively, perhaps the risk of WMD was not the real underlying motivation for the war; perhaps the real reason was liberating the Iraqi people, spreading democracy, deterring other rogue states, seizing control of oil resources, or something else. But critics of precaution in the health and environmental arena make the same complaint: that precaution is a cover for other motives, such as disguised trade protectionism. The basic point remains that the Bush National Security Strategy and the stated rationale for specific actions taken pursuant to it, including the war in Iraq, are the precautionary principle applied to terrorism.

The degree to which the Bush doctrine was highly precautionary is also evident from its controversial status under international law. Some authors distinguish "precautionary" regulation from "preventive" regulation, arguing that precaution applies to unknown risks whereas prevention applies to known risks (Sanderson and Peterson 2001; EEA 2002). Preemptive war (like preventive regulation) is anticipatory self-defense against an imminent (i.e., "known") threat. Preventive war (like precautionary regulation) is more aggressive: it is anticipatory self-defense without an imminent threat (Jervis 2003). Traditionally, under international law (Article 51 of the UN Charter), preemptive war is legal if in "self-defense" against an *imminent* attack, but not against highly uncertain threats (Ackerman 2003). The advent of WMD held by rogue states or terrorists is leading some legal experts to recognize more room for "anticipatory self-defense" (Ackerman 2003, 6). "In the twenty-first century, maintaining global peace and security requires states to be proactive rather than reactive" (Feinstein and Slaughter 2004). Yoo (2004) argues that national self-defense must be understood to allow preventive attacks against uncertain threats of WMD long before an armed attack occurs, but only if the preventive action yields positive expected net benefits. Others argue that precautionary "preventive war" against uncertain nonimminent threats may only be undertaken by the UN Security Council, not unilaterally by individual states (High-Level Panel 2004, 55). The point here is not to settle the legal question whether preemptive or preventive war by individual states violates international law, but merely to say that the Bush doctrine announced in 2002, calling for unilateral anticipatory military attacks against potential threats before evidence of an imminent threat has been shown, is a move to a substantially more precautionary strategy to combat the risks of terrorism and WMD, with uncertainty being no excuse for inaction (Jervis 2003).

Explanations for the Observed Pattern

The preceding section yields the following historical observation: in the arena of counterterrorism, there has been a shift toward greater relative U.S. precaution compared with the EU. The EU was more precautionary in 1970s, while the United States and the UK have become more precautionary since the 1990s and especially since 2001. This indicates a flip-flop or reversal in relative precaution, but in the opposite direction of Vogel's hypothesis described in Chapter 1. In addition, the history reveals divergence within Europe, especially regarding the war in Iraq.

The United States and other countries have used preemptive strikes in the past, but the adoption of an overall strategy of preemption and preventive war is a new frontier (Weeks 2003). Several factors drove this shift to a more precautionary approach in United States and British strategy.

Strategic Need

First, as noted above, experts sought the shift on the ground that the Cold War strategies of deterrence and containment would be far less effective against nonstate actors using suicide surprise attacks, and that such attacks could be catastrophic; hence the need for a more anticipatory strategy that incapacitates the threat before it occurs.

The end of the Cold War and the rise of nonstate threats to international security made the prior strategy of deterrence and containment (Kennan 1947) a less effective option. Nonstate actors with no base of operations are harder to deter militarily because it is unclear whom to threaten with massive retaliation, and where. Suicide bombers, in particular, cannot be deterred with military means because they do not fear death. (Still, there may be other things they fear, such as failure, a sullied reputation, or inability to enter heaven, which decisionmakers might try to exploit.) If such terrorists join forces with "rogue" states equipped with weapons of mass destruction (WMD)—as the Bush administration feared—the result could be catastrophic.

But the application of this strategy to specific places (such as Afghanistan and Iraq) depends on risk assessments—intelligence estimates and threat information—that appear to have overstated the risk of WMD in Iraq (a false positive). *The Economist* magazine initially urged "The Case for War" (on August 3, 2002), and later, after WMD failed to turn up, ventured "The Case for War—Revisited" (on July 19, 2003). It later ran two cover photos of George Bush and Tony Blair with the disillusioned headlines "Wielders of Mass Deception?" on October 4, 2003, and then "Sincere Deceivers" on July 17, 2004.

Risk Assessment and Its Errors

Second, then, was the overstatement of risk by expert risk assessors (the intelligence community) and by policy officials. For example, before the war, CIA Director George Tenet told President Bush that the case for finding WMD in Iraq was a "slam dunk" (Woodward 2004). (In 2005, he said those were "the two dumbest words I ever said" (Goldenberg 2005).) Relying on that assessment, President Bush said in 2003 in the State of the Union speech that Iraq was seeking materials for nuclear weapons from Niger, a claim that later appeared to have been false and based in part on a forged document. Secretary of State Colin Powell enumerated ostensible evidence of WMD in Iraq to the United Nations in February 2003. The British government said that Iraqi forces could deploy WMD within 45 minutes. Yet after the war, no WMD were found, and high-level panels called the prewar assessments "dead wrong" (Commission on the Intelligence Capabilities of the U.S. Regarding WMD 2005; Butler et al. 2004, 125–127). And the "45 minutes" claim, it turned out, was meant to refer to battlefield deployment in Iraq, not a strike in Europe, but that qualification was dropped as drafts of the dossier were edited, and in any case, the claim itself is now deemed doubtful (Butler et al. 2004, 125–127).

These overstatements were in part a reaction to the 9/11 surprise attacks and the intelligence failures they had represented—that is, an effort to avoid making the same false negative error a second time, especially if the second time could be with WMD. The claim of WMD in Iraq—the central premise of the precautionary strategy to wage preventive war in Iraq—so crucial in motivating both leaders and the public to go to war, appears in retrospect to have been a false positive. Past false negatives (neglect) can spur future false positives (overreaction). Analysts have been wrong about WMD programs many times in the past, including the Soviet Union in 1949, China in 1964, India in 1974, Iraq in 1991, North Korea in 1994, Iraq in 1995, India in 1998, Pakistan in 1998, North Korea in 2002, Iran in 2003, and Libya in 2003—all cases in which "the WMD program turned out to be more advanced than the intelligence community thought" (Feaver 2004). This list of false negative failures helps to explain why the intelligence community might have overstated its findings—determined to get it right this time—especially in the immediate aftermath of the surprise attacks of September 11. There had been warnings of al Qaeda's intent to strike in the United States—such as the famous Presidential Daily Briefing of August 6, 2001 ("Bin Laden Determined to Strike within the U.S.")—as well as the earlier National Intelligence Estimate (NIE) produced in 1995, warning that Islamist terrorists might try to blend into U.S. immigrant Muslim populations and use conventional weapons or civil aviation to attack landmarks such as Wall Street and the White House (Pillar 2004a). Also, clues to the hijackers' plans at regional FBI offices did not get adequate attention (9/11 Commission Report 2004). But it is easy in hindsight, knowing which attack actually occurred, to forget that before 9/11, these strands competed for attention amidst many other hints and threats; it was not simple to sort the true positives from the false ones. Still, the false negative of 9/11 was stunning. "Though analysts have been wrong on major issues in the past, no previous intelligence failure has been so costly as the September 11th attacks" (Select Committee on Intelligence 2004, 32). "It is a well-known phenomenon within intelligence communities that memory of past failures can cause overestimation next time around" (Butler et al. 2004, 15).

The Senate Select Committee on Intelligence concluded that most of the key judgments of the NIE of October 2002, *Iraq's Continuing Programs for Weapons of Mass Destruction*, were either "overstated or were not supported by the underlying intelligence reporting" (Select Committee on Intelligence 2004, 14). But President Bush, like advocates of precaution, had emphasized the opposite problem: "Our collection and analysis of intelligence will never be perfect, but in an age where our margin for error is getting smaller, in an age in which we are at war, the consequences of underestimating a threat could be tens of thousands of innocent lives" (Shane and Sanger 2005). This approach to uncertainty, as we have seen, is the precautionary principle in action. Its cognate in the health and environmental arena is the use of conservative default assumptions and methods in risk assessments—such as linear nonthreshold low-dose extrapolations, use of the most sensitive test species, extrapolation from test animals to humans, and use of the hypothetical maximum exposed individual—to overstate the risk estimate in order to avoid adopting regulations that are underprotective.

In his assessment of Israeli intelligence failures in regard to Iraq, retired Israeli general Shlomo Brom attributed the adoption of worst-case scenarios to a desire to avoid blame for underestimating threats. The intelligence failure prior to the Yom Kippur War created a culture of "assigning culpability and punishing those responsible." Analysts thus have an incentive to exaggerate the enemies' capabilities because they "feel that by giving bleak assessments they decrease the threat to themselves." If the assessment is correct, they will be treated as heroes, he wrote, and if it is wrong, no one will pay much attention "because everyone will be pleased that their bleak prophecies did not materialize" (Brom 2003). And it is worth recalling that Iraq itself had claimed it possessed WMD in the 1990s (Stern 1999). An internal CIA analysis insisted that although mistakes were evident in retrospect, the prewar assessment of Iraq's WMD was reasonable based on the information that was available at the time (Jehl 2004).

Psychology: Availability, Fear, and Dread

A third key driver of the shift to precaution was the psychological element: availability, fear, and dread. The availability heuristic is the tendency to respond aggressively to alarming events that are "available" or vivid in people's minds (Kahneman et al. 1982). People tend to exaggerate the likelihood of such events (relative to risks that are statistically more likely) because they are easy to imagine or recall, and so they support more stringent protective measures against available risks. Yet low-probability high-consequence catastrophic events—a major terrorist attack or, say, an asteroid collision—are by definition rare and so not easily available. In general, therefore, people tend to understate the risk of low-probability high-consequence events such as terrorist attacks or asteroid collisions, ignoring or lampooning remote chances of catastrophes even when such events warrant precaution on an expected value basis. Perhaps this is because people lack experience with such rare extreme events or because the mind avoids the mental burden of contemplating the horrific (Posner 2004a; Dana 2003). This leads to false negative errors, catastrophic surprise, and hindsight recriminations. But once such an event, or one similar to it, has recently occurred, the availability heuristic is triggered, and people tend to overstate the risk of another catastrophic event (Slovic 2000; Slovic and Weber 2003; Sunstein 2003). "U.S. citizens and their elected leaders respond far more readily to dramatic events in their midst than to warnings and analyses about threatening events yet to occur" (Pillar 2004b). "Experience has shown that major policy changes tend to come only from actual disasters" (Pillar 2004a). One available event can set in motion a cascade of public clamor for stringent protective measures against similar events even if they not causally connected, such as fear of genetically modified foods driven by mad cow disease, and even if other risks deserve more prospective attention (Sunstein and Kuran 1999). The adoption of major health and environmental legislation was similarly driven by crisis events such as the burning of the Cuyahoga River, pollution in Lake Erie, and the discovery of toxic waste in Love Canal (Andrews 1999; Percival 1998). Similarly, President Bush and Vice President Cheney justified the war in Iraq as a response to 9/11 despite no evidence linking the two. Although experts had been warning for years of the potential for mass-casualty terrorism and of al Qaeda's likely involvement in such attacks, with the highly visible 9/11 event terrorism suddenly rose to the top of the national agenda. The United States shifted from inattention to aviation risks before 9/11 (because there had been no hijackings of U.S. airplanes since 1986) to frantic efforts to safeguard aviation (Posner 2004b, 9). Yet it is unclear why the United States did not react more strongly to the 1993 World Trade Center bombing—perhaps because it was not highly damaging. Many proverbial barn doors were closed after 9/11, even if those barn doors had little to do with the likelihood of future horses escaping. Yet other barn doors such as ports and mass transit remained relatively open.

Meanwhile, across the Atlantic, "[i]t is only in those West European states which have suffered protracted and destructive campaigns of terror that the existence of special antiterrorist legislation has been accepted" (Chalk 1996, 99). This helps account for antiterror legislation adopted in the 1970s in Britain (against the IRA) and Spain (against the Basque separatists).

Here the availability heuristic was compounded by dread—the abject fear of sinister, mysterious, or unnatural risks (Stern 2002; Slovic 1987; Sunstein 2003). The envisioned threat—of WMD being wielded by suicidal foreign religious fanatics who hate America or the West—is a source of dread that can motivate decisionmakers to take particularly aggressive actions to avoid risk, and dread can lead the public to support leaders who are seen to take aggressive action. When dangers evoke a strong sense of dread, policymakers are particularly susceptible to implement risk-reduction policies with little regard to countervailing dangers (Stern 1999; Stern 2003a). It has long been observed that the things that frighten us most are often quite different from those most likely to harm us (Slovic 1987). Psychologists have found that fear is disproportionately evoked by certain qualitative attributes of risks, including involuntary exposure, unfamiliarity, invisibility, catastrophic potential, latency, and uncertainty (Slovic 1987; Sunstein 2005). Terrorism—especially with WMD—is unusual in that it possesses all of these characteristics.

Compounding and amplifying this dread is the element of evil. In the 9/11 terrorist attacks, many of the classic components of evil—including malice, premeditation, surprise attack without warning or ultimatum, the killing of thousands of innocent civilians, and suicide attack—have "rarely been so well combined" (Nieman 2002, 284–285). If a leader can persuade us we are fighting evil itself, we are more likely to make sacrifices and more prone to throw caution aside in regard to new risks introduced by our actions. Hence a war against evil is proclaimed by both sides—by the terrorists rallying jihad, and the target countries rallying the war on terror. Dread of evil cements societies, Jeremy Bentham observed, more than the hope for good (Bentham 1830, xviii, section 17). Thus, four days after the 9/11 terrorist strikes, President Bush announced that his administration would "rid the world of evil-doers" (Peres-Rivas 2001). He referred to rogue states seeking WMD as an "axis of evil."

Consequences of Precaution against Terrorism and WMD

In a companion paper (Stern and Wiener 2008) to this chapter, we attempt a comprehensive analysis of the consequences of precaution against terrorism. Here we summarize that analysis briefly.

A full portfolio analysis of precaution against a risk compares the reduction in target risk (TR) plus ancillary benefits (AB), versus the costs (C) plus increases in countervailing risks (CR) (Wiener 1998; Rascoff and Revesz 2002; Wiener 2004). Analyses should be undertaken both *ex ante* and *ex post*, first to decide and then to learn how to decide better next time. Such risk analysis can be a powerful guide to intelligent decisionmaking in counterterrorism.

At the same time, the case of counterterrorism can provide a lesson for risk analysts: the need to foresee subsequent moves taken by terrorists to respond to initial counterterrorism measures. Risk analysis has too often assumed a simple direct relationship between regulatory measures and the change in emissions or risk, neglecting responsive behavior by the regulated actors. Risk analysis could benefit from approaches (such as general equilibrium analysis and multiperiod games) that take account of responsive actors—actors who take evasive or reallocative steps in response to risk management interventions. Terrorists clearly respond strategically to defensive measures (Lakdawalla and Zanjani 2002; Keohane and Zeckhauser 2003), but this general approach will also be useful for analyzing the effects of measures directed at, for example, adaptive pathogens or law-abiding business firms.

Our analysis is necessarily limited to publicly available information, so we cannot assess impacts as fully as the government defense and intelligence agencies could if they chose to do so, but we can suggest a framework for analysis of the types and directions of impacts that the government agencies might neglect if they were not put to the challenge of such analysis. And although we unavoidably take account of information gleaned *ex post*, such as the apparent absence of WMD in Iraq, we also attempt to consider how an *ex ante* analysis would have looked before the decision to engage in preventive war. *Ex ante*, on expected value criteria, it is possible that even a low probability of WMD existing in Iraq, combined with high damages from their use, plus ancillary benefits, weighed against predictions of low cost and low countervailing risk, could have justified precautionary action. Yet we doubt that a careful analysis of these impacts was made *ex ante*, and we suggest that had it been, the calculus could well have shown that the decision should have been different because the likely costs and countervailing risks were quite significant.

Reduction in Target Risk

We take the target risk of concern to be an attack by terrorists on the United States (or its allies), particularly with weapons of mass destruction (WMD), though major damage could also be done without WMD (as on 9/11, or by an attack on a dam, computer network, chemical factory, or nuclear power plant). The Bush and Blair administrations clearly made reducing the risk of terrorism with WMD the primary public rationale for the new national security strategies and for the wars in Afghanistan and Iraq (Bush 2002a, 2002b; Zengerle 2003; Weeks 2003, postscript).

Risk is a combination of probability and severity. Low probability is not by itself a sufficient reason to neglect a risk with potentially severe consequences (Posner 2004a); what matters is the expected value of the risk. *Ex ante*, even if the probability of attack with WMD is low (e.g., 1% per year), as long as the impact is serious (e.g., 500,000 deaths), then the expected value of the risk is potentially large (here, 5,000 deaths per year). If the probability or the impact were higher, the expected value could rise.

Moreover, if (as seems to be the case) people are more upset by a mass disaster such as the loss of 3,000 lives on 9/11 than by the sum of the same or greater number of individual deaths occurring separately (e.g., in 40,000 different automobile accidents per year), then the expected utility loss from a 1% chance of 500,000 deaths in a single attack would be even larger than the expected utility loss from 5,000 (or perhaps even 50,000) deaths occurring individually; a "catastrophe premium" would need to be added.

A counterterrorism measure would achieve some percentage reduction in the expected value (plus catastrophe premium) of the target risk. *Ex ante*, if hardening targets, conducting surveillance, fortifying aviation, or the wars in Afghanistan or Iraq (or other precautionary measures) would reduce the probability or impact of a WMD attack, they could be justified despite the costs and countervailing risks. Davis et al. (2003) predicted that the war in Iraq would save direct expenses of continued containment of Iraq (naval, air, and troop deployment) of $13 billion/year, possibly up to $19 billion/year if intensified, lasting over 33 years (assuming a 3% per year likelihood of the Saddam Hussein regime ending); it would also save the costs of another 9/11-type (non-WMD) attack on the United States, assumed to cost $50 billion per attack in lost earnings, property damage, and reconstruction, assumed to be 5% likely per year (once every 20 years) if Saddam were left in power; it would save the costs of extra homeland security measures in the United States, assumed to be $10 billion/year (extra, part of a total of $80 billion/year the United States is estimated to spend on homeland security) over 33 years (as above); and it would yield improvement in Iraqi living standards of 50% over 20 years (net of economic damage due to war). Davis et al. calculated a total (discounted to present value) of $630 billion plus the improvement in Iraqi living standards.

Ex post, the war in Afghanistan appears to have reduced the target risk of attack by al Qaeda (Pillar 2004b), though by how much and for how long are not easy to quantify. The real actors behind the 9/11 attacks, Osama bin Laden and al Qaeda, remain at large. *Ex post*, WMD have not been found in Iraq (Duelfer 2004). Whatever WMD were thought to be in Iraq either did not exist or have escaped seizure. Perhaps Iraq had future plans to make WMD, which were thwarted by the war, so an earlier invasion was superior to waiting and attacking later despite the greater uncertainties (Pollack 2002). Acting early to forestall a growing but uncertain risk is, as we have seen, a key tenet of the precautionary principle. But this argument would authorize highly precautionary strikes against countries with no current capacity to attack based on conjecture about their future plans—going far beyond the doctrine of preemptive self-defense, and amidst far greater uncertainties about the reduction in target risk to be achieved, if any. The question therefore remains whether the war in Iraq was really part of the war against terrorism or instead a costly distraction—whether the war in Iraq has made the world safer or less safe from terrorism. Osama bin Laden is still at large. Many al Qaeda leaders may have been captured or killed, but others may have taken their place. With no WMD yet found in Iraq, the target risk reduction benefit now seems much smaller than had been anticipated before the war. It would not be implausible to find that the war in Iraq yielded *zero* reduction in target risk of WMD attack on the United States or Europe, although it would also not be implausible to find (based on evidence yet to be uncovered) that it did yield some beneficial reduction in this target risk, or on the contrary that it increased this risk (as we discuss below).

Ancillary Benefits

In addition to reducing the target risk, a policy intervention can also yield other unintended benefits such as by reducing other coincident risks (Graham and Wiener 1995; Rascoff and Revesz 2002; Wiener 2004). Several kinds of ancillary benefits may arise from counterterrorism measures:

- *Saving victims of oppressive regimes.* Civilians who would have been killed, abused, or oppressed by Saddam's regime would be spared. Davis et al. (2003) estimated that deposing Saddam would save 10,000 to 20,000 Iraqi civilian lives per year over 33 years (assuming a 3% per year chance of the regime ending), extrapolated from a history of over 200,000 deaths caused by the regime and sanctions against it in the decade from 1991 to 2002, and over 400,000 deaths in the preceding decade caused by the Iran-Iraq war and the Iraqi campaign against the Kurds. This assumes the successor regime would cause no such deaths.
- *Democracy.* Liberating Afghanistan and Iraq from tyranny could help spread democracy there and in other countries, such as Palestine and Lebanon (Jervis 2003, 367) (although independent internal events, chiefly the deaths of Yasser Arafat and Rafic Hariri, may have been more important factors). After WMD were not found in Iraq, the goals of liberating oppressed peoples and spreading democracy became the Bush and Blair administrations' primary stated rationales for the war in Iraq (Ignatieff 2005). "The war is hard to understand if the only objective was to disarm Saddam or even remove him from power. Even had the inflated estimates of his WMD capability been accurate, the danger was simply too remote to justify the effort. But if changing the Iraqi regime was expected to bring democracy and stability to the Middle East, discourage tyrants, and energize reformers throughout the world ... then as part of a larger project, the war makes sense" (Jervis 2003, 386). "If democracy plants itself in Iraq and spreads throughout the Middle East, Bush will be remembered as a plain-speaking visionary. If Iraq fails, it will be his Vietnam, and nothing else will matter much about his time in office" (Ignatieff 2005, 44). Yet democracy remains fragile at best in Afghanistan and Iraq, and has not yet spread to

Kuwait, Saudi Arabia, or Syria. In Iran, democracy has been restricted. Democracy may require a healthy domestic civil society, which in Iraq was depleted by the economic sanctions imposed in the 1990s (Zakaria 2005). Human rights abuses attributed to U.S. forces, such as at Abu Ghraib and Guantanamo, may undermine U.S. efforts to promote democracy and human rights in Iraq. And the transition from authoritarianism to democracy may cause terrorism to increase first and decline only later (Abadie 2004; Ignatieff 2005, 44–45).

- *Deterrence.* Attacking and deposing governments that support terrorism and WMD may deter other rogue states from potential violence. For example, soon after the war in Iraq, Libya admitted its nuclear weapons program and agreed to dismantle it. Bush administration officials credited the change in Libya to the example of Iraq (Wortzel 2004). Perhaps Iran and North Korea will be similarly deterred (Schmitt 2004). Others doubt that the war in Iraq is providing the impetus for these changes. They note that Muammar Qadaffi had reportedly been trying to strike a deal since the Clinton administration, and the deal became possible only when an agreement was reached to make his son immune from prosecution in the Lockerbie bombing trial; also, Iran and North Korea did not seem to be any more cooperative after the war in Iraq than before— indeed, the war may have induced them to rush even faster to bolster their nuclear arsenals in order to deter a potential U.S. strike.

- *Diversion.* Perhaps the continuing violent insurgency in Iraq is actually a benefit, on the theory that it diverts Islamist terrorists away from other targets (such as the U.S. homeland) to the fighting in Iraq. The claim is that the Islamist radicals care most about Muslim control of Muslim countries and less about attacking the United States per se; by this reasoning, the U.S. invasion of Iraq drew thousands of foreign fighters (and al Qaeda leader Abu Musab al Zarqawi, killed in 2006) into Iraq to combat U.S. troops, thereby diverting the terrorists from planning attacks elsewhere. On the other hand, the continuing war in Iraq may be serving as a recruiting and training ground for new jihadists who will thereby be better equipped to attack the United States and Europe in the future.

- *Resilience.* Hardening targets and infrastructure against terror, such as by improving security, strengthening buildings, developing vaccines, and improving response planning, could also help shield against risks unrelated to terrorism, such as crime, accidents, severe weather, and pandemic disease. On the other hand, counterterrorism measures could divert funding and attention away from these purposes, undermining resilience.

- *Transportation safety.* Aviation security systems could not only reduce aviation fatalities, but also reduce highway traffic fatalities by enhancing the perception that air travel is safe and by reducing the delay imposed by airport screening, thereby increasing air travel, reducing automobile travel, and reducing highway accidents. But aviation security systems that increase delay (or other costs) would have the opposite effect, inducing greater highway travel and highway fatalities.

Costs

Counterterrorism policies can be costly both in out-of-pocket expenses and in social costs imposed. This subsection focuses on financial outlays. Other adverse impacts of the war, such as military and civilian casualties, are discussed in the subsection below, "Increase in Countervailing Risks."

- *Out-of-pocket expenses. Ex ante*, the Bush administration was reluctant to name a number but appeared to predict costs for the war in Iraq of under $100 billion. Former economic adviser Lawrence Lindsey was evidently fired for stating publicly that the costs would be between $100 billion and $200 billion. Combining military, occupation, reconstruction, and humanitarian spending, Davis et al. (2003) estimated $125 billion in expenses, while Nordhaus (2002, 77) predicted expenses ranging from $156 to $745 billion per decade. But *ex post*, the total of such expenses from the beginning of the war in March 2003 through June 2005 (just over two years) had already reached over $200 billion and continued to grow. Wallsten and Kosec (2005) counted the direct expenses by United States and coalition countries through August 2005 at over $248 billion. Moreover, after two years of the war in Iraq, Wallsten and Kosec (2005) found, in contrast to Davis et al. (2003), that the actual costs substantially exceeded the benefits, both from 2003 to 2005 and forecast to 2015, including both direct expenses and human casualties (valued economically), comparing those incurred in the war and those avoided by the war (the latter by liberating Iraq from the Saddam regime; they do not assess the change in risk of terrorist attack on the United States). Bilmes and Stiglitz (2008) estimated the cost, including medical care for returning veterans and the cost of lost lives, at over $3 trillion.

- *Social costs.* Nordhaus (2002, 77) predicted other economic costs, largely related to oil prices, ranging from a savings of $57 billion to a cost of $1.169 trillion. Thus, in total, Nordhaus's estimates ranged from about $100 billion per decade in the "low" case (short war) to about $2 trillion per decade in the "high" case (in which "the war drags on, occupation is lengthy, nation-building is costly, the war destroys a large part of Iraq's oil infrastructure, there is lingering military and political resistance in the Islamic world to U.S. occupation, and there are major adverse psychological reactions to the conflict"). The effect of the war on the price of oil was a major component of both of Nordhaus's scenarios, accounting for almost half the net costs in each case. Nordhaus put the cost of oil in 2004 at about $25/barrel in the "low" scenario and about $65/barrel in the "high" scenario (drawing on work by George Perry) (Nordhaus 2002, 73 and Figure 1). In fact, the price of oil in August 2004 was about $40 to $45 per barrel, about halfway between Nordhaus's "low" scenario and his "high" scenario. By June 2005, the price had reached about $60/barrel. If this price increase is mostly due to the war in Iraq, then the cost of the war is nearer the high end of his range.

- *Duration.* A key uncertainty in Nordhaus's estimate is the duration of the occupation of Iraq and the intensity of the insurgency. The longer and more intense, the higher the costs. *Ex ante*, on February 7, 2003, Secretary of Defense Donald Rumsfeld predicted the war would last between six days and six months; by June 26, 2005, he said the insurgency might last up to 12 years.

Increase in Countervailing Risks

All risk management measures can have the perverse effect of increasing other risks (Wiener 1998). Such "risk-risk tradeoffs" are pervasive in human decisionmaking (Graham and Wiener 1995). The use of foreign policy and military force to reduce risks such as terrorism and WMD is not immune to risk-risk trade-offs (Stern 2002). Indeed, history is replete with military strategies that proved ineffectual or counterproductive— what Barbara Tuchman has called the "March of Folly" (Tuchman 1984).

Moreover, terrorism is a dynamic strategic risk. Because terrorists are strategic actors who respond to countermeasures, assessing the full consequences of a counterterrorism strategy must include attention to such responses (Bier and Abhichandani 2002). For example, hardening some targets against attack (if such defenses are observable) can induce terrorists to shift their attacks to other targets (Lakdawalla and Zanjani 2002; Keohane and Zeckhauser 2003; Clotfelter 1978). Or, when governments begin profiling a particular type of suspect, terrorists may recruit another type. For example, airline screening for particular passenger attributes may yield false negatives as terrorists deploy operatives selected to evade the profile (or switch to other targets such as trains or ports); likewise, screening may elicit false positives that snare innocent travelers and condition inspectors to relax their vigilance. A focus on men from Islamic countries may lead al Qaeda to turn increasingly to women and other recruits who do not fit the standard profile of a Middle Eastern male (Stern 2003b).

The countervailing risks of counterterrorism measures may include the following:

- *Collateral damage—civilian deaths.* Data on civilian and military deaths in war are not easy to find, and those data that are available may be disputed or unreliable. Raiding buildings where terrorists have taken hostages can kill both combatants and hostages, as occurred in a Moscow theatre in 2002 and at a school in Beslan, Russia, in September 2004. Bombing terrorist camps and military facilities, even with precision-guided munitions, can kill nearby civilians. In the Afghanistan and Iraq wars, *ex ante*, U.S. officials predicted that U.S. troops would be greeted as liberators and the wars could last just days with few civilian casualties. Davis et al. (2003) predicted up to 35,000 deaths from the war in Iraq. *Ex post*, these two wars have lasted longer and have killed thousands so far, including about 4,400 U.S. soldiers by 2010. The U.S. and UK militaries have not kept, or have not disclosed, counts of civilian deaths in Afghanistan and Iraq. Private analysts have attempted to keep such data. By May 2003, civilian deaths from the war in Afghanistan were roughly 3,300, with the vast majority occurring in the first four months of war, from October 2001 to February 2002, according to an accounting by University of New Hampshire economist Marc Herold (http://pubpages.unh.edu/~mwherold/). From March 2003 through October

2005, civilian deaths from the Iraq war were roughly 27,000, according to the website www.iraqbodycount.net, maintained by independent researchers drawing on Herold's methodology. But an estimate by public health researchers from Johns Hopkins University and their colleagues, based on surveys of a sample of households in Iraq and published in the peer-reviewed medical journal *The Lancet*, estimated that the number of civilian deaths resulting from the Iraq war was closer to 100,000 or more through October 2004, principally due to air strikes (Roberts et al. 2004), or up to 600,000 through July 2006 (Burnham et al. 2006). At the same time, the extent of collateral damage caused by U.S. forces appears to be declining over time, probably because of increased use of precision weapons technologies, and compared to earlier wars (such as World War II) in which civilian populations were deliberately targeted (Knickerbocker 2004).

- *Civil liberties.* Expanding surveillance and information collection, such as NSA surveillance of Americans' electronic communications, can intrude on privacy. Preventive detention of captured enemy fighters in military camps such as at Guantanamo Bay indefinitely, without trial, or with trial in military tribunals rather than civilian courts, may violate their civil liberties; that question has been debated in the courts—e.g., the Supreme Court's decision in *Boumediene v. Bush*, 553 U.S. 723 (2008), holding that detainees at Guantanamo are entitled to habeas corpus. Restricting suspected terrorists' access to the country can also impinge on innocent immigrants' civil liberties (Keeney 2001).

- *Accidents.* Giving airline pilots guns to stop terrorists may lead to in-flight accidents, theft, or misuse. Controlling access to information on pathogens in order to prevent bioterrorism can increase the impact of natural disease outbreaks (Stern 2003a).

- *Blowback: increased terrorist recruiting and reprisals.* The invasion and occupation of Iraq could increase terrorist recruiting by causing anger and humiliation among the Iraqi people and Muslims generally (Johnson 2004; Hutchins 2004). Ayman al-Zawahiri, bin Laden's second in command, appears to believe (as did Caribbean writer and revolutionary Frantz Fanon) that violence is a "cleansing force" that frees the oppressed youth from his "inferiority complex, despair, and inaction," restoring his self-respect (Fanon 1961). The U.S. and UK attack on Iraq, not aimed at al Qaeda, followed by the U.S. occupation of a Muslim country—accompanied by occasional religious rhetoric from U.S. generals and officials about a "crusade" to "rid the world of evil-doers," by images of U.S. soldiers humiliating Iraqi prisoners at Abu Ghraib, or by alleged desecration of the Koran by U.S. interrogators at Guantanamo—may all further the sense of humiliation and give credence to the Islamist nihilist view, thereby increasing the flow of recruits to radical Islamist terror cells (Pillar 2004b). The presence of foreign occupying troops has been identified as a particular factor in motivating suicide bombers (in both secular and religious movements) against the occupier's troops and home country (Pape 2005; Bloom 2005). Many advocates of the war on terrorism have criticized the invasion of Iraq as likely to strengthen terrorism by expanding the ranks of new recruits to al Qaeda (e.g., Pillar 2004b; Scheuer 2004; Fallows 2004; Clarke 2004; Cirincione et al. 2004, 58; Adams 2004). Cirincione et al. state: "It was almost inevitable that a U.S. victory would add to the sense of cultural, ethnic, and religious humiliation that is known to be a prime motivator of al Qaeda-type terrorists. It was widely predicted by experts beforehand that the war would boost recruitment to this network" (2004, 58). Observers of diverse political stripes worry about the impact of the war on support for America in the Islamic world. "Bush invaded Iraq, united the Arab world against us, isolated us from Europe, and fulfilled to the letter bin Laden's prophecy as to what we were about. We won the war in three weeks—and we may have lost the Islamic world for a generation," Pat Buchanan warned (2004, 84). Al Gore has made the same argument (Gore 2004). It bears noting that there is no disloyalty in recognizing that an aggressive precautionary strategy may be counterproductive. Refusing to recognize such consequences is classic military folly (Tuchman 1984). It is more loyal to our troops and the nation to deploy our forces effectively, not perversely. Israel, staunchly antiterrorist, recently chose to end its own practice of demolishing the homes of Palestinian militants' relatives, because Israeli analysts found that this policy inspired more terrorism, not less (Myre 2005).

- *Distraction from greater threats.* The extended attention and resource commitment to Iraq may have distracted the United States from al Qaeda in other countries such as Afghanistan, and from other rogue states such as Iran and North Korea—which are much closer to deploying WMD than Iraq was (Fallows 2004, 72). As the United States got bogged down in Iraq (which proved not to have WMD), it may have forfeited the ability to address the target risk of WMD where they really exist, such as in Iran and North Korea and perhaps elsewhere.

- *Reduced U.S. military recruiting.* The extended war in Iraq, and policies such as "stop-loss" to prevent soldiers from returning home after their originally agreed-upon service duty is completed, sharply reduced U.S. Army recruiting rates (Schmitt 2005; *New York Times* 2005). This deficit may undermine the ability of the United States to fight the next (more important) war.

- *Emboldened adversaries.* The war may be showing the insurgents and the world that the superpower U.S. military can be held at bay for months, thereby inspiring additional groups to be confrontational.

- *Underreaction next time.* The belief (accurate or not) that U.S. and UK claims of WMD in Iraq were a false positive—"crying wolf"—may lead other countries to disbelieve the United States and UK the next time they assert a WMD threat; and yet the next time may be tragically true—just as the wolf ultimately ate the sheep after no one would believe the boy shepherd. The present false positive and overreaction may yield a future underreaction, thereby incurring just the risk of a WMD attack on the United States or Europe that the precautionary Bush administration strategy was intended to prevent.

- *Dividing NATO.* The war in Iraq divided the NATO alliance, at least temporarily. The United States, UK, Poland, Italy, and Spain joined the war, but

France, Germany, Russia, and others opposed it. Spain later switched parties and withdrew. If the western alliance remains divided, that may do more to undermine the future ability to combat terrorism and WMD than the war in Iraq has done (if any) to advance that goal.

- *Tempting others to preempt.* The UN's High-Level Panel (2004) argued that authorizing unilateral preventive war is an invitation for all to do so—"allowing one to so act is to allow all." Setting the precedent of unilateral preventive war may induce fear of surprise attack, tempting others to attack first lest they be attacked. The result may be more frequent wars among other states, some of which entangle the United States; another might be the possibility that a country like North Korea might strike the United States first, not expecting strategic victory, but in the hopes of decapitating the U.S. government. The preemptive war "[s]trategy fails to acknowledge that a preemptive attack could precipitate the very attacks it seeks to prevent. An obvious danger is that the rogue state will use its weapons of mass destruction before it loses them—or deliberately give them to a group that will" (Daalder et al. 2002).

- *Dissemination of WMD and related materials.* Another countervailing danger in going to war in Iraq was the risk that WMD materials and expertise would be disseminated rather than destroyed. Indeed, attacking Iraq—without protecting its borders—may well have made it *more* likely that WMD components and expertise would end up in the hands of terrorists. Ironically, this countervailing danger would be higher if Iraq really had possessed the WMD that the Bush and Blair administrations argued it had, and if Saddam really had been prepared to share his WMD with terrorists. Although these assertions now appear to have been false, some dissemination of materials and expertise appears to have occurred. The buildup to the U.S.-UK invasion took several months, allowing ample time to hide or relocate WMD. After the war, no WMD were found, but Iraqi authorities informed the International Atomic Energy Association (IAEA) that 380 tons of high explosives under IAEA seal had been stolen—explosives that the IAEA had specifically warned the United States to guard, apparently in vain (Glanz et al. 2004). The IAEA reported to the UN Security Council that satellite imagery has shown many instances of the dismantlement of entire buildings that housed precision equipment, as well as the removal of equipment and materials. Biological materials may have been stolen as well, according to a report coauthored by Jessica Matthews, who visited Iraq to investigate; enough material to produce a "dirty bomb" was stolen (Cirincione et al. 2004, 58–59). Once scientists know how to grow and disseminate biological agents effectively, new stockpiles can be rapidly rebuilt. Perhaps some of Saddam's weaponeers, displaced or disaffected by the invasion and overthrow, provided their expertise to terrorists. Moreover, the strategy of preemption (or preventive war) could itself induce rogue states to use or pass on their nascent WMD. "An obvious danger is that the rogue state will ... deliberately give [its WMD] to groups that will [use them]. A less obvious danger is that terrorists will be able to use the chaos that accompanies war to buy or steal weapons of mass destruction" (Daalder et al. 2002).

Net Impacts

No simple quantitative bottom line can be calculated. It is more important to recognize the full set of consequences than to reach quantitative precision about each (Sunstein 2000). The two *ex ante* estimates were both incomplete: Nordhaus did not count military or civilian casualties due to the war, nor did he attempt to quantify or compare the benefits of the war. Davis et al. (2003) argued that the war would yield substantial net benefits, both to the United States and to the Iraqi people, but the Davis et al. calculation did not include the ancillary benefits of spreading democracy elsewhere, or of deterring other rogue states; nor did it even include the target risk reduction benefit of seizing Iraqi WMD (it counted only the avoided risk of additional low-technology terror attacks similar to 9/11); the Davis et al. estimate counted only out-of-pocket costs and did not appear to account for the effect of the war on oil prices and macroeconomic performance, which were the two largest items in Nordhaus's cost estimate; nor did Davis et al. include the countervailing risks that could increase the risk to the United States of new terror attacks.

Lessons

Events are still unfolding, so we must wait to evaluate the ultimate *ex post* consequences of present counterterrorism policies. It will take years to tell whether the war in Iraq and domestic counterterrorism measures will actually have reduced or increased the risk of terrorist attacks on the United States or will have had other impacts. The absence of a clear counterfactual scenario (what would have happened otherwise) may make it very difficult to say what the impact of these choices has been. Repeated analysis of consequences before, during, and after a policy is implemented will be essential to deciding, learning, updating, and adaptive improvement. And, of course, such analyses must compare alternative options for reducing the risk of terrorism, including precaution (preventive war), civil defense (target hardening and decentralization), undermining terrorist groups by infiltration and impeding financing and recruitment (including via competing carrots), and other alternatives. (For a useful economic analysis of alternatives, see Frey (2004), who concludes that military intervention and deterrence are likely to be less effective at reducing the risk of future terrorist attacks than are alternative strategies such as decentralizing targets and recruiting potential terrorists to other pursuits.) Here we have proposed an analytic framework and institutional mechanism for making such comparative evaluations in the future.

The risk of terrorist attacks is sufficiently serious (even if low probability) that it may warrant precaution. But precautionary measures may turn out to increase instead of decrease the risk, such as by fostering blowback, increased recruitment of terrorists, theft of WMD, displacement to softer targets, and impairment of U.S. military capabilities. While considering worst-case scenarios can be important for the development of sound policy, taking action based only on the worst-case scenario can introduce unforeseen dangers and costs (Cirincione et al. 2004, 54; Sunstein 2007). Successful precautionary counterterrorism measures require *ex ante* consideration of expected consequences—that is, full portfolio impact assessment. As we argue elsewhere (Stern and Wiener 2008), just as *ex ante* impact analysis of regulatory measures is routine in the health and environmental area, with White House oversight a similar analytic approach should be adopted for precaution in the national security arena. Along these lines, the 9/11 Commission urged that the United States needs "a forward-looking strategic plan systematically analyzing assets, risks, costs, and benefits" of counterterrorism options (9/11 Commission Report 2004, 391). Lieutenant Colonel Michael Weeks proposed that the new National Security Strategy be accompanied by the use of concepts from economic analysis to help make decisions:

> We must make new assessments of our capabilities and consider both direct and indirect costs [including] ... [c]ollateral damage. ... With precision weapons ... we have the ability to put a bomb through a particular window. What we don't always have is the technology to decide which window we should choose. ... If we are to make efficient decisions about where to intervene, we must be able to assess the costs and benefits of such actions. ... The primary point is that we should make a full accounting of the elements in the equation in order to arrive at the appropriate decision. (Weeks 2003)

As in other areas, the case of terrorism teaches that precaution driven by overstated risk assessments and fear of dreaded risks will not yield sound policies. Sensible *ex ante* analysis can identify foreseeable but unintended consequences. Many of the new risks introduced by the war were foreseeable, at least as plausible scenarios. Yet there does not seem to have been a systematic analysis of these benefits, costs, and risks before the decision to engage in preventive war. More generally, there does not appear to be an institutional process for *ex ante* or *ex post* review of the expected consequences of proposed counterterrorism measures. Such a process should be established in each government or intergovernmental body taking important counterterrorism decisions. The point here is not that the war in Iraq or domestic measures were clear mistakes—though, viewed *ex post*, the war in Iraq appears to have yielded a minimal reduction in target risk (especially given the absence of WMD in Iraq), unclear ancillary benefits (though Iraq has moved partially toward democracy), significant costs (trillions of U.S. expenses, not to mention great costs to coalition partners and to Iraq itself), and significant countervailing risks (including military and civilian lives lost, increased terrorist recruiting, neglect of other risks of WMD and other rogue states, impaired U.S. military capabilities, and potential loss of WMD from Iraq). The point here is larger: counterterrorism—especially precautionary counterterrorism—should draw valuable insights from risk analysis. Like other risk management interventions, it should be preceded by (and later appraised using) a serious, systematic analysis of the full portfolio of expected impacts. The Obama administration appears to be favoring this approach by emphasizing in its new National Security Strategy that "[w]hile the use of force is sometimes necessary, we will ... carefully weigh the costs and risks of action against the costs and risks of inaction" (Obama 2010, 22). This process should be established in appropriate institutional mechanisms (Stern and Wiener 2008). The alternative is repeated policy errors with potentially devastating adverse consequences.

Acknowledgments

We are grateful to Paul Bracken, Peter Feaver, Peter Jutro, Alexandra Lloyd, Ragnar Lofstedt, David Schanzer, Anthony Wiener, and participants at the Fourth Transatlantic Dialogue on Precaution, held at Duke University in September 2004, for helpful comments on prior drafts; and to Zia Cromer and Greg Andeck for excellent research assistance.

References

9/11 Commission Report. 2004. *Final Report of the National Commission on Terrorist Attacks against the United States: Authorized Edition.* New York: W.W. Norton.

Abadie, Alberto. 2004. Poverty, Political Freedom, and the Roots of Terrorism. NBER Working Paper 10859. October. www.nber.org/papers/w10859 (accessed July 27, 2010).

Ackerman, David M. 2003. International Law and the Preemptive Use of Force against Iraq. Congressional Research Service (CRS) Report RS21314 (updated April 11, 2003).

Adams, Christopher. 2004. Bush Described as al-Qaeda's "Best Recruiting Sergeant" by UK Ambassador. *Financial Times* Sept. 21, 1.

Alberto, Valerie, and Dominique Bogatz. 2004. Computer Assisted Passenger Prescreening System ("CAPPS II"): National Security versus Civil Liberties. www.maxwell.syr.edu/uploadedFiles/campbell/events/AlbertoBogatz.pdf (accessed July 27, 2010).

Albright, Madeleine. 2002. Interview with Margaret Warner on the PBS show *The News Hour with Jim Lehrer.* December 19. www.pbs.org/newshour/bb/middle_east/july-dec02/iraq_12-19.html (accessed July 27, 2010).

Andrews, Richard N. L. 1999. *Managing the Environment, Managing Ourselves: A History of American Environmental Policy.* New Haven, CT: Yale University Press.

Beck, Ulrich. 1992. *The Risk Society.* Newbury Park, CA: Sage Publications.

Bentham, Jeremy. 1830. *Principles of Legislation.* Boston, MA: Wells and Lilly.

Berman, Ilan. 2004. U.S. Plays Hardball with Syria. *Washington Times,* May 23. www.washingtontimes.com/op-ed/20040523-094452-1943r.htm (accessed July 27, 2010).

Bier, Vicki M., and Vinod Abhichandani. 2002. Optimal Allocation of Resources for Defense of Simple Series and Parallel Systems from Determined Adversaries. *ASCE Conference Proceedings* 129: 5. http://dx.doi.org/10.1061/40694(2003)5 (accessed May 12, 2010).

Bilmes, Linda, and Joseph Stiglitz. 2008. The Three Trillion Dollar War. *London Sunday Times,* Feb. 23. www.timesonline.co.uk/tol/comment/columnists/guest_contributors/article3419840.ece (accessed July 27, 2010).

Blix, Hans. 2003. Blix: U.S. Led Us Astray on Iraq. *Kathimerini* (Greece's international English language newspaper), Sept. 22. www.ekathimerini.com/4dcgi/_w_articles_politics_100014_22/09/2003_34326 (accessed July 27, 2010).

Bloom, Mia. 2005. *Dying to Kill: The Allure of Suicide Terror.* New York: Columbia University Press.

Brom, Shlomo. 2003. The War in Iraq: An Intelligence Failure? *Strategic Assessment* 6 (3).

Buchanan, Patrick J. 2004. *Where the Right Went Wrong.* New York: Thomas Dunne Books.

Burnham, Gilbert, Riyadh Lafta, Shannon Doocy, and Les Roberts. 2006. Mortality after the 2003 Invasion of Iraq: A Cross-Sectional Cluster Sample Survey. *Lancet* 368 (Oct. 12): 1421–1428.

Bush, George W. 2002a. Remarks by the President at 2002 Graduation Exercise of the United States Military Academy, West Point, New York. June 1. www.whitehouse.gov/news/releases/2002/06/20020601-3.html (accessed March 1, 2003).

———. 2002b. *The National Security Strategy of the United States of America.* September 17. Introduction and Part V. www.whitehouse.gov/nsc/nss.html (accessed March 1, 2003).

———. 2002c. Speech in Cincinnati. October 7.

Butler, Lord, Sir John Chilcot, Lord Inge, Michael Mates, and Ann Taylor. 2004. The Butler Report Review of Intelligence on WMD. July 14. www.archive2.official-documents.co.uk/document/deps/hc/.../898.pdf (accessed July 27, 2010).

Chalk, Peter. 1996. *West European Terrorism and Counter-Terrorism.* New York: St. Martin's Press.

Cirincione, Joseph, Jessica T. Matthews, George Perkovich, and Alex Orton. 2004. WMD in Iraq: Evidence and Implications. Carnegie Institute for International Peace. January. www.carnegieendowment.org/files/Iraq3FullText.pdf (accessed July 27, 2010).

Clarke, Richard. 2004. *Against All Enemies.* New York: Free Press.

Clotfelter, Charles T. 1978. Private Security and the Public Safety. *Journal of Urban Economics* 5: 388–402.

Commission on the Intelligence Capabilities of the U.S. Regarding WMD. 2005. Report to the President of the United States. March 31. www.gpoaccess.gov/wmd/index.html (accessed July 27, 2010).

Daalder, Ivo H., James M. Lindsay, and James B. Steinberg. 2002. The Bush National Security Strategy: An Evaluation. Brookings Institution Policy Brief 109 (October). www.brookings.edu/papers/2002/10defense_daalder.aspx (accessed July 27, 2010).

Dana, David. 2003. A Behavioral Economic Defense of the Precautionary Principle. *Northwestern University Law Review* 97: 1315.

Davis, Steven J., Kevin M. Murphy, and Robert H. Topel. 2003. War in Iraq versus Containment: Weighing the Costs. Unpublished paper. March 20.

DHS (U.S. Department of Homeland Security). 2003. CAPPS II: Myths and Facts. February 13. www.dhs.gov/xnews/releases/press_release_0348.shtm (accessed July 27, 2010).

DiPaolo, Amanda, and Bartosz H. Stanislawski. 2004. Information Sharing: The European Experience. http://insct.syr.edu/.../Information%20Sharing%20Conf/DiPaoloStanislawski.pdf (accessed July 27, 2010).

Duelfer, Charles. 2004. Comprehensive Report of the Special Advisor to the DCI on Iraq's WMD. September 30. https://www.cia.gov/lib/ (accessed July 27, 2010).

EEA (European Environment Agency). 2002. *Late Lessons from Early Warnings.* Copenhagen: European Environment Agency.

The Economist. 2005. The War on Terror: That Not-Winning Feeling. June 18, 27.

Fallows, James. 2004. Bush's Lost Year. *Atlantic Monthly* (October): 68–84.

Fanon, Frantz. 1961. *The Wretched of the Earth.* New York: Grove Press.

Feaver, Peter. 2003. Different Medicines for Different Maladies. *Raleigh News and Observer,* Jan. 12, Opinion section, 1.

———. 2004. The Fog of WMD. *Washington Post,* Jan. 28, A21.

Feinstein, Lee, and Anne-Marie Slaughter. 2004. A Duty to Prevent. *Foreign Affairs* 83 (1): 136–151.

Fischer, Joschka. 2002. Address by Joschka Fischer, Minister for Foreign Affairs of the Federal Republic of Germany, at the 57th Session of the United Nations General Assembly, New York. September 14, 2002. www.auswaertiges-amt.de/www/en/aussenpolitik/index_html (accessed March 6, 2003).

Fleischer, Ari. 2002. Briefing by White House Press Secretary Ari Fleischer. December 5. www.commondreams.org/headlines02/1205-10.htm (accessed July 27, 2010).

Frey, Bruno. 2004. *Dealing with Terrorism: Stick or Carrot?.* London: Edward Elgar.

Glanz, James, William J. Broad, and David E. Sanger. 2004. Tracking the Weapons: Huge Cache of Explosives Vanished from Site in Iraq. *New York Times,* Oct. 25.

Goldenberg, Suzanne. 2005. Ex-CIA Chief Eats Humble Pie. *Guardian,* April 29. www.guardian.co.uk/Iraq/Story/0,2763,1472826,00.html (accessed May 11, 2010).

Gore, Al. 1992. *Earth in the Balance.* Boston, MA: Houghton Mifflin.

———. 2004. Remarks. May 26. www.moveonpac.org/goreremarks052604.html (accessed May 29, 2004).

Graham, John D. 2002. The Role of Precaution in Risk Assessment and Management: An American's View. Remarks at the First Transatlantic Dialogue on Precaution, Bruges, Belgium, January 11–12. www.whitehouse.gov/omb/inforeg/eu_speech.html (accessed July 27, 2010).

Graham, John D., and Jonathan B. Wiener. 1995. *Risk vs. Risk: Tradeoffs in Protecting Health and the Environment.* Cambridge, MA: Harvard University Press.

High-Level Panel on Threats, Challenges, and Change. 2004. *A More Secure World: Our Shared Responsibility*, Report to the Secretary General, United Nations General Assembly, 59th Session, Agenda Item 55, December 2, 2004, A/59/565. www.un.org/secureworld/report.pdf (accessed May 11, 2010).

Hutchins, Robert. 2004. X+9/11. *Foreign Policy* 143 (July–August): 70–72.

Ignatieff, Michael. 2005. Who Are Americans to Think That Freedom Is Theirs to Spread? *New York Times Sunday Magazine*, June 26, 42–47.

Jehl, Douglas. 2004. CIA Review Is Critical of Prewar Analysis. *New York Times*, Sept. 22, A18.

Jervis, Robert. 2003. Understanding the Bush Doctrine. *Political Science Quarterly* 118: 365–388.

Johnson, Chalmers. 2004. *Blowback: The Costs and Consequences of American Empire.* 2nd ed. New York: Henry Holt (Owl Books).

Jordan, Andrew, and Timothy O'Riordan. 1999. The Precautionary Principle in Contemporary Environmental Policy and Politics. In *Protecting Public Health and the Environment: Implementing the Precautionary Principle*, edited by Carolyn Raffensperger and Joel Tickner. Washington, DC: Island Press, 15–35.

Kahneman, Daniel, Paul Slovic, and Amos Tversky. 1982. *Judgment under Uncertainty: Heuristics and Biases.* Cambridge: Cambridge University Press.

Kaplan, Eben. 2006. Targets for Terrorists: Post 9/11 Aviation Security. Council on Foreign Relations. www.cfr.org/publication/11397/targets_for_terrorists.html (accessed July 27, 2010).

Keeney, Ralph. 2001. Countering Terrorism: The Clash of Values. *Operations Research/Management Sciences Today* 28 (6): 20–22.

Kennan, George. 1947. The Sources of Soviet Conduct. *Foreign Affairs.* July.

Keohane, Nathaniel, and Richard Zeckhauser. 2003. The Ecology of Terror Defense. *Journal of Risk and Uncertainty* 26 (2–3): 201–229. http://ksghome.harvard.edu/~.RZeckhauser.Academic.ksg/ecology_of_terror.pdf (accessed June 16, 2004).

Knickerbocker, Brad. 2004. Who Counts the Civilian Casualties? *Christian Science Monitor*, March 31. www.csmonitor.com/2004/0331/p15s01-wogi.html (accessed July 5, 2004).

Koslowski, Rey. 2004. *International Cooperation on Electronic Advanced Passenger Information Transfer and Passport Biometrics.* Montreal: ISA, Mar. 17–20.

Krugman, Paul. 2003. Who's Accountable? *New York Times*, June 10, A27.

Lakdawalla, Darius, and George Zanjani. 2002. Insurance, Self-Protection, and the Economics of Terrorism (September). NBER Working Paper No. W9215. http://ssrn.com/abstract=332259 (accessed May 11, 2010).

Levin, Alan. 2002. Armed Pilots Are Months Away. *USA Today*, Nov. 24. www.usatoday.com/news/washington/2002-11-24-armed-pilots_x.htm (accessed July 27, 2010).

Lewis, Anthony. 2001. The Feelings of a Coup. *New York Times*, March 31, A15.

Loewenberg, Samuel. 2003. Precaution Is for Europeans. *New York Times*, May 19, 4.14.

Lott, John R., Jr. 2003. P.C. Air Security: When Will Our Pilots Be Armed? *National Review Online*, Sept. 2. www.nationalreview.com/comment/comment-lott090203.asp (accessed July 27, 2010).

Malkin, Michelle. 2004. *In Defense of Internment.* Washington, DC: Regnery Publishing.

Murphy, Rex. 2003. CBC Radio One. *Cross-Country Checkup.* Feb. 9. www.cbc.ca/checkup/archive/2003/intro030209.html (accessed July 27, 2010).

Myre, Greg. 2005. Israel Halts Decades-Old Practice of Demolishing Militants' Homes. *New York Times*, Feb. 18.

New York Times. 2003. Editorial. The Failure to Find Iraqi Weapons. Sept. 26, A24.

———. 2005. The Death Spiral of the Volunteer Army. May 29.

Nieman, Susan. 2002. *Evil in Modern Thought.* Princeton, NJ: Princeton University Press.

Nordhaus, William. 2002. The Economic Consequences of a War with Iraq. In *War with Iraq: Costs, Consequences, and Alternatives.* American Academy of Arts and Sciences. www.econ.yale.edu/~nordhaus/homepage/homepage.htm (accessed July 27, 2010).

Norris, Clive, Mike McCahill, and David Wood. 2004. Editorial. The Growth of CCTV: A Global Perspective on the International Diffusion of Video Surveillance in Publicly Accessible Space.

Surveillance and Society 2 (2–3): 110–135. www.surveillance-and-society.org/cctv.htm (accessed July 27, 2010).

Obama, Barack. 2010. National Security Strategy of the United States of America. May 27. Washington, DC: White House.

Pape, Robert A. 2005. *Dying to Win: The Strategic Logic of Suicide Terrorism.* New York: Random House.

Percival, Robert. 1998. Environmental Legislation and the Problem of Collective Action. *Duke Environmental Law and Policy Forum* 9: 9–28.

Peres-Rivas, Manuel. 2001. Bush Vows to Rid the World of Evil-Doers. Sept. 16. http://archives.cnn.com/2001/US/09/16/gen.bush.terrorism/ (accessed July 27, 2010).

Pillar, Paul. 2004a. A Scapegoat Is Not a Solution. *New York Times*, June 4.

———. 2004b. Counterterrorism after Al Qaeda. *Washington Quarterly* 27 (3): 101–113.

Pollack, Kenneth M. 2002. *The Threatening Storm: The Case for Invading Iraq.* New York: Random House.

Posner, Richard A. 2004a. *Catastrophe: Risk and Response.* New York: Oxford University Press.

———. 2004b. The 9/11 Report: A Dissent. *New York Times Book Review*, Aug. 29, 1, 9.

Powell, Colin. 2003. Remarks to the United Nations Security Council. March 7. www.un.org/News/Press/docs/2003/sc7658.doc.htm (accessed July 27, 2010).

Raffensperger, Carolyn and Joel, Tickner, eds. 1999. *Protecting Public Health and the Environment: Implementing the Precautionary Principle.* Washington, DC: Island Press.

Rascoff, Samuel, and Richard L. Revesz. 2002. The Biases of Risk Tradeoff Analysis: Towards Parity in Regulatory Policy. *University of Chicago Law Review* 89: 1763–1786.

Rio Declaration. 1992. Rio Declaration on Environment and Development. *International Legal Materials* 31: 876.

Robbins, James S. 2003. They Can't Handle the Truth: Assessing the Evidence. *National Review Online*, Feb. 6. www.nationalreview.com/robbins/robbins020603.asp (accessed July 27, 2010).

Roberts, Les, Riyadh Lafta, Richard Garfield, Jamal Khudhairi, and Gilbert Burnham. 2004. Mortality Before and After the 2003 Invasion of Iraq: Cluster Sample Survey. *Lancet* 364 (9448): 1857–1864. www.thelancet.com/journals/lancet/PIIS0140673604174412/fulltext.

Runciman, David. 2004. The Precautionary Principle. *London Review of Books* 26 (7), April 1. www.lrb.co.uk/v26/n07/runc01_.html (accessed July 27, 2010).

Saletan, William. 2003. Security Council Scorecard: How Powell Did at the UN. *Slate*, Feb. 5. http://slate.msn.com/id/2078209/ (accessed July 27, 2010).

Sanderson, Hans, and Soren Peterson. 2001. Power Analysis as a Reflexive Scientific Tool for Interpretation and Implementation of the Precautionary Principle in the European Union. *Environmental Science and Pollution Research* 8: 1–6.

Sandin, Per. 1999. Dimensions of the Precautionary Principle. *Human and Ecological Risk Assessment* 5: 889–907.

Scheuer, Michael. 2004. *Imperial Hubris: Why the West Is Losing the War on Terror.* New York: Potomac Books.

Schmitt, Eric. 2005. Army Officials Voice Concern over Shortfall in Recruitment. *New York Times*, March 4, A1.

Schmitt, Gary. 2004. Shooting First. *Los Angeles Times*, May 30.

SEHN (Science and Environmental Health Network). 2002. Frequently Asked Questions. www.sehn.org/ppfaqs.html (accessed March 1, 2003).

Select Committee on Intelligence (U.S. Senate Select Committee on Intelligence). 2004. *Report on the U.S. Intelligence Community's Prewar Intelligence Assessments on Iraq.* July 7. www.gpoaccess.gov/serialset/creports/iraq.html (accessed July 27, 2010).

Shane, Scott, and David E. Sanger. 2005. The Intelligence Critique: The Report; Bush Panel Finds Big Flaws Remain in U.S. Spy Efforts. *New York Times*, April 1, A1.

Slovic, Paul. 1987. Perception of Risk. *Science* 236: 280.

———. 2000. *The Perception of Risk.* London: Earthscan.

Slovic, Paul, and Elke Weber. 2003. Perception of Risk Posed by Extreme Events. Unpublished paper. Columbia University Center for Hazards and Risk Research. www.ldeo.columbia.edu/chrr/documents/meetings/roundtable/white_papers/slovic_wp.pdf (accessed July 27, 2010).

Stern, Jessica. 1999. *The Ultimate Terrorists*. Cambridge, MA: Harvard University Press.

———. 2002. Dreaded Risks and the Control of Biological Weapons. *International Security* 27 (3): 89–123.

———. 2003a. The Protean Enemy. *Foreign Affairs* 82 (4): 27–40.

———. 2003b. When Bombers Are Women. *Washington Post*, Dec. 18.

Stern, Jessica, and Jonathan B. Wiener. 2008. Precaution against Terrorism. In *Managing Strategic Surprise: Lessons from Risk Management and Risk Assessment*, edited by Paul Bracken. Cambridge: Cambridge University Press.

Sunstein, Cass R. 2000. Cognition and Cost-Benefit Analysis. *Journal of Legal Studies* 29: 1059–1103.

———. 2003. Terrorism and Probability Neglect. *Journal of Risk and Uncertainty* 26 (2–3): 121–136.

———. 2005. *The Laws of Fear: Beyond the Precautionary Principle*. Cambridge: Cambridge University Press.

———. 2007. *Worst-Case Scenarios*. Cambridge, MA: Harvard University Press.

Sunstein, Cass R., and Timur Kuran. 1999. Availability Cascades and Risk Regulation. *Stanford Law Review* 51: 683–768.

TSA (U.S. Transportation Security Administration). 2005. TSA Suspends 30-Minute Rule for Reagan National Airport. July 14. www.tsa.gov/press/releases/2005/press_release_0607.shtm (accessed July 27, 2010).

Tuchman, Barbara W. 1984. *The March of Folly: From Troy to Vietnam*. New York: Ballantine Books.

UN (United Nations Special Commission). 1999. Chronology of Main Events. www.un.org/Depts/unscom/Chronology/chronologyframe.htm (accessed July 28, 2010).

USEU (U.S. Mission to the EU). 2003. U.S., EU Agree on Air Passenger Data Transfer. December 16. www.useu.be/Terrorism/USResponse/Dec1603PNRAgreement.html (site now discontinued).

———. 2004. U.S., EU Sign Agreement on Transfer of Airline Passenger Data. May 28. ec.europa.eu/justice_home/fsj/.../2004-05-28-agreement_en.pdf (accessed July 27, 2010).

Vogel, David. 2003. The Hare and the Tortoise Revisited: The New Politics of Consumer and Environmental Regulation in Europe. *British Journal of Political Science* 33: 557–580.

Wallsten, Scott, and Katrina Kosec. 2005. The Economic Costs of the War in Iraq. Working Paper 05-19. Washington, DC: AEI-Brookings Joint Center for Regulatory Studies. September.

Wallstrom, Margot. 2002. U.S. and EU Environmental Policies: Converging or Diverging? Speech to the European Institute. April 25. http://europa.eu.int/rapid/start/cgi/guesten.ksh?p_action.gettxt=gt&doc=SPEECH/02/184|0|AGED&lg=EN&display= (accessed March 4, 2003).

Weeks, Michael. 2003. Cost-Benefit Economics: Enhancing National Security and Air and Space Power. *Air and Space Power Journal* (Fall). www.airpower.maxwell.af.mil/airchronicles/apj/apj03/fal03/weeks.html (accessed July 27, 2010).

Wiener, Jonathan B. 1998. Managing the Iatrogenic Risks of Risk Management. *Risk: Health Safety and Environment* 9: 49–82.

———. 2002. Precaution in a Multirisk World. In *Human and Ecological Risk Assessment: Theory and Practice*, edited by Dennis D. Paustenbach. New York: John Wiley and Sons, 1509–1531.

———. 2003. Whose Precaution After All? A Comment on the Comparison and Evolution of Risk Regulation Systems. *Duke Journal of Comparative and International Law* 13: 207–262.

———. 2004. Precaution, Risk and Multiplicity. Unpublished paper presented at Harvard Law School Conference on Environmental Law. November 7, 2003, Cambridge, MA.

Wiener, Jonathan B., and Michael D. Rogers. 2002. Comparing Precaution in the U.S. and Europe. *Journal of Risk Research* 5: 317–349.

Wildavsky, Aaron. 1995. *But Is It True?*. Cambridge, MA: Harvard University Press.

Woodward, Bob. 2004. *Plan of Attack*. New York: Simon and Schuster.

Wortzel, Larry M. 2004. Combating Weapons of Mass Destruction. Testimony delivered to the Armed Services Committee. U.S. House of Representatives. March 17.

Yoo, John. 2004. Using Force. *University of Chicago Law Review* 71 (3): 729–797.

Zakaria, Fareed. 2005. How to Change Ugly Regimes. *Newsweek*, June 27, 31.

Zengerle, Jason. 2003. Is Bush Serious about WMDs? Burden of Proof. *The New Republic*, May 12.

A complex interconnected society engaged in innumerable daily interactions is portrayed by Pieter Bruegel the Elder, *The Numbering at Bethlehem* (1566). See the discussion in the text on pages 5, 27, 520, 524, and 554–55.

A society unified behind an iconic idea is portrayed by Eugène Delacroix, *La Liberté Guidant le Peuple* (1830). See the discussion in the text on pages 5, 520, and 554.

PART III
PRECAUTION IN RISK INFORMATION
SYSTEMS

CHAPTER 13

Information Disclosure

Peter H. Sand

*P*recautionary environmental decisionmaking is crucially dependent on access to information—in particular, information on environmental risks. Yet traditional legal systems have tended to favor administrative and corporate secrecy, thereby monopolizing knowledge in the hands of governmental authorities or private stakeholders. This chapter describes innovative initiatives in the United States and Europe to establish an environmental "right-to-know" for civil society, by mandatory disclosure both of government-held information (from the 1966 U.S. Freedom of Information Act to the 1998 UNECE Aarhus Convention and the Council of Europe's 2009 Tromsø Convention) and of industry-held risk data (through pollutant release and transfer registers, and through court-enforced access to "privileged" documentation—for example, on tobacco-related health risks). These disclosure strategies to facilitate precautionary action have spread across the Atlantic and triggered a "third wave" of environmental regulation, replacing or supplementing command-and-control and market-based instruments. However, the chapter also highlights continuing transparency deficits (sometimes resulting in "manufactured uncertainty," prompted either by economic interests or by precaution against countervailing risks such as terrorism) with regard to risk-sensitive information of common concern.

Precaution is a way of coping with uncertainty. Most environmental policymaking and decisionmaking is typically plagued by uncertainty, with regard both to biogeophysical processes and to socioeconomic costs and benefits (Arrow and Fisher 1974; Thompson 1986; Iida 1993; Clyde 1997; Harremoës 2000; Young 2001; Stewart 2002; Gollier et al. 2004). Some of those uncertainties are exogenous, often incalculable, and we simply have to cope with them as risks and unknowns (Knight 1921, 19; Costanza and Cornwell 1992; Ladeur 1994; Cohen and Tallon 2000; Jaeger et al. 2001; Funtowicz and Ravetz 2001; Engel et al. 2002; von Schomberg 2003;

Wesseler et al. 2003).[1] Other information deficits, however, are manifestly endogenous, homemade—"manufactured uncertainties" (Beck 1996), "smokescreen uncertainty" (Lewis 1999, 242), or "strategically manipulated information" (Graham et al. 2009, 22). The sad reality is that we are all too often kept in the dark—through neglect or by design, by public officials or private stakeholders and "knowledge brokers" (Litfin 1994, 4; Sappington and Stiglitz 1987; Stiglitz 1999; Eigen 2003; Roberts 2006). To reduce that level of uncertainty—"information gap filling" (Esty 2004, 140)—therefore becomes a legitimate and crucial element of institutional design to facilitate precautionary action across all sectors, at the national and international levels (Chayes and Chayes 1995, 135; Mitchell 1998; Hansen 1999, 1060; Zoellner 2006).

At the same time, access to information may be viewed as an instrument of democratic governance (Bullinger 1985; van der Lek 1988; Graham 2002b; Hood and Heald 2006; Gupta 2008; Foti et al. 2008),[2] openness and transparency being a prerequisite of executive and corporate accountability to civil society.[3] Hence precautionary procedures and safeguards here also refer to precaution against encroachments on civil liberties, be they in the form of governmental attempts at withholding information as a source of political power or in the form of industry attempts at monopolizing information as a source of economic gain. The purpose of this chapter is to take a closer look at the solutions that different legal systems in North America and Europe have developed to deal with the problem of undisclosed or concealed risk information, i.e., citizen access to publicly held and privately held data on environmental risks, knowledge or ignorance of which is decisive for precautionary action.

Public Data Disclosure

Historically, there have been significant differences between and among national administrative laws with regard to government-held information. Most European countries (including Britain, France, and Germany) had a notorious tradition of secrecy with regard to a broad range of data kept by public authorities (Rowat 1966, 1979, 1980; Schwan 1984; Marsh 1987; Chevallier 1988; Rose-Ackerma 1995, 114; Vahle 1999; Höffler 2002), partly out of a legitimate concern with effective governance (Dahl 1994; Rowan-Robinson et al. 1996). The one major exception was Sweden. Starting with the Freedom of the Press Act of 1766 (*Tryckfrihets-Förordningen*) (Lamble 2002), Swedish citizens have had a general right of access to public data that is unmatched in

---

[1] Paradoxically, though, the "veil of uncertainty" (Brennan and Buchanan 1985, 30) may sometimes even facilitate collective response and decisionmaking (Helm 1998; Kolstad 2002).

[2] "I know of no safe depository of the ultimate powers of society, but the people themselves; and if we think them not enlightened enough to exercise their control with a wholesome discretion, the remedy is not to take it from them, but to inform their discretion" (Jefferson 1854; quoted in NRC 1989, 14).

[3] Compare EPA 2005 ("a steward operates with transparency"); and Fisher 2004.

any other legal system (Andersen 1973; Holstad 1979; Petrén 1987; Österdahl 1998). Other Nordic countries followed: Finland (formerly governed by Swedish law) adopted a Publicity of Documents Act in 1951 (superseded in 1999 by the Act on the Openness of Government Activities), Denmark a Public Access to Files Act in 1970 (*Offentligheds-Lov* 1970; Holm 1975). Even so, the open Scandinavian approach to government-held information remained unusual among the prevailing pattern of "arcane administration" (*arcana imperii*: Scherzberg 2003) in Europe, where access to files by citizens was long viewed as incompatible with the principle of representative—as distinct from "direct"—democracy (Bullinger 1979, 217).

Against that background came the U.S. Freedom of Information Act (FOIA) of 1966 (FOIA 1966; Bryant 1972; Foerstel 1999; as amended by the Open Government Act, OGA 2007). It had already been foreshadowed by the federal Administrative Procedure Act (APA 1946, § 3; Cross 1953) and at the state level by California's 1952 "Brown Act" (Singer 1979, 310). An avalanche of "sunshine statutes"[4] followed in its wake all over North America and in other common law countries (GSA 1976; Wallace 1987; McDonagh 2000; Smyth 2000; Roberts 2002a; CEC 2003), radically changing the global map of comparative administrative law. This remarkable legislative transplant (Wiener 2001) may actually have changed the universal catalogue of constitutional rights (Ivester 1977; Cossiga 1992; Sedley 2000; Calland and Tilley 2002; Banisar 2004; Birkinshaw 2006; Mendel 2008; Atlanta Declaration 2008; Kravchenko and Bonine 2008, 219).

Initially, European countries other than those in Scandinavia were slow to follow suit. Among the first examples in continental Europe were the 1978 French Act on Administrative Relations with the Public (*Loi 78-753*; Delaunay 2003; IFSA/CADA 2003) and the Netherlands' Administrative Transparency Act (*Openbaarheidswet* 1978; Luebbe-Wolff 1980). It was the Organisation for Economic Co-operation and Development (OECD), comprising both West European and North American Member States, that innovated by adopting a Declaration on Anticipatory Environmental Policies in 1976 and a Decision-Recommendation of the Council concerning "Provision of Information to the Public and Public Participation in Decisionmaking Processes Related to the Prevention of, and Response to, Accidents Involving Hazardous Substances" in 1988 (OECD 1988; Smets 1991). Two years later—after considerable debate in the European Commission and Parliament (Campbell 1994, 46)[5]—EU Council Directive 90/313/EEC on Freedom of Access to Information on the Environment mandated the enactment of transparency legislation in all member countries of the European Union (EU 1990; Winter 1990; Krämer 1991; Pallemaerts 1991; von Schwanenflügel 1991; Engel 1993; Fluck 1993; Fluck and Theuer 1994; Prieur 1997; Kloepfer 2004).

---

[4] The term goes back to U.S. Supreme Court Justice Louis D. Brandeis, who recommended "publicity ... as a remedy for social and industrial diseases. Sunlight is said to be the best of disinfectants" (Brandeis 1914, 62).

[5] Initiated by a legislative proposal introduced on November 10, 1987, by Ken Collins and Beate Weber in the European Parliament (Doc. PE/A2-208/87); cf. van der Lek 1988.

Even though "green" politicians and academics in Europe had long hailed FOIA as "the new Magna Carta of ecological democracy" (Fischer 1989, 152) and as evidence of a new "structural pluralism" (Giddens 2000, 55; Roberts 2001), reactions at the governmental level were anything but enthusiastic. Several EU Member States missed the prescribed deadline for the new statutory enactments and administrative reforms required,[6] and the Commission had to resort to judicial actions to make Germany comply (ECJ 1999; EU 2000b; Schoch 2002; Schmillen 2003). National implementation of the 1990 directive—superseded in 2005 by new EU Parliament/Council Directive 2003/4/EC (EU 2003a; Jahnke 2003; Butt 2003; Schrader 2004; Krämer 2004; Werres 2005; Beer and Wesseling 2006)—has been far from perfect (Hallo 1996; Kimber and Ekardt 1999; EU 2000a; Wilsher 2001; Schram 2001; Roll 2003; Strohmeyer 2003; Larssen 2003), with state courts and even the European Court of Justice interpreting it restrictively (ECJ 2003; van Calster and Lee 2004; Garcia Ureta and Lazcano Brotóns 2005; De Abreu Ferreira 2007). It seems as though old administrative habits, especially the entrenched reluctance of civil service departments to conduct their business in the open, are hard to break indeed.

Yet things began to change in the wake of the 1992 UN Conference on Environment and Development in Rio de Janeiro, which declared that "at the national level, each individual shall have appropriate access to information concerning the environment that is held by public authorities, including information on hazardous materials and activities in their communities" (Rio Declaration 1992, Principle 10). The Convention for the Protection of the Marine Environment in the North-East Atlantic (OSPAR 1992, Article 9) opened public access to government-held information regarding that particular maritime subregion of Europe, which extends beyond the EU (Sands 2003, 859; Dorman 2004).

The process of reform next reached the still wider geographic framework of the United Nations Economic Commission for Europe (UNECE), which also includes all of Central and Eastern Europe, the United States, and Canada. Freedom of access to environmental information—under the catchword of *glasnost*—had long been one of the political demands of civil-society opposition groups in the former socialist countries in particular, preceding and indeed precipitating the fall of the Berlin Wall (Stec 1998). Not surprisingly, therefore, it was an alliance of Northern and Eastern European nongovernmental organizations (NGOs) that played a key role in the preparation and negotiation of the 1995 UNECE Sofia Guidelines on access to information and public participation in environmental decisionmaking (Wates 1996; Agarwal et al. 2001, 148). They led to the adoption of the Aarhus Convention on June 25, 1998 (UNECE 1998; Scheyli 2000; Petkova and Veit 2000; Harrison 2000; Rose-Ackerman and Halpaap 2002; Bruch and Czebiniak 2002; Thurnherr 2003), one of whose "three pillars" is public access to environmental information—including so-called "passive

---

[6] For example, the Environmental Information (Scotland) Regulations (2004) were finally adopted by the Scottish Parliament on December 2, 2004, and entered into force in January 2005. See *Scottish Statutory Instruments* 2004, No. 520.

access," that is, the right to seek information from public authorities (under Article 4);[7] and "active access," that is, the duty of governments to collect, disclose, and disseminate such information regardless of specific requests, under Article 5 (Stec et al. 2000, 6; Butt 2001).[8] The Aarhus Convention now has 43 Member States. Among the first cases taken up by its Compliance Committee—established in 2002—were complaints for denial of access to environmental information (Article 4), brought by nongovernmental organizations (NGOs) against the governments of Armenia, Belgium, Kazakhstan, Poland, and the Ukraine (UNECE 2005b, §§ 15 and 21/a; Morgera 2005, 142; Koester 2007, 88). Its ripple effects are showing up in national constitutional law as well: the 2004 "environmental amendment" of the French Constitution now includes—in addition to the French variant of the precautionary principle—"the right, under the conditions and within the limits defined by law, to have access to information relating to the environment that is held by public authorities" (*Charte de l'Environnement* 2005, Article 7).

Finally, the Council of Europe—whose 1993 Lugano Convention on Environmental Liability had already provided for access to environmental information held by governments and "bodies with public responsibilities for the environment and under the control of a public authority" (Lugano Convention 1993, Article 15; Ebbesson 1997, 90)—adopted a Convention on Access to Official Documents at Tromsø, Norway, on June 18, 2009 (Tromsø Convention 2009). Although criticized by NGOs and parliamentarians for not going far enough, the new Tromsø Convention—which is expected to enter into force after a minimum of ten ratifications in 2011—introduces a number of innovative provisions, including the principle that standard exceptions such as national security or privacy rights must also be balanced against requirements of environment protection. Implementation of the convention will be monitored by a permanent Group of Specialists on Access to Official Documents, to be elected from an expert list by the Consultation of the Parties.

Simultaneously, in what may almost be characterized as a process of judicial "Scandinavization," the European Court of Human Rights at Strasbourg has begun to recognize public access to government-held documents as a fundamental right protected by Article 10 of the European Convention on Human Rights (ECHR 1950; Hins and Voorhoof 2007; *TASZ* case 2009; Voorhoof 2009; see also the earlier *Guerra* and *McGinley* cases 1998; Weber 1990; Gavouneli 2000; Fievet 2001, 173). Public access to government-held environmental information thus becomes an actionable right, subject to supranational judicial review well beyond the EU, especially in the countries of Central and Eastern Europe. As mentioned before, people in those countries are acutely sensitive to environmental risk information, which had been

---

[7] The general right to "seek, receive, and impart information" is already affirmed in Article 19 of the Universal Declaration of Human Rights (UNGA 1948).

[8] An amendment adopted on May 27, 2005 (new Article 6 *bis*), expressly extends application of the Convention to public information and participation prior to decisions on genetically modified organisms (UNECE 2005a).

denied to them in the past (Harman-Stokes 1995; Zaharchenko and Goldenman 2004, 234; Stec 2005; Jendrośka 2007).

From a comparative perspective, it is probably fair to say that Europe has begun to catch up with North America but still has a lot to learn in this field (Council of Europe 1988; Campbell 1994; Coliver et al. 1999; OECD 2000; Öberg 2000; Wilcox 2001; RFF 2001; Partsch 2002; Frost 2003). It would undoubtedly be worthwhile to study both the transcultural and psychological implications of that learning process and its impact on civic and administrative attitudes toward environmental risks and precaution (Wiener and Rogers 2002) and on the perceived balance of openness versus security (Steele 1975; Geiger 2000; Gassner and Pisani 2001; White 2003). Even though some information-based regulatory policies—such as environmental impact assessments, eco-labels, prior informed consent, and other "informational devices" (Jordan et al. 2003, 12)—are now globally accepted (Sand 1990, 25; Yeater and Kurukulasuriya 1995; Kern et al. 2000; Farber and Morrison 2000), "context-oriented" instruments for information rights and duties are still far from mainstream in EU environmental governance (Deckmyn and Thomson 1997; Burkert 1998; Bunyan 1999; Holzinger et al. 2003, 126; Kranenborg and Voermans 2005). One of the most difficult subtasks was to persuade the European Union itself (i.e., the bureaucracy in Brussels) that it, too, had a problem with information disclosure. It took years of litigation (ECFI 1997, 1998, 1999; ECJ 2001) to establish public access to EU Parliament, Council, and Commission documents (Kunzlik 1997; O'Neill 1998; Monédiaire 1999; Schiffauer and Jeffreys-Jones 1999; Travers 2000; Wägenbaur 2001; Broberg 2002; Roberts 2002b). Today access is guaranteed by the "Transparency Regulation" of May 30, 2001 (EU 2001a, EU 2004; Partsch 2001; Peers 2002; Krämer 2003; Schram 2005),[9] even though it has been interpreted rather restrictively by the EU Court in Luxembourg (ECFI 2004) and is currently under revision (EU 2007; EU 2008; EU 2010). If it is any consolation, some other intergovernmental bureaucracies like the multilateral development banks have had to go through a similar learning curve as regards information disclosure to the public (Shihata 1994, 28; Udall 1998, 404; Nelson 2001; Grigorescu 2003; IMF 2005; Moghadan 2009; Global Transparency Initiative 2009; Transparency International 2009).[10]

---

[9] Since the EU also ratified the 1998 Aarhus Convention (on February 17, 2005), its own institutions are now considered "public authorities" subject to the convention's disclosure requirements (Davies 2001; Rodenhoff 2002, 350; Jendrośka 2005), as implemented since 2007 by the "Aarhus Regulation" (EU 2006b; Guckelberger 2008; Bergkamp and Smith, Chapter 17 in this volume, 465). See also Article 15 (3) of the Lisbon Treaty on the Functioning of the EU.

[10] The World Bank's new Access to Information Policy became effective on July 1, 2010, replacing earlier directives and policies of 1985/2005 (World Bank 2009). On similar initiatives in the African, Asian and Inter-American Development Banks, the European Bank for Reconstruction and Development, the European Investment Bank, the International Finance Corporation, the International Monetary Fund, and the Multilateral Investment Guarantee Agency, see *Yearbook of International Environmental Law* 5:296 (1994), 7:262 (1996), 9:340 (1998), 14:721 (2003); Handl 2001, 47; Saul 2002; and FreedomInfo (2010).

Private Data Disclosure

The Atlantic divide looms larger still when it comes to questions of access to privately held environmental data, especially information on environmental and health-related risks. The turning point for North American regulatory history was the Bhopal accident in December 1984, which occurred at the local affiliate of a U.S. chemical company in India and killed more than 2,400 people (Desai 1993; Lapierre and Moro 2001). In the face of the magnitude of that tragedy—and also because it was followed in 1985 by another, albeit less catastrophic, accident in West Virginia (in a plant owned by the same corporation; Abrams and Ward 1990, 143), illustrating the risk of similar disasters at home—legislative reaction in the United States was swift and truly innovative.

The Toxics Release Inventory (TRI) established in 1986 by the federal Emergency Planning and Community Right-to-Know Act (EPCRA 1986; Schierow 1997; Weeks 1998; Khanna et al. 1998; Greenwood and Sachdev 1999; von Oppenfeld 1999; Volokh 2002) requires mandatory reporting of toxic industrial emissions. The information is then made publicly available (online) via a computerized database operated by the U.S. Environmental Protection Agency (EPA, at www.epa.gov/tri). U.S. NGOs use and publicize information from the database in networks such as the Chemical Scorecard (www.scorecard.org), kept by Environmental Defense, and the Right-to-Know Network (www.rtknet.org), operated by OMB Watch (Bass and MacLean 1993). As a result, anybody can download standardized, site-specific, up-to-date, and user-friendly data on specified toxic emissions from all facilities covered by TRI. At the state level, California's 1986 Safe Drinking Water and Toxic Enforcement Act (Proposition 65) imposed additional warning and disclosure requirements for toxic chemicals—as interpreted and applied by the courts (*Lungren* case 1996; Rechtschaffen 1996, 1999; Freund, 1997)—unless emitters can show that the level of exposure is low enough to pose "no significant risk" (§ 25249.10.c).

Although there had been earlier toxic-emission disclosure laws at the state and local levels since the 1970s, mainly in response to demands by labor leaders to alert employees to workplace risks (Chess 1984; Ashford and Caldart 1985; Hadden 1989), the near-instant success of TRI and Proposition 65 seems to have taken everyone by surprise (Wolf 1996; Konar and Cohen 1997; Stephan 2002). Both statutes began taking effect in 1988. Data for the 10-year period from 1988 to 1997 show that atmospheric emissions of some 260 known carcinogens and reproductive toxins from TRI-reporting facilities have been reduced by approximately 62% nationwide and by about 85% in the state of California (i.e., for all chemicals listed in California as known to cause either cancer or reproductive toxicity *and* reported as air emissions under TRI; Roe 2002, 10233).

Attempts at explaining this "accidental success story" (Fung and O'Rourke 2000, 116) variously emphasize the innovative use made of (a) "eco-information" via the Internet, by TRI and its NGO multipliers (Kennedy et al. 1994; Menell 1995; Jobe 1999); (b) reversal of the burden of proof for exemptions under Proposition 65 (Barsa 1997); (c) enforcement by citizen suits, under both schemes (Naysnerski and Tietenberg 1992; Grant 1997; Green 1999; Graf 2001, 669); (d) data standardization to facilitate comparison and "performance benchmarking" (Karkkainen 2001); and

(e) the "reputational" effects of such competitive ranking on the stock market and on a firm's behavior (Hamilton 1995; Graham 2001, 8; Graham and Miller 2001; Patten 2002; Driesen 2003, 147). While it will be important to learn the right lessons from all of this, the outcome is unlikely to be attributable to a set of isolated causes, let alone a single cause. A number of external driving forces certainly are plausible, and "success" more often than not rests on the right combination of information and regulation (Graham 2002a; Beierle 2003; Harrison and Antweiler 2003; Kraft et al. 2004; Weil et al. 2006; Bubna-Litic 2008), whereas "failure" may be caused by a combination of political inertia, lack of incentives for disclosers, and—most significantly, perhaps— lack of capacity on the side of disclosees to make optimal use of the information available (Ben-Shahar and Schneider 2010).

Many observers view the advent of "informational regulation" (Viscusi et al. 1986; Magat and Viscusi 1992; Grant and Downey 1996; Kleindorfer and Orts 1998; Sage 1999; Sunstein 1999; Case 2001; Cohen and Santhakumar 2002), "smart regulation" (Gunningham and Cornwall 1994; Gunningham et al. 1998, 63) or "regulation through revelation" (Florini 1998, 2007, 2008; Hamilton 2005) as viable alternatives to the stalemate of traditional environmental lawmaking and the kind of regulatory fatigue it seems to have spread (Pedersen 2001; Cohen 2001; Foulon et al. 2002). A number of academic analysts thus call for "mutual transparency" as a means of ensuring accountability and legitimacy (Brin 1998, 149; Wilmshurst and Frost 2000; Fung et al. 2004), and of promoting "environmental democracy in action" (Sarokin and Shulkin 1991; Lynn and Kartez 1994)—albeit at the risk of "technopopulism" (Graham 2002b; Fung et al. 2007). Lawyers and political scientists have identified "sunshine methods" as effective strategies to induce compliance with environmental laws and treaties (Weiss and Jacobson 2000, 549), pointing in the direction of the "disclosure model" as a new type of self-regulatory "reflexive environmental law" (Orts 1995, 1334; Orts 2001, 174; Gaines 2003) and "informational governance" (Ramkumar and Petkova 2007, 282; Mason 2008; Mol 2008). Others refer to "information provision devices" as part of a new generation of "third-way environmentalism" (Schroeder 2000, 19; Stewart 2001). Along the same lines, proponents of "information economics" (Lamberton 1971, 1984; Lyndon 1989; Stiglitz 2000) have hailed disclosure strategies as the "third wave" in pollution control (Tietenberg 1998; Tietenberg and Wheeler 2001; Henke 2004)—after the first generation of command-and-control (e.g., emissions standards and fines) and the second generation of market-based approaches (e.g., effluent charges and tradable permits).

Right-to-know laws have since been enacted in at least 25 U.S. states and in Canada (Zimmermann et al. 1995; Yu et al. 1998; CEC 2001, 2003; Antweiler and Harrison 2003). The North American pilot experience also prompted other countries to set up Pollutant Release and Transfer Registers (PRTRs), in response to recommendations by the 1992 UN Rio Conference (Agenda 21, § 19.61.c) and the Organisation for Economic Co-operation and Development (OECD 1996, 2005), as well as under technical assistance projects in the Third World (World Bank 2000). Further initiatives for worldwide dissemination of the concept have been launched by the UN Environment Programme (UNEP; see www.chem.unep.ch/prtr); the UN Institute for Training and Research (UNITAR 2000); the Inter-Organization Programme for the

Sound Management of Chemicals (IOMC 2001); and private-sector networks such as the International Right-to-Know Campaign, at www.irtk.org (Casey-Lefkowitz 2001; Bann 2002).

In July 2000, the European Union decided to establish a mandatory European Pollutant Emission Register (EPER 2000), operated by the European Environment Agency (EEA) in Copenhagen. The first EPER Review Report, based on data from 17 countries for the year 2001, was issued in June 2004. At the national level, the first operational system had already been introduced in 1974 by the Netherlands Ministry of Housing, Spatial Planning, and the Environment (VROM), on a voluntary basis. A mandatory system followed in Norway;[11] Sweden started mandatory reporting (after voluntary pilot studies initiated in 1994) under a new PRTR system operated by the Environmental Protection Agency in cooperation with the Chemical Inspectorate. The United Kingdom currently has a multiregister system operating in England and Wales, and one in Scotland. Other countries with integrated national systems in operation include Austria, Belgium, the Czech Republic, Denmark, Finland, Germany, Hungary, Ireland, Portugal, and Spain (UNECE 2000, Annex I).

Within the framework of the 1998 Aarhus Convention, a Protocol on Pollutant Release and Transfer Registers was adopted in Kiev on 21 May 2003 (UNECE 2003). Following its ratification by the EU on February 21, 2006, it was implemented by a regulation (EU 2006a) expanding and reorganizing the existing EPER (MacDonald 2008), with a first report—based on 2007 data—issued in 2009. The new European Pollutant Release and Transfer Register (E-PRTR) now collects and annually updates pollutant emissions data from over 25,000 industrial facilities in the 27 EU Member States plus Iceland, Liechtenstein, Norway, and Switzerland (http://prtr.ec.europa.eu).

The Kiev Protocol is open to all UN Member States (Article 26).[12] Its main purpose is to require all member countries to establish "publicly accessible national pollutant release and transfer registers" for pollutants and source categories to be listed in annexes and expected to be expanded over time, possibly also including "diffuse sources" such as agriculture and traffic (Article 2/11). A net effect therefore will be to bring important environmental data held by the private sector into the public domain (UNECE 2004) and thus "to render information less a private good (for enterprise) than a public one" (Farmer and Teubner 1994, 7).[13]

Among the most effective "multiplier" instruments for this purpose—because they affect all public companies listed on the stock market—are environmental disclosure requirements in corporate financial accounting (stakeholder/shareholder risk

---

[11] Regarding publicly held data, Norway also enacted an Environmental Information Act (modeled in part after the U.S. FOIA), in force January 1, 2004 (Jahnke 2003, 232).

[12] That is, regardless of their membership in the UNECE or the Aarhus Convention. In November 2002, however, the United States (which is a member country of the UNECE but not of the Aarhus Convention) withdrew from follow-up negotiations under the convention; see also the U.S. statement in UN Doc ECE/MP.PP/2 (Geneva, December 17, 2002), reprinted in *Environmental Policy and Law* 33 (2003) 178.

[13] See also Viscusi 1992, 154; Pildes and Sunstein 1995, 103; and Mock 1999, 1085.

disclosure: Abkowitz et al. 1999; Repetto and Austin 2000; CEC and UNEP 2003). The U.S. Securities and Exchange Commission (SEC) has since 1971 required SEC filings of environmentally relevant information as part of its regulations concerning mandatory annual reports under Form 10-K (Geltman 1992; Wallace 1993; Feller 1995; Kass and McCarroll 1997; Repetto et al. 2002; Mansley 2003, 33):[14]

> Appropriate disclosure shall also be made as to the material effects that compliance with federal, state, and local provisions which have been enacted or adopted *regulating the discharge of materials into the environment, or otherwise relating to the protection of the environment*, may have upon the capital expenditures, earnings, and competitive position of the registrant and its subsidies. (emphasis added)

SEC reporting has led to improved transparency (and hence, comparability of corporate performance), *inter alia* with regard to greenhouse gas emissions (Hancock 2005; Wallace 2008; McFarland 2009).[15] In January 2010, the SEC clarified that businesses should disclose to investors any serious risks due to climate change or climate change policy (Broder 2010; Schapiro 2010). Still, gaps and deficiencies remain (Bagby et al. 1995; Goodman and Little 2003; GAO 2004; Young et al. 2009; Latham 2009). Further to proposals for "globalizing" the SEC disclosure requirements (Romano 2000, 108), there also have been a number of transnational initiatives for voluntary reporting (UBA 2002; Gozali et al. 2002; Berthelot et al. 2003). These include the Global Reporting Initiative launched by UNEP and the "Coalition for Environmentally Responsible Economies" (CERES) in 1997 (GRI 2006; GRI 2009), now pushing for mandatory environmental risk disclosure in Europe (GRI 2010); the Greenhouse Gas Protocol Initiative promoted since 1998 by the World Resources Institute and the World Business Council for Sustainable Development (WRI and WBCSD 2004; WRI and WBCSD 2005); the Carbon Disclosure Project launched in 2000 (Kiernan and Dickinson 2005; Hesse 2006; CDP 2009a, 2009b); and the ISO Greenhouse Gas Standards 14064 and 14065 issued by the International Organization for Standardization (ISO 2006; ISO 2007). Mandatory reporting of fuel and emissions data was already required under U.S. state legislation for the electric utility industry;[16] and reporting of greenhouse gas emissions is now mandatory for all large sources and suppliers (including manufacturers of vehicles and engines, and for all facilities emitting 25,000 metric tons or more annually) under rules finalized by the EPA on September 22, 2009 (EPA 2009; Stolaroff et al. 2009).

Regulation of corporate financial reporting in Europe is beginning to follow the SEC lead, with mandatory disclosure of various types of environmental information now

---

[14] SEC Reg. § 229.101(c)(xii); for background, see Caron 1987; White 1992, 257; Villanova Symposium 1994.

[15] In some instances, reporting by European companies listed in the United States (under SEC Form 20-F) resulted in more extensive disclosure than in their respective home countries, e.g., British Petroleum's 1998 report to the SEC on potential impacts of the Kyoto Protocol (Hibbitt 2004, 36).

[16] For example, state-by-state summaries in the U.S. Department of Energy's Green Power Network. See also the comparative reports issued in 2002, 2004, and 2006 by CERES, *Benchmarking Air Emissions of the 100 Largest Electric Generation Owners in the U.S.* (CERES 2006; Delmas et al. 2006; Schatz 2008. For a comparison with Canadian regulations, see Erion 2009.

required in Denmark, France, the Netherlands, Norway, Spain, Sweden, and the United Kingdom (Bobbington 1999; Emtairah 2002; WRI 2003, 115; Hibbitt 2004; Villiers 2006, 234). Following an earlier recommendation to this effect by the EU Commission (EU 2001b) and a related directive on corporate accounts (EU 2003c), more specific environmental disclosure standards for financial accounting are to be anticipated, especially in the context of future EU emissions trading for greenhouse gases (Hesse 2004). At the same time, the Basel Committee on Banking Supervision—established by the central bank governors of the G-10 countries—has since 2004 required banks to "monitor the risk of environmental liability arising in respect of the collateral, such as the presence of toxic material on a property" (Basel II Framework 2005, 108 § 510).

To sum up, legal obligations to disclose environment-related risk information now exist at four distinct levels:

1. disclosure to **governments**, by environmental impact statements for the planning or licensing of specified projects,[17] categories of industries (*établissements classés*),[18] environmentally hazardous activities (*miljöfarlig verksamheter*),[19] or "dangerous goods";[20]
2. disclosure to **citizens**, under "right-to-know" schemes for specified workplace environments or for the benefit of communities adjoining industrial facilities;[21]
3. disclosure to **consumers**, through a variety of labeling schemes ranging from hazard warnings[22] to product-related or process-related certifications of contents or origin (yet another arena of transatlantic polarization in recent trade disputes);[23]

---

[17] Concept introduced by the 1970 U.S. National Environmental Policy Act (NEPA 1970) and a corresponding EU Directive (EU 1985; Sand 1990, 25).

[18] Precautionary licensing of environmentally hazardous industries dates back to nineteenth-century French legislation, Prussia's 1845 *Gewerbe-Ordnung*, and Britain's 1900 Alkali and Other Works Regulation (Sand 2000, 448).

[19] Concept introduced by the 1969 Swedish Environment Protection Act (Westerlund 1975, 1981).

[20] For example, for border-crossing carriage of dangerous goods by road, under the ADR Agreement (UNECE 1957); and for exports of banned or restricted hazardous chemicals (Basel Convention 1989; PIC Convention 1998; POPs Convention 2001).

[21] For example, labeling required under the "hazard communication standards" of the U.S. Occupational Safety and Health Administration (OSHA 1983; Viscusi 1983, 158); and the TRI and PRTR schemes discussed above.

[22] For example, for cigarette labeling (Godfrey 2004, 120); and pursuant to legislation on pesticides, polychlorinated biphenyls (PCBs), and other hazardous substances (McGarity and Shapiro 1980; Hilson 2005, 319).

[23] For example, the debates on labeling provisions for genetically modified food products in the context of the World Trade Organization, the Biosafety Protocol 2000, and the FAO/WHO Codex Alimentarius (Bernauer 2003; Thorpe and Robinson 2005; Sand 2006); and on the transatlantic spillover of information disclosure for toxic chemicals under the EU Regulation on Registration, Evaluation and Authorization of Chemicals (REACH 2006; Sachs 2009; Renn and Elliott, Chapter 10 in this volume).

4. disclosure to **investors**, as part of corporate financial accounting schemes (as described above).

Outlook

Let us remember, however, that this is only the tip of the iceberg. There is a huge mass of privately held environmental and health risk information that is woefully "asymmetric"—to use a somewhat euphemistic term from uncertainty economics (Arrow 1963; Baron 1984; Sandmo 1999; Cranor 1999; Coglianese et al. 2004, 4)—but is not covered by the Aarhus Convention, and where Europe still lags years behind North America in terms of public access rules that would facilitate precautionary environmental decisionmaking. A striking illustration is disclosure of the tobacco industry's "privileged" documents under the 1998 Minnesota settlement (*Humphrey* case 1998; Ciresi et al. 1999; Little 2001). Only now, after court-enforced electronic access to those corporate files, was a research team from the University of California able to document the multinationals' well-planned and highly successful sabotage of EU tobacco advertising legislation (Bitton et al. 2002; Neuman et al. 2002), culminating in the annulment of a 1998 Council Directive (EU 1998; Simma et al. 1999) by the European Court of Justice in October 2000 (ECJ 2000; Schroeder 2001; Tridimas and Tridimas 2002).[24] The documentation shows, in gruesome detail and transparency, how "captive" governments and top politicians (with Germany and the United Kingdom in front) were used,[25] and—to put it bluntly—corrupted, in a game that will have massive and measurable negative effects on environmental health for years to come (Barnes and Bero 1996; Godfrey 2004; Graham et al. 2009, 23; Blanke, Chapter 4 in this volume).

---

[24] On May 26, 2003, the EU Parliament and Council adopted—against German opposition—a new Directive 2003/33/EC to ban tobacco advertising by 2005 (EU 2003b). On September 10, 2003, the German government, under pressure from economic lobbyists, brought action before the ECJ in Luxembourg, hoping to have the Directive annulled once again under Article 230 of the EEC treaty (Case 380/03) (Nicola and Marchetti 2005). On December 12, 2006, however, the ECJ dismissed the action (Rauber 2007); a related action by *Nürburgring* Speedway Ltd, claiming adverse effects on its advertising revenues, had already been dismissed by the European Court of First Instance on June 29, 2006 (Case T-311/03). After the Commission brought further action in the ECJ against Germany on August 24, 2006 (Case C-351/06), for failing to implement Directive 2003/33/EC, the German federal Parliament finally amended the applicable legislation on November 9, 2006, accordingly.

[25] Simpson 2002; Didzoleit 2002; Collin et al. 2002, 271; Godfrey 2004, 208–210. In 2002, Germany earned the infamous "Marlboro Man Award" from the NGO Network for Accountability of Tobacco Transnationals (see www.infact.org/101702 mm.html) for its stalwart diplomatic efforts—in coalition with the United States and Japan—to water down the global ban on tobacco advertising, promotion, and sponsorship as formulated in Article 13 of the WHO's Framework Convention on Tobacco Control (FCTC 2003; Larsson Ortino 2004; Crow 2004; Jacob 2004; Roemer et al. 2005; Burci 2005).

More transparency might also help in some of the academic analysis concerned. For example, a collection of legal opinions on the 1998 EU ban on tobacco advertising by a respectable scholarly publisher in Germany (Schneider and Stein 1999) purported to demonstrate—according to the editors' preface—"striking conformity and unanimity" among the experts, to the effect that the ban had indeed been *ultra vires*. However, readers had to proceed as far as page 55 to discover that the learned book had been solicited and sponsored by the Confederation of European Community Cigarette Manufacturers (Kleine 2000). Given this abundance of "manufactured information" or disinformation, there clearly is a need for new disclosure rules—to be applied not only to government and industry, but also to captive scientific writers and law professors. Pending that, all I can recommend is a high degree of precaution when approaching German legal literature on this topic.[26]

Far more serious, however, are recent developments triggered by the tragic events of September 11, 2001. In the face of terrorist bombing threats against the most vulnerable "soft" targets—for example, major chemical factories—a large part of industrial risk data in the United States was reclassified as "critical infrastructure information" (Cha 2002; Cohen 2002; Costner 2002; Davis 2002; Penders and Thomas 2002; Siegel 2002; CEC 2003, 188; Dycus 2005; Moteff 2005). Not surprisingly, economic pressure groups that had always resisted the disclosure of environmental risks to the public—namely, the American Chemistry Council (ACC, formerly the Chemical Manufacturers Association, CMA), the Coalition for Effective Environmental Information (CEEI), and the Center for Regulatory Effectiveness (CRE)—lent enthusiastic support to the Bush administration's efforts to restrict access to such information (Greenwood 1999; Kennedy 2004, 156). They scored a first tactical victory with the "data quality rider" attached to the U.S. Treasury Department's appropriation bill in December 2001, labeled the Information Quality Act (DQA 2001; Adler 2001; Logomasini 2002; Conrad 2002; Shapiro 2004; O'Reilly 2007), which directed the U.S. Office of Management and Budget (OMB) to develop new "Guidelines for Ensuring and Maximizing the Quality, Objectivity, Utility, and Integrity of Information Disseminated by Federal Agencies" (OMB 2002; EPA 2002; Copeland and Simpson 2004; Shapiro 2007).

Substantive and procedural restrictions on environmental information disclosure have since been imposed under the Homeland Security Act of November 25, 2002 (HSA 2002; Gidiere and Forrester 2002; Blanton 2002; O'Reilly 2002; Echeverria and Kaplan 2002; Steinzor 2002; McDermott 2002; Jacobson 2003; Uhl 2003; Moteff and Stevens 2003; DHS 2004; Johnson 2004; Pack 2004; Salkin 2005; AALS 2005; Wheeler 2006; Robinson 2007, 132; Chekouras 2007).[27] Procedures for public

---

[26] Undisclosed industry influence on German medical and pharmaceutical publications is equally notorious (Grüning et al. 2006).

[27] Pursuant to section 892 of the act, Executive Order 13311 of July 29, 2003, instructed the U.S. Department of Homeland Security (DHS) also to develop procedures for identifying and safeguarding "sensitive but unclassified" information held by federal agencies. On the general attitude of the courts, see Harvard Law Review Note 1990 and Papandreou 2005.

access to chemical risk information—in particular, to risk management plans (RMPs) and off-site consequences analysis (OCA) for certain chemical facilities pursuant to section 112(r) of the Clean Air Act[28]—had already been curtailed before. The RMPs database had been removed from the EPA website with the stated intent of withholding the information also from NGO networks (Stephenson 2003, 4). Exemptions from FOIA had thus been conceded under the Chemical Safety Information, Site Security, and Fuels Regulatory Relief Act of 1999 (P.L. 106-40, U.S. Statutes at Large 113: 207 (1999)). In 2006, EPA substantially reduced TRI reporting requirements for industry (EPA 2006; Vladeck 2008, 1791). Moreover, pursuant to the Department of Homeland Security's Chemical Facility Anti-Terrorism Standards, effective June 8, 2007, "notwithstanding the Freedom of Information Act, the Privacy Act and other laws, records containing CVI ["chemical terrorism vulnerability information"] are not available for public inspection or copying, nor does DHS release such records without a need to know."[29] In the face of new security threats, the U.S. government thus sounded the retreat from a "right-to-know" approach toward a kind of "soft paternalism" (Sunstein and Thaler 2003; Thaler and Sunstein 2003; Jolls and Sunstein 2004; Glaeser 2006, 149), with a benevolent "avuncular state" (*Economist* 2006) to determine what citizens do or do not *need* to know (Podesta 2003).[30]

Right up to the 2002 Johannesburg World Summit on Sustainable Development, the United States—no matter how much fault critics may have found with its environmental record in other areas—had remained the undisputed champion of citizen access to environmental data, public or private. In his message to the Summit, Colin Powell, then U.S. secretary of state, had indeed highlighted the "access initiative" by 26 civil society organizations in nine countries to assess how well governments are providing access to risk information (Powell 2002, 10; Petkova et al. 2002; WRI 2002; Foti et al. 2008). Starting from Principle 10 of the 1992 Rio Declaration, the "Plan of Implementation" adopted by the Summit reaffirmed the need "to ensure access, at the national level, to environmental information," and in particular, "to encourage development of coherent and integrated information on chemicals, such as through national pollutant release and transfer registers"

---

[28] U.S. Code 42: § 7521; procedures for access to OCA information—mandated in 1990—had been laid down by an EPA Final Rule in August 2000, *U.S. Federal Register* 65: 48108. The U.S. Department of Justice supported changes that would "prohibit general, public access to OCA information in facility RMPs" (Stephenson 2003, 6).

[29] U.S. Code 6: § 27.400(g)(1), see Chemical Facility Anti-Terrorism Standards: Final Rule (April 9, 2007), issued by the U.S. DHS pursuant to Sec. 550 of the Homeland Security Appropriations Act of 2007; *U.S. Federal Register* 72: 17688, at 17716; for legislative background, see Shea 2005.

[30] Considering, though, that the *avunculus* in Roman law was the maternal rather than the paternal uncle (i.e., *patruus*; I owe this clarification to Anne Petitpierre), it would perhaps be more accurate for "soft paternalism" to be relabeled maternalism, or Big Mother Syndrome.

(Johannesburg Report 2002).[31] However, at the 2003 session of the UNEP Governing Council, the executive director's follow-up proposal for global guidelines to implement Rio Principle 10—including more specific rules on information access—ran into opposition from the United States in coalition with China and the Group of 77, and as a result was deferred "for review" until 2010.[32]

It had taken decades to establish procedures for mandatory information disclosure (public and private), to ensure transparency and thereby to reduce the range of uncertainties that often make precautionary action necessary. Ironically, precaution—against the new risk of terrorism (Stern and Wiener 2006; see Chapter 12 in this volume)—was now being invoked to reduce that very transparency. Ultimately, of course, it is for each society to determine which risks it can afford to trade off against which countervailing risks (Graham and Wiener 1995). Yet, in the course of this particular trade-off, the public's hard-won environmental "right to know" suddenly confronted the ugly claw of a zombie, resurrected from the dark ages of European administrative law: government's "hiding hand." There are signs, however, of a reversal of this ominous trend and a return to transatlantic convergence in this field. President Obama's memoranda on transparency and freedom of information, issued on the first day of his administration on January 21, 2009, thus call for "an unprecedented level of openness in government" (Transparency Memorandum 2009; FOIA 2009a). They were followed by comprehensive guidelines from the attorney general (FOIA 2009b), establishing a "presumption of openness" and rescinding the earlier administration's more restrictive guidelines dating back to October 2001.[33] Even so, an independent

---

[31] See Sections 23(f) and 128 (Gray 2003; Cordonnier Segger et al. 2003, 65). See also the Johannesburg Declaration's call on private sector corporations "to enforce corporate accountability, which should take place within a transparent and stable regulatory environment" (Report p. 4, Article 29), and the call for "public access to relevant information" in the work program for implementation of the Johannesburg Principles on the Role of Law and Sustainable Development, adopted by the Global Judges Symposium on August 20, 2002 (*Environmental Policy and Law* 32: 236–238, see Rehbinder 2003).

[32] "Enhancing the Application of Principle 10 of the Rio Declaration on Environment and Development," UN Doc. UNEP/GC.22/3/Add.2/B (2002), and decision UNEP/GC.22/17/II/B (2003) calling for a report to the Twenty-Third Session of the Governing Council in February 2005; *Earth Negotiations Bulletin* 16(30): 9 (February 10, 2003). After some governments (including the United States) requested more time "for consultation," the UNEP secretariat quietly postponed the report. Meanwhile, the Bangkok Congress of the World Conservation Union (IUCN) in November 2004 unanimously adopted Recommendation REC/WCC3.081 on the "Implementation of Principle 10 by Building Comprehensive Good Governance"—with the U.S. delegation alone abstaining, upon instructions from Foggy Bottom. Finally, the UNEP Governing Council adopted a set of voluntary "guidelines for the development of national legislation on access to information, public participation and access to justice in environmental matters," as part of its decisions on environmental law at the 11th Special Session/Global Environmental Forum in Bali, UN Doc. UNEP/GCSS.XI/4/I (February 26, 2010).

[33] See also recent legislative proposals for a commission on FOIA processing delays ("Faster FOIA Act"), unanimously passed by the U.S. Senate on May 5, 2010 (S 3111) and currently pending in the House of Representatives (HR 5087).

audit of agency-wide practice completed in March 2010 still shows uneven responses to these initiatives and concludes that "much more pressure and leadership will be necessary" (Blanton 2010).

Acknowledgments

This chapter, built on earlier work including Sand (2003, 2005), was written with research assistance by Devyani Kar and Joe Monfort, and helpful comments by John Graham, Aarti Gupta, Peter M. Haas, Kathryn Harrison, David Roe, Jeremy Wates, Jonathan B. Wiener, and John Zimmer. All are gratefully acknowledged.

References

AALS (Association of American Law Schools). 2005. *Democracies Die behind Closed Doors: Secrecy in the Age of Terrorism*, San Francisco, CA. AALS Annual Meeting Workshop. January 8, 2005.

Abkowitz, Mark D., Mark A. Cohen, Susan S. Buck, David W. Case, and Patricia A. Drake. 1999. Environmental Information Disclosure and Stakeholder Involvement: Searching for Common Ground. *Corporate Environmental Strategy* 6: 415–424.

Abrams, Robert, and Douglas H. Ward. 1990. Prospects for Safer Communities: Emergency Response, Community Right-to-Know, and Prevention of Chemical Accidents. *Harvard Environmental Law Review* 14: 135–188.

Adler, John. 2001. How EPA Helps Terrorists. *National Review*, September 27.

Agarwal, Anil, Sunita Narain, Anju Sharma, and Achila Imchen. 2001. *Global Environmental Negotiations 2: Poles Apart*. New Delhi: Centre for Science and Environment.

Agenda 21. 1992. Action Programme Adopted by the United Nations Conference on Environment and Development in Rio de Janeiro. June 3 to June 14. New York: UN Doc. A/CONF.151/26/Rev.1 (1993) 1: 9.

Andersen, Stanley V. 1973. Public Access to Government Files in Sweden. *American Journal of Comparative Law* 21: 419–473.

Antweiler, Werner, and Kathryn Harrison. 2003. Toxic Release Inventories and Green Consumerism: Evidence from Canada. *Canadian Journal of Economics* 36: 495–520.

APA (U.S. Administrative Procedure Act). 1946. Public Law 79-404. *U.S. Code* 5: § 501 (1946).

Arrow, Kenneth. 1963. Uncertainty and the Welfare Economics of Medical Care. *American Economic Review* 53: 941–973.

Arrow, Kenneth, and Anthony C. Fisher. 1974. Environmental Preservation, Uncertainty, and Irreversibility. *Quarterly Journal of Economics* 88: 312–319.

Ashford, Nicholas A., and Charles C. Caldart. 1985. The "Right-to-Know": Toxics Information Transfer in the Workplace. *Annual Review of Public Health* 6: 383–401.

Atlanta Declaration. 2008. Declaration and Plan of Action for the Advancement of the Right of Access to Information. International Conference on the Right to Public Information. February 28–29, Carter Center, Atlanta, GA.

Bagby, John W., Paula C. Murray, and Eric T. Andrews. 1995. How Green Was My Balance Sheet? Corporate Liability and Environmental Disclosure. *Virginia Environmental Law Journal* 14: 224–342.

Banisar, David. 2004. *Transparent Government: Developing Public Access to Government Information*. Washington, DC: National Democratic Institute for International Affairs.

Bann, Amy J. 2002. Development of an International Right-to-Know: Towards Public Disclosure of Multi-National Corporations' Environmental Practices through Legal Transparency Measures. *Law, Social Justice, and Global Development Journal* 1: 1–24.

Barnes, Deborah E., and Lisa A. Bero. 1996. Industry Funded Research and Conflict of Interest: An Analysis of Research Sponsored by the Tobacco Industry through the Center for Indoor Air Research. *Journal of Health Politics, Policy and Law* 21: 515–542.

Baron, David P. 1984. Regulatory Strategies under Asymmetric Information. In *Bayesian Models in Economic Theory*, edited by Marcel Boyer and Richard E. Kihlstrom. Amsterdam: North Holland, 155–180.

Barsa, Michael. 1997. California's Proposition 65 and the Limits of Information Economics. *Stanford Law Review* 49: 1223–1247.

Basel Convention. 1989. Basel Convention on the Control of Transboundary Movements of Hazardous Wastes and Their Disposal, adopted at Basel on March 22, 1989, in force May 5, 1992; ratified by 174 countries [not including the U.S.] and the EU. *United Nations Treaty Series* 1673: 57, *International Legal Materials* 28: 657.

Basel II Framework. 2005. *International Convergence of Capital Measurement and Capital Standards: A Revised Framework*. Basel, Switzerland: Basel Committee on Banking Supervision. (Orig. pub. June 2004, updated November 2005.).

Bass, Gary D., and Alair MacLean. 1993. Enhancing the Public's Right-to-Know about Environmental Issues. *Villanova Environmental Law Journal* 4: 287–310.

Beck, Ulrich. 1996. World Risk Society as Cosmopolitan Society? Ecological Questions in a Framework of Manufactured Uncertainties. *Theory, Culture, and Society* 13 (4): 1–32.

Beer, Julia, and Anke Wesseling. 2006. Die neue Umweltinformations-Richtlinie im Spannungsfeld von europäischer Eigentumsgewährleistung und privatem Informations-Interesse. *Deutsches Verwaltungsblatt* 121: 133–140.

Beierle, Thomas C. 2003. *The Benefits and Costs of Environmental Information Disclosure: What Do We Know about Right-to-Know?* RFF Discussion Paper 03-05. Washington, DC: Resources for the Future.

Ben-Shahar, Omri, and Carl E. Schneider. 2010. *The Failure of Mandated Disclosure*. University of Michigan Legal Working Papers No. 9. Ann Arbor, MI: Empirical Legal Studies Center.

Bernauer, Thomas. 2003. *Genes, Trade, and Regulation: The Seeds of Conflict in Food Biotechnology*. Princeton, NJ: Princeton University Press.

Berthelot, Sylvie, Denis Cormier, and Michel Magnan. 2003. Environmental Disclosure Research: Review and Synthesis. *Journal of Accounting Literature* 22: 1–10.

Biosafety Protocol. 2000. Cartagena Protocol (to the 1992 Convention on Biological Diversity) on Biosafety, adopted at Montreal on January 29, 2000, in force September 11, 2003; ratified by 159 countries [not including the U.S.] and the EU. *International Legal Materials* 39: 1027.

Birkinshaw, Patrick J. 2006. Freedom of Information and Openness: Fundamental Human Rights? *Administrative Law Review* 58: 177–218.

Bitton, Asaf, Mark David Neuman, and Stanton A. Glantz. 2002. *Tobacco Industry Attempts to Subvert European Union Tobacco Advertising Legislation*. San Francisco, CA: University of California San Francisco Center for Tobacco Control, Research, and Education.

Blanton, Thomas S. 2002. The World's Right to Know. *Foreign Policy* 131: 50–58.

Blanton, Thomas S., et al., eds. 2010. Introduction. In *Sunshine and Shadows: National Security Archive FOIA Audit*, edited by Thomas S. Blanton. Washington, DC: George Washington University.

Bobbington, Jan. 1999. Compulsory Environmental Reporting in Denmark: An Evaluation. *Social and Environmental Accounting* 19 (2): 2–4.

Brandeis, Louis D. 1914. *Other People's Money, and How the Bankers Use It*. 2nd ed. New York: Stokes. 1932.

Brennan, Geoffrey, and James M. Buchanan. 1985. *The Reason of Rules: Constitutional Political Economy*. Cambridge: Cambridge University Press.

Brin, David. 1998. *The Transparent Society: Will Technology Force Us to Choose between Privacy and Freedom?* Reading, MA: Addison-Wesley.

Broberg, Morten. 2002. Access to Documents: A General Principle of Community Law? *European Law Review* 27: 194–205.

Broder, John M. 2010. S.E.C. Adds Climate Risk to Disclosure List. *New York Times*, January 28, B1. www.nytimes.com/2010/01/28/business/28sec.html (accessed January 28, 2010).

Bruch, Carl, and Roman Czebiniak. 2002. Globalizing Environmental Governance: Making the Leap from Regional Initiatives on Transparency, Participation, and Accountability in Environmental Matters. *Environmental Law Reporter* 32: 10428–10453.

Bryant, Roscoe. 1972. History and Background of Public Law 90–23, the Freedom of Information Act. *North Carolina Central Law Journal* 3: 193–214.

Bubna-Litic, Karen. 2008. Environmental Reporting as a Communications Tool: A Question of Enforcement? *Journal of Environmental Law* 20: 65–85.

Bullinger, Martin. 1979. Western Germany. In *Administrative Secrecy in Developed Countries*, edited by Donald C. Rowat. New York: Columbia University Press, 217–236.

———. 1985. Freedom of Expression and Information: An Essential Element of Democracy. *German Yearbook of International Law* 28: 88–143.

Bunyan, Tony. 1999. *Secrecy and Openness in the European Union*. London: Kogan Page.

Burci, Gian Luca. 2005. La convention-cadre de l'OMS pour la lutte antitabac. *Journal du Droit International* 132: 77–100.

Burkert, Herbert. 1998. Informationszugang als Element einer europäischen Informationsrechtsordnung? Gegenwärtige und zukünftige Entwicklungen. In *Globalisierung und informationelle Rechtskultur in Europa*, edited by Siegfried Lamnek and Marie T. Tinnefeld. Baden-Baden, Germany: Nomos, 113–135.

Butt, Mark Eric. 2001. *Die Ausweitung des Rechts auf Umweltinformation durch die Aarhus-Konvention*. Stuttgart: Ibidem.

———. 2003. Erweiterter Zugang zu behördlichen Umweltinformationen: die neue EG-Umweltinformationsrichtlinie. *Neue Zeitschrift für Verwaltungsrecht* 22: 1071–1075.

Calland, Richard and Alison, Tilley, eds. 2002. *The Right to Know, the Right to Live: Access to Information and Socio-Economic Justice*. Cape Town: Open Democracy Advice Center.

Campbell, Dennis, ed. 1994. *Environmental Hazards and Duties of Disclosure*. London: Graham and Trotman.

Caron, Gerard E. 1987. Comment. SEC Disclosure Requirements for Contingent Environmental Liability. *Boston College Environmental Affairs Law Review* 14: 729–748.

Case, David W. 2001. The Law and Economics of Environmental Information as Regulation. *Environmental Law Reporter* 31: 10773–10789.

Casey-Lefkowitz, Susan. 2001. *International Right-to-Know: Strategies to Increase Corporate Accountability in the Midst of Globalization*. Washington, DC: Natural Resources Defense Council.

CDP (Carbon Disclosure Project). 2009a. *Europe 300 Report*. London: CDP.

———. 2009b. *Global 500 Report*. London: CDP.

CEC (North American Commission for Environmental Cooperation). 2001. *Taking Stock: North American Pollutant Releases and Transfers 1998*. Montreal: CEC.

———. 2003. *Public Access to Government-Held Environmental Information: Report on North American Law, Policy and Practice*. 2nd ed. North American Environmental Law and Policy Series No. 10. Montreal: CEC, 1–190.

CEC and UNEP (North American Commission for Environmental Cooperation and United Nations Environment Programme). 2003. *Environmental Disclosures in Financial Statements: New Developments and Emerging Issues*. Event Report, February 26, 2003. New York: UNEP Finance Initiative.

CERES (Coalition for Environmentally Responsible Economies). 2006. *Benchmarking Air Emissions of the 100 Largest Electric Generation Owners in the U.S.* Boston, MA: CERES, Natural Resources Defense Council, and Public Service Enterprise Group.

Cha, Ariana E. 2002. Risks Prompt U.S. to Limit Access to Data *Washington Post*, Feb. 24, A-1.

Charte de l'Environnement. 2005. French Constitutional Law No. 2005–205, promulgated on March 1, 2005. *Journal Officiel de la République Française*. March 2, 3697.

Chayes, Abram, and Antonia H. Chayes. 1995. *The New Sovereignty: Compliance with International Regulatory Agreements*. Cambridge, MA: Harvard University Press.

Chekouras, Katherine. 2007. Balancing National Security with a Community's Right-to-Know: Maintaining Public Access to Environmental Information through EPCRA's Non-Preemption Clause. *Boston College Environmental Affairs Law Review* 34: 107–142.

Chess, Caron. 1984. *Winning the Right to Know: A Handbook for Toxics Activists*. Philadelphia, PA: Delaware Valley Toxics Coalition.

Chevallier, Jacques. 1988. Le mythe de la transparence administrative. In *Information et Transparence Administratives*, edited by François Rangeon, Jean Laveissière, and Philippe Belin. Paris: Presses Universitaires de France, 273–284.

Ciresi, Michael V., Roberta B. Walburn, and Tara D. Sutton. 1999. Decades of Deceit: Document Discovery in the Minnesota Tobacco Litigation. *William Mitchell Law Review* 25: 477–566.

Clyde, Ian. 1997. Ignorance Is Not Bliss: The Importance of Environmental Information. *Asia Pacific Journal of Environmental Law* 2: 253–276.

Coglianese, Cary, Richard Zeckhauser, and Edward Parson. 2004. *Seeking Truth for Power: Informational Strategy and Regulatory Policy Making*. Publication 04–25. Washington, DC: American Enterprise Institute and Brookings Institution Joint Center for Regulatory Studies.

Cohen, Mark A. 2001. Information as a Policy Instrument in Protecting the Environment: What Have We Learned? *Environmental Law Reporter* 31: 10425–10431.

———. 2002. Transparency after 9/11: Balancing the "Right-to-Know" with the Need for Security. *Corporate Environmental Strategy* 9: 368–374.

Cohen, Mark A., and V. Santhakumar. 2002. *Information Disclosure as Environmental Regulation: A Theoretical Analysis*. Paper presented at the Second World Congress of Environmental and Resource Economists, Monterey, CA.

Cohen, Michèle, and Jean-Marc Tallon. 2000. Décision dans le risque et l'incertain: l'apport des modèles non-additifs. *Revue d'économie politique* 110: 631–682.

Coliver, Sandra, Paul Hoffman, Joan Fitzpatrick, and Stephen Bowen. eds. 1999. *Secrecy and Liberty: National Security, Freedom of Expression, and Access to Information*. The Hague: Nijhoff.

Collin, Jeff, Kelley Lee, and Karen Bissell. 2002. The Framework Convention on Tobacco Control: The Politics of Global Health Governance. *Third World Quarterly* 23: 265–282.

Conrad, James W., Jr. 2002. The Information Quality Act: Antiregulatory Costs of Mythic Proportions? *Kansas Journal of Law and Public Policy* 12: 521–557.

Copeland, Curtis W., and Michael Simpson. 2004. *The Information Quality Act: OMB's Guidance and Initial Implementation*. Report for Congress RL 32532. Washington, DC: U.S. Congressional Research Service.

Cordonnier Segger, Marie-Claire, Ashfaq Khalfan, Markus Gehring, and Michelle Toering. 2003. Prospects for Principles of International Sustainable Development Law after the WSSD: Common but Differentiated Responsibilities, Precaution, and Participation. *Review of European Community and International Environmental Law* 12: 54–68.

Cossiga, Francesco. 1992. *Umweltschutz und Informationsrecht: Der Verfassungsschutz der allgemeinen Interessen*. Bonn: Bouvier.

Costanza, Robert, and Laura Cornwell. 1992. The 4P Approach for Dealing with Scientific Uncertainty. *Environment* 34 (9): 12–20, 42.

Costner, Brian. 2002. Access Denied. *Bulletin of the Atomic Scientist* 58: 58–62.

Council of Europe. 1988. Secrecy and Openness: Individuals, Enterprises and Public Administration. *Proceedings, Seventeenth Colloquy on European Law*, October 21–23, Saragossa, Spain.

Cranor, Carl F. 1999. Asymmetric Information, the Precautionary Principle, and Burdens of Proof. In *Protecting Public Health and the Environment: Implementing the Precautionary Principle*, edited by Carolyn Raffensperger and Joel Tickner. Washington, DC: Island Press, 74–99.

Cross, Harold L. 1953. *The People's Right to Know: Legal Access to Public Records and Proceedings*. New York: Columbia University Press.

Crow, Melissa E. 2004. Smokescreens and State Responsibility: Using Human Rights Strategies to Promote Global Tobacco Control. *Yale Journal of International Law* 29: 209–250.

Dahl, Robert A. 1994. A Democratic Dilemma: System Effectiveness versus Citizen Participation. *Political Science Quarterly* 109: 23–34.

Davies, Peter. 2001. Public Participation, the Aarhus Convention, and the European Community. In *Human Rights in Natural Resource Development*, edited by Donald M. Zillmann, Alastair Lucas, and George Pring. Oxford: Oxford University Press, 155–185.

Davis, Ann. 2002. New Alarms Heat Up Debate on Publicizing Chemical Risks. *Wall Street Journal* May 30.

De Abreu Ferreira, Sofia. 2007. The Fundamental Right of Access to Environmental Information in the EC: A Critical Analysis of *WWF-EPO v. Council*. *Journal of Environmental Law* 19: 399–408.

Deckmyn, Veerle and Ian, Thomson, eds. 1997. *Openness and Transparency in the European Union*. Maastricht, Netherlands: European Institute of Public Administration.

Delaunay, Bénédicte. 2003. De la loi du 17 juillet 1978 au droit à l'information en matière de l'environnement. *Actualité Juridique: Droit Administratif* 25: 1316–1324.

Delmas, Magali, Maria Montes-Sancho, and Jay Shimshack. 2006. *Mandatory Information Disclosure and Environmental Performance in the Electricity Industry*. Seminar in Environmental Economics and Public Policy at John F. Kennedy School of Government, Harvard University. October, Cambridge, MA.

Desai, Bharat H. 1993. The Bhopal Gas Leak Disaster Litigation: An Overview. *Yearbook of International Law* 3: 163–179.

DHS (U.S. Department of Homeland Security). 2004. Procedures for Handling Critical Infrastructure Information (CII): Interim Rule. February 20. *Federal Register* 69: 8073–8089.

Didzoleit, Winfried. 2002. Tabakwerbung: Nagel im Sarg. *Der Spiegel*, Dec. 9, 40.

Dorman, Ted L. 2004. Case Note on the OSPAR Arbitration Award of July 2, 2003, in *Ireland vs. UK*. *American Journal of International Law* 98: 330–339.

DQA (U.S. Data Quality [Information Quality] Act). 2001. Consolidated Appropriations Act: Fiscal Year 2001 of 2000. *Public Law* 106–554, § 515.

Driesen, David M. 2003. *The Economic Dynamics of Environmental Law*. Cambridge, MA: MIT Press.

Dycus, Stephen. 2005. Osama's Submarine: National Security and Environmental Protection after 9/11. *William and Mary Environmental Law and Policy Review* 30: 1–54.

Ebbesson, Jonas. 1997. The Notion of Public Participation in International Environmental Law. *Yearbook of International Environmental Law* 8: 51–97.

ECFI (European Court of First Instance). 1997. Judgment by the European Court of First Instance of March 5, 1997 (T-105/95, *WWF UK vs. Commission*), *European Court Reports* [1997] II: 313.

———. 1998. Judgment by the European Court of First Instance of February 6, 1998 (T-124/96, *Interporc II vs. Commission*), *European Court Reports* [1998] II: 231.

———. 1999. Judgment by the European Court of First Instance of October 14, 1999 (T-309/97, *Bavarian Lager Co. Ltd. vs. Commission*), *European Court Reports* [1999] II: 3217.

———. 2004. Judgment by the European Court of First Instance of November 30, 2004 (T-168/02, *IFAW vs. Commission*), *Official Journal of the European Union* [2005] C 31: 18.

Echeverria, John D., and Julie B. Kaplan. 2002. Poisonous Procedural "Reform": In Defense of Environmental Right to Know. *Kansas Journal of Law and Public Policy* 12: 579–649.

ECHR (European Convention for the Protection of Human Rights). 1950. European Convention for the Protection of Human Rights and Fundamental Freedoms, adopted at Strasbourg on November 4, 1950, ratified by 47 countries. *Council of Europe Treaty Series* 005, *United Nations Treaty Series* 213: 222.

ECJ (European Court of Justice). 1999. Judgment by the European Court of Justice of September 9, 1999 (C-217/97, *Commission v. Germany*, *European Court Reports* [1999] I: 5087) [declaring the 1994 German Environmental Information Act (*Umweltinformationsgesetz/UIG, BGBl* I: 1490) inadequate for compliance with EU Directive 90/313/EEC].

———. 2000. Judgment by the European Court of Justice of October 5, 2000 (C-376/98, *Germany v. European Parliament and Council*: Tobacco Advertising), *European Court Reports* [2000] I: 8419; and Order of the Court of April 3, 2000, regarding removal of documents. *European Court Reports* [2000] I:2247.

———. 2001. Judgment by the European Court of Justice of December 6, 2001 (C-353/99 P., *Council v. Heidi Hautala et al.*), *European Court Reports* [2001] I: 09565.

———. 2003. Judgment by the European Court of Justice of June 12, 2003 (C-316/01, *Eva Glawischnig v. Austrian Ministry for Social Security and Generations*), *European Court Reports* [2003] I: 6009 [refusing to disclose the names of manufacturers and products not in compliance with EU regulations on the labeling of genetically modified foodstuffs under Directive 90/313/EC].

Economist. 2006. The New Paternalism: The Avuncular State. *Economist* 379 (8472): 75–79.

Eigen, Peter, ed. 2003. *Access to Information: Global Corruption Report.* Berlin: Transparency International.

Emtairah, Tarequation. 2002. *Corporate Environmental Reporting: Review of Policy Action in Europe.* Lund, Sweden: International Institute for Industrial Environmental Economics.

Engel, Christoph, Jost Halfmann, and Martin Schulte, eds. 2002. *Wissen, Nichtwissen, unsicheres Wissen.* Baden-Baden, Germany: Nomos.

Engel, Rüdiger. 1993. *Akteneinsicht und Recht auf Informationen über umweltbezogene Daten: die Informationsrichtlinie der EG im Vergleich zur bundesdeutschen Rechtslage.* Pfaffenweiler, Germany: Centaurus.

Environmental Information (Scotland) Regulations. 2004. *Scottish Statutory Instruments* 2004 No. 520.

EPA (U.S. Environmental Protection Agency). 2002. *Guidelines for Ensuring and Maximizing the Quality, Objectivity, Utility, and Integrity of Information Disseminated by the Environmental Protection Agency.* EPA/260R-02-008. October. Washington, DC: EPA.

———. 2005. Principles of Environmental Stewardship Behavior. Appendix B of Draft *Nanotechnology White Paper.* December 2. Washington, DC: EPA.

———. 2006. Toxics Release Inventory Burden Reduction: Final Rule. *Federal Register* 71: 76932 December 22. *Code of Federal Regulations* 40: 372 (2008).

———. 2009. Final Mandatory Greenhouse Reporting Rule (pursuant to FY 2008 Consolidated Appropriations Act, Public Law 110-161). *Federal Register* 74: 56260 October 30.

EPCRA (U.S. Emergency Planning and Community Right-to-Know Act). 1986. *U.S. Code* 42, § 11001, enacted as Title III of the Superfund Amendments and Reauthorization Act. Public Law 99-499, as amended and supplemented [e.g., by the Pollution Prevention Act of 1990].

EPER (European Pollutant Emission Register). 2000. Implementation of a European Pollutant Emission Register (EPER): Decision by the European Commission (2000/479/EC, July 17, 2000). *Official Journal of the European Communities* [2000] L 192: 36.

Erion, Graham. 2009. The Stock Market to the Rescue? Carbon Disclosure and the Future of Securities-Related Climate Change Litigation. *Review of European Community and International Environmental Law* 18: 164–171.

Esty, Daniel C. 2004. Environmental Protection in the Information Age. *New York University Law Review* 79: 115–211.

EU (European Union). 1985. Directive on the Assessment of the Effects of Certain Public and Private Projects on the Environment: Council of the European Communities (85/337/EEC, June 27, 1985). *Official Journal of the European Communities* [1985] L 175: 40; as amended by Directive 97/11/EC (March 14, 1997), *Official Journal of the European Communities* [1997] L 73: 5.

———. 1990. Directive on Freedom of Access to Information on the Environment: Council of the European Communities (90/313/EEC, June 7, 1990). *Official Journal of the European Communities* [1990] L 158: 56.

———. 1998. Directive on the Approximation of the Laws, Regulations and Administrative Provisions of the Member States relating to the Advertising and Sponsorship of Tobacco Products: Council of the European Communities (98/43/EC, July 6, 1998). *Official Journal of the European Communities* [1998] L 213: 9.

———. 2000a. Report by the European Commission on the Experience Gained in the Application of Council Directive 90/313/EEC. EU Doc. COM (2000)400/final (June 29, 2000).

———. 2000b. Action for Financial Penalties, Brought by the European Commission in the European Court of Justice on November 8, 2000 (C-408/00, *Commission vs. Germany, Official Journal of the European Communities* [2001] C 28: 13) [for noncompliance with several EU Directives; after new legislation was enacted by Germany in 2001 (*UIG, BGBl* I, 2218), the case was removed from the Court's register on February 22, 2002].

———. 2001a. Regulation (EC) 1049/2001 regarding Public Access to European Parliament, Council, and Commission Documents: European Parliament and Council of the European

Communities (May 30, 2001). *Official Journal of the European Communities* [2001] L 145: 43 [prior to the regulation, the matter had been covered by a Code of Conduct implemented by Council Decision 93/731 and Commission Decision 94/90].

———. 2001b. Recommendation on the Recognition, Measurement, and Disclosure of Environmental Issues in the Annual Accounts and Annual Reports of Companies: European Commission (2001/453/EC, May 30, 2001). *Official Journal of the European Communities* [2001] L 156: 33.

———. 2003a. Directive on Public Access to Environmental Information, and Repealing Council Directive 90/313/EEC: European Parliament and Council of the European Communities (2003/4/EC), January 28 2003. *Official Journal of the European Union* [2003] L 41: 26.

———. 2003b. Directive on the Approximation of the Laws, Regulations and Administrative Provisions of the Member States Relating to the Advertising and Sponsorship of Tobacco Products: European Parliament and Council of the European Communities (2003/33/EC), May 26, 2003. *Official Journal of the European Union* [2003] L 152: 16, corrigendum [2004] L 67: 34.

———. 2003c. Directive on the Annual and Consolidated Accounts of Certain Types of Companies, Banks and Other Financial Institutions and Insurance Undertakings: European Parliament and Council of the European Communities (2003/51/EC), June 18, 2003. *Official Journal of the European Union* [2003] L 178: 16.

———. 2004. *Council Annual Report on Access to Documents.* Luxembourg: Council of the European Communities. May.

———. 2006a. Regulation (EC) 166/2006 concerning the Establishment of a European Pollutant Release and Transfer Register and Amending Council Directives 91/689/EEC and 96/61/EC: European Parliament and Council of the European Communities (January 18, 2006, in force February 24, 2006). *Official Journal of the European Union* [2006] L 33: 1.

———. 2006b. Regulation (EC) 1367/2006 on the Application of the Provisions of the Aarhus Convention to European Community Institutions and Bodies: European Parliament and Council of the European Communities (September 6, 2006, in force June 28, 2007). *Official Journal of the European Union* [2006] L 264: 13.

———. 2007. Commission Green Paper on Public Access to Documents Held by the Institutions of the European Community: A Review (April 18, 2007). COM (2007) 185 final.

———. 2008. Commission Proposal for a Regulation of the European Parliament and of the Council Regarding Public Access to European Parliament. Council and Commission Documents (April 30 2008). COM (2008) 229 final.

———. 2010. European Parliament: Committee on Civil Liberties, Justice and Home Affairs. Draft Report on the Proposal for a Regulation of the European Parliament and of the Council Regarding Public Access to European Parliament. Council and Commission Documents (recast, May 12, 2010). COM (2008)0229-C6-0184/2008-2008/0090(COD).

Farber, Daniel A., and Fred L. Morrison. 2000. Access to Environmental Information. In *International, Regional and National Environmental Law,* edited by Fred L. Morrison and Rüdiger Wolfrum. The Hague: Kluwer Law International, 845–860.

Farmer, Lindsay, and Gunther Teubner. 1994. Ecological Self-Organization. In *Environmental Law and Ecological Responsibility: The Concept and Practice of Ecological Self-Organization,* edited by Gunther Teubner, Lindsay Farmer, and Declan Murphy. Chichester, UK: John Wiley and Sons, 3–13.

FCTC (Framework Convention on Tobacco Control). 2003. World Health Organization Framework Convention on Tobacco Control, adopted at Geneva by Resolution 56.1 of the World Health Assembly on May 21, 2003, in force February 27, 2005; ratified by 170 countries [not including the U.S.] and the EU. *United Nations Treaty Series* 2302: 166; *International Legal Materials* 42: 518.

Feller, Robert H. 1995. Environmental Disclosure and the Securities Laws. *Boston College Environmental Affairs Law Review* 22: 225–266.

Fievet, Gilles. 2001. Réflexions sur le concept de développement durable: prétention économique, principes stratégiques, et protection des droits fondamentaux. *Revue Belge de Droit International* 34: 128–184.

Fischer, Joschka. 1989. *Der Umbau der Industriegesellschaft: Plädoyer wider die herrschende Umweltlüge.* Frankfurt: Eichborn. English transl. in *Ecological Enlightenment: Essays on the Politics of Risk Society,* edited by Ulrich Beck. 1995. Atlantic Highlands, NJ: Humanity Press.

Fisher, Elizabeth. 2004. The European Union in the Age of Accountability. *Oxford Journal of Legal Studies* 24: 495–515.

Florini, Ann. 1998. The End of Secrecy. *Foreign Policy* 111: 50–63.

———, ed. 2007. *The Right to Know: Transparency for an Open World.* New York: Columbia University Press.

———. 2008. Making Transparency Work. *Global Environmental Politics* 8 (2): 14–16.

Fluck, Jürgen, eds. 1993. *Freier Zugang zu Umweltinformationen.* Heidelberg: Müller.

Fluck, Jürgen, and Andreas Theuer, eds. 1994. *Informationsfreiheitsrecht mit Umweltinformations-und Verbraucherinformationsrecht.* Heidelberg: Müller.

Foerstel, Herbert N. 1999. *Freedom of Information and the Right to Know: The Origins and Applications of the Freedom of Information Act.* Westport, CT: Greenwood Press.

FOIA (U.S. Freedom of Information Act). 1966. U.S. Freedom of Information Act of July 4, 1966. Public Law 89–554, 90-23. *U.S. Code* 5: § 552, as amended 2003 by Public Law 107–306, and 2007 by Public Law 110–175.

———. 2009a. White House Memorandum on the Freedom of Information Act (January 21, 2009). *Federal Register* (January 26) 74: 4683.

———. 2009b. U.S. Attorney General's Memorandum on the Freedom of Information Act (March 19, 2009) for Heads of Executive Departments and Agencies.

Foti, Joseph, Lalanath de Silva, Heather McGray, Linda Shaffer, Jon Talbot, and Jake Werksman. 2008. *Voice and Choice: Opening the Door to Environmental Democracy.* Washington, DC: World Resources Institute.

Foulon, Jérôme, Paul Lanoie, and Benoît Laplante. 2002. Incentives for Pollution Control: Regulation or Information? *Journal of Environmental Economics and Management* 44: 169–187.

FreedomInfo. 2010. IFTI. http://freedominfo.org/ifti (accessed June 1, 2010).

Freund, Michael. 1997. Proposition 65 Enforcement: Reducing Lead Emissions in California. *Tulane Environmental Law Journal* 10: 333–370.

Frost, Amanda. 2003. Restoring Faith in Government: Transparency Reform in the United States and Europe. *European Public Law* 9: 87–104.

Fung, Archon, Mary Graham, and David Weil. 2007. *Full Disclosure: The Perils and Promise of Transparency.* Cambridge: Cambridge University Press.

Fung, Archon, Mary Graham, David Weil, and Elena Fagotta. 2004. The Political Economy of Transparency: What Makes Disclosure Policies Sustainable? Faculty Research Working Paper. Cambridge, MA: John F. Kennedy School of Government, Harvard University.

Fung, Archon, and Dara O'Rourke. 2000. Reinventing Environmental Regulation from the Grassroots Up: Explaining and Expanding the Success of the Toxics Release Inventory. *Environmental Management* 25: 115–127.

Funtowicz, Silvio O., and Jerry R. Ravetz. 2001. Global Risk, Uncertainty, and Ignorance. In *Global Environmental Risk,* edited by Jeanne X. Kasperson and Roger E. Kasperson. Tokyo: United Nations University Press, 173–194.

Gaines, Sanford E. 2003. Reflexive Law as a Legal Paradigm for Sustainable Development. *Buffalo Environmental Law Journal* 10: 1–24.

GAO (U.S. Government Accountability Office). 2004. *Environmental Disclosure: SEC Should Explore Ways to Improve Tracking and Transparency of Information,* Washington, DC: GAO-04-808. July 14.

García Ureta, Agustín, and Iñigo Lazcano Brotóns. 2005. Access to Information on the Environment and Failure of a Public Authority to Respond within the Time-Limit for Reply. *Environmental Liability* 13: 60–64.

Gassner, Ulrich M., and Christian Pisani. 2001. Umweltinformationsanspruch und Geheimnisschutz: Zukunftsperspektiven. *Natur und Recht* 23: 506–512.

Gavouneli, Maria. 2000. Access to Environmental Information: Delimitation of a Right. *Tulane Environmental Law Journal* 13: 303–327.

Geiger, Gebhard, ed. 2000. *Sicherheit der Informationsgesellschaft: Gefährdung und Schutz informations-abhängiger Infrastrukturen.* Baden-Baden, Germany: Nomos.

Geltman, Elizabeth Ann Glass. 1992. Disclosure of Contingent Environmental Liabilities by Public Companies under the Federal Securities Laws. *Harvard Environmental Law Review* 16: 129–137.

Giddens, Anthony. 2000. *The Third Way and Its Critics.* Cambridge: Polity Press.

Gidiere, Stephen, and Jason Forrester. 2002. Balancing Homeland Security and Freedom of Information. *Natural Resources and Environment* 16: 139–145.

Glaeser, Edward L. 2006. Paternalism and Psychology. *University of Chicago Law Review* 73: 133–156.

Global Transparency Initiative (GTI). 2009. Comments on *Toward Greater Transparency through Access to Information: The World Bank's Disclosure Policy Revised Draft (October 16, 2009).* Washington, DC: Bank Information Center.

Godfrey, Fiona, ed. 2004. *Tobacco or Health in the European Union: Past, Present and Future.* Brussels: European Communities ASPECT Consortium.

Gollier, Christian, Hans-Peter Weikard, and Justus Wesseler. 2004. Risk and Uncertainty in Environmental and Resource Economics. *Journal of Risk and Uncertainty* 29: 5–6.

Goodman, Susannah B., and Tim Little. 2003. *The Gap in GAAP: An Examination of Environmental Accounting Loopholes.* Oakland, CA: Rose Foundation for Communities and the Environment.

Gozali, Nike O., Janice C. Y. How, and Peter Verhoeven. 2002. The Economic Consequences of Voluntary Environmental Information Disclosure. In *Integrated Assessment and Decision Support: Proceedings of the First Biennial Meeting of the International Environmental Modelling and Software Society,* edited by Andrea E. Rizzoli and Anthony J. Jakeman. Manno, Switzerland: IEMSS 2, 484–489.

Graf, Michael W. 2001. Regulating Pesticide Pollution in California under the 1986 Safe Drinking Water and Toxic Exposure Act (Proposition 65). *Ecology Law Quarterly* 28: 663–754.

Graham, John D., Beat Habegger, Belinda Cleveland, and Marie V. Florin, eds. 2009. *Risk Governance Deficits: An Analysis and Illustration of the Most Common Deficits in Risk Governance.* Geneva: International Risk Governance Council.

Graham, John D., and Jonathan B. Wiener. 1995. *Risk versus Risk: Tradeoffs in Protecting Health and the Environment.* Cambridge, MA: Harvard University Press.

Graham, Mary. 2001. *Information as Risk Regulation: Lessons from Experience.* Innovations in American Government Program, OPS-10-01. Cambridge, MA: Harvard University Press.

———. 2002a. Is Sunshine the Best Disinfectant? The Promise and Problems of Environmental Disclosure. *Brookings Review* 20 (2): 18–19.

———. 2002b. *Democracy by Disclosure: The Rise of Technopopulism.* Washington, DC: Brookings Institution.

Graham, Mary, and Catherine Miller. 2001. Disclosure of Toxic Releases in the United States. *Environment* 43 (8): 8–20.

Grant, Don Sherman II.. 1997. Allowing Citizen Participation in Environmental Regulation: An Empirical Analysis of the Effect of Right-to-Sue and Right-to-Know Provisions on Industry's Toxic Emissions. *Social Science Quarterly* 78: 859–873.

Grant, Don Sherman II, and Liam Downey. 1996. Regulation through Information: An Empirical Analysis of the Effects of State-Sponsored Right-to-Know Programs on Industrial Toxic Pollution. *Policy Studies Review* 14: 339–352.

Gray, Kevin. 2003. World Summit on Sustainable Development: Accomplishments and New Directions? *International and Comparative Law Quarterly* 52: 256–268.

Green, Krista. 1999. An Analysis of the Supreme Court's Resolution of the Emergency Planning and Community Right-to-Know Act Citizen Suit Debate. *Boston College Environmental Affairs Law Review* 26: 387–434.

Greenwood, Mark A. 1999. *White Paper from Industry Coalition to EPA on Concerns over Information Program.* Washington, DC: Coalition for Effective Environmental Information; reprinted in Bureau of National Affairs, *Daily Environment Reporter,* May 4, E-1.

Greenwood, Mark A., and Amit K. Sachdev. 1999. *A Regulatory History of the Emergency Planning and Community Right to Know Act of 1986: Toxics Release Inventory.* Washington, DC: Chemical Manufacturers Association.

GRI (Global Reporting Initiative). 2006. *Sustainability Reporting Guidelines G3.* Amsterdam: GRI.
————. 2009. *2007–2008 Sustainability Report.* Amsterdam: GRI.
————. 2010. *Beyond Voluntary Laissez-Faire Reporting: Towards a European ESG Disclosure Framework.* Amsterdam: GRI.
Grigorescu, Alexandru. 2003. International Organizations and Government Transparency: Linking the International and Domestic Realms. *International Studies Quarterly* 47: 643–667.
Grüning, Thilo, Anna P. Gilmore, and Martin McKee. 2006. Tobacco Industry Influence on Science and Scientists in Germany. *American Journal of Public Health* 96: 20–32.
GSA (U.S. Government in the Sunshine Act). 1976. Public Law 94-409. *U.S. Code* 5, § 552b.
Guckelberger, Annette. 2008. Die EG-Verordnung zur Umsetzung der Aarhus-Konvention auf der Gemeinschaftsebene. *Natur und Recht* 30: 78–87.
Guerra case. 1998. Judgment by the European Court of Human Rights of February 29, 1998 (App. No. 14967/89, *Anna Maria Guerra et al. v. Italy*). *European Human Rights Reports* 26: 357 reprinted in *International Environmental Law Reports* 3: 260, and in Kravchenko and Bonine 2008, 251–253.
Gunningham, Neil, and Amanda Cornwall. 1994. Legislating the Right to Know. *Environmental and Planning Law Journal* 11: 274–288.
Gunningham, Neil, Peter Grabosky, and Darren Sinclair. 1998. *Smart Regulation: Designing Environmental Policy.* Oxford: Clarendon.
Gupta, Aarti. 2008. Transparency under Scrutiny: Information Disclosure in Global Environmental Governance. *Global Environmental Politics* 8 (2): 1–7.
Hadden, Susan G. 1989. *A Citizen's Right-to-Know: Risk Communication and Public Policy.* Boulder, CO: Westview.
Hallo, Ralph E., ed. 1996. *Access to Environmental Information in Europe: The Implementation and Implications of Directive 90/313/EEC.* London: Kluwer Law International.
Hamilton, James T. 1995. Pollution as News: Media and Stock Market Reactions to the Toxics Release Inventory Data. *Journal of Environmental Economics and Management* 28: 98–113.
————. 2005. *Regulation through Revelation: The Origin, Politics, and Impacts of the Toxics Release Inventory Program.* Cambridge: Cambridge University Press.
Hancock, Elizabeth E. 2005. Red Dawn, Blue Thunder, Purple Rain: Corporate Risk of Liability for Global Climate Change and the SEC Disclosure Dilemma. *Georgetown International Environmental Law Review* 17: 233–251.
Handl, Günther. 2001. *Multilateral Development Banking: Environmental Principles and Concepts Reflecting General International Law and Public Policy.* London: Kluwer Law International and Asian Development Bank.
Hansen, Patricia I. 1999. Transparency, Standards of Review, and the Use of Trade Measures to Protect the Global Environment. *Virginia Journal of International Law* 39: 1017–1068.
Harman-Stokes, Katherine M. 1995. "Community Right-to-Know" in the Newly Independent States of the Soviet Union: Ending the Culture of Secrecy Surrounding the Environmental Crisis. *Virginia Environmental Law Journal* 15: 77–138.
Harremoës, Poul. 2000. *Scientific Incertitude in Environmental Analysis and Decision Making* (Heineken Lecture). The Hague: Royal Netherlands Academy of Arts and Sciences.
Harrison, John. 2000. Legislazione Ambientale Europea e Libertà di Informazione: La Convenzione di Aarhus. *Rivista Giuridica dell'Ambiente* 15: 27–36.
Harrison, Kathryn, and Werner Antweiler. 2003. Incentives for Pollution Abatement: Regulation, Regulatory Threats, and Non-Governmental Pressures. *Journal of Policy Analysis and Management* 22: 361–382.
Harvard Law Review Note. 1990. Keeping Secrets: Congress, the Courts, and National Security Information. *Harvard Law Review* 103: 906–925.
Helm, Carsten. 1998. International Cooperation behind the Veil of Uncertainty. *Environmental and Resource Economics* 12: 185–201.
Henke, Jan M. 2004. *Information as an Environmental Policy Instrument: Environmental Product Information Schemes.* St. Gallen, Switzerland: Oikos Foundation for Economy and Environment, University of St. Gallen.

Hesse, Axel. 2004. *Das Klima wandelt sich: Integration von Klimachancen und-Risiken in die Finanzberichterstattung.* 2nd ed. Bonn: Germanwatch.

———. 2006. *Climate and Corporations: Right Answers or Wrong Questions?* Bonn: Germanwatch.

Hibbit, Chris J. 2004. *External Environmental Disclosure and Reporting by Large European Companies.* Amsterdam: Limperg Instituut.

Hilson, Chris. 2005. Information Disclosure and the Regulation of Traded Product Risks. *Journal of Environmental Law* 17: 305–322.

Hins, Wouter, and Dirk Voorhoof. 2007. Access to State-Held Information as a Fundamental Right Under the European Convention on Human Rights. *European Constitutional Law Review* 3: 114–126.

Höffler, Imke. 2002. *Akteneinsichtsrechte des Bürgers bei Deutschen Verwaltungsbehörden: Amtsgeheimnis oder Aktenöffentlichkeit?* Berlin: dissertation. de verlag.

Holm, Nils E. 1975. The Danish System of Open Files in Public Administration. *Scandinavian Studies in Law* 19: 153–177.

Holstad, Sigvard. 1979. Sweden. In *Administrative Secrecy in Developed Countries,* edited by Donald C. Rowat. New York: Columbia University Press, 29–50.

Holzinger, Katharina, Christoph Knill, and Ansgar Schäfer. 2003. *Steuerungswechsel in der europäischen Umweltpolitik?.* In *Politische Steuerung im Wandel: Der Einfluss von Ideen und Problemstrukturen,* edited by Katharina Holzinger, Christoph Knill, and Dirk Lehmkuhl. Opladen, Germany: Leske and Budrich, 103–129.

Hood, Christopher and David, Heald, eds. 2006. Transparency: The Key to Better Governance? *Proceedings of the British Academy No. 135.* Oxford: Oxford University Press.

HSA (U.S. Homeland Security Act). 2002. Public Law 107-296. *U.S. Code* 6, § 131. November 25.

Humphrey case. 1998. Settlement Agreement and Stipulation for Entry of Consent Judgment. *State ex rel. Humphrey v. Philip Morris Inc.,* No. C1–94–8565, 1998 WL 394331. Minnesota District Court, May 8.

IFSA-CADA (Institut Français des Sciences Administratives and Commission d'Accès aux Documents Administratifs). 2003. *Transparence et secret: colloque pour le XXVe anniversaire de la loi du 17 juillet 1978 sur l'accès aux documents administratifs.* Paris: Documentation Française.

Iida, Keisuke. 1993. Analytic Uncertainty and International Cooperation: Theory and Application to International Economic Policy Considerations. *International Studies Quarterly* 37: 431–457.

IMF (International Monetary Fund). 2005. *Transparency: Publication Policies.* Decision No. 13564-(05/85), October 5. Washington, DC: IMF.

IOMC (Inter-Organization Programme for the Sound Management of Chemicals). 2001. Summary Record of the Seventh Meeting of the IOMC PRTR Coordinating Group, June. Paris. Geneva: World Health Organization.

ISO (International Organization for Standardization). 2006. *Greenhouse Gases: Specifications for the Quantification, Monitoring and Reporting of Emissions and Removals.* Technical Committee 207 on Environmental Matters. ISO Standard 14064. March. Geneva: ISO.

———. 2007. *Greenhouse Gases: Requirements for Greenhouse Gas Validation and Verification Bodies for Use in Accreditation or Other Forms of Recognition.* Technical Committee 207 on Environmental Matters. ISO Standard 14065. April. Geneva: ISO.

Ivester, David Mitchell. 1977. The Constitutional Right to Know. *Hastings Constitutional Law Quarterly* 109: 109–132.

Jacob, Gregory F. 2004. Without Reservation. *Chicago Journal of International Law* 5: 287–302.

Jacobson, Joseph D. 2003. Safeguarding National Security through Public Release of Environmental Information: Moving the Debate to the Next Level. *Environmental Lawyer* 9: 356–396.

Jaeger, Carlo, Ortwin Renn, Eugene A. Rosa, and Thomas Webler. 2001. *Risk, Uncertainty and Rational Action.* London: Earthscan.

Jahnke, Marlene. 2003. Right to Environmental Information. *Environmental Policy and Law* 33: 37.

Jefferson, Thomas. 1854. Letter to William Charles Jarvis, September 28, 1820 *The Writings of Thomas Jefferson.* Vol. 7, edited by H. A. Washington. Washington, DC: Taylor & Maury, 177.

Jendrośka, Jerzy. 2005. Aarhus Convention and Community Law: The Interplay. *Journal for European Environmental and Planning Law* 2: 12–25.

———. 2007. *Dostęp do Informacji o Środowisku i Jego Ochronie* [Access to Environmental Information]. Wrocław-Poznań, Poland: PZITS.

Jobe, Margaret M. 1999. The Power of Information: The Example of the U.S. Toxics Release Inventory. *Journal of Government Information* 26: 287–295.

Johannesburg Report. 2002. Report of the World Summit on Sustainable Development, Johannesburg, August 26–September 4, South Africa. New York: UN Doc. A/CONF.199/20.

Johnson, Stephen M. 2004. Terrorism, Security, and Environmental Protection. *William and Mary Environmental Law Review* 29: 107–158.

Jolls, Christine, and Cass R. Sunstein. 2004. *Debiasing through Law*. Olin Law and Economics Discussion Paper 495. Cambridge, MA: Harvard Law School. September; reprinted as Olin Law and Economics Working Paper 225, University of Chicago, March.

Jordan, Andrew, Rüdiger K. W. Wurzel, and Anthony R. Zito, eds. 2003. *"New" Instruments of Environmental Governance? National Experiences and Prospects*. London: Cass.

Karkkainen, Bradley C. 2001. Information as Environmental Regulation: TRI and Performance Benchmarking, Precursor to a New Paradigm? *Georgetown Law Journal* 89: 257–370.

Kass, Stephen L, and Jean M. McCarroll. 1997. Environmental Disclosure in Security and Exchange Commission Filings. *Environment* 39 (3): 2–4.

Kennedy, Peter W., Benoit LaPlante, and John W. Maxwell. 1994. Pollution Policy: The Role for Publicly Provided Information. *Journal of Environmental Economics and Management* 26: 31–43.

Kennedy, Robert F. Jr. 2004. *Crimes against Nature: How George W. Bush and His Corporate Pals Are Plundering the Country and Hijacking Our Democracy*. New York: Harper Collins.

Kern, Kristine, Helge Jörgens, and Martin Jänicke. 2000. *The Diffusion of Environmental Policy Innovations: A Contribution to the Globalisation of Environmental Policy*. Discussion Paper FS II/01-302. Berlin: Wissenschaftszentrum für Sozialforschung.

Khanna, Madhu, Wilma Rose H. Quimio, and Dora Bojilova. 1998. Toxics Release Information: A Policy Tool for Environmental Protection. *Journal of Environmental Economics and Management* 36: 243–266.

Kiernan, Matthew J., and Paul Dickinson. 2005. *Carbon Disclosure Project Report CDP3*. London: Innovest.

Kimber, Cliona J. M., and Felix Ekardt. 1999. Zugang zu Umweltinformationen in Grossbritannien und Deutschland. *Natur und Recht* 21: 262–268.

Kleindorfer, Paul R., and Eric W. Orts. 1998. Informational Regulation of Environmental Risks. *Risk Analysis* 18: 155–170.

Kleine, Maxim. 2000. Book Review of Schneider and Stein 1999. *Zeitschrift für ausländisches öffentliches Recht und Völkerrecht [Heidelberg Journal of International Law]* 60: 277–278.

Kloepfer, Michael. 2004. Umweltrecht als Informationsrecht. *Umwelt- und Planungsrecht* 25: 41–49.

Knight, Frank H. 1921. *Risk, Uncertainty and Profit*. Repr. Chicago: University of Chicago Press. 1985.

Koester, Veit. 2007. The Compliance Committee of the Aarhus Convention: An Overview of Procedures and Jurisprudence. *Environmental Policy and Law* 37: 83–96.

Kolstad, Charles D. 2002. International Environmental Agreements and the Veil of Uncertainty. Paper presented at the Conference on Risk and Uncertainty in Environmental and Resource Economics, Wageningen, Netherlands.

Konar, Shameek, and Mark A. Cohen. 1997. Information as Regulation: The Effect of Community Right-to-Know Laws on Toxic Emissions. *Journal of Environmental Economics and Management* 32: 109–124.

Kraft, Michael E., Troy D. Abel, and Mark Stephan. 2004. *Information Disclosure and Risk Reduction: The Sources of Varying State Performance in Control of Toxic Chemical Emissions*. Conference on Corporate Environmental Behavior and the Effectiveness of Government Intervention, April 26. Washington, DC: U.S. EPA National Center for Environmental Economics.

Krämer, Ludwig. 1991. La directive 90/313/CEE sur l'accès à l'information en matière d'environnement: génèse et perspectives d'application. *Revue du Marché Commun* [1991]: 866.

———. 2003. Access to Letters of Formal Notice and Reasoned Opinions in Environmental Law Matters. *European Environmental Law Review* 12: 197–203.

————. 2004. Access to Environmental Information in an Open Society: Directive 2003/4/EC. *Yearbook of European Environmental Law* 4: 1–28.

Kranenborg, Herke, and Wim Voermans. 2005. *Access to Information in the European Union: A Comparative Analysis of EC and Member State Legislation.* Groningen, Netherlands: Europa Law Publishing.

Kravchenko, Svitlana and John E., Bonine, eds. 2008. *Human Rights and the Environment: Cases, Law, and Policy.* Durham, NC: Carolina Academic Press.

Kunzlik, Peter. 1997. Access to the Commission's Documents in Environmental Cases: Confidentiality and Public Confidence. *Journal of Environmental Law* 9: 321–344.

Ladeur, Karl-Heinz. 1994. Coping with Uncertainty: Ecological Risks and the Proceduralization of Environmental Law. In *Environmental Law and Ecological Responsibility: The Concept and Practice of Ecological Self-Organization,* edited by Gunther Teubner, Lindsay Farmer, and Declan Murphy. Chichester: John Wiley and Sons, 299–336.

Lamberton, Donald M., ed. 1971. *The Economics of Information and Knowledge.* Harmondsworth, UK: Penguin.

————. 1984. The Emergence of Information Economics. In *Communication and Information Economics: New Perspectives,* edited by Meheroo Jussawalla and Helene Ebenfield. Amsterdam: North Holland, 7–22.

Lamble, Stephen. 2002. Freedom of Information: A Finnish Clergyman's Gift to Democracy. *Freedom of Information Review* 97: 2–8.

Lapierre, Dominique, and Javier Moro. 2001. *Il était minuit cinq à Bhopal: récit.* Paris: Laffont. English transl. 2002, *Five Past Midnight in Bhopal.* London: Scribner.

Larssen, Christine, ed. 2003. *Ten Years of Access to Environmental Information in International, European and Belgian Law.* Brussels: Bruylant.

Larsson Ortino, Maria. 2004. *Framework Conventions as Instruments to Address Health and Environmental Concerns in International Law: The Case of the Framework Convention on Tobacco Control.* Geneva: Graduate Institute of International Studies.

Latham, Mark. 2009. Environmental Liabilities and the Federal Securities Laws: A Proposal for Improved Disclosure of Climate Change Related Risks. *Environmental Law* 39: 647–728.

Lewis, Sanford J. 1999. The Precautionary Principle and Corporate Disclosure. In *Protecting Public Health and the Environment: Implementing the Precautionary Principle,* edited by Carolyn Raffensperger and Joel Tickner. Washington, DC: Island Press, 241–251.

Litfin, Karen T. 1994. *Ozone Discourse: Science and Politics in Global Environmental Cooperation.* New York: Columbia University Press.

Little, Margaret A. 2001. A Most Dangerous Indiscretion: The Legal, Economic, and Political Legacy of the Government's Tobacco Litigation. *Connecticut Law Review* 33: 1143–1205.

Logomasini, Angela. 2002. Toxic Road Map for Terrorists *Washington Post,* Sept. 4.

Loi 78-753 [French Act on Administrative Relations with the Public]. 1978. Loi No. 78-753 du 17 juillet 1978 portant diverses mesures d'amélioration des relations entre l'administration et le public et diverses dispositions d'ordre administratif, social et fiscal. *Journal Officiel de la République Française* (18 July 1978) 2851.

Luebbe-Wolff, Gertrude. 1980. Das niederländische Gesetz über die Verwaltungsöffentlichkeit. *Verwaltung* 13: 339–355.

Lugano Convention. 1993. Convention on Civil Liability for Damage Resulting from Activities Dangerous to the Environment, adopted by the Council of Europe at Lugano on June 21, 1993, signed by nine countries and ratified by three, not yet in force. *International Legal Materials* 32: 1228.

Lungren case. 1996. Judgment by the California Supreme Court in *People ex rel. Lungren vs. Superior Court (American Standard Inc.). California Reports,* 4th ser. 14: 294.

Lyndon, Mary L. 1989. Information Economics and Chemical Toxicity: Designing Laws to Produce and Use Data. *Michigan Law Review* 87: 1795–1861.

Lynn, Francis M., and Jack D. Kartez. 1994. Environmental Democracy in Action: The Toxics Release Inventory. *Environmental Management* 18: 511–521.

MacDonald, Kareen E. 2008. The European Pollutant Release and Transfer Register. *European Journal of Law Reform* 10: 21–40.

Magat, Wesley A., and W. Kip Viscusi. 1992. *Informational Approaches to Regulation*. Cambridge, MA: MIT Press. Repr. in *Foundations for Environmental Law and Policy*, edited by Richard L. Revesz. 1997. Oxford: Oxford University Press, 149.

Mansley, Mark. 2003. *Open Disclosure: Sustainability and the Listing Regime*. London: Friends of the Earth.

Marsh, Norman S., ed. 1987. *Public Access to Government-Held Information: A Comparative Symposium*. London: Stevens and Son.

Mason, Michael. 2008. Transparency for Whom? Information Disclosure and Power in Global Environmental Governance. *Global Environmental Politics* 8 (2): 8–13.

McDermott, Patrice. 2002. Withhold and Control: Information in the Bush Administration. *Kansas Journal of Law and Public Policy* 12: 671–692.

McDonagh, Maeve. 2000. Freedom of Information in Common Law Jurisdictions: The Experience and the Challenge. *Multimedia und Recht* 3: 251–256.

McFarland, Jeffrey M. 2009. Warming Up to Climate Change Risk Disclosure. *Fordham Journal of Corporate and Financial Law* 14: 281.

McGarity, Thomas O. and Sidney A. Shapiro. 1980. The Trade Secret Status of Health and Safety Testing Information: Reforming Agency Disclosure Policies. *Harvard Law Review* 93: 837–888.

McGinley case. 1998. Judgment by the European Court of Human Rights of June 9, 1998 (App. No. 21825/93, 23414/94, *McGinley and Egan vs. United Kingdom*). *European Human Rights Reports* 27: 1.

Mendel, Toby. 2008. *Freedom of Information: A Comparative Legal Survey*. 2nd ed. Paris: UNESCO.

Menell, Peter S. 1995. Structuring a Market-Oriented Federal Eco-Information Policy. *Maryland Law Review* 54: 1435–1474.

Mitchell, Ronald B. 1998. Sources of Transparency: Information Systems in International Regimes. *International Studies Quarterly* 42: 109–130.

Mock, William. 1999. On the Centrality of Information Law: A Rational Choice Discussion of Information Law and Transparency. *John Marshall Journal of Computer and Information Law* 17: 1069–1086.

Mohagdan, Reza. 2009. Freedom of IMFormation. International Monetary Fund Global Economy Forum, September 17, Washington, DC.

Mol, Arthur P. J. 2008. *Environmental Reform in the Information Age: The Contours of Informational Governance*. Cambridge: Cambridge University Press.

Monédiaire, Gérard. 1999. Les droits à l'information et à la participation du public auprès de l'Union européenne. *Revue Européenne de Droit de l'Environnement* 3: 129–156, 253–269.

Morgera, Elisa. 2005. An Update on the Aarhus Convention and Its Continued Global Relevance. *Review of European Community and International Environmental Law* 14: 138–147.

Moteff, John D. 2005. Critical Infrastructures: Background, Policy, and Implementation. Report for Congress RL30153. July 12. Washington, DC: U.S. Congressional Research Service.

Moteff, John D., and Gina Maria Stevens. 2003. Critical Infrastructure Information Disclosure and Homeland Security. Report for Congress RL31547. January 29. Washington, DC: U.S. Congressional Research Service.

Naysnerski, Wendy and Thomas H. Tietenberg. 1992. Private Enforcement of Environmental Law. *Land Economics* 68: 28–48. Repr. in *Innovation in Environmental Policy*, edited by Thomas H. Tietenberg (1991), Aldershot: Edward Elgar, 109–136; and in *Economics and Environmental Policy*, by Thomas H. Tietenberg (1994), Aldershot: Edward Elgar, 254–274.

Nelson, Paul J. 2001. Transparency Mechanisms in the Multilateral Development Banks. *World Development* 29: 1835–1847.

NEPA (U.S. National Environmental Policy Act). 1970. Public Law 91-190. *U.S. Code* 42: 4321 January 1.

Neuman, Mark A., Asaf Bitton, and Stanton Glantz. 2002. Tobacco Industry Strategies for Influencing European Community Tobacco Advertising Legislation. *Lancet* 359 (9314): 1323–1330.

Nicola, Fernanda, and Fabio Marchetti. 2005. Constitutionalizing Tobacco: The Ambivalence of European Federalism. *Harvard International Law Journal* 46: 507–525.

NRC (U.S. National Research Council). 1989. *Improving Risk Communication.* Committee on Risk Perception and Communication. Washington, DC: National Academy Press.

Öberg, Ulf. 2000. EU Citizens' Right to Know: The Improbable Adoption of a European Freedom of Information Act. *Cambridge Yearbook of European Legal Studies* 2: 303–328.

OECD (Organisation for Economic Co-operation and Development). 1988. *Decision-Recommendation of the Council concerning Provision of Information to the Public and Public Participation in Decisionmaking Processes Related to the Prevention of, and Response to, Accidents Involving Hazardous Substances.* July 8. C(88)85 final. Paris: OECD.

————. 1996. *Recommendation of the Council on Implementing Pollutant Release and Transfer Registers.* February 20, 1996. C(96)41 final; as amended on May 28, 2003, C(2003)87. Paris: OECD.

————. 2000. *Proceedings of the Seminar on Public Access to Environmental Information,* June 5–7, Athens. ENV/EPOC/GEP(2000)8. Paris: OECD.

————. 2005. *Uses of Pollutant Release and Transfer Register Data and Tools for Their Presentation: A Reference Manual.* ENV/JM/MONO(2005)3. January 26. Paris: OECD.

Offentligheds-Lov. 1970. Public Access to Documents in Administrative Files: Danish Act No. 280 of June 10, 1970, in force January 1, 1971.

OGA (U.S. OPEN Government Act). 2007. Public Law 110–175. *U.S. Statutes at Large* 121: 2524.

OMB (U.S. Office of Management and Budget). 2002. Guidelines for Ensuring and Maximizing the Quality, Objectivity, Utility, and Integrity of Information Disseminated by Federal Agencies. February. *Federal Register* 67: 8452–8460.

OMB Watch. 2005. *Dismantling the Public's Right to Know.* Washington, DC: OMB Watch. December.

O'Neill, Michael. 1998. The Right of Access to Community-Held Documentation as a General Principle of EC Law. *European Public Law* 4: 403–432.

Openbaarheidswet. 1978. Netherlands *Wet Openbaarheid van Bestuur* [WOB, Administrative Transparency Act] of November 9, 1978. Netherlands *Staatsblad* [1978]: 581, in force from May 1, 1980 [superseded by the Act of 31 October 1991 containing regulations governing public access to government information. English transl. in *Public Access to Environmental Information and Data: Practice Examples from the United States, the European Union, and Central and Eastern Europe* (2001). Washington, DC: Resources for the Future.

O'Reilly, James T. 2002. "Access to Records" versus "Access to Evil": Should Disclosure Laws Consider Motives as a Barrier to Records Release? *Kansas Journal of Law and Public Policy* 12: 559–578.

O'Reilly, Kirk T. 2007. Science, Policy, and Politics: The Impact of the Information Quality Act on Risk-Based Regulatory Activity at the EPA. *Buffalo Environmental Law Journal* 14: 249–287.

Orts, Eric W. 1995. Reflexive Environmental Law. *Northwestern University Law* 89: 1227–1340.

————. 2001. *Autopoiesis and the Natural Environment.* In *Law's New Boundaries: The Consequences of Legal Autopoiesis,* edited by Jiŕi Pribáň and David Nelken. Aldershot: Ashgate-Dartmouth, 159–178.

OSHA (U.S. Department of Labor Occupational Safety and Health Administration). 1983. Hazard Communication Standard (1983, as amended to 1994). *Federal Register* 59: 6126.

OSPAR (OSPAR Convention). 1992. Convention for the Protection of the Marine Environment of the North-East Atlantic [revising and consolidating the earlier 1972 Oslo and 1974 Paris Conventions], adopted at Paris on September 22, 1992, in force March 25, 1998; ratified by 15 European countries and the EU. *International Legal Materials* 32: 1068.

Österdahl, Inger. 1998. Openness versus Secrecy: Public Access to Documents in Sweden and the European Union. *European Law Review* 23: 336–356.

Pack, Bradley. 2004. FOIA Frustration: Access to Government Documents under the Bush Administration. *Arizona Law Review* 46: 815–842.

Pallemaerts, Marc, ed. 1991. *Het recht op informatie inzake leefmilieu/Le droit à l'information en matière d'environnement/The Right to Environmental Information.* Brussels: Story-Scientia.

Papandreou, Mary-Rose. 2005. Under Attack: The Public's Right to Know and the War on Terror. *Boston College Third World Law Journal* 25: 35–81.

Partsch, Christoph J. 2001. Die neue Transparenzverordnung (EG) Nr. 1049/2001. *Neue Juristische Wochenschrift* 54: 3154–3158.

———. 2002. *Die Freiheit des Zugangs zu Verwaltungsinformationen: Akteneinsichtsrecht in Deutschland, Europa und den U.S.A.* Cologne: Lohmar.

Patten, Dennis M. 2002. The Relation between Environmental Performance and Environmental Disclosure: A Research Note. *Accounting, Organizations and Society* 27: 763–773.

Pedersen, William F. Jr. 2001. Regulation and Information Disclosure: Parallel Universes and Beyond. *Harvard Environmental Law Review* 25: 151–211.

Peers, Steve. 2002. The New Regulation on Access to Documents: A Critical Analysis. *Yearbook of European Law* 21: 385–442.

Penders, Michael J., and William L. Thomas. 2002. The Specter of Ecoterror: Rethinking Environmental Security. *Natural Resources and Environment* 16 (3): 159–164, 207.

Petkova, Elena, Crescencia Maurer, Norbert Henninger, and Fran Irwin. 2002. *Closing the Gap: Information, Participation, and Justice in Decisionmaking for the Environment.* Washington, DC: World Resources Institute.

Petkova, Elena, and Peter Veit. 2000. *Environmental Accountability beyond the Nation State: The Implications of the Aarhus Convention.* Washington, DC: World Resources Institute.

Petrén, Gösta. 1987. Access to Government-Held Information in Sweden. In *Public Access to Government-Held Information: A Comparative Symposium,* edited by Norman S. Marsh. London: Stevens and Son, 35–54.

PIC Convention. 1998. Rotterdam Convention on the Prior Informed Consent Procedure for Certain Hazardous Chemicals and Pesticides in International Trade, adopted at Rotterdam on September 10, 1998, in force February 24, 2004; ratified by 138 countries [not including the U.S.] and the EU. *United Nations Treaty Series* 2244: 337; *International Legal Materials* 38: 1.

Pildes, Richard H., and Cass R. Sunstein. 1995. Reinventing the Regulatory State. *University of Chicago Law Review* 62: 1–129.

Podesta, John. 2003. Need to Know: Governing in Secret. In *The War on Our Freedoms: Civil Liberties in an Age of Terrorism,* edited by Richard C. Leone and Greg Anrig Jr. New York:. 220–236.

POPs Convention. 2001. Stockholm Convention on Persistent Organic Pollutants, adopted at Stockholm on May 22, 2001, in force May 17, 2004; ratified by 171 countries [not including the U.S.] and the EU. *International Legal Materials* 40: 531.

Powell, Colin L. 2002. Only One Earth. *Our Planet* 13 (2): 8–10.

Prieur, Michel, ed. 1997. *Le droit à l'information en matière d'environnement dans les pays de l'Union européenne.* Limoges: Presses Universitaires de Limoges.

Proposition 65. 1986. Safe Drinking Water and Toxic Enforcement Act. *California Health and Safety Code §*: 25249.5–25249.13.

Ramkumar, Vivek, and Elena Petkova. 2007. Transparency and Environmental Governance. In *The Right to Know: Transparency for an Open World,* edited by A. Florini. New York: Columbia University Press, 279–308.

Rauber, Markus. 2007. Das Tabakwerbeverbot des EuGH. *Zeitschrift für Europarechtliche Studien* 10: 151–160.

REACH. 2006. EU Commission Regulation 1907/2006 on the Registration, Evaluation, and Authorization of Chemicals. *Official Journal of the European Union* [2006] L 396 (1).

Rechtschaffen, Clifford. 1996. The Warning Game: Evaluation Warnings under California's Proposition 65. *Ecology Law Quarterly* 23: 303–368.

———. 1999. How to Reduce Lead Exposures with One Simple Statute: The Experience of Proposition 65. *Environmental Law Reporter* 29: 10581–10591.

Rehbinder, Eckard. 2003. World Summit on Sustainable Development. Environmental Law Network International. *ELNI Review* 1: 1–3.

Repetto, Robert, and Duncan Austin. 2000. *Coming Clean: Corporate Disclosure of Financially Significant Environmental Risks.* Washington, DC: World Resources Institute.

Repetto, Robert, Andrew MacSkimming, and Gustavo Carvajal Isunza, eds. 2002. *Environmental Disclosure Requirements in the Securities Regulations and Financial Accounting Standards of Canada, Mexico and the United States.* Montreal: Commission for Environmental Cooperation.

RFF (Resources for the Future). 2001. *Public Access to Environmental Information and Data: Practice Examples from the United States, the European Union, and Central and Eastern Europe.* Washington, DC: RFF.

Rio Declaration. 1992. Rio Declaration on Environment and Development, adopted by the United Nations Conference on Environment and Development. June 3–14, Rio de Janeiro. New York: UN Doc. A/CONF.151/26/Rev.1, 1: 3 *International Legal Materials* 31: 874.

Roberts, Alasdair. 2001. Structural Pluralism and the Right to Information. *University of Toronto Law Journal* 51: 243–271.

———. 2002a. New Strategies for Enforcement of the Access to Information Act. *Queen's Law Journal* 27: 647–682.

———. 2002b. Multilateral Institutions and the Right to Information. Experience in the European Union. *European Public Law* 8: 255–275.

———. 2006. *Blacked Out: Government Secrecy in the Information Age.* Cambridge: Cambridge University Press.

Robinson, Nicholas A. 2007. Terrorism's Unintended Casualties: Implications for Environmental Law in the U.S.A. and Abroad. *Environmental Policy and Law* 37: 125–139.

Rodenhoff, Vera. 2002. The Aarhus Convention and Its Implications for the "Institutions" of the European Community. *Review of European Community and International Environmental Law* 11: 343–357.

Roe, David. 2002. Toxic Chemical Control Policy: Three Unabsorbed Facts. *Environmental Law Reporter* 32: 10232–10239.

Roemer, Ruth, Allyn L. Taylor, and Jean Lariviere. 2005. Origins of the WHO Framework Convention on Tobacco Control. *American Journal of Public Health* 95: 936–938.

Roll, Sebastian. 2003. *Zugang zu Umweltinformationen und.* Freedom of Information. Berlin: Duncker and Humblot.

Romano, Patricia. 2000. Sustainable Development: A Strategy That Reflects the Effects of Globalization on the International Power Structure. *Houston Journal of International Law* 23: 91–121.

Rose-Ackerman, Susan. 1995. *Controlling Environmental Policy: The Limits of Public Law in Germany and the United States.* New Haven: Yale University Press. German transl.: *Umweltrecht und-Politik in den Vereinigten Staaten und der Bundesrepublik Deutschland,* Baden-Baden, Germany: Nomos.

Rose-Ackerman, Susan, and Achim A. Halpaap. 2002. The Aarhus Convention and the Politics of Process: The Political Economy of Procedural Environmental Rights. *Research in Law and Economics* 20: 27–64.

Rowan-Robinson, Jeremy, Andrea Ross, William Walton, and Julie Rothnie. 1996. Public Access to Environmental Information: A Means to What End? *Journal of Environmental Law* 8: 19–42.

Rowat, Donald C. 1966. The Problem of Administrative Secrecy. *International Review of Administrative Sciences* 32: 99–106.

———. 1979. *Administrative Secrecy in Developed Countries.* New York: Columbia University Press.

———. 1980. *The Right to Know: Essays on Governmental Publicity and Public Access to Information.* Ottawa: Carleton University Department of Political Science.

Sachs, Noah M. 2009. Jumping the Pond: Transnational Law and the Future of Chemical Regulation. *Vanderbilt Law Review* 62: 1817–1869.

Sage, William M. 1999. Regulating through Information: Disclosure Laws and American Health Care. *Columbia Law Review* 99: 1701–1825.

Salkin, Patricia E. 2005. GIS in an Age of Homeland Security: Accessing Public Information to Ensure a Sustainable Environment. *William and Mary Environmental Law and Policy Review* 30: 55–94.

Sand, Peter H. 1990. *Lessons Learned in Global Environmental Governance.* Washington, DC: World Resources Institute.

———. 2000. The Precautionary Principle: A European Perspective. *Human and Ecological Risk Assessment* 6: 445–458. Repr. in *Indian Journal of International Law* 40: 1–13.

———. 2003. Information Disclosure as an Instrument of Environmental Governance. *Zeitschrift für ausländisches öffentliches Recht und Völkerrecht [Heidelberg Journal of International Law]* 63: 487–502. Repr. in *Proceedings of the 2002 Berlin Conference on the Human Dimensions of Global Environmental Change: Knowledge for the Sustainability Transition,* edited by Frank Biermann, Sabine Campe, and Klaus Jacob (2004), Amsterdam and Potsdam: Global Governance Project, 292–301.

———. 2005. The Right to Know: Environmental Information Disclosure by Government and Industry. In *Making Law Work: Environmental Compliance and Sustainable Development,* edited by Durwood Zaelke, Donald Kaniaru, and Eva Kružíková, Vol. 2. London: Cameron May and Institute for Governance and Sustainable Development, 17–48.

———. 2006. Labeling Genetically Modified Food: The Right to Know. *Review of European Community and International Environmental Law* 15: 185–192.

Sandmo, Agner. 1999. Asymmetric Information and Public Economics: The Mirrlees-Vickrey Nobel Prize. *Journal of Economic Perspectives* 13: 165–180.

Sands, Philippe J. 2003. *Principles of International Environmental Law.* 2nd ed. Cambridge: Cambridge University Press.

Sappington, David E. M., and Joseph E. Stiglitz. 1987. Information and Regulation. In *Public Regulation: New Perspectives on Institutions and Policies,* edited by Elizabeth E. Bailey. Cambridge, MA: MIT Press, 3–43.

Sarokin, David, and Jay Shulkin. 1991. Environmentalism and the Right-to-Know: Expanding the Practice of Democracy. *Ecological Economics* 4: 175–189.

Saul, Graham. 2002. Transparency and Accountability in International Financial Institutions. In *The Right to Know, the Right to Live: Access to Information and Socio-Economic Justice,* edited by Richard Calland and Alison Tilley. Cape Town: Open Democracy Advice Center, 127–137.

Schapiro, Mary. 2010. Statement before the Open Commission Meeting on Disclosure Related to Business or Legislative Events on the Issue of Climate Change. Press Release, January 27. Washington, DC: U.S. Securities and Exchange Commission.

Schatz, Andrew. 2008. Regulating Greenhouse Gases by Mandatory Information Disclosure. *Virginia Environmental Law Journal* 26: 335–393.

Scherzberg, Arno. 2003. Von der *arcana imperii* zur *freedom of information*: der lange Weg zur Öffentlichkeit der Verwaltung. *Thüringer Verwaltungsblätter* 9: 193–203.

Scheyli, Martin. 2000. Die Aarhus-Konvention über Informationszugang, Öffentlichkeitsbeteiligung und Rechtsschutz in Umweltbelangen. *Archiv des Völkerrechts* 38: 217–252.

Schierow, Linda-Jo. 1997. Toxics Release Inventory: Do Communities Have a Right to Know More? Report for Congress 97–970 ENR. October 26. Washington, DC: U.S. Congressional Research Service.

Schiffauer, Peter, and Gwenda Jeffreys-Jones. 1999. *The Principle of Transparency: A Comparative Overview on the Legislation of the EU Member States and the Rules Applied by Community Institutions.* Working Paper POLI 106 EN. Luxembourg: European Parliament Directorate General for Research.

Schmillen, Markus. 2003. *Das Umweltinformationsrecht zwischen Anspruch und Wirklichkeit: Rechtliche und praktische Probleme des Umweltinformationsgesetzes unter Einbeziehung der UIG-Novelle und der neuen Umweltinformationsrichtlinie.* Berlin: Erich Schmidt.

Schneider, Hans P., and Torsten Stein, eds. 1999. *The European Ban on Tobacco Advertising: Studies Concerning Its Compatibility with European Law.* Baden-Baden, Germany: Nomos.

Schoch, Friedrich K. 2002. Informationsfreiheitsgesetz für die Bundesrepublik Deutschland. *Verwaltung* 35: 149–157.

Schrader, Christian. 2004. Neue Umweltinformationsgesetze durch die Richtlinie 2003/4/EG. *Zeitschrift für Umweltrecht* 15: 130–135.

Schram, Frankie. 2001. *Manuel Publicité de l'Administration/Handboek Openbaarheid van Bestuur.* Brussels: Politeia.

————. 2005. Public Access to Environmental Documents: Regulation (EC) No. 1049/2001. *Yearbook of European Environmental Law* 5: 23–65.

Schroeder, Christopher H. 2000. Third Way Environmentalism. *Kansas Law Review* 48: 1–30.

Schroeder, Werner. 2001. Vom Brüsseler Kampf gegen den Tabakrauch: 2 Teil. *Europäische Zeitschrift für Wirtschaftsrecht* 12: 489–495.

Schwan, Eggert. 1984. *Amtsgeheimnis oder Aktenöffentlichkeit?* Munich: Schweitzer.

Sedley, Sir Stephen. 2000. Information as a Human Right. In *Freedom of Expression and Freedom of Information: Essays in Honour of Sir David Williams*, edited by Jack Beatson and Yvonne Cripps. Oxford: Oxford University Press, 239–248.

Shapiro, Sidney A. 2004. The Information Quality Act and Environmental Protection: The Perils of Reform by Appropriations Rider. *William and Mary Environmental Law and Policy Review* 28: 339–374.

————. 2007. OMB and the Politicization of Risk Assessment. *Environmental Law* 37: 1083–1106.

Shea, Dana A. 2005. *Legislative Approaches to Chemical Facility Security.* Report for Congress RL33043. August 16. Washington, DC: U.S. Congressional Research Service.

Shihata, Ibrahim F. I. 1994. *The World Bank Inspection Panel.* Oxford: Oxford University Press.

Siegel, Joseph A. 2002. Terrorism and Environmental Law: Chemical Facility Site Security vs. Right-to-Know. *Widener Law Symposium Journal* 9: 339–385.

Simma, Bruno, Joseph H. H. Weiler, and Markus C. Zöckler. 1999. *Kompetenzen und Grundrechte: Beschränkungen der Tabakwerbung aus der Sicht des Europarechts.* Berlin: Duncker and Humblot.

Simpson, David. 2002. Germany: How Did It Get like This? *Tobacco Control* 11: 291–293.

Singer, Michael J. 1979. U.S.A. In *Administrative Secrecy in Developed Countries*, edited by Donald C. Rowat. New York: Columbia University Press, 309–356.

Smets, Henri. 1991. The Right to Information on the Risks Created by Hazardous Installations at the National and International Levels. In *International Responsibility for Environmental Harm*, edited by Francesco Francioni and Tullio Scovazzi. London: Graham and Trottman, 449–472.

Smyth, Gerry. 2000. Freedom of Information: Changing the Culture of Official Secrecy in Ireland. *Law Librarian* 31: 140–146.

Stec, Stephen. 1998. Ecological Rights Advancing the Rule of Law in Eastern Europe. *Journal of Environmental Law and Litigation* 13: 275–358.

————. 2005. "Aarhus Environmental Rights" in Eastern Europe. *Yearbook of European Environmental Law* 5: 1–22.

Stec, Stephen, Susan Casey-Lefkowitz, and Jerzy Jendrośka. 2000. *The Aarhus Convention: An Implementation Guide.* Geneva: United Nations Economic Commission for Europe.

Steele, Fritz. 1975. *The Open Organization: The Impact of Secrecy and Disclosure on People and Organizations.* Reading, MA: Addison-Wesley.

Steinzor, Rena. 2002. "Democracies Die behind Closed Doors": The Homeland Security Act and Corporate Accountability. *Kansas Journal of Law and Public Policy* 12: 641–670.

Stephan, Mark. 2002. Environmental Information Disclosure Programs: They Work, but Why? *Social Science Quarterly* 83: 190–205.

Stephenson, John B. 2003. *Homeland Security: EPA's Management of Clean Air Act Chemical Facility Data.* Report GAO-03-509R. March 14. Washington, DC: U.S. General Accounting Office.

Stern, Jessica, and Jonathan B. Wiener. 2006. Precaution against Terrorism. *Journal of Risk Research* 9: 393–447.

Stewart, Richard B. 2001. A New Generation of Environmental Regulation? *Capital University Law Review* 29: 21–141.

————. 2002. Environmental Regulatory Decision Making under Uncertainty. *Research in Law and Economics* 20: 71–126.

Stiglitz, Joseph. 1999. *On Liberty, the Right to Know, and Public Discourse: The Role of Transparency in Public Life.* Oxford Amnesty Lecture. January 27, Oxford University.

————. 2000. The Contribution of the Economics of Information to Twentieth Century Economics. *Quarterly Journal of Economics* 115: 1441–1478.

Stolaroff, Joshua K., Christopher L. Weber, and H. Scott Matthews. 2009. Design Issues in a Mandatory Greenhouse Gas Emissions Registry for the United States. *Energy Policy* 37: 3463–3466.

Strohmeyer, Jochen. 2003. *Das europäische Umweltinformationszugangsrecht als Vorbild eines nationalen Rechts der Aktenöffentlichkeit.* Berlin: Duncker and Humblot.

Sunstein, Cass R. 1999. Informational Regulation and Informational Standing: *Akins* and Beyond. *University of Pennsylvania Law Review* 147: 613–675.

Sunstein, Cass R., and Richard H. Thaler. 2003. Libertarian Paternalism Is Not an Oxymoron. *University of Chicago Law Review* 70: 1159–1199.

TASZ case. 2009. *Társaság a Szabadságjogokért (Hungarian Civil Liberties Union) v. Republic of Hungary.* Judgment of the European Court of Human Rights (2nd sec.), April 14 (Application No. 3734/05).

Thaler, Richard H., and Cass R. Sunstein. 2003. Libertarian Paternalism. *American Economic Review* 93: 175–179.

Thompson, Paul B. 1986. Uncertainty Arguments in Environmental Issues. *Environmental Ethics* 8: 59–76.

Thorpe, Andy, and Catherine Robinson. 2005. When Goliaths Clash: U.S. and EU Differences over the Labeling of Food Products Derived from Genetically Modified Organisms. *Agriculture and Human Values* 21: 287–298.

Thurnherr, Daniela. 2003. *Öffentlichkeit und Geheimhaltung von Umweltinformationen: Weiterentwicklung des Umweltvölkerrechts durch die Aarhus-Konvention und deren Bedeutung für das schweizerische Recht.* Zürich: Schulthess.

Tietenberg, Thomas H. 1998. Disclosure Strategies for Pollution Control. *Environmental and Resource Economics* 11: 587–602.

Tietenberg, Thomas H., and David Wheeler. 2001. Empowering the Community: Information Strategies for Pollution Control. In *Frontiers of Environmental Economics*, edited by Henk Folmer, H. Landis Gabel, Shelby Gerking, and Adam Rose. Cheltenham, UK: Edward Elgar, 85–120.

Transparency International. 2009. *Comments on the European Investment Bank's Public Disclosure Policy Dated May 2009.* July 23. Berlin: Transparency International.

Transparency Memorandum. 2009. White House Memorandum on Transparency and Open Government of January 21, 2009. *Federal Register* (January 26) 74: 4685.

Travers, Noel. 2000. Access to Documents in Community Law: On the Road to a European Participatory Democracy. *Irish Jurist* 35: 164–237.

Tridimas, George, and Takis Tridimas. 2002. The European Court of Justice and the Annulment of the Tobacco Advertisement Directive: Friend of National Sovereignty or Foe of Public Health? *European Journal of Law and Economics* 14: 171–183.

Tromsø Convention. 2009. Convention on Access to Official Documents, adopted at Tromsø (Norway) on June 18, signed by 12 countries and ratified by 3, not yet in force *Council of Europe Treaty Series* No. 205. *ASIL International Law in Brief.* July 10. Washington, DC: American Society of International Law.

UBA (*Umweltbundesamt*, German Federal Environmental Agency). 2002. *Global Voluntary Corporate Environmental Reporting: The Corporate Register Directory.* Berlin: Umweltbundesamt.

Udall, Lori. 1998. The World Bank and Public Accountability: Has Anything Changed? In *The Struggle for Accountability: The World Bank, NGOs, and Grassroots Movements*, edited by Jonathan A. Fox and L. David Brown. Cambridge, MA: MIT Press, 391–436.

Uhl, Kristen Elizabeth. 2003. The Freedom of Information Act Post-9/11: Balancing the Public's Right to Know. *American University Law Review* 53: 261–311.

UNGA (United Nations General Assembly). 1948. Universal Declaration of Human Rights. Article 19, adopted by UN General Assembly Resolution 217 A (III) of December 10.

UNECE (United Nations Economic Commission for Europe). 1957. European Agreement Concerning the International Carriage of Dangerous Goods by Road (ADR). Adopted at Geneva on September 30, 1957, in force January 29, 1968; ratified by 39 European countries and Morocco. *United Nations Treaty Series* 619: 77; as amended/consolidated, Geneva: UN Doc. ECE/TRANS/175, Vols. I–II (2005) and Corr.1.

———. 1998. Convention on Access to Information, Public Participation in Decisionmaking and Access to Justice in Environmental Matters [Aarhus Convention], adopted at the Fourth UNECE Ministerial Conference on "Environment and Europe" in Aarhus, Denmark on June 25, 1998, in force October 30, 2001; ratified by 43 European countries and the EU [though not by Canada and the U.S.]. *United Nations Treaty Series* 2161: 447; *International Legal Materials* 38: 517.

———. 2000. *Task Force on Pollutant Release and Transfer Registers: Report on the First Meeting.* February 21–23, Prague. Committee on Environmental Policy. Geneva: UN Doc. ECE/CEP/WG.5/2000/5.

———. 2003. Protocol [to the Aarhus Convention, UNECE 1998] on Pollutant Release and Transfer Registers. adopted by the Extraordinary Meeting of the Parties to the Aarhus Convention at Kiev on May 21; ratified by 25 countries and the EU, in force October 8, 2009. Geneva: UN Doc. ECE/MP.PP/2003/1.

———. 2004. *Working Group on Pollutant Release and Transfer Registers: Report on the First Meeting.* February 16–18, Geneva. UN Doc. ECE/MP.PP/AC.1/2004/2.

———. 2005a. *Report of the Second Meeting of the Parties to the Aarhus Convention.* [UNECE 1998], Decision II/1. Geneva: UN Doc. ECE/MP.PP/2005/2/Add.2.

———. 2005b. *Compliance Committee* [of the Conference of Parties to the Aarhus Convention, UNECE 1998]: *Report on the Ninth Meeting.* October 12–14, Geneva. UN Doc. ECE/MP.PP/C.1/2005/6.

UNITAR (United Nations Institute for Training and Research). 2000. *Designing and Implementing National Pollutant Release and Transfer Registers: A Compilation of Resource Documents.* CD-Rom. Geneva: UNITAR.

Vahle, Jürgen. 1999. Informationsrechte des Bürgers contra "Amtsgeheimnis". *Deutsche Verwaltungspraxis* 50: 102–106.

van Calster, Geert, and Maria Lee. 2004. Case note on ECJ 2003. *Yearbook of International Environmental Law* 14 (624) and *Review of European Community and International Environmental Law* 13: 107.

van der Lek, Bram. 1988. Democracy and the Right to Know. *Proceedings of the International Conference Guaranteeing the Right to the Environment.* February 4–6. Lisbon: Fundaçao Calouste Gulbenkian.

Villanova Symposium. 1994. Symposium on Disclosure of Environmental Liability in SEC Filings, Financial Statements, and Debt Instruments. *Villanova Environmental Law Journal* 5 (315).

Villiers, Charlotte. 2006. *Corporate Reporting and Company Law.* Cambridge: Cambridge University Press.

Viscusi, W. Kip. 1983. *Risk by Choice: Regulating Health and Safety in the Workplace.* Cambridge, MA: Harvard University Press.

———. 1992. *Fatal Tradeoffs: Public and Private Responsibilities for Risk.* New York: Oxford University Press.

Viscusi, W. Kip., Wesley A. Magat, and Joel Huber. 1986. Informational Regulation of Consumer Health Risks: An Empirical Evaluation of Hazard Warnings. *RAND Journal of Economics* 17: 351–365.

Vladeck, David C. 2008. Information Access: Surveying the Current Legal Landscape of Federal Right-to-Know Laws. *Texas Law Review* 86: 1787–1836.

Volokh, Alexander. 2002. The Pitfalls of the Environmental Right-to-Know. *Utah Law Review* 2002: 805–841.

von Oppenfeld, Rolf R. 1999. Emergency Planning and Community Right-to-Know Act *Environmental Law Handbook.* 15th ed., edited by Thomas F. P. Sullivan. Rockville, MD: Government Institutes, 629–644.

von Schomberg, René, ed. 2003. *Science, Politics and Morality: Scientific Uncertainty and Decision Making.* Dordrecht, Netherlands: Kluwer Academic Publishers.

von Schwanenflügel, Matthias. 1991. Das Öffentlichkeitsprinzip des EG-Umweltrechts. *Deutsches Verwaltungsblatt* 106: 93–104.

Voorhoof, Dirk. 2009. European Court of Human Rights: Case of *TASZ v. Hungary. IRIS Legal Observations* 7: 2/1.

Wägenbaur, Bertrand. 2001. Der Zugang zu EU-Dokumenten: Transparenz zum Anfassen. *Europäische Zeitschrift für Wirtschaftsrecht* 12: 680–685.

Wallace, Jill. 1987. The Canadian Access to Information Act 1982. In *Public Access to Government-Held Information: A Comparative Symposium*, edited by Norman S. Marsh. London: Stevens and Son, 122–171.

Wallace, Perry E. 1993. Disclosure of Environmental Liabilities under the Securities Laws: The Potential of Securities-Market-Based Incentives for Pollution Control. *Washington and Lee Law Review* 50: 1093–1140.

———. 2008. Climate Change, Fiduciary Duty, and Corporate Disclosure: Are Things Heating Up in the Boardroom? *Virginia Environmental Law Journal* 26: 293–334.

Wates, Jeremy. 1996. *Access to Environmental Information and Public Participation in Environmental Decision-Making: UN/ECE Guidelines from Theory to Practice*. Brussels: European Environmental Bureau.

Weber, Stefan. 1990. Environmental Information and the European Convention on Human Rights. *Human Rights Law Journal* 12: 177–185.

Weeks, Rebecca S. 1998. The Bumpy Road to Community Preparedness: The Emergency Planning and Community Right-to-Know Act. *Environmental Law* 4: 827–889.

Weil, David, Archon Fung, Mary Graham, and Elena Fagotto. 2006. The Effectiveness of Regulatory Disclosure Policies. *Journal of Policy Analysis and Management* 25: 155–181.

Weiss, Edith Brown and Harald K., Jacobson, eds. 2000. *Engaging Countries: Strengthening Compliance with International Environmental Accords*. Cambridge, MA: MIT Press.

Werres, Bettina. 2005. Information und Partizipation der Öffentlichkeit in Umweltangelegenheiten nach den Richtlinien 2003/4/EG und 2003/35/EG. *Deutsches Verwaltungsblatt* 120: 611–619.

Wesseler, Justus, Hans-Peter Weikard, and Robert D. Weaver, eds. 2003. *Risk and Uncertainty in Environmental and Natural Resource Economics*. Cheltenham, UK: Edward Elgar.

Westerlund, Staffan. 1975. *Miljöfarlig Verksamhet*. Stockholm: Norstedt.

———. 1981. Legal Antipollution Standards in Sweden. *Scandinavian Studies in Law* 25: 223–244.

Wheeler, Kristen D. 2006. Homeland Security and Environmental Regulation: Balancing Long-Term Environmental Goals with Immediate Security Needs. *Washburn Law Journal* 45: 437–466.

White, Laura A. 2003. The Need for Governmental Secrecy: Why the U.S. Government Must Be Able to Withhold Information in the Interest of National Security. *Virginia Journal of International Law* 43: 1071–1110.

White, Mark A. 1992. SEC Disclosure of Environmental Matters. In *The Greening of American Business: Making Bottom-Line Sense of Environmental Responsibility*, edited by Thomas F. P. Sullivan. Rockville, MD: Government Institutes, 255–268.

Wiener, Jonathan B. 2001. Something Borrowed for Something Blue: Legal Transplants and the Evolution of Global Environmental Law. *Ecology Law Quarterly* 27: 1295–1371.

Wiener, Jonathan B., and Michael D. Rogers. 2002. Comparing Precaution in the United States and Europe. *Journal of Risk Research* 5: 317–349.

Wilcox, William A. Jr. 2001. Access to Environmental Information in the United States and the United Kingdom. *Loyola of Los Angeles International and Comparative Law Review* 23: 121–247.

Wilmshurst, Trevor D., and Geoffrey R. Frost. 2000. Corporate Environmental Reporting: A Test of Legitimacy Theory. *Accounting, Auditing & Accountability Journal* 13: 10–26.

Wilsher, Daniel. 2001. Freedom of Environmental Information: Recent Developments and Future Prospects. *European Public Law* 7: 671–697.

Winter, Gerd, ed. 1990. *Öffentlichkeit von Umweltinformationen: Europäische und nordamerikanische Rechte und Erfahrungen*. Baden-Baden, Germany: Nomos.

Wolf, Sidney M. 1996. Fear and Loathing about the Public Right-to-Know: The Surprising Success of the Emergency Planning and Community Right-to-Know Act. *Journal of Land Use and Environmental Law* 11: 217–313.

World Bank. 2000. *Greening Industry: New Roles for Communities, Markets, and Governments*. Washington, DC: World Bank.

———. 2009. *Toward Greater Transparency through Access to Information: The World Bank's Disclosure Policy.* Washington, DC: World Bank Operations Policy and Country Services.

WRI (World Resources Institute). 2002. *Partnership for Principle 10,* www.pp10.org (accessed June 1, 2010).

———. 2003. *World Resources 2002–2004. Decisions for the Earth: Balance, Voice, and Power.* Washington, DC: WRI.

WRI and WBCSD (World Resources Institute and World Business Council for Sustainable Development). 2004. *The Greenhouse Gas Protocol: A Corporate Accounting and Reporting Standard.* Washington, DC, and Geneva: WRI and WBSCD.

———. 2005. *The Greenhouse Gas Protocol: The GHG Protocol for Project Accounting.* Washington, DC, and Geneva: WRI and WBCSD.

Yeater, Marceil, and Lal Kurukulasuriya. 1995. Environmental Impact Assessment Legislation in Developing Countries. In *UNEP's New Way Forward: Environmental Law and Sustainable Development,* edited by Sun Lin and Lal Kurukulasuriya. Nairobi: United Nations Environment Programme, 257–275.

Young, Beth, Suarez Celine, and Gladman Kimberly. 2009. *Climate Risk Disclosure in SEC Filings: An Analysis of 10-K Reporting by Oil and Gas, Insurance, Coal, Transportation and Electric Power Companies.* Boston: CERES.

Young, Richard. 2001. *Uncertainty and the Environment: Implications for Decisionmaking and Environmental Policy.* Cheltenham, UK: Edward Elgar.

Yu, Chilik, Laurence J. O'Toole Jr., James Cooley, Gail Cowie, Susan Crow, and Stephanie Herbert. 1998. Policy Instruments for Reducing Toxic Releases: The Effectiveness of State Information and Enforcement Actions. *Evaluation Review* 22: 571–589.

Zaharchenko, Tatiana R., and Gretta Goldenman. 2004. Accountability in Governance: The Challenge of Implementing the Aarhus Convention in Eastern Europe and Central Asia. *International Environmental Agreements: Politics, Law and Economics* 4: 229–251.

Zimmermann, Nils, Michael M'Gonigle, and Andrew Day. 1995. Community Right to Know: Improving Public Information about Toxic Chemicals. *Journal of Environmental Law and Practice* 5: 95–139.

Zoellner, Carl-Sebastian. 2006. Transparency: An Analysis of an Evolving Fundamental Principle in International Economic Law. *Michigan Journal of International Law* 27: 579–628.

CHAPTER 14

Frameworks for Risk Assessment, Uncertainty, and Precaution

Gail Charnley and Michael D. Rogers

*R*isk analysis is a portmanteau for the several risk-related disciplines grouped within the "risk labyrinth" (see Figure 14.1). This labyrinth has many overlapping components with strong feedback loops among them. This chapter focuses on the component of risk assessment (RA). Although the chapter focus is on RA, for policy, risk management (RM) has central importance. Furthermore, in most cases with regulatory significance, significant overlap and feedback exist between the two functions. For example, monitoring results obtained as a result of risk management decisions concerning a genetically modified organism (GMO) crop (see Chapter 2) can feed back to produce a revised risk assessment. Risk management goals should guide the nature and extent of a risk assessment. Consequently, attempts by regulators to artificially compartmentalize the two functions are likely to result in poorer risk regulation decisions except where the uncertainty in the RA is small. Because this book (and this chapter in particular) is concerned with the problem of significant uncertainty, some reference to this interface is inevitable.

Risk Assessment

Risk assessment (RA) is the practice of using observations about what we know to make predictions about what we do not know in order to draw conclusions about the likelihood of a risk or to make decisions about how best to control a particular risk. RA is a procedure informed by both science and judgment that, at its heart, consists of identifying hazard-harm pairs and then determining the relationship between exposure to the hazard and the likelihood of resultant harm (the dose-response relationship). A typical example would be identifying exposure to the sun as a risk factor

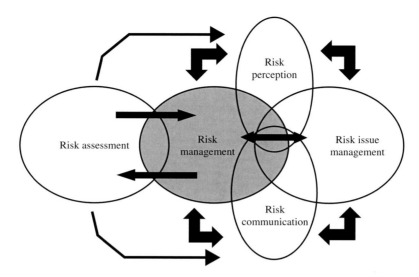

Figure 14.1 *The Risk Labyrinth*

(the hazard) for skin cancer (the harm) and then elucidating quantitatively the form of the relationship, perhaps through epidemiological studies (Rogers 2003).

RA is a procedure for including science in decisions about whether and to what extent risks to health, safety, or the environment should be limited. However, in nearly all cases the science, and hence the RA, is beset by uncertainties (as distinct from variability; see, for example, Hattis 2004). In general, we have only limited information about a population's varied exposures to chemicals (see Chapter 10), for example, or about the toxicological mode of action of a particular chemical once exposure occurs and how that might differ in different individuals, or about the interactions among multiple environmental and physiological characteristics.

Risk-related *uncertainties* are of three types:

- uncertainty about the effect (because the realization of the harm is stochastic in nature);
- uncertainty about the cause (because a realized harm may be due to any one of several hazards or a combination of hazards); and
- uncertainty about the given hazard-harm relationship (because of poor confidence in the hypothesized dose-response model or relationship).

The third type of uncertainty arises when there is insufficient knowledge about a postulated hazard-harm pair and is thus epistemic in nature. *Epistemic uncertainty has particular relevance to precaution* and the precautionary principle (see the section of this chapter on risk management).

For the risk assessor, details about exposures, effects, and interactions are generalized using assumptions and estimates of likelihood or estimates of the level of hazard that are likely to result in harm. Those assumptions are generally precautionary, and the estimates can be modified using uncertainty factors to identify conditions under which a level of risk realization is unlikely. Risk assessment is valuable because it provides a structured way to evaluate and draw conclusions from available scientific data, but it is at the same time limited by the nature and extent of the data. As the U.S. National Academy of Sciences report *Science and Judgment in Risk Assessment* (NAS/NRC 1994) puts it:

> The overall accuracy of a risk assessment hinges on the validity of the various methods and models chosen, which in turn are governed by the scope and quality of data. The degree of confidence that one can place in a risk assessment depends on the reliability of the models chosen and their input parameters (i.e., variables) and on how well the boundaries of uncertainty have been quantified for the input parameters, for the models as a whole, and for the entire risk-assessment process.

The European Commission has instituted a program to harmonize procedures for risk assessments in the human health and environmental protection fields. The First Report from this program of work (EC 2000a) acknowledges that the hazard-harm relationship consists of four steps: *hazard identification, hazard characterization, exposure assessment,* and *risk characterization,* and that this process is based on *Risk Assessment in the Federal Government: Managing the Process*—also called "the red book"—by the U.S. National Academy of Science's National Research Council (NAS/NRC 1983). In fact, most RA systems in use are based on this NRC report, although the NAS/NRC version refers to "dose-response assessment" instead of hazard characterization. However, there is continuing confusion about the hazard identification step, which involves identifying potential adverse effects of concern. The identification of a hazard per se does not translate into a risk unless exposure to the hazard results in a degree of harm. This is why the simpler hazard-harm formulation is to be preferred.

More recently, the European Food Safety Authority (EFSA) has issued a report on the RA of GMOs (EFSA 2005), which defines RA as:

> "a process of evaluation including the identification of the attendant uncertainties, of the likelihood and severity of an adverse effect(s)/event(s) occurring to man or the environment following exposure under defined conditions to a risk source(s)" (EC 2000a). A risk assessment comprises hazard identification, hazard characterization, exposure assessment and risk characterization. ... The sequential steps in risk assessment of GMOs identify characteristics which *may* cause adverse effects, evaluate their potential consequence, assess the likelihood of occurrence and estimate the risk posed by each identified characteristic of the GMOs. (emphasis added)

The ultimate purpose is essentially practical—namely, to set limits on exposure to a hazard so that the likelihood of the resultant harm is acceptable in a regulatory context. If there is little model uncertainty—that is, the hazard-harm or dose-response relationship is well characterized—and little data uncertainty, establishing acceptable exposure limits is straightforward. Where uncertainties abound, precautions may be taken. The nature and extent of those precautions are where the differences among jurisdictions may become apparent.

Risk Management

Risk management (RM) is the process of deciding what appropriate actions to take in order to avoid, reduce, or eliminate a risk when there is (or might be) one. The results of an RA can provide some qualitative and quantitative information about the nature, severity, and likelihood of a risk, but RAs do not dictate the appropriate risk management response. The RA may provide information useful for risk management decisionmaking, particularly in the context of regulatory policy, but the eventual risk management response also depends on many social, economic, legal, and other variables. The RA is necessary but not sufficient for regulatory action. The U.S. Presidential/Congressional Commission on Risk Assessment and Risk Management proposed a risk management framework that illustrates how the risk assessment stage of RM is part of a decisionmaking continuum, guided by RM goals and providing information that feeds into the stages displayed in Figure 14.2. The framework emphasizes the importance of defining a risk problem and the goals of RM prior to designing and conducting an RA (U.S. Risk Commission 1997).

The U.S. National Academy of Sciences report *Understanding Risk* (NAS/NRC 1996) describes RA as "a decision-driven activity, directed toward informing choices and solving problems. ... The purpose of risk [assessment] is to enhance practical understanding and to illuminate practical choices." In other words, RA exists at the pleasure of RM. If an RA does not provide useful information for the risk manager to

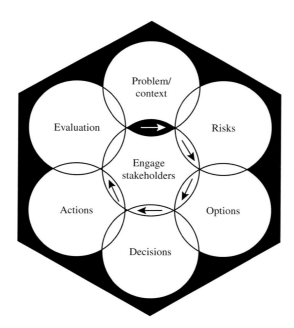

Figure 14.2 *Risk Management Decisionmaking Framework*

Source: U.S. Presidential/Congressional Commission on Risk Assessment and Risk Management (1997)

decide how to manage a population's or individual's risks, then the RA has little utility. So while RA and RM may be distinct activities, risk management problems and goals should guide how risk assessments are performed and the questions they seek to answer.

One approach to RM is to establish regulatory standards to control the risk in question. Regulatory standards may consist of exposure limits (e.g., the maximum allowed concentration of a specified chemical in potable water), process requirements (e.g., the requirement to use best available technology to limit pollutant releases), or complete bans on products or processes. The aim of regulatory standards is to protect human health, organizations, or the environment from a particular risk *to an agreed level of safety*—that is, to put in place regulations that will reduce the likelihood of a potential harm to a level considered insignificant or negligible. Other, nonregulatory approaches to RM are also possible. Some examples are voluntary substitution of less hazardous technologies or materials in manufacturing, providing tax incentives to encourage implementation of cleaner technologies, recycling and purchasing products that use recycled materials by communities and individuals, and upgrading sewage and municipal solid waste treatment facilities.

The choice of RM actions is dependent in part on scientific knowledge (the *a posteriori* facts) sufficient to determine the relationship between the hazard exposure and the harm realization to some agreed confidence level (say 95%). If this relationship is not understood with confidence, but some evidence of a possible causal link remains (say, on the balance of probabilities, i.e., greater than 50% confidence), then any RM actions may be considered precautionary in nature. In such cases, the interface of RA and RM is mediated through precaution, i.e., it is prospective in nature (acting in advance of a clearly demonstrated risk). This makes the approach postmodern in many respects (De Marchi and Ravetz 1998; de Sadeleer 2002), particularly perhaps in the European regulatory context.

The EU Approach to Precaution and the Precautionary Principle

The precautionary principle (PP) became part of European law in 1992, when the Treaty on European Union (the Maastricht Treaty) modified Article 130r of the treaty establishing the European Economic Community to include the phrase "Community policy on the environment ... shall be based on the precautionary principle ..." (EU 1999). The PP is an integral part of EU primary law (EU 1999). However, Article 174 does not define the PP. Consequently, in order to clarify the situation regarding the correct application of the PP, the European Commission (EC) issued a communication on the PP in February 2000 (EC 2000b) whose keystone is that the PP gives *permission to act under scientific uncertainty*. "To act or not to act," as the communication puts it (EC 2000b, 13). This permission-giving rule is in accordance with Principle 15 of the Rio Declaration from the 1992 UN Conference on the Environment and Development: "In order to protect the environment, the precautionary approach should be widely applied by States according to their capabilities. Where there are threats of serious or irreversible damage, lack of full scientific certainty shall not be used as a reason for postponing cost-effective measures to prevent environmental degradation."

For the EU, recourse to the PP presupposes that potentially dangerous effects deriving from a phenomenon, product, or process—*i.e., the hazard*—have been identified, and that scientific evaluation does not allow the risk—*i.e., the degree or likelihood of harm*—to be determined with sufficient certainty. If this is the case, then the implementation of an approach to RM based on the PP should be underpinned by a scientific evaluation done as completely as possible; that evaluation should characterize the degree of scientific uncertainty when feasible.

The communication's most important features are the criteria by which the resulting precautionary actions (PA) should be judged (once the PP has been invoked). These five criteria are as follows:

(1) The PAs should be *proportional* to the chosen level of protection.
(2) The PAs should be *nondiscriminatory* in their application.
(3) They should be *consistent* with similar measures that have been previously taken.
(4) The PAs should be *based on an examination of the potential benefits and costs* of action or lack of action (including, where appropriate and feasible, an economic cost–benefit analysis).
(5) They should be *subject to review,* in light of new scientific data. Furthermore, the PAs may include *assigning responsibility for producing the scientific evidence* necessary for a more comprehensive risk assessment; see Section 6.4 of the communication (EU 2000a).

The fifth criterion, namely that the PAs should be subject to review in light of new scientific data, is the only criterion that directly relates to the PP. It ensures that measures based on the PP should be maintained *only so long as scientific information is incomplete or inconclusive,* when the possible risk is still considered too high to be imposed on society in view of the chosen level of protection. Consequently, measures should be reviewed periodically in the light of scientific progress and amended as necessary (see Figure 14.3).

The communication on the PP was broadly endorsed by the European Council at its 2000 meeting in Nice (European Council 2000). It was also endorsed by the European Parliament (European Parliament 2000, Article 11 *et seq.*). Furthermore, the communication has been recognized by the European Court of Justice in a number of cases (de Sadeleer 2002).

The precautionary principle has now been explicitly incorporated into EU secondary law in a number of directives and regulations. It is a core element of the EU's General Food Law (Regulation 178/2002) and of the EU's GMO law (Directive 2001/18; see, e.g., Rogers 2004). This body of primary law (the treaties), secondary law (directives, regulations, and so on), and what might be termed "soft law" (such as the Communication on the Precautionary Principle) is being interpreted by the European Court of Justice in its case law.

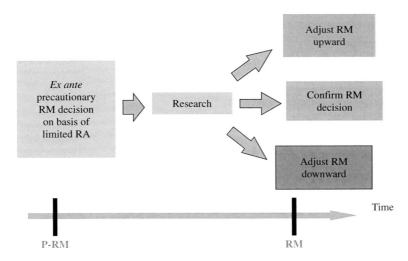

Figure 14.3 *A Possible Model for Precautionary Risk Management in the EU*

Source: Rogers (forthcoming)

A useful example of how the method displayed in Figure 14.3 operates in practice is the precautionary risk management of phthalates. Phthalates are chemicals widely used to soften the normally rigid plastic polyvinyl chloride (PVC). The resultant material is used in the manufacture of a range of products from soft toys to medical equipment. Studies have shown that some phthalates can produce liver and kidney damage in laboratory animals (SCTEE 1998). Furthermore, simple experiments have indicated that the phthalates could be leached out of the PVC by prolonged exposure to saliva (SCTEE 1998). Consequently, the European Commission took precautionary action to mitigate the postulated risk that children might be absorbing damaging quantities of phthalates from such toys. This action was promulgated in Decision 99/815/EEC of December 7, 1999, prohibiting the placing on the market of toys and childcare articles intended to be placed in the mouth by children under three years of age made of soft PVC containing one or more of certain specified phthalates (EC 1999). The Commission had previously requested an opinion on the risk from phthalates in toys from the Scientific Committee on Toxicity, Ecotoxicity, and the Environment (SCTEE), which delivered it on November 27, 1998 (SCTEE 1998). The Committee confirmed that there were grounds for concern with potentially low safety margins concerning the exposure of children to certain phthalates in connection with their use in soft PVC toys (liver and kidney and testicular damage).

The Decision was adopted on the basis of Article 9 of Directive 92/59/EEC on General Product Safety, which gives the Commission the power, under specified conditions, to adopt decisions that require the Member States to take measures regarding products that pose serious and immediate risks. Such measures are temporary (usual valid for three months); this particular Decision had been extended 18 times. Now that a full risk assessment has been carried out (SCTEE 2001), and in the light of more recent scientific data, permanent measures were proposed to Parliament and Council. It should be noted that the ban was temporary (pending more information); that it was specific to certain products (soft toys); and that it was taken in parallel with research actions to make the risk assessment more quantitative. Finally, the precautionary action was replaced by a permanent RM decision (European Parliament and Council 2005). This accords, more or less, with the decision process illustrated in Figure 14.3.

A second example illustrating the dynamic of scientific knowledge and the impact of this dynamic on the risk management process concerns bovine somatotropin, or BST. BST is a hormone that controls lactation in cows. For some years, BST has been commercially engineered as rBST, an agricultural pharmaceutical used to boost milk production. The U.S. Food and Drug Administration (FDA) approved the use of rBST in 1993 (see Chapter 3). However, the use of rBST was banned for 10 years in Europe in 1990 as a precautionary measure (European Council 1990) except for the purposes of carrying out scientific and technical trials. The risk-related reasons for this prohibition were that the various possible adverse effects of substances like BST were not sufficiently clear and that a period of time should be provided for in-depth studies. Plausible risk scenarios were postulated, in terms of both animal and human health, and thus the ban was limited to the time required to obtain further information on these risk scenarios.

This prohibition was made permanent in 1999, and the exception that had been available for scientific and technical trials was removed (European Council 1999). This second and final decision was based on research that had demonstrated that injecting rBST increased the risk of mastitis in cattle as well as the duration of necessary treatment for the affliction. Furthermore, foot and leg disorders in dairy cattle increased when rBST was administered, together with severe reactions at the injection site. Thus for animal welfare reasons, which were required under the European Convention for the Protection of Animals Kept for Farming Purposes, the prohibition was made permanent. Precautionary action under scientific and technical uncertainty (the time-limited prohibition of 1990) had been replaced by a risk management decision based on new knowledge.

These two examples relate strictly to the fifth criterion concerning precautionary actions described above: precautionary actions should be subject to review in light of new data. The examples may be compared with the U.S. leaded gasoline case described in the following section. However, other precautionary actions are also taken to account for model deficiencies, such as safety factors and linear extrapolation of dose-effect curves to low exposures (as with carcinogenic hazards).

The U.S. Approach to Precaution

In contrast to the EU, the United States has not explicitly embraced the PP in legislation or regulation. It is often the case, however, that U.S. regulatory agencies decide on a course of action to protect public health, safety, or the environment before science has resolved all the key factual questions about a suspected hazard and the effectiveness of prevention or mitigation efforts (OMB 2003). Different approaches to RA and RM are taken by different U.S. regulatory agencies depending on their statutory mandates and regulatory goals.

To a large extent, the body of U.S. statutory law that seeks to ensure public health, safety, and environmental quality—or at least mitigate risks to health and the environment—was established before quantitative RA was a well-recognized and codified discipline. Most of the methodology of RA was developed in reaction to the calls by these laws to define limits on potential risks such as chemical exposures, for example, that will protect the public health *with an adequate margin of safety* (42 U.S.C. § 7409(b)(1); the Clean Air Act) or similar precautionary language. That is, in passing the laws, the U.S. Congress called on the regulatory agencies to develop means to assess risks so as to make RM choices that would achieve the stated qualitative goals of health or environmental protection (Rhomberg 1997).

Although the PP has not been embraced in the United States as an explicit basis for regulation, it has guided U.S. regulatory RM decisionmaking for many years (Charnley and Elliott 2002). For example, in the 1950s, the Delaney Clause required the FDA to ban outright food and color additives that had been shown to produce tumors in humans or laboratory animals, whether or not they posed a risk to public health (Federal Food, Drug, and Cosmetic Act, 21 U.S.C.A. §§ 409(c)(3)(A), 706(b)(5)(B), and 512(d)(1)(H)). In the 1970s, a legal basis for a U.S. precautionary approach was established by the *Ethyl Corp. v. U.S. Environmental Protection Agency* decision (541 F.2d 1, 6 ELR 20267 (D.C. Cir.), cert. denied, 426 U.S. 941 (1976))—the ban of leaded gasoline. At the time, there was great debate about the wisdom of taking such a radical step when the benefits of doing so were unclear. But the U.S. Court of Appeals for the DC Circuit upheld the decision of the U.S. Environmental Protection Agency (EPA) decision to take a precautionary approach and ban leaded gasoline anyway, even in the absence of scientific evidence adequate to demonstrate exactly what risks from the lead existed or what the benefits of removing it would be. As it turned out, banning leaded gasoline was the single most important contributor to the virtual elimination of lead from air and from most children's blood. Today only 1.4% of U.S. children aged one to five years have blood lead levels equal to or above the level associated with learning deficits, 10 µg/dL blood, compared with 4.4% in the early 1990s (CDC 2010); in 1976, the mean lead level for the U.S. population was 12.8 µg/dL blood (ATSDR 1999).

In 1980, however, the U.S. Supreme Court's *Benzene* decision turned away from the precautionary policy of the *Ethyl* decision and substituted a fact-based principle focusing on the extent of risk (*Industrial Union Department v. American Petroleum Institute* 448 U.S. 607). The *Benzene* decision struck down a workplace standard for benzene exposure that was based on a policy of trying to reduce concentrations of benzene as far as technologically possible without considering whether existing concentrations posed a "significant risk" to health. The Supreme Court decided that benzene could be regulated only if it posed a *"significant risk of material health impairment."* Although the court did not define "significant risk of material health impairment" and stressed that the magnitude of the risk need not be determined precisely, the decision strongly implied that some form of quantitative RA is necessary as a basis for deciding if a risk is large enough to deserve regulation.

Relying on quantitative RA for scientific input to RM does not imply that precautionary considerations are excluded. Precaution plays a role in both RA methods and RM decisions in the United States, with decisionmakers relying on a number of different science-based precautionary approaches in assessing risks and taking protective regulatory actions (OMB 2003). In the case of chemical exposures, for example, EPA builds in conservative, precautionary measures by relying on assumptions about maximum exposures, choosing the most sensitive laboratory animal species and effect to represent human sensitivity, and using statistical upper bounds instead of maximum likelihood estimates of risk. In the interest of precaution, uncertainties about interspecies and interindividual variations in sensitivity to toxicity are compensated for through the use of uncertainty factors and safety factors to lower exposure limits. Such measures are meant to protect the most sensitive segments of an exposed population, where sensitivity may be attributed to either greater exposure or greater susceptibility to toxicity than the average individual. EPA has issued extensive guidance for assessing chemical risks, which has recently been summarized and critically evaluated (NAS/NRC 2005).

Regulation of hazardous air pollutants (HAPs) under the 1990 amendments to the Clean Air Act provides an example of how the PP has been implicitly incorporated into federal environmental legislation (Goldstein and Carruth 2003). After 18 years of relying on a procedurally cumbersome, risk-based approach to setting standards limiting air pollutant concentrations, EPA had promulgated standards for only 7 substances. In response, Congress passed amendments requiring a technology-based approach to limiting pollutant emissions regardless of the degree of risk and enumerating 189 substances that Congress considered hazardous, substituting legislative fiat for RA. By focusing attention on all HAPs regardless of risk, by measuring success in terms of tons of pollutants (not risk) reduced, and by mandating particular technologies, a focus on the most toxic pollutants is lost, potential impacts on public health cannot be assessed, and incentives to develop better technologies are eliminated (Goldstein and Carruth 2003). The Clean Air Act is thus an example of how purely risk-based or purely precautionary approaches to limiting risks may not achieve the intended goal of public health protection.

Another example is food safety in the United States, which is ensured in part by putting the precautionary burden of guaranteeing safety onto food processors through strict liability and regulation. In this way, a processor who sells a food that causes injury to a consumer is legally responsible even in the prior absence of actual knowledge of the hazard. Like EPA, the FDA incorporates precaution by employing conservative, health-protective assumptions and safety factors when assessing potential risks from, for example, food additives, food-borne pathogens, or chemical contaminants. For example, the FDA's Pathogen Reduction/Hazard Analysis and Critical Control Points (HACCP) regulation relies on risk-based precaution to prevent food-borne illness by placing the burden on industry to produce safe food and on the FDA to ensure industry meets its burden. Regulation of food additives also puts the onus of demonstrating safety on industry and uses safety factors to determine acceptable dietary exposure levels for individual substances.

The U.S. Department of Agriculture (USDA) also uses both risk assessment and precaution to ensure food safety. Importation of cattle from Canada was banned in 2003 as a precautionary measure against potential transmission of bovine spongiform encephalopathy (BSE), or "mad cow disease," after BSE-contaminated cattle were found there. The ban was lifted when the risk of letting BSE-infected cattle into the United States was characterized qualitatively as "low."

In contrast, disposal of low-activity nuclear waste in the United States is an area that is not guided by RA and is considered inadequately protective in some instances and unduly stringent in others (NAS/NRC 2003). Although U.S. statutory and institutional authority to ensure the safe management of such wastes is adequate, RM relies on a complex and confusing patchwork of regulations based on the *origin* of the waste and not on its *risk*. Disposal is regulated by at least 12 statutes and several different agencies, with precautionary approaches employed in some cases and not in others.

Thus, in general, the United States links precautionary and quantitative approaches to regulatory RM in order to fulfill both the qualitative goals of congressional statutes and the legal implications of judicial decisions such as *Benzene*. Because science is generally uncertain or incomplete, purely risk-based approaches are infeasible; precautionary measures, such as protective assumptions or safety factors, are included to help guide RM decisions. Finding the appropriate balance between risk and precaution continues to be a challenge.

Conclusions

Debates about the nature and extent of precaution associated with European and U.S. risk assessment practices often center on when the science available to characterize a particular risk is adequate and, consequently, on how much precaution is needed to ensure public health and environmental protection. The difference between science and regulatory science can be an important one. Although science informs risk assessment practices, when several possible interpretations of the science exist, the more precautionary choice is assumed to be appropriate for regulatory purposes, if not necessarily correct. Scientists and regulated parties often believe that the weight of the scientific evidence supports a different choice, but agencies mandated to protect health and the environment may believe that uncertainty about the science justifies precaution nonetheless.

Scientists and regulated parties also criticize agency risk assessors for confusing risk assessment and risk management. By making conservative assumptions and precautionary choices as part of the risk assessment process, risk assessors are de facto acting within the realm of risk management, thought to be the provenance solely of risk managers with greater public accountability. While it is true that making precautionary choices and assumptions as part of risk assessment does constitute risk management to some degree, it is impractical—and perhaps impossible—to completely disaggregate the two. The solution is to characterize and articulate clearly the nature and extent of relevant uncertainties and to make each corresponding precautionary assumption and its underlying justification or rationale as transparent as possible. Such transparency improves accountability and highlights areas where further research to reduce particular uncertainties may have the greatest impact on the outcome of a risk assessment.

The preceding discussion indicates that many similarities between the approaches to risk regulation in the EU and the United States exist. Acting before the consequences of a particular risk scenario are fully understood is accepted on both sides of the Atlantic. The EU and the United States also have parallel approaches for taking account of model deficiencies and uncertainties by means of safety factors, and so on. Where differences appear, these are not due to conflicting philosophies but to case-by-case differences in emphasis, as other chapters in this book illustrate. Differences may also be attributable in some cases to the different legal traditions found in the United States and EU, as described in Chapter 17.

References

ATSDR (Agency for Toxic Substances and Disease Registry). 1999. Toxicological Profile for Lead. Atlanta, GA: U.S. Department of Health and Human Services. www.atsdr.cdc.gov/toxprofiles/tp13.html (accessed July 27, 2010).

CDC (U.S. Centers for Disease Control and Prevention). 2010. National Report on Human Exposure to Environmental Chemicals. Atlanta, GA: U.S. Department of Health and Human Services. www.cdc.gov/exposurereport/Lead_FactSheet.html (accessed July 29, 2010).

Charnley, G., and E. D. Elliott. 2002. Risk versus Precaution: Environmental Law and Public Health Protection. *Environmental Law Reporter* 32: 10363.

De Marchi, B., and J. R. Ravetz. 1998. *Risk Management and Governance*. Report prepared for the European Commission by the Institute of International Sociology, Gorizia, Italy.

de Sadeleer, N. 2002. *Environmental Principles: From Political Slogans to Legal Rules*. Oxford: Oxford University Press.

EC (European Commission). 1999. Commission Decision (1999/815/EC) of December 7, 1999. Adopting measures prohibiting the placing on the market of toys and childcare articles intended to be placed in the mouth by children under three years of age made of soft PVC containing one or more of the substances di-iso-nonyl phthalate (DINP), di(2-ethylhexyl) phthalate (DEHP), dibutyl phthalate (DBP), di-iso-decyl phthalate (DIDP), di-n-octyl phthalate (DNOP), and butylbenzyl phthalate (BBP) (notified under document number C(1999) 4436). *Official Journal* L 315 09/12/1999: 0046–0049.

———. 2000a. First Report on the Harmonisation of Risk Assessment Procedures. European Commission report dated October 26–27, 2000. http://europa.eu.int/comm/food/fs/sc/ssc/out83_en.pdf (accessed July 18, 2005).

———. 2000b. Communication from the Commission on the Precautionary Principle. COM(2000)1. Brussels, February 2. http://europa.eu.int/comm/dgs/health_consumer/library/pub/pub07_en.pdf (accessed July 18, 2005).

EFSA (European Food Safety Authority). 2005. Guidance Document of the Scientific Panel on Genetically Modified Organisms for the Risk Assessment of Genetically Modified Plants and Derived Food and Feed, European Food Safety Authority report published March 2005. www.efsa.eu.int/science/gmo/gmo_guidance/660/guidance_docfinal1.pdf (accessed July 18, 2005).

EU (European Union). 1999. Treaty Establishing the European Community. Article 174 (ex 130r) in Selected Instruments Taken from the Treaties, 1:253–254. Luxembourg: Office for Official Publications of the European Communities.

European Council. 1990. Decision of April 25, 1990, concerning the Administration of Bovine Somatotropin. 90/218/EEC. *Official Journal* 1990/116: 27.

———. 1999. Decision of December 17, 1999, concerning the Placing on the Market and Administration of Bovine Somatotropin (and Repealing Decision 90/218/EEC). 99/879/EEC. *Official Journal* 1999/331: 71.

———. 2000. Presidency Conclusions. Nice European Council Meeting, December 7–9, 2000. Annex III: Council Resolution on the Precautionary Principle. http://ue.eu.int/ueDocs/cms_Data/docs/pressData/en/ec/00400-r1.%20ann.en0.htm (accessed July 18, 2005).

European Parliament. 2000. European Parliament Resolution on the Commission Communication on the Precautionary Principle. COM(2000) 1–C5-0143/2000–2000/2086 (COS). www.europarl.eu.int/home/default_en.htm (accessed July 18, 2005).

European Parliament and Council. 2005. Directive 2005/84/EC dated 14 December 2005 amending for the 22nd time Council Directive 76/69/EEC on the approximation of the laws, regulations and administrative provisions of the Member States relating to restrictions on the marketing and use of certain dangerous substances and preparations (phthalates in toys and childcare articles). http://eurlex.europa.eu/LexUriServ/LexUriServ.do?uri=OJ:L:2005:344:0040:0043:en:PDF (accessed July 27, 2010).

Goldstein, B. D., and R. S. Carruth. 2003. Implications of the Precautionary Principle to Environmental Regulation in the United States: Examples from the Control of Hazardous Air Pollutants in the 1990 Clean Air Act Amendments. *Law and Contemporary Problems* 66: 249–263.

Hattis, D. 2004. The Concept of Variability in Risk Analysis. In *Risk Analysis and Society*, edited by T. McDaniels, and M. J. Small. Cambridge: Cambridge University Press.

NAS/NRC (U.S. National Academy of Sciences/National Research Council). 1983. *Risk Assessment in the Federal Government: Managing the Process.* Washington, DC: National Academy Press.

———. 1994. *Science and Judgment in Risk Assessment.* Washington, DC: National Academy Press.

———. 1996. *Understanding Risk. Informing Decisions in a Democratic Society.* Washington, DC: National Academy Press.

———. 2003. *Improving the Regulation and Management of Low-Activity Radioactive Wastes. Current Regulations, Inventories, and Practices.* Interim report of the Committee on Improving Practices for Regulating and Managing Low-Activity Radioactive Wastes. Washington, DC: National Academy Press.

———. 2005. *Toxicity Testing for Assessment of Environmental Agents.* Washington, DC: National Academy Press.

OMB (U.S. Office of Management and Budget). 2003. *Informing Regulatory Decisions: 2003 Report to Congress on the Costs and Benefits of Federal Regulations and Unfunded Mandates on State, Local, and Tribal Entities.* Washington, DC: Office of Information and Regulatory Affairs.

Rhomberg, L. 1997. A Survey of Methods for Chemical Health Risk Assessment among Federal Regulatory Agencies. *Human and Ecological Risk Assessment* 3: 1029–1196.

Rogers, M. D. 2003. Risk Analysis under Uncertainty, the Precautionary Principle, and the New EU Chemicals Strategy. *Regulatory Toxicology and Pharmacology* 37: 370–381.

———. 2004. Genetically Modified Plants and the Precautionary Principle. *Journal of Risk Research* 7: 675–688.

———. Forthcoming. Risk Management and the Record of the Precautionary Principle in EU Case Law. *Journal of Risk Research.*

SCTEE (European Commission Scientific Committee of Toxicity, Ecotoxicity, and the Environment). 1998. Opinion on Phthalate Migration from Soft PVC Toys and Child-care Articles. Sixth CSTEE plenary meeting, Brussels, November 26–27. http://ec.europa.eu/health/scientific_committees/environmental_risks/opinions/sctee/sct_out19_en.htm (accessed May 14, 2010).

———. 2001. Opinion on the Results of the Risk Assessment of: 1,2-Benzenedicarboxylic Acid di-C9-11-branched Alkyl Esters, C10-rich and di-"isodecyl" Phthalate. CAS No. 68515-49-1 and 26761-40-0. EINECS No. 271-091-4 and 247-977-1. Report version (Human health effects). Final report, May. Opinion expressed at the 24th CSTEE plenary meeting, Brussels, June 12. http://ec.europa.eu/health/ph_risk/committees/sct/sct_opinions_en.htm (accessed May 15, 2010).

U.S. Risk Commission (U.S. Risk Commission on Risk Assessment and Risk Management). 1997. *Final Report,* Vol. 1, *Framework for Environmental Health Risk Management.* GPO #055-000-00567-2. Washington, DC.

PART IV
A BROADER EMPIRICAL TEST OF
RELATIVE PRECAUTION

A Quantitative Comparison of Relative Precaution in the United States and Europe, 1970–2004

Brendon Swedlow, Denise Kall, Zheng Zhou, James K. Hammitt, and Jonathan B. Wiener

*T*o review the premise of this book, we note that its many contributors explore here in detail the question of whether Europe or the United States adopts a more precautionary stance to the regulation of various potential risks. Some commentators have suggested that Europe is more risk-averse and precautionary, whereas the United States is seen as more risk-taking and optimistic about the prospects for new technology (Levy and Newell 2000). Others suggest that the United States is more precautionary because its regulatory process is more legalistic and adversarial, while Europe is more lax and corporatist in its regulations (Jasanoff 1986, 1998). The flip-flop hypothesis, suggested by Vogel (2001, 2003) and discussed in Chapter 1, asserts that the United States was more precautionary than Europe in the 1970s and early 1980s, but that Europe has become more precautionary since then. A variety of other patterns have also been suggested.

A significant body of literature compares the relative precaution embodied in European and U.S. risk regulation (e.g., Vogel 1986, 2001, 2002, 2003; Lynch and Vogel 2000; Lofstedt and Vogel 2001; Bernauer and Meins 2003; Kagan and Axelrad 2000; Breyer and Heyvaert 2000; Jasanoff 1986, 1998; Rose-Ackerman 1995; Brickman et al. 1985; Rehbinder and Stewart 1985; Kelman 1981; Vig and Faure 2004). Influential research on precaution has also focused on the consequences of adopting (and not adopting) the so-called "precautionary principle" for the United States, Europe, and the world (Harremoës et al. 2002; Lomborg 2001; Simon 1995; Wildavsky 1995; Worldwatch Institute 2004). However, past regulatory research, including that concerned with precautionary approaches, has suffered from shortcomings in the methods used to select cases, collect data, and draw overall comparisons (as discussed in Wiener 2003). Some authors chose to study only one policy area, such as cancer (Jasanoff 1986) or genetically modified (GM) food

(Bernauer and Meins 2003; Lynch and Vogel 2000), or one sector, such as workplace safety (Kelman 1981) or chemical regulation (Brickman et al. 1985), and then drew broad conclusions about a larger unit of analysis, often extending to the general characteristics of national regulatory approaches. Others tried to study diverse cases in one sector, such as environmental protection (e.g., Harrington et al. 2004; Vig and Faure 2004; Rose-Ackerman 1995; Vogel 1986), or various sectors (e.g., Jasanoff 2005; Worldwatch Institute 2004; Harremoës et al. 2002; Lomborg 2001; Hood et al. 2001; Kagan and Axelrad 2000; Wildavsky 1995; Graham and Wiener 1995; Simon 1995), but did not choose their cases according to an unbiased selection method.

Two studies of precautionary regulation and its consequences, one preceding the foregoing research and a second, contemporary investigation building on that study, begin to overcome the case selection problems of the regulatory research just described. Allan Mazur's *True Warnings and False Alarms: Evaluating Fears about the Health Risks of Technology, 1948–1971* (2004) is based on a sample of 31 cases systematically drawn from 45 risks that were studied in depth by Edward Lawless in *Technology and Social Shock* (1977). Lawless took his cases from more than 200 post-World War II instances where "technological information reported in the popular media had concerned or alarmed segments of the public." To arrive at 45 cases, Lawless generally excluded "routine problems such as transportation accidents and industrial fires," occupational hazards, and, with one exception, problems involving government security—but "no specific criteria for inclusion were closely followed." Mazur further excluded nine environmental risks and five about ethics or fraud, leaving him with 31 cases that "involve public warnings about technological threats to human health (and sometimes additionally to animals and the environment)" (Mazur 2004, 74–75; further reviewed in Swedlow 2005).

This exemplar of applied social science research on precaution and its consequences cannot, however, answer questions that animate unresolved scholarly and political debate about precautionary trends in the United States and Europe. Lawless's 200-plus cases only covered threats from technology, and only those technological threats that had been reported in the media and alarmed the public. Moreover, the reduction of the 200 cases to 45 is not sufficiently systematic to use the 45 cases (or any derived from them) to make reliable inferences about the larger set of cases. And while the reduction from 45 cases to 31 is systematic, Mazur's study only focuses on technological threats to human health. Also, both studies just assess risks arising in the period 1948–1971, and both are solely concerned with U.S. treatment of these risks.

This chapter, therefore, is intended to provide a more comprehensive and rigorous approach to comparing relative precaution in risk regulation than any of the studies just reviewed. It also overcomes the other limitations of Lawless's and Mazur's research to answer questions about U.S. and European precautionary trends (although our study of course has its own limitations, the most significant of which we hope to have identified below). As described in the next section, we developed a comprehensive list of almost 3,000 risks identified in the literature over the last three decades, categorized them by risk type and endpoint (ecological, health, or safety), and randomly selected 100 for analysis. For each of the 100 risks, we sought information on the stringency of regulation in Europe and the United States for each of the 35 years from 1970 through 2004, and we summarized the relative stringency of regulation in the form of a score for each risk and year. The information sources and scoring methods are described in the section titled "Characterizing Relative Precaution." We analyzed the distribution and trends in the scores across the sample of 100 risks, by risk type and by ecological, health, and safety endpoint, as described in the "Results" section, and our conclusions follow.

Our results suggest that (a) averaging over risks, there is no significant difference in relative precaution over the period; (b) weakly consistent with the flip-flop hypothesis, there is some evidence of a modest shift toward greater relative precaution of European regulation since about 1990; although (c) there is a diversity of trends across risks, of which the most common is no change in relative precaution—including cases where Europe and the United States are equally precautionary and where one of the two was consistently more precautionary. The overall finding is of a mixed and diverse pattern of relative transatlantic precaution over the period.

Constructing a Representative Sample of Risks

The objective of our research was to accurately characterize the observed pattern of relative precaution in U.S. and European risk regulation. In subsequent research (described in Swedlow et al. 2009), the data we collected may be used as the dependent variable to test the ability of various independent variables to explain the observed pattern; or it could serve as the independent variable in an explanation of precautionary consequences. Drawing broad conclusions about the regulatory pattern and the role of explanatory variables based on case studies selected by convenience or prominence is an invitation to bias and error (King et al. 1994). To guard against the selection bias evident in past studies requires a systematic method for developing a representative sample of risks that may be subject to regulation. As we were unable to identify a preexisting comprehensive list, we developed a risk matrix: a nearly comprehensive list of risks organized by two sets of categories (risk type and endpoint).

The matrix was constructed using an iterative search process. First, we identified lists of risks and pooled them. The task of finding risk lists began with a few well-known sources, such as Renn and Rohrmann (2000), the U.S. Environmental Protection Agency's *Unfinished Business* (EPA 1987), and numerous studies by Slovic and colleagues (e.g., Axelrod et al. 1999; Englander et al. 1986; Fischhoff et al. 1978; Goszczynska et al. 1991; Hohenemser et al. 1983; Kraus and Slovic 1988; Lichtenstein et al. 1978; McDaniels et al. 1995). Next, we attempted to expand the risk list using a snowball method to pursue sources cited by these original sources. Third, we pursued other search methods, including searching library databases and the World Wide Web, to ensure a thorough search for risk lists in the existing literature.

We attempted to find and include every study of risk perceptions and every risk-ranking exercise published in the United States or Europe since 1970. We focused on environmental, health, and safety risks, and ruled out sources that seemed to be exclusively about other kinds of risks. Although we did not include sources dealing exclusively with financial, business, or insurance risks, examples of these risks were included on some of the lists we looked at, so these types of risks are represented in our matrix (although not as diversely or frequently as if we had drawn lists from those literatures). The search was also limited to English-language sources and focused on sources from the United States and Europe. But again, our search methods led us to include sources that covered other countries or regions. Thus, our risk matrix includes risk lists from many areas outside the United States and Europe.

While we intended to draw on a population of risk lists produced by scholars, governments, think tanks, and advocacy groups, our search resulted in a population drawn primarily from academic sources, particularly the literature on risk perception. We assume (1) that the risks appearing on scholarly lists reflect risks that are of concern to the people and organizations that scholars studied, and (2) that the risk concerns of these people and organizations are representative of U.S. and European populations.

The search produced an original matrix of 11,992 "verbatim risks" (i.e., risks described exactly as on the list from which it was taken). These risks come from 403 risk lists[1] from 252 sources.[2] In almost all cases, the verbatim risks were associated with a geographic region. A total of 7,758 risks pertain to the United States, 1,712 to Europe, and 1,635 to both. The greater number of risks for the United States than for Europe may reflect the fact that the primary research was conducted in the United States with easier access to U.S. sources. It may also reflect a larger underlying volume of risk research produced in the United States than in Europe. We are unsure whether it could reflect a larger variety of risks having been of concern to scholars, policymakers, and the public in the United States than in Europe.

Since this study focuses on the United States and Europe, the 887 risks (from 29 risk lists and 24 sources) pertaining to other regions were deleted, leaving a total of 11,105 verbatim risks, 374 risk lists, and 228 sources. The final matrix includes only 10,869 risks because 122 unique risks were deleted when we decided they were not really risks or were too vague to study,[3] and 19 risks were inadvertently overlooked when transferring risks from one worksheet to another.

---

[1] The 403 risk lists are not unique, because some were replicated in articles or book chapters. We include not only tables of risks, but also multiple risks appearing in figures, tables of contents, and even risks appearing in text. Case studies including two or more risks were also included.

[2] Citations for these 252 sources can be found online at the Duke Center for Environmental Solutions (2004).

[3] We used strict criteria to eliminate as few risks as possible, but some initially included in the matrix appeared unsuited to regulation (e.g., friend does not appreciate a gift) or too broad or vague (e.g., lifestyle, children, all accidents, exposure) to permit study of regulation. We erred on the side of including risks if we believed it was at all possible to study their regulation, leaving many difficult-to-study risks in the matrix.

The matrix of 10,869 verbatim risks was condensed to 2,878 "unique risks" by combining essentially identical verbatim risks by reducing plurals and singulars to a common form, standardizing punctuation, and removing unique expressions.[4]

Although we attempted to develop as unbiased a process as practical for constructing the risk matrix, the snowball literature-search method we adopted may favor particular lines of research. We are confident, however, that if other researchers followed our procedures and criteria, they would produce a matrix substantively comparable to ours, albeit with some differences in distribution. While acknowledging the many constraints and weaknesses of our matrix, we believe that given the time and resources available to us, it represents a comprehensive list and a substantial improvement over previous studies.[5] We believe our method of comprehensive literature search is superior to other possible methods such as surveying risks that are currently regulated, compiling lists from governmental publications, or focusing only on visible, salient risks (e.g., from news media coverage), because those methods omit risks that could be of concern but are not yet regulated in one legal system or the other—precisely the kind of emergent risks that might in time be subject to precautionary regulation, or that might illustrate interesting contrasts across the legal systems.

Risk-Type Categories

No single method of categorizing risks can serve all useful purposes (Morgan et al. 2000). We developed two approaches to categorizing the universe of 2,878 unique risks: by type of source or cause; and by endpoint (ecological, health, or safety). The risk types are mutually exclusive, so that each risk appears in exactly one risk-type category. In contrast, the endpoint categories are not exclusive, as a risk may pose ecological, health, and/or safety consequences. The categorization of the risks was primarily of interest as a

---

[4] For example, "police work" became the common label for risks that appeared as "policework" and "being a policeman." More controversial relabeling collapsed different aspects of the same risk into the relabeled risk. For example, if nuclear power were selected, a reasonable person would consider nuclear power plants, nuclear power accidents, radiation from nuclear power plants, employees at nuclear power plants, residents living near nuclear power plants, and so forth. Therefore, any unique risk that would clearly be studied if one were studying nuclear power was labeled as nuclear power. (Nuclear waste risks were kept distinct from nuclear reactor risks.) Unique risks that were more specific and might be considered in a case study were labeled more specifically. More specific risks were usually hyphenated, with the more general risk first, followed by specifics. For example, the unique risk "East European nuclear power plants" was relabeled as "nuclear power-East European."

[5] Developing a workable approach to constructing a risk universe, assembling the list of 11,992 verbatim risks from 252 sources, reducing it to 2,878 unique risks, organizing these into 18 categories and 92 subcategories, coding the risks on various other characteristics (including environmental, health, and safety endpoints), and helping develop the sampling strategy took approximately one year of work by a full-time postdoctoral fellow (Swedlow) and six part-time research assistants (including Kall). Finalizing the assembly and categorization of risks, researching and scoring the sample of 100, and helping develop the sampling strategy took an additional year of work by two full-time graduate research associates (Kall and Zhou), plus a few additional temporary research assistants.

way to characterize the terrain of the universe of risks. The categories were not necessary to nor used in our random sampling and scoring of the 100 risks, though they could be used in a future stratified sampling exercise (as discussed in Swedlow et al. 2009).

To the best of our knowledge, ours is the first attempt to categorize the risk universe. Of course, no single or static set of risks could encompass the risk universe, because awareness of risks is continuously changing as technology, science, perceptions, and values change.

Initially, we read through the list from top to bottom, assigning number 1 to the first risk and every subsequent risk that appeared similar to it, the number 2 to the first risk that appeared different from category 1 and every subsequent risk that appeared similar to it, and so on. This helped us group similar risks together and allowed us to begin to see what subcategories might exist and how risks might have to be recategorized to gain the greatest logical coherence. This coding exercise also helped us to see that there was no one right way to code all risks, that there were trade-offs in different coding systems, and that some risks resisted categorization.

The coding effort required many judgment calls. For example, many risks could fall into more than one category (e.g., environmental tobacco smoke could be classified as tobacco or air pollution).[6] Many of the challenges involved whether to establish a new category or subcategory, what to name it, and how broad or specific to make it. We relied on our intuitions based on our knowledge of the world today, such as how different regulatory agencies deal with different risks.

The distribution of risks across risk categories, both in the sample and the matrix, is summarized in Table 15.1.[7] The categories are (1) crime and violence, (2) alcohol, tobacco, and other drugs, (3) medication and medical treatment, (4) transportation, (5) accident risks not classified elsewhere, (6) recreation, (7) war, security, and terrorism, (8) toxic substances, (9) food and agricultural, (10) pollution, (11) energy production, (12) political, social, and financial, (13) ecogeological, (14) global, (15) human disease/health, (16) occupational, (17) consumer products, and (18) construction. The smallest category (construction risks) includes only 1.4% of the unique risks, while the largest category (occupational risks) includes 15% of the unique risks. The mean fraction of risks per category is 5.6%, the standard deviation is 3.8%, and the median is 4.5%.

Endpoint Categories

We also categorized the risks according to whether they affect ecological, health, or safety endpoints. Although these terms are frequently used to describe risks, they are rarely defined, and definitions that do exist are often imprecise or conflicting.

---

[6] This issue is further discussed in Swedlow et al. 2009.

[7] For a listing of the 100 risks and their distribution across the 18 risk categories and 92 risk subcategories, see Table 15.1 in an earlier version of this chapter posted online at the Duke Center for Environmental Solutions (2004), and Table II in Swedlow et al. 2009.

Table 15.1 *Risks by Type*

Code	Category	Percentage in Matrix	Percentage in Sample
1	Crime and violence	1.8	3
2	Alcohol, tobacco, and other drugs	3.0	3
3	Medication and medical treatment	6.8	8
4	Transportation	8.2	13
5	Accident risks not classified elsewhere	2.4	2
6	Recreation	5.5	8
7	War, security, and terrorism	1.5	3
8	Toxic substances	9.8	8
9	Food and agriculture	9.5	9
10	Pollution	7.5	8
11	Energy production	5.0	3
12	Political, social, and financial	3.4	1
13	Ecogeological	4.0	2
14	Global	2.2	1
15	Human disease/health	9.7	9
16	Occupational	15.0	17
17	Consumer products	3.4	2
18	Construction	1.4	0
	Total percentage	100	100
	Total number	2,878	100

We categorized risks as ecological, health, or safety depending on the endpoint, not the agent or vector. By our definition, health and safety risks threaten humans directly, while ecological risks threaten nonhuman endpoints. The U.S. Environmental Protection Agency (EPA) defines an ecological impact as "the effect that a man-caused or natural activity has on living organisms and their nonliving (abiotic) environment" (EPA 2002).[8] We restate this definition as *ecological risks are risks that may harm nonhuman organisms and their supporting physical conditions*. We describe these risks as ecological rather than environmental to encompass risks to both the abiotic environment and its organisms. We restrict attention to nonhuman organisms because risks to humans are classified under health and safety. Examples of ecological risks include biodiversity loss, oil spills, acid rain, pesticide and chemical pollution, and hazardous waste sites.

Distinguishing between health and safety risks is more difficult because both are risks to humans. Drawing from the definitions of the Centers for Disease Control and

---

[8] EPA (2002) defines ecological/environmental risks as "the potential for adverse effects on living organisms associated with pollution of the environment by effluents, emissions, wastes, or accidental chemical releases; energy use; or the depletion of natural resources." This definition includes humans, but not the abiotic environment. Kolluru's (1996, 1.11) description of ecological/environmental risks focuses on habitat and ecosystem impacts. Risk characteristics include "subtle effects, myriad interactions among populations, communities, and ecosystems (including food chains) at micro and macro level."

Prevention (CDC 2003), Koren (1996), and Webster's Third International Dictionary (1993),[9] we define health as human physical, mental, and social well-being,[10] where well-being is the unimpaired ability to perform vital functions. Characteristics that differentiate health risks from safety risks are identified by Kolluru (1996). Health risks typically derive from "chronic (long-term) exposure to low-concentrations" (Kolluru 1996, 4.6) and have long-latency, delayed effects. However, diseases can manifest years later from acute (short-term) exposures as well. Therefore, we define health risks as *risks that may cause latent illness, disease, or other impairments of health to humans as a result of acute or chronic exposure.* Examples of health risks include AIDS, pesticides in food, hazardous-waste sites affecting humans, air pollution, cigarette smoking, and alcohol.

Kolluru (1996, 4.6) states that "safety risks stem from acute hazards"; are usually characterized by a low probability of high exposure, high-consequence accidents; and have acute, immediate effects. "The endpoints are well defined: fatalities, injuries, and economic losses" (1996, 1.13). We define safety risks as *risks that may cause injury or fatality to humans as an immediate result of acute (i.e., short-term) exposure.* Safety risks include workplace accidents, automobile crashes, airplane crashes, bridge collapses, and terrorism. Although these safety risks may impair one's health, these are immediate effects instead of long-latency, so for our purposes we classify them as safety risks.

Table 15.2 reports the distribution of the 2,878 unique risks by endpoint category. Most risks affect more than one endpoint category. More than one-third of the risks affect all three endpoints, one-quarter affect two endpoints (usually health and safety), and one-third affect only a single endpoint. About 2% of the risks are classified as affecting none of these endpoints.[11] About three-quarters of the risks affect health or safety, and almost half affect ecological endpoints.

Sample Selection

From the final matrix of 2,878 unique risks, we drew a simple random sample of 100 risks (without regard to category). Randomness in case selection is critical to controlling selection bias and permitting valid inference. While our sample is not randomly drawn from the universe of all known or possible risks—nor could any sample be—it is representative of the universe we constructed and will support inferences about that universe. Consequently, we believe our sample represents a substantial improvement

---

[9] Webster's Third International Dictionary (1993) defines health as "the condition of an organism or one of its parts in which it performs its vital functions normally or properly: the state of being sound in body or mind." Similarly, the Centers for Disease Control and Prevention (2003) define health as "a state of complete physical, mental, and social well-being and not merely the absence of disease or infirmity." Koren's (1996, 191) definition is comparable: "the avoidance of disease and injury and the promotion of normalcy through efficient use of the environment, a properly functioning society, and an inner sense of well-being."

[10] We include social and mental well-being for their own sake and where they influence physical well-being.

[11] Examples include burglary and social/ethical/cultural impacts of technology.

Table 15.2 *Risks by Endpoint Category*

Endpoint category	Matrix	Sample
0 None	2.2	2
1.1 Ecological	2.7	3
1.2 Health	17.7	16
1.3 Safety	15.3	21
Total: one category	35.6	42
2.1 Ecological and health	4.2	1
2.2 Ecological and safety	3.6	2
2.3 Health and safety	17.2	16
Total: two categories	25.0	19
3 Ecological, health, and safety	37.2	39
Total: All	100	100
Total: All Ecological (1.1, 2.1, 2.2, 3)	47.7	45
Total: All Health (1.2, 2.1, 2.3, 3)	76.3	72
Total: All Safety (1.3, 2.2, 2.3, 3)	73.2	78

Source: Hammitt et al. (2005)

over past studies relying on a few cases selected by convenience or prominence, or on one industry sector, to generalize about precautionary regulation.

The random sample appears to be highly representative of our universe of unique risks, as indicated by a chi-square test and by the sample's distribution across risk-type categories. A chi-square test provides no evidence to reject the hypothesis that the sample is a random draw from the final matrix ($\chi^2_{17} = 13.4, p = 0.7$).[12] As shown in Table 15.1, the sample includes risks from all 18 major risk-type categories except one, construction, which has the smallest number of unique risks and hence the smallest probability of being sampled. The largest number of risks (17) comes from the largest category, occupational risks. The difference between the percentage of the random sample of 100 and the percentage of the matrix of 2,878 is 2.5 percentage points or less for all categories except transportation, which includes 13% of the random sample but only 8.2% of the matrix, a difference of 4.8 percentage points. The randomly selected risks span about half of the 92 subcategories.

The random sample is also representative with respect to the endpoint categories shown in Table 15.2, although safety risks appear to be slightly overrepresented. The fractions of risks that affect ecological, health, or safety endpoints are 45%, 72%, and 78% in the sample, respectively, compared with 48%, 76%, and 73% in the matrix.

---

[12] The chi-square test statistic is the sum over the 18 categories of $(O - E)^2 / E$, where O is the observed number of risks drawn from that category and E is the expected number if the risks are drawn randomly. From Table 15.1, for category 1 (crime and violence), the observed number is 3, the expected number is 1.8, and so the calculation yields $1.2^2 / 1.8 = 0.8$. Doing the analogous calculation for the other 17 categories and summing yields $Z = 13.4$. Under the hypothesis of random sampling, Z has a chi-squared distribution with 17 degrees of freedom (18 bins minus 1, because the sum of the observed frequencies must be 100%). The p-value is about 0.71, so we cannot reject the hypothesis that the sample is a random draw from the population.

Characterizing Relative Precaution

To evaluate relative precaution between the United States and Europe, we compared regulation of the 100 randomly selected risks from 1970 through 2004. The first step was to gather all relevant regulatory information for each of the sampled risks in both regions over the past 35 years. The goal was to collect information about all major regulations, including date of enactment, quantitative measures of stringency, narrative legal language, expressions of or allusions to the "precautionary principle" or precaution, and other relevant information. Researchers scoured numerous sources for such information, including U.S. statutes, the *Federal Register*, and the Code of Federal Regulations; U.S. state laws and regulations; European Union legislation, directives, and regulations; European national (Member State) laws and regulations; judicial decisions (case law) in these jurisdictions; and scholarly commentaries, the World Wide Web, and library catalogs and databases. For each risk, a dossier was prepared synthesizing this research and scoring relative precaution over the 35-year period.

Several problems arose in this search process. One dilemma was the question of which jurisdictions to compare. Given our interest in precautionary behavior, we were interested in the first populous political entity to regulate a risk. We defined populous political entities as the federal government and state governments in the United States, and the EU and national governments in Europe, while recognizing that this definition omits cities or other local governments that have sometimes been the first to attend to particular risks.

For the United States, the federal government regulates many risks and sets minimum national standards, so information was sought at the federal level for all risks. State information was also gathered for risks that were regulated at the state level and might have been more precautionary than the federal regulations. In general, we used the federal laws and regulations for comparison unless a risk was regulated only at the state level, or was regulated earlier or more strictly at the state level.

For Europe, the task was more challenging, as many risks are regulated by the national governments of the EU Member States, and we were unable to investigate the regulation of all 100 risks in every Member State. Moreover, even the set of states that are "European" has changed over the 1970 to 2004 period we analyze (i.e., the number of states comprising what is now the European Union has grown from 6 in 1970 to 12 at the 1992 Treaty of Maastricht to 25 in 2004). We defined "Europe" as Western Europe, including the 15 Member States that comprised the EU in 2003 plus non-EU members such as Norway and Iceland. If a risk was regulated at the European Union level, we searched for directives and regulations by the EU institutions (i.e., Council, Commission) that prescribe basic actions and harmonized standards. We also attempted to find the most precautionary country in Europe for each risk, starting with Germany, Sweden, the United Kingdom, France, and the Netherlands, which are often said to be among the countries from which more precautionary standards emerge.

The quality of our data collection was also affected by several factors. First, our ability to collect information on European regulations was hindered by differences in language. We attempted to overcome this obstacle by enlisting several secondary researchers from Europe (including Europeans studying at Duke Law School) who provided additional information on countries such as Germany. Second, the quality of our data varies over time because of the advancing use of the World Wide Web. Information about recent regulations is much more easily accessed than information on regulations from the 1970s; hence our information is more complete for the latter part of the period. For 12 risks in the sample, we were unable to find scoreable information on regulation in Europe or the United States—possibly because these risks have not been regulated, regulations could not be found, or they are too broad, vague, or multidimensional to be scored sensibly.

Scoring

We evaluated the information on U.S. and European regulations to determine which polity was more precautionary in each year from 1970 to 2004. We measured precaution by two components: earliness and stringency (Wiener 2002, 1513–1514). The polity that regulates a risk earlier and more stringently than the other is considered more precautionary. We developed a comparison of the stringency of existing regulations in each year from 1970 through 2004. Regulations were analyzed by the date of enactment, not date of implementation. This choice reflects which region first took action. Neither compliance nor effectiveness of regulations was considered in this task due to the extreme time and effort required to evaluate those highly contextual attributes. Our results thus reflect announced standards more than actual standards in practice. If there is a systematic tendency of one legal system to use more precautionary language, but to enforce that language less stringently than the other legal system, our scoring results would reflect the language alone. Our comparison of regulatory stringency is purely categorical. In each year, we judge whether the United States or Europe has the more stringent regulation, but we did not attempt to distinguish cases where one regulation is only slightly more stringent than another from cases where one regulation is much more stringent than the other. We also did not attempt to determine the date at which information or awareness about a risk began to arise, and so we cannot compare earliness of regulation, relative to emerging information, across risks. Nor could we assess relative precaution in terms of earliness of regulation compared to the eventual manifestation of a risk.[13]

For each year, a polity received one point if its overall regulation of a particular risk is more stringent than regulation in the other polity in that year. The score for a year is +1 if the European regulations are more stringent, −1 if the U.S. regulations are more stringent, and 0 if the regulations are equally stringent or if we were unable to determine which are more stringent. Therefore, positive scores represent greater European precaution and negative scores represent greater U.S. precaution. Each risk

---

[13] These limitations of our quantitative study, which is broadly representative but shallow in its investigative detail, highlight the need for complementary research on comparative law in context and in action (Reitz 1998), and on case studies of the policy process over time (Blomquist 1999), which are narrower in scope but deeper in detail. Ways to use our matrix to accomplish comparative nested analysis of cases, combining quantitative and qualitative methods (Lieberman 2005; Coppedge 2005; Seawright and Gerring 2008), are discussed in Swedlow et al. 2009.

received a score for each of the 35 years from 1970 through 2004. The more stringent (and thus precautionary) polity receives one point every year until a change in regulation occurs. When a change occurs, we evaluate how the change influences relative stringency. This approach automatically incorporates the earliness component, because if one polity regulated a risk before the other, then until the second polity started to regulate that risk, the former is considered more precautionary. We calculated the average score for each risk over time, which is bounded between −1 and +1. An average score at the boundary of −1 or +1 would be achieved for a risk where the U.S. regulations were more stringent than the European regulations in *all* 35 years, and a risk where the European regulations were more stringent than the U.S. regulations in *all* 35 years, respectively.

The scoring of regulatory stringency in each year presented several challenges and required extensive judgment. Many risks are multidimensional and thus have many aspects to compare. In cases where we were able to obtain sufficient information, all aspects were compared, and the region that was more precautionary on the most important aspects was scored as the more precautionary. Some risks were too broad to compare all aspects and were scored as a tie by default.

Another challenge is that regulations may be difficult to compare for a variety of reasons. For example, regulations may use different strategies or approaches. One country may rely on command-and-control regulations while another uses a tax or a tradable-permit system. The default judgment in such cases is to score the regulations as a tie unless we have a solid reason to make a judgment about which regulation is more precautionary. Similarly, regulations may use different quantitative measures. For example, as noted by Haward (2004), U.S. and EU policy differ in the frequency with which concentrations of ozone in ambient air can exceed the legal standard, with the United States permitting only one exceedence per year and the EU permitting 26 exceedences per year but with the EU imposing a more stringent concentration standard. Without knowing the time distribution of ozone levels over a year, it is difficult to judge which standard is the more stringent.

The time resolution of our scoring is limited to calendar years, so that if both the United States and Europe regulated a risk in the same year (at the same level of stringency), they would be treated as equally precautionary. This limitation is probably not important to the interpretation of our results, because regulations typically require more than a year to develop, and it is unlikely that both polities would adopt regulations in the same year unless the risk had attracted significant concern in both of them.

We developed confidence weights to indicate our degree of assurance about which polity had the more stringent regulations in each year. The confidence weights range from zero to three, with zero representing no confidence and three representing very high confidence in the relative-precaution score. Weighted scores were calculated for each year as the product of the confidence weight and the precaution score and normalized so the weighted scores are bounded by −1 and +1. This approach gives less weight to precaution scores that may be less reliable due to incomplete information. We prefer to rely on the confidence-weighted scores rather than the unweighted scores, as the confidence-weighted scores provide a more accurate picture of our judgments about relative precaution.

We also entered codes to document missing information for each risk and year, distinguishing between cases where the information was missing for Europe, for the United States, and for both polities. In addition, we recorded the jurisdictional level at which the regulations were promulgated, whether it was at the U.S. federal level, U.S. state level, EU level, European national level, or any combination of these levels.

Scores were assigned by two of the authors (Kall and Zhou), working independently. As described in the following section, the two sets of scores are similar, which provides some evidence for the reliability of the scoring process. The two sets of scores and confidence weights were combined to provide a single set of consensus scores and confidence weights for analysis (consensus weighted scores for each risk and year are the product of the corresponding consensus confidence weight and consensus score). In cases where the researchers assigned the same score or weight, that value became the consensus value. In cases where they assigned different values, the consensus value was achieved by discussion. This method permitted sharing information and understanding between the researchers. Empirically, the consensus values are similar to a simple average of the two scores.

To evaluate overall precaution and trends in precaution, we averaged the weighted and unweighted scores across risks. This procedure gives equal weight to each risk: we made no attempt to account for the magnitude of the risks or the effectiveness of the regulation as measured, e.g., by the actual impact on health, safety, or ecosystems. If one region is systematically more precautionary with respect to large or important risks, and the other is systematically more precautionary with respect to small or less significant risks, our method would not allow us to identify this difference.

Results

In this section, we report our estimates of the extent to which one or the other region has exhibited more precautionary risk regulation. We analyze average relative precaution over the 35-year period, examine trends over the period, and conclude with an evaluation of the reliability of our scoring procedure.

Average Precaution, 1970–2004

To construct an aggregate measure of relative precaution over the entire period, we averaged both the unweighted and confidence-weighted annual consensus scores over each of the 35 years from 1970 through 2004. The resulting average scores are reported for the 18 major risk-type categories in Table 15.3 and for the endpoint categories in Table 15.4.

Table 15.3 *Relative Precaution by Risk Type*

Risk type		Number	Weighted		Unweighted	
			Score	t-statistic	Score	t-statistic
Greater U.S. precaution						
2	Alcohol, tobacco, and other drugs	3	−0.56	−10.51**	−0.79	−6.82**
10	Pollution	8	−0.17	−1.80	−0.50	−2.43**
5	Accident risks not elsewhere classified	2	−0.17	−1.00	−0.50	−1.00
6	Recreation	8	−0.13	−2.09*	−0.28	−2.53**
3	Medication and medical treatment	8	−0.01	−0.04	−0.10	−0.44
Equal precaution						
12	Political, social, and financial	1	0.00	NA	0.00	NA
17	Consumer product	2	0.00	NA	0.00	NA
Greater European precaution						
11	Energy production	3	0.01	1.00	0.02	1.00
9	Food and agriculture	9	0.03	0.33	−0.11	−0.64
15	Human disease/health	9	0.05	0.55	0.02	0.10
16	Occupational	17	0.09	1.62	0.12	1.12
1	Crime and violence	3	0.11	0.38	0.00	0.00
4	Transportation	13	0.15	1.61	0.14	0.91
8	Toxic substances	8	0.15	1.30	0.16	0.76
13	Ecogeological	2	0.25	1.00	0.50	1.00
7	War, security, and terrorism	3	0.41	1.83	0.60	1.68
14	Global	1	0.52	NA	1.00	NA
	Total	100	0.04	1.19	−0.02	−0.34

Notes: *, ** denote statistically significantly different from zero at 10% and 5% significance level, respectively. Scores are normalized so minimum and maximum possible scores are −1 and +1, respectively. NA when standard error = 0.
Source: Hammitt et al. (2005)

Table 15.4 *Relative Precaution by Endpoint Category*

Category	Number	Weighted		Unweighted	
		Score	t-statistic	Score	t-statistic
0 None	2	−0.17	−1.00	−0.50	−1.00
1.1 Ecological	3	0.00	−1.00	−0.01	−1.00
1.2 Health	16	0.01	0.10	−0.08	−0.53
1.3 Safety	21	0.13	1.60	0.14	1.01
2.1 Ecological and health	1	0.00	NA	0.00	NA
2.2 Ecological and safety	2	0.26	1.00	0.50	1.00
2.3 Health and safety	16	−0.06	−0.80	−0.16	−1.12
3 Ecological, health, and safety	39	0.04	0.92	−0.03	−0.29
All	100	0.04	1.19	−0.02	−0.34
All Ecological	45	0.05	1.17	0.00	−0.02
All Health	72	0.01	0.30	−0.05	−0.70
All Safety	78	0.05	1.36	0.00	0.06

Notes: *, ** denote statistically significantly different from zero at 10% and 5% significance level, respectively. Scores are normalized so minimum and maximum possible scores are −1 and +1, respectively. NA when standard error = 0.
Source: Hammitt et al. (2005)

Table 15.3 shows that the average relative precaution over the 35-year period differs across risk categories, with Europe apparently slightly more precautionary than the United States in a majority of categories. Using the weighted scores, Europe appears to have been slightly more precautionary than the United States for the average risk in 10 categories (68 risks), slightly less precautionary than the United States for the average risk in 5 categories (29 risks), and equally precautionary for 2 categories (3 risks).

To test whether the difference in apparent precaution for a risk category could be due to sampling variability, we construct t-statistics on the assumption that the scores assigned to risks in the same category are probabilistically independent. This test is likely to overstate the degree of statistical significance, because information about risks in the same category is likely to come from similar sources, and scoring errors resulting from limitations on the data we collected or misinterpretation of regulations are likely to be positively correlated across risks. Using the confidence-weighted scores, the difference in relative precaution appears to be statistically significant in two cases (alcohol, tobacco, and drugs; recreation). Using the unweighted scores, the difference appears to be statistically significant for these two cases plus a third (pollution). In all three cases, the United States appears be more precautionary than Europe. Because these tests are likely to overestimate the degree of statistical significance, we conclude that there is little evidence of any variation in relative precaution between broad risk categories.

Aggregating over all 100 risks, the average weighted and unweighted scores are both very close to zero, and neither differs from zero by a statistically significant amount. The average weighted score is slightly greater than zero (suggesting greater European precaution), and the average unweighted score is slightly less than zero (suggesting greater U.S. precaution).

Table 15.4 reports the average weighted and unweighted scores for the risks aggregated by endpoint categories. None of the t-statistics approach conventional significance levels, so we cannot reject the hypothesis of no transatlantic difference in relative precaution in any of the endpoint categories. As in Table 15.3, the t-statistics are calculated on the assumption that errors in coding are independent between risks, so these tests are likely to overstate the degree of statistical significance.

Average precaution scores mask variation in precaution within categories. For almost two-thirds of the risk categories, one or more risks are not regulated with greater precaution by the polity that on average regulates the risks in the category with greater precaution.[14] Within-category variation in regulatory precaution is probably even greater than this, however. Only one of five categories where all risks in the category are regulated with greater precaution by one polity—the United States' consistently greater precaution regarding alcohol, tobacco, and other drugs—may have enough risks in it (three) to generalize about the category.

---

[14] See Table 15.1 in an earlier version of this chapter posted online at the Duke Center for Environmental Solutions (2004).

Table 15.5 *Average Precaution, the United States Compared to Europe, 1970–2004*

For 100 risks	Weighted score	For 18 categories of risk
Greater U.S. Precaution (36 risks)		
Sake	−0.67	Alcohol, tobacco, and other drug
Vaccination − side effects	−0.57	Medications and medical treatment
Smoking regulations	−0.51	Alcohol, tobacco, and other drug
Pot smoking	−0.50	Alcohol, tobacco, and other drug
Carbon monoxide	−0.38	Pollution
Snowboarding	−0.34	Recreation
Burglary	−0.33	Crime and violence
Disaster preparedness	−0.33	Accident
Dredging and dredge disposal	−0.33	Pollution
Food coloring	−0.33	Food and agriculture
Genes − defects predisposing to illness	−0.33	Human disease/health
Air pollution	−0.33	Pollution
Smog	−0.33	Pollution
Polyvinyl chloride − living nearby	−0.30	Toxic substance
Charcoal-broiled steak	−0.29	Food and agriculture
Radiation therapy	−0.28	Medications and medical treatment
Roller coasters	−0.26	Recreation
Amusement park rides	−0.26	Recreation
Circuses and amusement and theme parks	−0.26	Recreation
Sulfur dioxide	−0.22	Pollution
Occupational carcinogens	−0.19	Occupational
Snowmobiles	−0.18	Transportation
Industrial chemical release	−0.16	Pollution
Unsuitable eating habits	−0.14	Food and agriculture
Shortage of medicines	−0.14	Medications and medical treatment
Neurologic malfunction	−0.13	Human disease/health
Nitrocompounds − aromatic	−0.13	Toxic substance
Woodworking	−0.12	Occupational
West Nile virus	−0.11	Human disease/health
Train accident	−0.10	Transportation
Laboratory worker	−0.07	Occupational
Work at high altitudes	−0.07	Occupational
Caffeine − chronic effects	−0.06	Medications and medical treatment
Health care facilities and services − exposure to physical agents	−0.06	Medications and medical treatment
War and terrorism	−0.04	War, security, and terrorism
Aviation − commercial − noise	−0.01	Transportation
Equal Precaution (21 risks)		
Transportation noise	0.00	Transportation
Airport and flight control	0.00	Transportation
Aviation − commercial − crashes	0.00	Transportation
Submarine − accidents	0.00	Transportation
Bus − transit	0.00	Transportation
Aerospace manufacturing and maintenance − environmental and public health issues	0.00	Transportation
Television	0.00	Consumer product
Carpets and rugs	0.00	Consumer product
Metal manufacturing	0.00	Toxic substance
Hazardous response personnel	0.00	Toxic substance

Table 15.5 (*Continued*)

For 100 risks	Weighted score	For 18 categories of risk
Semiconductor manufacturing	0.00	Occupational
Hotels and restaurants – health effects and disease patterns	0.00	Occupational
Oil refineries	0.00	Energy production
Transport of oil – transcontinental pipelines	0.00	Energy production
Sabotage	0.00	Crime and violence
Food processing and distribution	0.00	Food and agriculture
Health care facilities and services	0.00	Medications and medical treatment
Urban pollution	0.00	Pollution
Gallbladder	0.00	Human disease/health
Fire/explosion	0.00	Accident
Hang gliding	0.00	Recreation
*Unscoreable Risks (12)**		
CEO deaths	0.00	Occupational
Engineer deaths	0.00	Occupational
Safety and health training	0.00	Occupational
Safety culture and management	0.00	Occupational
Workplace – performance measures and compensation	0.00	Occupational
Rodeo performer	0.00	Recreation
Jogging	0.00	Recreation
Heat stroke	0.00	Human disease/health
Biological agents – pet hair, skin, and excreta	0.00	Human disease/health
Dieting	0.00	Food and agriculture
Termites attacking food crops	0.00	Ecogeological
Social/ethical/cultural impacts of technology	0.00	Political, social, and financial
Greater European Precaution (31 risks)		
Liquid propane trains	0.04	Energy production
Workplace violence	0.04	Occupational
Motor vehicle traffic	0.06	Transportation
Mononucleosis	0.10	Human disease/health
Hexachlorophene	0.11	Toxic substance
Horse riding – falls, including racing	0.11	Recreation
Forestry	0.14	Food and agriculture
Rubber manufacture – ergonomics	0.20	Occupational
Jewelry	0.21	Occupational
Biotechnology – ingredients in products	0.29	Food and agriculture
Genetic manipulation – animals	0.29	Food and agriculture
Deliberate release of genetic engineered organisms	0.29	Food and agriculture
Genetic engineering	0.29	Medications and medical treatment
Cognitive disorders	0.31	Human disease/health
Stone quarries	0.33	Occupational
Formaldehyde – workers	0.37	Toxic substance
Nonpoint-source discharges to surface water	0.41	Pollution
Flooding of dikes	0.50	Ecogeological
Sea level rise	0.52	Global
Timber preservatives	0.52	Toxic substance
Nuclear weapons – test	0.61	War, security, and terrorism
Sleep	0.63	Human disease/health

Table 15.5 (*Continued*)

For 100 risks	Weighted score	For 18 categories of risk
Ergonomics – sleep deprivation	0.63	Occupational
Occupationally acquired infections of the lung	0.63	Occupational
Ammonia	0.67	Toxic substance
Firearms	0.67	Crime and violence
Childbearing	0.67	Medications and medical treatment
Anti-ballistic missile	0.67	War, security, and terrorism
Automobile – bicycle accident	0.67	Transportation
Highway safety	0.67	Transportation
Drinking and driving	0.83	Transportation

*These 12 risks could not be scored for relative precaution because they have not been regulated, regulations could not be found, or they are too broad, vague, or multidimensional to be scored sensibly

Categorical and aggregate averages in precaution also mask several other noteworthy precautionary patterns. In Table 15.5, we take the 100 risks out of the 18 categories and array them from those where the United States is more precautionary than Europe to those where Europe is more precautionary than the United States using the weighted scores. Here we observe that the United States is more precautionary than Europe regarding a *greater number* of risks (36 versus 31), but that for those risks where Europe is more precautionary than the United States, Europe regulates a *larger proportion* with a greater number of years of greater precaution—what we will call "net duration of greater precaution"—than is the case for risks where the United States is the more precautionary polity. This may also be due in part to the use of weighted scores, since the coders gave greater confidence scores when they were more confident they had complete European information, as described below. Using the net duration of greater precaution measure, Europe not only regulates drinking and driving with greater precaution than the United States but regulates it earlier and/or more stringently than the United States in a greater number of years than either polity led the other in precaution regarding any other risk.

One way of identifying further precautionary patterns is to see whether risks regulated by the United States or Europe with equal precaution or with larger or smaller net durations of greater precaution are from the same risk categories. While the following analysis describes the patterns we found, we ask readers to remember our sample's great differences in the numbers of risks from different risk categories. Our sample included only one global risk but 17 occupational risks, for example. This distribution of risk types in our sample is surprisingly representative of their distribution in the risk universe we created, as previously discussed. However, as a result of some categories of risk being much more prevalent in our risk universe and sample than others, they are also more likely to take on a variety of precautionary patterns.

For example, of the risks that the United States regulates with more precaution than Europe, three of the five risks with the highest net duration of greater precaution are from the alcohol, tobacco, and drugs category. Since these three risks are also the only risks in the category in our sample, this pattern is easier to interpret than Europe's corresponding "top five," which includes 3 of 13 transportation risks—the other 10 of which were regulated with little or no differences in precaution. As we describe these varied precautionary patterns here and in the accompanying footnotes, it is therefore important to keep in mind the differences in numbers of risks in the 18 risk categories. Thus, while we can say that the United States' precautionary "top 10" included three alcohol, tobacco, and drug risks and two pollution risks,[15] and Europe's "top 10" included three transportation and two occupational risks,[16] readers should note that the United States and Europe also regulate many risks in these last two categories equally or with little difference in precaution (i.e., 10 transportation and 9 occupational risks).

Of the 21 risks the United States and Europe regulate with equal precaution, six are transportation risks and two are risks from each of the following categories: energy production, toxic substance, occupational, and consumer products.

Trends in Relative Precaution

To examine whether the degree of relative precaution has changed over the 35-year period, we average the relative precaution scores across risks for each year and plot the results as a function of time. Figure 15.1 shows the resulting patterns for the average of the 100 risks. The results are weakly consistent with Vogel's (2001, 2003) flip-flop hypothesis. The unweighted score suggests that the United States exhibited greater precaution than Europe from 1970 through the late 1980s, including increasing relative U.S. precaution during 1980–1989, and that Europe became relatively more precautionary during the 1990s and early 2000s. The confidence-weighted score suggests a relatively static balance of relative precaution from 1970 through the late 1980s, followed by increasing relative precaution in Europe during the 1990s and early 2000s. In contrast to the unweighted score, the weighted score is uniformly greater than zero, suggesting Europe was more precautionary on average in the 1970s as well as in later periods. Both scores, but especially the unweighted values, suggest a shift toward greater relative precaution in the United States during the 1980s, which is surprising because the Reagan administration (1981–1989) is not usually seen as an advocate of more stringent environmental, health, and safety regulation. Consistent with the slightly decreasing relative precaution of U.S. regulation we observe after 1990, Lazarus (2004) notes that voting on environmental bills in the U.S. Congress reflected

---

[15] The United States' precautionary "top 15" included four risks from the pollution category, three from alcohol, tobacco, and other drugs, and two from food and agriculture. Among the "top 20," the five following risk categories are most heavily represented: pollution (5 risks), alcohol, tobacco, and other drugs (3), recreation (3), food and agriculture (2), and medications and medical treatment (2).

[16] Europe's precautionary "top 15" include transportation (3), occupational (2), toxic substance (2), and war, security, and terrorism (2). Risks 19 through 22 were regulated with the same degree of precaution, so it is only possible to identify the "top 22" (rather than 20) most precautionary European risks. The precautionary "top 22" include transportation (3), occupational (3), food and agriculture (3), toxic substance (3), war, security, and terrorism (2), human disease/health (2), and medications and medical treatment (2) risks.

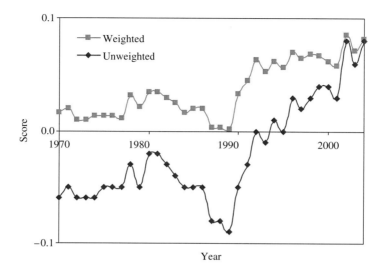

Figure 15.1 *Trends in Relative Precaution (All Risks)*

Source: Hammitt et al. (2005)

bipartisan support until 1990, after which voting increasingly diverged along partisan lines, with Democrats increasingly voting for, and Republicans increasingly voting against, more stringent environmental laws. This increasing polarization may have contributed to a decline in relative precaution in the United States if it impeded the enactment of new laws and regulations.

The estimated magnitude of the change in average relative precaution is quite modest. By the year 2004, European regulation is less than 0.1 points more precautionary on average than U.S. regulation (on a range from -1 to $+1$). Comparing average relative precaution in the last five years of the period to average relative precaution in the first five years, the weighted and unweighted scores increase by 0.06 and 0.12, respectively. To put these changes in perspective, note that a change of 0.06 in the weighted score would be achieved if the regulations of 3% of risks unambiguously changed from greater precaution in the United States to greater precaution in Europe, with no change in the relative precaution with which the remaining 97% of risks were regulated. A change of 0.12 in the unweighted score would be achieved by a shift in regulation of 6% of risks (from more precautionary in the United States to more precautionary in Europe) with no change to the remaining 94%.

A statistical test for the change in relative precaution is difficult to construct, because the annual scores for each risk are not independent, given that incomplete data on regulations about a risk along with errors in the coders' judgments about relative stringency will tend to be common across multiple years. Moreover, it is difficult to know how to model the dependence of scores across years. It seems reasonable to suppose that the degree of dependence declines with temporal distance, because changes in regulation are more likely to be introduced over a longer timespan. Hence, we test for the apparent change in trend by comparing the average scores across all 100 risks in 1970 and in 2004 with the average score in 1989. Under the assumption that the scores in 1970 and 2004 are independent of the scores in 1989, we cannot reject the hypothesis of no change in relative precaution between 1970 and 1989 (the t-statistic equals 0.32 for the weighted scores and 0.33 for the unweighted scores). Comparing 2004 with 1989, we cannot reject the hypothesis of no change using the weighted score and can reject this hypothesis at the 10% significance level using the unweighted scores (the t-statistic equals 1.46 for the weighted scores and 1.71 for the unweighted scores). Because these tests are likely to overstate the confidence with which we can reject the hypothesis of no trend, we conclude there is suggestive evidence of a slight trend between 1989 and 2004.

Figure 15.2 presents the time patterns for the risks classified by endpoint, using the weighted scores. The results suggest that the pattern observed for all risks in Figure 15.1 is also observed for risks having ecological, health, or safety effects. The apparent trend is strongest for ecological risks, where the mean weighted score increased by 0.19 between 1970–1974 and 2000–2004. For health and safety risks, the corresponding changes are 0.07 and 0.05, respectively.

In evaluating the trends by endpoint category, it is important to recognize that the endpoint categories are not independent, because many of the risks are included in more than one category. As Table 15.3 shows, 39 risks are included in all three endpoint categories, and 16 are included in both health and safety endpoint categories. The numbers of risks that are included in only a single endpoint category are 3 in ecological, 16 in health, and 21 in safety.

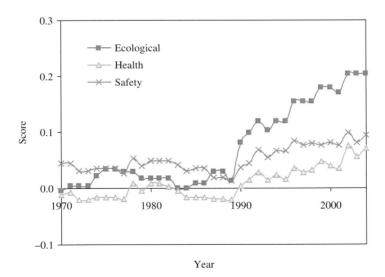

Figure 15.2 *Trends by Endpoint Category (Weighted Scores)*

Source: Hammitt et al. (2005)

A complementary method for evaluating time patterns of relative precaution is to identify a set of possible patterns and investigate how many risks are consistent with each pattern. Figure 15.3 reports the number of risks in our sample of 100 that are consistent with each of 12 alternative patterns (using the unweighted scores). The most common pattern, exhibited by 33 risks, is that Europe and the United States are equally precautionary over the entire period. To some extent, our analysis is biased in favor of finding no difference in precaution (or trend in relative precaution), because this is the default score in the absence of information to the contrary. Twelve (12) risks were scored as equally precautionary in every year because they have not been regulated, regulations could not be found, or they are too broad, vague, or multidimensional to be scored sensibly.

Excluding these 12 risks leaves 21 risks showing equal precaution across the full period—still almost twice as many as showing any other pattern. The second most frequent pattern is an oscillation or other complex pattern (12 risks). A total of 20 risks show a difference but no change in the direction of relative precaution. Of these, Europe is more precautionary in 11 cases and the United States is more precautionary in 9 cases.

The slight trend suggested in Figures 15.1 and 15.2 is generated by the difference between 21 risks for which Europe has become relatively more precautionary and the 14 risks where the United States has become relatively more precautionary. The 21 risks for which Europe has become relatively more precautionary include 9 for which the United States and Europe were originally equally precautionary and Europe has become more precautionary, 7 for which the United States was initially more precautionary and the two polities are now equally precautionary, and 5 for which the United States was more precautionary and Europe has become more precautionary. The 14 risks where the shift has gone the other direction include 11 for which the two polities were equally precautionary and the United States has become more precautionary, 2 for which Europe was more precautionary and the two polities are now

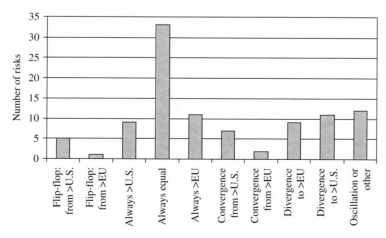

Figure 15.3 *Patterns of Relative Precaution*

Source: Hammitt et al. (2005)

equally precautionary, and 1 for which Europe was more precautionary and the United States has become the more precautionary.[17] As indicated in Figure 15.3, this is a diverse mixture of patterns and not a very strong overall trend.

We also note that the apparent modest shift toward greater relative precaution in Europe than in the United States may reflect an artifact of our data-collection methods. As discussed above, information on current regulations is much more frequently accessible through electronic means than is information on older regulations. To the extent that information on older U.S. regulations is more readily accessible to our U.S.-based research team than information on older European regulations, our results would be biased toward finding greater relative precaution in the United States in the earlier years we studied, i.e., the 1970s. This factor should have less effect on the weighted scores than on the unweighted scores, as the risks and years for which we have limited information on European regulations are given low confidence weights. Indeed, Figure 15.1 shows less relative U.S. precaution in the period 1970–1989 using the weighted scores than using the unweighted scores.

Finally, we turn to the question of which risks and which risk categories are exhibiting which trends, answered by Table 15.6. Consistent with the analysis so far, the most striking pattern here is the absence of a strong pattern. None of the trends we report here are dominated by particular categories of risk. Rather, diverse regulatory trends are created by diverse risks and risk types. As previously discussed, the probability of any category of risk taking on any particular trend is a function of the number of risks in the category. A single global risk can take on only one trend, while 17 occupational risks could conceivably be distributed across every possible trend (and in fact contribute to all but two trends).

Only five risks exhibit a flip-flop consistent with Vogel's hypothesis (2001, 2003). Two of the five flip-flop risks are in the pollution category. Three of these five flip-flops are risks from chemicals (sulfur dioxide, timber preservatives, and industrial chemical releases), although chemicals are not a matrix risk category.

The trends that have the greatest concentrations of particular kinds of risks occur for risks where Europe always has taken greater precaution, where the United States and Europe have diverged in the extent of precaution, and where precaution oscillates or exhibits some other complex pattern. The categories, number of risks in the category, and number of risks from the category creating these trends for categories where at least two risks from the category are part of the trend are summarized here:

- **Always greater European precaution (11 risks in trend):**
  - transportation (3 of 13)
- **Divergence: from tie to greater European precaution (9):**
  - food and agriculture (3 of 9)

---

[17] The effect of these changes on the unweighted score can be calculated as [9 (+1) + 7 (+1) + 5 (+2) + 11 (−1) + 2 (−1) + 1 (−2)] / 100 = 0.11. Note that this value is almost identical to the change in the unweighted score between the first and last five-year subperiods, 0.12.

   ○ occupational (2 of 17)
   ○ medications and medical treatment (2 of 8)
 • **Divergence: from tie to greater U.S. precaution (11):**
   ○ recreation (3 of 8)
   ○ occupational (2 of 17)
   ○ medications and medical treatment (2 of 8)
 • **Oscillation or other complex pattern (13):**
   ○ toxic substances (3 of 8)
   ○ occupational (2 of 17)
   ○ recreation (2 of 8)

While the most common risk type differs for each trend, the second most common risk types (occupational and medications and medical treatment) take on two or three of these four trends. Note also that in both instances where we found a diverging trend, the risks most heavily represented in the trend were not only from the same category, but very similar to each other. For example, the three food and agriculture risks that were regulated with greater European precaution by the end of the period were all biotechnology-related.

Pollution and transportation risks are somewhat concentrated in the two remaining patterns:

 • **Always greater U.S. precaution (9):**
   ○ pollution (2 of 8)
 • **Convergence: from greater U.S. precaution to tie (7):**
   ○ pollution (2 of 8)
   ○ transportation (2 of 13)

That particular categories of risk appear to be more responsible than others for creating particular precautionary trends suggests some patterning. However, these apparent patterns occur within an overall pattern of great within-category variation in precautionary trends. All but a few risk categories with only a couple of risks in them have experienced diverse precautionary trajectories over the past 35 years.

Reliability of Scoring

To evaluate the reliability of the scoring procedure, all 100 risks were scored independently by two of the authors. In cases where their scores or confidence weights differed, the coders discussed the cases and reached a consensus score and confidence weight, which are used in the main analysis. In this section, we compare the original scores with each other and with the consensus scores.

The time patterns for each of the two coders' scores, together with the average of their scores and the consensus score, are presented in Figure 15.4 (weighted scores). Both researchers' scores yield the same pattern of little change in relative precaution from 1970 through about 1990, and a reasonably steady albeit slight trend toward

Table 15.6 *Trends in Precaution for the U.S. and Europe, 1970–2004*

For 100 risks (number in pattern)	For 18 categories of risk (rank ordered from categories most to least represented in trend)
Flip-flop from > U.S. to > European (5)	
Sulfur dioxide	Pollution
Industrial chemical release	Pollution
Timber preservatives	Toxic substance
Woodworking	Occupational
Forestry	Food and agriculture
Flip-flop from > European to > U.S. (0)	
Always > U.S. (9)	
Dredging and dredge disposal	Pollution
Air pollution	Pollution
Sake	Alcohol, tobacco, and other drug
Food coloring	Food and agriculture
Genes – defects predisposing to illness	Human disease/health
Snowmobiles	Transportation
Radiation therapy	Medications and medical treatment
Burglary	Crime and violence
Disaster preparedness	Accident
Always > European (11)	
Drinking and driving	Transportation
Highway safety	Transportation
Automobile – bicycle accident	Transportation
Flooding of dikes	Ecogeological
Anti-ballistic missile	War, security, and terrorism
Stone quarries	Occupational
Sea level rise	Global
Ammonia	Toxic substance
Cognitive disorders	Human disease/health
Firearms	Crime and violence
Childbearing	Medications and medical treatment
Convergence: from > U.S. to tie (7)	
Smog	Pollution
Carbon monoxide	Pollution
Train accident	Transportation
Aviation – commercial – noise	Transportation
Polyvinyl chloride – living nearby	Toxic substance
Occupational carcinogens	Occupational
Neurologic malfunction	Human disease/health
Convergence: from > European to tie (2)	
Sleep	Human disease/health
Ergonomics – sleep deprivation	Occupational
Divergence: from tie to > European (9)	
Biotechnology – ingredients in products	Food and agriculture
Genetic manipulation – animals	Food and agriculture
Deliberate release of genetic engineered organisms	Food and agriculture
Genetic engineering	Medications and medical treatment

Table 15.6 (*Continued*)

For 100 risks (number in pattern)	For 18 categories of risk (rank ordered from categories most to least represented in trend)
Caffeine – chronic effects	Medications and medical treatment
Jewelry	Occupational
Occupationally acquired infections of the lung	Occupational
Motor vehicle traffic	Transportation
Mononucleosis	Human disease/health
Divergence: from tie to > U.S. (11)	
Amusement park rides	Recreation
Circuses and amusement and theme parks	Recreation
Roller coasters	Recreation
Laboratory worker	Occupational
Work at high altitudes	Occupational
Shortage of medicines	Medications and medical treatment
Vaccination – side effects	Medications and medical treatment
Pot smoking	Alcohol, tobacco, and other drug
West Nile virus	Human disease/health
War and terrorism	War, security, and terrorism
Unsuitable eating habits	Food and agriculture
Oscillation or other complex pattern (13)	
Formaldehyde – workers	Toxic substance
Nitrocompounds – aromatic	Toxic substances
Hexachlorophene	Toxic substances
Horse riding – falls, including racing	Recreation
Snowboarding	Recreation
Workplace violence	Occupational
Rubber manufacture – ergonomics	Occupational
Smoking regulations	Alcohol, tobacco, and other drug
Nuclear weapons – test	War, security, and terrorism
Nonpoint-source discharges to surface water	Pollution
Liquid propane trains	Energy production
Charcoal-broiled steak	Food and agriculture
Health care facilities and services – exposure to physical agents	Medications and medical treatment
Always equal/tie (21)	
Transportation noise	Transportation
Airport and flight control	Transportation
Aviation – commercial – crashes	Transportation
Submarine – accidents	Transportation
Bus – transit	Transportation
Aerospace manufacturing and maintenance – environmental and public health issues	Transportation
Television	Consumer product
Carpets and rugs	Consumer product
Metal manufacturing	Toxic substance
Hazardous response personnel	Toxic substance
Semiconductor manufacturing	Occupational
Hotels and restaurants – health effects and disease patterns	Occupational
Oil refineries	Energy production

Table 15.6 (*Continued*)

For 100 risks (number in pattern)	For 18 categories of risk (rank ordered from categories most to least represented in trend)
Transport of oil – transcontinental pipelines	Energy production
Sabotage	Crime and violence
Food processing and distribution	Food and agriculture
Health care facilities and services	Medications and medical treatment
Urban pollution	Pollution
Gallbladder	Human disease/health
Fire/explosion	Accident
Hang gliding	Recreation
*Unscoreable risks (12)**	
CEO deaths	Occupational
Engineer deaths	Occupational
Safety and health training	Occupational
Safety culture and management	Occupational
Workplace – performance measures and compensation	Occupational
Rodeo performer	Recreation
Jogging	Recreation
Heat stroke	Human disease/health
Biological agents – pet hair, skin, and excreta	Human disease/health
Dieting	Food and agriculture
Termites attacking food crops	Ecogeological
Social/ethical/cultural impacts of technology	Political, social, and financial

*These 12 risks could not be scored for relative precaution because they have not been regulated, regulations could not be found, or they are too broad, vague, or multidimensional to be scored sensibly

relatively greater precaution in Europe after about 1990. However, the researchers appear to differ systematically in their judgments about relative precaution, with Researcher 1 assigning higher scores on average (indicating greater European precaution). Over the 35 years, the average difference between the researchers' scores is 0.10 for the weighted score and 0.11 for the unweighted score.

For both weighted and unweighted scores, the consensus scores are similar to the average of the two researchers' scores, but are closer to Researcher 1's original scores than to Researcher 2's. The differences in scores appear to reflect a variety of factors. Some of the variation is simply random, as when one of the coders missed or misunderstood some information that the other noticed. Other variations were systematic. In cases where the researchers had limited information on European regulations but believed such regulations to exist—yet meanwhile had good information on U.S. regulations— Researcher 1 scored the risk as one of equal precaution (0) and Researcher 2 scored it as greater U.S. precaution (-1). This pattern appears to account for a significant part of the difference in unweighted scores, but it should have less effect on the weighted scores because Researcher 2 assigned small confidence weights in these cases.

In assigning confidence weights, Researcher 2 had a tendency to give higher confidence weights in general, and Researcher 1 had a tendency to give lower confidence

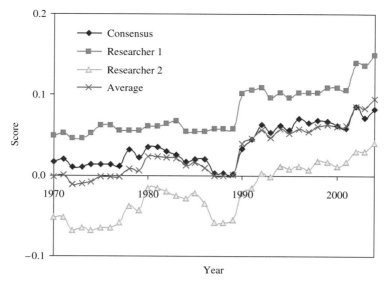

Figure 15.4 *Comparison of Individual and Consensus Scores (Weighted)*

Source: Hammitt et al. (2005)

weights when unsure whether all the European information was available. In cases where good European information was available, Researcher 1 typically assigned greater confidence weights, which tends to shift the weighted scores toward larger values (indicating greater European precaution). In general, Researcher 1 assigned lower confidence weights and more ties in cases where Researcher 2 judged the case one of greater U.S. precaution, a pattern that contributes to Researcher 1's higher average weighted scores.

Conclusions

This analysis represents the most methodologically rigorous attempt of which we are aware to investigate the relative extent of precautionary regulation of ecological, health, and safety regulations in Europe and the United States. In developing our methodology, we identified and developed workable answers to a number of challenges, including the need to describe the set of risks that might potentially be subjected to precautionary regulation; the need to assemble a database representing the universe of risks and draw a representative sample from that list; the difficulty of obtaining comprehensive and comparable information on regulation in the United States and Europe; and the difficulties in comparing the stringency of regulations at a point in time because of the multidimensional nature of risks and the differences among the structure, *locus*, and approach of counterpart regulatory measures.

Overall, our results suggest that the degree of precaution exhibited in European and American risk regulation is very similar. Averaging across the 100 randomly selected risks and 35-year period, we find no difference in relative precaution. Examining each of the 18 risk-type categories averaged over the period, we find that European regulations appear to have been more precautionary for 10 categories (including 68 risks), and U.S. regulations appear to have been more precautionary for 5 categories (including 29 risks). However, our statistical tests suggest that we cannot reject the hypothesis that these apparent differences are due to sampling variability—except, perhaps, for two or three of the risk categories in which the United States appears to have been more precautionary.

The results offer some limited support to the flip-flop hypothesis—that in general, the United States was more precautionary than Europe in the 1970s and 1980s, but Europe has become relatively more precautionary than the United States. Trends in both weighted and unweighted scores suggest little change in relative precaution from 1970 through about 1990, followed by a slight shift toward greater relative precaution in Europe from about 1990 through 2004. However, the magnitude of the shift is quite modest. It is less than a 10% overall edge by 2004, and it is equal to the change that would occur if regulation of 3% to 6% of risks shifted from more precautionary in the United States to more precautionary in Europe, with no change in the relative precaution with which other risks are regulated.

Our analysis of the patterns by individual risk suggests a much greater diversity of patterns. By far the most common pattern we identified (accounting for a third of the risks) is that the United States and Europe were equally precautionary over the 35-year period. To some extent, this finding of equal precaution reflects our inability to obtain full information about regulations in each region and to make confident judgments about which of two sets of multidimensional regulations is, on balance, more stringent. But even excluding those risks we could not score for lack of information, equal precaution remains the modal pattern. Patterns reflecting a difference but no change in the direction of relative precaution are also common, accounting for 20% of the risks we examined. These cases are almost exactly divided between the 11 cases where Europe appears to be more precautionary over the entire period and 9 cases where the United States appears to be more precautionary. Of the cases in which there was a change in relative precaution, the change is more often toward greater relative precaution in Europe, but even here many cases show the opposite result. The direction of movement was toward greater relative precaution in Europe for 21 cases, and toward greater relative precaution in the United States for 14 cases.

In summary, our results provide some support for the view that there has been a slight shift toward relatively greater precaution in European risk regulation compared with U.S. regulation, but also that patterns of regulation are quite diverse. This suggests that there are no simple or categorical national styles of regulation, but that regulation is highly contextual—with policy choices that are specific to the particular risk. The history of U.S. and European risk regulation over the period 1970–2004 has been one of selective precautionary particularity, not of overarching precautionary principle (Wiener 2003, 260–262). The broad but shallow quantitative comparison presented here should be complemented by more narrow but more detailed examination of specific risks and policy processes to shed light on the contextual factors that influence the timing, stringency, enforcement, and type of regulation selected to address particular risks (Swedlow et al. 2009).

Acknowledgments

This chapter provides additional information on relative transatlantic precaution beyond that found in Hammitt et al. 2005, much of which is concentrated in Tables 15.5 and 15.6 and their accompanying text. The authors thank JoAnn Carmin, Robert Keohane, Kathryn Saterson, and participants at a conference at Duke University, including our discussant, Richard "Pete" Andrews, for helpful suggestions, Joshua Cohen for assistance with data analysis, and Zia Cromer, Shannon Frank, Dylan Fuge, Lena Hansen, Clayton Jernigan, Chris Kocher, Chloe Metz, Jessica Regan, Caitlin Snyder, and Ivan Urlaub for invaluable research assistance. This research was supported by the Duke Center for Environmental Solutions.

References

Axelrod, L. J., T. McDaniels, and Paul Slovic. 1999. Perceptions of Ecological Risk from Natural Hazards. *Journal of Risk Research* 2 (1): 31–53.

Bernauer, Thomas, and Erika Meins. 2003. Technological Revolution Meets Policy and the Market: Explaining Cross-National Differences in Agricultural Biotechnology Regulation. *European Journal of Political Research* 42: 643–684.

Blomquist, William. 1999. The Policy Process and Large-N Comparative Studies. In *Theories of the Policy Process*, edited by Paul A. Sabatier. Boulder, CO: Westview Press, 201–224.

Breyer, Stephen, and Veerle Heyvaert. 2000. Institutions for Regulating Risk. In *Environmental Law, the Economy, and Sustainable Development: The United States, the European Union, and the International Community*, edited by Richard L. Revesz, Phillipe Sands, and Richard B. Stewart. Cambridge: Cambridge University Press.

Brickman, Ronald, Sheila Jasanoff, and Thomas Ilgen. 1985. *Controlling Chemicals: The Politics of Regulation in Europe and the United States*. Ithaca, NY: Cornell University Press.

CDC (Centers for Disease Control and Prevention). 2003. *Glossary of Epidemiology Terms*, www.cdc.gov/nccdphp/drh/epi_gloss.htm#H (accessed May 8, 2003).

Coppedge, Michael. 2005. Explaining Democratic Deterioration in Venezuela through Nested Induction. In *The Third Wave of Democratization in Latin America*, edited by Frances Hagopian and Scott Mainwaring. New York: Cambridge University Press.

Duke Center for Environmental Solutions. 2004. Reality of Precaution Project, www.env.duke.edu/solutions/precaution_project.html (accessed May 15, 2010).

Englander, Tibor, Klara Farago, Paul Slovic, and Baruch Fischhoff. 1986. A Comparative Analysis of Risk Perception in Hungary and the United States. *Social Behaviour* 1: 55–66.

EPA (U.S. Environmental Protection Agency). 1987. *Unfinished Business*. Washington, DC: U.S. EPA Office of Policy, Planning, and Evaluation.

———. 2002. Terms of the Environment, www.epa.gov/OCEPAterms/ (accessed May 21, 2003).

Fischhoff, Baruch, Paul Slovic, Sarah Lichtenstein, Stephen Read, and Barbara Combs. 1978. How Safe Is Safe Enough? A Psychometric Study of Attitudes towards Technological Risks and Benefits. *Policy Sciences* 9: 127–152.

Goszczynska, Maryla, Tadeusz Tyska, and Paul Slovic. 1991. Risk Perception in Poland: A Comparison with Three Other Countries. *Journal of Behavioral Decision Making* 4: 179–193.

Graham, John D., and Jonathan Baert Wiener, eds. 1995. *Risk versus Risk: Tradeoffs in Protecting Health and the Environment.* Cambridge, MA: Harvard University Press.

Hammitt, James K., Jonathan B. Wiener, Brendon Swedlow, Denise Kall, and Zheng Zhou. 2005. Precautionary Regulation in Europe and the United States: A Quantitative Comparison. *Risk Analysis* 25 (5): 1215–1228.

Harremoës Poul, David Gee, Malcolm MacGarvin, Andy Stirling, Jane Keys, Brian Wynne, and Sofia Guedes Vaz, eds. 2002. *The Precautionary Principle in the Twentieth Century: Late Lessons from Early Warnings.* London: Earthscan.

Harrington, Winston, Richard D. Morgenstern, and Thomas Sterner, eds. 2004. *Choosing Environmental Policy: Comparing Instruments and Outcomes in the United States and Europe.* Washington, DC: Resources for the Future Press.

Haward, Steven F. 2004. *2004 Index of Leading Environmental Indicators,* 9th ed. San Francisco: Pacific Research Institute for Public Policy. www.pacificresearch.org/pub/sab/enviro/04_enviroindex/Enviro_2004.pdf (accessed June 15, 2010).

Hohenemser, C., R. W. Kates, and P. Slovic. 1983. The Nature of Technological Hazard. *Science* 220 (4595): 378–384.

Hood, Christopher, Henry Rothstein, and Robert Baldwin. 2001. *The Government of Risk: Understanding Risk Regulation Regimes.* Oxford: Oxford University Press.

Jasanoff, Sheila. 1986. *Risk Management and Political Culture.* New York: Russell Sage Foundation.

———. 1998. Contingent Knowledge: Implications for Implementation and Compliance. In *Engaging Countries: Strengthening Compliance with International Environmental Accords,* edited by E. Brown Weiss and H. Jacobson. Cambridge, MA: MIT Press.

———. 2005. *Designs on Nature: Science and Democracy in Europe and the United States.* Princeton, NJ: Princeton University Press.

Kagan, Robert A. and Lee Axelrad, eds. 2000. *Regulatory Encounters: Multinational Corporations and American Adversarial Legalism.* Berkeley: University of California Press.

Kelman, Steven. 1981. *Regulating America, Regulating Sweden: A Comparative Study of Occupational Safety and Health Policy.* Cambridge, MA: MIT Press.

King, Gary, Robert O. Keohane, and Sidney Verba. 1994. *Designing Social Inquiry: Scientific Inference in Qualitative Research.* Princeton, NJ: Princeton University Press.

Kolluru, Rao V. 1996. Risk Assessment and Management: A Unified Approach. In *Risk Assessment and Management Handbook: For Environmental Health, and Safety Professionals,* edited by Rao Kolluru, Steven M. Bartell, Robin M. Pitblado, and R. Scott Stricoff. New York: McGraw-Hill, 1.3–1.41.

Koren, Herman. 1996. *Illustrated Dictionary of Environmental Health and Occupational Safety.* New York: Lewis Publishers.

Kraus, N. N., and Paul Slovic. 1988. Taxonomic Analysis of Perceived Risk: Modeling Individual and Group Perceptions within Homogeneous Hazard Domains. *Risk Analysis* 8: 435–455.

Lawless, Edward. 1977. *Technology and Social Shock.* New Brunswick, NJ: Rutgers University Press.

Lazarus, Richard. 2004. *The Making of Environmental Law.* Chicago, IL: University of Chicago Press.

Levy, David L., and Peter Newell. 2000. Oceans Apart? Business Responses to Global Environmental Issues in Europe and the United States. *Environment* 42 (9): 8–20.

Lichtenstein, Sarah, Paul Slovic, Baruch Fischhoff, Mark Layman, and Barbara Combs. 1978. Judged Frequency of Lethal Events. *Journal of Experimental Psychology: Human Learning and Memory* 4 (6): 551–578.

Lieberman, Evan S. 2005. Nested Analysis as a Mixed-Method Strategy for Comparative Research. *American Political Science Review* 99 (3): 435–452.

Lofstedt, Ragnar, and David Vogel. 2001. The Changing Character of Regulation: A Comparison of Europe and the United States. *Risk Analysis* 21: 399–405.

Lomborg, Bjorn. 2001. *The Skeptical Environmentalist: Measuring the Real State of the World.* Cambridge: Cambridge University Press.

Lynch, Diahanna, and David Vogel. 2000. Apples and Oranges: Comparing the Regulation of Genetically Modified Food in Europe and the United States. Paper prepared for the American Political Science Association annual meeting, August 31–September 3.

Mazur, Allan. 2004. *True Warnings and False Alarms: Evaluating Fears about the Health Risks of Technology, 1948–1971.* Washington, DC: Resources for the Future Press.

McDaniels, T., L. J. Axelrod, and Paul Slovic. 1995. Characterizing Perception of Ecological Risk. *Risk Analysis* 15 (5): 575–588.

Morgan, M. Granger, H. Keith Florig, Michael DeKay, Paul Fischbeck, Kara Morgan, Karen Jenni, and Baruch Fischhoff. 2000. Categorizing Risks for Risk Ranking. *Risk Analysis* 20 (1): 49–58.

Rehbinder, Eckard, and Richard Stewart. 1985. *Environmental Protection Policy: Legal Integration in the United States and the European Community.* New York: De Gruyter.

Reitz, John C. 1998. How to Do Comparative Law. *American Journal of Comparative Law* 46: 617–636.

Renn, Ortwin, and Bernd Rohrmann, eds. 2000. *Cross-Cultural Risk Perception: A Survey of Empirical Studies.* Dordrecht, Netherlands: Kluwer.

Rose-Ackerman, Susan. 1995. *Controlling Environmental Policy: The Limits of Public Law in Germany and the United States.* New Haven, CT: Yale University Press.

Seawright, Jason, and John Gerring. 2008. Case-Selection Techniques in Case Study Research: A Menu of Qualitative and Quantitative Options. *Political Research Quarterly* 61 (June): 294–308.

Simon, Julian. 1995. *The State of Humanity.* Oxford: Blackwell.

Swedlow, Brendon. 2005. Review of Allan Mazur's *True Warnings and False Alarms: Evaluating Fears about the Health Risks of Technology, 1948–1971* (2004). *Environmental Science and Policy* 8 (4): 432–435.

Swedlow, Brendon, Denise Kall, Zheng Zhou, James K. Hammitt, and Jonathan B. Wiener. 2009. Theorizing and Generalizing about Risk Assessment and Regulation through Comparative Nested Analysis of Representative Cases. *Law and Policy* 31 (2): 236–269.

Vig, Norman and Michael Faure, eds. 2004. *Green Giants: Environmental Policies of the United States and the European Union.* Cambridge, MA: MIT Press.

Vogel, David. 1986. *National Styles of Regulation: Environmental Policy in Great Britain and the United States.* Ithaca, NY: Cornell University Press.

———. 2001. Ships Passing in the Night: The Changing Politics of Risk Regulation in Europe and the United States. Working Paper 2001/16: 1. San Domenico di Fiesole, Italy: Robert Schuman Centre for Advanced Studies, European University Institute.

———. 2002. Risk Regulation in Europe and the United States. In *Yearbook of European Environmental Law*, Vol. 3. http://faculty.haas.berkeley.edu/vogel/ (accessed March 4, 2003).

———. 2003. The Hare and the Tortoise Revisited: The New Politics of Consumer and Environmental Regulation in Europe. *British Journal of Political Science* 33: 557–580.

Webster's Third International Dictionary (Unabridged). 1993. Published under License from Merriam-Webster, Inc, http://lion.chadwyck.com/works/search (accessed May 8, 2003).

Wiener, Jonathan B. 2002. Precaution in a Multirisk World. In *Human and Ecological Risk Assessment: Theory and Practice*, edited by Dennis D. Paustenbach. New York: John Wiley and Sons, 1509–1531.

———. 2003. Whose Precaution After All? A Comment on the Comparison and Evolution of Risk Regulatory Systems. *Duke Journal of International and Comparative Law* 13: 207–262.

Wildavsky, Aaron. 1995. *But Is It True? A Citizen's Guide to Environmental Health and Safety Issues.* Cambridge, MA: Harvard University Press.

Worldwatch Institute, Lester Brown, et al. 2004. *State of the World 2004.* New York: W.W. Norton.

PART V
CAN WE EXPLAIN THE OBSERVED
PATTERN OF PRECAUTION?

CHAPTER 16

Political Institutions and the Principle of Precaution

Giandomenico Majone

*B*oth the European Union and the United States rely on the precautionary principle in many of their risk regulations. It is true that the lack of a precise and generally accepted definition of the principle makes comparative analysis rather difficult. Regardless of the definition one uses, however, it is a fact that both political systems apply precaution to imported goods or services with particular vigor. The domestic application of the principle is of course a different story. The situation of the European authorities is particularly delicate in this respect. On the one hand, the European Commission, pushed by the Council and the European Parliament (EP), has been engaged in a sustained effort to promote the precautionary principle (PP) to the status of a central plank of Community policy and, more ambitiously, to the status of a general principle of international economic and environmental law. On the other hand, the major beneficiaries of this promotional effort could well be the Member States of the EU, which may be tempted to use the principle to regain significant portions of their regulatory autonomy in the management of environmental and health risks. And the "Better Regulation" initiative advanced by the European Commission and several Member States over the past decade has in part moderated the promotion of the precautionary principle by applying impact assessments and reviews to major regulatory policies.

At any rate, it would be surprising if any polity with a well-developed system of risk regulation did not use at least some version of the PP. Basically, the principle says that scientific uncertainty should not be used as an excuse for regulatory inaction. Since regulatory science is intrinsically uncertain, any responsible risk regulator may be said to use a precautionary approach. The danger is, rather, that the principle could be used too freely, even in cases where its application lacks rational justification—except perhaps as a protectionist device. Again, this danger has been clearly recognized by both American and European authorities. The possibility of abuse does not stem only from the populist refusal to compare opportunity costs and expected benefits of regulatory measures in the presence of risks, however hypothetical, to human life and health. Populist tendencies are reinforced by the natural risk aversion of regulators. It is well known that the structure of incentives facing risk regulators is quite asymmetric: while the decision not to approve a safe and potentially useful product entails difficult-to-quantify opportunity costs—the number of lives that could be saved, had the product been available—and does not usually cause political controversy, the reverse is true in case of an error of the second kind.

Aside from such general observations, not much can be said about the PP, or any other general regulatory principle, until one knows the political and institutional context in which the principle is invoked, implemented, and perhaps modified in the light of experience. This chapter explores the roles of those political institutions in shaping the degree of precaution in actual regulation in the United States and in Europe.

The Influence of Electoral Laws

Populist themes are particularly attractive to single-issue movements or parties, both on the right (e.g., immigration) and on the left (e.g., the precautionary approach to environmental and risk regulation) of the political spectrum. The reason is that such political groups, appealing only to narrow segments of the electorate, have no interest in balancing and trading off, at the margin, conflicting policy objectives. However, single-issue parties can only assume direct policy responsibility in coalition governments under electoral systems of proportional representation. In majoritarian, first-past-the-pole or "winner-take-all" electoral systems—the United States and the Westminster models—single-issue parties cannot usually take part in government. Social movements can affect public policy only indirectly through their influence on one of the major parties and on public opinion. It is true that when single-issue parties become members of a governing coalition, they tend to assume at least some of the characteristics of a "popular party" (*Volkspartei*), but as the German case shows, this transformation can be quite difficult because of the opposition of the party activists and the fear of losing the party's traditional electorate.

Thus, the nature of the electoral system can explain, in part, why the precautionary principle has never become a serious topic of political debate in the UK, while in continental Europe it has moved toward the top of the political agenda during the 1990s—in some countries even before. During this period, green parties were members of coalition center-left governments in most European countries with some form of proportional representation, generally wielding an influence on public policy out of proportion to their electoral strength. The Italian case is particularly striking in this respect. The Italian environmentalist party gathers between 2% and 4% of the popular vote at national elections, but for most of the 1990s it managed to be essential to the survival of various center-left coalition governments. As a consequence, the Italian government passed extremely strict legislation on certain types of low-probability risk—while doing very little to control other risks. For example, it did little to improve occupational health and safety—an area in which Italy, according to International Labor Office data, has one of the worst records in Europe. In another example, in the late 1990s, the risk connected with electromagnetic fields (EMFs, or "electrosmog") and towers/masts became a topic of intense political controversy, involving even the Vatican for certain radio transmitters located near Rome. Explicitly appealing to the PP, the minister of the environment persuaded the government to approve what are considered to be the most stringent exposure standards in the world. The minister of health of the same center-left government—a highly respected cancer specialist—argued that with the resources needed to implement the new standards, it would have been possible to save thousands of cancer patients—rather than the one death from leukemia per year that the standards are supposed to prevent—but to no avail.

This episode is strongly reminiscent of the case discussed in *Saving Two in a Billion*, a study published in 2000 by three World Bank economists (Otsuki et al. 2000). The study reported research done by the Joint Food and Agriculture Organization/World Health Organization Expert Committee on Food Additives, according to which the proposed European Community standard of 2 parts per billion (ppb) for B_1 aflatoxin— another standard based on the precautionary principle—would reduce deaths from liver cancer by 1.4 deaths per billion—i.e., by less than one death per year in the European Union (EU). For the purpose of this calculation, the Community standard was compared to a standard based on the international (Codex) guideline of 9 ppb. Since about 33,000 people die from liver cancer every year in the EU, the health gain produced by the precautionary standard is indeed minuscule. Its economic impact on some of the poorest African countries, however, would be devastating. The World Bank economists calculated that the precautionary aflatoxin standards proposed by the European Commission in the late 1990s would decrease African exports of cereals, dried food, and nuts to the EU by 64%, relative to a regulation set at the international standard (Otsuki et al. 2000). It should be noted that the proposed European standards are also significantly more stringent than the U.S., Canadian, and Australian standards.

The political and institutional system of the EU is significantly different from that of its Member States. Nevertheless, the fact that in the 1990s the majority of national governments were ruled by center-left coalitions was reflected in the composition of the EU Council of Ministers. Moreover, institutional factors tend to increase the influence of ministers coming from single-issue parties at the European level, relative to the national level. Although according to European law there is only one Council of Ministers, in practice the Council operates according to a principle of specialization and of effective monopoly of issues similar to that of standing parliamentary (or congressional) committees. Thus, only ministers of the environment meet in the Council when environmental issues are debated and decided upon. At the national level, the cabinet system ensures that all important decisions are taken collegially. This means that the minister of the environment, say, must be able to convince his or her colleagues—including the treasury or finance minister!—that the proposed measure makes economic and political sense. No such control exists at European level; hence even extreme proposals have a reasonable chance of being approved.

No substantive control is exercised by the European Parliament (EP), either. This body has little in common with the legislature of a parliamentary system. It has no power of legislative initiative, no taxing power, and its functions do not include the formation of a majority government. Because of its limited powers and low popular participation at European elections, the EP has serious legitimacy problems of its own. Hence, it constantly looks for occasions to assert its prerogatives vis-à-vis the other European institutions, and to enhance its role vis-à-vis the national parliaments (Majone 2005). These characteristics make the EP a favorable forum in which to debate populist themes. Thus, it is not surprising that the Commission Communication on the precautionary principle (CEC 2000) was prepared in response to separate requests from the Council and the EP. The political situation has changed, however. Now a majority of Member States of the EU have center-right governments, and in the EP conservatives have replaced socialists as the largest parliamentary group. Hence, it can be assumed that until the next round of national and European elections, at least, debate about the precautionary principle will be more subdued at both levels of governance. The situation may be different internationally because of the temptation to use the principle as a protectionist device, independently of any ideological justification. In the following pages, I argue that the influence of constitutional principles on various aspects of risk regulation runs even deeper than electoral rules.

Constitutional Principles: Separation of Powers versus Representation of Interests

Separation of powers is the centerpiece of modern constitutionalism. When countervailing branches of government are correctly arranged, then, in Montesquieu's words, "power arrests power." Elaborating on suggestive remarks by the French philosopher, James Madison clarified how separation of powers could be maintained by giving each branch of government a "constitutional control" over the others. This control consisted in "a partial agency in the acts of the others"—for instance, the presidential veto over measures passed by Congress, or the Senate's power of refusing consent to certain of the president's appointments (Beer 1993, 284). What separation of powers is to modern constitutionalism, institutional balance is to the much older type of polity known as "mixed government." As I have argued elsewhere (Majone 2005), the European Community is best understood, constitutionally, as a latter-day version of mixed government. Here it is sufficient to point out that the theory of separation of powers and the theory of mixed government both share the idea of using different "powers" (in the EU context, different institutions) to check and balance one another. But as Samuel Beer (1993, 285) has pointed out, the end served by these controls is quite differently conceived by the two models. While the modern theory refers to the separation of *branches of government*, in the model of mixed government the division of power among "estates," such as King, Lords, and Commons in England, was designed to balance *different social and political interests.* All the estates shared in the legislative power. "Balance" resulted since the consent of each was necessary to the exercise of that power. Each, therefore, was a check on the others because it could withhold its consent. Unlike the control by partial agency of Madison's scheme, however, this check was not intended to confine each to a certain function, but to prevent any of the social interests represented by the estates from becoming dominant.

It is hardly necessary to remind the reader that the constitutional architecture of the EC/EU is not based on the principle of separation of powers. One of its characteristic features is the impossibility of mapping functions onto specific institutions. Thus, the EU, like the previous EC, has no legislature but a legislative process in which the Council, the Parliament, and the Commission have different parts to play. Similarly, there is no identifiable executive because executive powers are exercised for some purposes by the Council acting on a Commission proposal, for other purposes by the Commission, and overwhelmingly by the Member States in implementing European policies on the ground.

Perhaps the most striking violation of separation of powers is the Commission's monopoly of legislative initiative: not a right—as in parliamentary systems where the executive has a right of legislative initiative—but an actual monopoly, so that the other institutions cannot legislate in the absence of a prior proposal by the Commission. Meanwhile, the Commission cannot be compelled to take a legislative initiative when it thinks that such initiative is not in the interest of the Community (or in its own institutional interest). This extraordinary grant of monopoly power should be understood as a form of precommitment to the process of European integration. If the Council had a right of legislative initiative, it could undo previous pro-integration legislation any time this appeared to be politically advantageous. By the same logic, but also to preserve the balance between Community institutions, the right of legislative initiative is denied also to the popularly elected EP—one of several instances where the value of integration trumps democratic values.

It seems unlikely that the framers of the treaties establishing the European Communities were directly inspired by ancient theories of government, but they did make a conscious choice between two distinct conceptions: that of separating the functional branches of government, and that of mixing the "estates" of the polity in the legislature—where the three "political" estates are not, of course, the Crown, Lords, and Commons, as in the classical English model of mixed government, but the national governments, the supranational institutions, and the "peoples of the States brought together in the Community" (Article 137 of the EEC Treaty) represented—at least virtually—in the European Parliament.

Jean Paul Jacqué (1991) has emphasized the fact that the organizing principle of the Community is not the separation of powers, but the representation of interests *cum* institutional balance. Each Community institution is the bearer of a particular interest, which it strives to protect and promote. The nature of the prevailing interest determines the structure of decisionmaking. Thus, when the framers of the treaty deemed that national interests should hold sway in a policy area of particular relevance to national sovereignty, such as fiscal harmonization, they required a unanimous vote in the Council. On the other hand, where it appeared that national interests had to be reconciled with the common interest, it was decided that the Council should legislate by qualified majority, thus enhancing the significance of the Commission proposal. Again, where it was thought that the common, rather than the national, interest should prevail, the Commission was given an autonomous power of decision. In short, each subject matter has its own decisionmaking procedure according to the nature of the interest receiving special protection. Finally, the European Court of Justice guarantees the maintenance of the balance among the European institutions, as defined in the treaties.

Institutional and Policy Implications

The contrast between separation of powers and representation of interests/institutional balance, in the sense just specified, is essential to a correct understanding of the difference between the constitutional model of the EC/EU and the more familiar presidential or parliamentary models existing at national levels. Thus, the model of mixed government explains the much deprecated "democratic deficit" of the European system of governance, as well as the peculiar politics of that system (Majone 2005). In the following, I shall limit myself to drawing some implications of direct relevance to risk regulation. More specifically, I intend to examine the influence of the two constitutional models—represented by the United States and the EC/EU—on the issue of delegation of regulatory powers and on attitudes toward policy learning.

The United States was the first country to develop a tradition of judicial review and to create independent regulatory bodies. Both developments are of course a direct consequence of the principle of separation of powers embedded in the U.S. Constitution. Statutory regulation by means of independent bodies combining legislative, executive, and judicial functions (rulemaking, adjudication, and enforcement, in the language of American administrative law) goes back to the Interstate Commerce Act of 1887 at the federal level, and even earlier in such states as New York, Massachusetts, and Wisconsin. With this act, the U.S. Congress delegated its own power to regulate an important part of interstate commerce—namely, interstate railway traffic—to an agency designed especially for the purpose: the Interstate Commerce Commission (ICC). This was a significant institutional innovation. As James Landis would comment 50 years later, the novelty with respect to traditional administration consisted not only in the precise definition of the scope of the activities of the ICC, but especially in regard to the responsibility given to the Commission for the exercise of those powers. In the words of Landis: "in the grant to it of that full ambit of authority necessary for it in order to plan, to promote, and to police, it represents an assemblage of rights normally exercisable by government as a whole" (1966 [1938], 15).

Faith in the power of expertise—technical expertise which neither legislators nor courts nor bureaucratic generalists presumably possess—has always been an important source of legitimacy for American regulators. However, faith in expertise is only a partial explanation of the willingness of legislators to delegate important regulatory powers to independent agencies. The origins of the Independent Regulatory Commissions (IRCs) must be understood in the context of separation of powers and of the resulting struggle over policymaking between the chief executive, on the one side, and Congress, and occasionally the Supreme Court, on the other. The IRCs were created by Congress not only to deal with some complex technical problems, but also to limit presidential control over important policy areas. In fact, the independence of the regulatory bodies created during the New Deal—the Federal Communications Commission, the Securities and Exchange Commission, and the Civil Aeronautics Board, among others—was the price President Roosevelt had to pay for acceptance by Congress and the Supreme Court of far-reaching public intervention in the economy. The president would have preferred to assign the new functions to executive departments under his immediate control, but the other branches of government were not willing to accept this.

In sum, in the United States, the propriety of delegating rulemaking powers to independent agencies is now regarded as having been settled by the practice of over one century. It is true that in the past a "non-delegation doctrine" enjoyed such widespread acceptance that it came to be regarded as the traditional model of administrative law. The model conceives of the regulatory agency as a mere transmission belt for implementing legislative directives in particular cases. Congress, according to the doctrine, should decide all questions of policy and frame its decisions in such specific terms that administrative regulation will not entail the exercise of broad discretion by the regulators. However, experience soon revealed the difficulty of deriving operational guidelines from general standards. By the time the Federal Trade Commission was established in 1914, the agency received essentially a blank check authorizing it to eliminate unfair competition. The New Deal agencies received even broader grants of power to regulate particular sectors of the economy "in the public interest" (Stewart 1975).

The last time the Supreme Court used the non-delegation doctrine was in 1935, when it held the delegation in the National Industrial Recovery Act unconstitutional. The doctrine has never been repealed, however. The question of whether and under what conditions Congress should be permitted to delegate legislative powers to other institutions remains central to the theory and practice of a constitutional democracy based on the principle of separation of powers. The U.S. Supreme Court's continued acceptance of the non-delegation principle, coupled with its very sparing use to strike down legislation, illustrates a continuing judicial effort to harmonize the modern regulatory state with traditional notions of separation of powers, representative government, and the rule of law (Mashaw et al. 1998). The situation is rather different in the EU.

Institutional Balance versus Delegation of Powers

As shown by the Communication proposing a new operating framework for the European regulatory agencies (CEC 2002), the Commission has changed its traditional position on a number of points concerning the organization and the functioning of such agencies. On the central issue of delegating rulemaking powers, on the other hand, its official position has hardly changed over the years: agencies may not be empowered to adopt legislative measures of general applicability. The only exception to a strict non-delegation doctrine is the admission that agencies may be allowed to adopt individual decisions in clearly specified areas of Community legislation "where a single public interest predominates and where they do not have to arbitrate on conflicting public interests, exercise powers of political judgment, or make complex economic assessments" (CEC 2002, 11). The Office of Harmonisation in the Internal Market, which deals with trademarks and industrial property, the Community Plant Variety Office, and the European Aviation Safety Agency have been deemed to satisfy these conditions and hence have been allowed to adopt legally binding decisions in the adjudication of particular cases.

The Agency for the Evaluation of Medicinal Products (EMEA) and the Food Safety Authority (EFSA) seem to satisfy the same conditions: EMEA is exclusively concerned with the safety and efficacy of new medical drugs; EFSA, with the safety of the food we eat. Yet these agencies have been denied any power of adjudication: in both cases, the Commission makes, at least formally, the final determinations. This lack of logical consistency reveals that institution's unwillingness to surrender politically and economically important powers. What interests us here is the arguments used in order to justify this unwillingness to follow the example of the United States, and indeed of the Member States of the EU, in delegating rulemaking powers to independent agencies. In fact, even within the Commission, not everybody accepts the non-delegation doctrine. A number of Commission officials now openly advocate the creation of European agencies with powers of rulemaking as well as adjudication. This internal opposition is particularly vocal in the Commission services dealing with policy areas such as transport, energy, telecommunications, and risk regulation, where the shortcomings of the traditional legal approach to market integration are most evident. The reformers are not yet strong enough to overcome the resistance of the traditionalists, but some feel that time is working in their favor.

A striking feature of the internal debate between opponents and advocates of independent European agencies is the importance both groups attach to the principle of institutional balance. The difference is that the opponents interpret the principle statically, while the second group tends to adapt it to the changing nature of Community tasks. Aside from differences in interpretation, the agreement on the principle itself is not surprising, since the European Court of Justice (ECJ) has always attached constitutional value to the notion of "balance of powers." In *Meroni* (case 9/56 *Meroni v. High Authority* [1957–1958], ECR 133), the Court justified the limitations on the lawful delegation of powers by referring to "the balance of powers which is characteristic of the institutional structure of the Community," and which must be seen as "a fundamental guarantee granted by the Treaty in particular to the undertakings ... to which it applies." The Court concluded that "to delegate a discretionary power, by entrusting it to bodies other than those which the treaty has established to effect and supervise the exercise of such power within the limits of its own authority, would render that guarantee ineffective." Thus, for the ECJ institutional balance or, equivalently, "balance of powers" plays in the Community system a role analogous to that of "separation of powers" in modern constitutional democracies. The interpretation is, however, much more rigid than in the case of the U.S. Supreme Court, and the practical consequences for the effectiveness and credibility of EU regulation in general, and risk regulation in particular, are quite serious.

Consider the case of the EMEA. As already mentioned, this agency has not been granted the power to authorize the marketing of new products: under present rules, such authorizations may be given only by the Commission, on the recommendation of EMEA and subject to the usual "comitology" or committee controls. This pragmatic solution can perhaps be defended as a reasonable compromise between the rigidity of the official non-delegation doctrine and the need for regulatory discretion in highly technical matters. However, such a compromise entails costs that a clearer assignment of responsibilities would avoid. First, as the agency itself complains, the need to wait for the Commission's formal decision means that precious time is lost before a new and possibly life-saving product reaches the market. Second, the present situation blurs the line of accountability, and because of its ambiguity presents some risks even for the Commission, which someday might be called to bear the responsibility of decisions in whose formation it played no substantive role.

In the case of the EFSA, the tension between the desire to improve the credibility of Community regulation by appealing to independent scientific expertise and the refusal to delegate regulatory powers to the agency has been temporarily resolved by the doubtful expedient of institutionally separating risk assessment (the task assigned to the Authority) and risk management (which remains the responsibility of the Commission). Experience shows that such institutional separation of functions tends to be counterproductive. Thus, the U.S. Occupational Safety and Health Act of 1970 created the National Institute for Occupational Safety and Health (NIOSH), directing it to perform research and risk assessments for the newly established regulatory agency, the Occupational Safety and Health Administration (OSHA). While NIOSH is an independent agency within the Department of Health and Human Services, OSHA has been placed within the Department of Labor—an institutional design largely dictated by political reasons. This organizational separation, however, yielded functional separation to only a limited extent. On the one hand, NIOSH criteria documents not only provided risk assessments, but also recommended occupational standards. On the other hand, OSHA tended to take on more of the risk-assessment function itself. NIOSH continued to assist OSHA in the preparation of risk assessments, but gradually OSHA asserted control over the entire standard-setting process (Greenwood 1984).

The institutional separation of risk assessment and risk management tends to be counterproductive because, while the two functions are conceptually distinct, they are closely intertwined in practice. Thus, the setting of rational regulatory priorities entails scientific, economic, and political judgments that are not easily separable. Again, under conditions of scientific uncertainty, the determinations of the risk analysts can effectively preempt the decisions of the risk managers. For example, it is often impossible to know whether a dose-response function follows a linear or a nonlinear (threshold) model, yet the scientist's choice in favor of one or the other model has a determining influence on the chosen level of the safety standard. If risk assessment and risk management are not separable in practice, then it follows that efficiency and accountability are best achieved when a single specialized agency—rather than a collegial body composed of generalists, such as the Commission—takes responsibility for the entire standard-setting process.

The Commission Communication on the PP

The second part of this chapter is devoted to a discussion of the importance of policy learning in risk regulation—and of the institutional factors that may facilitate or impede such learning. As an introduction to that discussion, it may be useful to briefly review the risk philosophy of the European institutions. With its Communication on the precautionary principle of February 2, 2000, the Commission intended to outline its own understanding of the principle; establish guidelines for applying it; build a common understanding of how to assess and manage risks under condition of scientific uncertainty; and avoid recourse to the PP as a disguised form of protectionism. In fact, the document fails to consider what would be the implications of adopting the principle, not as an exceptional temporary measure, but as a "key tenet" of Community policy, a "guide in preparing proposals for legislation," and a "full-fledged and general principle of international law." It does not even mention such key issues as the setting of rational regulatory priorities or the opportunity cost of precautionary measures. These are serious omissions: it should be obvious that the attempt to control poorly understood, low-level risks necessarily uses up resources that in many cases could be directed more effectively toward the reduction of well-known, large-scale risks. Since resources are always limited, it is impossible to control all actual and potential risks. Even if a society is willing "to pay a higher cost to protect an interest, such as the environment or health, to which it attaches priority" (CEC 2000, 20), it is still the case that some environmental or risk regulations might be too expensive. Hence, the choice of which risks to regulate and when to regulate them is crucially important for a rational allocation of resources and for consistency in policymaking. The "Better Regulation" initiative, advanced in Europe since 2001, attempts to correct these omissions by ensuring assessment of a policy's full impacts (Wiener 2006).

As already mentioned, the PP is often taken to mean that incomplete scientific knowledge is not a valid excuse for regulatory inertia, or, more explicitly, that it is legitimate to take regulatory measures to prevent possible risks even in the absence of strong scientific evidence of causal relationships or the extent of damage. The problem with statements such as these is not that they are wrong, but that they provide no practical guidance for taking regulatory decisions under uncertainty. This is because incomplete scientific knowledge is the rule, not the exception, in risk regulation. Extrapolation—a key element in the establishment of health and safety standards—is inherently an uncertain operation. Thus, scientists have developed several mathematical models for dose-response functions. The difficulty is that different models are compatible with the same data points. It may be argued—as many advocates of the PP do—that if there is no firm scientific basis for choosing among different dose-response models, then one should prefer the safest or most conservative procedure. The problem with this argument is that it is not clear where one should stop: it is difficult to be conservative in a consistent manner unless one is prepared to propose a zero level of exposure in each case.

The statement that incomplete knowledge is not a valid excuse for regulatory inertia is unhelpful rather than wrong. More problematic are suggestions that precautionary regulation should be based on "worst-case" scenarios, or that the approach is to be used when the probabilities of adverse events are "unknown." All such views, of which more than a trace can be found in the Commission's Communication, are ultimately rooted in fundamental misunderstandings about the logic of decisionmaking under uncertainty (Majone 2005, 138–142). Until not so many years ago, most risk regulators were unfamiliar with this logic, and precisely for this reason policy learning is so important. I submit that current differences in EU and US approaches to risk regulation are largely explainable by the different positions that the two systems occupy on the learning curve. If this is true, then this is another reason for assuming that the approaches will eventually converge.

The Evolution of Risk Regulation in the United States

In the remainder of this chapter, I consider the influence of constitutional principles (again, separation of powers versus institutional balance) on the incentives of policymakers to refine their approach to risk regulation in the light of theoretical advances and practical experience. A good deal of learning is required before a general policy principle may be applied by legislators, regulators, and courts in a reasonable and consistent way. This is especially true of the precautionary principle because of its unclear logical status and the uncertainty about its broad implications. The experience of the United States in the area of risk regulation suggests that separation of powers, whatever its problems in other respects, is particularly favorable to intense policy debate in a variety of forums, and thus conducive to policy learning.

To a large extent, policy learning means learning about the constraints and opportunity costs of alternative strategies. The slow but steady improvement in the conceptual foundations of risk regulation in the United States provides a good illustration. It is convenient to trace this development through a sequence of four regulatory principles: prohibitions; lowest feasible risk; elimination of significant risks; and balancing the costs and benefits of risk reduction. While this is not a linearly progressing, or monotone increasing, sequence—since different principles coexist even in the same area, such as food safety—I shall argue that a trend can be detected in the direction of a broader inclusion of relevant factors, with greater consistency in putting together the various elements of the regulatory problem.

Prohibitions

Prohibitions represent one of the earliest and least sophisticated approaches to risk regulation. This is not to deny that in some cases an outright ban may be the most appropriate regulatory response, but only to say that the appropriateness of such a radical measure has to be proved, rather than simply assumed.

One of the best-known illustrations of the problems raised by an apparently clear-cut prohibition is provided by the so-called Delaney Clause in the Federal Food, Drug, and Cosmetic Act. The clause appears in the provision of the act that empowers the Food and Drug Administration (FDA) to license food additives. The Food Additives Amendment was added to the law in 1958; it directs the FDA to refuse approval of any food additive not shown to be safe. To this general instruction, the Delaney Clause adds this proviso:

> No additive shall be deemed to be safe if it is found to induce cancer when ingested by man or animal, or if it is found, after tests which are appropriate for the evaluation of the safety of food additives, to induce cancer in man or animals.

According to FDA officials, this proviso authorizes the agency to exercise scientific judgment in determining whether a test is an appropriate one and whether the results demonstrate induction of cancer. Once the agency has made its determinations concerning these two matters, however, no further inquiry is allowed. For example, the agency may not establish a maximum level of safe use or authorize further use of an additive based on a judgment that the benefits of continued use outweigh the risks involved (Mashaw et al. 1998). For nearly 20 years, the Delaney Clause had little influence on the FDA's actions, since only very few additives had been shown to cause cancer in animal experiments. On March 9, 1977, however, the FDA announced its intention to ban the use of the artificial sweetener saccharin because of a recent Canadian study showing that saccharin—in doses equivalent to 800 cans of diet soft drinks a day!—induced cancer in test animals. At the time, no other nonnutritive sweetener was approved for use in the United States. Hence, the FDA announcement threatened the marketing of all artificially sweetened foods and beverages; consequently, it precipitated intensive public controversy. Representatives of health organizations testified at congressional hearings that saccharin provides enormous health benefits to persons, such as diabetics, who must restrict the intake of sugar.

Responding to these concerns, Congress, through the Department of Health and Human Services, commissioned two studies by the National Academy of Sciences, one to assess the scientific evidence concerning saccharin's safety, the other to evaluate the law's current food safety standards and suggest alternative approaches. The Academy's assessment of the scientific evidence confirmed that saccharin was a carcinogen in laboratory animals, although a weak one. It found no reliable evidence that saccharin caused cancer in humans, but it stressed that epidemiological methods were not capable of detecting increases in the incidence of bladder cancer of the magnitude the animal data suggested saccharin could cause.

The second Academy study found that the standards for regulating food additives were inadequate. One proposal was to amend the law to allow the FDA to rank additives in three risk categories: those so serious as to merit prohibition; those so trivial as to warrant no regulatory action; and those whose acceptability should depend on an assessment of benefits and on the availability of alternatives. The proposals did not lead to any radical amendment of the legislation, but the FDA found other means to avoid a ban if a food additive presented only slight risks or offered substantial benefits. Thus, the agency has sometimes concluded that a substance is not a "food additive," and thus subject to the Delaney Clause, even when it occurs in food, arguably through human agency (Mashaw et al. 1998, 129–134). For example, the FDA has refused to regulate compounds such as PCBs and aflatoxin. Proceeding in this fashion, by the mid-1980s the agency had effectively narrowed the application of the Delaney Clause to direct food additives.

In retrospect, we can see that the drafters of the clause believed that only a few additives caused cancer, but that those few were extremely dangerous. By the 1980s, it was clear that many substances are carcinogenic, but many of them create exceptionally minor risks. The new information severely undermined the assumptions of the clause, suggesting that it may well cause more deaths than it prevents. This is because vastly improved detection techniques prevent basically safe but weakly carcinogenic substances from coming on the market, whereas cruder and older technology used to test previously authorized substances allowed them to be approved. The result is less rather than more safety (Sunstein 1990).

Lowest Feasible Risk

According to the principle of "lowest feasible risk," human exposure to health risks should be reduced to the lowest possible level. This is a sort of "second-best" rule. The first-best regulatory policy would be one that ensures a risk-free working and living environment, but because of technical and economic constraints, a risk-free environment is unattainable, hence the need of a second-best rule. Thus, Section 6(b)(5) of the 1970 Occupational Safety and Health Act directs OSHA when regulating worker exposure to toxic substances to set standards that "most adequately assure, *to the extent feasible* ... that no employee will suffer material impairment of health or functional capacity even if such employee has regular exposure to the hazard ... for the period of his working life" (emphasis added).

Trade union representatives claimed that this instruction obliged OSHA to mandate the use of whatever available technology an industry could afford without bankrupting itself. U.S. Supreme Court Justice William Brennan expressed a similar view: "Congress itself defined the basic relationship between costs and benefits, by placing the 'benefits' of worker health above all other considerations save those making attainment of the 'benefit' unachievable" (cited in Graham et al. 1988, 97). The meaning of "feasibility" is crucial in the present context. A body of analysis and case law has thus emerged to clarify this term.

According to some court decisions, a standard may be considered technologically feasible even if no existing devices would allow industry to comply with the standard, as long as there is evidence that companies, "acting vigorously and in good faith," can develop the technology. This "technology forcing" approach implies that regulatory agencies are not limited to set standards based on existing devices, but they may require improvements in existing technology or even the development of new technology. This may be quite expensive, so the issue of technical feasibility is inseparable from the issue of economic feasibility. It is clear that regulators estimate the costs of proposed standards, but it is less clear which criteria they use to judge whether a given standard is "affordable." At least as far as the Occupational Safety and Health Act is concerned, American courts have ruled that an expensive standard is not necessarily economically infeasible. Although some firms may find safety standards particularly expensive or even financially prohibitive, courts have not excused individual firms from such standards. As one court put it in a 1978 case: "It would appear to be consistent with the purposes of the [OSH] Act to envisage the economic demise of an employer who has lagged behind the industry in protecting the health and safety of employees and is consequentially financially unable to comply with new standards as quickly as other employers" (cited in Graham et al. 1988, 99). Thus, economic feasibility has been interpreted quite strictly: a standard is to be considered "infeasible" only if it would cripple or bankrupt an entire industry, rather than some technologically backward firms.

It is clear that the lowest-feasible-risk approach is very far from any sort of balancing of marginal costs and benefits. In fact, marginal considerations are rejected on the ground that the two sides of the basic relationship are incommensurable. As the opinion of Justice Brennan cited above makes clear, health benefits have to be considered "above all other considerations." Even if one accepts this value judgment, however, serious conceptual problems remain. First, the approach fails to consider possible alternatives to standards, such as information disclosure or greater reliance on liability rules. It also omits any consideration of probabilities of possible events, so that standards are set without any knowledge of the expected number of deaths or accidents prevented. Second, setting standards strictly is a significant cause of the slow pace of the standard-setting process. This means that relatively few standards can be set, so that many hazards remain unregulated; hence, overregulation leads to underregulation (Mendeloff 1988). Third, the emphasis on industry viability means that very dangerous occupations in marginally profitable industries may be unregulated, while other jobs may be made so safe at such high cost that employment levels and wages shrink. Finally, by ignoring one of the key lessons of policy analysis—that decisions should be based on marginal, rather than total, costs and benefits—the approach wastes resources that could have been used to control more risks.

The Significant-Risk Doctrine

As was indicated above, federal courts generally upheld OSHA's standards. The striking exception was the benzene standard, which reduced the occupational exposure to this carcinogen from 10 parts per million (ppm) to 1 ppm. In the 1978 case *American Petroleum Institute v. OSHA*, the Fifth Circuit Court of Appeals held the regulation invalid on the ground that the agency had not shown that the new exposure limit was "reasonably necessary and appropriate to provide safe or healthful employment" as required by the statute. Specifically, the court argued that OSHA had failed to provide substantial evidence that the benefits to be achieved by the stricter standard bore a reasonable relationship to the costs it imposed. The court added: "This does not mean that OSHA must wait until deaths occur as a result of exposure levels below 10 ppm before it may validly promulgate a standard reducing the permissible exposure limit. Nevertheless, OSHA must have some factual basis for an estimate of expected benefits before it can determine that a one-half billion dollar standard is reasonably necessary" (cited in Mendeloff 1988, 116–117).

What the court required was some sort of quantification of benefits as a necessary step to carry out a cost–benefit test of the new standard. Without a quantification of risk, and hence of the expected number of lives saved by the regulation, it is clearly impossible to weigh the benefits against the costs. Unlike other agencies such as the Environmental Protection Agency (EPA) and the FDA, OSHA had always maintained that quantitative risk analysis is meaningless. Thus, in the preamble to the benzene standard, it stated that it was "impossible to derive any conclusions regarding dose-response relationships." As Mendeloff notes, OSHA's reluctance to follow the example of EPA and the FDA reflected trade union pressures, combined with staff preferences for protection to override any interest in the use of more analytic approaches. It was feared that if the agency performed quantitative risk assessments, these might be used as a weapon by those who opposed strict standards. On the other hand, an agency like EPA with a much broader mandate was aware that not every risk could be reduced to the lowest feasible level.

The Fifth Circuit Court's decision stunned OSHA's leaders, who viewed it as a total challenge to their regulatory philosophy and to their idea of the agency's mission. They decided to appeal the decision. In *Industrial Union Department (AFL-CIO) v. American Petroleum Institute* (1980), a badly split Supreme Court—the nine justices issued five separate opinions!—upheld the Fifth Circuit's decision, but not all parts of its argument. In particular, it expressed no opinion about the requirement of a cost–benefit assessment. Justice Lewis Powell, concurring in part and concurring in the judgment, did, however, note that "a standard-setting process that ignored economic considerations would result in a serious misallocation of resources and a lower effective level of safety than could be achieved under standards set with reference to the comparative benefits available at a lower cost" (cited in Mashaw et al. 1998, 815). Expressing the view of a four-judge plurality (in a separate opinion, Justice William Rehnquist provided the fifth vote for overturning the standard), Justice John Paul Stevens explicitly rejected the lowest-feasible-risk approach: "We think it is clear that the statute was not designed to require employers to provide absolute risk-free workplaces whenever it is technologically feasible to do so, so long as the cost is not great enough to destroy an entire industry. Rather, both the language and structure of the Act, as well as its legislative history, indicate that it was intended to require the elimination, as far as feasible, of *significant* risks of harm" (cited in Graham et al. 1988, 100; emphasis added).

In other words, zero risk cannot be the goal of risk regulation. Justice Stevens insisted that "safe" is not the same as risk-free, pointing to a variety of risks in daily life—ranging from driving a car to "breathing city air"—that people find acceptable. Hence, before taking any decision, the risk from a toxic substance must be quantified sufficiently to enable the agency to characterize it as significant "in an understandable way." Conceding the difficulty of quantifying risks, the plurality opinion emphasized the scientific elements of the significant-risk determination. In fact, OSHA was not required to support its finding that a significant risk exists with anything approaching scientific certainty. So long as the determination is supported by a body of reputable scientific thought, the agency is free to use conservative assumptions in interpreting the data, risking error on the side of overprotection.

The problem with the proposed regulation was procedural rather than substantive: the question was not whether the standard of 1 ppm was "correct," but whether sufficient justification for this determination had been provided. According to the plurality opinion, this had not been done, hence the standard-setting process was flawed. Thus, OSHA did not ask for comments as to whether or not benzene presented a significant health risk at exposures of 10 ppm or less. Rather, it asked for comments as to whether 1 ppm was the minimum feasible exposure limit. Also, the evidence of adverse health effects of benzene exposure at 10 ppm was sketchy at best. OSHA had not attempted to make any estimate, based on the available scientific studies, of how significant the risk would be at exposure of 10 ppm or less. Rather, it stated that a lack of data made it impossible to construct a dose-response curve at the time, even rejecting an industry witness's testimony that a dose-response curve could be constructed on the basis of the reported epidemiological studies. In short, the agency had simply concluded—from the government's generic carcinogen policy—that, in the absence of definitive proof of a safe level, it must be assumed that *any* level above zero presents *some* increased risk of cancer. But as the justices pointed out, "In view of the fact that there are literally thousands of substances used in the workplace that have been identified as carcinogens or suspect carcinogens, the Government's theory would give OSHA power to impose enormous costs that might produce little, if any, discernible benefit" (cited in Mashaw et al. 1998, 813).

Since the government's generic carcinogen policy provides no guidance as to which substances should be regulated first, an important merit of the significant-risk doctrine is to raise the crucial issue of regulatory priorities. Most risks are regulated in response to petitions or pressures from labor unions, public-health groups, environmentalists, and other political activists, with little analysis by the agency of other possible regulatory targets. Given that resources are always limited, the real (opportunity) cost of a regulation is the number of lives that could be saved by using the same resources to control other, perhaps more significant, risks. By requiring OSHA to show significant risk as a prelude to standard setting, the justices were insisting on some analysis in priority setting: regulatory priorities should be directed toward the most important risks—which are not necessarily those that are politically most salient.

In conclusion, the significant-risk doctrine places a higher analytical burden on regulators than the lowest-feasible-risk approach. Not all potential risks are treated equally; only those substances shown to pose a significant risk of cancer will be regulated, focusing limited agency resources on the most important health risks. In addition, the doctrine, without requiring a formal marginal analysis of benefits and costs, does place a constraint on the stringency of standards. If exposure to a carcinogen is reduced to the point that the residual risk is insignificant, then no further tightening of the standard is appropriate (Graham et al. 1988, 103–105). *Industrial Union Department (AFL-CIO) v. American Petroleum Institute* is a landmark case from the point of view of risk analysis methodology as well. The U.S. Supreme Court not only confirmed the legitimacy of quantitative risk assessment, but also effectively made reliance on the methodology obligatory for all American agencies engaged in risk regulation. In most subsequent disputes over regulatory decisions to protect human health, the question has not been whether a risk assessment was required, but whether the assessment offered by the agency was plausible (Mashaw et al. 1998, 823–825). This historical background may explain American advocacy of science-based risk assessment at the international level, as well as U.S. opposition to the precautionary principle as interpreted by the European Commission. In fact, risk assessment is the standard by which trade-restricting health regulations are evaluated as necessary and compatible with the rules of the World Trade Organization.

Balancing Costs and Benefits

Until the 1970s, judicial review was the only effective control on the quality of the decisionmaking process of American regulatory agencies. Congress can, of course, pass legislation requiring that an agency take a particular type of action. However, congressional oversight is output-oriented rather than process-oriented. At any rate, routine regulatory measures seldom receive congressional scrutiny. Most important, there is no need for congressional approval for a regulatory agency to take action, provided that it can survive judicial review. In contrast, the courts have been important agents of policy learning, as we just saw in the benzene case. Nevertheless, judicial oversight, too, suffers from serious shortcomings. First, it is only exercised *ex post*—even if it is true that a judicial doctrine like the significant-risk doctrine will influence a stream of future agency decisions. Also, the principle of separation of powers prevents any sustained interaction between courts and agencies before proceedings are formally initiated. Again, a serious mismatch between the leisurely time of judicial decisionmaking and the hectic pace of agency rulemaking exists. Also, according to some observers, heavy reliance on judicial review creates an adversarial atmosphere, which does not always facilitate the achievement of regulatory objectives.

From the point of view of policy learning, the most serious limitation of judicial review, however, is the unpredictability of court decisions. In the benzene case, for example, the Supreme Court criticized the logic of the lowest-feasible-risk decision rule and effectively mandated the use of quantitative risk assessment, while taking no position on the issue of whether an agency should undertake a formal cost–benefit analysis (CBA) to justify its decisions. More precisely, the question that was not answered in the benzene case was, is the use of CBA by OSHA required, permitted, or outlawed? At any rate, Justice Stevens's opinion strongly suggests that the plurality shared the belief that the benzene standard imposed high costs with limited benefits. But only a year later, the court—in the cotton-dust case, *American Textile Manufacturers v. Donovan*, 1981—held explicitly that OSHA standards need not show a positive cost–benefit ratio; they must only be shown to be technologically achievable and "affordable." Clearly, unpredictable court decisions do not help systematic policy learning. The decision on the cotton-dust standard seemed to interrupt an ongoing learning process, and for this reason, it has been severely criticized by students of the regulatory process. No judicial decision, however, could conceal the growing economic impact of risk regulation.

With the great expansion of environmental, health, and risk regulation in the 1970s, the need to calculate more precisely the costs of the proliferating regulations, as well as their corresponding benefits, became increasingly evident. According to many advocates of regulatory reform, only the executive branch could provide a continuous and systematic oversight of the regulatory process. Important steps to improve the quality of federal regulation were taken under President Jimmy Carter, when the notion of a "regulatory budget" was first introduced. The oversight mechanism was perfected in the late 1980s, during the second term of the Reagan administration. The Office of Management and Budget (OMB), in the president's Executive Office, was given responsibility for setting the budgets of all regulatory agencies and for monitoring the rulemaking process. Instead of simply imposing a cost-effectiveness requirement, as previous presidents had done, Reagan moved to a fully fledged cost–benefit test with his Executive Order No. 12291 of 1981. It stated that regulatory action was not to be undertaken unless the potential benefits to society outweigh the potential costs; among alternative approaches to any given regulatory objective, the alternative involving the least net costs to society had to be chosen; and finally, agencies are required to set regulatory priorities with the aim of maximizing the aggregate net benefits, taking into account the condition of the particular industries affected by regulations, the condition of the national economy, and other regulatory measures contemplated for the future. If the cost–benefit test conflicts with the agency's legislative mandate—as it did at the time for most risk and environmental regulations—the test is not binding, in the sense that the standard need not be based on the result of the cost–benefit calculations; a complete analysis must be submitted to the OMB nevertheless. Executive Order No. 12498 of 1985 added to the oversight process—the review by the OMB of the regulation proposed by an agency, and of the analysis supporting it—the development of a formal planning process whereby the agencies would have to clear a regulatory agenda (a "regulatory calendar") with the OMB. In 1993, President Clinton issued Executive Order No. 12866, reaffirming presidential oversight of regulation through the OMB and using cost–benefit analysis (while drawing greater attention to qualitative measures, distributional equity, and transparency). In 1995, regulatory legislation in the form of the Unfunded Mandates Reform Act was passed by Congress, and although not subject to judicial review, its net effect was to reinforce the test that must be passed by new regulations. The key congressional concerns were that regulations be based on an accurate assessment of the risks involved, rather than on worst-case scenarios, and that regulatory agencies proceed with regulations only if the benefits exceed the costs.

Policy Learning: A Comparative Institutional Perspective

The foregoing survey of policy and institutional developments in the United States reveals a steady improvement in the understanding of the various dimensions of risk regulation—scientific, economic, legal, and political—and of the methodologies for fitting together these partial analyses in a coherent manner. The progress from the early reliance on outright bans or simple "feasibility" tests—similar in spirit to the precautionary approach—to the applications of key principles of policy analysis not only to agency rulemaking but also to the enabling legislation is an outstanding example of policy learning. Compared with these developments, risk regulation in Europe is still at a rather primitive stage. Indeed, the examples mentioned at the beginning of this chapter—the Italian standards for exposure to electromagnetic fields, and the proposed Community standards for aflatoxins—are in the spirit of the early U.S. approach to risk regulation. Conceptual advances in the United States were made possible by several factors, including interactions among partly cooperating but partly competing institutions, policy entrepreneurship, and a style of policy discourse that puts a high premium on reliable quantitative information and analytic sophistication. While American institutions and political culture cannot be replicated on the other side of the Atlantic, it is important to make a serious effort to understand the factors, historical and institutional, that have contributed to a slower rate of policy learning in the EU.

After the failure of political integration in the 1950s, the only way to move forward seemed to be the functionalist method advocated by Jean Monnet: European integration was to be achieved not by direct political means, but through legal harmonization and the development of common policies. Economic integration and regulatory harmonization, it was believed, would eventually produce political integration. In spite of some remarkable accomplishments in the economic sphere, the limitations of both the functionalist approach and its legal basis, the Community method, are becoming increasingly clear. Under the Community method, the Commission will never propose a policy that does not also contribute, directly or indirectly, to an expansion of EU, and its own, powers. As a result, EU policies are often by-products of efforts to advance the integration process, rather than attempts to solve a specific problem in the best possible way. It is of course true that at the national level, public policy also is often made less to solve concrete problems than to serve party political or other interests. Electoral competition, however, gives the voters the opportunity to evaluate policy outcomes. Too wide a gap between objectives and actual outcomes invites punishment at the hand of the voters. Except on the rare occasions where people are given the chance to express their feelings in a referendum, such direct democratic controls do not exist at EU level, where suboptimal policy outcomes can persist, unscrutinized and unchallenged, for decades.

If policy is epiphenomenal, and what really matters is the acquisition of additional policymaking powers, then policy learning is largely irrelevant. This explains, for example, why Article I-11 of the proposed Constitutional Treaty still lists the conservation of marine biological resources under the Common Fisheries Policy (CFP) among the exclusive competencies of the Union. Yet over its more than 15-year history, the CFP has largely failed in its aim to conserve fishery resources. The problem, which has been recognized by several independent experts, is that the CFP was shaped more by concerns about the competence of Community institutions than by concern for effective conservation measures. Elsewhere (Majone 2005), I have provided a number of examples of extremely slow or nonexistent policy learning. Also, the Commission Communication on the PP seems to be driven more by integration objectives and institutional self-interest than by a serious attempt to define a logically defensible approach to risk regulation. The "Better Regulation" initiative, meanwhile, offers promise for transatlantic policy learning about regulatory review (Wiener 2006).

Institutional balance—another key principle of the Community method—is the distinctive feature of a polity based on the representation of interests. Each European institution is the bearer of a particular interest, national or supranational, which it strives to protect and promote. Hence, the main theme of political conflict is not the formulation and implementation of policy, but the defense of the respective prerogatives of Council, Parliament, and Commission. As we saw, institutional balance is invoked in support of a strict non-delegation doctrine. This convenient doctrine allows the Commission to be the sole regulator in matters in which it has no substantive expertise, and thus prevents the emergence of institutional arrangements, such as independent European regulatory agencies, which would enhance the level of expertise and facilitate policy learning. The point is that for significant institutional innovations to occur, the Commission, as well as the other European institutions, would have to give up some of their prerogatives, and this is unlikely to happen, since it goes against the grain of the Community method.

Conclusions

Perhaps no other area of regulation involves so many and such difficult conceptual and scientific problems as risk regulation. The precautionary approach currently advocated by the European institutions appeals to many people who are increasingly concerned about the "globalization of risk"—the transmission of environmental and health risks through the channels of free trade. As a general approach to environmental and risk regulation, however, the PP suffers from a number of serious shortcomings: it lacks a sound logical foundation; it distorts regulatory priorities; and it can have undesirable distributive consequences. In short, when it is critically examined and compared with the best international practice, risk regulation in the EU is seen to correspond to an early stage of conceptual and technical development—a time when the principles of decisionmaking under uncertainty were not yet part of the tool kit of risk regulators. For this reason, the present chapter emphasizes the importance of policy learning and the politico-institutional conditions that may facilitate or impede such learning. We conclude that institutional competition, political entrepreneurship, substantive judicial review, and a style of policy discourse that favors formal, quantitative analyses—all features associated with U.S.-style separation of powers—accelerate the learning process. In contrast, the current institutional framework of the EU provides few incentives for institutional innovation and policy learning. Are there reasons to expect improvements in the reasonably near future?

In 2005, the ratification process of the proposed new Constitutional Treaty for Europe was suspended as a result of its rejection by the French and Dutch voters. This rejection by two founding members of the Community of what was meant to become the new constitutional basis of the enlarged Union marks a turning point in the history of European integration. The subsequent adoption of the Lisbon Treaty on the Functioning of the EU (TFEU) in 2009 was a partial effort to salvage some of the constitutional proposals. It is too early to understand the full implications of this development, but one lesson that emerges with sufficient clarity is that in the future, political aims will have to be pursued by overtly political means—and thus they will be open to public scrutiny—rather than by roundabout economic and legal strategies. Symmetrically, policy measures should be undertaken to solve concrete problems, not to serve integration or other political aims. Such a change of method would signify the end of the functionalist approach and of integration by stealth (Majone 2005). If the arguments presented in this chapter are correct, then the abandonment of an obsolete approach to integration should be seen as a positive development, favoring policy learning and helping to depoliticize issues such as the proper use of the precautionary principle.

Concerning the range of application of the PP, the Constitutional Treaty had nothing new to say. Article III-233(2), now Article 191 of the TFEU and where the principle is mentioned, reproduces the wording of Article 174 of the prior EC Treaty—except for a few linguistic modifications. In both treaties, the PP appears only in the Environment Section and remains undefined. With reference to the EC Treaty, the Commission and some legal scholars have argued that the principle applies beyond the area of environmental policy. This is because Article 6 of the EC Treaty provides that environmental protection requirements be integrated into the definition and implementation of other Community policies and activities. Insofar as the PP is considered to be one of the core principles of EC environmental policy, it is concluded that it should be integrated, as appropriate, into other Community (now, Union) policies. Thus, even if the Constitutional Treaty had been eventually ratified, nothing would have changed, as a direct consequence, in the implementation of the PP: all the ambiguities and pitfalls discussed in the present chapter would also remain.

Even a nonratified treaty can provide information about the thinking of its drafters. In institutional terms, the Constitutional Convention had to choose among three possibilities: (a) to continue with the present arrangements, whereby the executive function at the European level is effectively divided between the Council of Ministers and the Commission, with one institution more in the lead on some policy issues and the other on other issues; (b) a Commission-led executive; and (c) an executive led by the European Council (Wallace 2003). Following the arguments of the "Feasibility Study" (code name Penelope) contributed by the Commission to the debate on the Constitutional Treaty, a Commission-led executive would have meant, *inter alia,* a generalization of the Community method, including the Commission's monopoly of legislative initiative and generalized qualified majority voting in the Council. It would have meant strong Commission powers in all policy domains and a Commission president elected by the European Parliament and confirmed by the European Council.

The final agreement reached by the Member States moved definitely beyond the status quo, and it just as definitely rejected the model proposed by the Commission in favor of a European executive led by the European Council. This institution, consisting of the heads of state or government of the Member States, provides the Union with the necessary impetus for its development and defines its general political directions and priorities. Its president is elected by qualified majority of the Council, for a term of two and a half years, renewable once. He or she drives forward the work of the Council, ensuring proper preparation and continuity, and the external representation of the Union on issues concerning its Common Foreign and Security Policy. The institutional architecture chosen by the framers of the Constitutional Treaty, and partly reflected in the TFEU, is an important indication of the progressive erosion of the Community method and the weakening of the Commission's role in EU policymaking.

This tendency—which is highly unlikely to be reversed in future treaties—raises the problem of how the Member States can credibly commit themselves without delegating powers to the supranational institutions. However, it may eventually facilitate reforms and innovations that the old institutional arrangements have impeded. To illustrate, at the beginning of this chapter it was pointed out that the Council of Ministers of the EU in practice operates according to a principle of specialization based on the monopoly of issues. For example, only ministers of the environment meet in the Council when environmental issues are discussed. This situation—the equivalent of single-issue politics at the European level—is largely responsible for the fragmentation of EU policymaking and for the failure to consider the costs and benefits of alternative measures. Council presidents rotating every six months have been unable to do anything to correct this situation. An EU Council president governing for several years, on the other hand, should be able to introduce much-needed mechanisms of coordination and control.

References

Beer, S. H. 1993. *To Make a Nation: The Rediscovery of American Federalism.* Cambridge, MA: Belknap Press.

CEC (Commission of the European Communities). 2000. *Communication from the Commission on the Precautionary Principle.* COM(2000) 1. Brussels: CEC.

———. 2002. *Communication from the Commission: The Operating Framework for the European Regulatory Agencies.* COM(2002) 718 final. Brussels: CEC.

Graham, J. D., L. C. Green, and M. J. Roberts. 1988. *In Search of Safety.* Cambridge, MA: Harvard University Press.

Greenwood, T. 1984. *Knowledge and Discretion in Government Regulation.* New York: Praeger.

Jacqué, J. P. 1991. Cours Général de Droit Communautaire [General Course on EU Law]. In *Collected Courses of the Academy of European Law,* edited by A. Clapham, Vol. 1, Book 1. Dordrecht, Netherlands: Martinus Nijhoff Publishers, 247–360.

Landis, J. M. 1966. *The Administrative Process.* New Haven, CT: Yale University Press. (Orig. pub. 1938.).

Majone, G. 2005. *Dilemmas of European Integration: The Ambiguities and Pitfalls of Integration by Stealth.* Oxford: Oxford University Press.

Mashaw, J. L., R. A. Merrill, and P. M. Shane. 1998. *Administrative Law.* 4th ed. St. Paul: West Group.

Mendeloff, J. M. 1988. *The Dilemma of Toxic Substance Regulation.* Cambridge, MA: MIT Press.

Otsuki, T., J. S. Wilson, and M. Sewadeh. 2000. *Saving Two in a Billion: A Case Study to Quantify the Trade Effect of European Food Safety Standards on African Exports.* Washington, DC: World Bank.

Stewart, R. B. 1975. The Reformation of American Administrative Law. *Harvard Law Review* 88: 1667–1813.

Sunstein, C. R. 1990. *After the Rights Revolution.* Cambridge, MA: Harvard University Press.

Wallace, H. 2003. Designing Institutions for an Enlarging European Union. In *Ten Reflections on the Constitutional Treaty for Europe,* edited by B. de Witte. E-book. Florence: European University Institute, 85–106.

Wiener, Jonathan B. 2006. Better Regulation in Europe. *Current Legal Problems* 59: 447–518.

CHAPTER 17

Legal and Administrative Systems: Implications for Precautionary Regulation

Lucas Bergkamp and Turner T. Smith, Jr.

*L*egal and administrative systems can be viewed as the vehicles a society uses for transmitting risk preferences to public decisionmakers, and for enabling those preferences to be reflected in public policy. This chapter deals with the "crosscutting" issue of whether such legal and administrative systems have implications, in and of themselves and independent of the substantive area of regulation involved, for the degree of precaution in risk regulation that results. We intend "degree of precaution" to encompass the timing and stringency of preventive regulation against future risks (Wiener 2002), but to be an entirely descriptive phrase and to imply no value or merits judgment as to the appropriateness or adequacy of such regulation. We illustrate our conclusions by reference to both *ex ante* and *ex post* regulation, in the context of the legal and administrative systems of the United States and the EU.

The chapter consists of three parts. The first main section contains our general conclusions. The second sets out our analytical framework. The remaining bulk of the chapter, the section titled "Key Features and Differences in U.S. and EU Legal and Administrative Systems," provides the body of our analysis of these systems' design, structure, functions, actors, incentives, and procedural and substantive rules, with emphasis on those that may, *prima facie*, have implications for precautionary regulation. We address generic substantive rules governing degree of precaution, the structure and functioning of *ex ante* lawmaking institutions and processes, and the nature of *ex post* remedial systems. In each case, we discuss and compare the pertinent provisions of the U.S. and EU legal and administrative systems.

Conclusions

A fundamental driver, perhaps the most fundamental driver, of degree of precaution in risk regulation in a governmental system is the risk preferences held by those controlling that system. These risk preferences are, in our judgment, largely independent of the legal and administrative system through which they are expressed. The key question, however, is who controls the governmental system, and thus whose risk preferences drive both the design and the operation of that system, and the results produced by it.[1]

In a representative democracy, it should be, and in many cases actually is, the risk preferences of individual citizens that control degree of precaution, whether those risk preferences are transmitted to government decisionmakers through the voting process or through lobbying or other methods of persuasion. These preferences may stem from cultural and other factors (e.g., recent societal risk experience). Their transmission to government decisionmakers can be facilitated, or impeded, by the nature of the specific legal and administrative tools or processes used to create risk regulation. Further, many other sources of group and institutional influence, expressed through the legal and administrative system, impinge on the result in risk regulation. Finally, the public's risk preferences can themselves be significantly affected by government actions and attitudes, although as indicated above, it seems likely to us that risk preferences are mostly independent of the legal and administrative system through which they are expressed.

Of the two legal and administrative systems we examine, the U.S. governmental system is created by a constitution—an agreement among individual citizens. U.S. citizens are directly represented, as individuals, in both chambers of the federal legislature. While groups and institutions of all sorts, both public and private, play important roles in the shaping of legislation and regulation, the conceptual model is that of a representative democracy where public decisions are to be controlled by citizen preferences.

The EU, on the other hand, is a "representative" governmental system (Lindseth 1999). Debate exists as to whether the EU is best assessed as a new or unfolding "constitutional policy in its own right" system or as a "supranational body exercising delegated normative power" (Lindseth 1999, 628, 636). The EU, established by treaty among sovereign Member States, is a system in which those Member States are "represented" in the EU Council, where the EU legislative institution has final and decisive authority over legislation. Individual EU citizens are thus only indirectly represented in the EU Council, although they are directly represented in the EU Parliament, a directly elected legislative-style body with increasing power to shape legislation. This situation would not have been changed in its broad essentials by the proposed European Constitution, itself actually still only a treaty among sovereign

---

[1] To the extent that those controlling a governmental system believe that its design (either overall or in specific details), or the way in which it is operated, can have an independent effect on the degree of precaution in the regulatory result, their risk preferences may influence their choice of governmental structure or operation, independent of the degree of precaution that they choose to build directly into any specific regulatory result.

states. While there would have been evolution toward granting individual citizens more power and influence, the EU would have remained largely a governmental system with Member States firmly in command of the legislative results.

Thus, while risk preferences drive degree of precaution in representative governmental systems, it should be no surprise when we conclude that, overall, public risk preferences, defined as those of individual citizens, have a more direct impact on degree of precaution in the United States than they do in the EU. That being said, however, the actual interplay of influences through the legal and administrative systems on degree of precaution in both jurisdictions is extremely complex. In both jurisdictions, the paradigm, whether of representative democracy or of representation of Member States, breaks down and requires qualification as detail is examined. In all cases, the key is to focus not only on whether risk preferences are facilitated or impeded by various aspects of the legal and administrative systems being examined, but also on whose risk preferences are being facilitated or impeded.

Legal and Administrative Systems' Effect on Degree of Precaution

Legal and administrative systems and provisions have the potential for important impacts on degree of precaution. First, of course, they frame the universe of risks needing regulation. The corpus of existing law determines which risks are already regulated, and some risks are themselves created by activities required or authorized by law. These facts could have an effect on the timing or stringency of further regulation. We consider below, for example, the potential impact of existing tort law on degree of precaution. Second, such systems and provisions themselves sometimes prescribe, as a generic matter, the degree of precaution to be achieved where risks are regulated. We examine below, for example, the extent to which the U.S. or EU systems contain legal provisions with generic standards governing the timing or stringency of risk regulation.

Third, and most important, various aspects of legal and administrative systems can affect, both directly and indirectly, the timing and stringency of precautionary regulation. Since, however, virtually all aspects of these systems can seem to have such an impact because they act as a vehicle for the expression of risk preferences, it is critical to distinguish the effects of the "message" from those of the "message vehicle." That is, the first question is whether, and if so, when and how, a given aspect of the legal or administrative system can impact the timing or stringency of risk regulation. The second question is whether it does so in and of itself—that is, independently of the risk preferences that it transmits—and independently of other apparent causal factors. The third question is whether the direction of its effect on timing or stringency is systematic and predictable, an inquiry that is frequently central to determining whether the effect is in fact that of the "message vehicle," not that of the "message" being transmitted by whoever then happens to control that vehicle.

The situation is complicated, however, because there are aspects of the legal and administrative system that may influence or determine not just timing or stringency of particular pieces of regulation, but may also influence or determine whose risk preference agendas, as between the public generally and various private and public actors with special access or power, actually drive precautionary regulation, which in turn may affect *either timing or stringency*, the direction and extent depending on the agendas of the actors involved and their ability to affect the decisional process.[2] Furthermore, the design and structure of such aspects may be capable of manipulation by those private or public actors, either so that they can control them, or so that the aspects in question will have a desired general result in terms of timing or stringency, or a tendency toward such a result regardless of who controls them at a given point in time. (This may well be true where the specific structure of the legal or administrative system determines, systematically and predictably, the *timing* of regulation.)

As a result of our analysis, we suggest that some aspects of legal and administrative systems predictably and systematically affect the *timing* of risk regulation, either lengthening or shortening the time to its adoption. We suggest, however, it is only infrequently that legal and administrative systems determine, predictably and systematically, the *stringency* of precautionary regulation, independent of public or private risk preferences however transmitted through the decisional process.

We conclude that the most fundamental causal factor in risk regulation is risk preferences (even if not always the preferences of the "public" as transmitted through the voting system). The legal and administrative system plays a contributing role in the result, of course, since it provides the structure relating to the governmental decisional process that may largely determine whose preferences get registered with decisionmakers and to what extent. It is in a sense, however, normally just a tool, and of itself does not yield systematic or predictable results in terms of stringency. It is the preference agendas expressed through it that drive the result, whether that be more or less timely or stringent precautionary regulation, even though it may be the structure of the legal or administrative system that allows them to do so. Indeed, the structure of the legal or administrative system itself may have been determined by the very preferences whose transmission it subsequently favors. Thus, while it is a difficult and tricky issue on which to generalize, it seems to us that it is normally the risk preferences at play, not the nature of the legal or administrative system in and of itself, that make risk regulation either more or less timely or stringent.

General Conclusions about U.S. and EU Legal and Administrative Systems

Our analysis deals with whether, and how, a number of the main elements of the legal and administrative systems in the United States and the EU influence the timing or level of stringency of precautionary regulation.

---

[2] We do not attempt to address the normative questions involved in whether, when, and the extent to which, in a representative democracy, transmission of risk preferences on the part of individual citizens or groups of citizens should be allowed or limited. Rather, we chiefly examine the effects of the normal voting process and of formal participation in the legislative or administrative processes found in the United States and the EU, labeling other expression of risk preferences "extrinsic," and commenting where it seems useful on the extent to which the legal or administrative processes favor or disfavor the expression of risk preferences by individuals or groups of individuals (both public and private) with common personal interests, of whatever stripe, and whether or not "extrinsic."

As a general matter, we conclude that the U.S. systems, while problematic in many ways,[3] have formal mechanisms designed to transmit public risk preferences of individuals and groups relatively efficiently and accurately to public officials, both in the case of enacting legislation[4] and in the case of promulgating administrative regulation, resulting in earlier precautionary regulation, and regulation that more accurately aggregates public risk preferences (but not regulation that is necessarily more or less stringent), than would be the case were this not true.

We conclude that, for understandable reasons at the present stage of the evolution of the EU, the EU systems for both legislation and implementing provisions—being designed to reflect EU institutional agendas instead of the direct views of individual EU citizens, being quite complex and not transparent in many ways, and being not fully politically and judicially accountable—result in public officials being freer to bring to bear on decisionmaking both their own extrinsic institutional or private agendas and the agendas of third parties,[5] rather than those of the public expressed through voting for legislators or through open public participation in formal administrative processes. While this may result in risk regulation that does not directly (and may not accurately) reflect public risk preferences, however, it is not clear that it necessarily results in predictable or systematic bias toward more or less timely or stringent regulation. That question likely turns, rather, on whatever more general aims may exist in the relevant extrinsic agendas (e.g., the institutional aims of the Member States and of the main EU institutions).

Thus, we reach no general conclusion as to which legal and administrative system, as such, results in a greater or lesser degree of precaution in promulgated regulation. We do conclude, however, that the U.S. system is relatively well implemented and enforced, while the EU system suffers from a significant continuing implementation and enforcement deficit, with the overall result that in many areas of regulation, particularly

---

[3] For example, as noted earlier, the personal or institutional agendas of government decisionmakers, or third-party agendas adopted by them, may frequently trump efforts to determine accurately the aggregated public risk preferences through formal legal or administrative structures. We do not attempt in this chapter to deal with the important questions of when the risk preference agendas of third parties are (at least in the United States) simply a constitutionally protected part of the transmission of public risk preferences to the government, and when, if ever, they are in some sense illegitimate. Nor do we tackle the question of how to control the personal or institutional agendas of government decisionmakers.

[4] The recent initiative by the EU Commission to use structured regulatory impact analysis, with public input, for developing legislative proposals may, however, be thought to be a formal mechanism that is more efficient and accurate in aggregating public risk preferences than the largely unstructured, open-ended, and "political" processes used in the U.S. Congress for developing proposals for legislation. See further discussion below.

[5] In the past, the third-party agendas of businesses and business groups have predominated. More recently, as environmental, health, and safety issues have become more salient and as European governments have lost the trust of their publics due to failures of regulation, the agendas of environmental or other "public interest" nongovernmental organizations (NGOs) have become key drivers of risk regulation.

relating to the environment, the United States is likely to be *actually achieving* more timely and stringent precautionary regulation.[6]

Other General Conclusions

Wiener and Rogers have argued that risk regulation actions must be disaggregated in order to understand causal factors with any specificity, writing, "issue-specific context is crucial" (2002, 3). We believe that they are generally correct. We have certainly found this to be the case in thinking about the influence of legal and administrative systems on degree of precaution. The range of risks and risk regulatory actions, and of the factors influencing them, is so broad and complex that, at this stage of the maturity of causal analysis in this area, generalization as to impact on degree of precaution in regulatory systems *as a whole* is very difficult.[7]

There has been much posturing on both sides of the Atlantic about differences in levels of precaution in U.S. and EU regulation. Wiener and Rogers have made a persuasive case that generalizations in this regard can easily be misleading (Wiener and Rogers 2002; Wiener 2003). They have argued that both systems engage in precautionary regulation; that neither system is generically more precautionary than the other in the regulation it has adopted; that in specific situations each system is sometimes more precautionary and sometimes less precautionary than the other, but frequently with regard to different risks; that the variation (as among particular risks and within different levels of government) within each system is significant; and that each case of regulation of each type of risk must be examined on its own merits to determine how precautionary each system has been, and why. They may well be right as to the levels of precaution *aimed at* in the legislation and rules in question (and are certainly right as to the complexity of the situation and the need for careful, case-specific analysis). It is our view, however, that, at the least, real differences exist in the levels of precaution *actually achieved* in the United States and the EU in the past and to date—in environmental regulation in particular, due to the EU's continuing deficit in implementation and enforcement.

Further, notwithstanding the views of Wiener and Rogers with regard to the difficulty of generalization, we believe that some overall generalizations can be made, and are useful, as to U.S. and EU risk regulation from 1970 to 2004. We are convinced

---

[6] Even in this regard, we know of no systematic studies of the levels of voluntary compliance achieved in either system, and we have not attempted to evaluate studies of results actually achieved with regard to various possible end result parameters (e.g., air or water quality measures in the environmental context).

[7] How risk is regulated—that is, the direction of development of the legal and administrative systems themselves, and their likely convergence or divergence—is a separate issue from (a) their respective influences on degree of precaution, and (b) the degree of precaution that each in fact produces. We believe that fruitful generalizations *are* possible on *how* risk is regulated at this point, and that the U.S. and EU legal and administrative systems are, for functional reasons, on slowly converging evolutionary paths in this regard, notwithstanding the very different social and political contexts within which each is embedded.

that both citizens and officials in the respective legal and administrative systems are on a learning curve with regard to understanding risks and how to regulate them, but that they are at different points on that learning curve and have been since the 1970s. We find it useful to view the process from 1970 to 2004 as one in which the progressive development of better understanding of risks, and their regulation by both citizens and officials in each system, plays an important part in determining their risk preferences, and thus the timing and degree of precautionary regulation (see Chapter 16).

The United States has been ahead on the learning curve, at least until recently. The U.S. public's period of irrational fears as to most of the risks currently at issue peaked 10 or more years ago (but by no means disappeared entirely), while the EU public has focused more strongly on such risks in the last 10 years and is in the midst of a similar period of public irrationality, prompted by some significant regulatory failures and driven by environmental NGO advocacy. Additionally, the earlier U.S. period of irrationality was also prompted to a large extent by regulatory failure, or the perception of regulatory failure, and driven by environmental NGO advocacy. Because public concern peaked early in the United States, the United States developed comprehensive and detailed environmental, health, and safety legislation much earlier than the EU did.

The EU is catching up, however, and has now taken the lead in forms of regulation relating to products (a particular concern in a "common" market) and in some other areas such as greenhouse gas emissions. Notwithstanding this, the United States remains ahead on the curve as to implementation and enforcement of risk regulation. The United States is also ahead as to the sophistication of governmental procedures to assess risks, costs, and benefits, but Europe is making progress here as well. We discuss below the EU regulatory reform efforts and efforts to incorporate into precautionary regulation the use of risk assessment and cost–benefit analysis. We regard the current EU penchant for indiscriminate use of the precautionary principle—in place of factual support or structured analysis of why it is "worth it" to society to act in the face of uncertainty—as probably a passing phase, reflecting the current lack of sophistication by the European public, national politicians, and judges in making rational risk choices, coupled with aggressive, opportunistic special pleading to take advantage of the current situation by environmental NGOs and some sections of domestic EU industry and agriculture. The U.S. lead on the learning curve in all of the regards noted above may well have been driven by a more efficient social learning process inherent in the contentious, competitive, and vigorous public debate and political, administrative, and judicial review processes characteristic of the United States.[8]

---

[8] See Chapter 16 on "policy learning." Thus, we agree with some parts of the David Vogel (2003) "flip-flop" hypothesis, but we see it much more as a matter of late maturation in the EU, believe that the EU remains well behind the United States in many areas of regulation (e.g., environmental regulation in the areas of air, water, and waste regulations; soil and groundwater contamination; and wetlands regulation), and believe that the EU is way behind the United States in terms of effective implementation and enforcement across the board.

The Analytical Framework

Precautionary regulation is established in a representative democracy through collective societal decisions made by government in the face of uncertainty. Legal and administrative systems are the formal governmental framework—the vehicle—by which such collective decisions are made, most fundamentally through the processes of voting for legislators. Put another way, legal and administrative systems constitute the tools and processes by which democratic government aggregates individual risk preferences and transforms them into precautionary regulation.[9] Thus, it is important, as a normative matter, that these systems *transmit* public risk preferences *efficiently* and *accurately*, and ensure the public officials *aggregate* those preferences *efficiently* and *accurately* into public decisions that they then *effectively implement and enforce*. However, we do not address the important question of whether citizen risk preferences should be respected and implemented in all cases, even if those preferences are "irrational" by some definition (Wiener 1997).

It might be thought, at first impression, that such "tools and processes" would play a neutral role as to timing and stringency of precautionary regulation. The design, structure, and functions of legal and administrative systems can, however, have a direct and immediate influence on some elements of the extent of precaution in the resulting regulation, particularly its timing. Those same characteristics can also act indirectly, creating incentives for those operating through or within the legal and administrative system, with important indirect effects on precaution. In both cases, the effect may or may not be systematic and predictable.

There is, of course, a wide range of ways in which the design, structure, and functions of legal and administrative systems can and do have an effect on the precaution of the resulting regulation. Most obviously, the whole purpose of many aspects of design and structure is to facilitate transmission of public risk preferences (e.g., most aspects of access to information and opportunity to participate). These

---

[9] The legal and administrative system also serves other functions, such as to shape and filter public preferences (e.g., through protections for minority rights and limitations on majority rights set forth in constitutions). Further, we recognize that the "transmission" process is much more complex than the text may seem to suggest. It operates continuously, and acts through lobbying both the legislative and the administrative processes as well as through periodic voting to elect legislators and some executive and judicial officials. It is also two-way, since government and government officials communicate with the public on risk matters, and these communications can, in turn, have a major influence on the public's risk perceptions. We recognize our model of the lawmaking system in a representative democracy is simplified. See, e.g., Sunstein 1991 (critique of what the author calls "subjective welfarism"); Sunstein 1988 (critique of what the author calls "pluralism"); Aranson et al., 1982 (critique of "welfare (public-interest) rationales" for delegation in collective decisionmaking, observing that agency budget maximizing behavior tends to cause agencies to overstate the dangers of activities they regulate or propose to regulate, and that agencies with a mission of reducing risks should have an incentive to make type-II errors, since the public notices type-I errors more; both phenomena would result in more precautionary regulation). Nonetheless, given the scope limitations of this chapter, it seems to be an appropriate and useful starting place for analysis.

provide formal mechanisms to enable both the public individually, and the public acting through groups and organizations, to register preferences, both as to stringency and as to timing, that can influence the extent of precaution in the resulting government decision. In most cases, however, it is not possible to say in advance that these aspects of design or structure will have any systematic or predictable influence in one direction or another. Generally, the legal or administrative system is simply acting, as it should, as a neutral transmission tool. The result is determined by the content of the risk preferences registered and transmitted, whether as to timing or as to stringency.

With regard specifically to the element of timing, the design and structure of the systems themselves sometimes can have a direct effect on timing of precautionary regulation, by either advancing or delaying transmission of public risk preferences. For example, provision for public participation in the decisionmaking process through notice and comment rulemaking may cause delays in making decisions, even though it promotes fuller and more accurate transmission of public risk preferences to government decisionmakers. Delay results in a lesser degree of precaution, as we use that term, because precautionary rules will be less timely. But other public participation rights (e.g., the right to petition for rulemaking) can so facilitate transmission of public pressure for action that the result may be earlier risk regulation than would otherwise occur; however, this could also lead to delay when the public pressure is for inaction. As another example, judicial review by affected individuals, while essential to accountability of government decisionmakers, achieves this benefit only at some cost in delay. This can either happen directly because the appeal takes up time, or indirectly because administrative officials take more time to document administrative decisions out of concern for the risks of potential court review. But rights to challenge agency inaction through judicial review can also result in more timely precautionary regulation than would otherwise occur. In such cases, the effect flows from the nature of the element of the legal or administrative system itself, can thus be termed direct, and would seem to have a systematic and predictable impact on timing (and thus on the extent) of precautionary regulation.[10]

Another example deals with both timing and stringency. The design and structure of legal and administrative systems may be such as to fail to ensure adequate implementation and enforcement. Real precaution is a matter of enforced result, not mere "hortatory" law (that is, legal requirements that are not implemented or enforced, or "soft law" that is not legally binding). To the extent that a legal or administrative system provides for efficient application and enforcement, this can have a decisive and predictable favorable result on whether (a question of stringency), and when (a question of timing), the degree of precaution announced is actually achieved. To the extent that such a system does not provide for efficient application and enforcement, there will

---

[10] Note the caution with which we express this and similar conclusions. Even where we can suggest plausible potentially significant impacts, and even if we are correct in that appraisal, we may have identified only one among many causal factors at play in any given situation, where relative impact among them may vary in different situations. Further, while we may suggest plausible associations, we have no way of testing systematically for actual causation.

likely be an unfavorable effect on both whether and when the objectives announced in the regulatory proclamation are actually achieved. Here again, the effect seems to be systematic and predictable on both scores.

In addition to these situations, there are some other situations where it can be thought that the design or structure of legal and administrative systems causes systematic and predictable effects on the degree of precaution. This class of indirect effects can occur because the design or structure creates incentives for both private and public actors in the regulatory process, incentives that may favor or disfavor such actors as they try to influence the resulting precaution in specific cases. In many identifiable types of situations, it may be thought that specific incentives are created for one or another type of private or public actor, or that one or another is systematically and predictably favored or disfavored, and that the orientation of such actor to the extent of precaution in the resulting regulation is also systematic and predictable. In such situations, it can be argued that the design or structure of one or more aspects of the legal or administrative system will, as a result, have an indirect effect on the extent of precaution in the resulting regulation, either in terms of timing or in terms of stringency. In these cases, however, while the design and structure of legal and administrative systems may determine what incentives various private and public actors have, and thus whose agenda drives the resulting regulation in specific situations or generally, the impact, if any, on the degree of precaution in the substance of the regulation actually adopted will normally turn at base on the values and risk preferences of the participants in the process who are favored, not solely on characteristics of the process itself.[11]

In short, legal and administrative systems, as frameworks for action and as tools and processes, sometimes and in some respects can, and sometimes do—but more frequently do not, in and of themselves—have any predictable and systematic generic bias toward either more or less precautionary results.

---

[11] For example, in any given political context, government officials may, for whatever reasons, have personal or institutional agendas driven by personal or institutional risk preferences, separate from their perceptions of aggregated public risk preferences (and thus labeled by us as "extrinsic"), that are allowed or facilitated by the design or structure of the existing legal and administrative systems. They may also respond to agendas advanced by third parties, whether public or private, which are themselves driven by risk preferences held or responded to by those parties. These third-party agendas we do not label as "extrinsic," since they reflect the risk preferences of certain parts of the "public." Both of these types of agendas may result in more or less precautionary regulation. When one knows those agendas or likely agendas, one may be able to generalize in a useful predictive manner, in light of the extent to which the design or structure of the legal or administrative system facilitates their expression about the result on the degree of precaution in regulation. These risk preferences, however, seem to be a more fundamental influence on outcome than the design or structural aspects of the legal or administrative systems that create the incentives or facilitate the agendas, although there is certainly concurrent causation where design or structural aspects tend systematically and predictably to favor groups that generally hold stronger or weaker precautionary preferences than those of the public as a whole.

Key Features and Differences in U.S. and EU Legal and Administrative Systems

This section discusses some of the key features of U.S. and EU legal and administrative systems (see Bergkamp (2003) for an extensive discussion of EU legal issues in risk regulation) that might be thought to influence the choice of the risks regulated and the degree of precaution in the risk choices in each system.[12]

Generic Rules Governing Level of Precaution

Among the questions about generic rules this section explores are issues of regulating uncertain risks, generic substantive requirements as to degree of precaution, and risk assessment versus cost–benefit analysis requirements.

Does the Legal and Administrative System Allow Regulation of Uncertain Risk?
Regulation in the face of uncertainty, which is allowed in both the U.S. and EU systems, was resolved in the United States 25 years earlier than in the EU. In 1976, the D.C. Circuit opined in *Ethyl Corp. v. EPA*, 541 F.2d 1 (D.C. Cir. 1976): "Where a statute is *precautionary in nature* . . . we will not demand rigorous step-by-step proof of cause and effect. Such proof may be impossible to obtain if the *precautionary purpose* of the statute is to be served." For the EU, regulation under uncertainty was addressed in *Pfizer Animal Health S.A. v. Council*, Case T-13/99, 2002 WL 31377, and *Alpharma v. Council*, T-70/99, 2002 WL 31388.

Generic Substantive Requirements as to Degree of Precaution.
Both the U.S. and the EU legal and administrative systems have enacted substantive provisions that purport, in various ways, to govern the degree of precaution in regulation as a generic matter. The EU system, however, establishes few useful decision criteria with regard to stringency, while the U.S. system establishes a plethora of different, uncoordinated, and sometimes vague or general criteria. Further, generic decision criteria in either system that require a given degree of precaution—while apparently governing the degree of

---

[12] Many of the legal and administrative features discussed here, and their differences, are structural (i.e., they do not vary much over time and are inherent to the particular legal and administrative system). Thus, one might have thought that if they have any effect, they tend to have the same "net" effect on the degree of precaution (in either direction) in all cases. This is not always true, however. Even if they have an effect, a particular structural parameter or feature may have a varying influence. For instance, a strong and deterrent civil liability system might be thought to have an influence on the general need for *ex ante* precautionary regulation, but not in cases where the potential damage greatly exceeds the assets of the actors being regulated. Further, where structural characteristics have their effect by creating incentives or disincentives for use of personal, institutional, or specific third-party agendas in place of aggregated public risk preferences, the effect turns on the nature of those agendas, which will respond to many factors in addition to any incentives created by the design and structure of the legal and administrative systems, and in any case, the agendas themselves may change over time.

stringency (if not timing) of precautionary regulation directly and expressly—are analytically unhelpful in explaining the choice of that level of precaution, since the necessary inquiry is simply pushed back one step—to an analysis of how and why the criteria in question was adopted in the first place.

The U.S. legal system has no constitutional requirement specifying the level of precaution required in legislative or administrative enactments. The "substantive due process" concept has the potential to impose substantive limits on the level of precaution, but as currently interpreted by the Supreme Court, it does not significantly constrain federal government decisionmaking (*Nebbia v. New York*, 291 U.S. 502 (1934); *Usery v. Turner Elkhorn Mining Co.*, 428 U.S. 1 (1976)).

The EU Treaty (adopted in Maastricht in 1992) set forth general "principles" that should guide EU institutions in pursuing the EU's policies, a number of which are specific to environmental and health and safety legislation. The most important example in the context of this book is the "precautionary principle" of EU Treaty Article 130r, since renumbered as Article 174(2) of the Treaty of Nice signed in 2001, and now as Article 191 of the 2009 Lisbon Treaty on the Functioning of the European Union (TFEU). That article requires that "[c]ommunity policy on the environment shall be based on the precautionary principle" but contains no definition of that principle. As Stone (2001), Wiener (2003), and others have noted, the precautionary principle has been defined in many different and inconsistent ways, some of which are not useful in guiding decisionmaking, and some of which would stymie rational decisionmaking if adopted. The European Commission issued a communication (European Commission 2000) that interprets the precautionary principle to require risk management procedures in decisionmaking and effectively extends the scope of the precautionary principle to all risk regulation, but the communication does not define the principle and thus provides little or no useful substantive guidance as to the required level of precaution.

Another "principle," articulated in Article 5 of the EU Treaty, is the "proportionality" principle, which provides that "[a]ny action by the Community shall not go beyond what is necessary to achieve the objectives of this Treaty." In theory, this allows the EC to impose on EC citizens only such legislative or administrative obligations, restrictions, and penalties as are strictly necessary for the attainment of the purposes pursued, and then only if the objectives pursued fall within the treaty's objectives. There must always be a "reasonable relationship" between the measures taken and the objective pursued by the EC—that is, measures may not exceed what is appropriate and necessary to attain the objective (*Internationale Handelsgesellschaft v. Einfuhr*). In applying the proportionality principle, the European Court of Justice (ECJ) has developed two tests—an "efficacy" test (is the measure reasonably likely to achieve its objective?) and a "necessity" test (is the measure's adverse impact justified in view of the importance of the objective it pursues?). The proportionality principle, however, has no well-defined substantive content, imposes no concrete decision criteria on the legislative branch, and is applied sparingly by the courts in judicial review.

A third treaty provision, Article 191(3) of the 2009 TFEU (formerly Article 174(3), EC Treaty), requires the EC to "take account of" costs and benefits in setting environmental policy. This provision may well establish only a procedural requirement to perform some form of cost–benefit analysis, but it does state expressly that costs and benefits must be "taken into account" in environmental decisions. Any actual decision criteria, however, are only implicit, and undefined, so it seems to provide no real guidance as to level of precaution.

A fourth treaty principle—applicable when legislation is based on Article 114 of the 2009 TFEU (formerly Article 95 (internal market), EC Treaty) or Article 192 of the 2009 TFEU (formerly Article 175, EC Treaty) on environmental protection—is found in Articles 114(3) and 191(2) of the 2009 TFEU (formerly Articles 95(3) and 174(2), EC Treaty). It requires that EC environmental policy be "based on"[13] a "high level of protection," again with no definition of this term. Similar "high level of protection" language is also found, e.g., in Articles 168(1) on human health and 169(1) on consumer protection of the 2009 TFEU (formerly Articles 152(1) and 153(1), EC Treaty). As with the other principles, unless this requirement is defined or made concrete through administrative action or judicial interpretation, it imposes no specific or discernible level of precaution in regulatory decisionmaking (Cases C-157/96 and C-180/96, May 5, 2008; European Commission 1997).

In short, the EU Treaty specifies no usable requirement (nor even usable guidance) as to level of precaution.[14]

The second level for consideration is the statutory level. There is no *across the board* generic requirement as to degree of precaution at the statutory level, either in the

---

[13] The proposed EU Constitution stated that "Union policy on the environment shall *aim at* a high level of protection, taking into account the diversity of situations in the various regions of the Union" (Article III-233, paragraph 2; emphasis added).

[14] Some commentators have argued that at least some of these principles are "hard law" (e.g., Douma 2000), and that these principles provide all the decision criteria necessary to resolve environmental issues through balancing one principle against the other (Sadeleer 2003, examining their legal force and offering a novel theory of norm formation by courts in environmental law). Others recognize that they are only "general guidelines for Community environmental policy that do not constitute binding rules of law which apply to each individual Community measure" (Kraemer 2002). In any case, it is problematic for courts to resort to unguided balancing of values drawn from vague undefined "principles" for deciding cases—especially in areas of risk regulation, which normally involve economic policy choices and trade-offs or complex scientific or technical evaluation. In these areas, courts are not institutionally well suited to be the decisionmakers, much less to make the value and policy trade-offs involved. Perhaps for these reasons, the proposed EU Constitution stated expressly that "principles" could be implemented by legislative and executive acts, but that they should "be judicially cognizable only in the interpretation of such acts and in the ruling on their legality," but should apparently not be given independent life by the judges (see the proposed EU Constitution, Article II-112).

United States or in the EU.[15] Each system, however, does specify levels of precaution required under specific pieces of legislation that address specific types of risks.[16]

Requiring Risk Assessment or Cost–Benefit Procedures.

While a procedural requirement to use risk assessment or cost–benefit procedures would not seem, absent associated decision criteria, to govern degree of precaution directly, such a requirement might be thought to do so indirectly. Since 1982, the United States has had executive branch requirements that agencies perform risk assessments and cost–benefit analysis, and that "significant" agency rules (defined objectively and quantitatively) be reviewed by a branch of the Office of the President, the Office of Management and Budget (OMB). (See Wiener (2003) on the history and provisions of OMB.) In 1993, Executive Order 12866 required comprehensive executive branch review of the covered agency rules by OMB's Office of Information and Regulatory Affairs (OIRA); 3 C.F.R.

---

[15] The U.S. National Environmental Policy Act does not contain such a generic requirement, since it is procedural only, not substantive. The Sixth Community Environment Action Programme refers to the precautionary principle but does not set forth a generic requirement as to the degree of precaution (other than to repeat the treaty language "a high level of protection"; see Decision 1600/2002 of July 22, 2002, laying down the Sixth Community Environment Action Programme, OJ L 242/1, September 10, 2002). Likewise, the EU's Environmental Impact Assessment (EIA) Directive provides no substantive criteria, since it merely requires *assessment* of various factors. The provisions of the EU Commission's "Better Regulation" impact assessment initiatives are discussed below. They list several possible criteria for decisionmaking among alternatives, e.g., cost–benefit analysis involving identification and evaluation of "expected economic, environmental, and social benefits and costs of proposed public initiatives," with a measure considered "justified where net benefits can be expected"; cost-effectiveness analysis using a "cost per unit of effectiveness" technique as an alternative to cost–benefit analysis in cases where it is difficult to value benefits in money terms; "multi-criteria analysis" (covering "a wide range of techniques that share the aim of combining a range of positive and negative impacts in a single framework to allow easier comparison or scenarios and decisionmaking," but which also allows criteria, perhaps multiple criteria, to be chosen to compare options, as long only as the criteria are "measurable, at least in qualitative terms"); "risk analysis"; and "sensitivity analysis." No one criterion is required for use. Commission bureaucrats are enjoined that "*final choice is always left to the College of Commissioners*" (emphasis added), and the Commission's guidelines are not in any case legally binding.

[16] In the U.S. system, statutory formulations of the required level of precaution are common. They range from the more general ("in the public interest") to the more specific ("lowest achievable emission rate"), and from the less stringent ("best practicable technology") to the more stringent ("best available technology"). There is also extensive administrative and judicial gloss on the required level of precaution, with some cases of administrative gloss providing highly quantified criteria. In the EU, the Integrated Pollution Prevention and Control (IPPC) Directive imposes relevant substantive requirements, requiring that permit conditions reflect "best available technology" and prevent "significant" pollution (Article 3(a) and (b), Directive 96/61, concerning integrated pollution prevention and control, OJ L 257/26 October 10, 1996, of the IPPC Directive). There are also various decision criteria in directives and regulations that purport to govern level of precaution, but they tend to be more general and nonspecific than such criteria in U.S. statutes, thus providing even less useful guidance on the required level of precaution than do their frequently problematic U.S. counterparts.

§ 638 (1994) established "principles of regulation" that require each agency, *inter alia*, to "design its regulation in the most cost-effective manner to achieve the regulatory objective" and in doing so to "consider ... distributive impacts, and equity." There is much further detailed written guidance in the rules and guidelines of OIRA and various agencies on how this is done, and highly quantified analyses are routinely prepared by agencies and reviewed by OIRA. The OIRA requirements are, however, essentially procedural and are not judicially enforceable.

These U.S. procedural requirements have certainly made the articulated reasons for agency decisions more transparent, and they have helped to structure and focus the debate over those decisions within and without government (and, it is hoped, made that debate—even if not the resulting decisions—more rational). Whether they have changed actual agency decisions, however, making them either more or less precautionary, or resulting in more elaborate *ex post facto* justification, is an empirical question.[17] The major impact of these requirements may be simply that they ask the right questions and by doing so have changed the terms of the public and governmental debate,[18] bringing all participants up the learning curve (Hahn and Litan 2004, 5–13).

Article 191(3) of the 2009 TFEU (formerly Article 174, EC Treaty) imposes a requirement that costs and benefits be "taken into account" in making environmental policy decisions, but it does not expressly call for the conducting of cost–benefit analysis prior to the adoption of environmental measures. Since 1996, this provision has been implemented in nonbinding "Regulatory Policy Guidelines" issued by the president of the European Commission.

In June 2002, the Commission issued a communication on regulatory impact assessment (RIA) for "major initiatives." That communication, which is not legally binding on the Commission, provided for an integrated assessment of all economic, social, and environmental impacts of "major initiatives," replacing a number of sector-specific impact analyses that preceded it. It defines impact assessment as "the process of systematic analysis of the likely impacts of intervention by public authorities." The Commission goes out of its way to note that impact assessment is "an aid to decisionmaking, not a substitute for political judgment," stressing that while impact analysis provides "an important input by informing decisionmakers of the consequences of policy choices," "political judgment involves complex considerations

---

[17] The fact that the executive branch is judge in its own case may cause skepticism as to the rigor with which these requirements will be applied. On the other hand, review by agents of a directly elected president may be thought to exercise salutary executive control over actions by other bureaucrats that respond to individual or institutional agendas that may diverge from efficient aggregation of individual citizen risk preferences as identified by the president.

[18] Mere use of the tools may have had the effect of helping to educate both the public and officials in how to think rationally about the issues, resulting in more accurate and efficient transmission of public risk preferences and perhaps altering those preferences themselves, although it may not be possible to generalize about the direction or strength of any such impact. It could be argued persuasively that the EU Commission's recent "Better Regulation" Impact Assessment Guidelines, discussed below, will have the same effect.

that are go [*sic*] far beyond the anticipated impacts of a proposal." It notes that impact assessment overlaps to some degree with the *ex ante* budgetary evaluation required by the Financial Regulation of all proposals involving budgetary expenditures, but that the two can be melded into a single evaluation where both apply (European Commission 2002a, 3–5).

Subsequently, the Barroso Commission issued a major policy announcement on March 16, 2005, on the need for regulatory reform to ensure the success of the "Better Regulation" initiative aimed at promoting economic growth (European Commission 2005a). On June 15, 2005, the Commission issued new Impact Assessment (IA) Guidelines (European Commission 2005b), replacing the Commission's 2002 guidelines. It later revised these IA Guidelines in 2006 and issued new guidelines in 2009 (European Commission 2009). These 2005 guidelines, which again are not legally binding, provide much useful new analysis and detail as to the *process* that Commission bureaucrats should use in developing the IA, and provides that the IA will accompany the legislative proposal through the decisionmaking process. They do not, however, prescribe the process or criteria that the Commissioner's or the other EU institutions will use *in actually making a decision.*

Interestingly, IAs are required only for the development by the Commission of proposals for legislation (only the Commission in the EU can originate legislation). They do not apply to the subsequent legislative process, although the Commission is trying to persuade other EU institutions and states to adopt IAs, nor to the administrative regulatory process—the Commission's actions as to the latter being expressly "normally exempted" (European Commission 2005b, 6). Of course, more of the important precautionary decisions are made at the legislative stage in the EU, as noted below, than in the United States, where the real regulatory action normally takes place at the administrative level. They also apply only to a class of the most significant legislative proposals, the makeup of which is not defined objectively, since the Commission controls unilaterally the projects it places in the designated categories.

They contain no binding decision criteria, referring instead to three "generic evaluation criteria that apply to all proposals of the Commission," criteria set by the EU treaties (e.g., the subsidiarity and proportionality principles), and five alternative sets of criteria that can be used by the Commission bureaucrats to compare impacts (European Commission 2005b, 43, and Annexes, 42–44).

Once again, as in its 2002 Communication, the Commission takes pains to subordinate impact assessment in the actual decisional process, noting that it is not the same thing as the "policy proposal or … the explanatory memorandum which precedes the proposal." It says that "[t]he College of Commissioners will take the IA findings into consideration in its deliberations. The IA will not, however, dictate the contents of its final decision. The adoption of a policy proposal is a political decision that belongs solely to the College, not to officials or technical experts" (European Commission 2005b, 4).

While the guidelines are not legally binding and do not seem to establish an EU equivalent to the U.S. OIRA, they do provide for administrative policing of their provisions, even indicating institutional and structural methods for doing so. There is mention of use of Intra-Service Steering Groups to ensure broad participation by other affected parts of the bureaucracy (establishment of such a group is "compulsory for all items of a cross-cutting nature," and "valid reasons must be provided" if a directorate general does not plan to establish such a group), and of centralized supervision of the process by the secretariat general (which will "consider the quality of the IA report as part of the formal Inter-Service Consultation procedure" and apparently may issue "a suspended or unfavorable opinion" if the IA report "does not reach a satisfactory level of quality"). Further, the Commission notes that "it is also possible that one or more of the Groups of Commissioners will examine the draft proposal and the impact assessment prior to the College's deliberation," and, quoting an earlier document, that one such group is the "Competitive Group of Commissioners," whose mandate allows it, "at the request of the President, [to] consider the impact of significant draft Commission proposals outside the Competiveness Council's remit, and in particular, to ensure that the impact assessments accompanying such proposals adequately take account of competitiveness" (European Commission 2005b, 7, 9, 14–15).

There is also a requirement that "stakeholder" consultation during the IA process be undertaken "according to the Commission's general principles and minimum standards for consultation," as well as instruction on collection and use of expertise (European Commission 2005b, 11–12).

The scope of action covered by impact assessment includes all legislative and other policy proposals that the Commission includes in its Annual Policy Strategy or Work Program, "provided that they have a potential economic, social and/or environmental impact and/or require some regulatory measure for their implementation" (because the Commission controls which proposals are subject to IA opportunity for strategic maneuvering, and if an independent, quantitative definition of "major initiatives" existed, similar to Executive Order 12866, it would reduce this problem significantly). These actions include "[a]ll regulatory proposals, White Papers, expenditure programmes and negotiating guidelines for international agreements (with an economic, social, or environmental impact)." The Commission may also decide "on a case-by-case basis … to carry out an impact assessment of a proposal which does not appear on the WP." Green Papers and proposals for consultation with "Social Partners" are exempted, as are "periodic Commission decisions and reports, proposals following international obligations and Commission measures deriving from its powers of controlling the correct implementation of EC law and executive decisions" (European Commission 2005b, 6).

The 2002 Communication called for two stages in the IA process. All major initiatives were subject to a preliminary assessment, which served as a "filter." Certain policy initiatives were then chosen by the Commission for an "extended impact assessment." This structure seems to have given way in the 2005 IA Guidance to a requirement for an IA Report in all cases covered by the communication—but with such a report subject to "proportionate analysis," under which "[t]he impact assessment's depth and scope will be determined by the likely impacts of the proposed action. … " (European Commission 2005b, 6, 8).

Under the 2005 IA Guidelines, the IA process has six basic steps:

- What is the problem?
- What are the objectives?
- What are the policy options?
- What are the likely economic, social, and environmental impacts?
- How do the options compare?
- How could future monitoring and evaluation be organized? (European Commission 2005b, 2–3)

The IA Report can be no more than 30 pages (excluding annexes) and must follow a set format (European Commission 2005b, 14).

Neither the 2002 Communication nor the 2005 IA Guidelines calls expressly for either risk assessments or cost–benefit analyses, and the 2002 Communication specifically notes the following:

> A number of analytical methods can be used to assess impacts. They differ in concept and coverage (e.g., cost-benefit analysis, compliance cost analysis, multi-criteria analysis and risk assessment). The choice of method and the level of detail will vary with the nature of the problem and judgments about feasibility.

> When assessing impacts, strict cost-benefit analysis may not always supply the most relevant information; for example, the degree of irreversibility should also be considered. The precautionary principle should be applied when appropriate. The impact on established policy objectives where available, should be assessed (European Commission 2002a, 15–16).

The 2002 Communication, however, does not supply any single or binding decision criterion. Neither do the 2005 IA Guidelines, noting as they do that IA is a decision *tool*, but that it will not govern the "political" decision of the Commission, much less that of the Parliament or the Council. The new guidance does, however, go much further than prior guidance both in "screening" to arrive at a shortlist of options (using the criteria of "effectiveness, efficiency, and consistency") and in structuring the consideration and ranking of options. It requires that for all options considered (which must include the "no action" option), the IA Report must "consider all the relevant positive and negative impacts alongside each other, regardless of whether they are expressed in qualitative, quantitative, or monetary terms." While the Commission presents this approach as a "simple multi-criteria analysis" and carefully distinguishes it from the alternative approaches of "cost-benefit analysis, which compares positive and negative impacts expressed in the same units, normally in monetary terms, and cost-effectiveness analysis, which compares the costs of achieving a given objective," in fact, the approach suggested by the Commission is compatible with what is commonly considered cost–benefit analysis in the United States. Here, the term "formal" or "quantified" cost–benefit analysis is normally properly reserved for the fully quantified type of assessment. On the other hand, when the Commission defines "multi-criteria analysis," it does not require that a "net benefits" hurdle or a "maximizing net benefits" test be used for multi-criteria analysis (European Commission 2005b, 39, 42–43).

In short, if implemented rigorously and consistently, the EU 2005 IA Communication and the IA process it requires potentially represent a significant move by the EU Commission toward more rigorously institutionalizing impact assessment (and thus, perhaps in due course, toward a broad and flexible cost–benefit analysis, properly understood, as opposed to insistence on fully quantified cost–benefit analysis). It is true that it deals only with executive branch review of EU risk legislative proposals—which in the EU contain much more detailed precautionary regulation than legislation alone does in the United States[19]—and that the process will not cover implementing administrative actions: what would in the United States be called administrative regulation, and where much of the real regulatory action in the United States takes place. It is also true that it remains nonbinding, highly discretionary, and not subject to any rigorous (that is, judicial rather than political) accountability through judicial review at the behest of generally affected private parties (except perhaps for much more rigorous internal policing of the quality of IA Reports by the secretariat general of the Commission and perhaps by those commissioners sitting on the Competitiveness Group). Nonetheless, it is a significant new development. Still, because both the 2002 Communication and the 2005 IA Guidance are relatively new, it is chiefly their precursors that will have influenced prior risk regulation during the period 1970 to date. These precursors were of lesser scope and much less rigor (see Hahn and Litan 2004, 13–19, for an assessment of the EU RIA process). The 2006 and 2009 revisions to the IA Guidelines largely reaffirmed the basic approach to impact assessment we have described here (European Commission 2009).

Ex Ante *Lawmaking Institutions and Processes*

This section will compare how nine *ex ante* institutions and processes shape risk regulation in the United States and the EU. They are institutional design and authority, issues of vertical structure, the electoral process, the legislative process, rulemaking,

---

[19] Further, the 2005 IA Guidance is full of much practical wisdom on this process, like the suggestions (a) that problem definition is the key first step, (b) that understanding why the problem is a problem is crucial, (c) that one must distinguish among the problem, the objective (indeed, three levels of objectives—the general overall goals of a policy, expressed in terms of its outcome or ultimate impact; the specific objectives, expressed in terms of the direct and short-term effects of the policy; and the operational objectives, normally expressed in terms of outputs, that is, goods or services that the policy should produce), and the proposed policy before fine-tuning the proposed policy in consideration of alternatives, and (d) that how you express the problem (e.g., as a "lack of something") can bias the whole subsequent analysis. Perhaps the greatest blind spot, however, is illustrated by asking "why the problem is a problem," without specific focus on why, if the policy is such a good idea, rational people operating in a market system have not already implemented the policy, and then letting that analysis of cognitive or market failure guide the further analysis of what needs to be, and can be, done. See Smith (1994).

choosing policy instruments and integrating policies, administrative implementation, enforcement, and judicial review.

Institutional Design and Authority. The overall structural design of the U.S. federal government, while it allows ample opportunity for the play of public and private institutional agendas that may impact on degree of precaution, has significant formal elements of political and judicial accountability that tend to allow aggregated public risk preferences to play a major role in the degree of precaution in risk regulation. The overall structural design of the EU government at its present state of evolution remains, however, largely a division of power among institutions that reflect primarily institutional agendas, with little direct political or judicial accountability to the public as such.[20] This results in dominance, as to issues of degree of precaution, by the Member States acting through the Council. The EU degree of precaution at any point in time reflects primarily the outcome of institutional struggles among institutional actors whose risk preference agendas do not necessarily accurately reflect aggregate EU public risk preferences.

United States. The U.S. legislature is bicameral, consisting of two bodies—the Senate and House of Representatives. Both senators and representatives are directly elected by popular vote, so the states of the Union are not themselves represented as institutions in the federal legislature (although originally senators were selected by the state legislatures, an arrangement akin to the current selection method for the EU Council). Any legislation that passes the Senate and House must be presented to the president for signature. Any presidential veto of legislation can be overridden by a two-thirds majority of both Houses of Congress. Proposals for legislation may be introduced by any member of either body, but only by them.

In the United States, there is a clear distinction between legislation ("statutes") and implementing measures (administrative "rules" and "regulations"). Legislation, adopted by the Senate and the House in the form of statutes, normally establishes general requirements, such as that air quality must protect public health and welfare with an adequate margin of safety, or that chemicals must not pose an unreasonable risk. Statutes normally authorize a federal administrative agency, generally an executive

---

[20] The recently proposed European Constitution, which was replaced by the 2009 Lisbon Treaty on the Functioning of the European Union (TFEU), introduced a number of provisions aimed at creating more democratic, transparent, and accountable EU institutions. For example, the Constitution would provide citizens with the right to invite the Commission to submit a proposal, if they manage to collect one million signatures in a significant number of Member States. Also, the proceedings of the Council, when exercising its legislative function, would be open to the public. Nonetheless, the major structural aspects that result in domination by Member States acting as such would remain in place.

branch agency rather than an independent agency,[21] to issue detailed administrative regulations spelling out the more specific requirements necessary to implement the statutory requirements. Thus, specific detailed or quantitative requirements—say, ambient air quality standards or emissions limits—are normally set out in regulations or in individual source permits, not in statutes.

The U.S. federal governmental system is based on the separation of powers doctrine, with clearly delineated legislative, executive, and judicial branches and constitutional checks and balances among them. This structure can have important effects on how risk regulation takes place.[22] While the power of each branch to check another can simply be used to impose one branch's institutional agenda on another, it can also be used to check use by another branch of institutional agendas that the first branch views as diverging from its perception of transmitted aggregate public risk preference.[23]

European Union. The EU legislature is made up of the Council of Ministers and the European Parliament, with the Council of Ministers decidedly the senior partner. The Parliament's power depends on the applicable legislative procedure, and under the ordinary legislative procedure of the 2009 TFEU (formerly known as "co-decision" procedure), the Parliament has the power to block (and thus indirectly affect) the adoption of legislation. The Council is not directly elected and represents Member States—indeed, Member State *governments*—as such. It has no fixed membership; its membership varies with the issue being acted on. The members of the Council for any

---

[21] While independent agencies were popular early in U.S. regulatory history, their lack of political accountability and other characteristics have been much debated in the United States over time. Most significant U.S. risk regulation is now handled by executive branch agencies, and independent agencies are of less importance than they once were.

[22] Because of the separation of powers doctrine, Congress has limited power over the executive branch through legislative oversight and generally has no standing to sue for judicial review as an institution. Thus, Congress "enlists" private parties to force the executive branch to properly implement its legislation by authorizing judicial review of agency action to be brought by such parties. As a result, Congress has a strong incentive, when enacting statutes delegating substantive rulemaking authority to administrative agencies, to specify statutory decision criteria, even if in fairly general terms (e.g., requiring agency action to be "in the public interest," or to ensure "protection of the public health and welfare with an adequate margin of safety," or to prevent "significant risk"), so as to limit agency discretion in ways that courts can enforce during judicial review at the behest of private litigants with standing. There is not the same incentive in parliamentary systems, where the legislative branch controls the executive branch. There, the legislators tend to write statutes with very broad, general decision criteria, allowing themselves, acting as the executive branch, much discretion and at the same time depriving the judicial branch of clear criteria for holding executive action to account for compliance with legislative commands. See Smith (1986).

[23] The same need for checks and balances exists *within* the major institutions, which helps explain the usefulness of the different institutional sensitivity to transmission of public risk preferences of the House (more sensitive to short-term swings in public feeling) and the Senate (less sensitive to such short-term swings), as well perhaps as indicating the usefulness of presidential staff (OIRA) review of risk measures proposed by agency bureaucrats within the executive branch.

given piece of legislation consist of the ministers from each Member State responsible in their own Member State government for the issue at hand. Thus, when acting on environmental issues, the Council consists of the environment ministers from the Member States.

The European Parliament, directly elected from the Member States, is the only EU institution composed of directly elected officials. It has traditionally had only advisory power, but it has taken on a much more active and powerful role in the evolution of the EU's complex legislative procedures and now has effective veto power over certain issues.

The EU Commission, effectively the EU Executive, also has an important role in the EU legislative process. First, only the Commission can initiate legislation. Thus, the Commission, not the Council or the Parliament, largely governs the initial timing and choice of subject matter for regulation, as well as the initial form, structure, and content of proposals for the regulatory scheme itself.[24] The Commission also has a consultative role during various stages of the EU legislative processes and can shape the final content of legislation by withholding its consent to changes in the legislation in various ways and at various stages. Its influence can be, and in some cases is, used to push more precautionary legislation.

EU government is said not to be based on a separation of powers (see Chapter 16). While this may be true in some senses, that does not mean that there are no checks and balances. In the EU, the checks and balances are chiefly institutional. They are built into the complex interplay between the EU institutions of the legislative and executive branches (and between them and the Member States) in the legislative process, and into the ability of the various EU institutions (including the Member States) to obtain judicial review of the actions of the others in the ECJ. Given the apparent influence of Member States in EU legislation, given that they are acting in their institutional capacity in the Council, and given their only indirect accountability to their national publics when doing so, these relationships and the checks and balances they embody are likely to have a distorting effect—possibly a major distorting effect—on the accurate and efficient transmission and integration of aggregated public risk preferences into risk regulation.[25]

---

[24] One by-product is that EU legislation is drafted initially by Commission bureaucrats, not by legislative staff. This results in more intellectually coherent and sometimes more rational legislation than is found in the United States. At least partially because these bureaucrats are normally not lawyers, however, EU legislation has in the past frequently been so general and loosely drafted as to impede rigorous implementation and enforcement—a tendency that Member States acting in the Council have had no incentive to discourage, because it leaves them with more discretion over the actual applied degree of precaution during implementation.

[25] A further issue: Member States acting in Council represent only the interests of their own national publics, even when and if they do operate as accurate transmitters of public risk preferences. On the other hand, any legislator in a representative democracy is an agent representing the interests of his or her own constituents, however that constituency is defined.

The structural predominance of the Member State governments in the EU legislative and policy process has led to that process traditionally resembling a treaty negotiation among sovereign states more than the dynamics of legislation in national-level parliaments. EC policy is set chiefly on the basis of the results of negotiated political deals that involve trade-offs of national interests across a wide range of issues (Radaelli 2003, 12–13).

The treaty-like process in the Council has had important implications for the resulting degree of precaution in EU legislation over time. It has also had impacts on the functionally useful distinction between legislation (imposing relatively general standards through directives or regulations) and implementing measures (imposing specific, detailed requirements through rules or other instruments). Both of these issues have gotten swept up in the struggle over the vertical distribution of power in the EU, with varying results over time in terms of degree of precaution (e.g., ineffective and less precautionary legislation early on, with real control over degree of precaution retained at Member State level; then lately more and better legislation, with a recent trend to more precaution due partly to the impact of the Nordic countries).

Further, the Commission has thus generally tended to push for more precautionary legislation than some Member States felt comfortable with, and the EU has tended to enact more precautionary legislation as the Parliament increased in power and cooperated more with the Commission. That tendency has recently become more pronounced as the EU has expanded. The Nordic Member State governments, reflecting the sentiment of their populations, have joined the German government—traditionally more green than other Member States—to push greener legislation within the Council. It remains to be seen, however, what impact the addition of Central and Eastern European countries to the EU will make in the balance of power on risk regulation in the Council. It seems likely to have a tendency to diminish the degree of precaution due to their lower standard of living and thus their desire for economic development, along with their current less advanced status of environmental protection.

Issues of Vertical Structure. The institutional structures for, and the political struggles concerning, the vertical distribution of power in both the United States and the EU have had important impacts on the degree of precaution in risk regulation, but have done so chiefly by reflecting the risk preferences of the institutions involved in the struggle. In the United States, federal legislation tended, in the early years, to be more stringent than state legislation; EU-level legislation has tended to reflect the desires of Member States to retain real control over the degree of precaution at the Member State level.

United States. The United States has a federal system, with a strong federal government and with residual power resting in the states. The bulk of U.S. precautionary risk legislation is driven by federal-level statutes and rules (Bergkamp 2003, 651–658). In the areas of *product* regulation (e.g., regulation of hazardous chemicals, food, drugs, cosmetics, pesticides, and insecticides), factory health and safety regulation, soil and groundwater contamination cleanup (at sites "listed" under the federal legislation), some forms of natural resource regulation (e.g., migratory wildfowl and mining law), and some forms of energy regulation (e.g., nuclear and hydroelectric power plant regulation), U.S. law has tended to establish nationally uniform requirements directly applicable to the regulated community. In other areas of environmental regulation—especially air, water, and waste regulation—U.S. law more frequently sets a substantive and procedural framework under federal law that makes many of the basic risk decisions but leaves implementation and enforcement against the regulated community to the states. Of course, outside the area of preemptive product regulation (and some standards like uniform national ambient air quality standards for criteria pollutants), these federal laws normally allowed states to be more stringent if they chose to do so. In these regards, the applicable U.S. statutes resemble EU directives in their structure. U.S. land use regulation mostly takes place at the local municipal level of government, although many aspects of federal and state risk regulation have important land use regulatory implications.

U.S. federal requirements have traditionally been more precautionary, on the whole, than state-level provisions. For years, green NGOs, driven by efficiency considerations and the view that national legislators are less parochial than those in the states, concentrated their efforts at the national level. Now that there is an effective deadlock in Congress on many environmental issues, however, environmental NGOs have turned to the states to promote more precautionary regulation. They are having success in doing so. Thus, the vertical distribution of authority in the United States has likely had a strong impact on the degree of precaution in U.S. risk regulation, chiefly by being exploited on an opportunistic basis by environmental NGOs to achieve their desires for more precautionary results.

European Union. The EU is, in effect, a confederation at this stage of its development, and as noted above, it is dominated by the Member State governments. The EU has treaty authority to legislate in the environment, health and safety, and other risk-related areas, and when it does so, its law preempts those of the Member States. The preemptive effect of EU law is founded on a line of ECJ rulings establishing that all national authorities, including regional and local subdivisions of the national governments, along with publicly owned companies, regardless of national constitutional structure, must implement and apply Community law. The treaty and secondary legislation (e.g., through a so-called "safeguard" clause pursuant to which, under certain conditions, Member States may temporarily restrict activities permitted by EU legislation) do give the Member States some leeway to impose requirements going beyond EU legislation (Articles 114(5) and 193 of the 2009 TFEU; formerly Articles 95(5) and 176, EC Treaty). The treaty "principle" of subsidiarity requires, at least in theory, that legislation must be adopted at the lowest practicable level, restricting EU legislation to those matters that must be resolved at the EU level for various functional reasons (Article 5, TFEU; formerly Article 5, EC Treaty). In fact, the pattern of regulation of various types of risks in the vertical dimension in the EU does not differ significantly from that found in U.S. risk regulation—as to product and factory health and safety regulation, at least. There is, however, little EU-level risk regulation in the natural resource and energy production categories, and the new EU Environmental Liability Directive governing soil and groundwater cleanup leaves many crucial details of substance, as well as all implementation and enforcement, to Member State governments.

Further, notwithstanding EU authority to regulate in various areas of risk reduction, the Member States continue to have full national-level risk regulatory systems. The result is greater scope, both *de jure* and de facto, for more stringent regulation at the Member State level than in the United States. In addition, because the EC government (except for Parliament) is not chosen by direct democratic election, EU risk regulation tends to be reactive, rather than proactive. It follows either developments at the Member State level or the Member States' perceptions of what their publics want.[26] Thus, the degree of precaution adopted at the EU level tends to mimic that at the national level, with such changes as result from the domination of that process by the Member States through the Council.

The Electoral Process. The design or structure of the electoral process does not seem to affect degree of precaution in the United States, but use of proportional voting may have some impact in the EU, although again, it is the Member States through the Council, not the (elected) Parliament, that exercise the real political power.

United States. The United States uses first-past-the-post plurality voting at both federal and state (but not necessarily municipal) levels, which results in a strong two-party system. The theory of the median voter suggests that both parties will tend toward centrist positions on risk issues, but both parties seem currently to respond strongly to extreme factions.[27] The Democratic Party, the party of the left, tends consistently to favor more risk-averse policies and legislation. On balance, however, it is not clear that the electoral process, in and of itself, affects the net result as to degree of precaution in the United States.

---

[26] In some cases, however, the EU structure allows enactment of more precautionary EU legislation than would have been adopted at the national level, since the Commission views itself as protecting the larger "European" interest when it proposes legislation, and since it is Member State environment ministers who sit as the EU Council for dealing with environmental issues, without the necessity or check of "cabinet government" approval of the resulting EU legislation by industry or other ministers, as would normally occur at the national level, and without direct public accountability to voters.

[27] See the extensive literature on incentives, voting, and the incoherence of legislative outcomes due to cycling and strategic behavior, e.g., Arrow (1963) and Riker (1982). More recent models suggest stable and predictable voting outcomes, and empirical studies show "a strong tendency" in actual voting to favor "balanced compromise outcomes" (Farber and Frickey 1988). It is beyond the scope of this chapter to comment on current voting patterns in light of these analyses.

European Union. Most (14) EU Member States use the proportional voting system for selection of EU Parliament representatives. Wiener and Rogers (2002) have suggested that this method of voting may empower green partisans, despite their representing only a narrow segment of the population, to elect enough members to the Parliament to hold the balance of power in some cases and to have their leaders attain positions as ministers in the governing coalition. It is also plausible that the fact that members of the EU Parliament are not yet well known or well respected in their national-level jurisdictions frees them to be less responsive to voter sentiment. A corollary might be that green partisans, for whom the risk issues are highly salient, can organize and elect greener Parliament members than would otherwise be the case. The Parliament does tend to be greener than the Council, with the Commission in the middle. Even with the new influence the Parliament has obtained, however, it is often the Member States, through the Council, not the Parliament, that ultimately drive the degree of precaution in EU legislation. That does not mean that the Parliament does not try to push (and sometimes effectively pushes) the Council toward more precautionary legislation by threatening to use its veto power and by other exercises of political influence.

The Legislative Process. The legislative process does not seem to affect degree of precaution in the United States, but it does do so in the EU, where it reflects the struggles for power among, and the institutional agendas of, the main EU political institutions.

United States. Federal legislative procedure is, on the whole, the same for any bill, without regard to its subject matter or legal basis,[28] and the type of legislation used is primarily a statute, which imposes legally binding requirements directly on the regulated entity, or requires states to do so. In some cases, risk policy is made indirectly rather than directly, by attaching "riders" (that is, amendments) to fiscal legislation that deprive an agency of funds if it does not follow some policy requirement in the rider. The legislative committee process means that risk regulation is subject to specialist committees, which makes integration of risk policy in the U.S. Congress difficult. Legislative review of risk regulation by administrative agencies has been tried, and found constitutionally wanting in certain forms: *INS v. Chada,* 426 U.S. 919 (1983) (one-house veto); *Process Gas Consumer Group v. Consumer Energy Council of America,* 463 U.S. 1216 (1983) (two-house veto). The U.S. legislative process itself, however, does not seem likely to have much predictable and systematic independent impact on the level of precaution.

---

[28] The rules of the House and Senate with regard to legislative organization and procedure are complex and beyond the scope of this chapter. They can, of course, affect the outcome of legislation, but it is not clear to us that they have, either individually or in aggregate, any systematic and predictable impact in and of themselves, in one direction or the other, on degree of precaution.

European Union. Two major types of EC lawmaking result from the EU legislative process: regulations and directives. (Other EC measures include recommendations, opinions, resolutions, and decisions.) Regulations are "directly applicable" throughout the Community, which means that they impose legally binding requirements directly on the regulated entities throughout the EU, just as U.S. statutes normally do. Regulations do not require any legislative action by the Member States (although Member States often do enact their own implementing legislation or regulations in connection with EC regulations). Directives, on the other hand, do not impose binding requirements directly on the regulated entities. Rather, they bind the Member States, frequently requiring them to enact legal requirements applicable directly to regulated entities. The rule that directives are not directly effective is subject to an important court-created exception. The ECJ has ruled that certain provisions of directives, as well as some treaty articles, may, even in the absence of adequate implementing national legislation, create individual rights—in other words, have "direct effect" (*Van Gend en Loos v. Nederlandse Administratie der Belastingen*, Case 26/62, 1963 ECR 10; *Marshall v. South-West Hampshire Area Health Authority*, Case 152/84, 1986 ECR 723).[29]

Most EC legislation comes in the form of directives; regulations are rare, but their use is increasing in the area of risk regulation (e.g., Regulation (EC) No. 1013/2006 of the European Parliament and of the Council of 14 June 2006 on shipment of waste). Member States are frequently more reluctant to agree to EC regulations than to directives, precisely because regulations remove much of their national-level discretion, normally exercised during implementation of a directive, over the degree of precaution.

Four ways in which the EU legislative process, per se, influences the degree of precaution have been discussed above in the context of institutional structure. First is the dominance of EU policy and legislation by the Member States in the Council, which at least until recently has tended to result in less precautionary regulation. Second is the right of the Commission to initiate legislation, which frequently results in more precautionary regulation. Third is the fact that there traditionally has been no forum,

---

[29] See, e.g., *Van Gend en Loos v. Nederlandse Administratie der Belastingen*, Case 26/62, 1963 ECR 10, which held for the first time that Community law differed from "ordinary" international law and could therefore have direct effect in the Member States' legal order; *Marshall v. South-West Hampshire Area Health Authority*, Case 152/84, 1986 ECR 723; *Comitato de Coordinamento per la Diffesa della Cava v. Regione Lombardia*, Case C-236/92, 1994 ECR I-484. For a case finding a direct effect in the case of an obligation to prepare an environmental impact assessment for projects "where member states consider that their characteristics so require," see *Kraaijenveld and Others v. Gedeputeerde Staten van Zuid-Holland*, Case C-72/95, 1996 E.C.R. I-5431. The "direct effect" doctrine is similar to the doctrine in international law of "directly effective" treaties or provisions thereof, and could be said to reflect the continuing underlying connections of the EU legislative process to treaty-making processes. In addition, a theory of "indirect effect" has been developed by the European Court. This doctrine stipulates that "a national court is required to interpret its national law in the light of the wording and the purpose" of an applicable directive: *Marleasing SA v. Le Comercial Internacional de Alimentacion SA*, Case C-106/89, 1990 ECR I 4153, at I-4158, para. 7.

such as is found in "cabinet government" at the national level, through which other ministries can moderate the views of the environmental ministers acting as the EU Council—which frequently results in more stringent legislation than would otherwise have been enacted.[30] Fourth is the increasing power of the Parliament, almost always exerting pressure for more precautionary legislation.

A fifth important way in which the legislative process can influence risk regulation, both as to substance and as to procedure, involves the legal basis in the treaty chosen as the authority for legislation. First, the legal basis chosen governs the legislative process used during enactment. This in turn governs the modes of participation, voting rules, and powers, during that process of the various EU institutions—the Council, the Parliament, the Commission, and the Member States. Second, the legal basis chosen arguably can affect the level of precaution required. For example, if the legislation to be adopted has more than an "incidental" effect on harmonizing market conditions in the EU (or if its "center of gravity" does, where it has more than one objective), then Article 114 of the 2009 TFEU (formerly Article 95, EC Treaty), a section dealing with the establishment of an internal market, must be chosen in lieu of some other specialized provision governing specific types of risk regulation such as Article 192 of the 2009 TFEU, empowering the EU to adopt environmental legislation. Where these Article 114 "internal market" measures concern "health, safety, environmental protection and consumer protection," Article 114(3) requires that Commission proposals must "take as a base a high level of protection, taking account in particular of any new development based on scientific facts." (As noted earlier, the term "high level of protection" is not defined.) While Article 192 imposes a similar requirement (Articles 168(1) and 169(1) of the 2009 TFEU), the environment ministers and the green parties in the Parliament can exercise greater control under Article 192 of the 2009 TFEU, meaning internal market considerations have less weight there. As a result, Article 192 legislation tends to be more precautionary, in the sense of more stringent. By way of exception to qualified majority voting pursuant to Articles 192 and 294 of the TFEU (formerly Articles 175 and 251, EC Treaty), when environmental measures are "primarily of a fiscal nature," regulate land use or water resource management, or significantly affect energy supply, they must be adopted by a unanimous vote, not by qualified majority, with the normal result being a *lower* degree of precaution (Article 192(2) of the 2009 TFEU; formerly Article 175, EC Treaty).

Third, the legal basis chosen will also govern to what extent, and how, existing more stringent Member State risk regulation is preempted, as well as to what extent,

---

[30] There is, however, a consultation process within the Commission, which takes place before draft legislation is presented, and there is now a Competitiveness Council, which is intended to check the power of specialist ministers sitting as the Council and to guard the competitiveness of EU industry. Note also that in Denmark, a minister must get cabinet approval before voting on proposed EU legislation. These mechanisms, while not terribly successful in the past in broadening the perspectives brought to bear on risk regulation, may have some effect in the future. See, e.g., *ENDS Environment Daily* (2004).

and how, Member States can enact more stringent legislation in the future on the same subject. For example, under Article 114(4) of the 2009 TFEU, Member States may "maintain" more stringent national law provisions, and only under the strict conditions of Article 114(5) (formerly Article 95(5), EC Treaty), they may "introduce" more stringent requirements, whereas Article 193 of the 2009 TFEU (formerly Article 176, EC Treaty) permits them to "maintain *or introduce*" more stringent provisions.

In short, to the extent that the legal basis is chosen (where there is discretion to do so) based on risk preferences in the various institutional agendas of the legislating institutions, particularly that of the Council vis-à-vis the Parliament and the Commission, the structure of the legislative process may have a major influence on the degree of precaution in the resulting risk legislation. Even where, however, the institutional agendas driving a choice of legal basis are focused on factors other than a desired impact on degree of precaution in the resulting legislation, the choice of legal basis may have an important incidental impact on degree of desired precaution. In either case, it is still difficult to generalize about the direction of overall impact on degree of precaution, since that direction will be a result of the outcome of the political struggle among EU institutions with specific risk preferences in specific situations.

Rulemaking. The U.S. rulemaking process can delay precautionary rulemaking. While it can be susceptible to various degrees of regulatory "capture" (by NGOs as well as by industry), the impact on stringency will be a function of which group does the capture. In any case, various safeguards may ameliorate the impact of such capture on either timing or stringency of resulting precautionary regulation. The EU rulemaking process is not open to public scrutiny, is less politically and judicially accountable, and is more susceptible to capture by public or private institutional actors with agendas that diverge from any transmitted aggregate risk preferences of citizens. Lacking as it does some of the U.S. system's formal safeguards, we believe that this tendency can have a decisive impact on degree of precaution, depending on which such agendas capture and drive the process in specific directions in specific instances.

United States. The U.S. administrative process uses "notice and comment" rulemaking under the U.S. Administrative Procedure Act (APA) to promulgate implementing measures (ABA 2006). This process serves notice on the public generally, and the regulated community specifically, of federal agency initiation of precautionary rulemaking. The process gives a highly structured opportunity for interested persons to have access to the regulatory action proposed and the agency reasoning and factual record supporting its proposals so that such interested parties may comment on both the factual basis and the policy embodied in it. The APA also requires that agencies produce a reasoned written explanation for their choices and decisions, and it provides standards for judicial review. Specific risk regulatory statutes may also prescribe supplementary or substitute administrative or judicial procedures. We suspect, however, that the impact of this process, while it tends to promote efficient and accurate transmission of public risk preferences to, and accountability of, officials, is neutral as to level of stringency in the resulting regulation.[31]

The APA rulemaking process may, however, affect timing in several ways. First, it facilitates the transmission of public risk preferences to officials, which may make such transmission speedier than it otherwise would be. The APA also provides for petitions to agencies to initiate rulemaking actions that are within their statutory authority, which can force agencies to take more timely precautionary action. Further, many specific statutes require agencies to take regulatory action, and both those statutes (in citizen suit mandamus provisions) and the APA (in provisions allowing judicial review for agency failure to act, in the face of a duty or a request to act, where the agency inaction can be construed as "final agency action") allow persons with standing (liberally construed under U.S. law) to bring a judicial review action in the relevant federal district or appeals court to force the agency to initiate rulemaking or to defend its decision not to do so. These tools have been used to great effect by NGOs to influence the timing of precautionary regulation, sometimes forcing agencies to act before they would otherwise have done so. As a result, EPA has at times been effectively in judicial receivership in federal district court in the implementation of some of its programs under, for example, the Clean Water Act, when it has been unable to keep up with congressionally mandated statutory deadlines for its actions. Finally, however, the APA rulemaking process can slow down government decisionmaking, particularly in conjunction with the judicial review process. The relevant question is whether any delay in government decisionmaking is worth the gain in better transmission of public risk preferences and in agency accountability.

European Union. The European administrative law system at the EU level is considerably less well developed than in the United States. No EU APA with judicially enforceable rights exists, and no judicial review of EU policy, legislation, and implementing measures takes place other than at the behest of Community institutions.[32] The process of adopting implementing measures takes place in the EU in

---

[31] It may be argued that the protracted building of an administrative record by agencies, thought necessary by them to satisfy intensive judicial review by courts, results in less stringent regulation, as well as just in delay (Charnley and Elliott 2002). We believe, however, that any effect here, whether by delay or stringency, may be as much caused by overreaction by risk-averse bureaucrats as by the stringency of judicial review. See the section of this chapter below titled "Judicial Review."

[32] The proposed EU Constitution did not provide for a private right to judicial review and did not require the adoption of APA-like legislation (Treaty establishing a Constitution for Europe, OJ C 310/1, December 16, 2004); also see Article II-107 and Article 47 of the Charter of Fundamental Rights: "everyone whose rights and freedoms guaranteed by the law of the Union are violated has the right to an effective remedy before a tribunal"—but not necessarily through an independent court. While some movement toward citizen suit rights appeared in proposed legislation implementing the Aarhus Convention, the rights contemplated are more in the nature of limited environmental and citizen group enforcement rights against Member States or regulated industry than any generalized right to challenge EU government action through judicial review.

two main ways: through the so-called "comitology" process and through the so-called "standards" process. Neither is as straightforward and transparent as the U.S. APA rulemaking process. Further, the legal power to delegate "legislative" (as opposed to "implementation") powers is unclear in EU law (see Chapter 16 of this volume and Yataganas 2001 for discussions of legal issues associated with EU legislative delegation). The questions as to whether and when to delegate, pursuant to what instructions, and how broadly or narrowly have been caught up in both the horizontal and vertical power struggles among the EU institutions.

EU risk legislation originally tended to be vague and general, thus retaining real discretion over risk levels at the Member State level during implementation. When it became clear that such legislation was resulting in an implementation and enforcement "deficit," the EU changed course. In light of the lack of a well-defined process for adopting implementing measures at the EU level—as well as Member State reluctance to give the Commission powers to elaborate general legislative provisions through implementing rules—EC legislation became more specific, incorporating into legislation details that would have been reserved for implementing administrative regulations in the United States. Finding such legislative specificity difficult if not unworkable in a dynamic environment, EU legislation has now become again more general, frequently being limited to establishing a "framework" for regulation. "The supposed advantage of this New Approach," Hunter (2001, 7) explains, "is twofold. For industry, it gets to write the detailed rules applying to it. For the Commission, the New Approach frees it of a burdensome task; it also allows the Commission to claim that it has nothing to do with writing the standards, and hence cannot be held accountable." Under such legislation, the EC legislature typically delegates the tasks of filling in detail, implementing, and updating legislation (so-called "adaptation to technological progress") to one of two processes. Each is under the *supervision* of the Commission, but each is conducted by entities independent of the Commission but over each of which Member States have carefully retained strong elements of Member State control or influence. The two processes are "comitology," using technical or regulatory committees of Member State government bureaucrats,[33] or the "standards" process, using, for example, European standardization bodies like the Comité Européen de Normalisation (CEN), on which both Member State bureaucrats and industry

---

[33] Perhaps to reduce to some extent the EC's reliance on comitology, in which Member State bureaucrats can have a strong hand, the Commission is in favor of establishing new regulatory agencies that would operate under a clearly defined mandate (European Commission 2001b). Some suggest use of independent agencies that are not accountable to the Commission (Chapter 16 of this volume). As Commissioner Bolkestein observes, however, separate regulatory agencies raise accountability issues. "We cannot have officials who are accountable to no one. They can only be accountable to the Commission." Perhaps in an effort to minimize this issue, and perhaps to ensure its own control, the Commission proposes that independent agencies would not be empowered to "arbitrate between conflicting public interests, exercise political discretion, or carry out complex assessments." (Bolkestein 2002, 24). So neutered, it is hard to see how they could play any useful role in adopting risk regulation.

representatives sit. Thus, the Member States have attempted to ensure in each case that they retain much control over the process of delegated legislation. It is not clear that in fact, however, the Commission does not get its way most of the time, at least with regard to comitology (European Commission 2003a). Both processes are complex and confusing. They lack transparency, lack clear political and judicial accountability— indeed the "standards" process delegates decisionmaking to essentially private, nongovernmental standards bodies—and have been strongly criticized on these grounds (Christiansen and Kirchner 2000, 1). The Commission's response to such criticism has not been to propose structural change, but rather to include environmental groups in the process,[34] which is likely to lead increasingly to standards that reflect the agendas of all of the special interest groups granted participation rights.

The EU institutions have recognized the need to improve the quality of both legislation and administrative regulation. In the area of environmental regulation, the EU ratified the Aarhus Convention on Access to Information, Public Participation in Decision-Making and Access to Justice in Environmental Matters, providing for public participation in procedures such as decisionmaking on specific activities; the preparation of environmental plans, programs, and policies; and the preparation of executive regulations and other generally applicable legally binding normative instruments (Aarhus 1998). In 2003, the EU adopted two directives to implement Aarhus with respect to Member State governments, dealing with public access to environmental information in Member States and with regard to public participation in Member States (European Parliament 2003a, 2003b). On October 24, 2003, the Commission proposed a "package" of three legislative proposals to complete implementation of Aarhus by dealing with access to information and public participation at the level of the EU institutions, and with judicial review at both the EU and Member State levels (European Parliament 2003c). The EC has since adopted regulation EC/1367/2006 (September 6, 2006, in force since June 28, 2007) implementing the Aarhus Convention (for more details, see Sand, Chapter 13 of this volume). A Commission proposal for a "recast" Aarhus regulation, which has just passed Parliament, is currently in the legislative process.

Both the Aarhus Convention and its EU implementing measures apply only to precautionary regulation in the environmental field. Further, even in the area of environmental regulation, neither the Aarhus Convention itself nor the proposed EU implementation of it provides strong judicial review rights for affected individuals, especially regarding illegality of government action in general, as opposed to regarding access to information

---

[34] A recent Commission communication is aimed at "improving the participation of environmental experts and representatives of environmental interests in the Technical Committees that develop standards." The Commission notes that "participation in these committees is open, but some groups may need more encouragement to get involved. For example, the Commission funds the European Environmental Citizens Organisation for Standardisation (ECOS) to ensure that environmental concerns are expressed and considered when standards are developed" (European Commission 2004).

or "citizen enforcement" of environmental law.[35] This lack of provision for strong executive branch and administrative accountability through broad and widely available judicial review will seriously weaken the effectiveness of the other, more specifically provided public participation rights, even in the limited area of environmental regulation.

The Commission has also produced a 2001 report on improving and simplifying the regulatory process and a White Paper on European Governance (European Commission 2001a, 2001b). In June 2002, the Commission issued a "Better Lawmaking" package of communications (European Commission 2002b). None of these, however, provides for real accountability at the EU level through broad public rights to judicial review. Where the EU does grant standing rights to initiate judicial review of government decisions, it tends to limit challenge to lack of enforcement of existing law (as opposed to challenging to the validity of law), and to provide a legislative right to challenge only in an asymmetrical manner, by granting such privileges solely to environmental groups, not to regulated industry.[36]

The EU administrative rulemaking process, in short, is more complex, less responsive to public input, and less accountable than that in the United States. Thus, since the EU process lacks effective judicial enforceability by the public of many of the safeguards found in the APA, we conclude that it likely does a worse job of transmitting public risk preferences efficiently and accurately than is the case in the United States, and that it likely gives greater scope to public officials to advance their own agendas, whether institutional, personal, or borrowed from third parties, without regard to the public's aggregated risk preferences.[37] Whether this process results in more or less

---

[35] In addition to requiring opportunities for national-level review in "a court of law" or "other independent and impartial body established by law" (but not necessarily a court) of its access to information and public participation obligations as those have been transmuted into national law, the Convention requires that national law allow judicial *or administrative* challenge to "acts and omissions by private persons and public authorities *which contravene provisions of its national law relating to the environment*" (thus, only to violations of substantive environmental law, not as to the validity of such law) by entities that "meet the criteria, if any, laid down in … national law" (thus requiring no change in national standing law) (Article 9(1)–(3); emphasis added).

[36] Regulation (EC) 1367/2006 implementing the Aarhus Convention on environmental matters provides that so-called "qualified entities" (basically, environmental groups meeting certain conditions) do not have to show a sufficient interest or impairment of a right for obtaining standing to initiate review of administrative acts or omissions *in breach of* environmental law (European Parliament and Council 2006). Likewise, the Environmental Liability Directive provides, in connection with standing, to initiate judicial review by "approved" environmental NGOs of the procedural and substantive legality of decisions, acts, or failures to act by the authorities under the directive, by providing that "the interest of *any non-governmental organization promoting environmental protection and meeting requirements under national law* shall be deemed sufficient for [standing] purposes" (Article 12(1), Directive, 2004/35; emphasis added).

[37] This conclusion should not, of course, be surprising. The current institutional design of the EU is driven largely, and is very expressly intended to be so driven, by concepts of institutional balance and control, with "sovereign" Member States playing an anchor role. It is not driven mainly by notions of direct representation of the EU public, although this paradigm is slowly evolving as the Parliament gains more power and as the proposed EU Constitution has been drafted.

timely and stringent risk regulation depends on which institutional or interest group agenda captures the process and drives it at any point in time and on specific issues. The EU's tendency to grant privileged standing rights to environmental groups, however, will likely increasingly result in judicial review of certain types of government acts that are less precautionary than these groups prefer, which in turn may well cause government decisions to gravitate toward higher levels of precaution than would otherwise be the case, and perhaps than aggregated public preferences would support.

Choosing Policy Instruments and Integrating Policy.   It may be argued that choice of policy instrument can have an effect on degree of precaution (e.g., that "ambient air quality regulation," which allows use of "tall stacks," is less precautionary or stringent than "best technology" emissions limit requirements). That argument seems unpersuasive, however, in terms of causation, because policy instruments are just that—instruments or tools through which policy choices about degree of precaution are implemented. They generally simply reflect those choices. They do, however, have different costs and different effectiveness in different situations. Choosing the most apt and the least socially expensive method of regulation thus may allow earlier regulation, or higher levels of stringency, for a given cost, because such a choice will lower the overall social cost of regulation at any time or level of stringency, everything else being equal.

Both the United States and the EU are, on the whole, free to use, and in fact largely do use, a relatively full panoply of policy instruments in different situations and in executing different choices as to degree of precaution, especially as to level of stringency. The EU system, however, does not provide for use of administrative civil penalties to the same extent as does the United States, and both systems have political difficulties using fiscal measures, such as taxes, as market regulatory instruments. The fact that one system has chosen one policy instrument in a specific situation, however, and the other has chosen a different one in the same situation, may be indicative of different risk choices, but it is not normally likely to have useful explanatory power in and of itself. The real issue is why the differing choices of policy instruments were made in each case.

What is true of choice of policy instrument may or may not be true of the extent of policy integration. It seems possible that fragmentation of jurisdiction over various risks or sources may impede effective implementation of any given choice of degree of precaution, either because it delays adoption of, or simply renders ineffective, a coordinated approach to a problem when a coordinated approach is necessary to the success of the degree of precaution chosen. Both U.S. and EU systems have "stovepipe" problems at both the legislative and the administrative levels, and both within and among the institutional actors in each case. We doubt that there is any decided overall advantage in either system, and thus suggest that this factor does not have any real power to explain, on a generic basis, the observed degree of precaution. The possible exception relates to precaution as actually achieved, rather than as promulgated on the face of the relevant requirement. Here, the continuing EU deficit in implementation at the Member State level and its similar deficit in uniform and effective enforcement against the regulated community can to some extent be explained by lack of effective vertical integration (see discussion above). These implementation and enforcement deficits result in different levels of achieved precaution in some risk areas—air, water, and waste regulation at a minimum. It might also be argued that the tendency toward more stringent regulation due to the traditional dominance of the EU Council by national *environment* ministers, unchecked by their cabinet peers, also represents an example of impact on degree of precaution, here due to a lack of horizontal integration (see above).

Administrative Implementation.   Unimplemented risk legislation does not achieve the desired degree of precaution. U.S. risk regulation is much better implemented than EU risk regulation. To that extent, it tends to be more precautionary.

United States. U.S. risk regulation requirements tend, in our judgment, to be well implemented. The administrative and judicial processes at the federal level give interested parties many tools to ensure that federal agencies take the implementing steps required by Congress, and that they enforce regulatory requirements against the regulated parties once they are set.

Some of U.S. federal risk regulation, however, especially in the environmental area, is required, to a large degree, to be implemented at the state level. Ensuring adequate legislative and administrative implementation at the state level is more difficult, but nonetheless it is reasonably well assured by the U.S. federal legislation, through a series of devices well illustrated in U.S. air, water, and waste legislation (Smith 1992).

European Union. The situation is quite different in the EU. First, to the extent that implementation is to be done at the EU level, there are few if any of the private party administrative, judicial review, and citizen suit mandamus rights that are key to adequate implementation at the federal level in the United States.[38]

Second, much more of the implementation of EU legislation has traditionally been left to the authorities of the individual Member States through use of directives rather than regulations. The implementation of EU legislation at the Member State level is perhaps the weakest element of the EU risk regulatory framework. For example, EU law and the Commission lack virtually all of the mechanisms used by the U.S. Environmental Protection Agency (EPA) in the more centralized U.S. federal system to ensure adequate and relatively uniform implementation and enforcement of the many

---

[38] There are, of course, many nonbinding declarations of policy and intent and regulatory reform proposals by EU bureaucrats as to, e.g., transparency and accountability, many of which have been referred to above. These do not, however, have binding effect and could not be enforced by judicial review in any case, except perhaps by other EU institutions, which may have little incentive to do so if their institutional powers or jurisdictions are not imperiled, or if they would themselves be threatened by any precedents established.

aspects of U.S. environmental law that are required to be implemented and enforced, as a primary matter, by the states. There is no reason in principle that these mechanisms could not be used under even existing EU law. What has been lacking is political will by the Member States.

The degree to which EU directives are effectively implemented has varied widely from country to country, and there is a widely acknowledged and documented enforcement deficit in this regard (European Council 2004). While some Member States do not give full effect to directives until long after adoption, other states adopt even stricter measures than those adopted at the Union level. The environmental law systems of the new Member States that joined the EU on May 1, 2004, now generally transpose the EU's environmental "acquis," or corpus of law and requirements, albeit with various forms of temporal derogations. To what extent this legislation is effectively implemented and enforced in the newest Member States at this point, however, is an entirely different matter.

Enforcement.   As with lack of implementation, lack of enforcement against the regulated party prevents risk regulation from achieving its intended degree of precaution. Here again, risk regulation is much better enforced against regulated parties in the United States than in the EU, and thus is more precautionary.

United States. Enforcement in the United States is vigorous and takes a number of forms. Nearly all of the major U.S. environmental regulatory statutes, for example, require some form of publicly available self-monitoring and reporting by the regulated party. Civil and criminal penalties for failure to report in the U.S. system provide significant incentives for compliance with such requirements. The system thereby automatically highlights lapses in compliance and the need for enforcement. When EPA deems state enforcement against regulated parties to be inadequate, it normally has the authority at any time to override the state's failure and to issue an administrative order or, in some situations, to assess civil penalties on an administrative basis. In either case, EPA may enforce its administrative action in federal court, or it can bypass administrative action in the first place and take the underlying violation directly into federal court for injunctive relief or civil or criminal penalties. Should EPA fail to enforce, citizens and environmental groups can themselves normally prosecute the violations in federal court under citizen enforcement suit provisions.

European Union. Even where EU directives are timely and correctly transposed, enforcement in the EU against the regulated community is a different matter. The EU does not have the power to enforce national implementing legislation; that is up to the Member State authorities. Even EU regulations, while directly applicable to regulated entities, must normally be enforced by Member States in Member State courts. Thus, at the level of enforcement of specific standards, requirements, or permit conditions against an individual regulated facility, the EU plays virtually no role.[39] Enforcement is sometimes difficult, even when attempted by Member States, since clear and precise regulatory requirements and self-monitoring and reporting obligations have not always been uniformly imposed, either by regulation or by permit conditions. Since 1992, the EU has vigorously promoted information exchange among Member State environmental regulatory authorities to improve standards of permitting, inspection, monitoring, and enforcement, through the IMPEL network (Fifth Annual Survey 2003). Government failure to prosecute generally cannot effectively be challenged except through publicity and the political process. In some Member States, citizens may have enforcement powers, in particular where criminal violations are involved.

Judicial Review.   As long as courts do not impose their own agendas on the other branches of government, strong and effective judicial review should not in principle affect degree of stringency in risk regulation, although a lengthy or complex process of judicial review might cause delay in all forms of regulation, including risk regulation, thus affecting degree of precaution in terms of timeliness. There may be some effect on timing due to judicial review in the United States, but little impact in the EU, where judicial review is much weaker and is normally only available (due to narrowly framed standing rules) to institutions, not the public, in challenging the legality of legislation and regulations.

United States. Under U.S. law, judicial review of administrative agency action is available in the federal courts under broad rules of standing that allow affected private parties to challenge agency decisions and receive injunctive relief. Errors of law are reviewed *de novo* under all circumstances. As to errors of "policy"—that is, errors with regard to matters of statutory interpretation where Congress has not "directly spoken to the precise question at issue"—"the question for the court is whether the agency's answer is based on a permissible construction of the statute" (*Chevron v. NRDC*, 467 U.S. 837, 841–843 (1984)). Errors of fact in rulemaking, under the "hard look" approach, are reviewed for support by substantial evidence in the record taken as a whole, and when such substantial evidence is found lacking, the agency action is judged to be arbitrary, capricious, and an abuse of discretion. Agencies are required to properly interpret the scope or ambit of their delegated discretion, and errors in doing so are reviewed *de novo* as errors of law. Errors in the exercise (but not the permitted ambit) of

---

[39] As Hunter has reminded us, in the debate in the 1780s about a proposed U.S. federal government, Alexander Hamilton commented on the characteristics of a confederation as follows: "The great and radical vice in the construction of the existing Confederation is in the principle of legislation for states or governments, in their corporate or collective capacities, and as contradistinguished from the individuals of which they consist" (Hunter 1995, 6, quoting Hamilton in The Federalist No. 15 (1996, 161); see Ketcham 1986). Hamilton added that "[i]f ... the measures of the Confederacy cannot be executed without the intervention of the particular administrations, there will be little prospect of their being executed at all."

policy or discretion are reviewed under an arbitrary, capricious, or abuse of discretion standard, in which agencies are required to have actually exercised their permitted discretion, and to have used reasoned decisionmaking in the way in which they exercised their permitted discretion. Failure as to these last two constraints constitutes agency action that is arbitrary, capricious, and an abuse of discretion. An agency rulemaking action can be reversed, reversed and remanded, or simply remanded for some specific defect without being reversed.

Thus, while U.S. courts have struggled with how they should deal with judicial review of risk management decisionmaking, they have not to date second-guessed either Congress or the executive branch as to stringency of risk regulation. They have insisted only that agency exercise of discretion under statutes remain within the bounds set by Congress; that delegated discretion be actually exercised; and that when it is exercised, it constitute reasoned decisionmaking—that is, be a reasonable (nonarbitrary) choice within the ambit of permitted discretion. Most policy judgments inherent in risk management decisions, as long as they are within the bounds set by Congress in the language of the statute, will thus be governed by a relatively lenient test of arbitrariness. U.S. federal judicial review law has always maintained, however, and continues to require, that agencies must provide substantial evidence in the record as a whole to support fact determinations, since failure to do so constitutes arbitrary agency action.

Charnley and Elliot (2002) have argued that judges have in some cases required "factual support in the administrative record for deciding that a risk to health is 'significant' enough to merit regulation." They argue that this "significance" test conceives of "risk assessment as fundamentally an issue of fact," which results in subordinating "policy considerations to 'facts.'" This, they say, "misunderstand[s] the nature of risk assessment and undervalue[s] expert judgment and policy considerations." The argument seems to be that "more demanding" judicial review requiring a "demonstrated factual basis for risk-based decisions" leads to less precautionary decisionmaking, because agencies are put to extensive work to prepare adequate factual records to support risk decisions.

It may well be that agencies put an inordinate amount of time and energy into preparing an administrative record with support for the facts underlying a risk decision, and that they shy away from more precautionary regulation as a result. All most courts seem to require, however, is that they provide substantial evidence in the record as a whole to support the factual determinations *that underpin their risk choices*, not the risk choices themselves. Making relevant and material factual determinations without adequate factual support would constitute a paradigm of arbitrary agency behavior. The risk policy choices made in light of the facts, however, especially where facts are uncertain, are normally (and properly) reviewed under a relatively more deferential reasoned decisionmaking standard to determine whether they are arbitrary, capricious, and an abuse of discretion, as long as they remain *within the boundaries* set by Congress in the language of the statute, and as long as the permitted discretion is actually *exercised* by the agency. Thus, any significant impact on either the timing or stringency of agency risk decisions would seem chiefly to lie not at the feet of the reviewing courts or the judicial review process as such, but perhaps rather more at the feet of risk-averse bureaucrats.[40] Still, the end result may be the same—that judicial review may cause reactions by the bureaucrats whose decisions are being reviewed that tend to cause not just delay in precautionary regulation, but also, perhaps, less stringency.

European Union. EU institutions have a right of judicial review of EU actions in the European Court of Justice.[41] Such actions are sparingly brought (except for Commission enforcement actions against Member States over implementation of EU legislation). When actions other than Commission enforcement actions are brought, the institutions are normally intent on vindicating their own institutional interests, which revolve around institutional jurisdiction and authority, rather than challenging the validity under the treaties of substantive provisions of EU legislation, or the legal or policy conformity of EU administrative actions with implementing legislation.

Private parties, as a general rule, do not have standing to challenge binding EC regulations or directives (as opposed to "decisions," which can be appealed by those to whom they are addressed), even where such legislation violates the treaty, fundamental rights, or general principles of EU law. Subject to a limited exception—when a regulation is said to be a disguised decision—private rights of action against generally binding rules cannot be asserted under EU rules of standing, unless an individual is both "directly" and "individually" affected (Article 263, TFEU; formerly Article 230,

---

[40] Bureaucrats, being human, may heap mountains of facts into the record in an overreaction to judicial review decisions, or in an effort to gloss over an unwillingness to spell out with precision but brevity the core of the matter—their permitted ambit of discretion and how they have exercised that discretion in making their risk policy choice in light of the facts in the record.

[41] This institutional right to judicial review is a major element of the checks and balances in the EU system, performing in some ways the same function as separation of powers in the United States. For the reasons outlined in text above and below, however, this tool is not necessarily used by EU institutions to prevent use by other EU institutions of institutional agendas that are separate from, and extraneous to, the accurate and timely implementation of aggregated public risk preferences, although it could be used for that purpose if an EU institution had an incentive to do so. In addition to such traditional, formal legal remedies as it contains, EU law also provides for certain informal "remedies," such as filing a complaint with a national government or the Commission, or with the European ombudsman. Private parties damaged by failure of Member States to properly implement EU directives can also sue Member States for damages under the *Francovich* case (*Francovich v. Italy*, Cases C-6, 9-90, [1991] ECR I-5357). This amounts, in effect, to an indirect form of judicial review of Member State implementation of EU law and can be used by a party who has suffered damages to test and deter various forms of Member State failure to implement EU law properly. Its direct purpose, however, is to ensure reparation for such damages. The *Francovich* doctrine does not provide for injunctive relief against the government, either alone or in addition to damages.

EC Treaty).[42] This lack of adequate private action rights against generally binding legislation and regulation is a severe defect in the architecture of the EU's institutional system that is not generally recognized in Europe as such.

The Commission's recent regulatory reform initiatives, listed above, tend to deal with the front end of the lawmaking and rulemaking process generally, and public participation particularly, championing such concepts as impact assessment, access, transparency, and stakeholder involvement. They tend not to deal with issues like standing to invoke, and accountability through judicial review of EU government decisions at the behest of affected individuals (as opposed to judicial review initiated by EU institutions, judicial review of Member State actions for conformity with EU law, and citizen enforcement actions against regulated entities). Such a failure will weaken effective implementation of those reform measures they do provide for. They are so recent that it is difficult to say whether they are having any impact in making more efficient or accurate the transmission and integration into EU risk regulation of aggregated public risk preferences and in controlling use of private or institutional agendas by EU public officials. They may have had some impact on the former, and may have more in the future, but the extent of the impact is not likely to be as great as if EU officials were held accountable for the legality and quality of their decisions through widely available judicial review. Any impact on the latter point—control of official EU abuse of power—is likely to be nil in the absence of real public accountability through strong and effective judicial review at the behest of private interested parties.

Ex Post *Remedial Systems*

The nine comparisons above detailed *ex ante* lawmaking institutions and processes. The final section of this chapter looks at *ex post* systems for remedying inadequate policy.

---

[42] The language of Article 230 of the EU Treaty says "of direct and individual concern." A person is not individually concerned if he or she is affected only as a member of a general class (Hartley 2003, 360–361). To be individually concerned, a person must be affected "by reason of certain attributes which are peculiar to them or by reason of circumstances in which they are differentiated from all other persons and by virtue of these factors distinguishes them individually just as in the case of the person addressed" (*Plaumann v. Commission*, Case 25/62, [1963] ECR 95 at 107). A substantial body of ECJ jurisprudence since the *Plaumann* case details the meaning of "individual concern" (see the above discussion of EU implementation of the Aarhus Convention). The proposed EU Constitution would have expanded standing for private parties by creating a right of action with respect to "a regulatory act which is of direct concern to him or her and does not entail implementing measures" (Article III-365(4), Treaty establishing a Constitution for Europe, OJ C 310 (December 16, 2004)). The term "regulatory act," however, is defined to exclude legislative acts (Article I-33(1)). This explicit grant of standing in respect of "regulatory acts" might have the effect of persuading the courts to use a stricter definition of "individual concern" in the case of regulations that constitute disguised decisions. Further, Articles I-29(1) and II-207 might initiate an EU constitutional law right to have at the national law level a judicial review cause of action and standing going beyond "individual" concern, but Article I-29(1)'s limitation to "remedies . . . sufficient to ensure effective legal protection" may be interpreted to exclude standing rights.

Civil Liability/Tort Systems.   The United States has a strong—perhaps too strong—tort system, but also a strong regulatory system. The EU has a strong civil liability system that provides more accurate compensation than does the U.S. tort system, but a less strong regulatory system. It is not clear that either tort/civil liability system has any real impact on the degree of precaution in *ex ante* risk regulation, despite good theoretical arguments that it might have.

Liability of Private Persons for Causing Harm.   The United States has a strong tort liability system—indeed, one that we and others believe overcompensates and is in many ways out of control (Bergkamp 2003, 413–465; 2001, 67–154). Being part of the common-law tradition, tort law in the United States is predominantly state law, but for a number of reasons, state tort laws have converged to a significant extent. The EU has no comprehensive EU-level tort liability system, although it has adopted some liability law, including a product liability directive (Directive 85/374) and an environmental liability directive (Directive 2004/35). Thus, as in the United States, where state, not federal, tort law predominates, civil liability in Europe is largely governed by Member State law, but European Member State civil liability systems have not converged to the same extent as the U.S. state-level tort liability systems.

While many of their applicable substantive rules are similar, the two civil liability systems differ significantly on institutional and procedural matters. In the United States, the existence of contingent fees for counsel, class actions, extensive discovery rights, trial by jury (with the jury frequently determining both the outcome and the extent of the damage award), damages for pain and suffering, and punitive damages, among other things, all make the system highly volatile and unpredictable, especially as to the amount of the awards of damages. European civil liability systems have none of these mechanisms, are much more in the control of the judges, are more stable, and produce smaller and more predictable damage awards that are far more likely to reflect actual damages suffered (Bergkamp and Hunter 1996, 399–418).

Wiener (2003) has suggested that the existence of a strong civil liability system that can step into provide compensation for risks once they have matured into damage may be an incentive for legislators to provide less stringent *ex ante* risk reduction. Indeed, if a liability system generates adequate incentives for prevention of a particular category of risks, regulation of that category of risks may not be deemed necessary. Because liability's deterrent effect results from the obligation to compensate for harm caused, however, liability does not provide adequate deterrence where defendants' assets are insufficient, causation cannot be proved, harm is conceptually or practically difficult to measure in terms of monetary damages, or it is inefficient to prove causation (e.g., where many small harms are involved). In these situations, legislators may want to supplement the liability system with specific *ex ante* regulation, no matter how good the tort or civil liability system is. Further, for liability to generate appropriate incentives, the outcomes of lawsuits must be sufficiently predictable and foreseeable, in terms of both whether liability will be imposed and, if so, how much compensation will be due. If liability judgments are to some degree a "lottery," or the awards do not accurately reflect the actual size of losses caused, liability will generate random incentives that are unlikely to lead to adequate damage prevention. For these reasons, a strong liability system, like the U.S. tort system, does not necessarily lead to adequate, let alone optimal, damage prevention.

Consequently, where the liability system fails to create adequate incentives, a rational *ex ante* regulator would want to use direct or market-based regulation (assuming such regulatory processes work reasonably well), to reduce the externalization of costs to the point that marginal social costs (including the cost of *ex ante* regulation) and benefits were equal, without regard to the liability system. To the extent that a particular risk is "unavoidable" (however defined), or it is not "socially efficient" to reimpose costs through *ex ante* regulation, society faces the issue of who should bear the cost associated with such risks. In these situations, compensation can be made available to victims through the liability system. Some argue that the liability system should be used only to compensate, not to prevent, damage (van Dunné 1993, 175–189; Slagter 1952) or some social insurance program. Even in situations where "socially efficient" *ex ante* regulatory measures have been imposed, however, the government, on distributional grounds, may still want to use the liability regime to reimpose the *residual* costs of the risky activity on the actor. In a perfect world, such full "internalization" of costs will give actors a continuing incentive to engage in further risk reduction if cost and benefit factors should change (Bergkamp 2001, 271–76, raising the issue as to whether regulatory compliance should preclude or be a defense to civil liability).

While Wiener is clearly right, in theory, as to the incentives that a strong tort/civil liability system provides to *ex ante* legislators and regulators, we do not see a clear indication, in either the U.S. or the EU legal or administrative system, of any actual significant impact on degree of precaution in the resulting risk regulation. There is little, if any, empirical evidence to support an argument that liability, in fact, results in adequate prevention, and that regulators, in fact, forgo or reduce regulation on the grounds that the liability system adequately handles risks causing losses.

Liability of the State in Damages for Regulation Failures.

Recognizing the *ex ante* effect of liability regimes, Wiener (2003) has also hypothesized that "*ex ante* precaution may be *greater* where *ex post* remedies against the *regulator* are *stronger*." He notes that government policymaking in the United States is not normally subject to liability for damages, while this is not true in some European countries and the EU. He suggests that "European regulators may seek to employ stringent *ex ante* regulation in order to shield themselves from lawsuits that could be filed against them if they left small risks unregulated."[43] *Prima facie,* this theory has a certain plausibility. Under U.S. law, there

---

[43] It is not entirely clear whether Wiener refers to liability of individual regulators or liability of a government institution. However, whether it is one or the other would not appear to change the analysis in relevant respects. The same argument would apply to both the regulator in his or her individual capacity and the regulating government as an institution. Depending on institutional structure, however, the incentives of regulators to protect the government may not be as sharp as their incentives to protect themselves in their individual capacity.

is a strong barrier to tort actions against the government, since sovereign immunity normally bars damages liability for the government. In Europe, sovereign immunity is not a generally recognized doctrine, although in some jurisdictions and in some situations, some institutions may have immunity from suit. Thus, potential liability exposure might have an effect on European regulators but not on U.S. regulators.

Liability's incentive effects against regulators under EU law should not be exaggerated, however. At the EU level, private parties have standing to initiate actions for damages grounded in the Community's extra-contractual liability under Article 340, TFEU (formerly Article 288, EC Treaty)—although such actions have generally failed. Moreover, failure to regulate cannot be a ground for liability unless the EU had an obligation to regulate. Actions for failure to regulate under national law would also likely be unsuccessful, unless there is a positive obligation to regulate.

We should note that Member State liability under the *Francovich* doctrine would not appear to have much effect on European Member State regulators' incentives to adopt precautionary regulation. Because *Francovich* liability requires breach of an individual right granted by EU law (*Denkavit and Other v. Bundesamt für Finanzen*), Member States are not exposed to liability for failure to regulate where there is no EU directive that requires that they do so (and even then, the directive at issue must confer rights on individuals). *Francovich* liability is an instrument intended to ensure Member States' compliance with EU law obligations, not to create a comprehensive Member State liability system covering all forms of government failure. In short, while we agree in principle with Wiener's analysis of incentives, we do not see any apparent significant or systematic effect of state liability for damages *vel non* on resulting degree of precaution in risk regulation in either the United States or the EU.

Social Welfare or Private Insurance Systems.

Europe has strong, comprehensive government systems that cover out-of-pocket health care costs and loss of income due to disability, whatever the source of the personal injury or damage. The United States has less comprehensive coverage and relies on private insurance to a much larger degree. (For some extraordinary risks, the U.S. system provides for a mix of private and public insurance, such as the Price-Anderson Act in the case of nuclear risks.) In either case, however, to the extent that government social welfare programs or government or private insurance programs provide *ex post* compensation for damage due to risks materializing, it could be suggested that they would have the same influence on the incentives of *ex ante* regulators as does the ability of a civil liability/tort system to perform the same function. Indeed, it is generally believed that the existence of pervasive and comprehensive governmental health care systems in Europe, which compensate for out-of-pocket costs from personal injury from risks just as they do from other causes, helps explain why Europe has traditionally relied less heavily on a strong civil liability system dealing with product liability than has the United States, which has no pervasive or comprehensive government coverage of health costs and loss of income. To the extent, however, that social welfare or insurance systems perform primarily a compensation function because they do not fully recover from the actor causing the risk the amount of the loss in question (either directly, or indirectly through subrogation), there may be no real incentive for "rational" *ex ante* regulators to alter their assessment as to how much precaution to provide. The full amount of the external costs are not internalized to that actor—the person who needs an incentive to reduce the risk to economically efficient levels.

Thus, the theoretical basis for an impact from social welfare/private insurance systems on the resulting actual degree of precaution in risk regulation seems largely missing, and we see no apparent impact in any case.

References

Aarhus (Aarhus Convention on Access to Information, Public Participation in Decision-Making and Access to Justice in Environmental Matters). 1998. Articles 6, 7, and 8. Convention on Access to Information, Public Participation in Decision-Making and Access to Justice in Environmental Matters, Aarhus, June 23–25.

ABA (American Bar Association). 2006. *A Guide to Federal Rulemaking.* 4th ed. Washington, DC: ABA.

Aranson, Peter H., Ernest Gellhorn, and Glen O. Robinson. 1982. A Theory of Legislative Delegation. *Cornell Law Review* 68: 1.

Arrow, Kenneth. 1963. *Social Choice and Individual Values.* 2nd ed. New York: John Wiley and Sons.

Bergkamp, Lucas. 2001. *Liability and Environment: Public and Private Law Aspects of Civil Liability for Environmental Harm in an International Context.* The Hague: Kluwer Law International.

———. 2003. The State and Future of EC Government. In *European Community Law for the New Economy.* Antwerp: Intersentia, 641–746.

Bergkamp, Lucas, and Rod Hunter. 1996. Product Liability Litigation in the U.S. and Europe: Diverging Procedure and Damage Awards. *Maastricht Journal of International and Comparative Law* 3: 399–418.

Bolkestein, Frits. 2002. Interview by Jackie Davis. E-Sharp: 17. February.

Charnley, Gail, and Donald E. Elliott. 2002. Risk versus Precaution: Environmental Law and Public Health Protection. *Environmental Law Reporter* 32: 10363.

Christiansen, T., and E. Kirchner (eds). 2000. Introduction. In *Europe in Change: Committee Governance in the European Union.* Manchester: Manchester University Press.

Denkavit and Other v. Bundesamt für Finanzen. 1996. Joined Cases C-283/94, C-291/94, and C-292/94, 1996 ECR I-5063, paras. 47–50.

de Sadeleer, Nicholas. 2003. *Environmental Principles: From Political Slogans to Legal Rules.* Oxford: Oxford University Press.

Directive 85/374. 1985. Directive 85/374 Concerning Liability for Defective Products. *Official Journal* L 210. August 7.

Directive 2004/35. 2004. Directive 2004/35 on Environmental Liability with Regard to the Prevention and Remedying of Environmental Damage. *Official Journal* L 143/56. April 30.

Douma, W. 2000. The Precautionary Principle in the European Union. *Review of European Community and International Environmental Law* 9 (2): 132, 141.

ENDS Environment Daily. 2004. EU Competitiveness Council Focuses on Economic Factors to Achieve Social Cohesion and Sustainable Development. Issue 1777, November 26.

European Commission. 1997. Green Paper on the General Principles of Food Law in the European Union. COM (97) 176.

———. 2000. Communication on the Precautionary Principle. COM (2000) 1, 2. February. http://ec.europa.eu/dgs/health_consumer/library/pub/pub07_en.pdf (accessed May 18, 2010).

———. 2001a. Interim Report to the Stockholm European Council: Improving and Simplifying the Regulatory Environment. COM (2001) 130. March 7: 5.

———. 2001b. White Paper on European Governance. COM (2001) 428. July 25.

———. 2002a. Communication on Impact Assessment. COM (2002) 276. June 6: 5.

———. 2002b. Communication on European Governance: Better Lawmaking. COM (2002) 275. June 5. [The "Better Lawmaking" package includes four documents: a communication on European governance, an action plan on simplifying and improving the regulatory environment, a communication on impact assessment, and a document on consultation and dialogue.]

———. 2002c. Action Plan "Simplifying and Improving the Regulatory Environment." COM (2002) 278. June 5.

———. 2002d. Communication: Towards a Reinforced Culture of Consultation and Dialogue – Proposal for General Principles and Minimum Standards for Consultation of Interested Parties by the Commission. COM (2002) 277. June 5.

———. 2003a. Communication: Updating and Simplifying the Community Acquis [stating that the provisions of "Better Lawmaking" are not intended to be binding]. COM (2003) 71. February 11.

———. 2003b. Report on the Working of Committees during 2003. COM (2004) 860, 2005/C 65 E/01.

———. 2004. Commission Communication. Integration of Environmental Aspects into European Standardisation. SEC (2004) 206. http://eur-lex.europa.eu/LexUriServ/site/en/com/2004/com2004_0130en01.pdf (accessed May 18, 2010).

———. 2005a. Communication from the Commission to the Council and the European Parliament, Better Regulation for Growth and Jobs in the European Union. COM (2005) 97. March 16.

———. 2005b. Impact Assessment Guidelines. SEC (2005) 791. June 15.

———. 2009. Impact Assessment Guidelines. SEC (2009) 92. January 15.

European Council. 1993. Regulation 259/93/EEC of February 1 on the Supervision and Control of Shipments of Waste within, into and out of the European Community. *Official Journal* L 30. February 6.

———. 2004. Presidency Conclusions. March 26. http://ue.eu.int/ueDocs/cms_Data/docs/pressData/en/ec/79696.pdf (accessed May 18, 2010).

European Parliament. 2003a. Public Access to Environmental Information Repealing Council Directive 90/313/EEC. *Official Journal* L 41. February 14: 26. January 28.

———. 2003b. Providing for Public Participation in Respect of the Drawing Up of Certain Plans and Programmes relating to the Environment and Amending with regard to Public Participation and Access to Justice Council Directives 85/337/EEC and 96/61/EC. *Official Journal* L 156. June 25: 17. May 26.

———. 2003c. Proposal for a Directive on Access to Justice in Environmental Matters. COM (2003) 624. October 24; Proposal for a Regulation on the Application of the Provision of the Aarhus Convention to EC Institution and Body. COM (2003) 622. October 24.

European Parliament and Council. 2001. Decision on the Conclusion, on Behalf of the European Community, of the Convention on Access to Information, Public Participation in Decisionmaking and Access to Justice regarding Environmental Matters. COM (2001) 130. March 7.

———. 2006. Regulation (EC) 1367/2006 of 6 September 2006 on the application of the provisions of the Aarhus Convention on Access to Information, Public Participation in Decision-making and Access to Justice in Environmental Matters to Community Institutions and Bodies. *Official Journal* L 264/13, 25 September.

Farber, D. A., and P. P. Frickey. 1988. Legislative Intent and Public Choice. *Virginia Law Review* 74: 423.

Fifth Annual Survey (Fifth Annual Survey on the Implementation and Enforcement of Community Environmental Law). 2003. Brussels, July 27. SEC (2004) 1025: 23–28.

Hahn, Robert W., and Robert E. Litan. 2004. Counting Regulatory Benefits and Costs: Lessons for the U.S. and Europe. Regulatory Analysis 04-07. Washington, DC: AEI-Brookings Joint Center for Regulatory Studies.

Hamilton, A. 1996. The Federalist No. 15. In *The Federalist: The Famous Papers on the Principles of American Government*, edited by F. B. Wright. New York: Barnes and Noble, 161.

Hartley, T. C. 2003. *The Foundations of European Community Law*. 5th ed. Oxford: Oxford University Press.

Hunter, R. D. 1995. The EU's Great and Radical Vice. *Wall Street Journal Europe*, Aug. 18–19, 6.

———. 2001. Harmonic Convergence at the Commission? *Wall Street Journal Europe*, February 22, 7.

Ketchum, R., ed. 1986. *The Anti-Federalist Papers and the Constitutional Debates.* New York: Penguin.

Kraemer, Ludwig. 2002. Precaution, the Protection of Health and the Environment, and the Free Circulation of Goods within the European Union. In *The Role of Precaution in Chemicals Policy,* Elisabeth Freytag et al. (eds), Vienna: Diplomatische Akademie, 42–54.

Lindseth, Peter L. 1999. Democratic Legitimacy and the Administrative Character of Supranationalism: The Example of the European Community. *Columbia Law Review* 99: 628–738.

Radaelli, Claudio C. 2003. *Getting to Grips with the Notion of Quality in the Diffusion of Regulatory Impact Assessment in Europe.* Paper prepared for the Conference on Regulatory Impact Assessment: Strengthening Regulation Policy and Practice. November 26–27, Chancellors Conference Centre, University of Manchester, Manchester, UK.

Riker, W. 1982. *Liberalism against Populism.* New York: W.H. Freeman and Company.

Slagter, W. J. 1952. *De rechtsgrond van de schadevergoeding bij onrechtmatige daad.* Leiden: Dissertatie.

Smith, Turner T., Jr. 1986. Approaches to Environmental Legislation: A Comparison between British and U.S. Practice. CEED/NERA Conference, Environmentalism Today—The Challenge for Business. April 16.

———. 1992. Designing Enforceable Environmental Requirements. EEC International Conference on Environmental Enforcement. September 22–25, Budapest, Hungary.

———. 1994. Environmental Law: Old Ways and New Directions. *Loyola of Los Angeles Law Review* 27 (April): 1077.

Stone, Christopher D. 2001. Is There a Precautionary Principle? *Environmental Law Reporter* 31: 10790.

Sunstein, Cass R. 1988. Beyond the Republican Revival. *Yale Law Journal* 97: 1539.

———. 1991. Preferences and Politics. *Philosophy and Public Affairs* 20 (Winter): 3.

van Dunné, J. M. 1993. Het beginsel van slachtofferbescherming: zo oud als de weg naar Kralingen. In *Beginselen van vermogensrecht,* edited by M. E. Franke et al. Arnhem: Gouda Quint BW-Krant Jaarboek, 175–189.

Vogel, David. 2003. The Hare and the Tortoise Revisited: The New Politics of Consumer and Environmental Regulation in Europe. *British Journal of Political Science* 33: 557–580.

Wiener, Jonathan B. 1997. Risk in the Republic. *Duke Environmental Law and Policy Forum* 8: 2.

———. 2002. Precaution in a Multi-Risk World. In *Human and Ecological Risk Assessment: Theory and Practice,* edited by Dennis D. Paustenbach. New York: John Wiley and Sons, 1509–1531.

———. 2003. Whose Precaution After All? A Comment on the Comparison and Evolution of Risk Regulatory Systems. *Duke Journal of Comparative and International Law* 13: 207.

Wiener, Jonathan B., and Michael D. Rogers. 2002. Comparing Precaution in the United States and Europe. *Journal of Risk Research* 5 (4): 317–349.

Yataganas, X. A. 2001. Delegation of Regulatory Authority in the European Union. *Jean Monnet Working Paper* 3/01.

CHAPTER 18

Risk Perceptions and Risk Attitudes in the United States and Europe

Elke U. Weber and Jessica S. Ancker

*P*ublic policies related to health and safety risks in Europe and the United States show different patterns of precaution, yet in complex ways that make simple explanations elusive (Wiener and Rogers 2002). Among the factors identified as possible explanations for these differences in precautionary concern are cultural differences in risk perception and preferences. In this chapter, we review the literature of behavioral decision theory and cross-cultural research that compares risk perceptions and preferences in different countries. We show that there are cross-cultural differences in the perception of risks and thus in people's apparent willingness to take such risks. But we also find that this phenomenon has not yet been systematically explored and that much research on the topic remains to be done.

The Precautionary Principle

Public policy and public health researchers generally quantify health and safety risks as the relative frequency of known instances of morbidity, mortality, or other adverse impacts. However, conclusive evidence of adverse impacts is lacking for many potential risks, especially those that are novel, uncertain, or require extrapolating from known to unknown situations (e.g., from animal experiments to human health). In such situations, waiting for deaths or cases of disease to accrue before making decisions may be politically and morally unacceptable. In light of this problem, advocates of the precautionary principle favor anticipatory regulation of possible risks. The precautionary principle arises primarily in the public policy arena (Wiener and Rogers 2002) but has also been discussed in other areas, including medical decisionmaking and public health (Cranor 2004; Resnik 2004; Weed 2004). The precautionary principle has been formulated in a number of ways, ranging from very weak (e.g., "regulation is permissible in the absence of complete evidence") to strong (e.g., "potentially risky activities should be prohibited until they can be proven to pose minimal risk"). It has been adopted in a highly issue-specific fashion in both the United States and the European Union. Wiener and Rogers (2002) and Sunstein (Chapter 19 of this volume) have argued convincingly that the patterns of precaution are so complex that neither the EU nor the United States can be described globally either as precautionary or risk-averse. For example, European countries have taken a precautionary stance on regulating genetically modified foods, whereas American policies on teenage drinking or new drug approvals can be seen as precautionary (Wiener and Rogers 2002). In Chapter 19, Sunstein revives an argument by proponents of risk-risk analysis (Lave 1981; Keeney 1997; Graham and Wiener 1995), namely, that it is in fact logically impossible to be globally precautionary with respect to all risks, because taking measures to prevent one hazard may increase the chances of another. For example, as Sunstein points out in Chapter 19, banning DDT to prevent ecosystem damage may result in increased malaria rates as mosquito populations rebound. The only way to think of one's actions as precautionary is thus to take a myopic view of the problem or issue at hand. Cognitive myopia has, of course, been observed in many areas, from investment decisionmaking (Benartzi and Thaler 1999) to the consideration of consequences of multiple, related decisions (Lave 1981; Keeney 1997; Read et al. 1999).

Decomposing Risk-Taking into Risk Perception and Risk Attitude

Because the precautionary principle focuses on preventing possible losses, including losses that have not yet happened, invocation of the precautionary principle would seem to be a sign of risk aversion at the individual or societal level.

In popular thought, risk attitude (defined as propensity for risk aversion or risk-taking) is typically thought of as a personality trait. In this view, some individuals are risk seekers across a broad range of situations and contexts, while others prefer safer options. This view, however, is undermined by a wealth of research on framing and domain effects. Framing effects refer to the finding that people's risk-taking and thus apparent risk attitudes are strongly affected by whether outcomes are framed in terms of losses ("10 out of 100 patients will die") or gains ("90 out of 100 patients will survive"). Explanations of framing effects draw on prospect theory (Kahneman and Tversky 1979), which posits different utility functions for gains and losses. Namely, a concave function for gains predicts risk-averse choices, and a convex function for losses predicts risk-seeking choices. Furthermore, risk-taking behavior varies across content domains. An individual's apparent risk-taking in the context of gambling does not predict risk-taking in other domains such as health, recreation, financial investing, business decisions, social choices, and ethical decisions (MacCrimmon and Wehrung 1986; Weber et al. 2002).

Together, these results suggest that risk attitudes inferred from choice (or, equivalently, from the shape of utility functions describing choice) are not stable personality attributes (Weber 2001a). A promising alternative model of risk-taking, adopted from finance, describes risk-taking as a function of three variables: (1) the perceived return of available choice options; (2) the perceived riskiness of those options; and (3) the decisionmaker's attitude toward perceived risk—that is, his or her willingness to trade perceived risk for possible return, or perceived-risk attitude (Brachinger and Weber 1997; Weber and Milliman 1997). When individual or group differences in risk-taking are examined closely, they are typically the result of differences in perceived risk and not of differences in willingness to take on perceived risk. For example, the characteristic that distinguishes entrepreneurs from other businesspeople is not a more positive attitude toward risk, but an overly optimistic perception of the risks involved (Brockhaus 1982; Cooper et al. 1988). Although there are individual differences in perceived-risk attitude, they are far smaller than individual and group differences in perceived risk, making perceived-risk attitude a credible candidate for a stable personality trait (Weber and Milliman 1997; Weber 2001a).

Culture and Risk Perception

The fact that individual and situational differences in apparent risk-taking are mediated by differences in the perception of the relative risks of choice options raises the possibility that national differences in preference for precautionary policies might be caused by national or cultural differences in the perceived risks of precautionary and other policies. Before discussing cross-cultural differences in risk perception and perceived-risk attitudes, we provide a brief overview of some developments in the psychological study of risk perception. As discussed in this section, perceptions of risk have been studied within three different research paradigms: measurement-theoretical, psychometric, and cultural theory.

Measurement-Theoretical Paradigm

Normative models of risk-taking—from finance (Markowitz 1959) to biology (Caraco 1980)—characterize the riskiness of a risky choice option as the variance of possible outcomes, i.e., the square of the average deviation of outcomes around the mean (Weber et al. 2004). Sure options thus carry no risk, while a widening distribution of possible outcomes increases risk. The perception of risk, however, has long been known to differ from the variance of outcomes. For example, the possibility of outcomes below the mean affects perceived risk far more than the possibility of outcomes above the mean (Weber and Bottom 1989, 1990). One model that attempts to capture such asymmetry of the effects of outcomes above and below the mean is Luce and Weber's conjoint expected risk (CER) model (Luce and Weber 1986). In this model, the perceived risk of a choice option is a linear combination of the probabilities of neutral, positive, and negative outcomes, and of the conditional expected values of positive outcomes and negative outcomes, raised to power functions. Model parameters allow for different weights of these different contributors to perceived risk, providing a way of explaining individual and group differences in risk perception.

In a study of business students and security analysts in Hong Kong, Taiwan, the Netherlands, and the United States, Bontempo et al. (1997) fit the CER model to judgments of the riskiness of monetary lotteries. The *probability* of a loss had a larger effect on perceived risk for the two Western samples, but the *magnitude* of losses had a larger effect on the two culturally Chinese samples. Cross-cultural differences in risk perception were greater than differences due to profession, suggesting that cultural upbringing and environment are more important in shaping financial risk perceptions than professional training and experience.

Psychometric Paradigm

Another research approach, the psychometric paradigm, arose to explain lay perceptions of the risks of technological and health hazards (Fischhoff et al. 1978; Slovic et al. 1986; Slovic 1987; Peters and Slovic 1996), which were found to differ from the risk estimates of experts who generally based their assessments on the relative frequency of negative outcomes such as death or disability, e.g., the list of mortality risks in Slovic (1997, 281). The primary question underlying this research agenda was why some hazards with low probability of negative outcomes (such as airplane travel) were perceived as riskier than others that carried a much higher probability (such as car travel). The psychometric paradigm decomposes risk perception into a set of psychological risk dimensions that can be reduced to two factors: dread and risk of the unknown. The dread of an event is heightened when a hazard has severe consequences (even if rare), provoking a gut-level "dread" reaction, and effects that are perceived as catastrophic and sudden (rather than gradual or chronic). The risk of the unknown is heightened by characteristics such as novelty, delayed impact, or undetectability (e.g., exposure to carbon monoxide is frightening in part because the gas cannot be seen or smelled). Additional variables that may also contribute to the two psychological risk factors include the origin of the hazard (man-made versus natural), voluntariness of the exposure to the risk, and real or perceived controversy in the scientific community. As a result, when lay judgments are compared with expert judgments, lay people tend to overweight risk associated with infrequent, catastrophic, and involuntary events, and underweight risk associated with frequent, familiar, and voluntary events. As Slovic has said, the public's perception of risk is "much richer" than that of the expert (Slovic 1997).

Psychometric researchers have thus sought to persuade health and environmental risk assessment experts to define risk not simply as the probability of adverse consequences, but to add some measure of the uncertainty of outcomes, as has long been accepted in financial definitions of risk (Markowitz 1959), in addition to other psychological dimensions. While the psychometric model has extensively documented the ways in which risk perception departs from probability, probabilities do contribute to risk perception, increasing for example the vividness and salience (and thus the availability) of the risk. Availability has been identified as one of the heuristics that is generally used to estimate the frequency of an event (Tversky and Kahneman 1974), including the frequency of adverse consequences as a measure of risk.

Holtgrave and Weber (1993) found that subjects' judgments of financial and health and safety risks were best explained by a hybrid model that integrated the "dread" risk dimension with probabilities and utilities drawn from a simplified version of the conjoint expected risk model. The hybrid model provides additional evidence that risk perception (even about monetary risks) has emotional elements that are not captured by purely consequentialist models (Loewenstein et al. 2001).

The two-factor structure of the psychometric paradigm of risk perception has been validated in studies using respondents from a variety of different countries, including Canada (Slovic et al. 1991), France (Bastide et al. 1989; Slovic et al. 2000), Hong Kong (Keown 1989), Hungary (Englander et al. 1986), Japan (Kleinhesselink and Rosa 1994), Norway (Teigen et al. 1988), the Soviet Union (Mechitov and Rebrik 1989), and Sweden (Slovic et al. 1989). Renn and Rohrmann (2000) provide a review. Only minor deviations from the standard two-factor risk dimension pattern emerged, with Americans, for example, rating high-tech hazards and risks high on the unknown axis as the most serious, whereas Hungarians rated everyday and familiar hazards such as driving cars as posing higher risks (Englander et al. 1986). Specific hazards in these studies often fell into different parts of the two-dimensional risk space in ways that were sometimes attributable to historical effects. For example, in a study conducted shortly after a Hong Kong public awareness campaign about heroin, Hong Kong students rated illicit drugs as more hazardous than did Americans (Keown 1989). Japanese students considered nuclear hazards to be old and well-known, unlike American students—a difference attributed to Japan's unique experience as the target of nuclear weapons at the end of World War II (Kleinhesselink and Rosa 1994).

Because of its success at capturing differences in perceptions of risk within a society, the psychometric paradigm has also been invoked to examine apparent differences in perceived risk across societies. For example, Wiener and Rogers (2002) invoke the psychometric paradigm of risk to suggest that Europeans' distrust of genetically modified foods may stem from their perception of such items as "unnatural." However, additional information would have to be provided to explain why American consumers do not share the European perception distrust of genetically engineered products as "unnatural." Sunstein suggests in Chapter 19 that the availability heuristic and the dynamics of social groups in combination with differences in national history may explain cultural differences in risk behavior. For example, the vividness of a severe acute respiratory syndrome (SARS) outbreak in Toronto and of the 9/11 terrorist attacks in the United States can help explain why Canadians have been more concerned with SARS than with terrorism, whereas American citizens show the opposite pattern of concern.

Cultural Theory

Both the measurement-theoretical and the psychometric paradigms were originally developed to explain individual differences in decisionmaking and risk perception, especially differences between lay and expert risk judgments. By contrast, a body of work originating in anthropology and sociology suggests that risk is not decided at an individual level, but instead is culturally constructed (Douglas and Wildavsky 1982; Douglas 1992). In the cultural theory model, a risk is an event that threatens values held to be important at the cultural or societal level. Such societal values serve as a frame through which members of a culture tend to view current events and future possibilities. As Douglas (1992) puts it, "A risk is not only the probability of an event, but also the probable magnitude of its outcome, and everything depends on the value that is set on the outcome. The evaluation is a political, aesthetic, and moral matter." In this view, providing information about probabilities fails to change risk judgments "not because the public does not understand the sums, but because many other objectives which it cares about have been left out of the risk calculation." Risk perception reflects what a society or community fears and seeks to blame for individual or group misfortune (Douglas 1992, 31, 40).

The cultural theory of risk has been operationalized through an instrument that categorizes individuals according to their preferred cultural worldview or "orienting disposition" (Dake 1991). Cultures and individuals that value both rigid societal structures and strong social group loyalties are termed *hierarchists*. Those who value neither societal rigidity nor group solidarity are *individualists*. *Egalitarians* view group solidarity as valuable while disapproving of rigid social hierarchies. *Fatalists* feel trapped in a social hierarchy without feeling strong social bonds, whereas *hermits* renounce social connections altogether. (Most researchers restrict their attention to the first three categories, as fatalists and hermits are rare, and when fatalists are identified, they tend to behave like hierarchists.)

The orienting disposition categorization predicts differences in risk preferences (Dake 1991; Weber 2001b). Members of hierarchical cultures tend to appear risk-tolerant toward industrial and technological risks because they trust the competency of the technocratic elites who handle risky decisions; social deviance is feared more than technological hazards because social change, unlike technological change, threatens the social order. Individualists are likely to see economic risk as opportunity, being willing to chance poor outcomes in order to reap the benefits of possible good ones. By contrast, egalitarians are distrustful of technological risks that may threaten equality by disproportionately harming the poor or the environment (Douglas and Wildavsky 1982; Dake 1991).

Palmer (1996) used the orienting dispositions questionnaire to identify hierarchists, individualists, and egalitarians from a multiethnic population of Southern Californian students. Respondents also rated the riskiness of a set of monetary and health/safety hazards, and their responses were assessed through the CER model. As predicted, Palmer found that the risk judgments of people with different worldviews were described by different components of the CER model. Hierarchists were predicted to be comfortable with risk–benefit methods of determining acceptable levels of risk for technologies (Thompson et al. 1990). In agreement with this prediction, Palmer found that hierarchists' risk judgments reflected all predictor variables of the CER model, where gains offset possible losses, and outcome levels as well as probabilities were considered. Egalitarians, by contrast, were predicted to be suspicious of technology and to view nature as a fragile shared resource in need of protection (Thompson et al. 1990). In agreement with this prediction, egalitarians viewed risk in terms of possible harms and provided risk judgments that reflected only the loss/harm predictor variables of the CER model. Finally, individualists have been described as viewing risk as opportunity, as long as the risk does not interfere with market mechanisms (Thompson et al. 1990). In agreement with this prediction, individualists provided the lowest risk judgments for almost all of the risky investments and activities.

Specifics of the cultural theory of risk have been debated. For example, Dake's categories have been criticized as "polemical abstractions" too rigid to adequately capture the complex and dynamic experience of either cultural dispositions or risk perception in the real world (Wilkinson 2001), and for being flawed by problematic data collection and statistical analyses (Rippl 2002; Sjöberg 2002). The adequacy of the Dake instrument as a measurement of culture has been called into question (Marris et al. 1998; Rippl 2002). Although ad hoc models have been proposed as alternatives to the cultural theory, no overarching theoretical framework appears to have emerged. Sjöberg (2002), for example, argues that in the case of perceived risk of nuclear waste, both the psychometric model and cultural theory should be jettisoned in favor of a regression model combining attitude toward nuclear power, risk attitude as a trait, attitude toward nature (the "tampering with nature" factor), perception of moral aspects of risk, and several attributes of the nuclear and radiation risk itself. Rohrmann (2000) suggests that globalization of the economy and media means that professional or political groups may have more in common with similar groups in other countries than with others of their own country, i.e., that social group differences may have larger effects than other cultural distinctions.

Risk Perception: Integrating Individual, Cultural, and National Factors

Among the factors shown to influence risk perception, several are likely to be cultural-specific. Two examples are sex and race (Slovic 1997; Slovic et al. 2000). For example, in the United States, the subset of white males with good educations, high incomes, and conservative political tastes tend to perceive risks to be markedly smaller and more manageable than do other men, women, or members of minority races (Slovic 1997). This "white male effect"—also confirmed by other researchers (see Weber et al. 2002)—may be attributable to the high status of white men in America, which tends to give them more real as well as perceived control over hazards. Such gender and race effects are likely to vary across nations as culture establishes the relative equality or inequality between the sexes and various racial groups.

A related factor identified by Slovic as affecting risk perception is the degree of trust in institutions (particularly those performing risk management), which can vary across cultures as well as from individual to individual (Slovic 1997; Renn and Rohrmann 2000). Impaired trust in social institutions implies suspicion about their willingness or ability to protect citizens, which could thus enhance the negative affective response to potential hazards. In studies in Europe (Sweden, Spain, the United Kingdom, and France), Viklund (2003) has confirmed that trust significantly predicted perceived risk within countries and across countries, but that the relationship was fairly weak. Public trust may be enhanced or attenuated by a country's mass media (Sjöberg et al. 2000).

A large study of sexual behavior (Realo and Goodwin 2003) in Estonia, Georgia, Hungary, Poland, and Russia contrasted individual perceptions of HIV risk in different countries. Participants were given a "collectivism scale" to assess the extent of their orientation toward their families as a source of authority and strength ("familism"). Across countries and occupations, high familism scores were associated with more conservative sexual behavior and with lower perceived vulnerability to HIV, but neither national origin nor profession had significant effects. This study can be interpreted to suggest that any national differences in risk perception are attributable to differences in familial attitude. However, because individual sexual history was so strongly correlated with familism and is also strongly correlated with both objective and subjective HIV risk, other effects of nationality may simply have been overwhelmed. It also seems possible that the Eastern European countries targeted in this series of studies were not different enough to produce large cultural effects, despite the authors' argument to the contrary.

Culture and Risk Preference

In contrast to risk perception (the perceived importance or magnitude of a risk as assessed by self-reports), risk preference is conceptualized as the willingness to take risks and can be measured by behavior. In a variety of financial gamble experiments, Weber and Hsee (1998, 1999) have repeatedly found that respondents from the People's Republic of China are less risk-averse in their financial choices than are U.S. respondents. The finding contradicts cultural stereotypes and, in one case, the predictions of the participants themselves (Weber and Hsee 1999). The difference in apparent risk preference between American and Chinese business students was attributed to differences in risk perception: Chinese participants tended to perceive financial risks as smaller than Americans did. The authors' cushion hypothesis attributes this phenomenon to the collectivism of Chinese culture: individuals who lose money are confident that they can turn to familial and social networks to "cushion" the blow. By contrast, members of America's individualist culture expect to shoulder the impact of adverse financial events themselves. The situation-specific element of risk-taking (that is, the perceived risk) resembles other theorists' formulation of risk perception as the severity of the *consequences* of a risk (Douglas and Wildavsky 1982; Sjöberg 2002). Another study by Weber and Hsee (1998) in the People's Republic of China, the United States, Germany, and Poland involved willingness to pay for financial investment options and perceived riskiness of these options. The Chinese respondents considered the risks to be the lowest and paid the highest prices. Americans considered risks to be highest and were willing to pay the least. The cross-national differences in willingness to pay were completely accounted for by differences in risk perception. That is, there were no national differences in perceived-risk attitude or people's willingness to take on risks after controlling for the difference in the perceived magnitude of the risks. Risk perceptions and risk preferences of German respondents were closer to those of Chinese respondents than those of American respondents, even though Germany's socioeconomic and political system is more similar to that of the United States. Consistent with attributing observed national differences to the cushion hypothesis, however, German culture has socially collectivist elements (such as strong family and group ties and extensive social safety nets) that resemble China's.

Additional support for the cushion hypothesis that attributes cross-cultural differences in risk preferences to differences in social networks was found by Hsee and Weber (1999). They found that Chinese had larger social networks than Americans, and that when social network measures were added to a regression model of risk preferences, the nationality variable was no longer significant. This suggests that social networks could be the means through which culture affects risk preference. The cushion hypothesis moreover predicts that risk preferences should differ with the type of risk. A member of a collectivist culture could expect that his or her social network would cushion the impact of losses on dimensions where interpersonal transfer is possible (e.g., money), but not of losses where no such transfer is possible (e.g., honor, academic grades, life expectancy). Hsee and Weber confirmed this prediction in an experiment in which Chinese and American participants were asked to make a financial decision (to invest money in a safe savings account or in risky stocks), an academic one (whether to write a term paper on a safe topic or a provocative one), and a medical one (whether to take a pain reliever with a known moderate effect or another one with an effect that could vary from high to low). The Chinese were significantly more risk-seeking than the Americans only in the financial choice (Hsee and Weber 1999). This work also calls attention to the domain-specificity of risk perception. Risk attitude does not appear to be a global trait; people express different thresholds for financial risks, health and safety risks, recreational risks, ethical risks, and social risks such as angering colleagues or friends (Weber et al. 2002).

Proverbs reflect cultural attitudes toward risk-taking (Weber et al. 1998). In a content analysis of proverbs from Chinese and American proverbial expressions, Weber et al. (1998) found that American and Chinese raters agreed that Chinese proverbs were more likely to promote risk-taking than were American ones. Because the Chinese proverbs are in many cases centuries old, this finding suggests the more risk-seeking behavior reported in the studies described above may have a long-standing cultural origin rather than reflecting merely current economic or political conditions. A larger proportion of American proverbs were judged to be applicable to financial-risk decisions than to social-risk decisions, whereas Chinese proverbs were judged to be roughly equally applicable to the two domains. The proverbs produced by these two cultures may reflect the fact that a collectivist culture considers social concerns to be as important as materialistic ones, whereas an individualist culture privileges material concerns.

Conclusions

Numerous cross-national and cross-cultural differences in risk perception have been identified, and it is these differences in the perception of risk—rather than attitudes toward (perceived) risk, proper—that seem to be responsible for cultural differences in risk-taking. A variety of explanations have been provided for observed cultural differences in risk perception: differences in the evaluation of specific risks on the psychological risk dimensions identified by the psychometric paradigm (including differences in perceived control as the result of power differentials or differences in institutional trust), as well as differences in objective circumstances (the cushion of collectivist risk diversification). The adoption of precautionary measures by governments may reflect, in part, the responses of policymakers to the vicissitudes of public perceptions of risk. Further research is necessary to explain how these identified cultural differences can contribute to the understanding of differences in patterns of precaution between Europe and the United States.

Acknowledgments

Preparation of this chapter was facilitated by funding provided by the National Science Foundation under Grant No. SES-0345840. Any opinions, findings, and conclusions or recommendations expressed here are those of the authors and do not necessarily reflect the view of the National Science Foundation.

References

Bastide, S., J. P. Moatti, J.-P. Pages, and F. Fagnani. 1989. Risk Perception and Social Acceptability of Technologies: The French Case. *Risk Analysis* 9: 215–223.

Benartzi, S., and R. Thaler. 1999. Risk Aversion or Myopia? Choices in Repeated Gambles and Retirement Investments. *Management Science* 45: 364–381.

Bontempo, R. N., W. P. Bottom, and E. U. Weber. 1997. Cross-Cultural Differences in Risk Perception: A Model-Based Approach. *Risk Analysis* 17: 479–488.

Brachinger, H. W., and M. Weber. 1997. Risk as a Primitive: A Survey of Measures of Perceived Risk. *OR Spectrum* 19: 235–250.

Brockhaus, R. 1982. The Psychology of the Entrepreneur. In *The Encyclopedia of Entrepreneurship*, edited by C. Kent, D. L. Sexton, and K. Vesper. Englewood Cliffs, NJ: Prentice Hall.

Caraco, T. 1980. On Foraging Time Allocation in a Stochastic Environment. *Ecology* 6: 119–128.

Cooper, A., C. Woo, and W. Dunkelberg. 1988. Entrepreneur's Perceived Chances for Success. *Journal of Business Venturing* 3: 97–108.

Cranor, C. F. 2004. Toward Understanding Aspects of the Precautionary Principle. *Journal of Medicine and Philosophy* 29 (3): 259–279.

Dake, K. 1991. Orienting Dispositions in the Perception of Risk: An Analysis of Contemporary Worldviews and Cultural Biases. *Journal of Cross-Cultural Psychology* 22 (1): 61–82.

Douglas, M. 1992. *Risk and Blame: Essays in Cultural Theory*. London: Routledge.

Douglas, M., and A. Wildavsky. 1982. *Risk and Culture: An Essay on the Selection of Technological and Environmental Dangers*. Berkeley, CA: University of California Press.

Englander, T., K. Farago, P. Slovic, and B. Fischhoff. 1986. A Comparative Analysis of Risk Perception in Hungary and the United States. *International Journal of Social Psychology* 1: 55–66.

Fischhoff, B., P. Slovic, S. Lichtenstein, S. Read, and B. Combs. 1978. How Safe Is Safe Enough? A Psychometric Study of Attitudes towards Technological Risks and Benefits. *Policy Sciences* 9: 127–152.

Graham, John D., and Jonathan B. Wiener, eds. 1995. *Risk vs. Risk: Tradeoffs in Protecting Health and the Environment.* Cambridge, MA: Harvard University Press.

Holtgrave, D., and E. U. Weber. 1993. Dimensions of Risk Perception for Financial and Health and Safety Risks. *Risk Analysis* 13: 553–558.

Hsee, C. K., and E. U. Weber. 1999. Cross-National Differences in Risk Preference and Lay Predictions. *Journal of Behavioral Decision Making* 12: 165–179.

Kahneman, D., and A. Tversky. 1979. Prospect Theory: An Analysis of Decision under Risk. *Econometrica* 47: 263–291.

Keeney, R. 1997. Estimating Fatalities by the Economic Costs of Regulations. *Journal of Risk and Uncertainty* 14: 5–23.

Keown, C. F. 1989. Risk Perceptions of Hong Kongese versus Americans. *Risk Analysis* 9: 401–405.

Kleinhesselink, R. R., and E. A. Rosa. 1994. Cognitive Representation of Risk Perceptions: A Comparison of Japan and the United States. *Journal of Cross-Cultural Psychology* 22: 11–28.

Lave, L. 1981. *The Strategy of Social Regulation: Decision Frameworks for Policy.* Washington, DC: Brookings Institution.

Loewenstein, G., E. U. Weber, and C. K. Hsee. 2001. Risk as Feelings. *Psychological Bulletin* 127 (2): 267–286.

Luce, R. D., and E. U. Weber. 1986. An Axiomatic Theory of Conjoint Expected Risk. *Journal of Mathematical Psychology* 30: 188–205.

MacCrimmon, K. R., and D. A. Wehrung. 1986. *Taking Risks: The Management of Uncertainty.* New York: Free Press.

Markowitz, H. M. 1959. *Portfolio Selection.* New York: Wiley.

Marris, C., I. H. Langford, and T. O'Riordan. 1998. A Quantitative Test of the Cultural Theory of Risk Perceptions: Comparison with the Psychometric Model. *Risk Analysis* 18 (5): 635–647.

Mechitov, A. I., and S. B. Rebrik, eds. 1989. Studies of Risk and Safety Perception in the USSR. *Contemporary Issues in Decision Making.* Amsterdam: North Holland.

Palmer, C. G. S. 1996. Risk Perception: An Empirical Study of the Relationship between Worldview and the Risk Construct. *Risk Analysis* 16: 717–724.

Peters, E., and P. Slovic. 1996. The Role of Affect and Worldview as Orienting Dispositions in the Perception and Acceptance of Nuclear Power. *Journal of Applied Social Psychology* 26: 1427–1453.

Read, D., G. Loewenstein, and M. Rabin. 1999. Choice Bracketing. *Journal of Risk and Uncertainty* 19: 171–197.

Realo, A., and R. Goodwin. 2003. Family-Related Allocentrism and HIV Risk Behavior in Central and Eastern Europe. *Journal of Cross-Cultural Psychology* 34 (6): 690–701.

Renn, O., and B., Rohrmann, eds. 2000. *Cross-Cultural Risk Perception: A Survey of Empirical Studies.* Boston: Kluwer Academic.

Resnik, D. B. 2004. The Precautionary Principle and Medical Decisionmaking. *Journal of Medicine and Philosophy* 29 (3): 281–299.

Rippl, S. 2002. Cultural Theory and Risk Perception: A Proposal for a Better Measurement. *Journal of Risk Research* 5 (2): 147–165.

Rohrmann, B. 2000. Cross-Cultural Studies on the Perception and Evaluation of Hazards. In *Cross-Cultural Risk Perception: A Survey of Empirical Studies*, edited by O. Renn and B. Rohrmann. Boston: Kluwer Academic, 103–144.

Sjöberg, L. 2002. Are Received Risk Perception Models Alive and Well? *Risk Analysis* 22 (4): 665–669.

Sjöberg, L., D. Kolarova, A. A. Rucai, and M. L. Bernstrom. 2000. Risk Perception in Bulgaria and Romania. In *Cross-Cultural Risk Perception: A Survey of Empirical Studies*, edited by O. Renn and B. Rohrmann. Boston: Kluwer Academic, 146–183.

Slovic, P. 1987. Perception of Risk. *Science* 236: 280–285.

————., ed. 1997. Trust, Emotion, Sex, Politics, and Science: Surveying the Risk-Assessment Battlefield. In *Environment, Ethics, and Behavior: The Psychology of Environmental Valuation and Degradation*, edited by M. H. Bazerman, D. M. Messick, A. E. Tenbrunsel, and K. A. Wade-Benzoni. San Francisco, CA: New Lexington Press, 277–313.

Slovic, P., B. Fischhoff, and S. Lichtenstein. 1986. The Psychometric Study of Risk Perception. In *Risk Evaluation and Management*, edited by V. T. Covello, J. Menkes, and J. Mumpower. New York: Plenum Press.

Slovic, P., J. Flynn, C. K. Mertz, M. Poumadere, and C. Mays. 2000. Nuclear Power and the Public: A Comparative Study of Risk Perception in France and the United States. In *Cross-Cultural Risk Perception: A Survey of Empirical Studies*, edited by O. Renn and B. Rohrmann. Boston: Kluwer Academic, 56–102.

Slovic, P., N. Kraus, H. Lappe, H. Letzel, and T. Malmfors. 1989. Risk Perception of Prescription Drugs: Report on a Survey in Sweden. In *The Perception and Management of Drug Safety Risks*, edited by B. Horrisberger and R. Dinkel. Berlin: Springer, 91–111.

Slovic, P., N. Kraus, H. Lappe, and M. Major. 1991. Risk Perception of Prescription Drugs: Report on a Survey in Canada. *Canadian Journal of Public Health* 82: S15–S20.

Teigen, K. H., W. Brun, and P. Slovic. 1988. Societal Risk as Seen by a Norwegian Public. *Journal of Behavioral Decision Making* 1: 111–130.

Thompson, M., R. Ellis, and A. Wildavsky. 1990. *Cultural Theory*. Boulder, CO: Westview Press.

Tversky, A., and D. Kahneman. 1974. Judgment under Uncertainty: Heuristics and Biases. *Science* 185: 1124–1130.

Viklund, M. J. 2003. Trust and Risk Perception in Western Europe: A Cross-National Study. *Risk Analysis* 23 (4): 727–738.

Weber, E. U. 2001a. Personality and Risk Taking. In *International Encyclopedia of the Social and Behavioral Sciences*, edited by N. Smelser and P. Baltes. Oxford: Elsevier, 11274–11276.

————. 2001b. Risk: Empirical Studies on Decision and Choice. In *International Encyclopedia of the Social and Behavioral Sciences*, edited by N. Smelser and P. Baltes. Oxford: Elsevier, 13347–13351.

Weber, E. U., A. R. Blais, and N. E. Betz. 2002. A Domain-Specific Risk-Attitude Scale: Measuring Risk Perceptions and Risk Behaviors. *Journal of Behavioral Decision Making* 15: 1–28.

Weber, E. U., and W. P. Bottom. 1989. Axiomatic Measures of Perceived Risk: Some Tests and Extensions. *Journal of Behavioral Decision Making* 2: 113–131.

————. 1990. An Empirical Evaluation of the Transitivity, Monotonicity, Accounting, and Conjoint Axioms for Perceived Risk. *Organizational Behavior and Human Decision Processes* 45: 253–276.

Weber, E. U., and C. K. Hsee. 1998. Cross-Cultural Differences in Risk Perception, but Cross-Cultural Similarities in Attitude towards Perceived Risk. *Management Science* 44: 1205–1217.

————. 1999. Models and Mosaics: Investigating Cross-Cultural Differences in Risk Perception and Risk Preference. *Psychonomic Bulletin Review* 6 (4): 611–617.

Weber, E. U., C. K. Hsee, and J. Sokolowska. 1998. What Folklore Tells Us about Risk and Risk Taking: A Cross-Cultural Comparison of American, German, and Chinese Proverbs. *Organizational Behavior and Human Decision Processes* 75: 170–186.

Weber, E. U., and R. Milliman. 1997. Perceived Risk Attitudes: Relating Risk Perception to Risky Choice. *Management Science* 43: 122–143.

Weber, E. U., S. Shafir, and A. R. Blais. 2004. Predicting Risk Sensitivity in Humans and Lower Animals: Risk as Variance or Coefficient of Variation. *Psychological Review* 111 (2): 430–445.

Weed, D. L. 2004. Precaution, Prevention, and Public Health Ethics. *Journal of Medicine and Philosophy* 29 (3): 313–332.

Wiener, J. B., and M. D. Rogers. 2002. Comparing Precaution in the United States and Europe. *Journal of Risk Research* 5 (4): 317–349.

Wilkinson, I. 2001. Social Theories of Risk Perception: At Once Indispensable and Insufficient. *Current Sociology* 49 (1): 1–22.

CHAPTER 19

Precautions against What?
Perceptions, Heuristics, and Culture

Cass R. Sunstein

*B*ecause risks are all on sides of social situations, it is not possible to be globally "precautionary." Hence the precautionary principle runs into serious conceptual difficulties; any precautions will themselves create hazards of one or another kind. When the principle gives guidance, it is often because of the availability heuristic, which can make some risks stand out as particularly salient, whatever their actual magnitude. The same heuristic helps to explain differences across groups, cultures, and even nations in the perception of risks, especially when linked with such social processes as cascades and group polarization. One difficulty here is that what is available is sometimes a result of predispositions, cultural and otherwise. There are complex links among availability, social processes for the spreading of information, and predispositions.

> Many Germans believe that drinking water after eating cherries is deadly; they also believe that putting ice in soft drinks is unhealthy. The English, however, rather enjoy a cold drink of water after some cherries; and Americans love icy refreshments. (Henrich et al. 2001, 353–354)[1]

> The most important factor contributing to the increased stringency of health, safety and environmental regulation in Europe has been a series of regulatory failures and crises that placed new regulatory issues on the political agenda and pressured policy makers to adopt more risk averse or precautionary policies. ... The regulatory failure associated with BSE significantly affected the attitude of the European public toward GM foods. ... Consumer and environmental regulations are likely to become more innovative, comprehensive and risk averse as a response to a widespread public perception of regulatory failures. (Vogel 2003, 557, 568–569, 580)

---

[1] See Henrich et al. (2001) for an entertaining outline in connection with food choice decisions.

It has become standard to say that with respect to risks, Europe and the United States can be distinguished along a single axis: Europe accepts the precautionary principle, and the United States does not.[2] On this view, Europeans attempt to build a "margin of safety" into public decisions, taking care to protect citizens against risks that cannot be established with certainty. By contrast, Americans are reluctant to take precautions, requiring clear evidence of harm in order to justify regulation. These claims seem plausible in light of the fact that the United States appears comparatively unconcerned about the risks associated with global warming and genetic modification of food; in those contexts, Europeans favor precautions, whereas Americans seem to require something akin to proof of danger. To be sure, the matter is quite different in the context of threats to national security. For the war in Iraq, the United States (and England) followed a kind of precautionary principle, whereas other nations (most notably France and Germany) wanted clearer proof of danger (see Chapter 12). But for most threats to safety and health, many people believe that Europe is precautionary and the United States is not.

But as others have demonstrated (Wiener and Rogers 2002; Chapter 1 of this volume), this opposition between Europe and America is false, even illusory. It is simply wrong to say that Europeans are more precautionary than Americans. As an empirical matter, neither is "more precautionary." Europeans are not more averse to risks than Americans. They are more averse to particular risks,[3] such as the risks associated with global warming; but Americans have their own preoccupations as well. My larger point, a central claim of this chapter, is conceptual. No nation can, even in principle, commit itself to precaution as such (Sunstein 2003a, 2005). The real problem with the precautionary principle, at least in its strongest forms, is that it is incoherent; it purports to give guidance, but it fails to do so, because it condemns the very steps that it requires. Was the war in Iraq precautionary? Is it precautionary to ban cellular telephones, nuclear power plants, genetically modified food, and airplanes? These questions should be enough to suggest that precautions always give rise to risks of their own—and that the operation of the precautionary principle is inextricably intertwined with social risk perceptions.

Nations can regard themselves as "precautionary" only if they blind themselves to many aspects of risk-related situations and focus on a narrow subset of what is at stake. That kind of self-blinding is what makes the precautionary principle seem to give guidance; and I shall have a fair bit to say about why people and societies are selective in their fears. My major hypothesis is that the *availability heuristic* is often the source of people's fears about certain risks.[4] If a particular incident is cognitively "available"— both vivid and salient—then people will have a heightened fear of the risk in question.

---

[2] On some of the complexities here, see Applegate (2000); Sand (2000).

[3] See Vogel (2003) for many examples in the context of health, safety, and the environment.

[4] Undoubtedly a great deal can be learned from use of the psychometric paradigm, stressed in Rohrmann and Renn (2000). I stress the availability heuristic here because of its comparative simplicity, but the heuristic interacts in complex ways with psychometrics and with culture; I try at least to scratch some of the surfaces here.

If people in one nation fear the risks associated with terrorism, and people in another nation fear the risks associated with "mad cow disease," the availability heuristic is likely to be the reason. Hence, cultural differences, with respect to application of the precautionary principle, are often rooted in availability. But this point misses some complexities, about both social influences and cultural predispositions; I shall turn to these in due course. The availability heuristic does not operate in a social or cultural vacuum.

In short, I aim here both to show that the precautionary principle is not quite what it seems, and that its operation is underwritten by an identifiable heuristic with social and cultural foundations. The result is a hypothesis to the effect that cross-cultural differences both in risk perception and in precautions are produced, in large part, by availability. I shall not be able to prove that hypothesis in this space, but I hope to be able to say enough to prove that the hypothesis is plausible, illuminating, and worth further exploration.

Weak and Strong

Begin with the precautionary principle.[5] There are 20 or more definitions, and they are not compatible with one another (Morris 2000; Chapter 1 of this volume). We can imagine a continuum of understandings. At one extreme are weak versions to which no reasonable person could object. At the other extreme are strong versions that would require a fundamental rethinking of regulatory policy.

The most cautious and weak versions suggest, quite sensibly, that a lack of decisive evidence of harm should not be a ground for refusing to regulate. Controls might be justified even if we cannot establish a definite connection between, for example, low-level exposures to certain carcinogens and adverse effects on human health. Thus, the 1992 Rio Declaration states, "Where there are threats of serious or irreversible damage, lack of full scientific certainty shall not be used as a reason for postponing cost-effective measures to prevent environmental degradation" (Lomborg 2001, 347). The Ministerial Declaration of the Second International Conference on the Protection of the North Sea, held in London in 1987, is in the same vein: "Accepting that in order to protect the North Sea from possibly damaging effects of the most dangerous substances, a Precautionary Principle is necessary which may require action to control inputs of such substances even before a causal link has been established by absolutely clear scientific evidence" (Morris 2000, 3). Similarly, the United Nations Framework Convention on Climate Change offers cautious language: "Where there are threats of serious or irreversible damage, lack of full scientific certainty should not be used as a reason for postponing [regulatory] measures, taking into account that policies and measures to deal with climate change should be cost-effective so as to ensure global benefits at the lowest possible cost" (Goklany 2001, 6).

---

[5] This and the following sections draw extensively from Sunstein (2005).

The widely publicized Wingspread Declaration, from a meeting of environmentalists in 1998, goes somewhat further: "When an activity raises threats of harm to human health or the environment, precautionary measures should be taken even if some cause and effect relationships are not established scientifically. In this context the proponent of the activity, rather than the public, should bear the burden of proof" (Goklany 2001, 6). The first sentence just quoted is more aggressive than the Rio Declaration because it is not limited to threats of serious or irreversible damage. And in reversing the burden of proof, the second sentence goes further still. Of course, everything depends on what those with the burden of proof must show in particular.

In Europe, the precautionary principle is sometimes understood in a still stronger way, suggesting that it is important to build "a margin of safety into all decision making" (Lomborg 2001, 348). According to one definition, the precautionary principle means "that action should be taken to correct a problem as soon as there is evidence that harm may occur, not after the harm has already occurred" (McFedries 2005). The word "may" is the crucial one here. In a comparably strong version, it is said that "the Precautionary Principle mandates that when there is a risk of significant health or environmental damage to others or to future generations, and when there is scientific uncertainty as to the nature of that damage or the likelihood of the risk, then decisions should be made so as to prevent such activities from being conducted unless and until scientific evidence shows that the damage will not occur" (Blackwelder 2002). The words "will not occur" seem to require proponents of an activity to demonstrate that there is no risk at all—often an impossible burden to meet. The Cartagena Protocol on Biosafety to the Convention on Biological Diversity, adopted in 2000, appears to adopt a strong version as well (Goklany 2001). The Final Declaration of the First European "Seas at Risk" conference says that if "the 'worst case scenario' for a certain activity is serious enough then even a small amount of doubt as to the safety of that activity is sufficient to stop it taking place" (Final Declaration of the First European "Seas at Risk" Conference 1994).

Safe and Sorry?

The weak versions of the precautionary principle are unobjectionable and important. Every day, individuals and nations take steps to avoid hazards that are far from certain. We do not walk in moderately dangerous areas at night; we exercise; we buy smoke detectors; we buckle our seatbelts; we might even avoid fatty foods (or carbohydrates). Sensible governments regulate risks that, in individual cases or even in the aggregate, have a well under 100% chance of coming to fruition. An individual might ignore a mortality risk of 1/500,000, because that risk is quite small, but if 100 million citizens face that risk, the nation had better take it seriously. With respect to the weak version of the precautionary principle, there are significant cross-cultural variations; but no serious person rejects that version.

For the moment, let us understand the principle in a strong way, to suggest that regulation is required whenever there is a possible risk to health, safety, or the environment, even if the supporting evidence remains speculative and even if the economic costs of regulation are high. To avoid absurdity, the idea of "possible risk" will be understood to require a certain threshold of scientific plausibility. To support regulation, no one thinks that it is enough if someone, somewhere, urges that a risk is worth taking seriously. But under the precautionary principle as I shall understand it, the threshold burden is minimal, and once it is met, there is something like a presumption in favor of regulatory controls. This version, as we shall see, helps to clarify a significant problem with the idea of precaution, and also to illuminate the existence of cross-national differences.

Why the Precautionary Principle Is Paralyzing

Why might the precautionary principle, understood in its strong sense, have such widespread appeal? At first glance, the answer is simple, for the principle contains some important truth. Certainly we should acknowledge that a small probability (say, 1 in 25,000) of a serious harm (say, one million deaths) deserves extremely serious attention. It is worthwhile to spend a lot of money to eliminate that risk. An economically oriented critic might observe that our resources are limited, and that if we spend large amounts of resources on highly speculative harms, we will not be allocating those resources wisely. In fact, this is the simplest criticism of the precautionary principle (Graham 2001). If we take costly steps to address all risks, however improbable they are, we will quickly impoverish ourselves. On this view, the precautionary principle "would make for a dim future" (Morris 2000, 1, 17). It would also eliminate technologies and strategies that make human lives easier, more convenient, healthier, and longer.

But there is something both odd and revealing about these claims. The precautionary principle is designed to decrease morbidity and mortality; how could it possibly make the future "dim"? I suggest that the real problem with the principle is that it offers no guidance—not that it is wrong, but that it forbids all courses of action, including regulation. Taken seriously, it bans the very steps that it requires. To understand the difficulty, it will be useful to anchor the discussion in some concrete problems.

- Genetic modification of food has become a widespread practice (McHughen 2000). The risks of that practice are not known with any precision. Some people fear that genetic modification will result in serious ecological harm and large risks to human health; others believe that genetic modification will result in more nutritious food and significant improvements in human health.
- Scientists are not in accord about the dangers associated with global warming,[6] but there is general agreement that global warming is in fact occurring. It is possible that global warming will produce, by 2100, a mean temperature increase

---

[6] For discussion, see Posner (2004); Lomborg (2001); Nordhaus and Boyer (2000).

of 4.5°C (the high-end estimate of the International Panel on Climate Change); that it will result in $5 trillion or more in monetized costs; and that it will also produce a significant number of deaths from malaria. The Kyoto Protocol would require most industrialized nations to reduce greenhouse gas emissions to 92% to 94% of 1990 levels. A great deal of work suggests that significant decreases in such emissions would have large benefits; but skeptics contend that the costs of such decreases would reduce the well-being of millions of people, especially the poorest members of society.

- Many people fear nuclear power, on the ground that nuclear power plants create various health and safety risks, including some possibility of catastrophe. But if a nation does not rely on nuclear power, it might well rely instead on fossil fuels, and in particular on coal-fired power plants. Such plants create risks of their own, including risks associated with global warming. China, for example, has relied on nuclear energy in a way that reduces greenhouse gases and a range of air pollution problems.[7]
- In the first years of the twenty-first century, one of the most controversial environmental issues in the United States involved the regulation of arsenic in drinking water. There is a serious dispute over the precise level of risks posed by low levels of arsenic in water, but in the "worst-case" scenario, over 100 lives might be lost each year as a result of the 50 part per billion (ppb) standard that the Clinton administration sought to revise. At the same time, the proposed 10 ppb standard would cost over $200 million each year, and it is possible that it would save as few as 6 lives annually.

In these cases, what kind of guidance is provided by the precautionary principle? It is tempting to say, as is in fact standard, that the principle calls for strong controls on genetic engineering of food, on greenhouse gases, on arsenic, and on nuclear power. In all of these cases, there is a possibility of serious harms, and no authoritative scientific evidence demonstrates that the possibility is close to zero. If the burden of proof is on the proponent of the activity or processes in question, the precautionary principle would seem to impose a burden of proof that cannot be met. Put to one side the question whether the precautionary principle, understood to compel stringent regulation in these cases, is sensible. Let us ask a more fundamental question: Is that more stringent regulation therefore compelled by the precautionary principle?

The answer is that it is not. In some of these cases, it should be easy to see that in its own way, stringent regulation would actually run afoul of the precautionary principle. The simplest reason is that such regulation might well deprive society of significant benefits, and hence produce serious harms that would otherwise not occur. In some

---

[7] See Zhong (2000). Of course, it is possible to urge that nations should reduce reliance on both coal-fired power plants and nuclear power and move instead toward environmentally preferred alternatives such as solar power. For general discussion, see Boyle (1996); Collinson (1991); Arvizu (2001). But these alternatives pose problems of their own, involving feasibility and expense. See Lomborg (2001, 118–148).

cases, regulation eliminates the "opportunity benefits" of a process or activity, and thus causes preventable deaths. If this is so, regulation is hardly precautionary. Consider the "drug lag," produced whenever the government takes a highly precautionary approach to the introduction of new medicines and drugs onto the market. If a government insists on such an approach, it will protect people against harms from inadequately tested drugs; but it will also prevent people from receiving potential benefits from those very drugs. Is it "precautionary" to require extensive premarketing testing, or to do the opposite?

In the context of medicines to prevent AIDS, those who favor "precautions" have asked governments to reduce the level of premarketing testing, precisely in the interest of health. The United States, by the way, is more precautionary about new medicines than are most European nations. But by failing to allow such medicines on the market, the United States fails to take precautions against the illnesses that could be reduced by speedier procedures.

Or consider the continuing debate over whether certain antidepressants impose a (small) risk of breast cancer (Kelly et al. 1999; Sharpe et al. 2002). A precautionary approach might seem to caution against use of such antidepressants because of their carcinogenic potential. But the failure to use those depressants might well impose risks of its own, certainly psychological and possibly even physical (because psychological ailments are sometimes associated with physical ones as well). Or consider the decision by the Soviet Union to evacuate and relocate more than 270,000 people in response to the risk of adverse effects from the Chernobyl fallout. It is not clear that on balance, this massive relocation project was justified on health grounds: "A comparison ought to have been made between the psychological and medical burdens of this measure (anxiety, psychosomatic diseases, depression, and suicides) and the harm that may have been prevented" (Tubiana 2000). More generally, a sensible government might want to ignore the small risks associated with low levels of radiation, on the ground that precautionary responses are likely to cause fear that outweighs any health benefits from those responses.[8]

Or consider a more general question about how to handle low-level toxic agents, including carcinogens. Do such agents cause adverse effects? If we lack clear evidence, it might seem "precautionary" to assume that they do, and hence to assume, in the face of uncertainty, that the dose-response curve is linear and without safe thresholds.[9] In the United States, this is the default assumption of the U.S. Environmental Protection Agency (EPA). But is this approach unambiguously precautionary? Considerable evidence suggests that many toxic agents that are harmful at high levels are actually beneficial at low levels (Calabrese and Baldwin 2003a, 2003b). Thus, "hormesis" is a dose-response relationship in which low doses stimulate desirable effects and high doses inhibit them. When hormesis is involved, government use of a linear dose-response

---

[8] For some counterevidence in an important context, see Hardell et al. (2003), discussing evidence of an association between cellular telephones and cancer.

[9] For criticism of the linearity assumption, see Tubiana (2000).

curve, assuming no safe thresholds, will actually cause mortality and morbidity effects. Which default approach to the dose-response curve is precautionary? To raise this question is not to take any stand on whether some, many, or all toxic agents are beneficial or instead harmful at very low doses. It is only to say that the simultaneous possibility of benefits at low levels and of harms at low levels makes the precautionary principle paralyzing. The principle requires use of a linear, nonthreshold model; but it simultaneously condemns use of that very model. For this and other reasons, unreflective use of the precautionary principle, it has been argued, threatens to increase rather than decrease the risks associated with food (Hanekamp et al. 2003).

Or consider the case of genetic modification of food. Many people believe that a failure to allow genetic modification might well result in numerous deaths, and a small probability of many more. The reason is that genetic modification holds out the promise of producing food that is both cheaper and healthier—resulting, for example, in "golden rice," which might have large benefits in developing countries. My point is not that genetic modification will likely have those benefits, or that the benefits of genetic modification outweigh the risks. The claim is only that if the precautionary principle is taken literally, it is offended by regulation as well as by nonregulation.

The example suggests that regulation sometimes violates the precautionary principle because it gives rise to *substitute risks*, in the form of hazards that materialize, or are increased, as a result of regulation.[10] Consider the case of DDT, often banned or regulated in the interest of reducing risks to birds and human beings. The problem with such bans is that in poor nations, they eliminate what appears to be the most effective way of combating malaria—and thus significantly undermine public health (Goklany 2001). Or consider EPA's effort to ban asbestos (*Corrosion Proof Fittings v. EPA* 1991), a ban that might well seem justified or even compelled by the precautionary principle. The difficulty, from the standpoint of that very principle, is that substitutes for asbestos also carry risks. The problem is pervasive. In the case of arsenic, the administrator of EPA expressed concern that aggressive regulation, by virtue of its cost, will lead people to cease using local water systems and to rely on private wells, which have high levels of contamination.[11] If this is so, stringent arsenic regulation violates the precautionary principle no less than less stringent regulation does. This is a common situation, for opportunity benefits and substitute risks are the rule, not the exception.[12]

It is possible to go much further. A great deal of evidence suggests the possibility that an expensive regulation can have adverse effects on life and health (Keeney

---

[10] See the discussion of risk-related trade-offs in Graham and Wiener (1995); Sunstein (2002).

[11] "But we have seen instances, particularly in the West and Midwest, where arsenic is naturally occurring at up to 700 and more ppb, where the cost of remediation has forced water companies to close, leaving people with no way to get their water, save dig wells. And then they are getting water that's even worse than what they were getting through the water company" (Whitman 2001).

[12] Note also that some regulation will have ancillary *benefits*, by reducing risks other than those that are specifically targeted. For a valuable discussion, see Rascoff and Revesz (2002).

1990; Lutter and Morrall 1994). It has been urged that a statistical life can be lost for every expenditure of $7 million (Keeney 1990); one study suggests that an expenditure of $15 million produces a loss of life (Hahn et al. 2000). Another suggests that poor people are especially vulnerable to this effect—that a regulation that reduces wealth for the poorest 20% of the population will have twice as large a mortality effect as a regulation that reduces wealth for the wealthiest 20% (Chapman and Hariharan 1996). To be sure, both the phenomenon and the underlying mechanisms are disputed (Lutter and Morrall 1994). I do not mean to accept any particular amount here, or even to suggest that there has been an unambiguous demonstration of an association between mortality and regulatory expenditures. The only point is that reasonable people believe in that association. It follows that a multimillion-dollar expenditure for "precaution" has—as a worst-case scenario—significant adverse health effects, with an expenditure of $200 million leading to perhaps as many as 20 to 30 lives lost.

This point makes the precautionary principle hard to implement not merely where regulation removes "opportunity benefits," or introduces or increases substitute risks, but in any case in which the regulation costs a significant amount. If this is so, the precautionary principle, for that very reason, raises doubts about many regulations. If the principle argues against any action that carries a small risk of imposing significant harm, then we should be reluctant to spend a lot of money to reduce risks, simply because those expenditures themselves carry risks. Here is the sense in which the precautionary principle, taken for all that it is worth, is paralyzing: it stands as an obstacle to regulation and nonregulation, and to everything in between.

It should now be easier to understand my earlier suggestion that despite their formal enthusiasm for the precautionary principle, European nations are not "more precautionary" than the United States. Simply as a logical matter, societies, like individuals, cannot be highly precautionary with respect to all risks. Each society and each person must select certain risks for special attention. In these respects, the selectivity of precautions is not merely an empirical fact; it is a conceptual inevitability. Comparing Europe with the United States, Wiener and Rogers (2002) have demonstrated this point empirically. In the early twenty-first century, for example, the United States appears to take a highly precautionary approach to the risks associated with abandoned hazardous waste dumps and terrorism, but not to take a highly precautionary approach to the risks associated with global warming, indoor air pollution, poverty, poor diet, and obesity. It would be most valuable to attempt to see which nations are especially precautionary with respect to which risks, and also to explore changes over time.

A nation-by-nation study commissioned by the German Federal Environmental Agency goes so far as to conclude that there are two separate camps in the industrialized world: "precaution countries" (Germany, Sweden, the Netherlands, and the United States) and "protection countries" (Japan, France, and the United Kingdom) (Sand 2000, 448). But this conclusion seems to me ludicrously implausible. The universe of risks is far too large to permit categorizations of this kind. The most general point is that no nation is precautionary in general, and costly precautions are inevitably taken against only those hazards that seem especially salient or insistent.[13] The problem with the precautionary principle is that it wrongly suggests that nations can and should adopt a general form of risk aversion.

The Availability Heuristic

I suggest that the precautionary principle becomes operational if and only if those who apply it wear blinders—only, that is, if they focus on some aspects of the regulatory situation but downplay or disregard others. But this suggestion simply raises an additional question: What accounts for the particular blinders that underlie applications of the precautionary principle? Which peoples' attention is selective, and why is it selective in the way that it is? Might different nations, with quite different policies, all believe that they are being precautionary? Much of the answer, I contend, lies in an understanding of behavioral economics and cognitive psychology, which provide important clues to cross-cultural differences in risk perception. The *availability heuristic* is the place to start.

It is well established that in thinking about risks, people rely on certain heuristics, or rules of thumb, which serve to simplify their inquiry (see Kahneman et al. 1982). Heuristics typically work through a process of "attribute substitution," in which people answer a hard question by substituting an easier one (Kahneman and Frederick 2002). Should we be fearful of nuclear power, terrorism, abduction of young children, mad cow disease, contaminated blood, or pesticides? When people use the availability heuristic, they assess the magnitude of risks by asking whether examples can readily come to mind (Tversky and Kahneman 2002). If people can easily think of such examples, they are far more likely to be frightened than if they cannot. The availability heuristic illuminates the operation of the precautionary principle, by showing why some hazards will be on-screen and why others will be neglected. The availability heuristic also tells us a great deal about differences in risk perceptions across groups, cultures, and even nations.

For example, "a class whose instances are easily retrieved will appear more numerous than a class of equal frequency whose instances are less retrievable" (Tversky and Kahneman 2002, 11). Consider a simple study showing people a list of well-known people of both sexes, and asking them whether the list contains more names of women or more names of men. In lists in which the men were especially famous, people thought that there were more names of men, whereas in lists in which the women were the more famous, people thought that there were more names of women (Tversky and Kahneman 2002).

This is a point about how *familiarity* can affect the availability of instances. A risk that is familiar, like that associated with terrorism, will be seen as more serious than a risk that is less familiar, like that associated with sunbathing. But *salience* is important as

---

[13] See Vogel (2003, 570–571) for a demonstration of this point for Europe.

well. "For example, the impact of seeing a house burning on the subjective probability of such accidents is probably greater than the impact of reading about a fire in the local paper" (Tversky and Kahneman 2002, 11). So, too, will recent events have a greater impact than earlier ones. The point helps explain differences across time and space in much risk-related behavior, including decisions to take precautions. Whether people will buy insurance for natural disasters is greatly affected by recent experiences (Slovic 2000). If floods have not occurred in the immediate past, people who live on floodplains are far less likely to purchase insurance. In the aftermath of an earthquake, insurance for earthquakes rises sharply—but it declines steadily from that point, as vivid memories recede. Note that the use of the availability heuristic, in these contexts, is hardly irrational.[14] Both insurance and precautionary measures can be expensive, and what has happened before seems, much of the time, to be the best available guide to what will happen again. The problem is that the availability heuristic can lead to serious errors, in terms of both excessive fear and neglect.

What, in particular, produces availability? An intriguing essay attempts to test the effects of ease of *imagery* on perceived judgments of risk (Sherman et al. 2002). The study asked subjects to read about an illness, Hyposcenia-B, that "was becoming increasingly prevalent" on the local campus. In one condition, the symptoms were concrete and easy to imagine, involving muscle aches, low energy, and frequent severe headaches. In another condition, the symptoms were vague and hard to imagine, involving an inflamed liver, a malfunctioning nervous system, and a general sense of disorientation. Subjects in both conditions were asked to imagine a three-week period in which they had the disease and to write a detailed description of what they imagined. After doing so, subjects were asked to assess, on a 10-point scale, their likelihood of contracting the disease. The basic finding was that likelihood judgments were very different in the two conditions, with easily imagined symptoms making people far more inclined to believe that they were likely to get the disease.

The availability heuristic helps to explain the operation of the precautionary principle and cross-national differences for a simple reason: sometimes a certain risk, said to call for precautions, is cognitively available, whereas other risks, including those associated with regulation itself, are not. In many cases where the precautionary principle seems to offer guidance, the reason is that some of the relevant risks are available while others are barely visible. And if one nation is concerned with the risk of sunbathing and another is not, availability is likely to provide a large part of the reason. This, then, is my central hypothesis: differences across nations, in the perception of risks, have a great deal to do with the operation of the availability heuristic.

---

[14] Tversky and Kahneman emphasize that the heuristics they identify "are highly economical and usually effective," but also that they "lead to systematic and predictable errors" (1986, 38, 55). Gigerenzer et al. (1999) and Gigerenzer (2000), among others, have emphasized that some heuristics can work extremely well; they use this point as a rejoinder to those who stress the errors introduced by heuristics and biases. I do not mean to take a stand on the resulting debates. Even if many heuristics mostly work well in daily life, a sensible government can do much better than to rely on them.

To be sure, those differences are also motivated in large part by actual differences in risk levels. Fortunately, reality matters. Nations suffering from high levels of malaria are likely to perceive malaria risks as far greater than nations in which malaria is not a problem. Countries that face serious risks from contaminated blood will probably show greater fear of contaminated blood than countries in which contaminated blood is not a problem. But availability produces differences in perceptions that do not track differences in reality.

The study of cross-cultural risk perceptions remains in its infancy (Renn and Rohrmann 2000), and hence my claim must remain only a hypothesis, one that I cannot establish to be true. What is necessary, and what is lacking, is anything like comprehensive information about cross-cultural risk perceptions that would allow us to test the role of availability. And we shall shortly see some complexities that bear on the adequacy of the availability hypothesis. But for now, consider some supportive evidence.

- Within the United States, public concern about risks usually does track changes in the actual fluctuations in those risks. But public concern outruns actual fluctuations in the important case of "panics," bred by vivid illustrations that do not reflect changes in levels of danger (Loewenstein and Mather 1990). At certain points in the 1970s and 1980s, there were extreme leaps in concern about teenage suicides, herpes, illegitimacy, and AIDS—leaps that did not correspond to changes in the size of the problem. Availability, produced by "a particularly vivid case or new finding that receives considerable media attention," played a major role in those leaps in public concern (Loewenstein and Mather 1990, 172). Sometimes the concern led to unjustified precautions, as in the behavior of some parents who refused to allow their children to attend classes alongside students with signs of herpes.

- Availability helps to explain the findings of a cross-national study of perceptions of risk associated with terrorism and severe acute respiratory syndrome (SARS) (Feigenson et al. 2004). In that study, Americans perceived terrorism to be a far greater threat, to themselves and to others, than SARS; Canadians perceived SARS to be a greater threat, to themselves and to others, than terrorism. Americans estimated their chance of serious harm from terrorism as 8.27%, about four times as high as their estimate of their chance of serious harm from SARS (2.18%). Canadians estimated their chance of serious harm from SARS as 7.43%, significantly higher than their estimate for terrorism (6.04%). Notably, the figures for SARS were unrealistically high, especially for Canadians; the best estimate of the risk of contracting SARS, based on Canadian figures, was .0008% (and the chance of dying as a result was less than .0002%). For obvious reasons, the objective risks from terrorism are much harder to calculate, but if it is estimated that the United States will suffer at least one terrorist attack each year with the same number of deaths as on September 11, 2001, the risk of death from terrorism is about .001%—a speculative number under the circumstances, but not an implausible place to start.

The availability heuristic helps to account for these cross-national differences and for the generally exaggerated risk perceptions. In the United States, risks of terrorism have (to say the least) received a great deal of attention, producing a continuing sense of threat. But there have been no incidents of SARS, and the media coverage has been limited to events elsewhere—producing a degree of salience, but far lower than that associated with terrorism. In Canada, the opposite is the case. The high degree of public discussion of SARS cases, accompanied by readily available instances, produced an inflated sense of the numbers—sufficiently inflated to exceed the same numbers from terrorism (certainly a salient risk in Canada, as in most nations post-9/11).

- What accounts for people's perception of their risk of being infected with HIV? Why are some people and some groups largely unconcerned about that risk, while other people and groups are highly focused on it? A study of rural Kenya and Malawi by Behrman et al. (2003) suggests that availability plays a critical role. The authors find that risk perception is a product of discussions that "are often provoked by observing or hearing about an illness or death." People "know in the abstract how HIV is transmitted and how it can be prevented," but they are unclear "about the advisability and effectiveness of the changes in sexual behavior that are recommended by experts" (Behrman et al. 2003, 10, 18). Perceptions of the risk of HIV transmission are very much a function of social networks, with pronounced changes in belief and behavior resulting from interactions with other people expressing a high level of concern. The effects of social networks are thus asymmetric, with substantial effects from having "at least one network partner who is perceived to have a great deal of concern about AIDS" (Behrman et al. 2003). The authors do not refer explicitly to the availability heuristic, but their findings are compatible with the suggestion that with respect to AIDS, risk perceptions are produced by availability.
- A study of Bulgaria and Romania by Sjöberg et al. (2000) concludes that differences in levels of perceived risk "cannot be explained by differences in levels of real risk." Indeed, the content of media are "a more potent determinant of perceived risk than real risk." Cultural variables were not found to be crucial. In general, "perceived risk is a function of real risk and perhaps media risk rather than culturally contingent values and belief" (Sjöberg et al. 2000, 147, 178).
- There are many commonalities between the risk perceptions of Americans and those of citizens of France. But such differences as there are have a great deal to do with availability. Hence, there is far more concern in France with genetically engineered bacteria, a risk with a high degree of publicity. By contrast, Americans show far more concern in the United States with coal-fired power plants, with radon in the home, and with suntanning—three much-publicized sources of risk (Slovic et al. 2000).
- What accounts for the recent rise of precautionary thinking in Europe? Why have certain environmental and health risks achieved so much salience in England, France, and the European Union generally? A comprehensive study (Vogel 2003) suggests that a few readily available incidents played a large role. In the 1990s, a

"wave of crises" involving food safety—above all, mad cow disease—led to the deaths of about 100 people, with especially large effects on public attitudes. In a tribute to the operation of availability, the "regulatory failure associated with BSE significantly affected the attitude of the European public toward GM foods." An additional "scandal was the apparent failure of French government officials and doctors to protect haemophiliacs from blood contaminated with AIDS" virus, in a way that had large repercussions for public opinion in France. The conclusion is that differences between European and American policies are not a product of deep-rooted cultural differences, but instead have a great deal to do with "widespread public perception of regulatory failures," often based on particular, vivid, and widely salient events (Vogel 2003, 569, 570–571, 580).

Social Influences

Thus far, my emphasis has been on individual cognition. But, to say the least, the availability heuristic does not operate in a social vacuum. What is readily "available" to some individuals, groups, cultures, and nations will not be available to all. Within the United States, many of those who favor gun control legislation have "available" a set of incidents in which such legislation would have avoided unnecessary deaths; many of those who reject such legislation are alert to incidents in which private gun ownership allowed people to fend off criminal violence (Kahan and Braman 2003). Obviously, both government and the media make some risks appear particularly salient. Consider President George W. Bush's plea: "Imagine those 19 hijackers [involved in the 9/11 attacks] with other weapons and plans, this time armed by Saddam Hussein. It would take one vial, one canister, one crate slipped into this country to bring a day of horror like none we have ever known." Environmentalists, in and out of government, operate in the same way, focusing public attention on potentially catastrophic harms. Well-organized private groups play a central role in activating public concern.

The question suggests the need to attend to the social and cultural dimensions of fear and risk perception. In many cases of high-visibility, low-probability dangers, such as sniper attacks, shark attacks, contaminated blood, and the kidnapping of young girls, the sources of availability are not obscure. The mass media focus on those risks; people communicate their fear and concern to one another; the widespread fact of fear and concern increases media attention; and the spiral continues until people move on. Hence the "risk of the month" syndrome, familiar in many societies, stems from the interaction between availability and social influences. Much of the time, however, what is available and salient to some is not available and salient to all. For example, many of those who endorse the precautionary principle focus on cases in which the government failed to regulate some environmental harm, demanding irrefutable proof, with the consequence being widespread illness and death. To such people, the available incidents require strong precautions in the face of uncertainty. But many other people, skeptical of the precautionary principle, focus on cases in which the government overreacted to weak science, causing large expenditures for little gain in terms of health or safety. To such people, the available incidents justify a measure of restraint in the face of uncertainty. Which cases will be available and to whom?

In any case, people and cultures have different *predispositions*. These predispositions play a large role in determining which, of the numerous possibilities, is salient. If you are predisposed to be fearful of genetic modification of food, you are more likely to seek out, and to recall, incidents in which genetic modification was said to cause harm. If you are predisposed to fear electromagnetic fields, you will pay attention to apparent incidents in which electromagnetic fields have produced an elevated incidence of cancer. If you are predisposed to believe that most media scares are false or trumped up, you will find cases in which public fears have been proved baseless. These are examples of individual predispositions, but undoubtedly cultural forces, some deep and some less so, help account for differences across nations.

Availability helps to determine beliefs, to be sure; but beliefs help to determine availability as well. Both beliefs and availability are endogenous to one another. When social and cultural forces interact with salience, to produce concern about one set of problems but not another, predispositions are crucial. It is in this sense that availability can be a product of forces that must be explained independently. But let us now turn to how availability spreads.

Cascades

Sometimes availability and salience are produced through social bandwagons or cascades, in which apparently representative anecdotes and gripping examples move rapidly from one person to another (Heath 1996; Heath et al. 2001). Consider a stylized example. Andrew hears of a dangerous event, which he finds to be revealing or illustrative. (The event might involve crime, terrorism, pesticides, environmental hazards, or threats to national security.) Andrew tells Barry, who would be inclined to see the event as not terribly informative, but who, learning Andrew's reaction, comes to believe that the event does indeed reveal a great deal, and that a serious threat exists. Carol would tend to discount the risk, but once she hears the shared opinion of Andrew and Barry, she is frightened as well. Deborah will have to have a great deal of private information to reject what has become the shared opinion of Andrew, Barry, and Carol (Hirshleifer 1995). Stylized though it is, the example shows that once several people start to take an example as probative, many people may come to be influenced by their opinion, giving rise to cascade effects. Cultural and even national differences can be explained partly in this way.

Among doctors dealing with risks and precautions, cascades are common. "Most doctors are not at the cutting edge of research; their inevitable reliance upon what colleagues have done and are doing leads to numerous surgical fads and treatment-caused illnesses" (Hirshleifer 1995, 204). Thus, an article in the prestigious *New England*

Journal of Medicine explores "bandwagon diseases" in which doctors act like "lemmings, episodically and with a blind infectious enthusiasm pushing certain diseases and treatments primarily because everyone else is doing the same" (Burnham 1987). Some medical practices, including tonsillectomy, "seem to have been adopted initially based on weak information," and extreme differences in tonsillectomy frequencies (and other procedures) provide good evidence that cascades are at work (Bikhchandani et al. 1998). Cross-cultural differences in medical practices can be explained in significant part through this route.

A distinctive feature of social cascades is that the people who participate in them are simultaneously amplifying the very social signal by which they are being influenced. By their very participation, those who join the cascade increase its size, making it more likely that others will join too. Unfortunately, cascades can lead people in mistaken directions, with a few "early movers" spurring social fear that does not match reality. In the example I have given, Andrew is having a large influence on the judgments of our little group, even though he may not, in fact, have accurate information about the relevant event. Barry, Carol, and Deborah might have some information of their own, perhaps enough to show that there is little reason for concern. But unless they have a great deal of confidence in what they know, they are likely to follow those who preceded them. The irony is that if most people are following others, then little information is provided by the fact that some or many seem to share a certain fear. Most are responding to the signals provided by others, unaware that those others are doing exactly the same thing. Of course, corrections might well come eventually, but sometimes they are late.

In the domain of risks and precautions, "availability cascades" are responsible for many social beliefs (Kuran and Sunstein 1999). A salient event, affecting people because it is available, tends to be repeated, leading to cascade effects as the event becomes available to increasingly large numbers of people. The point is amplified by the fact that fear-inducing accounts, with high emotional valence, are especially likely to spread (Heath et al. 2001). There is a general implication here. Because different social influences can be found in different communities, local variations are inevitable, with different examples becoming salient in each. Hence, such variations—between, say, New York and Ohio, or England and the United States, or Germany and France—might involve coincidence or small or random factors, rather than large-scale cultural differences. Different judgments within different social groups, with different "available" examples, owe their origin to social processes of this sort. Indeed, the different reactions to nuclear power in France and the United States can be explained in large part in this way. And when some groups concentrate on cases in which guns increased violence, and others on cases in which guns decreased violence, availability cascades are a large part of the reason. Return to my earlier quote: "Many Germans believe that drinking water after eating cherries is deadly; they also believe that putting ice in soft drinks is unhealthy. The English, however, rather enjoy a cold drink of water after some cherries; and Americans love icy refreshments" (Henrich et al. 2001, 353–354).

Group Polarization

There is a closely related phenomenon. When like-minded people deliberate with one another, they typically end up accepting a more extreme version of the views with which they began (Sunstein 2003b). This is the process known as *group polarization*. Consider a few examples:

- After discussion, citizens of France become more critical of the United States and its intentions with respect to economic aid (Brown 1985).
- A group of moderately profeminist women becomes more strongly profeminist after discussion (Myers 1975).
- After discussion, whites predisposed to show racial prejudice offer more negative responses to the question of whether white racism is responsible for conditions faced by African Americans in American cities (Myers and Bishop 1971).
- After discussion, whites predisposed not to show racial prejudice offer more positive responses to the same question; that is, they are more likely to find white prejudice to be the source of conditions faced by African Americans in American cities (Myers and Bishop 1971).
- Juries inclined to award punitive damages typically produce awards that are significantly higher than the awards chosen, before deliberation, by their median member (Sunstein et al. 2002).

Group polarization will inevitably occur in the context of perceptions of risk, and hence group polarization helps to account for cultural and even national differences. If several people who fear global warming or terrorism speak to one another, their fear is likely to increase as a result of internal discussions. If other people believe that nuclear power is probably safe, their belief to that effect will be fortified after they speak with one another, to the point where they will believe that nuclear power is no reason for concern. If some groups seem hysterical about certain risks, and other groups treat those risks as nonexistent, group polarization is likely to be a reason. Hence group polarization provides another explanation for the different fears of groups, localities, and even nations. Internal discussions can make Berliners fearful of risks that do not bother New Yorkers, and vice versa; so, too, the citizens of London may fear a supposed danger that does not much bother the citizens of Paris—even if the danger is not greater in the former than in the latter.

Group polarization undoubtedly occurs in connection with the availability heuristic. Suppose, for example, that several people are discussing mad cow disease, or a recent wave of sniper attacks, or cases involving the kidnapping of young girls, or situations in which the government has wrongly ignored a serious foreign threat. If the particular examples are mentioned, they are likely to prove memorable. And if the group has a predisposition to think that one or another risk is serious, social dynamics will lead the group to believe that the example is highly revealing. An initial predisposition toward fear is likely to be aggravated after collective deliberations. Within groups, a tendency toward fear breeds its own amplification.

Consider in this light the 2004 report of the U.S. Senate Select Committee on Intelligence, which contended the predisposition of the Central Intelligence Agency (CIA) to find a serious threat from Iraq led it to fail to explore alternative possibilities or to obtain and use the information that it actually held. Falling victim to group polarization in the particular context of fear, the agency showed a "tendency to reject information that contradicted the presumption" that Iraq had weapons of mass destruction (U.S. Senate Select Committee on Intelligence 2004, 6). This claim is a remarkable echo of one that followed the 2003 investigation of failures at the National Aeronautics and Space Administration (NASA), in which the Columbia Accident Investigation Board explicitly attributed the accident to NASA's unfortunate culture, one it said did too little to elicit information. In the board's words, NASA lacked "checks and balances" and pressured people to follow a "party line" (Columbia Accident Investigation Board 2003). The result was a process of polarization that led to a dismissal of serious risks.

Media, Interest Groups, and Politicians

It should be clear that in the real world, some voices are more important than others, especially when availability and salience are involved. In particular, the behavior and preoccupations of the media play a large role. Many perceived "epidemics" are in reality no such thing, but instead a product of media coverage of gripping, unrepresentative incidents. Attention to those incidents is likely to ensure availability and salience, promoting an inaccurately high estimate of probability and at the same time some degree of probability neglect. And in the face of close media attention, the demand for legal responses will be significantly affected. Changes within and even across nations are a natural result.

Knowing the importance of media coverage, well-organized private groups work extremely hard to promote public attention to particular risks. Some of these groups are altruistic; others are entirely self-interested. The common tactic is to publicize an incident that might trigger both availability and salience. Terrorists themselves are the most extreme and vicious example, using high-visibility attacks to convince people that "they cannot be safe anywhere." But many illustrations are less objectionable and sometimes even benign. In the United States, consider the abandoned hazardous waste at Love Canal, an event used to promote hazardous waste cleanup, or the Exxon *Valdez* disaster, an event used by the Sierra Club and other environmental organizations to promote more stringent safeguards against oil spills. Showing at least a working knowledge of the availability heuristic, private groups seize on selected incidents and publicize them to make them generally salient to the public. In all of these examples, the use of particular instances might be necessary to move the public, and legislatures, in the right directions. Certainly the social processes that interact with salience and availability can promote reform where it is needed. But there is no assurance here, particularly if social influences are leading people to exaggerate a problem or to ignore the question of probability altogether.

Politicians engage in the same basic project. By its very nature, the voice of an influential politician comes with amplifiers. When public officials bring an incident before the public, a seemingly illustrative example is likely to spread far and wide. A legal enactment can itself promote availability; if the law responds to the problems associated with hazardous waste dumps or "hate crimes," people might well come to see those problems as readily available. The terrorist attacks of September 11, 2001, would inevitably loom large no matter what President George W. Bush had chosen to emphasize. But the president, and his White House generally, referred to the attacks on countless occasions, frequently as a way of emphasizing the reality of seemingly distant threats and the need to incur significant costs to counteract them (including the 2003 Iraq war, itself fueled by presidential speeches including vivid narratives of catastrophic harm). No doubt the salience of these attacks played a large role in affecting political behavior—and this role cannot be understood without reference to social influences. The implications for cultural differences should be clear. If leaders in different nations draw attention to different risks, there will be large-scale differences in risk perceptions.

Predispositions and Culture

But all this does not provide the full picture. Beliefs and orientations are a product of availability, and social influences ensure both availability and salience. But as I have suggested, what is available is also a product of antecedent beliefs and orientations, both individual and social. In other words, availability is endogenous to, or a product of, predispositions, whether individual, cultural, or national. A great deal of further work remains to be done on this topic.[15]

Why do some people recall and emphasize incidents in which a failure to take precautions led to serious environmental harm? A likely reason is that they are predisposed to favor environmental protection. And why do some people recall and emphasize incidents in which environmental protection led to huge costs for little gain? A likely reason is that they are predisposed to oppose environmental controls. Here is an interaction between the availability heuristic and confirmation bias—"the tendency to seek information to confirm our original hypotheses and beliefs" (Aronson 1995), a tendency that reviewers have found in the judgments by the CIA and NASA described above. Confirmation bias plays a large role in different risk perceptions across individuals and groups. If members of a culturally distinct group are predisposed to believe that new technologies are risky, or that genetically modified organisms are hazardous, or that cell phones produce cancer, apparently supportive illustrations will be memorable, and contrary ones will be discounted.

---

[15] On culture, an influential treatment is Douglas and Wildavsky (1984); a natural reading of work by, and inspired by, Douglas and Wildavsky is that availability is a product of cultural orientations, rather than vice versa. But see Vogel (2003) for a contrasting view.

Of course, predispositions are not a black box, and they do not come from the sky. They have sources. Among their sources are availability and salience. After incidents of mad cow disease in England, many Europeans lost trust in the relevant authorities and acquired a predisposition to fear, and to take and urge precautions against, associated and analogous threats. In Europe, the growth of precautionary thinking across certain domains had a great deal to do with particular salient incidents (Vogel 2003). Hence, a complex set of interactions, with heuristics helping to constitute predispositions, is in turn responsible for the real-world operation of heuristics. All this happens socially, not merely individually; and predispositions are not static. When people are in a group that is predisposed in a particular direction, the salient examples will be quite different from those that are salient in a group with an opposite predisposition. Here group polarization is especially important. What is sometimes described as "culture," or as "deep-rooted cultural differences," may be no such thing. Cascade effects and polarization, interacting with availability, can be responsible for inclinations and variations that might well have taken another form.

On the other hand, different cultural orientations can play a large role in determining what turns out to be available. For example, the United States is highly diverse, and for some purposes, it is plausible to think of different regions and groups as having different cultures. Within African American communities, the available instances are sometimes quite different from those that can be found within all-white communities. Across nations, the differences are even more striking, in part because different worldviews play such a dominant role. And what is true for individuals is true for nations as well. Just as predispositions are in part a function of availability, so too availability is in part a function of predispositions. Social influences operate at both levels, affecting what is available and also moving predispositions in one or another direction. The problem is that both individuals and societies may be fearful of nonexistent or trivial risks—and simultaneously neglect real dangers.

Conclusions

In this chapter, I have ventured a conceptual claim and a psychological hypothesis. The conceptual claim is that it is not possible to be "precautionary" in general. An individual or a nation can take precautions against particular risks, to be sure, but no individual or nation can be precautionary as a general proposition. The reason is that risks are on all sides of social situations. If a person or state purports to be precautionary, it is almost certainly taking steps that create risks of their own. The point certainly holds for aggressive regulation of genetic modification of food and greenhouse gases; it holds as well for preemptive wars.

The psychological hypothesis is that the operation of the precautionary principle and differences in risk perception among nations have a great deal to do with the availability heuristic. If people can think of cases in which a risk has come to fruition, they are far more likely to think that the risk should be taken seriously. "Availability bias," in the form of excessive fear, and "unavailability bias," in the form of unjustified neglect, are unfortunate results. All cultures suffer from both of these. But they suffer from them in different ways, because what is available in one culture is often less available, or unavailable, in others.

Of course, availability is a product of social influences. Cascade effects and group polarization play substantial roles in making one or another incident available to many or most. There are multiple equilibria here: it is hardly inevitable that SARS would have great salience in Canada but not in the United States. Single incidents and small shocks can make an extraordinary difference. Moreover, what is available to some will not be available to all, in part because of social influences, and in part because of individual, cultural, and national predispositions. Hence, I have emphasized that some cultures will find some risks "available" not because of simple facts, but because the relevant citizens are predisposed to focus on some risks rather than others.

I believe that the availability heuristic provides many clues about the operation of the precautionary principle and cross-cultural risk perceptions. But a great deal of empirical work remains to be done, not least in exploring the complex interactions among individual cognition, cascade effects, the behavior of those who spread information, and cultural predispositions.

Disclaimer

This essay was completed long before the author entered federal employment, where he now serves as administrator of the Office of Information and Regulatory Affairs. Nothing said here reflects in any way an official position of the U.S. government.

References

Applegate, John S. 2000. The Precautionary Preference: An American Perspective on the Precautionary Principle. *Human and Ecological Risk Assessment* 6: 413–443.

Aronson, Elliott. 1995. *The Social Animal*. 7th ed. New York: W. H. Freeman.

Arvizu, Dan E. 2001. Advanced Energy Technology and Climate Change Policy Implications. *Florida Coastal Law Journal* 2: 435.

Behrman, Jere R., Hans-Peter Kohler, and Susan Cotts Watkins. 2003. Social Networks, HIV/AIDS, and Risk Perceptions. Penn Institute for Economic Research Working Paper No. 03-007. February 18.

Bikhchandani, Sushil, David Hirshleifer, and Ivo Welch. 1998. Learning from the Behavior of Others: Conformity, Fads, and Informational Cascades. *Journal of Economic Perspective* 12 (3): 151–170.

Blackwelder, Brent. 2002. Testimony before the Senate Appropriations Committee, Subcommittee on Labor, Health, and Human Services. January 24.

Boyle, Godfrey. ed. 1996. *Renewable Energy: Power for a Sustainable Future*. Oxford: Oxford University Press in association with the Open University.

Brown, Roger. 1985. *Social Psychology*. 2nd ed. New York: Free Press.

Burnham, John F. 1987. Medical Practice a la Mode: How Medical Fashions Determine Medical Care. *New England Journal of Medicine* 317: 1220–1202.

Calabrese, Edward J., and Linda A. Baldwin. 2003a. Hormesis: The Dose-Response Revolution. *Annual Review of Pharmacology and Toxicology* 43: 175–197.

———. 2003b. The Hormetic Dose-Response Model Is More Common Than the Threshold Model in Toxicology. *Toxicological Sciences* 71: 246–250.

Chapman, Kenneth S., and Govind Hariharan. 1996. Do Poor People Have a Stronger Relationship between Income and Mortality Than the Rich? Implications of Panel Data for Health-Health Analysis. *Journal of Risk and Uncertainty* 12: 51–63.

Collinson, Allan. 1991. *Renewable Energy*. Austin: Steck-Vaughn Library.

Columbia Accident Investigation Board. 2003. Report of the Columbia Accident Investigation Board. www.nasa.gov/columbia/home/CAIB_Vol1.html (accessed May 20, 2010).

Corrosion Proof Fittings v. EPA, 947 F.2d 1201 (5th Cir., 1991).

Douglas, Mary, and Aaron Wildavsky. 1984. *Risk and Culture*. Berkeley, CA: University of California Press.

Feigenson, Neal, Daniel Bailis, and William Klein. 2004. Perceptions of Terrorism and Disease Risks: A Cross-National Comparison. *Missouri Law Review* 69: 991–1012.

Final Declaration of the First European "Seas at Risk" Conference. 1994. Annex 1. Copenhagen.

Gigerenzer, Gerd. 2000. *Adaptive Thinking: Rationality in the Real World*. New York: Oxford University Press.

Gigerenzer, Gerd, Peter M. Todd, and the ABC Research Group. 1999. Simple Heuristics That Make Us Smart. New York: Oxford University Press.

Goklany, Indur. 2001. *The Precautionary Principle*. Washington, DC: Cato Institute.

Graham, John D. 2001. Decision-Analytic Refinements of the Precautionary Principle. *Journal of Risk Research* 4: 127–141.

Graham, John, and Jonathan Wiener. 1995. *Risk versus Risk*. Cambridge, MA: Harvard University Press.

Hahn, Robert W., Randall Lutter, and W. Kip Viscusi, eds. 2000. *Do Federal Regulations Reduce Mortality?*. Washington, DC: American Enterprise Institute.

Hanekamp, J. C., G. Frapporti, and K. Olieman. 2003. Chloramphenicol, Food Safety, and Precautionary Thinking in Europe. *Environmental Liability* 11 (6): 209–221.

Hardell, Lennart, Mild K. Hansson, and M. Carlberg. 2003. Further Aspects on Cellular and Cordless Telephones and Brain Tumours. *International Journal of Oncology* 22: 399–407.

Heath, Chip. 1996. Do People Prefer to Pass Along Good or Bad News? Valence and Relevance as Predictors of Transmission Propensity. *Organizational Behavior and Human Decision Processes* 68: 79.

Heath, Chip, Chris Bell, and Emily Sternberg. 2001. Emotional Selection in Memes: The Case of Urban Legends. *Journal of Personality and Social Psychology* 81: 1028–1041.

Henrich, Joseph, Wulf Albers, Robert Boyd, Gerd Gigerenzer, Kevin A. McCabe, Axel Ockenfels, and H. Peyton Young. 2001. Group Report: What Is the Role of Culture in Bounded Rationality? In *Bounded Rationality: The Adaptive Toolbox*, edited by Gerd Gigerenzer and Reinhard Selten. Cambridge, MA: MIT Press, 353–454.

Hirshleifer, David. 1995. The Blind Leading the Blind: Social Influence, Fads, and Informational Cascades. In *The New Economics of Human Behavior*, edited by Mariano Tommasi and Kathryn Ierulli. Cambridge: Cambridge University Press, 188–215.

Kahan, Dan M., and Donald Braman. 2003. More Statistics, Less Persuasion: A Cultural Theory of Gun-Risk Perceptions. *University of Pennsylvania Law Review* 151: 1291.

Kahneman, Daniel, and Shane Frederick. 2002. Representativeness Revisited: Attribute Substitution in Intuitive Judgment. In *Heuristics and Biases: The Psychology of Intuitive Judgment*, edited by Thomas Gilovich, Dale Griffin, and Daniel Kahneman. Cambridge: Cambridge University Press, 49–53.

Kahneman, Daniel, Paul Slovic, and Amos Tversky. 1982. *Judgment under Uncertainty: Heuristics and Biases*. New York: Cambridge University Press.

Keeney, Ralph. 1990. Mortality Risks Induced by Economic Expenditures. *Risk Analysis* 10: 147.

Kelly, Judith P., L. Rosenberg, J. R. Palmer, R. S. Rao, B. L. Strom, P. D. Stolley, A. G. Zauber, and S. Shapiro. 1999. Risk of Breast Cancer According to Use of Antidepressants, Phenothiazines, and Antihistamines. *American Journal of Epidemiology* 150: 861.

Kuran, Timur, and Cass R. Sunstein. 1999. Availability Cascades and Risk Regulation. *Stanford Law Review* 51: 683.

Loewenstein, George, and Jane Mather. 1990. Dynamic Processes in Risk Perception. *Journal of Risk and Uncertainty* 3: 155–175.

Lomborg, Bjorn. 2001. *The Skeptical Environmentalist*. New York: Cambridge University Press.

Lutter, Randall, and John F. Morrall III. 1994. Health-Health Analysis: A New Way to Evaluate Health and Safety Regulation, *Journal of Risk and Uncertainty* 8 (1): 43–49.

McFedries, Paul. 2005. Precautionary Principle. www.wordspy.com/words/precautionaryprinciple.asp (accessed June 9, 2005).

McHughen, Alan. 2000. *Pandora's Picnic Basket*. New York: Oxford University Press.

Morris, Julian. 2000. Defining the Precautionary Principle. In *Rethinking Risk and the Precautionary Principle*, edited by Julian Morris. New York: Butterworth-Heinemann, 1–21.

Myers, David G. 1975. Discussion-Induced Attitude Polarization. *Human Relations* 28: 699.

Myers, David G., and George D. Bishop. 1971. The Enhancement of Dominant Attitudes in Group Discussion. *Journal of Personality and Social Psychology* 20: 386.

Nordhaus, William D., and Joseph Boyer. 2000. *Warming the World: Economic Models of Global Warming*. Cambridge: MIT Press.

Posner, Richard A. 2004. *Catastrophe: Risk and Response*. New York: Oxford University Press.

Raffensperger, Carolyn, and Peter L. deFur. 1999. Implementing the Precautionary Principle: Rigorous Science and Solid Ethics. *Human and Ecological Risk Assessment* 5: 933–934.

Rascoff, Samuel J., and Richard L. Revesz. 2002. The Biases of Risk Tradeoff Analysis. *University of Chicago Law Review* 69: 1763.

Renn, Ortwin and Bernd Rohrmann, eds. 2000. *Cross-Cultural Risk Perception: A Survey of Empirical Studies*. Boston: Kluwer Academic.

Rohrmann, Bernd, and Ortwin Renn. 2000. Risk Perception Research: An Introduction. In *Cross-cultural Risk Perception: A Survey of Empirical Studies*, edited by O. Renn and B. Rohrmann. Boston: Kluwer Academic, 11, 17–18.

Sand, Peter H. 2000. The Precautionary Principle: A European Perspective. *Human and Ecological Risk Assessment* 6: 445–458.

Sharpe, C. R., J.-P. Collet, E. Belzile, J. A. Hanley, and J.-F. Boivin. 2002. The Effects of Tricyclic Antidepressants on Breast Cancer Risk. *British Journal of Cancer* 86: 92–97.

Sherman, Steven J., Robert B. Cialdini, Donna F. Schwartzman, and Kim D. Reynolds. 2002. Imagining Can Heighten or Lower the Perceived Likelihood of Contracting a Disease: The Mediating Effect of Ease of Imagery. In *Heuristics and Biases: The Psychology of Intuitive Judgment*, edited by Thomas Gilovich, Dale Griffin, and Daniel Kahneman. Cambridge: Cambridge University Press, 82.

Sjöberg, L., D. Kolarova, A. A. Rucai, and M. L. Bernström. 2000. Risk Perception in Bulgaria and Romania. In *Cross-Cultural Risk Perception: A Survey of Empirical Studies*, edited by Ortwin Renn and Bernd Rohrmann. Boston: Kluwer Academic, 146–183.

Slovic, P., J. Flynn, C. K. Mertz, M. Poumadere, and C. Mays. 2000. Nuclear Power and the Public: A Comparative Study of Risk Perception in France and the United States. In *Cross-Cultural Risk Perception: A Survey of Empirical Studies*, edited by O. Renn and B. Rohrmann. Boston: Kluwer Academic, 56–102.

Slovic, Paul. 2000. *The Perception of Risk*. London: Earthscan.

Sunstein, Cass R. 2002. Health-Health Tradeoffs. In *Risk and Reason*, edited by Cass R. Sunstein. Cambridge: Cambridge University Press, 133–152.

———. 2003a. Beyond the Precautionary Principle. *University of Pennsylvania Law Review* 151: 1003.

———. 2003b. *Why Societies Need Dissent*. Cambridge, MA: Harvard University Press.

———. 2005. *Laws of Fear: Beyond the Precautionary Principle*. Cambridge: Cambridge University Press.

Sunstein, Cass R., Reid Hastie, John W. Payne, David A. Schkade, and W. Kip Viscusi. 2002. *Punitive Damages: How Juries Decide*. Chicago, IL: University of Chicago Press.

Tubiana, Maurice. 2000. Radiation Risks in Perspective: Radiation-Induced Cancer among Cancer Risks. *Radiation and Environmental Biophysics* 39 (1): 3–10.

Tversky, Amos, and Daniel Kahneman. 1986. Judgment under Uncertainty: Heuristics and Biases. In *Judgment and Decision Making: An Interdisciplinary Reader*, edited by Hal R. Arkes and Kenneth R. Hammond. New York: Cambridge University Press, 38, 55.

———. 2002. Judgment under Uncertainty: Heuristics and Biases. In *Heuristics and Biases: The Psychology of Intuitive Judgment*, edited by Thomas Gilovich, Dale Griffin, and Daniel Kahneman. Cambridge: Cambridge University Press.

U.S. Senate Select Committee on Intelligence. 2004. Report on the U.S. Intelligence Committee's Prewar Intelligence Assesments on Iraq. http://intelligence.senate.gov/iraqreport2.pdf (accessed June 10, 2005).

Vogel, David. 2003. The Hare and the Tortoise Revisited: The New Politics of Consumer and Environmental Regulation in Europe. *British Journal of Political Science* 33: 557–580.

Whitman, Christine Todd. 2001. Interview by Robert Novak and Al Hunt. *Evans, Novak, Hunt, and Shields.* CNN (Cable News Network). April 21.

Wiener, Jonathan B., and Michael D. Rogers. 2002. Comparing Precaution in the United States and Europe. *Journal of Risk Research* 5: 317.

Zhong, Ling. 2000. Note: Nuclear Energy: China's Approach towards Addressing Global Warming. *Georgetown International Environmental Law Review* 12: 493.

PART VI
CONCLUSIONS

CHAPTER 20

The Real Pattern of Precaution

Jonathan B. Wiener

*T*he debate over precaution and the "precautionary principle" (PP) has riveted policymakers, scholars, business leaders, advocacy groups, and citizens. As we detailed in Chapter 1, this debate has been fought on both normative and descriptive terms: as a battle over the best approach to regulating risks, and as a transatlantic contest for leadership. Is Europe the new global regulator? Which is "more precautionary," the United States or Europe? This book has attempted to answer that question, and to critique it. We have sought to respond to the rhetoric of precaution with the reality of precaution.

Over the past decade, the oft-repeated claim is that Europe has become "more precautionary" than the United States across the broad arena of risk regulation addressing health, safety, environmental, and security risks. In this book, we examined that claim, testing the descriptive pattern of precaution in the United States and Europe, across a wide array of risks, from about 1970 to the present. To our knowledge, this project compiles the most comprehensive assessment to date of the risk regulation standards in Europe and America over the past four decades.

Through qualitative case studies, quantitative data analysis, and cross-cutting explanatory chapters, we considered four basic accounts of the history of regulatory precaution in Europe and America: *convergence* (driven by globalization and the pressure to harmonize standards); *divergence* (driven by different cultures and by regulatory competition); *reversal or "flip-flop"* (from greater U.S. precaution in the 1970s to greater European precaution since the 1990s, driven by shifts in internal politics and by international rivalry); and *"hybridization"* (the exchange of ideas and interweaving of diverse regulatory systems, driven by learning from experience with responses to particular risks). These hypotheses were detailed in Chapter 1.

The first three of these accounts treat the United States and Europe as discrete entities or rival blocs, painting a romantic image of competing clans each led by a heroic standard-bearer for a coherent approach. As detailed in Chapter 1, observers and advocates speak of a contest for "leadership" with countries "trading places" as "ships passing in the night." This imagery of rivalry among discrete political blocs is nicely illustrated by Eugène Delacroix's painting *La Liberté guidant le peuple* (1830) (though it is somewhat ironic to depict liberty as an icon of centralized leadership, when many people think of liberty as freedom from centralized direction). By contrast, the fourth account treats America and Europe as large and diverse, increasingly interconnected and intermingled, more like complex communities in ecosystems. It evokes an image that is chronologically older and yet politically more modern: the busy multitudes at work in the paintings of Pieter Bruegel the Elder, notably *The Numbering at Bethlehem* (1566). In Bruegel's rendering, villagers go about their innumerable quotidian tasks—paying taxes, preparing food, and seeking warmth (all related to risk and regulation)—with apparent indifference to Joseph and Mary arriving at the inn (while these religious icons are virtually indistinguishable from the industrious folk all around).

Much of the literature, both academic and popular, has seized on salient examples of particular policies, such as climate change, chemicals, and biotechnology. But this selective sample reflects a kind of "political availability heuristic" that overlooks many other important risks and policies. To move beyond claims based on just a few celebrated examples, in the present volume we assessed a much wider array of U.S. and European policies from 1970 to the present. Our evidence comes in two types. First, in Chapters 2 through 14, we examined over a dozen case studies in depth, regarding risks such as food safety (including genetically modified foods, beef hormones, and mad cow disease), air pollution, climate change, nuclear power, tobacco, chemicals, marine and terrestrial biodiversity, medical safety, and terrorism, as well as precaution embodied in risk information disclosure and risk assessment systems. Second, in addition to these detailed qualitative case studies, in Chapter 15 we conducted a broad quantitative analysis of relative precaution in a sample of 100 risks that we drew from our dataset of all 2,878 risks we identified over the period 1970 to the present. Our hope and expectation is that, taken together, our more numerous case studies of law in action, and our broad quantitative analysis of law on the books, offer a more thorough and more representative picture of the *real* pattern of precaution than has been captured by prior studies that focused narrowly on selected risks. Building on these descriptive inquiries, in Chapters 16–19, our project then investigated the causes and the consequences of the observed pattern of precaution. Finally, in this chapter, we offer a synthesis of our findings on risks, precaution, causes, and consequences. We assess several causal explanations for the observed pattern of precaution, and we highlight the growing role of the "Better Regulation" initiative and systems of regulatory impact assessment. We then close with recommendations for desirable regulatory policies, challenges to the traditional methods of comparative research, and a proposal for a transatlantic laboratory of ideas.

Our key findings and conclusions are the following:

- The methodology of comparison matters. Much prior research has suffered from narrow or unrepresentative selection methods and other limitations. In order to attain greater accuracy and clarity, we have expanded the number and diversity of case studies, and we have conducted quantitative analysis of large datasets.

- The real pattern of precaution is not purity of principle, but parity and particularity. In contrast to claims that Europe has become "more precautionary" across the board, we find that Europe and the United States have maintained rough parity across all risks over the past four decades. And we find that the pronounced differences that do occur are located in highly particular controversies over particular cases. Europe has been more precautionary about some risks, while the United States has been more precautionary about other risks, both in recent years and in previous decades. There is substantial internal variation in the degree of precaution in risk regulation across risks, agencies, and Member States, both within the United States and within Europe.

- "Better Regulation" has swept both the United States and Europe. In the United States since the 1970s, and the EU since 2001, presidents have required *ex ante* policy analysis and have established regulatory oversight bodies to supervise this process. There is now a transatlantic consensus in favor of executive oversight of the regulatory state using impact assessment and centralized review. The debate over precaution cannot be understood without appreciation of these developments, melding oversight and precaution into more comprehensive, pragmatic, and mature approaches to regulation.

- Hybridization is a more accurate depiction of the reality of precaution than are hypotheses of convergence, divergence, or reversal of positions. There has been substantial exchange or borrowing of ideas across the Atlantic and among Member States and U.S. states, in a process of "hybridization" that produces a complex and dynamic pattern of regulation. Stark contrasts drawn between the United States and Europe, as if they were discrete and rival systems, are belied by the growth of transnational networks across and within the United States and Europe. Among the many examples of such exchange of regulatory ideas are precaution itself, market-based incentives such as allowance trading, and better regulation programs using impact assessment and executive oversight.

- The causes of the complex pattern of precaution are likewise complex. Because the real pattern of precaution is not dichotomous (United States versus Europe), dichotomous causal theories will not suffice. Accounts of distinct cultures of risk aversion, or distinct political or legal systems, on one side of the Atlantic versus the other, do not offer strong predictions of the observed complex pattern of precaution. More satisfactory accounts must be more nuanced, attending to each risk, context, and institution, including the availability heuristic, trade protectionism, and transnational networks sharing regulatory ideas. The complex pattern that we observe presents a challenge to the traditional distinctions drawn (or presumed) in comparative law, between discrete national "legal systems," "legal origins," and "national styles of regulation." Increasing interconnectedness and exchange (hybridization) of legal ideas across transnational networks are piercing the national boundaries presumed by traditional comparative law. Comparative law and economics need to account for this interconnected reality by studying particular rules and institutions as modular elements that may be exchanged and adapted across interconnected legal systems.

- The consequences of regulatory policy are also complex and interconnected. Precaution against one risk can generate new risks. Regulators should consider full portfolio impact analyses, and should seek optimal or prudent precaution rather than maximal precaution. In practice, precaution is often moderated by such concerns. Indeed, the adoption of programs of "better regulation" in both the United States and Europe illustrates the normative advantages and the actual positive pressures to meld precaution into systems of impact assessment and executive oversight.

- Transatlantic regulatory relations are best seen not as conflict or competition, but as a collaborative process of exchanging ideas. Leadership can and should mean showing the way not just to more aggressive policies, but to better policies. Learning can occur over time (by observation and *ex post* evaluation) and across space (through comparison and borrowing). Hybridization enables regulators to adopt the elements and approaches that they find desirable from other jurisdictions. Further, purposeful experimentation and evaluation of alternative regulatory approaches can be carried out in what we term a transatlantic—or even global—policy laboratory.

The Claim of Greater European Precaution

In Chapter 1, we described the view that Europe became "more precautionary" than the United States after about 1990 by adopting the PP in formal laws and in regulatory policies applied to salient risks. Without repeating that discussion here, we turn now to the synthesis of the evidence we have amassed in our research.

In the face of the widespread view of a "more precautionary" Europe and the often acrimonious debate between U.S. and European officials over the normatively desirable degree of precaution in domestic policies and international agreements, we undertook the present research project to test these claims. Our objectives included improving the methods and accuracy of comparison by opening a wider scope onto a broader landscape of risks; overcoming the impasse in transatlantic debates over precaution as an abstract principle by looking at the reality of precaution as applied in concrete cases; and furnishing a better basis for policymaking by illuminating the actual pattern, causal factors, consequences, and impacts of alternative approaches to precaution. To do so, we organized a series of four Transatlantic Dialogues on Precaution, two each in the United States and in Europe, and we assembled a multidisciplinary team of leading experts to contribute to this book.

As noted in Chapter 1, an extensive prior literature has compared U.S. and European risk regulation. The present book goes beyond this literature in several ways. We explored these differences in Chapter 1; here we recap briefly.

First, we study the degree of precaution in standard-setting, rather than comparing approaches to federalism (e.g., Rehbinder and Stewart 1985; Kelemen 2004), administrative agency procedure (e.g., Rose-Ackerman 1995; Breyer and Heyvaert 2000; Lindseth et al. 2008; Rose-Ackerman and Lindseth 2010), judicial review (e.g., Marchant and Mossman 2004; Lindseth et al. 2008), or selection of policy instruments (Harrington et al. 2004). Our comparison of precautionary regulation touches on some of these areas but concentrates on the degree of precaution in the substance of regulatory policies. We also examine the evolution of regulation, in both the United States and Europe, from precaution to "better regulation" via impact assessment and executive oversight (Wiener 2006). This evolution illustrates the transatlantic exchange of ideas through borrowing and hybridization, along with the importance of institutional structures and powers to the design of regulatory oversight (Wiener and Alemanno 2010).

Second, we attempt to overcome limitations in the methods used by prior research to select cases and draw overall comparative assessments. Many past studies have focused narrowly on one product or sector, or on just a few highly visible examples of cases selected by convenience or with the purpose of demonstrating particular insights. These methods, though useful in uncovering the details of the specific issue studied, did not select an array of cases according to an unbiased representative sampling method and thus cannot support generalized comparative conclusions about the span of risk regulation overall (King et al. 1994). For example, Brickman et al. (1985) looked just at chemical regulation; Pollack and Shaffer (2009) looked just at genetically modified foods; and Vogel (forthcoming) generalized from four types of risks regulated by two U.S. agencies, despite numerous counterexamples (both outside his four areas, and even within those areas). Kagan and Axelrad (2000, 18) candidly declared: "This volume of case studies, therefore, cannot support unqualified generalizations about any of the national legal systems as a whole or about the across-the-board impact of national styles of law and regulation." As Kagan (2007, 100) forthrightly observed: "Generalizing about entire legal systems, each of which is pervaded by complexity and contradictory features, is a risky business." Studying just the visible cases—or worse, just the highly celebrated cases—yields a misleading picture of the wider reality.

Third, we attempt to avoid exaggerating transatlantic differences that are small in a global context—a "narcissism of minor differences" (Baldwin 2009). Commenters drawing sharp contrasts between U.S. and European regulatory systems may be falling into this tendency. The notion of the U.S.-EU precaution gap may persist because people imbue it with their own normative slants—even if it does not actually exist or is far more textured.

Fourth, we look beyond large categorical groupings of legal systems, legal origins, families of law, and national styles of law or regulation. Scholars of comparative law have written at length on the asserted differences among legal systems (e.g., Zweigert and Kötz 1998; Kagan 2007; La Porta et al. 2008). Generalizations about national traits can serve as models that help distill insight from detail, but they can also become stereotypes that mislead. Rather than try to force our data into the presumed existence of distinct U.S. and European approaches to regulation and precaution, we have tried, like Bruegel, to appreciate the variety and complexity of real life.

Our Findings

Our book combines two comparative methodologies: both a set of case studies of specific risks and policies, canvassing a broad range of types of risks and policies, and a quantitative analysis of a sample of 100 risks drawn from a database of nearly 3,000 risks. The case studies are each "deep but narrow"; the quantitative analysis is "broad but shallow." The case studies address both law on the books and law in action in each setting; the quantitative analysis assesses a larger number of risk policies but scores only the law on the books. Neither methodology is perfect or sufficient by itself, but taken together, they offer an improved capacity to characterize the risk regulation regimes overall and to observe the variations across specific policies.

We find that, over the broad array of risks, neither the United States nor Europe can claim to be "more precautionary" across the board. The reality of precaution has not been principle, it has been parity and particularity. Both the United States and Europe apply precaution to many risks, but in a highly variegated pattern over risks, space, and time. Formal adoption of the PP is not the whole story: the United States often takes a precautionary approach without formally endorsing the PP (Applegate 2000; de Sadeleer 2007), and Europe formally endorses the PP without applying precaution to every risk (Marchant and Mossman 2004). There is substantial spatial variation in the degree of precaution in actual policies, both among U.S. states (some of which apply precaution to some risks more than do others, such as California's policies on air pollution), and among the Member States of the Europe Union (where, for example, different states take different and sometimes conflicting stances on risks such as food contamination, nuclear power, chemicals, and cell phone transmissions) (Sand 2000; Zander 2010). And there is considerable variation across risks within each polity.

Even if Europe has become more precautionary than the United States since the 1990s on specific risks such as genetically modified foods (Jasanoff 2005; Cantley and Lex, Chapter 2 of this volume), chemicals (Selin and VanDeveer 2006; Renn and Elliott, Chapter 10 of this volume [though they question the accuracy of this claim]), and climate change (Hammitt, Chapter 7 of this volume), these are only a few of the many risks subject to regulation. Many claims of greater European precaution across the board have been based on only these examples (coupled with the EU's adoption of the PP in its treaties). Yet these are not a representative sample of the universe of risks and regulation. Assessing the wider array of risks presents a far different picture.

(It may also be true, though we cannot yet say definitively, that both the United States and Europe have been growing progressively more precautionary over time. Testing such a proposition requires an analysis of the full universe of risks and of the degree of early anticipation and stringency in regulatory systems taken as a whole, including the risks induced by precaution.)

We find precaution on both sides of the Atlantic. Based on the case studies in this book and on other literature, Europe appears to have been more precautionary than the United States regarding, for example, the following risks (each with some degree of uncertainty about cause and effect):

- marine pollution (Freestone, Chapter 8 of this volume);
- genetically modified foods (Cantley and Lex, Chapter 2 of this volume; Jasanoff 2005);
- beef hormones including rBST (Gray et al., Chapter 3 of this volume; Wiener and Rogers 2002);
- antibiotics in animal feed (Wiener 2003, 217–220);
- greenhouse gases and climate change (Hammitt, Chapter 7 of this volume);
- toxic chemicals (Renn and Elliott, Chapter 10 of this volume, although they argue that the EU's REACH policy emphasizes collecting evidence about old chemicals, rather than precautionary restrictions on new technologies in the absence of evidence);
- phthalates (Charnley and Rogers, Chapter 14 of this volume; Wiener 2003, 225);
- teenage use of marijuana and other drugs (Wiener 2003, 226); and
- guns (Wiener 2003, 226, 232–239).

Meanwhile, the United States appears to have been more precautionary than Europe regarding, for example, the following risks:

- new drug approval and adverse side effects (Miller, Chapter 11 of this volume);
- fisheries depletion (Freestone, Chapter 8 of this volume);
- endangered species (Saterson, Chapter 9 of this volume);
- choking hazards in food (Wiener 2003, 227);
- embryonic stem cell research (Jasanoff 2005);
- chlorofluorocarbons (CFCs) and stratospheric ozone protection (Hammitt, Chapter 7 of this volume);
- nuclear power (Ahearne and Birkhofer, Chapter 5 of this volume);
- "mad cow disease" (BSE and vCJD), especially in blood donations (Gray et al., Chapter 3 of this volume; Wiener 2003, 230–232; Wiener and Rogers 2002);
- air pollution, notably lead in gasoline in the 1970s and 1980s and fine particulate matter (PM) pollution from electric power plants, industry, and diesel engines in the decades since 1990 (Walsh, Chapter 6 of this volume; Wiener 2003, 227);
- cigarette smoking (tobacco) (Blanke, Chapter 4 of this volume);
- information disclosure systems ("right to know" laws) (Sand, Chapter 13 of this volume);
- risk assessment assumptions (Charnley and Rogers, Chapter 14 of this volume);
- teenage use of alcohol (Wiener 2003, 228);

- youth violence and potential violence by the mentally ill (Wiener 2003, 229, 232–239); and
- terrorism and weapons of mass destruction (Stern and Wiener, Chapter 12 of this volume; Wiener 2003, 239–241; Stern and Wiener 2008).

The relative length of these lists is not important; as discussed below, neither set of examples is a representative sample of the full population of cases, and thus neither set fully proves a general characterization. The counterexamples can undermine a theory but do not suffice to confirm an alternative theory. This broader set of examples merely indicates that neither the United States nor the EU can claim to be the more precautionary actor across the board, whether today or in the past. Simplistic contrasts—that "Americans are risk-takers while Europeans are risk-averse"—are not supported by actual regulatory experience. Nor are claims that "Americans are individualistic and antiregulation, while Europeans are collectivist and proregulation," in the face of greater U.S. precaution in regulatory policies that restrict the freedom to smoke and that limit freedom and privacy in order to combat terrorism.

Nor do these examples match the flip-flop account. To be sure, some of the above examples do reflect greater European precaution since the 1990s, including genetically modified foods, hormones in beef, toxic chemicals, and climate change. But many of the above examples are instances of the contrary trend, namely, greater relative U.S. precaution since the 1990s—e.g., fine PM air pollution, smoking tobacco, mad cow disease (especially in blood donations), information disclosure systems, embryonic stem cell research, youth violence, and terrorism and weapons of mass destruction. Notably, fine PM air pollution and smoking tobacco are two of the most serious risks among these examples, estimated (despite uncertainties about specific cause-effect relation-ships) to kill hundreds of thousands of people annually (as noted in Chapter 1 of this volume), and both characterized by greater relative U.S. precaution since the 1990s—especially regarding diesel PM emissions and secondhand tobacco smoke (though, to be sure, with variations across hazards, regulatory polities, and time, and with important European policies as well, as discussed in Chapters 4 and 6 of this volume). Many experts would add terrorism with weapons of mass destruction as another highly serious but highly uncertain risk of mass calamity, with greater relative U.S. precaution since 2001. Mad cow disease in blood is noteworthy because the U.S. policy, adopted in 1999, was markedly more precautionary than European policies (despite greater availability of mad cow disease in Europe), was expressly termed "precautionary" by the U.S. Food and Drug Administration, and has been described as one of most pure examples of precaution by European risk expert Michel Setbon (2004) in light of the absence of clinical evidence of prion transmission by blood when the U.S. policy was adopted. Further, the increasing use of information disclosure policies in the United States (Sand, Chapter 13 of this volume) represents an institutional implementation of precaution across an array of risks, yet one that is often neglected by studies aimed at specific sectors or products. All of these examples deeply undercut the flip-flop claim of greater European precaution since 1990. Meanwhile, some of the above-listed examples are instances of greater European precaution back in the 1970s—e.g., marine pollution, teenage use of marijuana and other drugs, and guns (for there was, and continues to be, debate over the cause-effect relationship—whether an increase in guns yields more or less violence). These examples, too, are contrary to the flip-flop claim.

These counterexamples do not prove the counterclaim that the United States has become more precautionary than Europe since 1990 (the opposite of the standard flip-flop account). Rather, what they show is that the flip-flop account of greater European precaution since about 1990 is based on selective citation of a few cases and is not sustainable once a broader array of cases is examined (see our further discussion of Table 20.1 below). It is difficult or untenable to claim that Europe has become more precautionary than the United States since the 1990s regarding serious risks. The better assessment is that both the United States and Europe have been precautionary, both before and after 1990, but sometimes against different risks.

Even within the category of environmental risks, where the PP was initially applied, the reality does not support the claim that U.S. policy has substantially slowed and the two sides have "traded places" (Kelemen and Vogel 2010), nor that the conflicts between the EU and the United States reflect "une culture de contrôle a priori [in Europe] et une autre a posteriori [in America]" (Kourilsky 2001, 34–35). In the last three decades, while Europe indeed adopted many important measures, the United States, spanning presidencies and Congresses of both major political parties, adopted a series of major precautionary measures, including but not limited to the 1984 Hazardous and Solid Waste Amendments (including tough new controls on older waste treatment and disposal sites); the 1986 Superfund Amendments (including tough waste site cleanup standards and the pathbreaking Toxics Release Inventory); the 1990 Oil Pollution Act (including new technology requirements and liability standards for oil shipping); the 1990 Clean Air Act Amendments (including tight technology controls on air toxics, and the very successful national SO_2 allowance trading system for sharply reducing acid rain); the 1996 Safe Drinking Water Act amendments; the 1996 Food Quality Protection Act; state laws restricting smoking in public places and the 2009 federal Family Smoking Prevention and Tobacco Control Act; the reauthorization of the Magnuson-Stevens Fishery Conservation Act in 2006; and numerous stringent agency regulations, including the 1989 ban on British beef, the 1997 and 2006 national ambient air quality standards for fine particulate matter (PM2.5), the 1997 and 2008 national ambient air quality standards for ozone, the 1999 and 2001 Food and Drug Administration (FDA) limits (expressly called "precautionary") on blood from Europe, the 2001 standard on arsenic in drinking water, the 2005 Clean Air Interstate Rule (CAIR) issued by the U.S. Environmental Protection Agency (EPA) to dramatically reduce sulfur and nitrogen oxide air pollution, and the very stringent standards on diesel engine air pollution emissions promulgated by EPA in 2001 (trucks and buses), 2003 (ocean vessels), 2004 (nonroad engines), and 2008 (trains and boats), as well as additional EPA air pollution rules promulgated in 2009–2010. This is not to say that all of these policies have been desirable, nor that countries should compete to enact more laws; nor is it to ignore differences among presidencies. It is just to say that U.S. regulatory inactivity is not the reality. Likewise, there may have been more policy action in Europe in the 1970s than is typically recognized today. That decade is, after all, when the notion of precaution blossomed in German, Swedish, and Swiss environmental law.

In order to compare relative precaution in the United States and Europe, in both the case studies and the quantitative analysis, one needs a way to measure relative precaution. This is complicated by the fact that there are multiple versions of the PP. The Rio Declaration (paragraph 15) is a standard version, but there are many more. Sandin (1999) found 19 versions, with significant differences regarding the level of threat, uncertainty, action, and command; VanderZwaag (1999) identified 14 formulations; Stone (2001) found no coherent statement; Bodansky (2004, 391) found key differences among versions of the PP on multiple dimensions, including reasons not to postpone action, license to act, duty to act, trigger of application, and what action should be taken, and concluded that the PP has "not moved ... towards consensus" and "the only point of overlap is a truism." Two experts sympathetic to the PP observe: "Paradoxically, we conclude that the application of precaution will remain politically potent so long as it continues to be tantalizingly ill-defined and imperfectly translatable into codes of conduct, while capturing the emotions of misgiving and guilt. ... [I]t is neither a well-defined nor a stable concept. Rather, it is has become the repository for a jumble of adventurous beliefs that challenge the status quo of political power, ideology, and environmental rights" (Jordan and O'Riordan 1999, 15). Wiener (2007) surveys the different elements of the PP that appear to vary across versions. Peel (2004) discusses the different characterizations of the precautionary idea as a principle, an approach, or a process.

Wiener and Rogers (2002) and Wiener (2007) identified three archetypal alternative formulations of the PP:

- *Version 1: Uncertainty does not justify inaction.* In its most basic form, the PP permits regulation in the absence of complete evidence about the particular risk scenario. This version is expressed in the 1992 Rio Declaration: "Where there are threats of serious or irreversible damage, lack of full scientific certainty shall not be used as a reason for postponing cost-effective measures to prevent environmental degradation." But there is never "full scientific certainty"; decisions must always be made under uncertainty. This version of the PP rebuts the contention (often urged by those about to be regulated) that uncertainty precludes regulation, but it does not answer the harder question: *what* action to take, given inevitable uncertainty.

- *Version 2: Uncertainty justifies action.* This version of the PP is more aggressive. "When an activity raises threats of harm to human health or the environment, precautionary measures should be taken even if some cause and effect relationships are not fully established" ("Wingspread Statement 1998" in Raffensperger and Tickner 1999, 353). But cause-and-effect relationships are never "fully established." And if it is unclear what causes the harm, it is unclear which "measures" would prevent it. Again, the real question is what action to take, given the uncertainty.

- *Version 3: Uncertainty requires shifting the burden and standard of proof.* This version of the PP is the most aggressive. It holds that uncertain risk requires forbidding the potentially risky activity until the proponent of the activity demonstrates that it poses no risk (or no unacceptable risk). For example: "the applicant or proponent of an activity or process or chemical needs to demonstrate that the environment and public health will be safe. The proof must shift to the party or entity that will benefit from the activity and that is most likely to have the information" (Raffensperger and Tickner 1999, 345–346). This shift in the burden of proof may simply elicit needed risk information from the least-cost provider (industry), which may be optimal. But if the standard of proof (here, the undefined term "safe") is too demanding, it may amount to a de facto ban or overregulation or bias against what is "new."

Our approach in this book has been to convert these narrative conceptions of the PP into a measure of the degree of relative precaution, stated as a continuous variable (as suggested in Wiener and Rogers 2002; and as employed in Hammitt et al. 2005; Wiener 2007; Swedlow et al., Chapter 15 of this volume). This avoids anchoring our comparisons on one contested version of the PP, or on binary classifications of whether a policy somehow "is" or "is not" precautionary. It recognizes the reality that some policies are incrementally more precautionary than others, which is indeed inherent in the claims made about relative U.S. and European precaution. The concept of degrees of relative precaution is illustrated in Figure 20.1, where the decisionmaker stands at a point early in time and does not know the eventual manifestation of the risk, which might trace any of the three curves into the future (or others)—a normal rise and fall (curve A), or an apparently sharply rising risk that turns out to wane into obscurity (curve B, a false positive), or an apparently minor risk that turns out to rise sharply into catastrophe (curve C, a false negative). Thus, in this illustration, greater precaution is represented by action in the face of greater uncertainty—action earlier along the

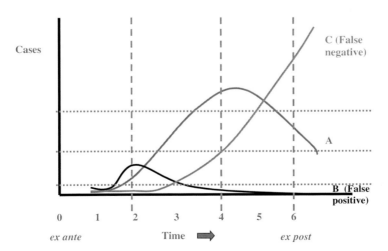

Figure 20.1 *Degrees of Precaution*

timeline of unfolding awareness. And, as indicated by the range of "weaker" to "stronger" versions of the PP described above, greater precaution means more stringent regulatory limits on the risk. The earlier in time a policy is adopted, the greater the uncertainty about the future manifestation of the risk, and the more stringent the policy, the greater the prevention of future risk. These two dimensions translate the narrative versions above into a continuous measure of degrees of relative precaution.

We also avoid the distinction occasionally drawn between "precaution" and "prevention." The Rio Declaration (quoted above) makes no such distinction; it uses "prevent" as the operative verb in its official statement of precaution. Harremoës et al. (2002) argued that precaution applies against "uncertain" risks, whereas prevention applies against "known" risks. It is unclear, however, what could be meant by a "known" risk. Either there is no such thing (because all risks are uncertain), in which case prevention is an empty set and the PP applies to all risks, or there are many "known" risks (in the sense of well-understood cause-and-effect relationships), in which case the PP is only about risks for which there is fundamental ("deep") uncertainty about the cause-and-effect or hazard-and-harm relationship, and the PP applies only to those few rare and temporary cases of utter mystery that then become understood as science advances (yet it remains mysterious how can one tell when that line has been crossed). We avoid this quagmire by speaking of degrees of precaution.

Thus, we treat precaution as a strategy, and measure its degree as a continuous variable in terms of two factors: timing and stringency. In the face of risks that are inescapably probabilistic, uncertain, and latent, government has two basic strategies: *ex post* remedies and *ex ante* precautions (or both). *Ex post* remedies include cleanups and civil liability administered by the courts. *Ex ante* precautions include preventive regulations administered by agencies. Such *ex ante* regulations are precautionary measures taken to avoid uncertain future harms. On the time path over which a risk is forecast to become manifest and better understood, a regulation is thus "more precautionary" the earlier it takes effect, and the more stringently it restricts the suspected source of the risk. Earliness is a measure of precaution because it measures the willingness to act in the face of greater uncertainty about future outcomes and understanding (Setbon 2004). Stringency is a measure of precaution because it measures the degree of aggressiveness, weight, or sacrifice that society is willing to bear to prevent the risk; it measures the shift entailed by moving from narrative version one to two to three. Christoforou (2004, 17), for example, refers to "more stringent regulation of risk" as a key indicator of precaution.

What we have done in this book is to combine "deep but narrow" longitudinal case studies (of the policy history over four decades of each risk across paired cross-national settings) with "broad but shallow" large N data collection (of numerous risks over four decades across paired cross-national settings). This helps overcome the shortcomings of each. The case studies by themselves would not be representative of the full universe (King et al. 1994), but the quantitative analysis by itself would miss important context and depth (Brady and Collier 2004) and could be enormously time-consuming to ensure it represents the full universe (as indeed it was) (Blomquist 2007).

Our methodology goes a step beyond prior research based on either case studies or large-N quantitative data analysis alone, and a step along the way to the kind of "nested mixed-method" approach recommended by Lieberman (2005). (See also Levi-Faur (2004), advocating a "medium-N" and "compound" approach.) Lieberman advocates the integration of both small-N in-depth case studies and large-N statistical studies as the best solution to the shortcomings of each; in his approach, the broad statistical analysis would be used to help select and frame the case studies, and the narrow case studies would be used to help identify hypotheses and processes to test in the broader statistical analyses. He writes:

> [S]tatistical analysis can guide case-selection for in-depth research, provide direction for more focused case studies and comparisons, and be used to provide additional tests of hypotheses generated from small-N research. Small-N analyses can be used to assess the plausibility of observed statistical relationships between variables, to generate theoretical insights from outlier and other cases, and to develop better measurement strategies. This integrated strategy improves the prospects of making valid causal inferences in cross-national and other forms of comparative research by drawing on the distinct strengths of two important approaches. (Lieberman 2005, 435)

Our approach used both case studies and large-N quantitative data analysis to inform one another: we used our accumulated case studies to help frame the design of the large-N study, and we used the results of the large-N study (Swedlow et al., Chapter 15 of this volume; Hammitt et al. 2005) to inform our qualitative discussion of causal variables. But we did not select the case studies based on the large-N analysis, nor have we yet used the large-N dataset to run regression analyses that would test the association between the degree of precaution (the dependent variable) and explanatory factors (independent variables). The debate over the real pattern of precaution is a debate, initially, over the contours of the dependent variable; just pinning that down has taken extensive effort. We hope to do so in future work (see Swedlow et al. 2009). In the meantime, our combined approach is a significant improvement over selecting case studies by convenience or because they are highly visible—an invitation to bias akin to the availability heuristic in risk perception—and over large-N statistical studies that lack detail on context and evolution. Subject to the limitations of our methods of sampling and scoring the data, we can situate case studies on precaution—our own or those by others—among our dataset and characterize their location across the larger distribution. There we find not divergence, flip-flop, or convergence, but a heterogeneous set of multiple trends that is highly variable across risks and types of risks (Swedlow et al., Chapter 15 of this volume). Moreover, by comparing our case studies to our large-N analysis, we can suggest tentatively that our set of case studies, in its greater diversity of trends, is more representative of the trends in our risk universe dataset than cases selected by authors arguing for convergence, divergence, national styles, or flip-flop accounts. Consequently, our cases should offer a stronger basis for interpreting and understanding the diverse causes and consequences of these trends than do other sets of cases that account for only a small segment of the real pattern.

The diversity of the case studies in this book is summarized in Table 20.1. Notably, while a few cases correspond to the flip-flop account, most do not.

Case studies, as discussed above, are limited by sample selection problems. We therefore undertook an extensive large-N quantitative study (Swedlow et al., Chapter 15 of this volume; Swedlow et al. 2009; Hammitt et al. 2005). This quantitative study of risk regulations adds to the body of quantitative research comparing national regulatory systems (Scruggs 1999, 2001, 2003, 2009; Esty and Porter 2005; La Porta et al. 2008; cf. Hinich and Munger 1998), and to the body of quantitative research on legal systems in general (Miles and Sunstein 2008; Cross 1997). As described more fully in Swedlow et al. (Chapter 15 of this volume), we compiled a dataset of the nearly 3,000 risks we

Table 20.1 *Comparing U.S. and EU Precaution by Case*

Case study	Authors	Author home	Category	More precautionary in 1970–1990	More precautionary in 1990–present	Flip-flop from U.S. to EU?
Genetically modified foods	Cantley and Lex	EU	Environment, health	?	EU	Yes
Beef hormones and Mad Cows	Gray, Rogers, and Wiener	U.S. and EU	Health	?	U.S.	No
Smoking tobacco	Blanke	U.S.	Health	U.S.	U.S.	No?
Nuclear power	Ahearne and Birkhofer	U.S. and EU	Environment, health	U.S.	?	No
Automobile emissions	Walsh	U.S.	Environment, health	U.S.	U.S.	No
Stratospheric ozone and climate change	Hammitt	U.S.	Environment, health	U.S.	EU	Yes
Marine	Freestone	EU	Environment	EU re pollution, U.S. re fish	U.S.?	No
Biodiversity	Saterson	U.S.	Environment	U.S.	U.S.	No
Chemicals	Renn and Elliott	EU and U.S.	Environment, health	U.S.	EU	Yes?
Medical	Miller	U.S.	Health, safety	U.S.	U.S.	No
Terrorism	Stern and Wiener	U.S.	Safety, security	EU	U.S.	No
Information disclosure	Sand	EU	All	U.S.	U.S.	No
Risk assessment methods	Rogers and Charnley	EU and U.S.	All	U.S.	U.S.	No

found mentioned in the literature from 1970 to 2004; from that dataset, we drew a random sample of 100 risks, which on inspection were appropriately representative of the diverse categories of types of risks in the larger dataset. We then researched and scored the degree of relative U.S. versus European precaution in each of the 100 risks for each year and calculated the trend in relative precaution on average and within the sample. We found no evidence of general convergence or divergence. We found weak evidence of a slight shift consistent with the flip-flop account, but representing less than 10% of the sample—far smaller than the wholesale "trading places" claims made by flip-flop advocates (see Figure 20.2). We found the data splintered by a variety of subtrends pointing in different directions—some to greater European precaution, some to greater U.S. precaution, some to convergence, some to divergence, and the modal trend to no change over the period (see Figure 20.3). We found, overall, average parity between the United States and EU over the period, and particularity—risk selection—in the differences that do arise.

In sum, both our case studies and our quantitative study find little or no support for the hypotheses of U.S.-European convergence, divergence, or reversal (flip-flop) in relative precaution over the past four decades. Instead, both our case studies and our quantitative study find rough transatlantic parity in overall precaution over the last four decades, with some visible examples of particular risk selection for greater precaution—but those outliers were not grouped on one side of the Atlantic, nor trending to one side. Sometimes Europe has been more precautionary about a particular risk, and sometimes the United States has been more precautionary—both in the 1970s and

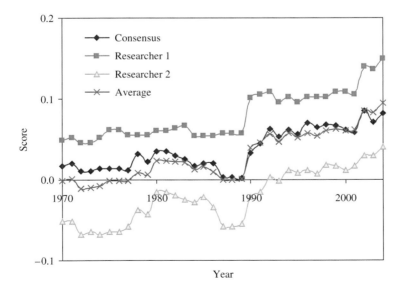

Figure 20.2 *Comparing U.S. and EU Precaution by Quantitative Scores*

Source: Hammitt et al. (2005); and Chapter 15 in this volume

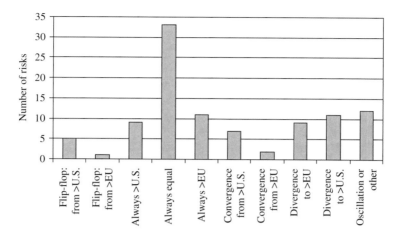

Figure 20.3 *Patterns of Relative Precaution in the Quantitative Sample*

Source: Hammitt et al. (2005); and Chapter 15 in this volume

1980s and since the 1990s. There has been much internal variation within both the United States and Europe across risks, agencies, Member States, and time.

One implication of this variation is that, in reality, precaution has been more a strategy than a principle. It does not manifest the kind of consistent state practice that could give rise to customary international law (cf. McIntyre and Mosedale 1997; Sands 1995).

We hasten to add that even longer and broader historical analyses may be warranted: of relative transatlantic precaution not just over the past four decades, but over, say, the past four centuries; and of relative precaution around the world.

Causes of Precaution: Explaining the Pattern

The observed complex pattern of precaution is difficult to explain through broad generalizations, because it does not lend itself to variables that differ dichotomously (the United States versus Europe). To be clear: our challenge here is not to explain why the United States approaches risks one way while Europe approaches risks another way, because that is not the pattern we observe. Instead, our task is to explain why a complex and varied pattern occurs, of both parity and particularity, varying more by specific risk than by side of the Atlantic. We did not observe a simple convergence (pressed to harmonize by globalization), divergence (driven to specialize by comparative advantage, or driven apart by conflicting worldviews), or flip-flop (reversal) of American and European risk policies. In trying to develop causal explanations for the complex observed pattern, then, the question is not who is more precautionary across the board, but why do different societies choose to worry more about different particular risks?

Wiener and Rogers (2002, 334–342) assessed multiple hypotheses to explain the observed pattern—policymaking on the merits, politics, culture, perceptions, protectionism, and legal system features—and found none highly probative. For example, they asked whether proportionate representation in European elections might favor green third parties more than do U.S. electoral systems, or the structure of EU institutions such as the Council might favor single-issue decisionmaking, or more potent civil liability (tort) law in the United States might reduce the felt need for *ex ante* precaution in America. But those hypotheses, they noted, would tend to predict greater European precaution throughout the period, not the flip-flop reversal claimed by others, nor the complex pattern that we observe.

In this section, we collect and assess the several kinds of causal factors that have been advanced to explain the pattern of precaution.

Culture

Assertions of European versus American cultures—of risk aversion versus risk-taking, respectively—were recounted in Chapter 1. They date from at least Oscar Wilde's parody to the present. For example, Kourilsky (2001, 34–35), in an otherwise lucid treatment, speaks of a European culture of *ex ante* precautions versus an American culture of *ex post* remedies. But these kinds of cultural claims are stereotypes, not reality—or at least not the reality of modern regulatory systems. The reality of precaution is diverse and particular, and it does not fit a presumed set of regional cultural types. Claims that Europe has a more risk-averse culture than does the United States are belied by the extensive *ex ante* precautions in American law discussed above, and indeed by the flip-flop account's characterization of greater U.S. precaution in the 1970s. For example, one often hears the claim that Europeans are more risk-averse, trusting in government, and accepting of collective order, whereas Americans are more risk-taking, distrustful of government, and enamored of individual freedom of choice; yet the tougher American regulation of individuals' cigarette smoking in public places exhibits the opposite (as detailed by Blanke, Chapter 4 of this volume). The science of cross-cultural risk perception indicates much more nuanced reactions to particular cues and contexts (Renn and Rohrmann 2000; Weber and Ancker, Chapter 18 of this volume). And if culture is coproduced dynamically with risk decisions (Jasanoff 2005; Douglas and Wildavsky 1982), then culture would be as variable and dynamic as the complex pattern of particularity in actual precaution. Moreover, whatever the role of cultural differences may have been in the past, the increasing interconnectedness of modern societies, at least across the Atlantic, is eroding those differences.

Politics

In trying to explain relative precaution, the first answer one hears is typically political leadership: changes from left to right in electoral succession, especially by the head of government (president or prime minister). On this view, American precaution grew under Democratic presidents Jimmy Carter, Bill Clinton, and Barack Obama and waned under Republican presidents Ronald Reagan, George H. W. Bush and George W. Bush; and parallel changes occurred under left-leaning and right-leaning leaders in

Europe. But this view does not match the history of risk regulation. Just to note a few major counterexamples, the Reagan administration adopted the Montreal Protocol on CFCs and the phaseout of lead in gasoline (years ahead of Europe); the two Bush administrations, father and son, were highly precautionary regarding air pollution (adopting the 1990 acid rain and air toxics laws, and the early 2000s restrictions on diesel PM and interstate air pollution). The move to much more aggressive precaution against terrorism—homeland security, through both foreign and domestic policies—occurred under the younger Mr. Bush (Stern and Wiener, Chapter 12 of this volume; Stern and Wiener 2008). In Europe, similarly, conservative leaders appear to have been just as likely to promote precaution as have left-leaning leaders. And the initiatives for "Better Regulation" (discussed further below) have been bipartisan on both sides of the Atlantic. In an era of increasing executive branch authority over risk regulation (Kagan 2001), the reality of specific leaders' administrations has been the selective application of precaution to particular risks, not broad trends up and down in precaution across the board.

A deeper look at politics focuses on the structures of power, notably the parliamentary systems in Europe, the separation of powers structure in the United States, and the structure of the EU. Majone (Chapter 16 of this volume) examines political systems and precaution, including the role of green parties in Europe, which enjoy greater representation than in the United States; the structure of EU institutions (e.g., the Council, which tends to give voice to single-issue coalitions of the ministers from each Member State); and related aspects. Although these features may point to greater precaution in Europe, he nonetheless finds them insufficient to account for the observed complex pattern of particular precautions. These broad political features do not account for the cases of greater American precaution on mad cow disease, air pollution, and smoking, for example. Vogel (2001, 2003) has suggested that Europe has become more precautionary than the United States because business lobbies are now more influential in politics in the United States than in Europe, but the influence of business in politics varies considerably by issue; Blanke (Chapter 4 of this volume) finds that the tobacco industry has been more influential in Europe than in the United States. Nor do the broad political features examined by Majone account for the variations in precaution regarding different risks in Europe, and in different countries within Europe. This is not surprising, because even within one polity such as the United States, theories of politics have proven very limited in their ability to account for actual regulatory policy outcomes (Wiener and Richman 2010). Standard theories of special interest group politics have failed to predict the observed adoption of general-interest regulation. More complex theories of interest group coalitions pairing activists with industry segments (dubbed "Baptists and bootleggers" by Yandle (1989)), and of both supply and demand for regulation, including the often pivotal role of policy entrepreneurs who champion innovative regulatory strategies, come closer to predictive accuracy but still require more nuance and more empirical validation (Wiener and Richman 2010).

One caveat here is that the EU institutions gained strength over the period of our study—both in terms of EU enlargement from 15 to 27 Member States and in terms of the authority of EU-level regulators to act on risks to health, safety, environment, and security. If one's dataset looked only at EU-level regulation, this trend would appear to indicate rising precaution over the past four decades (as in the flip-flop hypothesis), when in fact all that might be occurring is a relocation of the same regulatory authority from the Member States to the EU level. That is, the institutional trend in the EU may bias researchers into finding a greater rise in EU precaution than has actually occurred. The fact that our own quantitative analysis, described above and in Chapter 15, shows almost no change in aggregate relative precaution in the EU and United States over the period—*despite* this institutional trend toward stronger EU regulation—reinforces our view that no major change or reversal has occurred.

Legal Systems

Several hypotheses can be offered to explain the interaction of legal systems and precaution, with unclear implications (Wiener and Rogers 2002). For example, stronger *ex post* tort liability could render precaution less needed, and hence countries with weaker *ex post* tort liability could see *ex ante* precaution as more desirable. Alternatively, however, stronger tort liability might motivate industry to seek uniform preemptive precautionary regulation from the legislature (but such regulation does not always preempt tort law; and many strong uses of tort law are not followed by preemptive legislation). But these broad legal system influences would appear to predict precaution overall, and differing across the Atlantic, rather than the pattern of precaution we observe as applied to each specific risk (unless perhaps the tort liability system is highly variegated to apply differently to different risks).

Bergkamp and Smith (Chapter 17 of this volume) carefully dissect differences in legal systems—including administrative law, judicial review of agency action, and civil liability law—and find that these factors do not predict the observed complex variety of risk policies. In contrast to studies finding strong differences in the regulation of business associated with countries' "legal origins" (La Porta et al. 2008), Smith and Bergkamp do not find such a relationship accounting for differences in regulation of risk. This finding is more consistent with Roe (2006), who finds that, contrary to La Porta et al. (2008), legal origins do not explain patterns of corporate financial markets regulation because contemporary politics plays a major role. Notably, La Porta et al. recognize that specific regulations may diverge from legal origins in what they call "new spheres of social control," and especially following crisis events (2008, 307, 326). Other studies have also found that contemporary politics, not (only) legal origins, explains current regulation of business (Berkowitz et al. 2003; Nicoletti and Pryor 2006). Moreover, if the claim made by the "legal origins" studies that the U.S. legal system is more hospitable to business than Europe's (La Porta et al. 2008) were uniformly true, then the difficult period to render consistent with the flip-flop hypothesis would be the 1970s, when the United States allegedly was more precautionary than Europe. In short, explanations based on the "legal system" are too coarse to account for the observed complex variation in particular precautions.

Economic Analysis of Regulation

Some authors tie the degree of precaution inversely to the use of benefit–cost analysis (BCA) in regulatory decisionmaking. Krämer (2004) and Christoforou (2004) attribute lesser U.S. precaution in part to greater U.S. reliance on BCA. But this account faces objections. First, it does not match the observed pattern of parity and complex particularity in precaution. Second, the EU is also adopting BCA. Although Christoforou (2004, 38) said that "[u]nlike the situation in U.S. law, there is no general guideline in [European] Community law that obliges the regulatory authorities to systematically analyze the economic impact or cost of risk management measures," this is no longer accurate; now there are such Impact Assessment (IA) Guidelines, adopted by the European Commission in 2005, revised in 2006 and again in early 2009, and now overseen by the EU's Impact Assessment Board (IAB) created in late 2006 (see Renda 2006; Radaelli and De Francesco 2006, 2008; Wiener and Alemanno 2010). Moreover, the proportionality principle in EU law calls for a version of BCA (Alemanno 2008; Sweet and Matthews 2008); Article 174 of the EU's 2001 Nice Treaty (now Article 191 of the 2009 Lisbon Treaty on the Functioning of the EU) calls for BCA in the sentence just after it calls for the PP; and the European Commission's Communication on the PP in February 2000 itself called for BCA as part of the PP (belying the alleged conflict between the two that is the premise for this hypothesis) (see Wiener 2006). Indeed, sometimes European law uses BCA when U.S. law does not: for example, federal air pollution control in Germany uses BCA but federal ambient air quality standards in the United States do not (Dwyer et al. 2000), and new drug approval in the UK uses BCA but in the United States does not (Harris 2008). Even earlier, the origins of BCA lie in both Europe and America: Benjamin Franklin, Joseph Priestley, Cesare Beccaria, and Jeremy Bentham exchanged the basic idea across the Atlantic in the late 1700s, and French engineer-economists like Jules Dupuit developed it further in the early 1800s.

Trade Protectionism

Another possibility is that trade protectionism to shield domestic producers from foreign competition explains relative precaution. There has long been concern that the PP is used as disguised protectionism. James Whitman has characterized American law as more typically (though not always) "consumerist," meaning protecting consumers through low prices, and continental European law as more typically (though not always) "producerist," meaning protecting workers and firms against competition; he adds that where European law is moving to protect consumers, it is chiefly in consumer safety—that is, precaution (Whitman 2007). Kelemen and Vogel (2010), citing Yandle and Buck (2002), point to the motivation of protecting domestic producers as partly explaining the early U.S. affinity for precaution in international agreements and the recent shift in Europe they see toward relative enthusiasm for precaution. As indicated in our case study chapters, trade protectionism helps explain several examples of national regulatory precaution, such as restrictions on CFCs (when U.S. producers sought global restrictions to seize a competitive advantage), restrictions on GM foods and beef hormones (as European farmers sought protection against imports), and measures to prevent the spread of mad cow disease (as several countries with domestic beef industries took steps to bar imports of beef from afflicted areas). Local economic interests also played some role in the pattern of precaution seen in our chapters on nuclear energy, automobile emissions, and marine biodiversity. But trade protectionism is not so helpful in explaining other major examples of regulatory areas where precaution was used, such as mad cow disease in blood, smoking tobacco, climate change, and terrorism. As our chapters on those cases show, precautionary policies in these areas often tended to burden rather than favor domestic producers. To be sure, tighter domestic standards are sometimes urged, despite their initial costs, as a way to spur longer-term innovation in new technologies, but that gambit is not often backed by domestic industry incumbents. And perhaps rivalry *within* domestic industries can explain some precautionary policies; for example, European restrictions on genetically modified foods may reflect rivalry between traditional farmers and newer agribusiness interests, and the U.S. restrictions on blood donations by people who have lived in Europe may reflect rent-seeking behavior by the large blood banks, seeking to restrict supply from smaller blood banks and thereby raise market prices for blood purchased by hospitals.

Perceptions, Crisis Events, and "Availability"

Public perceptions of risk may spur regulation. But broad national contrasts in risk perception do not correspond closely to the observed complex pattern of precaution (cf. Renn and Rohrmann 2000). A more promising account is that the general parity in precaution, punctuated by occasional differences on particular risks, reflects the scattered sparks that spawn those particular policies (Repetto 2006). That is, there are occasional local stimuli—cognitively "available" events—that spur public perceptions and then political responses. And when people do respond to such available risks, they respond with their prior normative views of apparent causes and likely remedies in mind (Kahan 2007).

This account invokes the behavioral sources of risk perception and links them to politics. The availability heuristic is the phenomenon that memorable salient events, especially when experienced directly, loom much larger in one's perception than do predictions of probable harms in the future (Weber and Ancker, Chapter 18 of this volume; Sunstein, Chapter 19 of this volume; Sunstein and Kuran 1999). Its implication is that sporadic events trigger outsize public concern and political response. If so, then the particular cases of heightened precaution may be political responses to unusual events. The mad cow disease epidemic in Britain is often cited as having spurred precautionary food safety policies in Europe. (On the other hand, it is harder to use the availability heuristic to explain the U.S. policy restricting blood donations, and the comparative lack of such policies in Europe, because there was no mad cow epidemic in the United States, and the more serious scandal of HIV-contaminated blood had occurred in France.) Other precautionary policies may also have derived from crisis events, such as the phaseout of CFCs following the discovery of the ozone hole (Hammitt, Chapter 7 of this volume), or the Sarbanes-Oxley law enacted after the Enron scandal (Milhaupt et al. 2008; Hart 2009), or the U.S. counterterrorism measures after the 9/11 attacks.

In a world of greater safety and lower risks, those risks that do occur are seen as more scandalous by the public. As Godard et al. (2002, 29) put it, "*Plus la société est sûre, plus les poches résiduelles et les résurgences d'insécurité, plus les atteintes accidentelles à la vie ou à la santé sont considérées comme scandaleuses.*"[1] Psychologist Steven Pinker (2009) has seen the same phenomenon in our response to risks of violence:

> [O]ur ancestors were far more violent than we are today. Indeed, violence has been in decline over long stretches of history, and today we are probably living in the most peaceful moment of our species' time on earth. ... Given these facts, why do so many people imagine that we live in an age of violence and killing? The first reason, I believe, is that we have better reporting. ... There's also a cognitive illusion at work. Cognitive psychologists know that the easier it is to recall an event, the more likely we are to believe it will happen again. ... Gory war zone images from TV are burned into memory, but we never see reports of many more people dying in their beds of old age. And in the realms of opinion and advocacy, no one ever attracted supporters and donors by saying that things just seem to be getting better and better. Taken together, all these factors help create an atmosphere of dread in the contemporary mind...

Thus, risk perceptions sparked by occasional crisis events and amplified by the availability heuristic may explain a significant share of what we have termed precautionary particularity—the unusual policies adopted in response to unusual events. Percival (1998, 20–22) argues that a "trigger" event is needed to spur new legislation. Yet not every crisis event spurs regulation (Kahn 2007). Processes of social amplification are triggered in only some cases. Moreover, cognitive focus on "available" crisis events arguably leads the public to neglect both routine familiar risks (Slovic 1987), and also very remote catastrophic risks (Posner 2004; Slovic 2007)—yet the latter are just the types of risks that, normatively, precaution ought to be addressing.

Ironically, the widespread claim that Europe has become "more precautionary" than the United States, as noted in Chapter 1, may itself be a kind of "political availability heuristic." It reflects the visibility of particular risks and policies in the news media, at academic conferences, and in activity at the EU level (as noted above in the section on "Politics").

This process of crisis event and precautionary response may be abetted by activists who sound the alarm (Slovic et al. 1991; Chateauraynaud and Torny 1999; Harremoës et al. 2002), sometimes accurately and sometimes not (Wildavsky 1997; Mazur 2004). In any case, the role of crisis events, availability heuristics, and political response could help explain some of the observed particularity in relative precaution: why the United

---

[1] This might be translated as "The safer a society is, the more it harbors residual and resurgent insecurities, the more accidental injuries to life or health are seen as scandalous."

States is sometimes more precautionary about one risk, while Europe is more precautionary about another.

Hybridization

A further strand in the complex pattern of precaution relates to transnational exchange: the diffusion, borrowing, and "hybridization" of regulatory systems (Wiener 2003; Wiener 2006; Delmas-Marty 2006, 101–112). The reality of international relations is interconnectedness and the transnational diffusion of ideas, both within the EU (Thatcher and Coen 2008) and worldwide. Slaughter (2009) argues:

> We live in a networked world. ... In this world, the measure of power is connectedness. ... The twentieth-century world was, at least in terms of geopolitics, a billiard-ball world, described by the political scientist Arnold Wolfers as a system of self-contained states colliding with one another. ... The emerging networked world of the twenty-first century, however, exists above the state, below the state, and through the state. In this world, the state with the most connections will be the central player, able to set the global agenda and unlock innovation and sustainable growth.

Interconnectedness poses at least three challenges. First, it means more rapid propagation of risks across political borders and economic systems—such as pollution (e.g., greenhouse gases), disease (e.g., avian and swine flu), terrorism (e.g., the 9/11 attacks and cyberspace attacks), and financial crisis (e.g., the global credit collapse of 2008). Second, it multiplies the ancillary impacts of policy interventions—risk-risk tradeoffs—because our policy responses to risk also must operate in an interconnected world (Wiener 2002). But third, interconnectedness also enables the more fluid spread of ideas, and thereby offers increased opportunities to borrow and collaborate on solutions to the first two challenges. Regulatory ideas are increasingly being borrowed across the Atlantic, and worldwide, in an evolving web of global administrative law (Kingsbury et al. 2005; Rose-Ackerman and Lindseth 2010). Levi-Faur (2005, 20) writes:

> [T]he new order [of regulatory capitalism] is diffused rather than reproduced independently as a discrete event in each country and sector. Diffusion is a reflection of an increasingly interdependent world. Beyond economic interdependencies, there is a growth of "horizontal" channels of diffusion and an increase in the export and import of institutions and knowledge. ... A diffusion perspective allows us to endogenize change, to see it in a social and network context and, most important, to look at the role of "knowledge actors" in its diffusion.

The notion of the diffusion of policy ideas is much studied (see Rose 1993; Dolowitz and Marsh 2000; James and Lodge 2003; Berry and Berry 2007). Closely related concepts of diffusion as an evolutionary process have been developed in sociology (Hägerstrand 1968), economics (Rogers 2003, first published in 1963), law (Sand 1971 [using the term "interfusion"]; Watson 1993; Tushnet 1999), political science (Walker 1969; Weyland 2005; Simmons et al. 2008), biology (Arnold 1997; Grant 1999;

Deakin 2002), and history of science (Galison 1997). In biology, evolution was first understood to occur through competition among individuals within a species; later, through field studies, biologists began to appreciate that evolution also occurs through the exchange of genetic material across species via interbreeding (called "hybridization") (Arnold 1997; Grant 1999). Likewise, in law and political science, evolution was initially understood to occur through competition among individual rules within a legal system (Priest 1977; Elliott 1985; Farber 1994; but for doubts about the efficiency of such legal evolution, see Hadfield 1993; Roe 1996); later, through the equivalent of field studies, legal scholars came to appreciate that legal evolution also occurs through the exchange of legal concepts across legal systems via borrowing (Watson 1993; Elliott 1997; Wiener 2001, 2003, 2006; Deakin 2002), also called "hybridization" (Wiener 2003, 254–261; Wiener 2006; Delmas-Marty 2006, 101–112). Whereas evolution within a group selects for fitness that overcomes past selection pressures and may thus yield path-dependence (Roe 1996), hybridization across groups or systems may produce new kinds of hybrid offspring that do not always succeed in past conditions but that may promise improved fitness to withstand new pressures and fill new niches as conditions change.

Diffusion of law and policy does not just happen automatically; someone must take action to identify an approach and add or adapt it. Legal borrowing depends on borrowers (Watson 1993; Graziadei 2009). For example, Sweet and Mathews (2008) depict the diffusion, driven by key jurists, of "proportionality" as a constitutional principle of judicial review. In the present study, we see the diffusion of regulatory ideas across administrative institutions. Environmental law and risk regulation have been subject to considerable diffusion and borrowing, with many important policy ideas exchanged and spread internationally, including precaution (borrowed among European countries and by the United States), environmental impact assessment (EIA), regulatory impact assessment (RIA), information disclosure requirements, and emissions trading (cap and trade) (Busch and Jörgens 2005; Wiener 2003, 254–255; Wiener 2006; Wiener and Richman 2010; Ellerman et al. 2010). This process of hybridization, as in biology (Arnold 1997; Grant 1999), creates hybrid offspring that are neither convergent with nor divergent from the prior population, but new; they prosper when environmental change opens niches for which they are well adapted.

When diffusion is observed, the mechanism may be learning and borrowing, but it might also be constructivism, coercion, or competition (Simmons et al. 2008) or merely fads (Lazer 2005). Successful learning depends on some form of evaluation of performance. "Like constructivists, learning theorists trace changes in policy to changes in ideas. But rational learning theory implies a kind of cost-benefit analysis. ... People may draw lessons by observing the effects of policies other countries adopt, and they may engage in Bayesian updating, in which they constantly add new bits of evidence to the existing knowledge base. Policymakers can draw the wrong lessons from observation, but the overarching theme here is that countries learn to pursue effective policies" (Dobbin et al. 2007, 463). A similar point is that successful legal borrowing involves a kind of cost–benefit evaluation, both horizontally among countries and vertically between national and international levels of governance (Wiener 2001). But

Dobbin et al. (2007, 462) lament: "One weakness of many of the studies in this arena is that they take simple diffusion to be evidence of learning, without looking at whether there was evidence of the efficacy of a policy innovation before second- and third-movers adopted it."

Some evidence that policy approaches to risk regulation have actually been borrowed, based on learning about efficacy, comes from express references to the act of borrowing. Research on the emergence of "global administrative law," with its plural and multifaceted elements, reflects both hybridization and the role of purposive actors consciously borrowing ideas (Kingsbury et al. 2005). More specifically, the initiative for "Better Regulation" via impact assessment and executive oversight (discussed further below) provides a good illustration. In 2004, the prime minister of Ireland said:

> Better Regulation is a core theme of our EU Presidency and featured prominently at the recent Spring Economic Council. ... There is a long tradition in American Public Administration of focusing on the quality and impact of regulation. Many of the policies, institutions, and tools that support Better Regulation have their origins in the U.S.A. For example, a lot of very significant antitrust and consumer protection measures were put in place in the U.S.A. in the first decades of the 20th century. There is much that we have learned from the United States in relation to regulatory management and, through occasions like this, much that we can continue to learn. ... We hope too that there will be shared learning. While we in the European Union are newer to the game, I hope that we have moved beyond our rookie season! The Union is making up ground quickly in respect of Better Regulation. This is as it should be. There is a deeper understanding within the European Institutions and Member States of the need for regulatory reform. (Ahern 2004)

A second example of diffusion through learning is the adoption by Europe of an allowance trading system to regulate greenhouse gas emissions. Historically, the EU had preferred environmental taxes over allowance trading (Andersen 1994; Harrington et al. 2004; Ellerman et al. 2010). In the 1990s, the EU proposed a carbon tax and denounced the U.S. proposal of allowance trading for greenhouse gases (GHGs) as ineffective and immoral. But no EU carbon tax was adopted, and starting in 2001, the EU instead adopted allowance trading for GHGs. It has now implemented the EU Emissions Trading System (ETS), the largest cap-and-trade system in the world (Ellerman et al. 2010). Several factors help explain this dramatic shift in regulatory approach. First, substantial learning about the performance of allowance trading occurred during the 1990s: by 2001, the EU had been able to learn from the successful U.S. experience with SO_2 allowance trading to reduce acid rain under the 1990 Clean Air Act. Second, specific transatlantic conversations helped communicate to EU leaders the successes of allowance trading in the United States and the benefits of this instrument for GHG control. For example, U.S. government officials (including Richard Stewart, Richard Schmalensee, and Jonathan Wiener) organized a seminar in 1990 for EU and other officials on the merits of market-based environmental policies. Policy entrepreneurs such as Peter Zapfel (who studied with Robert Stavins and Richard Newell at Harvard's Kennedy School, and then became one of the key staffers at the European Commission running the EU ETS) brought the theory and evidence of allowance trading systems from the United States to the European Commission. Leading European economists and EU officials also made the case for allowance trading (Ellerman et al. 2010, 13–31). Third, symbolic politics had some impact. The EU had criticized allowance trading in the 1990s in part because that policy was favored by the United States, but after President George W. Bush withdrew the United States from the Kyoto Protocol in 2001, the EU could easily criticize the United States for this withdrawal without disparaging allowance trading itself. Fourth, EU voting rules also played an important role. EU law required unanimity among EU Member States to adopt an EU tax, but poorer EU Member States objected to a uniform carbon tax and blocked adoption. An allowance trading system, by contrast, could be implemented without unanimity. And, in any event, allowance trading could more successfully attract Member States' consent because extra allowances (more lenient caps) could be assigned to poorer Member States without undermining the aggregate effectiveness of the cap-and-trade system. Allowance trading enables the distribution of burden to be decoupled from the stringency of the cap and the cost of the program, whereas a tax could not be adjusted as easily to accommodate the comparative needs of the poorer Member States. Hence a voting rule requiring unanimity or consent favors trading over taxes (as hypothesized by Wiener 1999a, 1999b). Taken together, these factors—learning about performance, policy entrepreneurs, symbolic politics, and voting rules—strongly influenced the diffusion of allowance trading from the United States to Europe, overcoming Europe's initial opposition.

Thus, the process of diffusion, borrowing, and hybridization in an interconnected world is consistent with, and could explain, the observed complex pattern of general parity and occasional particularity in precaution. It strikes much closer to the mark than a generalized claim of divergent cultures or wholesale flip-flop. Delmas-Marty (2006) argues that hybridization is an essential feature of an emerging international legal pluralism. Sweet and Sandholtz (1997) argue that transnational exchanges in markets across Europe have driven the creation of supranational rules (by the EU) to foster such trade (see also Thatcher and Coen 2008). A similar observation could be made about the evolution of legal rules across the 50 states of the United States (Walker 1969; Lazer 2005). In the present study, we find transatlantic exchanges of regulatory ideas (as well as of marketed goods and services) yielding international hybridization, yet without an overarching governance institution such as the EU or the U.S. federal government. Many of the borrowings are destined for domestic use, such as the PP and RIA—not for harmonizing and fostering transatlantic trade.

Consequences of Precaution

The observed pattern of precaution is mixed across the Atlantic, making it more difficult to discern clear differences in outcomes than if precaution were neatly bifurcated into European and American versions. And the definition of the PP is unclear or heterogeneous. The optimal degree of precaution varies across risks and contexts, as is evident from the diverse normative views of precaution expressed among the case study chapters in this book. More generally, we lack good indicators of the consequences of regulation. Just as health care systems are moving to "evidence-based medicine" and employing comparative effectiveness research, regulatory systems need to develop routine programs of retrospective (*ex post*) outcomes evaluation, and we need to use this research to improve regulatory choices and *ex ante* impact assessments (Coglianese and Bennear 2005; Wiener 2006, 513–516).

The promise of precaution is better protection against emerging risks (Harremoës et al. 2002; Butti 2007; Kysar 2010). Given the aim of precaution to prevent emerging risks, it will usually take some time to observe the effects of precautionary measures. And it will require the extrapolation of counterfactual scenarios of what risks would have come to pass had the precautionary measure not been adopted (Butti 2007), or comparative evidence from jurisdictions where the measure was not imposed (controlling for confounding factors).

In short, the real choice is not "better safe than sorry," because one would always prefer "safe" to "sorry." The real choice is which of several risks faced *ex ante* to address, and with what side effects (Wiener 2007). Risk management is increasingly recognized to be increasingly complex (Graham and Wiener 1995; Wiener 2002; Sunstein 2005; Hassid 2005; Renn 2008). Decisionmakers need to appreciate not only the mix of quantitative and qualitative attributes of risks that make them worth addressing (Kahan 2008), but also the complex consequences of addressing each risk in a world that is a web of interconnected risks.

A long-standing concern about precaution is that it may beget new risks (Graham and Wiener 1995; Cross 1996; Wiener 1998, 2002; Goldstein 2001; Sunstein 2005; Frison-Roche 2005; Butti 2007). Because of such countervailing risks or ancillary impacts, excessive or misplaced precaution may turn out to be not so protective, or even perverse. (Some ancillary effects may be beneficial, and these too should be assessed; see Graham and Wiener 1995, 2; Revesz and Livermore 2008.) For this reason, strong versions of the PP, requiring "proponents of an activity" to demonstrate that it poses low or no risk before moving ahead, would block the PP itself. Thus, the PP as a categorical principle may be too rigid. It may yield high costs, stifle innovation, and spawn countervailing risks. Precaution against some emerging risks may even distract attention from more remote but more catastrophic risks (Posner 2004).

Our case studies illustrate this concern. Bans on GM foods may yield hunger in poor countries and greater use of land and chemical inputs. Restrictions on blood donations for fear of mad cow disease may lead to blood shortages in hospitals. Restricting diesel emissions may reduce PM but increase CO_2. Precautionary counterterrorism interventions may curtail some threats but also kill civilians, increase terrorist recruitment and divert efforts from other threats.

Chapter 5 of this volume (Ahearne and Birkhofer), on nuclear power, among others, illustrates these points. In terms of standards set, the United States and EU are comparable in precaution; in terms of dependence on nuclear power, the United States was more precautionary about nuclear power than was the EU. The U.S. policy was a de facto moratorium based on labyrinthine regulatory hurdles, analogous to the EU de facto moratorium on GM foods—neither is a formal ban, but in both cases, so many hurdles were erected that the technology could not proceed smoothly. These precautionary limits on new nuclear power were based in large part on perceived risks, and lobbying by activists, after the Three Mile Island incident in 1979 captured public attention. Even though the public perceived nuclear power to be equally risky in the United States and France, the French respondents perceived the benefits (avoidance of climate change and energy insecurity) as greater, and they put more trust in the institutions and experts running the nuclear industry than did the U.S. respondents (Slovic et al. 1991). One consequence of greater precaution against nuclear power is a risk-risk trade-off: reduced nuclear waste and accident risks versus increased coal burning, hence increased PM and CO_2 emissions. As Chapter 6 (Walsh) on vehicle emissions and Chapter 7 (Hammitt) on climate show, Americans have adopted more stringent controls on PM than have Europeans, whereas Europeans have adopted more stringent controls on CO_2. The asymmetry on nuclear power shows another vantage on this complex pattern of different worries about multiple risks—that is, of context-specific precautionary particularity rather than of broad precautionary principle.

Moreover, uncertainty—the predicate for the PP—is not the key issue, because we always face uncertainty. There are risks and uncertainties on all sides of each policy choice. Countervailing risks are also beset by uncertainty, so avoiding uncertainty does not necessarily counsel action against target risks; put another way, if precaution holds that uncertainty is no excuse for inaction (or demands action), that applies equally to the uncertain countervailing risks as to the uncertain target risks (Wiener 1998; Sunstein 2005). Indeed, if policies are easily reversible, uncertainty can enable greater learning and policy improvement over time (Listokin 2008).

Rather, the key issue is multiplicity: interconnectedness in the web of risk; choosing among multiple conflicting risks; and seeking risk-superior moves to reduce multiple risks in concert (Graham and Wiener 1995; Wiener 2002). We live in a networked world (Castells 2000), a web of risks rather than a world of separate risks each taken one at a time. We must envision the future consequences of our current choices, understanding that we weave the web of our own interconnections (Jonas 1984).

Some go further, arguing that no society can ever truly be "more precautionary" across the board, because the generation of new countervailing risks by precautionary measures means that being "more precautionary" is impossible (Sunstein 2005; Sunstein, Chapter 19 of this volume). All we can do, on this view, is select among risks. On this view, even if one country adopted more precaution in one area, such as food safety, it would be generating new countervailing risks in other areas; and if one country shifted away from, say, environmental precaution, it would be shifting toward precaution on another domain, such as terrorism. The issue is risk selection—why societies choose different risks to worry about more. But it seems possible for societies to "reduce overall risk" (Graham and Wiener 1995); we do not live in a Panglossian best of all possible worlds in which no improvement is possible.

Thus, although precaution as a universal principle has its shortcomings, precaution as a strategy may be appropriate and even urgently needed to address specific risks. The key point is that the desirability of precaution depends on a full portfolio impact assessment of alternative measures, including their effects on the target risk, costs, ancillary benefits, and ancillary harms or countervailing risks (Wiener 2006; Godard et al. 2002). Notably, several European scholars have called for a more moderate application of the PP that accommodates its potential costs and ancillary impacts (Godard et al. 2002; Butti 2007; Kourilsky 2001; Kourilsky and Viney 2000; cf. Frison-Roche 2005). For example, Kourilsky (2001, 77) offers "ten commandments of precaution" that include risk assessment, economic benefit–cost analysis, and provisional application pending further research. The European Commission (2000) likewise incorporated these concepts into its explication of the PP.

In practice, the PP is neither salvation nor apocalypse. The reality of precaution is not the pure principle that both advocates and detractors imagine. It is more moderate. Indeed, the more binding the legal rule, the more moderate the PP typically becomes (Wiener 2002). For example, the European Commission's Communication on the PP of February 2000 stressed that precaution must be proportionate, considering benefits and costs, and provisional so that it may be revised in light of new science. The French Environment Charter of 2004 emphasizes that precautionary measures are to be provisional and proportionate. The lesson is that we must seek optimal precaution, not maximal (or minimal) precaution.

Paths Forward

Given this history of a complex pattern of relative precaution, with particular causes and consequences, how can U.S. and European risk policy make progress? In this section, we highlight the promise of networks for exchanging regulatory ideas. First, we examine a major development in such hybridization: the Better Regulation initiatives in both Europe and the United States. These initiatives emphasize regulatory impact assessment, both *ex ante* and *ex post*, using benefit–cost analysis. Their rise on both sides of the Atlantic, notably in the EU since 2001, reinforces our rebuttal of the flip-flop claim of increasing relative European precaution in recent years. The Better Regulation initiatives also illustrate the integration of both precaution and impact assessment into criteria and institutions for sensible decisionmaking in risk policy. Second, we suggest that transatlantic regulatory relations can move beyond transatlantic rivalry to construct a "policy laboratory" that makes use of the observed diversity in risk policies to more accurately evaluate specific policy successes and failures across risks, space, and time. Third, we argue that comparative law should evolve beyond its standard focus on national legal systems or families (or sharp contrasts between the U.S. and EU), to appreciate the extensive variation in regulatory policies within and across countries, legal traditions, risks, agencies, and time.

From Precaution to Better Regulation

A major development too often left unaddressed by research on precaution is the simultaneous move to Better Regulation. Even if the flip-flop account were true, it focuses on the specific regulations that have been promulgated and neglects the important systems of regulatory oversight that have grown up along with risk regulation. At the same time that the EU has undertaken highly precautionary policies on GM foods, chemicals, and climate change, it has also rolled out the Better Regulation initiative (Lofstedt 2004). As noted above, the Better Regulation program borrows significantly from the U.S. model, while also incorporating important European elements and, arguably, improvements. It harks back to Benjamin Franklin's "prudential algebra" for sensible decisionmaking, explained by Franklin in his letter to his European friend, the chemist Joseph Priestley, in 1772 (see discussion in Wiener 2006). And it reflects the move in Europe, as in America, toward stronger executive oversight of the regulatory system (Majone 1996; Kagan 2001; Wiener 2006).

Better Regulation includes the requirement of Impact Assessment for all major items in the European Commission's Work Programme, review by the Commission's Impact Assessment Board (IAB), efforts to reduce administrative costs and to simplify legislation, and increased consultation both across the services of the Commission and with stakeholder groups (Renda 2006; Wiener 2006). The treaties of the EU have called for *both* the precautionary principle (PP) and benefit–cost analysis (BCA) since 1992, in the very same article (see Article 130r of the 1992 Maastricht Treaty, Article 174 of the 2001 Nice Treaty, and Article 191 of the 2009 Lisbon Treaty on the Functioning of the EU). The European Commission's Communication on the PP of February 2000 defined the PP as incorporating BCA (see Wiener 2006; Butti 2007). The Better Regulation initiative was then launched with a White Paper in 2001. The IA Guidelines have been revised twice since their first version in 2005, most recently in January 2009. The IAB was created in late 2006.

The EU's IA Guidelines and oversight system are increasingly comparable to the U.S. system of regulatory review by the U.S. Office of Management and Budget (OMB) via its Office of Information and Regulatory Affairs (OIRA), creating a platform for deeper transatlantic collaboration and for some degree of convergence in regulatory methods (if not in the choices of which risks to regulate) (Wiener 2006; Wiener and Alemanno 2010). Under Executive Order 12866, issued by President Clinton in 1993 (building on and replacing President Reagan's EO 12291 of 1981 and President Carter's EO 12044 of 1978), which remains in force today, OIRA reviews the regulatory impact assessments of major new federal regulations. The possibility of a new U.S. executive order on regulatory oversight, suggested by the Obama administration soon after it took office in early 2009, portends further interaction and possibly borrowing by the United States of some elements of European IA methods. Further, IA methods are being developed in the Member States as well as in the EU institutions (Radaelli and De Francesco 2006, 2008). The IAB is overseeing the quality of IAs prepared by services of the Commission, and it is beginning to be more rigorous in its review. In addition, the European courts are starting to pay increased attention to IA and even to require IA under the proportionality principle of EU law (Alemanno 2009, citing Case C-310/04, *Kingdom of Spain v. Council of the European Union* (European Court of Justice 2006)).

The Better Regulation initiative in Europe, following closely on the adoption of the PP, is analogous to similar moves in U.S. regulatory history. On the heels of the New

Deal expansion of the regulatory state, the U.S. Congress enacted the Administrative Procedure Act (APA) in 1946, authorizing judicial review of agency action. Following the Great Society expansion of the regulatory state and the adoption of several precautionary regulatory statutes in the 1970s, Congress enacted the Paperwork Reduction Act of 1980, creating OIRA. Meanwhile, Presidents Carter, Reagan, and Clinton issued a suite of executive orders on regulatory review, as noted just above. As then-professor Elena Kagan has demonstrated, executive oversight of the regulatory state has become firmly established in the United States, not only to check agency action, but also to promote presidential priorities (Kagan 2001). After the launch of Better Regulation in Europe since 2001, we can now say that a transatlantic consensus exists in favor of executive regulatory oversight using IA and some version of BCA. This consensus is reflected in its support and implementation by every president of the United States for the last four decades, of both Democratic and Republican political parties, and by the European Commission for the last decade under both center-left President Romano Prodi and center-right President José Manuel Barroso. And, as Figure 20.4 demonstrates, the Organisation for Economic Co-operation and Development (OECD) reports that since the 1970s, an ever-increasing number of its member countries have adopted RIAs, with increasing requirements for full portfolio analysis of risks, benefits, and costs (OECD 2009, 15–16).

Still, differences in approach remain between the U.S. and EU systems of impact assessment. Among these are the leadership of the oversight body (OIRA is a centralized office headed by a single administrator; the IAB is a five-member board with members drawn from the directorates it oversees), its power to influence decisions (OIRA can return proposed regulations to agencies, whereas the IAB comments on the quality of impact assessments), its scope of oversight (OIRA reviews agencies' proposed rules, whereas the IAB reviews proposals for legislation in the Commission's Work

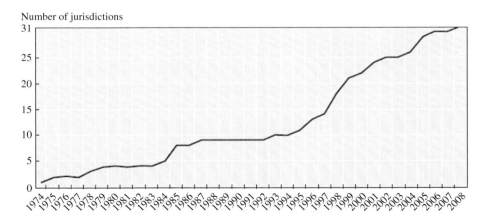

Figure 20.4 *Trend in Number of OECD Jurisdictions with Formal RIA Requirement (beyond a Simple Budget or Fiscal Impact)*

Source: OECD (2009, 15)

Programme), its staffing and expertise, its timing to review proposals, its criteria for undertaking review (dollar thresholds versus "proportionate analysis"), the valuation methods it employs (such as the value of a statistical life—usually about $6 million in the United States, but currently only about $1.5 million in the EU), and other features (Wiener and Alemanno 2010). These differences relate, in part, to the different constitutional systems in which each sits: OIRA is an executive branch body positioned to use technical analysis to oversee agencies that are charged to regulate by the more political legislative branch. In contrast, the IAB is a European Commission body positioned to help improve the quality of proposals for legislation that are developed by the technical directorates of the European Commission itself, before such proposals go to the more political branches for adoption and implementation (see Wiener and Alemanno 2010). But these differences are not intractable. Indeed, they present opportunities to test and compare approaches and thereby gain valuable learning for future iterations on both sides of the Atlantic (cf. Fabbrini 2007). For example, the EU could consider giving the IAB more staff, time, and authority to influence decisions; and the United States could consider using the proportionate analysis test, and applying impact assessment to proposals for legislation as well as to proposed agency rulemakings.

These institutional developments accompany an effort by scholars to interpret the PP as a form of decision analysis—that is, to reconcile and meld the PP and BCA. Talbot Page (1978) argued that precaution is warranted because the cost of neglecting a false negative is lost health, while the cost of acting on a false positive is just money; but this framing overlooks that acting (whether on a false or true positive) can also induce countervailing risks to health (as well as complacency or cynicism if the public senses "crying wolf" as alarms sound too often). More recent efforts have incorporated precaution into decision analysis by treating precaution as a heavier weight placed on catastrophic or irreversible impacts (Keeney and von Winterfeldt 2001; Graham 2001; Godard et al. 2002; DeKay et al. 2002; Stewart 2002; Gollier and Treich 2003; Sunstein 2007), as a form of real options analysis (Farrow 2004), or as a way to design policies that will be robust across numerous scenarios of the uncertain future (Barrieu and Sinclair-Désgagné 2006).

Among the Member State governments of Europe, there has been a range of enthusiasms for Better Regulation; the UK, Ireland, and the Netherlands have been leading voices, while France, for example, has been more circumspect. A survey of the Better Regulation efforts by all EU Member States, conducted by the European Commission in 2005, gave France a score of zero (largely for declining to answer the questionnaire). This is curious, given that core concepts of BCA were developed in France by engineer-economists like Jules Dupuit in the early 1800s. Perhaps they were inspired by Benjamin Franklin's "prudential algebra" mentioned above, brought to Paris by Franklin when he was the U.S. ambassador to France from 1776 to 1785? Or by Jeremy Bentham, whose *Theory of Legislation* was published in French by Etienne Dumont in 1802? (Bentham credited Joseph Priestley, as well as Cesare Beccaria, with the idea of the greatest happiness of the greatest number, and it was Priestley to whom Franklin had written his prudential algebra in 1772.) And today, leading scholars of benefit–cost economics (and precaution) include French economists Claude Henry, Olivier Godard, Jean Tirole, Christian Gollier, Nicolas Treich, and others such as public health experts Philippe Kourilsky, Michel Setbon, and Antoine Flahault. The lead author of the report to the European Commission that launched the Better Regulation initiative in 2001, Dieudonné Mandelkern, is French. There has been a great deal of interaction and exchange of ideas on BCA and IA among experts from America, Britain, France, Italy, and other countries across Europe. And France has a well-developed approach to technocratic decisionmaking in government. So it remains puzzling that France had done less to implement Better Regulation; perhaps this is changing.

The overall point here is that precaution and 'better regulation' can learn from each other. Although precaution can be an important and valuable strategy for anticipating and combating emerging (and especially catastrophic) risks, the "precautionary principle"—at least in its stronger versions—neglects important considerations such as cost, innovation, false positives, and risk-risk trade-offs (Wiener 2002; Sunstein 2005; Wiener 2007). These considerations need to be integrated with precaution to achieve successful risk policy. "Better Regulation" with full portfolio impact assessment is a move to incorporate these important considerations into a more thorough and holistic evaluation of policy choices (with, ideally, both *ex ante* and *ex post* assessments). Given the potential countervailing risks of precautionary measures, strong versions of the PP would block themselves; Better Regulation can thus save precaution from itself, and from the adverse side effects of narrow decisions. That is why the European Commission's Communication on the PP (2000) incorporated explicit consideration of benefits and costs into its framework, and its Better Regulation initiative paired precaution with impact assessment. And that is why the Health Council of the Netherlands (2008) report on "prudent precaution" urged that application of the PP must include consideration of the anticipated beneficial and adverse consequences of each policy option. Indeed, if policy impact assessments take on board the value of precaution in preventing extreme catastrophic risks (Sunstein 2007), and if policy impact assessments are used evenhandedly not only to discourage undesirable new policies but also to "prompt" desirable new policies (Wiener 2006; Graham 2007; Revesz and Livermore 2008), then Better Regulation will embrace precaution in truly *better* regulation and can obviate reliance on a special principle of precaution.

Transatlantic Regulatory Relations: Toward a Global Policy Laboratory

A central lesson of our research is that scholars and politicians should get past transatlantic one-upmanship and focus instead on pragmatic improvements to specific concrete policies. The real pattern of precaution is not dichotomous; there is not a European adherence to and American rejection of precaution as a principle; both the United States and Europe employ precaution in some but not all risk regulations. Hence, precaution should not be a dividing line for transatlantic discord. Instead, the United States and Europe should collaborate on exchanging ideas to improve regulation. As discussed above, these exchanges, diffusion, borrowing, and hybridization are indeed ongoing—this too is the reality of precaution.

Further, despite the large influence of the United States and EU in international patterns of economic activity and risk regulation, the world is not just the United States and EU. We are witnessing the rise of China—in a sense, its return to great power status, recalling that before the European industrial revolution, China accounted for almost a third of world economic output—as well as of India, Brazil, and others. The world is becoming multipolar and increasingly interconnected (Slaughter 2009). Risk policy over the coming decades will not take place in yesterday's or today's setting of world power. Looking back at U.S.-European regulatory relations over the past five decades is instructive but not predictive. Risk policy must be conceived as one element of the larger multipolar, multi-issue regime. Two European observers have put this point tendentiously:

> The rise of China and India is de facto leading to a multipolar power constellation. By 2025 at the latest, Washington, Beijing, and Delhi will be the most important centres of power in world politics. In comparison, all European nation states are merely small actors with limited sources of power. Europe will no longer play a key role, unless it comes up with a coherent EU strategy shared by all members. (Humphrey and Messner 2006)

The international promotion by the EU of its strategies of precaution and Better Regulation evince such an ambition to world influence. Meanwhile, in a multipolar world with different priorities in different countries, regulatory competition may prevail over attempts to achieve regulatory convergence (Esty and Geradin 2001; Breggin et al. 2009).

We see both diversity and hybridization in risk regulation occurring across the Atlantic, and in our view, this offers an opportunity for the United States and Europe to undertake collaboration, rather than conflict. Such collaboration can emphasize evaluation and learning from past experience with diverse policy approaches (Farber 1994) or even purposive experimentation with differing approaches to regulation (Greenstone 2009), rather than insistence on convergence. By examining actual risk regulation as applied in concrete experience across diverse settings, testing new approaches, and developing innovations and improvements, the United States and Europe can set examples of leadership that foster learning and diffusion worldwide. Where there is disagreement over particular options, rather than descending into acrimony, the United States and Europe can purposefully experiment with alternative approaches, collect and share data, and test outcomes. This would create a transatlantic policy laboratory, which could quickly become a global policy laboratory (Wiener 2009). It could achieve progress toward "evidence-based risk regulation" (learning from efforts at evidence-based medicine) that tests how well it delivers on its promise. As President Obama said in his first inaugural address, what matters is "not whether our government is too big or too small, but whether it works."

Beyond Comparative Law?

Comparative law has traditionally taken national "legal systems," "families of law," "legal origins," or "national styles of regulation" as the starting point for comparative analysis (Zweigert and Kötz 1998; Vogel 1986; Reitz 1998; La Porta et al. 2008). Perhaps this tendency is strongest in the economic analysis of "legal origins" (La Porta et al. 2008), where broad generalizations about modern business rules are based on grouping countries into a few ancient legal families (for related critiques of the "legal origins" literature, see Curran 2009; Michaels 2009). Comparative law scholars have long recognized the possibilities for legal transplants (Watson 1993), though whether such transplants truly take root in the other system, or remain isolated, or spur divergent responses, remains much debated. Overall, the presumption is that these transplants are rare grafts from one discrete legal system into another, and that their reception in the second legal system is precarious. But as David Kennedy (1997, 605) has observed, it's "more complicated than you thought." As we showed in Chapter 1, generalizations about national traits can be misleading. Culture, economics, politics, and governance interact (Kennedy 2003), such that legal rules are endogenous, not exogenous, and evolve along with culture, democracy, and identity (Jasanoff 2005). Even La Porta et al. recognize that "legal origins" may not account for regulations in "new spheres of social control," nor for regulations adopted following crisis events (2008, 307, 326)—two of the leading characteristics of precautionary risk regulation. Vogel (forthcoming) now finds national regulatory systems more open to change than he had previously seen (which is essential to his claim of a reversal in U.S. and European relative precaution, though he does recognize some counterexamples as exceptions to this asserted trend). Diffusion and hybridization, as discussed above, are powerful forces in that evolution. Hybridization, in law as in biology, interpenetrates and blurs the boundaries of legal "systems," "families," and "styles." Hybridization is not the same as convergence; rather than coalescence on the same legal rule or doctrine, hybridization can entail mixed exchanges of diverse ideas that create overlapping clouds with continued diversity at the level of particular rules and policies (Wiener 2003, 254–261; cf. Radaelli 2005, observing that the diffusion of better regulation systems need not mean policy convergence). Hybrids do not always succeed: hybrid offspring are often less fit, but they can thrive in new niches opened as the environment changes. Our research indicates that U.S. and European systems of risk regulation are undergoing hybridization, exchanging ideas on many topics including precaution, better regulation, impact assessment, economic incentive instruments, information disclosure, and other key elements. Risk regulation lives in an unfolding network society (Castells 2000; Slaughter 2004). The result is that it becomes increasingly difficult to distinguish or generalize about separate regulatory systems. Each is a dynamically evolving mix of ideas and compound institutions (see Fabbrini 2007).

Do the reality of detail and the fragility of generalizations mean that comparing national legal systems is impossible? Is this the end of comparative law? Not necessarily. We have argued that the generalizations often used to compare U.S. and European regulatory systems are hasty and incomplete. But we do not argue that no comparisons can be made. (Such a claim would itself be a hasty generalization drawn from inadequate data.) We do not adopt the view that comparative law is impossible because legal systems are so intrinsically different from each other that rules cannot be compared—what Siems (2007) critiques as the "strong form" of the claim of the "end of comparative law." This view is unsatisfactory both because it is self-negating (it depends on the very kind of sharp comparison that it purports to deny), and because our point is that the United States and Europe have shared legal ideas (not veered off on separate paths). We argue that comparisons can and must be made, but on the basis of much more systematic empirical study, rather than cherry-picking—selecting a few examples, especially those receiving recent news media attention under the proverbial streetlamp—and generalizing to "national styles" based on that small and biased sample. An improved approach will involve comparison of rules and institutions as modules or memes that can be exchanged across interconnected legal systems, rather than of categorical generalizations about national legal systems or legal origins. We aspire to a more robust empiricism in comparative law and policy, not a call to cease comparing. We seek a comparative law that is pragmatically applicable (Markesinis 2003, 53) to major public policy questions faced by legislative and regulatory institutions (Whitman 2007).

We argue that where legal systems are involved in high rates of borrowing, diffusion, and hybridization, it will be increasingly difficult and unhelpful to draw stark generalized contrasts among them. As Reimann (2001) pointed out, extensive diffusion of legal ideas can erode the traditional categories of comparative law that are based on discrete national legal systems. Amidst such intense hybridization, claims of discrete national legal systems or families become stereotypes of an era that is past (if it ever existed). In reality, the ideal types are not sorted neatly into separate polities or legal families, U.S. and European, or civil law and common law. The reality is that different legal rules and concepts can be compared, but they do not line up neatly in national boxes (or in discrete U.S. and EU domains). The reality is not the romantic depiction of conflicting clans led by heroic standard-bearers—Delacroix's *La Liberté*. The reality instead is a complex and evolving landscape that defies easy generalization—Bruegel's busy, busy world.

Even if one clings to the view that Europe and the United States evolved from greater American precaution in the 1970s to greater European precaution in the 1990s (as the flip-flop account maintains), our research suggests that they have now moved to a post-precaution period in which they are developing mutually borrowed systems of Better Regulation. Here again we see particularized decisionmaking based on the merits of each case, rather than categorical generalizations.

We are, indeed, convinced of the value of comparing: the project of comparing is itself a crucial route to understanding and learning. Claims of incommensurability are often efforts to assert the primacy of some preferred category over another—another comparison!—while neglecting that in reality, people must and do make trade-offs. As Hiram Chodosh has nicely shown, those who assert that "comparing apples and oranges" is impossible are committing three errors: first, people do in fact compare apples and oranges at the grocery store every day (in terms of taste, color, shape, price, and so on); second, using the phrase "apples and oranges" itself requires a comparison between the two fruits (to deem them so different); and third, such an assertion itself rests on a comparison between the degree of contrast between the two fruits and the degree of contrast between the other two items sought to be compared (Chodosh 1999). We do not reject comparisons. We seek better comparisons.

Conclusions

Our research indicates that the reality of precaution is particularity, not principle. The real pattern of precaution across the Atlantic since the 1970s (the period of our study) has been general parity, punctuated by occasional differences over particular risks, some of which become high-visibility disputes. Looking at both law on the books and law in action, we find that the reality of precaution has been neither convergence, divergence, nor reversal (flip-flop), but rather has been hybridization through exchange of ideas. The risk regulatory systems of the United States and Europe have not been "trading places" or "ships passing in the night"; they are not separate blocs, and they are far more diverse and intermingled than these metaphors imply. The evidence paints a Bruegel landscape of innumerable complex interactions, not a romanticized image of iconic heroes or rivals.

In reality, the precautionary principle has not been as aggressive as its advocates urge and its critics fear. It is moderated in practice. And in reality, precaution is being melded into the sensible agenda of Better Regulation, in both Europe and the United States.

Strong versions of the precautionary principle can create countervailing risks, in which case the PP would either spawn adverse side effects or block itself. The way out of this dilemma is full portfolio analysis of both the target and ancillary impacts of the policy options—that is to say, sensible impact assessment.

Rather than rivalry and reversal, our analysis (above in this chapter, and throughout this volume) suggests that risk regulation in the United States and Europe has followed an interactive evolutionary path, along the following lines. First, economic growth brings prosperity, which reduces immediate risks to survival and extends longevity. But this economic advance also supplies two sources of greater appreciation of risk: the scientific means to detect more subtle and latent risks, and new technologies that reduce some risks but may create new risks. These two factors, along with prosperity itself, help foster an increasing demand for precautionary policies. (Although much of the demand for precaution has been about the risk of new technologies, a significant share of the demand for precaution has been spurred not by new technology, but by new attention to other (older) sources of risk, such as overfishing, tobacco, chemicals, food contaminants, and conventional terrorism.)

Second, economic advance and greater longevity also shift the demand for risk protection toward greater emphasis on latent risks. Even though greater longevity reflects decreasing risks, longer lifespans also lead people to care more about risks that may arise farther into the future. And, in a decreasing-risk world, those risks that do occur are seen as more unusual and more outrageous by the public, spurring greater demand for protective measures. If so, it is not surprising that the PP first arose in wealthier, safer societies in the 1960s and 1970s, such as Switzerland, Sweden,

Germany, and the United States. This is consistent with the view that rising income yields rising demand for risk protection (Esty and Porter 2005). At the same time, this process implies that countries do not adopt the PP (or reject it) across the board, but rather that some risks are selected to be regulated in each polity because of episodic crisis events, public perceptions, cultural predispositions, and political responses. The observed pattern is one of particularity—occasional and selective application of precaution to different risks in different places and times.

Third, countries that are moving to adopt the PP then seek to have it adopted by their trade partners to avoid competitiveness losses (Kelemen and Vogel 2010). But, fourth, as the PP is applied with more teeth, it imposes costs and ancillary impacts. It thereby encounters resistance and becomes moderated. This occurred in the United States with the APA in 1946, and the presidential executive orders on regulatory impact assessment from Carter to Reagan to Clinton to the present; and it occurred in Europe as the PP of the 1990s was met by the Better Regulation initiative after 2001. Moreover, as the PP is applied, it inevitably poses further questions that it does not answer, including which of the multiple risks facing society are worthy of action (that is, the question of risk selection just noted), which actions should be taken to address those risks, and how to balance and overcome ancillary risk impacts in the complex web of risks. Expert inquiry, public perceptions such as the availability heuristic (Weber and Ancker, Chapter 18 of this volume; Sunstein, Chapter 19 of this volume), cultural processes for risk selection and social response (Chapters 18 and 19 of this volume; Douglas and Wildavsky 1982), and governance mechanisms (Wiener and Richman 2010) operate simultaneously to modulate how these questions will be answered. Programs of "Better Regulation" and regulatory impact assessment speak directly to these questions left open by the PP. And because risks, whether target or ancillary, do not respect political borders, both risks and precautionary measures in one country may have effects in others.

Fifth, then, demand grows for international coordination, hybridization, learning, diffusion, and borrowing of ideas about how best to address these interconnected risks. Simultaneously, a growing supply of policy ideas and evaluative experience spreads through transnational networks (Slaughter 2009) among regulators, experts, businesses, and nongovernmental organisations (NGOs) (including, perhaps, through our own four Transatlantic Dialogues on Precaution). The path leads beyond traditional comparative law: not just two "legal systems" with discrete "national styles of regulation," but an interwoven network of hybrid approaches. That is the reality of precaution.

To be sure, there is ample room for normative and iterative improvements in precaution, in regulation, and in impact assessment. These improvements may include greater transparency; better stakeholder engagement; more use of proportionate analysis; assessment and integration of distributional impacts into policy decisions; analysis of the full portfolio of important policy consequences, including ancillary impacts such as countervailing risks (risk-risk trade-offs) and ancillary benefits; the use by regulatory oversight bodies of policy "prompts" to agencies to undertake needed new regulations, as well as the more traditional policy "returns" to agencies to reconsider proposed regulations; and routine conduct of not only *ex ante* impact assessments (to choose new policies), but also *ex post* evaluations (both to help revise existing policies and to identify improvements in subsequent *ex ante* impact assessment methods).

One may also foresee that as a society becomes even safer due to the joint effects of prosperity, precaution, and better regulation, that society will come to confront even lower-probability, higher-consequence risks—that is, extreme catastrophic risks that would otherwise escape attention but that could be highly worth preventing (Posner 2004; Sunstein 2007). Scientific detection capabilities improve with prosperity and continuing research. Longer lifespans mean that extreme risks become more plausible within one's own lifetime and the lifetime of one's children and grandchildren. And the bequest value to the living of protecting future generations may increase with foresight, wealth, and present safety. But these rare extreme risks may go neglected where they are so rare that no present or memorable incident triggers the availability heuristic and adaptive learning in human cognition (Slovic and Weber 2002; Gilbert and Wilson 2007; Schachter et al. 2008). Furthermore, they tend to be neglected where short-term incentives cloud long-term losses (in both business and politics), where the losses would be so large that the public becomes numb (Slovic 2007), and where the catastrophe would wipe out the very institutions meant to provide remedies and *ex post* sanctions (thus weakening *ex ante* incentives for prevention). Beyond ordinary "tragedies of the commons", there are "tragedies of the uncommons" (Wiener 2005, 2008) that pose the best case for precaution. They warrant not only a modified version of benefit–cost analysis to add weight to catastrophic losses (Sunstein 2007), but also a corrective to the psychological and institutional failures of political systems to anticipate and prepare for rare extreme risks. Still, precaution against tragedies of the uncommons must confront the twin challenges of priority-setting (choosing which extreme scenario to address, even as such scenarios multiply as the probability worth worrying about becomes ever smaller) and risk-risk trade-offs (because measures to prevent one catastrophic risk might induce another). Thus, even in cases where precaution is strongly warranted against uncertain catastrophic risks, the full portfolio impact assessment of better regulation remains crucial.

To succeed, societies must manage both emerging risks (through precaution) and the ancillary impacts of their own risk protection measures (through impact assessment). Both are forms of foresight. A complex world demands that we open both our eyes to appreciate the busy details we are painting on the canvas of our future. This imperative is reflected, both descriptively and normatively, in the reality of precaution.

References

Ahern, Bertie. 2004. Speech by the Taoiseach (head of government of Ireland), Bertie Ahern, at the IBEC Conference on EU-U.S. Perspectives on Regulation. April 19, Dublin. www.betterregulation.ie/index.asp?docID_57_ (accessed May 24, 2010).

Alemanno, Alberto. 2007. *Trade in Food: Regulatory and Judicial Approaches in the EC and the WTO*. London: Cameron May.

———. 2008. Quis Custodet Custodes dans le cadre de l'initiative "Mieux Légiférer"? *Revue du Droit de l'Union Européenne* 1: 43–86.

————. 2009. The Better Regulation Initiative at the Judicial Gate: A Trojan Horse within the Commission's Walls or the Way Forward? *European Law Journal* 15: 382–401.

Andersen, Mikael Skou. 1994. *Governance by Green Taxes.* Manchester: Manchester University Press.

Applegate, John. 2000. The Precautionary Preference: An American Perspective on the Precautionary Principle. *Human and Ecological Risk Assessment* 6: 413–443.

Arnold, M. L. 1997. *Natural Hybridization and Evolution.* Oxford: Oxford University Press.

Baldwin, Peter 2009. *The Narcissism of Minor Differences: How America and Europe are Alike.* Oxford: Oxford University Press.

Barrieu, Pauline and Bernard Sinclair-Dégagné. 2006. On Precautionary Policies. *Management Science* 52: 1145–1154.

Berkowitz, Daniel, Katharina Pistor, and Jean-Francois Richard. 2003. Economic Development, Legality, and the Transplant Effect. *European Economic Review* 47: 165.

Berry, Frances Stokes, and William D. Berry. 2007. Innovation and Diffusion Models in Policy Research. In *Theories of the Policy Process*, edited by Paul A. Sabatier. Boulder, CO: Westview Press. 223.

Blomquist, William. 2007. The Policy Process and Large-N Comparative Studies. In *Theories of the Policy Process.* 2nd ed., edited by Paul A. Sabatier. Boulder, CO: Westview Press, 261–291.

Bodansky, Daniel. 2004. Deconstructing the Precautionary Principle. In *Bringing New Law to Ocean Waters*, edited by D. D. Caron, and H. N. Scheiber. Leiden, Netherlands: Koninklijke Brill NV.

Brady, Henry E., and David Collier eds. 2004. *Rethinking Social Inquiry: Diverse Tools, Shared Standards.* Berkeley, CA: Rowman and Littlefield and Berkeley Public Policy Press.

Breggin, Linda, Robert Falkner, Nico Jaspers, John Pendergrass, and Read Porter. 2009. *Securing the Promise of Nanotechnologies: Towards Transatlantic Regulatory Cooperation.* London: Chatham House/Royal Institute for International Affairs. www.lse.ac.uk/nanoregulation (accessed May 24, 2010).

Breyer, Stephen and Veerle Heyvaert. 2000. Institutions for Regulating Risk. In *Environmental Law, the Economy, and Sustainable Development: The United States, the European Union, and the International Community*, edited by Richard L. Revesz, Phillipe Sands, and Richard B. Stewart. Cambridge: Cambridge University Press.

Brickman, Ronald, Sheila Jasanoff, and Thomas Ilgen. 1985. *Controlling Chemicals: The Politics of Regulation in Europe and the United States.* Ithaca, NY: Cornell University Press.

Busch, Per-olof, and Helge Jörgens. 2005. The International Sources of Policy Convergence: Explaining the Spread of Environmental Policy Innovations. *Journal of European Public Policy* 12: 860–884.

Butti, Luciano. 2007. *The Precautionary Principle in Environmental Law: Neither Arbitrary nor Capricious If Interpreted with Equilibrium.* Milan: Giuffré Editore.

Castells, Manuel. 2000. *The Information Age: Economy, Society, and Culture.* 2nd ed., Vols. 1–3 Oxford: Blackwell.

Chateauraynaud, Francis, and Didier Torny. 1999. *Les Sombres Precurseurs: Une Sociologie Pragmatique de l'Alerte et du Risque.* Paris: School for Advanced Studies in the Social Sciences (EHESS).

Chodosh, Hiram. 1999. Comparing Comparisons: In Search of Methodology. *Iowa Law Review* 84: 1025.

Christoforou, Theofanis. 2004. The Precautionary Principle, Risk Assessment, and the Comparative Role of Science in the European Community and the United States Legal Systems. In *Green Giants? Environmental Policies of the United States and the European Union*, edited by Norman J. Vig and Michael G. Faure. Cambridge, MA: MIT Press.

Coglianese, Cary, and Lori Snyder Bennear. 2005. Program Evaluation of Environmental Policies: Toward Evidence-Based Decision Making. In *Social and Behavioral Science Research Priorities for Environmental Decision Making.* Washington, DC: National Research Council, National Academies Press, 246–273.

Cross, Frank. 1996. Paradoxical Perils of the Precautionary Principle. *Washington and Lee Law Review* 53: 851–925.

———. 1997. Political Science and the New Legal Realism: A Case of Unfortunate Interdisciplinary Ignorance. *Northwestern University Law Review* 92: 251.

Curran, Vivian G. 2009. Comparative Law and the Legal Origins Thesis. *American Journal of Comparative Law* 57: 863–876.

Deakin, Simon. 2002. Evolution for Our Time: A Theory of Legal Memetics. *Current Legal Problems* 55: 1–42.

DeKay, Michael, Mitchell Small, Paul Fischbeck, Scott Farrow, Alison Cullen, Joseph B. Kadane, Lester Lave, Granger Morgan, and Kazuhisa Takemura. 2002. Risk-Based Decision Analysis in Support of Precautionary Policies. *Journal of Risk Research* 5: 391–417.

Delmas-Marty, Mirelle. 2006. *Le Pluralisme Ordonné.* Paris: Seuil.

de Sadeleer, Nicholas. 2002. *Environmental Principles: From Political Slogans to Legal Rules.* Oxford: Oxford University Press.

———. ed. 2007. *Implementing Precaution: Approaches from Nordic Countries, the EU, and the U.S.A..* London: Earthscan.

———. 2009. The Precautionary Principle as a Device for Greater Environmental Protection: Lessons from the EC Courts. *Review of European Community and International Environmental Law.* 18 (April): 3–10.

Dobbin, Frank, Beth Simmons, and Geoffrey Garrett. 2007. The Global Diffusion of Public Policies: Social Construction, Coercion, Competition, or Learning? *Annual Review of Sociology.* 33 (August) www.wjh.harvard.edu/~dobbin/cv/articles/2007_ARS_Dobbin_Simmons.pdf: 449–472 (accessed May 24, 2010).

Dolowitz, David, and David Marsh. 2000. Learning from Abroad: The Role of Policy Transfer in Contemporary Policy Making. *Governance* 13 (1): 5–24.

Douglas, Mary, and Aaron Wildavsky. 1982. *Risk and Culture: An Essay on the Selection of Technological and Environmental Dangers.* Berkeley, CA: University California Press.

Dwyer, John P., Richard W. Brooks, and Alan C. Marco. 2000. The Air Pollution Permit Process for U.S. and German Automobile Assembly Plants. In *Regulatory Encounters: Multinational Corporations and American Adversarial Legalism,* edited by Robert A. Kagan, and Lee Axelrad. Berkeley, CA: University of California Press, 173–224.

Ellerman, A. Denny, Frank Convery, and Christian de Perthuis. 2010. *Pricing Carbon: The European Union Emissions Trading Scheme.* Cambridge: Cambridge University Press.

Elliott, E. Donald. 1985. The Evolutionary Tradition in Jurisprudence. *Columbia Law Review* 85: 38.

———. 1997. Law and Biology: The New Synthesis? *St. Louis University Law Journal* 41: 595.

Esty, Daniel C., and Damien Geradin eds. 2001. *Regulatory Competition and Economic Integration: Comparative Perspectives.* Oxford: Oxford University Press.

Esty, Daniel, and Michael Porter. 2005. National Environmental Performance: An Empirical Analysis of Policy Results and Determinants. *Environment and Development Economics* 10: 391–434.

European Commission. 2000. Communication from the Commission on the Precautionary Principle. COM (2000)1. Brussels, February 2.

Fabbrini, Sergio 2007. *Compound Democracies: Why the United States and Europe are Becoming Similar.* Oxford: Oxford University Press.

Farber, Daniel A. 1994. Environmental Protection as a Learning Experience. *Loyola of Los Angeles Law Review* 7: 791.

Farrow, Scott. 2004. Using Risk-Assessment, Benefit-Cost Analysis, and Real Options to Implement a Precautionary Principle. *Risk Analysis* 24: 727.

Frison-Roche, Marie-Anne, eds. 2005. *Les Risques de Régulation.* Paris: Presses de Sciences Po et Dalloz.

Galison, Peter. 1997. *Image and Logic: A Material Culture of Microphysics.* Chicago, IL : University of Chicago Press.

Gilbert, Daniel T., and Timothy D. Wilson. 2007. Prospection: Experiencing the Future. *Science* 317: 1351–1354.

Godard, Olivier. 2006. The Precautionary Principle and Catastrophism on Tenterhooks: Lessons from Constitutional Reform in France. In *Implementing the Precautionary Principle: Perspectives and Prospects*, edited by Elizabeth Fisher, Judith Jones, and René von Schomberg. Northampton, MA: Edward Elgar.

Godard, Olivier, Claude Henry, Patrick Lagadec, and Erwann Michel-Kerjan. 2002. *Traité des Nouveaux Risques: Précaution, Crise, Assurance.* Paris: Gallimard.

Goldstein, Bernard D. 2001. The Precautionary Principle Also Applies to Public Health Actions. *American Journal of Public Health* 91 (9): 1358–1361.

Gollier, Christian, and Nicolas Treich. 2003. Decision Making under Uncertainty: The Economics of the Precautionary Principle. *Journal of Risk and Uncertainty* 27: 77.

Graham, John D. 2001. Decision-Analytic Refinements of the Precautionary Principle. *Journal of Risk Research* 4: 127.

———. 2007. The Evolving Regulatory Role of the U.S. Office of Management and Budget. *Review of Environmental Economics and Policy* 1: 171–191.

Graham, John D., and Jonathan B. Wiener. eds. 1995. *Risk vs. Risk: Tradeoffs in Protecting Health and the Environment.* Cambridge, MA: Harvard University Press.

Grant, Peter R. 1999. *Ecology and Evolution of Darwin's Finches.* Princeton, NJ: Princeton University Press.

Graziadei, Michele. 2009. Legal Transplants and the Frontiers of Legal Knowledge. *Theoretical Inquiries in Law* 10 (2) Article 15.

Greenstone, Michael. 2009. Toward a Culture of Persistent Regulatory Experimentation and Evaluation. In *New Perspectives on Regulation*, edited by David Moss and John Cisternino,, www.tobinproject.org/twobooks (accessed May 24, 2010).

Hadfield, Gillian. 1993. Bias in the Evolution of Legal Rules. *Georgetown Law Journal* 80: 583.

Hägerstrand, Torsten. 1968. The Diffusion of Innovations. *International Encyclopedia of Social Sciences* 4: 194.

Hall, Peter A., and David Soskice. eds. 2001. *Varieties of Capitalism: The Institutional Foundations of Comparative Advantage.* Oxford: Oxford University Press.

Hammitt, James K., Jonathan B. Wiener, Brendon Swedlow, Denise Kall, and Zheng Zhou. 2005. Precautionary Regulation in Europe and the United States: A Quantitative Comparison. *Risk Analysis* 25: 1215–1228.

Harremoës, Poul, David Gee, Malcolm MacGarvin, Andy Stirling, Jane Keys, Brian Wynne, and Sofia Guedes Vaz. eds. 2002. *The Precautionary Principle in the Twentieth Century: Late Lessons from Early Warnings.* London: Earthscan.

Harrington, Winston, Richard D. Morgenstern, and Thomas Sterner. eds. 2004. *Choosing Environmental Policy: Comparing Instruments and Outcomes in the United States and Europe.* Washington, DC: Resources for the Future Press.

Harris, Gardiner. 2008. Balance Benefit vs. Cost of Latest Drugs. *New York Times*, Dec. 3, A1. www.nytimes.com/2008/12/03/health/03nice.html (accessed May 22, 2010).

Hart, Oliver. 2009. Regulation and Sarbanes-Oxley. *Journal of Accounting Research* 47: 437–445.

Hassid, Olivier. 2005. *La Gestion des Risques.* Paris: Dunod.

Health Council of the Netherlands. 2008. *Prudent Precaution*, Publication No. 2008/18E. The Hague: Health Council of the Netherlands. www.gezondheidsraad.nl/en/publications/prudent--precaution (accessed July 29, 2010).

Hinich, Melvin, and Michael Munger. 1998. Empirical Studies in Comparative Politics. *Public Choice* 97: 219–227.

Hood, Christopher, Henry Rothstein, and Robert Baldwin. 2001. *The Government of Risk: Understanding Risk Regulation Regimes.* Oxford: Oxford University Press.

Humphrey, John, and Dirk Messner. 2006. Self-Serving Giants in a Multipolar World. *D+C Magazine for Development and Cooperation* (May). www.inwent.org/E+Z/content/archive-eng/05-2006/foc_art4.html (accessed May 24, 2010).

James, Oliver, and Martin Lodge. 2003. The Limitations of "Policy Transfer" and "Lesson Drawing" for Public Policy Research. *Political Studies Review* 1: 179–193. http://people.exeter.ac.uk/ojames/psr_3.pdf (accessed May 24, 2010).

Jasanoff, Sheila. 2005. *Designs on Nature: Science and Democracy in Europe and the United States.* Princeton, NJ: Princeton University Press.

Jonas, Hans. 1984. In *The Imperative of Responsibility: In Search of Ethics for the Technological Age.* Translation of *Das Prinzip Verantwortung,* by Hans Jonas and David Herr. Chicago, IL: University of Chicago Press.

Jordan, Andrew, and Timothy O'Riordan. 1999. The Precautionary Principle in Contemporary Environmental Policy and Politics. In *Protecting Public Health and the Environment: Implementing the Precautionary Principle,* edited by Carolyn Raffensperger and Joel Tickner. Washington, DC: Island Press.

Kagan, Elena. 2001. Presidential Administration. *Harvard Law Review* 114: 2245–2385.

Kagan, Robert. 2003. *Of Paradise and Power: America and Europe in the New World Order.* New York: Knopf.

Kagan, Robert A. 2007. Globalization and Legal Change: The "Americanization" of European Law? *Regulation and Governance* 1: 99–120.

Kagan, Robert A., and Lee Axelrad. eds. 2000. *Regulatory Encounters: Multinational Corporations and American Adversarial Legalism.* Berkeley, CA: University of California Press.

Kahan, Dan. 2007. The Cognitively Illiberal State. *Stanford Law Review* 60: 115–154.

———. 2008. Two Conceptions of Emotion in Risk Regulation. *University of Pennsylvania Law Review* 156: 741.

Kahn, Matthew E. 2007. Environmental Disasters as Risk Regulation Catalysts? The Role of Bhopal, Chernobyl, Exxon Valdez, Love Canal, and Three Mile Island in Shaping U.S. Environmental Law. *Journal of Risk and Uncertainty* 35: 17–43.

Keeney, Ralph L., and Detlof von Winterfeldt. 2001. Appraising the Precautionary Principle: A Decision Analysis Perspective. *Journal of Risk Research* 4: 191.

Kelemen, R. Daniel. 2004. Environmental Federalism in the United States and the European Union. In *Green Giants: Environmental Policies of the United States and the European Union,* edited by Norman Vig, and Michael Faure. Cambridge, MA: MIT Press.

Kelemen, R. Daniel, and David Vogel. 2010. Trading Places: The Role of the United States and the European Union in International Environmental Politics. *Comparative Political Studies* 43: 427–456.

Kelman, Steven. 1981. *Regulating America, Regulating Sweden: A Comparative Study of Occupational Safety and Health Policy.* Cambridge, MA: MIT Press.

Kennedy, David. 1997. New Approaches to Comparative Law: Comparativism and International Governance. *Utah Law Review* 2: 545–637.

———. 2003. The Methods and Politics of Comparative Law. In *Comparative Legal Studies: Traditions and Transitions,* edited by Pierre Legrand and Roderick Munday. Cambridge: Cambridge University Press, 345–433.

King, Gary, Robert O. Keohane, and Sidney Verba. 1994. *Designing Social Inquiry: Scientific Inference in Qualitative Research.* Princeton, NJ: Princeton University Press.

Kingsbury, Benedict, Nico Krisch, and Richard B. Stewart. 2005. The Emergence of Global Administrative Law. *Law and Contemporary Problems* 68 (3): 15–62.

Kourilsky, Philippe. 2001. *Du Bon Usage du Principe de Précaution.* Paris: Editions Odile Jacob.

Kourilsky, Philippe, and G. Viney. 2000. *Le Principe de Précaution.* Paris: Editions Odile Jacob.

Krämer, Ludwig. 2004. The Roots of Divergence: A European Perspective. In *Green Giants? Environmental Policies of the United States and the European Union,* edited by Norman J. Vig and Michael G. Faure. Cambridge, MA: MIT Press.

Kysar, Douglas. 2010. *Regulating from Nowhere.* New Haven, CT: Yale University Press.

La Porta, Rafael, Florencio Lopez-de-Silanes, and Andrei Shleifer. 2008. The Economic Consequences of Legal Origins. *Journal of Economic Literature* 46: 285–332.

Lazer, David. 2005. Regulatory Capitalism as a Networked Order. *Annals of the American Academy.* (March) 52–66.

Levi-Faur, David. 2004. Comparative Research Designs in the Study of Regulation: How to Increase the Number of Cases without Compromising the Strengths of Case-Oriented Analysis. In *The Politics of Regulation: Institutions and Regulatory Reforms for the Age of Governance,* edited by Jacint Jordana and David Levi-Faur. Cheltenham, UK/Northampton MA: Edward Elgar, 177–199.

———. 2005. The Global Diffusion of Regulatory Capitalism. *The Annals of the American Academy of Political and Social Science* 598: 12–32. http://poli.haifa.ac.il/~levi/levifaur-framework.pdf (accessed May 22, 2010).

Lieberman, Evan S. 2005. Nested Analysis as a Mixed-Method Strategy for Comparative Research. *American Political Science Review* 99: 435–452.

Lindseth, Peter L., Alfred C. Aman, Jr., and Alan C. Raul. 2008. Oversight. In *Administrative Law of the European Union*, edited by George A. Bermann et al. Washington, DC: American Bar Association.

Listokin, Yair. 2008. Learning through Policy Variation. *Yale Law Journal* 118: 480–553.

Loewenberg, Samuel. 2003. Precaution Is for Europeans. *New York Times*, May 18.

Lofstedt, Ragnar. 2004. The Swing of the Regulatory Pendulum in Europe: From Precautionary Principle to (Regulatory) Impact Analysis. *Journal of Risk and Uncertainty* 28: 237–260.

Majone, Giandomenico D. 1996. *Regulating Europe*. London: Routledge.

Marchant, Gary E., and Kenneth L. Mossman. 2004. *Arbitrary and Capricious: The Precautionary Principle in the EU Courts*. Washington, DC: AEI Press.

Markesinis, Basil. 2003. *Comparative Law in the Courtroom and Classroom*. Oxford: Hart Publishing.

Mazur, Alan. 2004. *True Warnings and False Alarms*. Washington, DC: Resources for the Future Press.

McIntyre, O., and T. Mosedale. 1997. The Precautionary Principle as a Norm of Customary International Law. *Journal of Environmental Law* 9: 221.

Michaels, Ralf. 2009. Comparative Law by Numbers? Legal Origins Thesis, Doing Business Reports, and the Silence of Traditional Comparative Law. *American Journal of Comparative Law* 57: 765–795.

Miles, Thomas J., and Cass R. Sunstein. 2008. The New Legal Realism. *University of Chicago Law Review* 75: 831–851.

Milhaupt, Curtis, and Katharina Pistor. 2008. *Law and Capitalism: What Corporate Crises Reveal about Legal Systems and Economic Development around the World*. Chicago, IL: University of Chicago Press.

Nicoletti, Giuseppe, and Frederic Pryor. 2006. Subjective and Objective Measures of Governmental Regulations in OECD Nations. *Journal of Economic Behavior and Organization* 59: 433–449.

OECD (Organisation for Economic Co-operation and Development). 2009. *Regulatory Impact Assessment as a Tool for Policy Coherence*. Paris: OECD.

Page, Talbot. 1978. A Generic View of Toxic Chemicals and Similar Risks. *Ecology Law Quarterly* 7: 207–244.

Peel, Jacqueline. 2004. Precaution: A Matter of Principle, Approach, or Process? *Melbourne Journal of International Law* 5: 483–501.

Percival, Robert. 1998. Environmental Legislation and the Problem of Collective Action. *Duke Environmental Law and Policy Forum* 9: 9–27.

Pinker, Steven. 2009. Why Is There Peace? *Greater Good* magazine (April). http://greatergood.berkeley.edu/greatergood/2009april/Pinker054.php (accessed May 22, 2010).

Pollack, Mark A., and Gregory C. Shaffer. 2009. *When Cooperation Fails: The International Law and Politics of Genetically Modified Foods*. Oxford: Oxford University Press.

Posner, Richard A. 2004. *Catastrophe: Risk and Response*. Oxford: Oxford University Press.

Priest, George L. 1977. The Common Law Process and the Selection of Efficient Rules. *Journal of Legal Studies* 6 (October): 65.

Radaelli, Claudio M. 2005. Diffusion without Convergence: How Political Context Shapes the Adoption of Regulatory Impact Assessment. *Journal of European Public Policy* 12: (October) 924–943.

Radaelli, Claudio M., and Fabrizio De Francesco. 2006. *Regulatory Quality in Europe: Concepts, Measures, and Policy Processes*. New York: Manchester University Press.

———. et al. 2008. Regulatory Impact Assessment. In *Oxford Handbook of Regulation*, edited by Martin Cave. Oxford: Oxford University Press. Chapter 15.

Raffensperger, Carolyn, and Joel Tickner, eds. 1999. *Protecting Public Health and the Environment: Implementing the Precautionary Principle*. Washington, DC: Island Press.

Rehbinder, Eckard, and Richard Stewart. 1985. *Environmental Protection Policy: Legal Integration in the United States and the European Community*. New York: De Gruyter.

Reimann, Mathias. 2001. Beyond National Systems: A Comparative Law for the International Age. *Tulane Law Review* 75: 1103.

Reitz, John C. 1998. How to Do Comparative Law. *American Journal of Comparative Law* 46: 617–636.

Renda, Andrea. 2006. *Impact Assessment in the EU*. Brussels: Center for European Policy Studies.

Renn, Ortwin. 2008. *Risk Governance: Coping with Uncertainty in a Complex World*. London: Earthscan.

Renn, Ortwin, and Bernd Rohrmann. eds. 2000. *Cross-Cultural Risk Perception: A Survey of Empirical Studies*. Dordrecht, Netherlands: Kluwer.

Repetto, Robert, ed. 2006. *Punctuated Equilibrium and the Dynamics of US Environmental Policy*. New Haven, CT: Yale University Press.

Revesz, Richard L., and Michael A. Livermore. 2008. *Retaking Rationality: How Cost-Benefit Analysis Can Better Protect the Environment and Our Health*. Oxford: Oxford University Press.

Roe, Mark J. 1996. Chaos and Evolution in Law and Economics. *Harvard Law Review* 109: 641.

———. 2006. Legal Origins, Politics, and Modern Stock Markets. *Harvard Law Review* 120: 460.

Rogers, M. Everett. 2003. *The Diffusion of Innovations*. 5th ed. New York: Free Press.

Rose, Richard. 1993. *Lesson-Drawing in Public Policy*. Chatham, NJ: Chatham House.

Rose-Ackerman, Susan. 1995. *Controlling Environmental Policy: The Limits of Public Law in Germany and the United States*. New Haven, CT: Yale University Press.

Rose-Ackerman, Susan, and Peter Lindseth, eds. 2010. *Comparative Administrative Law*. Northampton, MA: Edward Elgar.

Sand, Peter H. 1971. Current Trends in African Legal Geography: The Interfusion of Legal Systems. *African Legal Studies* 5: 1–27.

———. 2000. The Precautionary Principle: A European Perspective. *Human and Ecological Risk Assessment* 6: 445–458.

Sandin, Per. 1999. Dimensions of the Precautionary Principle. *Human and Ecological Risk Assessment* 5: 889.

Sands, Philippe. 1995. *Principles of International Environmental Law*. New York: Manchester University Press.

Schachter, Daniel L., Donna Rose Addis, and Randy L. Buckner. 2008. Episodic Simulation of Future Events: Concepts, Data, and Applications. *Annals of the New York Academy of Sciences* 1124: 39–60.

Scruggs, Lyle. 1999. Institutions and Environmental Performance in Seventeen Western Democracies. *British Journal of Political Science* 29: 1–31.

———. 2001. Is There Really a Link between Neo-Corporatism and Environmental Performance? Updated Evidence and New Data for the 1980s and 1990s. *British Journal of Political Science* 31: 686–692.

———. 2003. *Sustaining Abundance: Environmental Performance in Industrialized Democracies*. New York: Cambridge University Press.

———. 2009. Democracy and Environmental Protection: An Empirical Analysis. Draft of April 2009. http://sp.uconn.edu/~scruggs/mpsa09e.pdf (accessed May 22, 2010).

Selin, Henrik, and Stacy VanDeveer. 2006. Raising Global Standards. *Environment* 48 (10): 6–17.

Setbon, Michel. 2004. *Risques, Sécurité Sanitaire, et Processus de Decision*. Amsterdam: Elsevier.

Siems, Mathias M. 2007. The End of Comparative Law. *Journal of Comparative Law* 2: 133–150.

Simmons, Beth A., Frank, Dobbin, and Geoffrey Garrett, eds. 2008. *The Global Diffusion of Markets and Democracy*. Cambridge: Cambridge University Press.

Slaughter, Anne-Marie. 2004. *A New World Order*. Princeton, NJ: Princeton University Press.

———. 2009. The Networked Century. *Foreign Affairs* 88 (January–February): 94.

Slovic, Paul. 1987. Perception of Risk. *Science* 236 (4799): 280–285.

———. 2007. "If I Look at the Mass I Will Never Act": Psychic Numbing and Genocide. *Judgment and Decision Making* 2 (2): 79–95.

Slovic, Paul, James Flynn, and Mark Layman. 1991. Perceived Risk, Trust, and the Politics of Nuclear Waste. *Science* 254: 1603–1607.

Slovic, Paul, and Elke Weber. 2002. *Perception of Risk Posed by Extreme Events.* New York: Columbia University Center for Hazards and Risk Research.

Stern, Jessica, and Jonathan B. Wiener. 2008. Precaution against Terrorism. In *Managing Strategic Surprise*, edited by Paul Bracken, Ian Bremmer, and David Gordon. Cambridge: Cambridge University Press. 110.

Stewart, Richard B. 2002. Environmental Regulatory Decisionmaking under Uncertainty. *Research in Law and Economics* 20: 71–152.

Stone, Christopher D. 2001. Is There a Precautionary Principle? *Environmental Law Reporter* 31: 10790.

Sunstein, Cass R. 2005. *The Laws of Fear: Beyond the Precautionary Principle.* Cambridge: Cambridge University Press.

———. 2007. *Worst-Case Scenarios.* Cambridge, MA: Harvard University Press.

Sunstein, Cass R., and Timur Kuran. 1999. Availability Cascades and Risk Regulation. *Stanford Law Review* 51: 683–768.

Swedlow, Brendon, Denise Kall, Zheng Zhou, James K. Hammitt, and Jonathan B. Wiener. 2009. Theorizing and Generalizing about Risk Assessment and Regulation through Comparative Nested Analysis of Representative Cases. *Law and Policy* 31: 236–269.

Sweet, Alec Stone, and Jud Mathews. 2008. Proportionality Balancing and Global Constitutionalism. *Journal of Transnational Law* 47: 73–165. http://works.bepress.com/alec_stone_sweet/11 (accessed May 22, 2010).

Sweet, Alec Stone, and Wayne Sandholtz. 1997. Integration and Supranational Governance. *Journal of European Public Policy* 43: 297–317. http://works.bepress.com/alec_stone_sweet/20 (accessed May 22, 2010).

Thatcher, Mark, and David Coen. 2008. Reshaping European Regulatory Space: An Evolutionary Analysis. *Western European Politics* 31: 806–836.

Tushnet, Mark. 1999. Possibilities of Comparative Constitutional Law. *Yale Law Journal* 108: 1225.

VanderZwaag, David. 1999. The Precautionary Principle in Environmental Law and Policy: Elusive Rhetoric and First Embraces. *Journal of Environmental Law and Practice* 8: 355.

Vig, Norman and Michael, Faure, eds. 2004. *Green Giants: Environmental Policies of the United States and the European Union.* Cambridge, MA: MIT Press.

Vogel, David. 1986. *National Styles of Regulation: Environmental Policy in Great Britain and the United States.* Ithaca, NY: Cornell University Press.

———. 2001. Ships Passing in the Night: The Changing Politics of Risk Regulation in Europe and the United States. Working Paper 2001/16. Robert Schuman Centre for Advanced Studies, European University Institute.

———. 2002. Risk Regulation in Europe and the United States. In *Yearbook of European Environmental Law.*, Vol. 3.

———. 2003. The Hare and the Tortoise Revisited: The New Politics of Consumer and Environmental Regulation in Europe. *British Journal of Political Science* 33: 557–580.

———. Forthcoming. *The Politics of Precaution: Regulating Health, Safety and Environmental Risks in the United States and Europe.* Princeton, NJ: Princeton University Press.

Walker, Jack L. 1969. The Diffusion of Innovation among the American States. *American Political Science Review* 63: 880–889.

Watson, Alan. 1993. *Legal Transplants: An Approach to Comparative Law.* 2nd ed. Athens, GA: University of Georgia Press.

Weyland, Kurt. 2005. Theories of Policy Diffusion. *World Politics* 57: 262–295.

Whitman, James Q. 2007. Consumerism versus Producerism: A Study in Comparative Law. *Yale Law Journal* 117: 340.

Wiener, Jonathan B. 1998. Managing the Iatrogenic Risks of Risk Management. *Risk: Health Safety and Environment* 9: 39–82.

———. 1999a. Global Environmental Regulation: Instrument Choice in Legal Context. *Yale Law Journal* 108: 677–800.

———. 1999b. On the Political Economy of Global Environmental Regulation. *Georgetown Law Journal* 87: 749–794.

———. 2001. Something Borrowed for Something Blue: Legal Transplants and the Evolution of Global Environmental Law. *Ecology Law Quarterly* 27: 1295–1371.

———. 2002. Precaution in a Multirisk World. In *Human and Ecological Risk Assessment: Theory and Practice*, edited by Dennis D. Paustenbach. New York: Wiley and Sons, 1509–1531.

———. 2003. Whose Precaution After All? A Comment on the Comparison and Evolution of Risk Regulatory Systems. *Duke Journal of International and Comparative Law* 13: 207–262.

———. 2005. Reviews of *Catastrophe* by Richard Posner and *Collapse* by Jared Diamond. *Journal of Policy Analysis and Management* 24: 885–890.

———. 2006. Better Regulation in Europe. *Current Legal Problems* 59: 447–518.

———. 2007. Precaution. In *Oxford Handbook of International Environmental Law*, edited by Daniel Bodansky, Jutta Brunnee, and Ellen Hey. Oxford: Oxford University Press, 597–612.

———. 2008. The Tragedy of the Uncommons. Remarks at the Conference on Global Catastrophic Risks. July 16–20, Oxford University.

———. 2009. Toward a Global Policy Laboratory. Remarks at the SRA-RFF Conference on New Ideas for Risk Regulation. June 22. www.rff.org/Events/Pages/New-Ideas-for-Risk-Regulation.aspx (accessed May 21, 2010).

Wiener, Jonathan B. and Alberto Alemanno. 2010. Comparing Regulatory Oversight Bodies across the Atlantic: The Office of Information and Regulatory Affairs in the U.S. and the Impact Assessment Board in the EU. In *Comparative Administrative Law*, edited by Susan Rose-Ackerman and Peter Lindseth. Northampton, MA: Edward Elgar.

Wiener, Jonathan B., and Barak D. Richman. 2010. Mechanism Choice. In *Public Choice and Public Law*, edited by Daniel Farber and Anne Joseph O'Connell. Northampton, MA: Edward Elgar.

Wiener, Jonathan B., and Michael D. Rogers. 2002. Comparing Precaution in the U.S. and Europe. *Journal of Risk Research* 5: 317–349.

Wildavsky, Aaron. 1997. *But Is It True? A Citizen's Guide to Environmental Health and Safety Issues.* Cambridge, MA: Harvard University Press.

Yandle, Bruce. 1989. Bootleggers and Baptists in the Market for Regulation. In *The Political Economy of Government Regulation*, edited by Jason F. Shogren. Boston: Kluwer Academic, 29–54.

Yandle, Bruce, and Stuart Buck. 2002. Bootleggers, Baptists, and the Global Warming Battle. *Harvard Environmental Law Review* 26: 177–229.

Zander, Joakim. 2010. *The Application of the Precautionary Principle in Practice: Comparative Dimensions.* Cambridge: Cambridge University Press.

Zweigert, Konrad, and Hein Kötz. 1998. *An Introduction to Comparative Law.* 3rd ed. Translated by Tony Weir. Oxford: Oxford University Press.

Acknowledgments

We are grateful for the deep and broad support this project has enjoyed. The project as a whole received in-kind and financial support from a diverse set of sources, spanning the public, private, and philanthropic sectors.

Both the European Commission and the U.S. Mission to the European Union provided major support to the Transatlantic Dialogues on Precaution. For helping to organize these dialogues, we acknowledge the valuable efforts of the European Commission's Group of Policy Advisers (later called the Bureau of European Policy Advisers), in particular Guy Wilmes; and of the U.S. Mission to the EU, in particular Larry Wohlers, Elisabeth Cramaussel, Csaba Chikes, and Michelle Dastin.

In addition to this transatlantic official support, we were fortunate to receive nonprofit philanthropy: the German Marshall Fund–U.S. and the Smith Richardson Foundation made the lead grants to the Duke Center for Environmental Solutions to support the Transatlantic Dialogues and this research project. We are grateful to Marianne Ginsburg at the German Marshall Fund and Mark Steinmeyer at the Smith Richardson Foundation, who gave us strong and enduring support, both financial and intellectual. Meanwhile, from the private sector, the American Chemistry Council and the ExxonMobil Foundation made unrestricted grants to the Duke Center for Environmental Solutions to support work on risk and regulation. Further, the European Policy Centre (Brussels) and the Duke Center for European Studies each helped host the Transatlantic Dialogues; and Duke Law School and Resources for the Future helped fund student research assistants. Throughout, Duke University, chiefly through its Provost, Peter Lange, gave essential operating support to the Duke Center for Environmental Solutions (which in 2005 was expanded into the Nicholas Institute for Environmental Policy Solutions at Duke).

I personally benefited from support that enabled me to spend significant time in Europe during the research and refinement of this project. These visits included a sabbatical year in 2005–2006 at l'École des Hautes Études en Sciences Sociales (l'EHESS) and at le Centre International de Recherches sur l'Environnement et le Développement (CIRED) in Paris (hosted there by Jean-Charles Hourcade, and supported by Duke Law School through the Eugene T. Bost, Jr., Research Professorship of the Charles A. Cannon Charitable Trust No. 3 at Duke University, thanks to Dean Kate Bartlett and Theresa Newman). I also benefited from many shorter visits to speak on this project and received helpful comments from European colleagues, notably at Sciences Po (Paris), Collège de France (Paris), IDDRI (Paris), the OECD (Paris), the U.S. Embassy–Paris, the France-Amériques society (Paris), the Republic of France in its rotation in 2008 as presidency of the European Union (Paris), the French Ministry of Finance Economy and Industry (Paris), Université Paris X (Nanterre), Université de Strasbourg, Université de Toulouse, the U.S. Mission to the EU (Brussels), the EU-U.S. High-Level Regulatory Cooperation Forum (Brussels), the European Policy Centre (Brussels), the European Risk Forum (Brussels), University College London, Ecologic (Berlin), the University of Zurich and ETH Zurich, Venice International University, the Society for Risk Analysis–Europe meetings in The Hague, Valencia, and London, and many others.

On the west side of the Atlantic, I also benefited from helpful feedback on this work offered by participants at many U.S. conferences and seminars, including at Cornell, Duke, Harvard, Pittsburgh, Vanderbilt, William and Mary, and Yale Universities, and at numerous meetings held by Resources for the Future (RFF), the Society for Risk Analysis (SRA), the American Association for the Advancement of Science (AAAS), the Toxicology Forum, and others.

We thank the many colleagues who generously gave comments on parts of this project, including Alberto Alemanno, Lorenzo Allio, Mikael Skou Andersen, Richard "Pete" Andrews, Sara Beale, Rick Belzer, Lucas Bergkamp, Herbert Bernstein, Francesca Bignami, Frederic Bouder, Joanne Caddy, Marie-Pierre Camproux-Duffrène, Mark Cantley, Luigi Carbone, Joann Carmin, Gail Charnley, Steve Charnovitz, Cary Coglianese, Phil Cook, Roger Cooke, Stanley Crossick, Heidi Dawidoff, Deborah DeMott, Bertrand du Marais, E. Donald Elliott, Dan Esty, Michael Faure, Barry Feld, Baruch Fischhoff, Ilya Fischhoff, Elizabeth Fisher, William Floyd, Marie-Anne Frison-Roche, David Gee, Olivier Godard, Bernie Goldstein, Christian Gollier, John Graham, George Gray, Robert Hahn, Jay Hamilton, Winston Harrington, Jane Holder, Donald Horowitz, Jean-Charles Hourcade, Stephane Jacobzone, Bruce Jentleson, Judith Kelley, Robert Keohane, Benedict Kingsbury, Josef Konvitz, Gert-Jan Koopman, Andreas Kraemer, Alan Krupnick, Howard Kunreuther, Doug Kysar, Helen Ladd, Peter Lindseth, Ragnar Lofstedt, Jonathan Losos, Richard Macrory, Giandomenico Majone, Nikolai Malyshev, Richard Merrill, Patrick Messerlin, Ralf Michaels, Marie-Lynn Miranda, Charles-Henri Montin, Granger Morgan, Richard Morgenstern, Madeline Morris, Joost Pauwelyn, Lars Mitek Pederson, Shainila Pradhan, Ray Purdy, Cornelia Quennet-Thielen, Jeff Rachlinski, Ortwin Renn, Susan Rose-Ackerman, Andrzej Rudka, Jim Salzman, Manuel Santiago dos Santos, Kathryn Saterson, Robert Scharrenbourg, Chris Schroeder, Peter Secor, Michel Setbon, Greg Shaffer, Bernard Sinclair-Désgagné, Turner Smith, David Soskice, Richard Stewart, Andy Stirling, Christopher Stone, Cass Sunstein, Robert Sussman, Tim Swanson, Alec Stone Sweet, Nicolas Treich, Matti Vainio, Norman Vig, David Vogel, Guy Wilmes, Katrina Wyman, and Franklin Zimring.

For very constructive comments on the penultimate draft of the entire book manuscript, we particularly thank John Graham of Indiana University.

And for insightful comments on nearly final drafts of the concluding Chapter 20, we thank participants in the Law and Globalization workshop at Yale Law School (December 2009), notably Alec Stone Sweet, Doug Kysar, Susan Rose-Ackerman, Peter Lindseth, Dan Esty, and their students; and participants in the faculty workshop at Harvard Law School (April 2010), notably Martha Minow, Mark Roe, John Goldberg, Jed Shugerman, Mort Horowitz, Jonathan Marx, Maximo Langer, and Anne Joseph O'Connell.

We want to thank as well the many students at Duke University who provided excellent research assistance for this project over several years. Brendon Swedlow spent a postdoctoral year at Duke working on this project and shaping the quantitative data project. Denise Kall led the team of student research assistants during her doctoral program in sociology. Zheng (Jonathan) Zhou obtained two master's degrees at Duke, and then worked for two years on the quantitative coding and scoring project. And the outstanding student research assistants who worked on aspects of the project included Greg Andeck, Deserai Anderson-Utley, Mark Axelrod, Zia Cromer Oatley, Xin Dai, Anthony Del Rio, Salwa Elshazly, Shannon Frank, Dylan Fuge, Lena Hansen, Amy Horner, Clayton Jernigan, David Jones, Chris Kocher, Mark Marvelli, Chloe Metz, Natasa Pajic, Rocio Perez, Jessica Regan, Leah Russin, Emily Schilling, Caitlin Snyder, Nicolle Snyder, and Ivan Urlaub.

Thanks also to the staff of the Duke Center for Environmental Solutions: Kathryn Saterson (its executive director from 2000 to 2005), Carolyn Leith, and Kristen Dubay. And to the staff at Duke Law School who helped in numerous aspects: Joan Ashley, Neylan Gurel, Kim Lott, Ann McCloskey, Karen Novy, Debbie Upchurch, and Renee Valade.

Our publishers at RFF Press/Earthscan—Don Reisman, Gina Mance, Andrea Titus, Claire Lamont, Anna Rice, and Joyce Bond, and the communications staff at Resources for the Future, Pete Nelson and Lisa Mihalik, and their colleagues—were simply terrific in helping us refine our text, put our manuscript in print, and publicize our product.

Most of all, I am deeply grateful to my superb fellow co-editors and co-project leaders, Michael Rogers, Jim Hammitt, and Peter Sand, with whom it has been a joy and an education to collaborate. And my gratitude is endless to my family, Ginger, Alex, Cal, and Carrie, who supported, endured, and shared my work and travel on this project over many years.

Jonathan B. Wiener

Index

For Product Safety Concerns and Information please contact our EU
representative GPSR@taylorandfrancis.com Taylor & Francis Verlag GmbH,
Kaufingerstraße 24, 80331 München, Germany

Printed and bound by CPI Group (UK) Ltd, Croydon, CR0 4YY
08/05/2025
01864553-0002